P9-DZY-844

HANDBOOK OF MIDDLE AMERICAN INDIANS, VOLUME 11

Archaeology of Northern Mesoamerica, Part 2

HANDBOOK OF MIDDLE AMERICAN INDIANS

EDITED AT MIDDLE AMERICAN RESEARCH INSTITUTE, TULANE UNIVERSITY, BY

ROBERT WAUCHOPE, *General Editor*

MARGARET A. L. HARRISON, *Associate Editor*

MARJORIE S. ZENGEL, *Research Associate*

INIS PICKETT, GYPSIE E. STEARNS, *Administrative Assistants*

DAVID S. PHELPS, FRANK T. SCHNELL, JR.,

ARDEN E. ANDERSON, JR., *Art Staff*

JAMES C. GIFFORD AND CAROL A. GIFFORD, *Indexers*

Editorial Advisory Board

ASSEMBLED WITH THE AID OF A GRANT FROM THE NATIONAL SCIENCE
FOUNDATION, AND UNDER THE SPONSORSHIP OF THE NATIONAL RESEARCH
COUNCIL COMMITTEE ON LATIN AMERICAN ANTHROPOLOGY

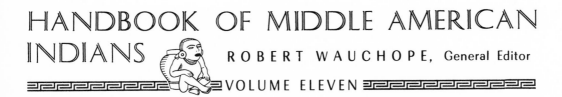

HANDBOOK OF MIDDLE AMERICAN INDIANS
ROBERT WAUCHOPE, General Editor

VOLUME ELEVEN

Archaelogy of Northern Mesoamerica

PART TWO

GORDON F. EKHOLM
IGNACIO BERNAL

Volume Editors

UNIVERSITY OF TEXAS PRESS AUSTIN

Published in Great Britain by the
University of Texas Press, Ltd., London

International Standard Book Number 0-292-70150-0
Library of Congress Catalog Card No. 64–10316
Copyright ©1971 by the University of Texas Press
All rights reserved.

The preparation and publication of
The Handbook of Middle American Indians
has been assisted by grants from
the National Science Foundation.

Typesetting by G&S Typesetters, Austin, Texas
Printing by The Meriden Gravure Company, Meriden, Connecticut
Binding by Universal Bookbindery, Inc., San Antonio, Texas

CONTENTS (*Continued from Vol. 10*)

HANDBOOK OF MIDDLE AMERICAN INDIANS, VOLUME 11

Archaeology of Northern Mesoamerica, Part 2

GENERAL EDITOR'S NOTE

Manuscripts for articles in all volumes of the *Handbook of Middle American Indians* were submitted at various dates over a period of several years. These Volumes 10 and 11 required by far the longest time to assemble, and as a result some of the articles were written more than ten years ago. As only minor revisions are possible at this stage of production, it is difficult to assign a date to each article. The reader can sometimes have an approximate indication of when an article was completed by noting the latest dates in the list of references at the end of each contribution, but an author should not be faulted if more current publications are not cited or if recent findings are not included.

19. The Peoples of Central Mexico and Their Historical Traditions

PEDRO CARRASCO

MEXICAN HISTORICAL traditions, like the Book of Genesis, gradually merge mythology into history, and it is difficult to separate one from the other. Most of the oldest traditions of clearly historical content refer to a period when the Toltec were the dominant people, ruling from their capital Tollan. This is described as a period of cultural florescence, and the archaeological data support the idea that this was a time when the Mesoamerican northern frontier extended farther north than it did at the time of the Spanish conquest. Most traditions about the Toltec describe their downfall caused by the tricks played by Tezcatlipoca against their priest ruler Quetzalcoatl. Then follow the abandonment of their city and a series of migrations throughout the 13th century toward the valleys of Mexico and Puebla and beyond.

Some of these migrating groups had the Mesoamerican culture of the Toltec, others were food-gathering barbarians from the outer fringes of the Toltec empire who now moved into previously Mesoamerican areas. In the wake of these migrations political fragmentation prevailed in central Mexico. Some political units were established by groups of Toltec culture, others by groups of barbarian ancestry. A merging of both types of peoples took place, with the barbarians gradually adopting the Mesoamerican culture and with the coexistence of groups of different origin in most political units.

A trend toward the development of larger political units first became established under the Tepanec of Azcapotzalco in the late 14th century. Their power was replaced in 1428 by the confederation led by the Mexica Tenochca that is usually labeled the Aztec empire.

There is a native tradition, however, which reaches farther into the past. It is one recorded by Sahagún (bk. 10, ch. 29, par. 12) as part of his account of the Mexica and is here summarized.

In the distant past the people who first arrived in this land came over the water in boats; they landed in Panotla or Pantla (the Huasteca) and moved along the coast as far as Quauhtemallan (Guatemala). They were led by their priests, who counseled with their god. Then they came to Tamoanchan and there they stayed. Their wise men (*tlamatinime*) were called book men (*amoxuaque*); they soon left and took with them the old books and the art of casting metals; when they left they announced the eventual return of their god. Four of the old wise men remained—Oxomoco, Cipactonal, Tlaltecui, and Xochicauaca—and devised the calendar.

From Tamoanchan the people went to Teotihuacan. Their leaders were elected there and when they died they buried them there and built a pyramid over them. There they also built the pyramids of the Sun and the Moon, very large like the pyramid of Cholollan.

The people called Olmec Uixtotin then left Tamoanchan; they followed those who went to the east and they went to the coast; they are now called Anauac Mixtec.

The boring of the maguey and the making of pulque were then devised at the mountain called Chichinahuia and Pozonaltepetl by Mayauel (the maguey goddess) and the pulque gods. Cuextecatl, the ruler of a group of people, got drunk and took off his loincloth; his people in shame left and settled in Panotla; they are the Cuextec (Huastec).

After the kingdom had lasted for a long time at Tamoanchan it moved to Xomiltepec. There the old men, rulers, and priests conferred and they decided that they should move in search of land. They first settled in Teotihuacan and then they departed. The Toltec took the lead. The leader of the Otomi left them at Coatepec and settled his people in the mountains. Then different people moved on: the Toltec, the Mexica, the Nahua; they wandered in the desert and they went to a place where there were seven caves (Chicomoztoc). There the god of the Toltec spoke and told them to go

back to the place from which they had come. They left and went to Tollantzinco and Tollan. Then the Teochichimec followed, and then the Michuaque. Then the Nahua followed: the Tepanec, Acolhuaque, Chalca, Huexotzinca, and Tlaxcaltec. The Mexica were the last; they traveled farther on to a place called Colhuacan; no one knows how long they were there but their god spoke to them and ordered them to return to their place of origin. Thus starts the movement of the Mexica to their settlement in the Valley of Mexico.

A much briefer view of these events is given in Origen de los mexicanos (3:259). After the creation of man in Teotihuacan people move to Teocolhuacan from where they later come south.

Thus, unlike most traditions which start with migrations from the barbarian areas of the north, Sahagún's tradition refers to a period of typical Mesoamerican culture centered in the central highlands and carried by people who arrived from the sea. There is mention of rulers and priests, pyramids, the calendar, books and metalwork, the cultivation of maguey and the making of pulque. Specific gods are not mentioned except those connected with maguey and pulque; otherwise general terms for the deity are used such as teotl, Tloque Nahuaque, Yohualli Ehecatl. The area concerned is defined by the reference to Teotihuacan. The pyramid of Cholollan is also mentioned but it is not clear whether as having been built by these people or by way of comparison. A mountain Chichinauhtzin still exists near Tepoztlan, and Xomiltepec is nearby south of Popocatepetl. Tamoanchan is a term of largely mythical meaning. As far as this tradition is concerned Jiménez Moreno (1942, p. 133), following the Histoire du Mechique, places it in the Cuernavaca area. Paul Kirchhoff (in still unpublished work) favors its identification with Cholollan.

A number of ethnic categories were used in ancient Mexico which, although often

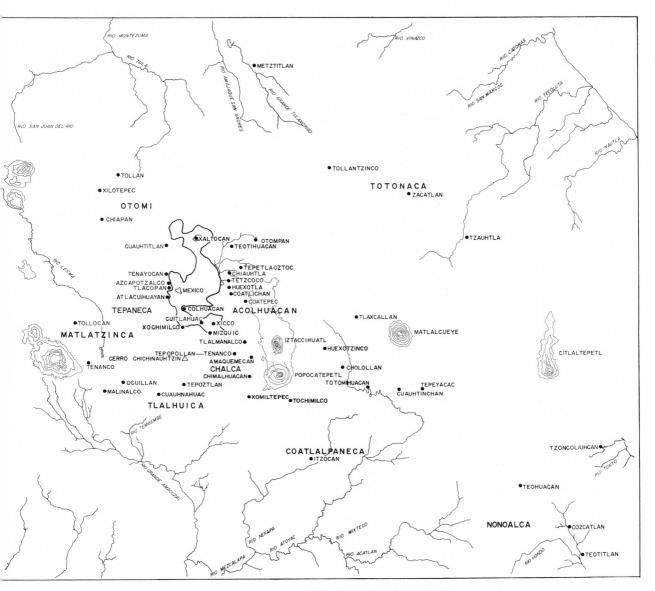

Fig. 1—MAP OF CENTRAL MEXICO BEFORE THE SPANISH CONQUEST

elusive in the complexity of their meaning, can best be defined on the basis of the overall historical process outlined above.

The term Chichimec is the most complex one. Linguistically it could be expected to be a gentile name applied to people from a place Chichiman (cf. Colimec and Chalmec from Coliman and Chalman) but no such place is ever mentioned. It can also be interpreted to mean dog lineage (*chichi*, 'dog'; *mecatl*, 'rope,' 'lineage') and this is the meaning usually accepted, although Chichimecatl is a singular (plural Chichimeca) and not a collective noun.

The concepts recorded by Sahagún in his Book 10, together with the tradition summarized above, allow the best general definition. First, Chichimec is applied to

461

the northern food-gathering nomads. Second, it is applied to a number of Mesoamerican groups who, having moved into that northern Chichimec country, moved back to the south; this includes the different Nahuatl groups, the Otomi, and even the Toltec. In contrast to both types of Chichimec were some people who, Sahagún says, were not called Chichimec: the Olmec, Huixtotin, and Nonoalca. These we may define as the old Mesoamerican peoples from the early period of Sahagún's tradition who did not receive cultural influences from the northern nomads.

The term Chichimec can then be applied to all the groups migrating toward the south after the downfall of Tollan, including the Toltec themselves. But a contrast can also be made between Chichimec and Toltec. In this case the term Toltec is applied to people of Mesoamerican culture who formed the Toltec empire, and the term Chichimec is restricted to groups with a food-gathering culture or to people of such an origin but already acculturated to Mesoamerican culture (Ixtlilxochitl, 1952, 1: 106). This contrast can be used in slightly different ways by a single author (*ibid.*, 1: 106, 295, 457), and each source may use the term Chichimec for a particular group to which it is applicable in the area whose history it describes.

These ethnic categories do not have a neat correspondence with language groups. The main languages of the central highlands were Nahuatl and the various languages of the Otomian family. At the time of the conquest Otomi-speakers were considered Chichimec, but Nahuatl was the language spoken by people who were considered to be Chichimec, Toltec, or Olmec. Some of these Nahuatl-speakers may have spoken formerly other languages whose identity it is not possible to ascertain, for instance the Chichimec of Xolotl (see below) or the Nonoalca of Chalco (Chimalpahin, 1965b, p. 166).

Most regions and political units of central Mexico include ethnic groups of different origin. At some times they appear as groups in process of acculturation and assimilation but, even beyond that, they constituted different subdivisions each with a different cultural tradition and a different role in the social division of labor which made up the various political units (see Article 14).

Before we review each particular region and political unit, the main ethnic components of the whole of central Mexico can be listed on the basis of the native ethnic categories given above as they were found throughout the area.

The groups named by Sahagún as not being Chichimec from any point of view were largely located beyond the area covered in this article. Some of them, however, are mentioned in some traditions as the original inhabitants of areas later occupied by peoples that moved south after the downfall of Tollan. Thus in Cholollan and Tlaxcallan the Olmec and Xicalanca were displaced by the Toltec and Chichimec. In Chalco the original population were Olmec, Xicalanca, Xochmec, Quiahuiztec, and Cocolca. An older Huixtotin population had once existed in Xaltocan. From what little is said about all these people it seems as if they were outside the circle of the Toltec empire. We may consider these Olmec and related groups as old Mesoamerican peoples who did not take part in the migration to the northern steppes and whose culture was not influenced by that of the northern nomads. We may also relate them to the people of Tamoanchan in Sahagún's old tradition. It goes without saying that these Olmec of historical traditions should not be identified with the early culture labeled Olmec by the archaeologists (Jiménez Moreno, 1942).

Another group of peoples are those who had formed part of a Toltec empire and consequently had a Mesoamerican culture even if they had cultural elements relating them to the northern barbarians in whose country their ancestors had settled. On this basis, as Sahagún tells us, they could all be called Chichimec.

The Toltec of native traditions, the people of Tollan, have a typical Mesoamerican culture and they can definitely be identified with the archaeological remains of Tula, Hidalgo. The Toltec excelled in crafts and building, so much so that the term *toltecatl* also has the meaning of skilled craftsman. Of their achievements in agriculture the legend says that they grew oversize fruits and cotton of various colors. Descriptions of the Toltec center on their downfall related to the misfortunes of the priest Quetzalcoatl, instigated by the gods Titlacahuan (or Tezcatlipoca), Huitzilopochtli, and Tlacahuepan. The cult of the supreme couple of the Omeyocan is also mentioned, as well as Tlaloc. Fast and penance were the required activities of Quetzalcoatl; he is also said to have opposed human sacrifice and to have offered instead snakes, birds, and butterflies. At the time of their downfall human sacrifice and the sacrificial stone (*techcatl*) are mentioned. The shooting with arrows of the victim and flaying are introduced at the end of the Tolteca period. It is difficult to say what the political hierarchy might have been because the different sources disagree about the contemporaneity of the main characters. A dual organization of secular ruler and high priest is most probable (Kirchhoff, 1955). It is also difficult to plot the extent of the Tolteca empire, a task that Kirchhoff (1961a) has undertaken. He includes as main centers Tollan, Tollantzinco, and Tenanco as well as parts of the Bajío where he locates Colhuacan and Aztlan, localities from which start the later migrations when the Bajío was abandoned to the hunting nomads. It would thus leave outside the Toltec realm most of the Valley of Mexico and the Valley of Puebla where the Olmec

would have been a continuation of the people described in Sahagún's tradition.

(The main sources on the Toltec are Sahagún, bk. 3; bk. 10, ch. 29; Códice Chimalpopoca; Chimalpahin; Ixtlilxochitl; Historia Tolteca-Chichimeca; Relación de la genealogía y linaje; Origen de los mexicanos; Historia de los mexicanos por sus pinturas.)

It is the downfall of Tollan that starts the migration movements which were the basic historical traditions of the people in all political units of central Mexico at the time of the Spanish conquest. Groups with very different culture are described as starting their migration to their 16th-century home country. They are usually given in different traditions in lists of a varying number of migratory groups called towns (*altepeme*) or wards (*calpultin*) in Nahuatl. The lists vary widely according to the area to which they apply, some covering the whole of the central highlands (e.g., Códice Ríos, fol. 66v), others only smaller regions such as the Valley of Mexico (e.g., Historia de los mexicanos por sus pinturas, 3 : 219).

A special case is that of the Nonoalca. They are described as present in Tollan at the time of its downfall and from there they moved south with the name Nonoalca Chichimec, according to the Historia Tolteca-Chichimeca in spite of Sahagún's statement given above that the Nonoalca were not Chichimec. The Nonoalca settled in the region of Itzocan (Izucar de Matamoros), known as the country of the Coatlalpanec and in the region of Tzoncoliuhcan (Zongolica), Teohuacan, Teotitlan, and Cozcatlan. The Nonoalca were also one of the major elements in the population of Chalco, and a Nonoalca group is also known from Michoacan (Seler, 1908, pp. 49 ff.; Jiménez Moreno, 1948, pp. 151–55). Localities or wards named Nonoalco existed in a number of towns in the Valley of Mexico, and we may assume that they were or had been occupied by Nonoalca. Such is the case in Tlatelolco, Atlacuihuayan (Tacubaya), Chiauhtla, and Coatlichan. Nonoalca are also reported to have been in Xaltocan. The Nonoalca seem to be people of typical Mesoamerican culture like the Olmec, who became part of the Toltec empire, i.e., of the political units established during the expansion to the north, but whose culture, however, was not affected by the people of the northern steppes (cf. Kirchhoff, 1940; Jiménez Moreno, 1942, pp. 136–40).

Other peoples most directly connected with the cultural centers of the Toltec period are the Toltec Chichimec who moved from Tollan to Chololan, and the Colhua who, originally from an older Colhuacan or Teocolhuacan beyond Tollan, moved to Tollan and on to Colhuacan in the southern Valley of Mexico where they became the main center of Toltec culture in the valley.

Other of the migrating groups originated in what had probably been provincial centers of the Toltec empire. Some may have had a more typical Toltec culture, others one more influenced by Chichimec contributions. Among these peoples are the Tepanec who settled in Azcapotzalco, other groups in the southern part of the valley such as the Tenanca of Chalco and the Mexica. Outside the Valley of Mexico the Matlatzinca to the west and the Tlalhuica and Couixca to the south also had probably a Toltec cultural background. Groups with more influence from the northern nomads were the Acolhua who settled in Coatlichan in the eastern part of the valley and the various Otomi groups.

In contrast with all the foregoing peoples are those Chichimec who enter the valleys of Mexico and Puebla with a culture of northern type epitomized in the traditional descriptions by ignorance of cultivation, reliance on hunting, ignorance of boiling in pots, clothes made of skins, and absence of idols and temples. What language these different Chichimec may have spoken is

not clear; it seems they may have spoken languages of their own, different from standard Nahuatl and Otomi although in the course of their acculturation to Mesoamerican culture they acquired one or the other of these languages even before they entered the valleys of Mexico and Puebla. At the time of the conquest most of their descendants spoke Nahuatl and some Otomi. A Chichimec language is reported in a very few localities but no linguistic data exist to identify this language (Carrasco, 1950, pp. 32, 34, 35, 38).

In this category of Chichimec with a hunting culture are found the people who enter the Valley of Mexico under the leadership of Xolotl, who established their center first in Tenayocan and later in Tetzcoco. In the northwestern part of the valley, Chichimec of the same type had their center in Cuauhtitlan and similar people also settled in the southern valley, as in Chalco where they went by the name of Totolimpanec. In the Puebla area a number of Chichimec groups settled who had their main centers in Tlaxcallan, Huexotzinco, Totomihuacan, and Cuauhtinchan. The historical traditions of all these groups differed in many points but they all show not only cultural similarities but also relationships in the course of their migrations that connect them as branches of a single movement of people.

Although these Chichimec are contrasted with other peoples on the basis of their hunting culture, they must have been at all times subject to influences of Mesoamerican societies and cultures. This appears in the fact that from the beginning they make Tollan a stopping place on their way south, that they have leaders who establish marriage alliances with rulers of Toltec ancestry, and that their patron gods, though typical of Chichimec groups, are nevertheless part of the Mesoamerican pantheon. The main Chichimec gods were Itzpapalotl (Obsidian Butterfly) and Mixcoatl (Cloud Snake), also called Camaxtli in the Puebla

464

region. At the time of the Spanish conquest all these Chichimec groups were fully acculturated to Mesoamerican culture.

Let us now review the main political units of central Mexico.

The Colhua are the people who settled in Colhuacan in the southern part of the valley. Their tradition places their origin beyond Tollan in Teocolhuacan (Relación de la genealogía, 3: 241) from where they went to Tollan to participate in the later events of Toltec history.

They were one of the most important groups that transmitted the Toltec culture into the later historical period, and most important in this respect is that they maintained dynastic continuity from Toltec days so that leaders of later newcomers established marriage alliances with the Colhua or obtained Colhua rulers. Long lists of Colhua rulers are given but no clear account of the kin relations among them; a system of collateral succession seems to have prevailed (Relación de la genealogía, 3: 246; Origen de los mexicanos, 3: 267; García Granados, 1952–53, 3: 414–15).

When the Colhua settled in Colhuacan, they became one of the main powers in the valley. They established dominion over other towns such as Ocuillan, Malinalco, Xochimilco, and Cuitlahuac, and they may have formed a triple alliance, perhaps similar to that of the later Aztec empire, together with the Tepanec of Azcapotzalco and the Acolhua of Coatlichan (Códice Chimalpopoca, par. 235; Chimalpahin, 1958, pp. 3–5, 14). The Mexica became their subjects when they settled in the lake area, and their first king derived his Toltec ancestry from the Colhua lineage. Colhuacan, however, collapsed at the time when Azcapotzalco became the main power in the valley; at that time is described an exodus of Colhua people who went mainly to many areas of the Acolhuacan, to Azcapotzalco, and to Cuauhtitlan where they introduced Toltec culture. After this, Colhuacan became of secondary importance as a subject

of Tenochtitlan (Códice Chimalpopoca, pars. 125–27, 131; Ixtlilxochitl, 1952, 2: 70–75).

As patron gods of the Colhua are mentioned Cinteotl, the maize god, and Cihuacoatl, wife of the god of hell. During their stay at Tollan the Colhua are said to have worshipped Huitzilopochtli and Tezcatlipoca (Historia de los mexicanos por sus pinturas, 3: 219, 225; Relación de la genealogía, 3: 243).

Of all the Chichimec groups who enter the central valleys with a hunting culture the most important are those who arrive under the leadership of Xolotl and establish a dynasty that eventually came to rule the eastern part of the valley with its capital in Tetzcoco and formed one of the three parties of the Aztec empire. Important sources such as Ixtlilxochitl, Codex Xolotl, and other pictorials report the traditional history of this group (Dibble, 1951; Aubin, 1885).

Xolotl is said to have arrived from the neighborhood of the Huasteca country married to a princess of Tamiyauh and Panuco. From Chicomoztoc they went to Tollantzinco and Tollan, which they found deserted, and moved on to the valley. Their first center was Tenayocan, but other related Chichimec also settled in the eastern part of the valley especially in the Tepetlaoztoc area.

The Chichimec are described in the written sources and depicted in the codices as having a hunting-gathering culture, living in caves, dressing in skin clothes, hunting with bows and arrows, and eating mezquite cakes. They spoke a Chichimec language different from Nahuatl and had no idols. The acculturation of these hunters took place under the influence of their more civilized neighbors, especially the people of Chalco, and also as the result of the settlement in their midst of other peoples of more advanced culture. The Chichimec started learning Nahuatl, the cultivation of corn, and the worship of the gods. Some

465

Chichimec, refusing to accept the new culture, rebelled and moved out, some going north to Metztitlan, others moving on to Huexotzinco and Tlaxcallan (Ixtlilxochitl, 1952, 1: 95; 2: 46–9, 65; León-Portilla, 1967).

Among the people who settled in the eastern valley with the Chichimec of Xolotl were the Acolhua, who arrived shortly after Xolotl and established their capital at Coatlichan, with their ruler Tzontecomatl marrying a Chalca princess of Toltec ancestry. The relationship of Chichimec and Acolhua was very close and the name Acolhuacan was applied to the larger area under the rule of Tetzcoco. Ixtlilxochitl describes the Acolhua as originating from the far northwest beyond Michoacan and with a culture characterized by the use of bow and arrow and skin clothes like the people of Xolotl but with temples and idols; their patron god was named Cocopitl (Ixtlilxochitl, 1952, 1: 94; 2: 41).

Under Xolotl's great-grandson Quinatzin the Chichimec capital was moved to Tetzcoco. Also during his reign two groups of Toltec culture moved into the area, the Chimalpanec and the Tlailotlaque. They came from the Mixteca area after having been for some time in Chalco. The Tlailotlaque were experts in picture writing and their god was Tezcatlipoca. The Chimalpanec are said to have been connected with Xolotl's lineage. Later, during the reign of Quinatzin's son Techotlalatzin, four other groups of Toltec culture moved in after the collapse of Colhuacan: the Colhua, Mexiti, Huitznahua, and Tepanec. These people generalize the use of Nahuatl in the region and introduce idolatry. Tezcatlipoca, who became the patron god of Tetzcoco, was brought by the Huitznahua. All these six immigrant groups were established in all the main towns of the Acolhuacan, each in their own separate wards. Tetzcoco was divided into six wards named after those six groups (Ixtlilxochitl, 1952, 1: 235; 2:

69–75; Torquemada, 1943–44, 1: 89; Pomar, 1941, pp. 13–14).

Thus, although the ruling dynasty of the Acolhuacan was of Chichimec origin, the bulk of the population and its culture was similar to that of other parts of the valley. As its counterpart in Mexico Tenochtitlan, the main temple of Tetzcoco contained the shrines of Huitzilopochtli and Tlaloc. Within the Acolhuacan the main point in the cult of Mixcoatl-Camaxtli, the Chichimec god, was at Coatepec on the Chalco and Huexotzinco borderland, where some of its relics were kept (Pomar, 1941, pp. 12–13; Durán, 1951, 2: 129).

A lineal father-to-son succession rule prevailed in the Chichimec dynasty. The son of Xolotl, Nopaltzin took as wife a Toltec princess. Later rulers established their marriage alliances with Coatlichan and Huexotla, the main towns of the Acolhuacan, and from Ixtlilxochitl on (the sixth ruler) with Tenochtitlan. Some traditions in Ixtlilxochitl's histories mention the ancestors of Xolotl, connecting him with the Toltec (García Granados, 1952–53, 3: 427; Ixtlilxochitl, 1952, 1: 78–79, 263–65).

In later times Tetzcoco became one of the three constituent parties of the Aztec empire (see Article 15).

The Tepanec, according to Ixtlilxochitl, were received by Xolotl together with the Acolhua and Otomi and they settled in Azcapotzalco under their ruler Acolnahuacatl, who married Xolotl's daughter. The Tepanec tradition from Tlatelolco, however, gives the Tepanec dynasty an older start under Matlaccoatl, grandfather of Acolnahuacatl (Anales de Tlatelolco, par. 207).

The Tepanec had close cultural connections with Otomian-speaking peoples immediately to their north and west. The sling is mentioned as their distinctive weapon, as with the Matlatzinca, and their tribal god Otontecuhtli, Ocotecutli, or Cuecuex is also the patron god of the Otomi (Carrasco, 1950, pp. 14–15).

Azcapotzalco first shared power in the valley with Colhuacan and Coatlichan (Códice Chimalpopoca, par. 221) but, under Acolnahuacatl's successor Tezozomoc, the Tepanec gradually dominated the whole valley and areas beyond. Tezozomoc established his sons as kings in a number of towns and brought other local rulers into his alliance, giving his daughters in marriage to some of them. Forming part of this Tepanec empire were the Mexica. Tlatelolco obtained as king a son of Tezozomoc; Tenochtlitlan, which had acquired a king from Colhuacan, succeeded to the leadership of the Colhua and became one of the main allies of Azcapotzalco. This short-lived empire of Tezozomoc is important as an antecedent of the Aztec empire and it is through their participation in it that the Mexica first joined the group of the great powers (Carrasco, 1950, pp. 268–73).

The ethnic composition of the Tepanec region was also mixed although detailed information is not available. Azcapotzalco was divided into two parts, Tepanecapan and Mexicapan, each with a king, and Tezozomoc was king of Mexicapan. Colhua people also settled in Azcapotzalco after the downfall of Colhuacan. A Nonoalco ward existed in Atlacuihuayan, and the linguistic situation was very complex (Códice Chimalpopoca, par. 127; Chimalpahin, 1965b, p. 182; Historia de los mexicanos por sus pinturas, 3: 228; Carrasco, 1950, pp. 32, 111).

The Otomi are the third group which, in Ixtlilxochitl's history, moved into the valley shortly after Xolotl. The Otomi leader married one of the daughters of Xolotl and settled in Xaltocan. The Otomi kingdom of Xaltocan was an important power for some time; it included areas in the northern Valley of Mexico and beyond, up to and including Metztitlan. This kingdom, however, fell under the Tepanec of Azacapotzalco and was incorporated into Tezozomoc's empire. A number of Otomi migrated at this time. Some went to Metztitlan where they

remained independent from the powers in the valley, others migrated to Otompan in the Acolhuacan, and others to Tlaxcallan.

The kingdom of Xaltocan was the only important political unit in the history of the Valley of Mexico which was ruled by the Otomi. The center of the Otomi population was always the region of Xilotepec and Chiapan, areas about which we have no important historical traditions. This was probably the region from which they moved into Xaltocan, a town for which tradition also mentions older populations of Huixtotin, Nonoalca, and Toltec (Nazareo, 1940, p. 123). The Otomi were settled in their heartland from the times of the Mesoamerican movement toward the north as reported in Sahagún's tradition, which places them in Coatepec. The Otomi were also numerous in the north of the valley, in the Valley of Tollocan, in the Mezquital, and in a few areas of the Puebla highlands, especially Tlaxcallan, where many had been accepted as refugees to serve as military defense against the Aztec empire. For the most part they were a peasant population. The Aztec considered the Otomi uncouth, improvident, and stupid. Some features of their culture such as tattooing and tooth blackening may point to a connection with the cultures of the Gulf Coast.

The patron god of the Otomi, Otontecuhtli, is described as being a form of the fire god; he seems to be also a form of the cult of the souls of the dead warriors. He was also the patron god of the Tepaneca and Mazahua (see Article 16). Other typical Otomi deities were the Moon and Yocippa, probably another name of the Chichimec god Mixcoatl.

The Otomi are always considered Chichimec. Their language, however, was widely spread and it is probable that, like Nahuatl, it was spoken by people that represented different cultural traditions. The people of the Otomi heartland and those of Xaltocan are not described as having a hunting culture, but some of the hunting Chichimec such as the Totomihuaque and related peoples may have spoken Otomi (Jiménez Moreno, 1939; Kirchhoff, 1940, p. 96).

(Data on Otomi culture and history are compiled in Carrasco, 1950.)

Linguistically related to the Otomi were the Matlatzinca of the Valley of Tollocan. At the time of their conquest by the Aztec they were governed by a hierarchy of three rulers with the titles Tlatoani, Tlacatecatl, and Tlacochcalcatl, in which each of them was succeeded by the ruler of lower rank, a son of the deceased succeeding to the lowest title—a system similar to that of the Tenochca themselves. The patron god of the Matlatzinca was Coltzin, about whom little is known (Carrasco, 1950).

A Chichimec group about which a fair amount of information is available is that of Cuauhtitlan. The cultural process in this area is similar to that of the Acolhuacan. A Chichimec group settled here characterized by hunting with bow and arrow, wearing clothes made of skins, and living without houses. Their gods were Mixcoatl and Itzpapalotl. They maintained their identity in conflict with Xaltocan and the Tepaneca but after the downfall of Colhuacan they received as immigrants Colhua and Mexicatzinca people who introduced the Toltec culture with the cult of Toci, 9 Monkey, and Xochiquetzal. The great celebration of the month Izcalli, which attracted to Cuauhtitlan people from many places (Motolinia, 1903, p. 62), must be part of this Colhua cultural influence. (The source on Cuauhtitlan is Códice Chimalpopoca.)

In the southern part of the Valley of Mexico the area best known is that of Chalco. Thanks to the writings of Chimalpahin we have a fair picture about the different ethnic elements in its population. The country of Chalco extended from the eastern shores of Lake Chalco to the mountain ridge of the Iztaccihuatl and Popocatepetl. During the migration period an important center was Xicco, an island in the lake, but the main political centers became Tlalmanalco and Amaquemecan with secondary centers in Tenanco-Tepopollan and Xochimilco-Chimalhuacan. Typical of Chalco were different ethnic groups occupying different wards within a given settlement and with a different ruler, each of whom had a distinct tecuhtli title. Although the political organization of Chalco changed at different periods of its history, there usually were several of such tecuhtli holding positions of tlatoani or king.

According to the traditional histories, the aboriginal population of Chalco were the Xochtec, Olmec, Xicalanca, Quiyahuizteca, and Cocolca. Their center was at the site of the later Amaquemecan. The local sacred mountain, then called Chalchiuhmomozco (Jade Shrine) and Tamoanchan, was the site of a water cult to Chalchiuhmatlalatl (Jade Green Water). This old population had the reputation of being sorcerers and rain-makers. These people left the area when it was conquered by the Chichimec Totolimpanec. The Olmec, Xochtec, and others can probably be identified with the Olmec of Sahagún's tradition given above and with the Olmec of Cholollan and Tlaxcallan (Jiménez Moreno, 1942).

The Olmec and related peoples disappear from the later history of Chalco. All the other peoples of this area are described as immigrants after the Toltec collapse. Some are groups with a Toltec culture, others are Chichimec who enter the region with a hunting culture.

The older settlers are said to be the Acxotec who came from Tollan. Their patron god was Acollacatl Nahualtecuhtli. They were traders and brought their market with them. Their chief had the title tecuachcuauhtli and he ruled over one of the wards of Tlalmanalco. Together with the Acxotec came other groups without a nobility of their own; they were the Mihuaque, Tlaltecahuaque, Contec, and Tlailotlaque.

Another group of Toltec ancestry were

the Teotenanca. Their ultimate origin was Aztlan but their point of departure in their later migration was Teotenanco, probably the present Tenango del Valle, state of Mexico, where they were fought by Topiltzin Quetzalcoatl of Tollan. The patron god of the Teotenanca was Nauhyotecuhtli Xipil, probably a form of the fire god. The Teotenanca were subdivided into six calpulli. In Chalco they eventually settled in Amaquemecan, where they occupied two wards: Tzacualtitlan Tenanco ruled by the Teohuatecuhtli, and Atlauhtlan Tenanco ruled by the Tlailotlactecuhtli.

The Nonoalca Teotlixca Tlacochcalca originated from Huehuetlapallan Nonoalco. They crossed the sea and after a long route arrived at Tollan. From there they moved into the Chalco region, where they arrived after the Acxotec, Mihuaque, and others, over whom they ruled in Tlalmanalco. In this city there were two Nonoalca rulers: the Teohuatecuhtli of Opochuacan Tlacochcalco, and the Tlatquictecuhtli of Itzcahuacan Tlacochcalco. The patron god of the Nonoalca was Tlatlauhqui Tezcatlipoca. During their stay at Tollan their use of the sacrificial stone (*techcatl*) and the round stone (*temalacatl*) for the gladiatorial sacrifice is mentioned. Another Nonoalca group settled in Amaquemecan, where they occupied the ward of Panohuayan and were ruled by the Tlamaocatl tecuhtli. These Nonoalca are clearly related to the Nonoalca of the Puebla region.

The main Chichimec group in Chalco was called Totolimpanec. Their point of origin was Aztlan Chicomoztoc. They arrived in Chalco after the Nonoalca and, in contrast with the latter who were agriculturalists, the Totolimpanec did not cultivate but hunted with bow and arrow. They are also described as going about naked and they offered to the Sun the game they shot with their arrows. Their patron gods were 1 Flintknife (Mixcoatl), 9 Monkey (Itzpapalotl) and 9 Wind (Ehecatl Quetzalcoatl). The Totolimpanec wrested Amaquemecan

from the Olmec. Their ruler had the title Chichimeca tecuhtli and was the leader of the ward Itztlacozauhcan.

Another Chichimec group that joined the Totolimpanec were the Tecuanipantlac, who occupied two wards of Amaquemecan. Their patron god was Citecatl, their name for Mixcoatl.

(The main source for Chalco is Chimalpahin. Of the different editions Zimmermann, 1960, is the best selection of data about the different ethnic groups. Cf. also Kirchhoff, 1956b.)

Much less is known about other areas in the southern part of the valley. Cuitlahuac has a population similar to that of Chalco, some of its people also coming from Xicco. The rulers were of Chichimec origin; they had the name of *tzompanteteuctin nahualteteuctin* (sorcerer chiefs) and traced their ancestry from Mixcoatl. They were credited with the founding of the four subdivisions of Cuitlahuac, each of which at the time of the conquest was ruled by its own tlatoani. The main gods of Cuitlahuac were Mixcoatl, Itzpapalotl, Amimitl, and Atlahua (Códice Chimalpopoca, pars. 84–85, 186, 209, 218, 222). Less is known about Mizquic. Its rulers claimed Toltec affiliation and the patron god was Quetzalcoatl (Durán, 1951, 1: 85; Historia de los mexicanos por sus pinturas, 3: 219).

The Xochimilca occupied a large area. In addition to Xochimilco itself, a number of towns along the southern slopes of the valley's mountain rim, from Tepoztlan to Tochimilco, were of Xochimilca affiliation (Durán, 1951, 1: 10-11, 113). The city of Xochimilco at the time of the conquest was divided into three parts, each with its own tlatoani. A long list of rulers exists, and collateral succession was practiced (Ixtlilxochitl, 1952, 1: 455–56), but little is known about the origin of the dynasty or its connections with the different local subdivisions or ethnic composition of the population. The patron goddess of Xochimilco was Quilaztli, another name of Cihuacoatl, described as the deer of Mixcoatl (Durán, 1951, 2: 171; Tezozomoc, 1944, p. 528; Historia de los mexicanos por sus pinturas, 3: 219). The fine-stone workers of Tenochtitlan claimed a Xochimilco origin (Sahagún, bk. 10, ch. 17).

The Mexica, the people who were to become the dominant power in central Mexico, are described in traditional histories as the latest in-migrants. Their culture during the migration period is clearly Mesoamerican, but their social standing was low as is shown by their lack of political power and their lack of a ruling lineage.

The place of origin of the Mexica was Aztlan, which is described as an island within a lake and from which the gentile name Azteca is derived. The culture of the migration Mexica included cultivation, the building of chinampas, clothes made of cloth, the building of temples, and a well-developed pantheon. Their patron god Huitzilopochtli was carried by four god-carriers (*teomama*); the building of his shrine was the main task at each stopping point in their migration. Huitzilopochtli spoke as an oracle, leading his people on, and the god is sometimes identified with an ancestral leader; he is also mentioned, however, as one of the four sons of the creating pair of gods and thus part of the basic Mesoamerican pantheon. From the beginning the Mexica are described as subdivided into calpulli, each devoted to the cult of a different god.

Like many other groups, the Mexica moved from their original home to Tollan and thence to the Valley of Mexico. In the neighborhood of Tollan the Mexica were located at Coatepec, where they fought the 400 Huitznahua, an event that was commemorated at Panquetzaliztli, one of the great monthly rituals.

The migration legends emphasize the search for a permanent settlement, which finally takes place in Mexico City, but it is also clear that other Mexica or people related to them settled in other areas. Early

in the migration the Michuaque and the Malinalca branched off; and, especially important, the settlement of the Mexica in Colhuacan was not only the source from which came the founders of Mexico City but also, after the downfall of Colhuacan, Mexica groups migrated together with the Colhua to the Acolhuacan and Cuauhtitlan.

The association of the Mexica with Colhuacan was of the greatest importance. The rituals of the cult of Toci in the month Ochpaniztli can be traced to this association. The final Mexica settlement in Mexico City comprised the twin cities of Tenochtitlan and Tlatelolco. Tenochtitlan obtained its first king and founder of its ruling lineage, Acamapichtli, from the Colhua. Although there are different versions about the precise ancestry of Acamapichtli, it is clear that the Mexica rulers derived their Toltec ancestry from the Colhua. When Colhuacan declined, Mexico Tenochtitlan took its place and the lineage of Acamapichtli became the main branch of the Colhua ruling line—a shift of capital and ruling lineage similar to that of the Tepanec from Azcapotzalco to Tlacopan, at the time when the Aztec empire was formed. Tenochtitlan also became one of the main partners in the Tepanec empire of Azcapotzalco. Tlatelolco, which had obtained as king a son of Tezozomoc, was another constituent city of the empire. The political development of the Mexica was thus not an independent evolution but the taking over of the older institutions of the Colhua and Tepanec.

The organization and growth of the Mexica-dominated Aztec empire is described in Article 15.

(The main sources on the Mexica are Tezozomoc, 1944, 1949; Durán, 1951; Chimalpahin; Relación de la genealogía; Origen de los mexicanos; Historia de los mexicanos por sus pinturas.)

In the eastern part of the central highlands, the areas around the Matlalcueye Volcano, the main ethnic components of the population were similar to those of the Valley of Mexico. Here again we read about an old Olmec population displaced by more recent waves of immigrants, among whom are groups of Toltec culture as well as Chichimec who arrive with a hunting economy.

The main cultural center of this region was the great city of Cholollan. The oldest population mentioned here is that of the Olmec Xicalanca, who were ruled by the Aquiach (Elder of the Above) and the Tlalchiach (Elder of the Ground). People from Tollan called Toltec-Chichimec moved to Cholollan as subjects of the Olmec but later took the city from them and assumed the name Chololtec. In order to consolidate their power and beat off the Xochimilca and Ayapanca, allies of the defeated Olmec, they brought in as allies Chichimec who helped them to defeat their enemies and settled in surrounding areas.

The Toltec-Chichimec arrived subdivided into a number of calpulli, which are the basis for five of the six major subdivisions of the city in conquest times. The sixth subdivision was that of the Colomochca, a people who moved in from the Mixteca. At the time of their migration to Cholollan the main gods and oracles of the Toltec-Chichimec were Quetzalcoatl and Tezcatlipoca. Although the two rulers, Aquiach and Tlalchiach, are first attributed to the Olmec, the same double rulership persisted until the conquest. The importance of the merchants and of the cult of Quetzalcoatl were distinctive features of Chololtec life.

(The main sources on Cholollan are Historia Tolteca-Chichimeca; Rojas, 1927; Durán, 1951, 1: 118 ff.; Torquemada, 1943–44, 2: 350–51. Cf. Kirchhoff, 1940.)

The Historia Tolteca-Chichimeca explains the arrival of Chichimec with a hunting culture to the Puebla area as a result of the trip of the Toltec-Chichimec leaders of Cholollan to Colhuatepec Chicomoztoc in order to bring them as helpers in their fight against the allies of the defeated Ol-

mec. Seven groups are mentioned as coming. The emphasis of this chronicle is placed on the Totomihuaque and Cuauhtinchantlaca who, after the defeat of the Olmec, settled in Totomihuacan, Cuauhtinchan, and Tepeyacac; but the seven groups also include the Texcaltec of Tlaxcallan and the Acolchichimec who settle in Huexotzinco.

These Chichimec are described as having no knowledge of cultivation in their original habitat (Historia Tolteca-Chichimeca, 1947, pp. 210–12, 263), but they were soon brought into the Toltec culture. The Chichimec leaders were invested with their offices by the two leaders of the Toltec officiating as Aquiach and Tlalchiach and they were given Toltec wives (ibid., p. 278). As in the Acolhuacan, groups of Toltec culture also settled among the Chichimec. Here there was a movement of Mixtec-Popoloca into the area; Toltec-Chichimec also came from Cholollan and established their own wards in Cuauhtinchan (ibid., pp. 322 ff., 338). As with other Chichimec groups of Puebla, Camaxtli is mentioned as the patron god of Tepeyacac (Papeles de Nueva España, 5: 29). (For these Chichimec tribes, see Kirchhoff's introduction to Historia Tolteca-Chichimeca.)

The historical traditions of the Tlaxcaltec were recorded by Muñoz Camargo. An older population of Olmec Xicalanca in this area were defeated and driven to the Zacatlan region (Muñoz Camargo, 1948, pp. 60–64). The Tlaxcaltec placed their origin at Chicomoztoc and they had the name Teochichimec. They settled for some time in Poyauhtlan in the southern Acolhuacan, where they were defeated by the Tepanec, Colhua, and Mexica, and started on a new migration that took some to Chalco (cf. the Totolimpanec of Chalco), others to Tollantzinco, and others beyond the mountains to Huexotzinco and Tlaxcallan (Muñoz Camargo, 1948, pp. 50–51). This tradition also connects these people with the Chichimec Poyauhtec of Ixtlilxochitl's history, who left the valley to settle in

Tlaxcallan and the Sierra de Puebla in order to escape the efforts of king Quinatzin of Tetzcoco to force upon them the civilized way of life (Ixtlilxochitl, 1952, 2: 56–57). The patron god of the Tlaxcaltec was Mixcoatl Camaxtli, who spoke to his people during their migration (Muñoz Camargo, 1948, pp. 45, 47, 50).

Tlaxcallan was subdivided into four parts, each ruled by a tlatoani. The first was Tepeticpac, from which the second, Ocotelolco, was established by a brother of the Tepeticpac ruler, who received half of the realm and of the relics of the patron god Camaxtli. The rulership of Ocotelolco, however, was later obtained in a revolt by people of Chichimec origin who had been for some time in Chololllan. Tizatlan was established by a member of the Tepeticpac dynasty at the time of the dynastic change in Ocotelolco. Quiahuiztlan was the last to be founded by later Chichimec arrivals from Tepetlaoztoc (Muñoz Camargo, 1948, pp. 81–82, 89–90, 95, 111). Because of the existence of four rulers in Tlaxcallan, it has often been called a republic. This is not different, however, from many other city states with several rulers of tlatoani rank such as Chalco and Xochimilco.

Another important city-state where the dominant population was of Chichimec origin is Huexotzinco. Unfortunately we have no native chronicle from this town, but it is clear that before falling to the Aztec empire it was a most important power in the Puebla area and as such had been allied to Tezozomoc of Azcapotzalco. The Tlaxcaltec tradition describes the settlement of Huexotzinco by Chichimec from Poyauhtlan, the same migration as that of the Tlaxcaltec, and Ixtlilxochitl derives the rulers of Huexotzinco from the Acolhua dynasty of Coatlichan (Muñoz Camargo, 1948, p. 60; Ixtlilxochitl, 1952, 1: 110). Again, as with other Chichimec, the patron god was Mixcoatl Camaxtli. Huexotzinco kept part of the relics of the god and had

a most important image and temple of the god (Muñoz Camargo, 1948, p. 82; Durán, 1951, 2: 127).

(The main glimpses into Huexotzinco history are reported in Códice Chimalpopoca. Cf. also Barlow, 1948c.)

The Nonoalca, after leaving Tollan, settled in areas of the south-central highlands: in the region of Itzocan (Izucar de Matamoros) that was known as the country of the Coatlalpanec, in the Tzoncoliuhcan area (Zongolica, Veracruz), and in the region that includes Teohuacan, Cozcatlan, and Teotitlan del Camino, a region that at the time of the conquest spoke Mazatec as well as Nahuatl. This latter area is one for which some fair ethnographic accounts are available. The main deities mentioned in the sources about Cozcatlan and Teotitlan are Cihuacoatl, Coatl (perhaps Quetzalcoatl), and Teiztapalli, a form of Xipe. The priests of this area were famous for the strictness of their abstinences. Teotitlan had three rulers of priestly titles and functions: a main one Teuctlamacaz (Lord Priest), Ecatlamacaz (Wind Priest), and Tetzatlamacaz (Priest of Tetzahuitl, Omen).

(The main sources for the Nonoalca of Puebla are Historia Tolteca-Chichimeca; Papeles de Nueva España, 4: 213–31; 5: 46–54; Motolinia, 1903, 69–72. Cf. Kirchhoff, 1940; Jiménez Moreno, 1942.)

To the north of Tlaxcallan, the Sierra de Puebla had a mixed population. The defeated Olmec of Chololllan and Tlaxcallan settled in this area, and because Zacatlan was one of their main locations the term Zacatec was applied to them. But Chichimec also settled in the area; two of the groups brought by the Chololtec, according to the Historia Tolteca-Chichimeca, were the Zacatec and the Tzauhtec (Kirchhoff, 1940).

The area of Zacatlan and beyond to the coast was also inhabited by the Totonac. According to a tradition from Zacatlan recorded by Torquemada (1943–44, 1: 278–

80) the Totonac left Chicomoztoc, went to Teotihuacan where they built the pyramids, and later settled in Zacatlan and expanded over the mountains to the coast. Later, Chichimec arrived, naked and eating raw meat, who were civilized by the To-tonac and took possession of part of the country.

(For Totonac history and ethnography see Krickeberg, 1933; Kelly and Palerm, 1952, pp. 16–23; Palerm, 1953.)

REFERENCES

Alva Ixtlilxochitl, 1952
Alvarado Tezozomoc, 1944, 1949
Anales de Tlatelolco, 1948
Aubin, 1885
Barlow, 1948c
Carrasco Pizana, 1950
Chimalpahin, 1889, 1949–52, 1958, 1965b
Codices: Chimalpopoca, 1945; Ríos, 1900
Dibble, 1951
Durán, 1951
García Granados, 1952–53
Historia de los mexicanos por sus pinturas, 1941
Historia Tolteca-Chichimeca, 1937–38, 1947
Ixtlilxochitl, see Alva Ixtlilxochitl
Jiménez Moreno, 1939, 1941, 1942, 1948
Kelly and Palerm, 1952
Kirchhoff, 1940, 1955, 1956b, 1961a
Krickeberg, 1933

Lehmann, 1938
León-Portilla, 1967
Motolinia, 1903
Muñoz Camargo, 1948
Nazareo, 1940
Olivera Sedano, 1956
Origen de los mexicanos, 1941
Palerm, 1953
Papeles de Nueva España, 1905–06
Pomar, 1941
Relación de la genealogía y linaje, 1941
Rojas, 1927
Sahagún, 1905–07, 1938, 1950–69
Seler, 1908
Tezozomoc, see Alvarado Tezozomoc
Torquemada, 1943–44
Zimmermann, 1960

20. Native Pre-Aztec History of Central Mexico

ROBERT CHADWICK

Toltec history, I shall try to prove, was copied from Mixtec codices (Jiménez Moreno, 1941, 1942, 1953a, 1953b, 1954–55). Evidence indicates that the story of Quetzalcoatl and Huemac in Tollan in the Códice Chimalpopoca is actually the history of the First and Second Dynasties of Tilantongo, which is related in Codices Bodley 2858, Selden 3135 (A.2), Vindobonensis (reverse), Nuttall, Becker, and Colombino, and the "Mapa de Teozacoalco."

We are assuming in this article that Caso's interpretations of the Mixtec codices are basically valid (1949, 1950b, 1951, 1954b, 1955a, 1955b, 1956b, 1958a, 1958b, 1958c, 1958d, 1960b, 1960c, 1960d, 1961a, 1961b, 1962b, 1963, 1964a, 1964b, 1964c, 1966a, 1966b, 1966c, 1967, 1969). Should this assumption be proved to be untenable, some of the correctness of my hypothesis would, of course, be undermined.

Other investigators have also recognized that the Toltec and Mixtec histories probably have a common denominator. Not only has Jiménez Moreno, the scholar who has concerned himself most with Toltec history, voiced the opinion that this is so, but he has also pointed out the possibility that Mixcoatl of the Aztec chronicles (Quetzalcoatl's father in some versions) might be the person called 8 Deer "Tiger's Claw" by Caso in the Mixtec codices (cited by Dahlgren de Jordán, 1954, p. 85). I shall attempt to show that the "Topiltzin" (i.e., Quetzalcoatl) of Ixtlilxochitl, not Mixcoatl, is the person called 8 Deer in the codices.

The common foundation of Mixtec and Toltec history has been mentioned by Covarrubias (1957, pp. 293–94), Robertson (1959), Dahlgren de Jordán (1954, p. 84), Bernal (1958a, pp. 6–7), Ruz (1945, p. 45), and Paddock (1966d, p. 380). I have previously shown that the Mixtec not only participated in Toltec culture, but also probably formed one of the ethnic groups in Teotihuacan (Chadwick, 1963, 1966, 1967, 1970, in press *a*, *b*).

To the best of my knowledge, the idea that the story of Quetzalcoatl in the chronicles also appears in the Mixtec codices in the story of the "war against the stone men"

474

(also called the "war that comes from heaven") was first stated by Spinden (1935, p. 439). This version of the Quetzalcoatl story is the one related by Torquemada (1943–44; 1964, pp. 13–17; see also Paddock, 1966d).

Spinden suggested that the "stone men" in the Mixtec codices "may be the *Tepehuani* or Toltecs who conquered the Mixtec region" (cited by Caso, 1960b, p. 29). Caso has stated that Spinden's idea is "a chronological possibility since the Toltec or inhabitants of Tula had already appeared upon the Mesoamerican scene by 859" (*ibid.*).

Beginning in 1949, Caso described, in most of his interpretations of the Mixtec documents, the various appearances of Quetzalcoatl (for example, Caso, 1960b, pp. 51–58; 1963; 1964a, p. 74, genealogical chart).

THE CHRONICLED VERSION

The Jiménez Moreno reconstruction of Toltec history is based mainly on the account given in the Aztec document called Anales de Cuauhtitlan or Códice Chimalpopoca, dating from 1570 (Kirchhoff, 1955, p. 164; 1964; Lehmann, 1938; Velázquez, 1945; Garibay K., 1953–54, 1: 53–54). Earlier documents which contain similar versions are the "Relación de la Genealogía y Linaje de los Señores de la Nueva España" (possibly written in 1531–32) and the "Origen de los Mexicanos," dated 1532 (García Icazbalceta, 1891, 1942). The writers of the last two documents are unknown. Garibay believes that possible authors of the Anales de Cuauhtitlan are Pedro de San Buenaventure and Alonso Begerano, natives of Cuauhtitlan who collaborated with Sahagún (Garibay, 1953–54, 2: 278). One other source, similar in content but not used by Jiménez Moreno in his reconstruction, is "Das 'Memorial breve acerca de la fundación de la ciudad de Culhuacan' von Domingo de S. Antón Muñon Chimalpahin" Lehmann, 1958).

Briefly, the story related in these documents with which we are concerned tells of Quetzalcoatl's being enthroned as both priest and king of a place called Tollan (Velázquez, 1945, par. 33); his subsequent vicissitudes as ruler (par. 34–50), which include incest with his sister Quetzalpetlatl while drunk; and his struggles against three "demons" called Tezcatlipoca, Ihuimecatl, and Toltecatl. Finally, Quetzalcoatl leaves Tollan in disgrace and proceeds to the coast, where he is said to have committed suicide (par. 50). It is also stated that he became the planet Venus.

Following the banishment of Quetzalcoatl, Códice Chimalpopoca lists five other rulers over a period of 168 years. At the end of this time the incumbent, Huemac, migrated from Tollan during a war begun in A.D. 1063. Huemac served first as priest of Quetzalcoatl and then as king, at which time he took the name Atecpanecatl (Velázquez, 1945, par. 58; Kirchhoff, 1964, pp. 84–85).

Since Huemac, according to such sources as Sahagún, Torquemada, Muñoz Camargo, Chimalpahin, the "Histoire du Mechique," and the "Leyenda de los Soles" (see Kirchhoff, 1955, 1964), is identified with Tezcatlipoca and is said to have lived during the life of Quetzalcoatl, this situation has caused Kirchhoff to comment that the Códice Chimalpopoca version is "found to be dismembered into two parts and therefore appears totally disfigured" (Kirchhoff, 1964, pp. 84–85; see also Kirchhoff, 1955; Jiménez Moreno, 1953a; 1954–55). Códice Chimalpopoca places persons considered as contemporaries in other sources nearly a hundred years apart. In Jiménez Moreno's reconstruction, the Quetzalcoatl-Tezcatlipoca battle occurs during the early period of Tollan, whereas the Huemac tale is placed at the end of the city's history. He has stated that Huemac was first a priest of Quetzalcoatl, but later became a partisan of the forces of Tezcatlipoca, thus indicating that these two "dynasties" lasted for a considerable period of time (Jiménez Mo-

475

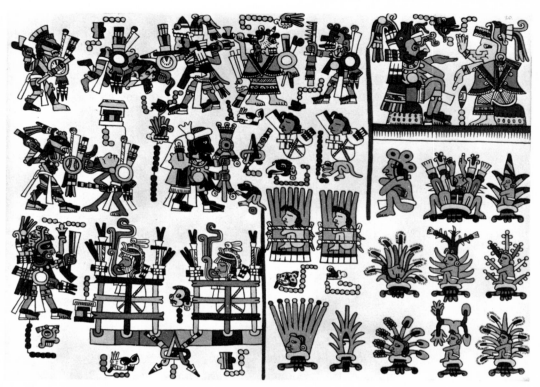

FIG. 1—WAR OF THE STONE MEN. 9 Grass "Skull," aided by 9 Wind "Flint" (Tezcatlipoca), fights against the "stone men," led by 9 Wind "Stone Skull" (Quetzalcoatl). (Codex Nuttall, pl. 20, top center.)

reno, 1953a). He thus rejects the idea that they were contemporaries. Kirchhoff (1955, 1964) tries to explain these discrepancies as due to the use of different native calendars.

I shall try to show that the Códice Chimalpopoca version is basically correct, but actually tells the histories of the First and Second Dynasties of Tilantongo in the Mixteca Alta, not Tollan.[1] The identification of Tollan will be dealt with in the final section of this article.

TOLLAN AND TILANTONGO

Evidence indicating that the Tezcatlipoca-Quetzalcoatl battle of Códice Chimalpopoca and Torquemada also appears in Codex Nuttall on page 20 has been published (Chadwick, 1967, pp. 17–39; in press a, pp.

1–32; in press b, pp. 1–84; Codex Nuttall). According to my interpretation, one of the two "Quetzalcoatls" shown on page 20 of the Nuttall, called 9 Wind "Stone Skull," may be identified with the dynasty of Quetzalcoatl; the other, called 9 Wind "Flint," may be identified with the dynasty of Tezcatlipoca. These persons appear in combat in what Caso calls the "war with the stone men" in the Nuttall and the "war which comes from heaven" in the Bodley (fig. 1).

To substantiate my further hypothesis that the Códice Chimalpopoca version was

[1] I wish to express my appreciation to Alfonso Caso and Wigberto Jiménez Moreno, from whom I learned Mexican documentary history. Without their work, no hypothesis such as is presented here would have been possible. It is they who are *los maestros de todos nosotros en estos asuntos.*

476

copied from Mixtec codical accounts of the First and Second Dynasties of Tilantongo, I note that, according to the Chimalpopoca, the Toltec began their career in a year 1 Rabbit, or A.D. 726 (Acosta, 1956–57, chart, p. 106). The Mixtec, according to the reverse of the Vindobonensis, began their history in 720 (Caso, 1950b, p. 12).[2] Torquemada begins Toltec history in 700 (1964, p. 13).

Further, according to the Chimalpopoca, Quetzalcoatl was born in a year 1 Reed, or 843 (Acosta, *ibid.*; Jiménez Moreno, 1941, chart facing p. 82). The Vindobonensis (reverse) and the Nuttall give the date of birth of 9 Wind "Stone Skull" (i.e., Quetzalcoatl) as 838 and 841, respectively, the latter date being only two years earlier than that given in the Chimalpopoca (Caso, 1960b, p. 29). The founder of the First Dynasty of Tilantongo is 9 Wind "Stone Skull," who previously engaged in a battle against 9 Wind "Flint" during which the rulers of a place called "Mountain-that-Opens-Bee-Sun" were slaughtered. It is this event, according to Caso (1960b, p. 58), "which permitted *Tilantongo* to establish itself as the metropolis of the Northern Mixteca."[3]

Other similarities between the Aztec and Mixtec versions include the fact that Quetzalcoatl became king of Tollan in a year 5 House, or 873, according to the Chimalpopoca (Jiménez Moreno, 1941, chart facing p. 83; Acosta, 1956–57, chart, p. 106), and we know that 9 Wind "Stone Skull's" enthronement in Tilantongo took place immediately after the defeat of the rulers of Mountain-That-Opens in 875, a year 6 Reed, or two years later than the Aztec date (Caso, 1960b, pp. 30, 57; see Table 1).

In Codex Bodley the "war with the stone men" began in 868 and ended seven years later. It may be more than coincidental then that the "Historia de los mexicanos por sus pinturas" of 1530–40 (Garibay, 1953–54, 1: 51; 1965a) states that Quetzalcoatl (here called Ce Acatl) did seven years

of penance before becoming king in Tollan. Also, according to Chimalpahin, Topiltzin Acxitl Quetzalcoatl left Tollan in 882 (Rendón, 1965, p. 65), seven years after 9 Wind "Stone Skull's" victory in the Bodley. According to the Relación de la genealogía, Quetzalcoatl became king of Tollan in 883, a year 2 Reed (Jiménez Moreno, 1941).

Further evidence that the dynasty of Tollan in Códice Chimalpopoca is connected with the First Dynasty of Tilantongo in Mixtec codices comes from the fact that the second rulers of both Tollan and Tilantongo also have the same calendrical name (as did the first pair of rulers). Quetzalcoatl is succeeded by a Matlacxochitl (who reigned 895–930), according to the Chimalpopoca; 9 Wind "Stone Skull" is succeeded by his son, 10 Flower "Tiger," in Codex Bodley (Acosta, 1956–57; Caso, 1960b, p. 30). Ma-

---

[2] The correlation of the native dates in the chronicles with dates in our calendar was accomplished by Jiménez Moreno (Jiménez Moreno and Mateos Higuera, 1940). Jiménez Moreno, however (1954–55, p. 222) believes that the dates in the Anales de Cuauhtitlan should be corrected by the addition of three cycles of 52 years in some cases, two 52-year cycles in others. I see no good reason for this correction, and accept the chronicle dates in this paper (cf. Jiménez Moreno, 1953b, for his chronology of the Historia Tolteca-Chichimeca). The correlation of the Mixtec and Christian chronologies is that of Caso (1951).

[3] I have interpreted the element "Mountain-that-Opens," which alternately shows a man or two hands opening a hill glyph, as the probable glyph for Tepeji de la Seda not only because a similar glyph for that place is recorded in Codex Mendocino (without a man or hands, however); but also because Tepeji means "hill of the hand" or *Po.tha²'hna²'* in Chocho-popoloca (Fernández de Miranda, 1961, p. 446). The "Staircase" element, which appears in the Bodley 36-35-34-I and Nuttall 22, I have identified as Cholula partly because Cholula is "Ñundiyo" in Mixtec or "Town of Stairs" (cf. Caso, 1960b, p. 28). The "Bee" element possibly is the glyph for Magdalena Jicotlan (Byers, 1967, fig. 19) northeast of Coixtlahuaca. There is a gloss, Xicotla, with the Bee glyph in the Lienzo de Santiago Ihuitlan (Caso, 1961a, p. 242); *Bee* or *Xicotla* can be located in the general area of Coixtlahuaca (*ibid.*). Thus, "Mountain-that-Opens-Bee-Sun-Staircase" seems to refer to a confederation, probably to the area conquered by Tezcatlipoca (Torquemada, 1964, p. 17).

TABLE 1—GENEALOGIES OF TOLLAN AND TILANTONGO

TOLLAN CHIMALPOPOCA LIST	*TILANTONGO* FIRST DYNASTY
Birth of Quetzalcoatl, 843 Reign of Quetzalcoatl, 873–895 Reign of Matlacxochitl, 895–930 Reign of Nauhyotzin, 930–946 Reign of Matlaccoatzin, 946–973 Reign of Tlicehuatzin, 973–994	Birth of 9 Wind "Stone Skull," 841 Reign of 9 Wind "Stone Skull," 875?—? (886?, marriage) Reign of 10 Flower "Tiger" (birth, 888; marriage, 909) Reign of 12 Lizard "Arrow Legs" (birth, 939) Reign of 5 Movement "Falling Smoke" 972–994? Life of heir apparent 2 Rain 971–992 SECOND DYNASTY
Huemac, 994–1063 (Chimalpopoca) Topiltzin, 1031–1063 (Clavijero, Ixtlilxochitl)	Reign of 5 Alligator, 994–1030 Reign of 8 Deer, 1031–1063
Interregnum, 983–1031 (Clavijero)	5 Alligator, 983–1030 (see text)
A "Quetzalcoatl," co-regent with Huemac, 1029–1051 (Chimalpahin)	12 Movement, regent in Tilantongo, 1030–1051
Huemac, 994–1051 Cuauhtli, priest of Quetzalcoatl, 1029–1051 (Chimalpahin, cf. Kirchhoff, 1964, p. 88; Velázquez, 1945, par. 58)	5 Alligator, 994–1030 10 Cuauhtli, 1029, defeats protector of 2 Rain; he is married to a "Quetzalcoatl" (9 Wind) and is the father of a "Quetzalcoatl" (1 Reed); see Table 2. 1051, first marriage of 8 Deer. (1051–1029=22 years, reign of first "Quetzalcoatl" in Chimalpopoca)
Clavijero	*Caso* FIRST DYNASTY
Totepeuh, 823–875 (father of Quetzalcoatl in several sources) Nacaxoc, 875–927 Mitl, 927–979 Queen Xiuhtzaltzin, 979–983	Birth of 9 Wind "Stone Skull," 841 Reign of 9 Wind, 975?—? Birth of 10 Flower, 888 Birth of 12 Lizard, 939 Coronation of 5 Movement, 972 Life of 2 Rain, 971–992 1 Buzzard "Tlaloc Skirt" (see text); she is the mother of the first king of the Second Dynasty, and a member of the royal family of Tilantongo SECOND DYNASTY
Interregnum, 983–1031 (in other sources Tecpancaltzin is said to be the ruler following the four-year reign of Queen Xiuhtzaltzin: Topiltzin [1031–1063] is the natural son of Tecpancaltzin)	5 Alligator, 983–1030 (see text) 8 Deer, 1031–1063

NOTE: The dates for the kings of Tollan through Huemac are from the Códice Chimalpopoca (Acosta, 1956–57). The dates for the Mixtec kings are from Caso (various). The second part of the table compares the king list from Clavijero (1964) with that of the Mixtec kings. I believe that the king list in the Chimalpopoca is that of the "Quetzalcoatl dynasty"; that in Clavijero (1964), Ixtlilxochitl (1952), and Veytia (1944) is that of the "Tezcatlipoca dynasty." Correlations are explained throughout this article. See note 10.

tlacxochitl means 10 Flower (Jiménez Moreno, 1953a, p. 29). In 888, 10 Flower of Tilantongo was born and in 909 began to reign (or was married) (Caso, 1960b, Table VI).[4]

Another indication that Toltec history as recorded in the Chimalpopoca was copied from Mixtec codices is the fact that the fourth ruler of Tollan was named Matlaccoatzin or 10 Snake (see Table 1). The importance of this to our argument is that the fourth ruler of Tilantongo, 5 Movement "Smoke Descending from Heaven," began his reign on the day 10 Snake—the name of the fourth ruler of Tollan who ended his reign a year after 5 Movement began to rule (Caso, 1960b, p. 31; Acosta, 1956–57, p. 106). Although this is not a one-to-one correlation, I believe it may explain why, during the reigns of the third and fourth rulers of Tollan (Nauhyotzin, who reigned 930–946, and Matlaccoatzin, 946–973), there was only one king in Tilantongo, 12 Lizard "Arrow Legs," who was born in 939.

The dates of the reigns of the fifth and fourth rulers of Tollan and Tilantongo, Tlicehuatzin and 5 Movement, respectively, are almost identical. Tlicehuatzin ruled 973–994; 5 Movement, 972–994 (Acosta, 1956–57; Caso, 1960b, p. 31). Although we do not know the date of 5 Movement's death, the first king of the Second Dynasty, 5 Alligator (who defeated 5 Movement) was finally confirmed as king in 994, a year 8 Rabbit (Caso, 1960b, p. 32; Codex Nuttall, p. 42). These concordances of dates again indicate that the histories of the two cities are related.

[4] It is important to note that in the Histoire du Mechique of 1543, Quetzalcoatl is said to have been accompanied by Matlacxochitl (10 Flower) to Quauhquechollan where the latter remained (cf. Kirchhoff, 1955, p. 167; Garibay, 1965a, p. 115). Since 10 Flower's wife came from a town called Temple of White Flowers in the Bodley (Caso, 1960b, p. 30), and since a white flower is part of the glyph for Cuauhquecholan-Macuilxochitepec in the Codex Mendocino, I believe that this might indicate a connection between the Temple of White Flowers (*Yucuita* in Mixtec) in the codices and Cuauhquecholan in the chronicles.

Further evidence that leads to the same conclusion is provided by the story of 5 Movement's son, 2 Rain "20 Tigers," who should have become the fifth king of the First Dynasty of Tilantongo. The son 2 Rain was born in 971 and died in 992 at the age of 21, the same length of time that Tlicehuatzin ruled in Tollan (Caso, 1960b). The first Quetzalcoatl ruled 22 years.

According to Caso (1960b, p. 76), "The second crisis in the history of the Mixtecs occurred at the death of the last king of the First Dynasty of *Tilantongo*. . . . The succession did not normally pass to his son 2 Rain '*Ocoñaña*,' the child of another wife; instead *Tilantongo* was conquered by 5 Alligator '*Tlaloc-Sun*' or '*Tlachitonatiuh*,' who became its king and founded the Second Dynasty. . . . '*Oconaña*' was sacrificed in 992." (See Table 2.)

Probably the most impressive evidence that the Tollan story in Códice Chimalpopoca is the same as that of the First Dynasty of Tilantongo is the fact that 2 Rain dies in the same manner as Quetzalcoatl: he commits suicide and then goes to heaven as the planet Venus (Velázquez, 1945, par. 50; Caso, 1960b, p. 32; fig. 2.)

Fig. 2—2 RAIN "TWENTY TIGERS" GOES TO HEAVEN AS THE PLANET VENUS. (From Codex Bodley, 1960, p. 5-I. Drawn by Colin Bibler.)

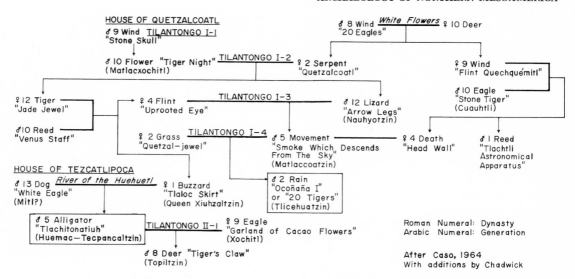

TABLE 2—Genealogical Correlation of "Toltec" and Mixtec Royalty. (Drawn by Colin Bibler.)

It is important to note here that the Bodley scene, in which 2 Rain kills himself before the lord 7 Vulture "Xolotl" at a place called "River of the Tree and the Serpent," shows a painted red band in the water-tank element in the place glyph (Codex Bodley, pp. 5–6–I). This may be why other sources say that Quetzalcoatl disappeared into the Red Sea (Caso, 1961b, p. 93).

It seems possible, too, that the place glyph read by Caso as "River of the Tree and Serpent" might be the glyph of Coatzacualco where Mendieta (1945, 1: 92) says Quetzalcoatl finally disappeared. Although I am not certain of the exact translation of Coatzacualco, it probably could be translated as "River of the Serpent," since "coatl" in Nahuatl means "serpent." Jiménez Moreno (1953a, p. 27) has pointed out that today in Coatzacualco the memory of Quetzalcoatl probably remains in the folklore about "un señor católico."

I am unable to understand, however, why this story appears with the first "Quetzalcoatl" in the Chimalpopoca, and not with Tlicehuatzin whose dates coincide with those of 2 Rain "Ocoñaña." This problem should be explored further. In any event,

the dates and other similarities in the careers of 2 Rain and Tlicehuatzin, in addition to the manner of death of 2 Rain and Quetzalcoatl, indicate that more than coincidence is involved.

Before proceeding with the similarities between the careers of Huemac of Tollan, the successor of Tlicehuatzin, and 5 Alligator of Tilantongo, the usurper who becomes the first king of the Second Dynasty, I must point out that the main reason behind the death and conquest of 2 Rain "Ocoñaña" was that "the second marriage of his father gave succession rights to the descendant of a queen who did not belong to the dynasty. Her son could rightfully be challenged as hereditary king by the other pretenders who were the sons of princesses belonging to the *Tilantongo* dynasty. . . ." (Caso, 1960b, p. 32; see Table 2).

The next and perhaps most important correlation between the dynasties of the two cities comes with the last king of Tollan, Huemac, and the first king of the Second Dynasty of Tilantongo, 5 Alligator. First, both kings began their rule in the same year, 994: 9 Rabbit in Códice Chimalpopoca, 8 Rabbit in the "Mapa de Teoza-

480

coalco" (Acosta, 1956–57, p. 106; Caso, 1960b, p. 36).[5] Second, both 5 Alligator and Huemac were usurper kings. Although Códice Chimalpopoca does not provide this evidence about Huemac, it does tell us that his name as king was Atecpanecatl (Velázquez, 1945, par. 58). Therefore, since the versions of the Relación de la genealogía and the Origin de los mexicanos both state that Quetzalcoatl's (here called Topiltzin) father Totepeuh (elsewhere called Mixcoatl) was killed by his brother-in-law Atecpanecatl, we see that Huemac was also a usurper (García Icazbalceta, 1891; 1942, pp. 242, 261–62).

This person is called Apanecatl in the Leyenda de los soles of 1558 (Paso y Troncoso, 1903; Lehmann, 1938; Velázquez, 1945; Yáñez, 1964). Although some discrepancies remain in correlating all the events and persons in the various chronicles, we believe that Chimalpahin's statement that Totepeuh, the king of Culhuacan, placed his son Huemac on the throne of Tollan probably can be considered an official version which covered up the murders and usual political "sins" inherent in any palace revolt (Kirchhoff, 1964, p. 88).[6]

Many other similarities between the histories of the two cities may be found. For example, we know that Huemac first was a priest of Quetzalcoatl, but when he lost that position and became king, taking the name Atecpanecatl, he was a partisan of the Tezcatlipoca forces (Velázquez, 1945, par. 58; Jiménez Moreno, 1953a, p. 29). Since the First Dynasty of Tilantongo belonged to the House of Quetzalcoatl (Chadwick, 1967), the validity of our reconstruction depends on proof in the codices that the Second Dynasty of Tilantongo had Tezcatlipoca as its patron (see Table 2).

The only other appearance of 9 Wind "Flint" (i.e., Tezcatlipoca) in Codex Nuttall after page 22 occurs on page 42 *immediately preceding the appearance of 5 Alligator*, thus indicating that the Second Dynasty was connected with the House of

Tezcatlipoca (Codex Nuttall, p. 42; see Caso, 1966a, fig. 3c). Caso has pointed out (1950b, p. 17) that 9 Wind "Flint" was the *"conquistador de Tilantongo."*

There is other evidence which equates Huemac (5 Alligator) with the dynasty of Tezcatlipoca. According to Chimalpahin (Lehmann, 1958, p. 8), Huemac was born from the earth. Thus, he was not one of the overlords born from trees who conquered the region. Lévi-Strauss (in Leach, 1966) has pointed out that autochthonous heroes are very commonly lame. One of the attributes of Tezcatlipoca in the ritual codices of the Borgia group is a mirror substituted for a foot (fig. 8). Caso (1964a, p. 85) suggested that the nickname of a personage in Codex Selden 3135 (A.2), "Lame Tiger," perhaps should be translated as Tezcatlipoca. I have shown (1967, pp. 24–25, 30–31) by another procedure that this translation probably is correct. (Jiménez Moreno [1953a, p. 29] states that Huemac was another name for the god Tezcatlipoca.)

Caso's interpretations verify and explain our view of this change in dynasties. First of all, 5 Alligator was a descendant of 9 Wind "Stone Skull" (Quetzalcoatl) on his mother's side since she (1 Buzzard "Tlaloc Skirt") was the niece of the third king of the First Dynasty (Caso, 1960b, p. 33; Tables 1 and 2). As Caso has stated (1964a, p. 81), "5 Alligator '*Tlachitonatiuh*,' who manages to become lord and founds the Second Dynasty in *Belching Mountain* (*sic*), establishes his claims through the female side of his family." This probably can

---

[5] Jiménez Moreno has demonstrated that in the Mixtec system the year name has the same sign as in the Aztec system, but the coefficient is one less (Caso, 1951, p. 49). Elsewhere Jiménez Moreno (1954–55, p. 224) has observed that the Mixtec system was 12 years earlier than the Mexican system. He states that it is difficult to know which system the Toltec followed. I accept the chronicle dates at face value in this article (see Article 8).

[6] It is only in Chimalpahin's "Memorial Breve" that Totepeuh is said to be the father of Huemac. In other versions, Totepeuh is said to be the father of Topiltzin, generally considered to be the same as Quetzalcoatl.

be correlated with Códice Chimalpopoca's statement (Velázquez, 1945, par. 45, 58) that Huemac married Coacueye, identified in the same chronicle as the mother of Quetzalcoatl.[7]

As further proof that the change in dynasty involved a shift of power to the Tezcatlipoca side of the family is the fact that 1 Buzzard's husband, an outsider, came from a place called "River of the Drum-Tiger Throne and Stone Leg" (Caso, 1960b, p. 33); this is the place glyph shown with the grandchildren of 9 Wind "Flint" in the Bodley 2-I. It is important to note also that one of 9 Wind "Flint's" grandchildren appears in the Vindobonensis (reverse) II–2–3, with the name "Smoking Mirror," which means "Tezcatlipoca" (Caso, 1960b, p. 27).

As pointed out above, both Huemac and 5 Alligator began to rule in the same year, 994, 9 Rabbit in Códice Chimalpopoca; 8 Rabbit in the Mapa de Teozacoalco (see note 5). Although Huemac lived until 1070, his reign was effectively ended in 1063 when war began in Tollan (Acosta, 1956–57). Since 5 Alligator's son, 8 Deer "Tiger's Claw," died in the same year that Huemac fled from Tollan (Caso, 1960b, p. 42), the actual reign of Huemac covers the same time span as the combined reigns of 5 Alligator and 8 Deer. It is for this reason that we suspect that the story of Huemac in Códice Chimalpopoca actually is a compilation of the histories of the two Mixtec kings. This idea perhaps is corroborated by Torquemada (1964, p. 10) who states that Tecpancaltzin (another name for 5 Alligator–Huemac) was also called Topiltzin (another name for 8 Deer; see below).

5 Alligator–Huemac and the Tututepec Glyph

The most important evidence which shows that the persons in the Aztec documents with whom we are concerned are protagonists copied from Mixtec codices, is presented in the following paragraphs.

Smith (1963, 1966) has shown convincingly that 8 Deer ruled the province of Tututepec on the south coast of Oaxaca. In her translation of the Mixtec annotations on Codex Colombino she has added to our knowledge of the Mixtec place glyphs, although there is almost no direct tie-in between the glosses and the glyphs in the pre-Hispanic pictorial. According to Nicholson (1968, p. 285), only three of the annotations seem to relate directly to the place glyphs: Yucudzaa-Tututepec, Jicayan-Tulixtlahuaca, and Santa Maria Acatepec. Smith's identification of Santa Maria Acatepec as "Yucuyoò" or "Hill of the moon" I question.

One of the most important Colombino place glyphs for our purposes is the one with the gloss "Yucudzaa," which is the Mixtec name for San Pedro Tututepec or "Hill of the Bird" (Nicholson, 1968, p. 281; Smith, 1963, 1966). Since there is evidence in the Aztec documents that Huemac, considered here to be 5 Alligator, the father of 8 Deer, received that name in a place called "Yucudzaa" in the same year in which 5 Alligator was invested with "royal insignia," i.e., 987, we believe that our argument is greatly strengthened (Caso, 1960b, p. 79; Lehmann, 1958, p. 8; Jiménez Moreno, 1962a, p. 98).

First of all, Chimalpahin (Lehmann, 1958, p. 8) states that Huemac received that name in Tototepec, and that he was also married there. Jiménez Moreno (1962a, p. 98), in his study of the Mixtec place glyphs, gives the Mixtec name of Yucudzaa for Tototepec. This is apparently the same annotation read by Smith, and identified by her as Tututepec. Tototepec means, she says, "en (el) cerro (de los) pájaros," and

---

[7] This might indicate why the Quetzalcoatl Venus story appears with the first Quetzalcoatl in the Chimalpopoca, and not with 2 Rain's counterpart, Tlicehuatzin. It is interesting that Coacueye means "Snake Skirt" whereas 1 Buzzard's nickname is "Tlaloc Skirt."

Yucudzaa has a similar meaning—"Cerro (de) pájaros." Peñafiel also (1967, p. 222) translates Tototepec in an identical manner—"Lugar de las aves." The illustrated Peñafiel glyph shows one bird posed on top of a hill glyph. The glyph identified by Smith as Tututepec in several codices is also a hill and/or temple with one bird. The Colombino glyph, quite complicated, has been described by Smith (1963, 1966).

"Yucu" means hill in Mixtec, and "dzaa" means beard or "el mentón" (Caso, 1962b, pp. 115, 151). Smith has explained why the annotation "Yucudzaa" should be translated as Tututepec, and since Tototepec in Mixtec is also "Yucudzaa," we accept her identification because the substitution of o in Tototepec for u in Tututepec provides no linguistic problem. Garibay (1961, p. 25) has stated that "en las vocales . . . el sistema de representación es uniforme en los manuscritos. Sólo por lo que toca a la o-u hay variedad, pero esto no depende de que se siga diverso sistema, sino de su carácter intermedio. Es la razón de que se halle en el mismo autor. Sahagún, por ejemplo: *uncan, oncan, ompa, umpa,* etcétera."

Therefore, we believe that Huemac's receiving his name in a place which can be translated as Yucudzaa in the same year in which 8 Deer's father received royal insignia must be more than coincidental. This is particularly true since 8 Deer himself ruled from a place called Yucudzaa, generally believed to be Tututepec.

Further indications in the chronicles support the suggestions made here. Later in this article we show that Ixtlilxochitl's Tecpancaltzin (see Table 2) can be equated with both Huemac and 5 Alligator, and that his son, Topiltzin, is the great Mixtec warrior, 8 Deer "Tiger's Claw." Since Ixtlilxochitl (1952, 1: 55, 88–89) states that Topiltzin's subjects fled to a place called Tototepec following his death, this indicates that we are not dealing merely with coincidences. Further, the two rulers who supported Topiltzin as king rather than the

more legitimate heirs were from Totolapan (also spelled Totolopan), which we believe is the former Cuitlatec province (Ixtlilxochitl, 1952, 1: 54, 72). Topiltzin's mother (here equated with Ixtlilxochitl's "Xochitl") was also killed in Totolapa (Ixtlilxochitl, 1: 70; see note 8), and we know that Mixcoatl (here equated with 5 Alligator–Huemac–Tecpancaltzin; see below) conquered Pochutla on the southern Oaxacan coast not far from Tututepec (Jiménez Moreno, 1966, map 7, fig. 4). Finally, Ixtlilxochitl states that one of Topiltzin's armies was garrisoned in the southern land of the Tlahuicas in a nearby region (Ixtlilxochitl, 1952, 1: 52).

Chimalpahin (Lehmann, 1958, p. 8) gives the names of Huemac's father- and mother-in-law. As we shall show below (see also Table 2), there is great confusion in the codices regarding the wives of 5 Alligator-Huemac. Chimalpahin gives the names of the parents of Huemac's wife (he does not give the name of the wife) as Teton and Maxio. To the best of my knowledge, these names appear in no other Aztec chronicle.

What is important to our argument here is that Chimalpahin informs us that Teton and Maxio were given these names in a place called Metztitlan, which in Mixtec is Ñuu-yoo or "Lugar o tierra (de la) luna" (Jiménez Moreno, 1962a, p. 92; Caso, 1962b, p. 128). Another of Smith's translations of the glosses in the Colombino "is that which identifies a temple (XII–36) just before a place-glyph representing the moon on a hill (XIII–37) as 'yucu yoo'" (Nicholson, 1968, p. 285). According to Smith (1966), Yucu-yoò was and is the Mixtec name for Santa Maria Acatepec, northeast of Tututepec. She suggests that this place might have rivaled Tututepec, and that therefore it was conquered by 8 Deer.

Although I am well aware of Smith's ability, and know that she collected most of her data on the south coast of Oaxaca, I believe that her identification of Santa

F<small>IG</small>. 3—"CULHUACAN" PLACE GLYPH SHOWN AT LEFT. The "Culhuacan" or "Twisted Hill" glyph is one of the elements in the toponym for Cuilapan, Oaxaca. (Codex Nuttall, pl. 19,*a*.)

Maria Acatepec as the Hill of the Moon in the codices may be in error.

In the first place, Acatepec in Mixtec is Yucutnuyoo (Yucu, 'hill'; tnu, 'of'; yoo, 'reed' or 'tule'; Caso, 1962b, p. 152; Jiménez Moreno, 1962a, p. 87). Yucutnuyoo means "Cerro del carrizal" or Hill of the Reeds; i.e., it is actually another name for Tollan just as are the names of such cities as Acatlan, Teotihuacan, Tula, and Toluca.

Therefore, if I am correct in assuming that Huemac ruled from Tututepec, and that his parents-in-law received their names in Metztitlan, it would seem more logical that this "Ñuu-yoo" is the Hill of the Moon which played such an important role not only in Codex Colombino, but also in Bodley and perhaps Selden, and therefore is not Santa Maria Acatepec as proposed by Smith. The Peñafiel "Catálogo Alfabético" (1967, p. 40) shows Acatepec as a hill glyph with what appear to be two tules or espadañas in addition to the acatl or reed sign: "El signo *acatl*, caña, sobre la terminación *tepec*, 'en el lugar poblado acatl,' 'en el cerro del carrizo.'" I suggest solely as an hypothesis that the important city where 5 Alligator–Huemac's in-laws lived, Metztitlan or "Ñuu-yoo," possibly is the

Hill of the Moon glyph in the codices; it could therefore be the present-day pueblo of Nuyoó just south of the Trique region and east of Putla (cf. Nader, 1969, fig. 1). Although I am aware of Smith's statement that Santa Maria Acatepec is today called Yucuyoò, some further investigation is needed to explain why the meaning of Acatepec and Yucu-tnu-yoo is the same both in Nahuatl and in Mixtec, and why neither means Hill of the Moon, according to the Reyes dictionary. It may be that we are dealing with dialect differences, and we know that among the Mixtec, according to Caso (1967b, p. 196, citing Alvarado, 1593, fol. 139v), the moon was called *Yyacaa huiyu* or the Lord 2 Reed, which is the calendrical name of Tezcatlipoca on page 14 of Codex Nuttall. According to Alvarado (*ibid.*), the word for moon was "yoo, y en su gentilidad la llaman los Indios yyacaa huiyu." Today there is a town called S. L. Yucuyoo southeast of Tulixtlahuaca, the place Smith considers to be the Tollan of Codex Colombino (Donald Robertson, unpublished information, 1969).

As noted above, Huemac was born from the earth, and therefore would be one of the (tay) nisino nuhu (Caso, 1962b, p. 124;

Lehmann, 1958, p. 8), or ancient Mixtec, and not a member of the group of overlords (born from trees) who conquered the Mixtec region around A.D. 700, and who may have been Cuicatecs (Jiménez Moreno, 1962a, p. 54). Since Tututepec or Tototepec (there are two Tututepecs on the south coast of Oaxaca) may at one time have been populated by Chatino (DeCicco, 1969, fig. 1), and since Nuyoò, our postulated home of Huemac's in-laws, is near the Trique region (Nader, 1969, fig. 1), it is possible that the change of dynasties discussed in this article may have involved the replacement of one linguistic royal family by another. There is the fascinating possibility, too, that 5 Alligator and 8 Deer may have been Zapotec; I discuss below the stela depicting a person called 8 Deer at Monte Alban. What is now clear is that the Mixtec codices obviously depict persons in many instances of linguistic affiliations other than Mixtec.

8 Deer and the Culhuacan-Cuilapan Glyph

Huemac in the Chimalpopoca can also be connected with 8 Deer in the Mixtec codices by showing that a place name associated with Huemac can be identified with the glyph in the codices where 8 Deer meets his death. This can be shown in the following way: the Códice Chimalpopoca states that the "Tezcatlipoca" who came to beleaguer Huemac Atecpanecatl once lived in Tzapotlan (Velázquez, 1945, par. 58). Since this is apparently the Tzapotlan of the Leyenda de los soles, mentioned as one of the conquests of Mixcoatl and his son 1 Reed, we know that this place is Zaachila (ancient Teotzapotlan) in the Valley of Oaxaca (fig. 4; Jiménez Moreno, 1966, p. 107; Yáñez, 1964, p. 26). The importance of this to our argument is that Caso has provided evidence that the place where 8 Deer died in 1063 probably was Cuilapan near Zaachila (Caso, 1966b, p. 329). The relación of Cuilapan tells us that this place was given as a dowry to the ruler of Teotzapotlan

(Zaachila) (ibid.). Jiménez Moreno suggested previously that Mixcoatl, the conqueror of Zaachila, might be 8 Deer. Mixcoatl also conquered Pochutla on the south coast of Oaxaca, in the same general region as Tututepec, 8 Deer's south coast capital (cited in Dahlgren de Jordán, 1954; Jiménez Moreno, 1966, p. 78, map 7; see fig. 4). Totepeuh means "nuestro conquistador" (Jiménez Moreno, 1954–55, p. 222). Totepeuh is generally considered to be another name for Mixcoatl.

The validity of our idea that the Tzapotlan of the Chimalpopoca may be equated with Cuilapan-Zaachila in the codices is strengthened when it is pointed out that one glyphic element in the toponym for Cuilapan is the Culhuacan or "twisted hill" element, and we know that Huemac's father, Totepeuh, ruled in a "Culhuacan" (Paddock, 1966c, pl. 12, which depicts the probable glyph for Cuilapan-Culhuacan, according to Caso; Kirchhoff, 1964, p. 88; see fig. 5; see note 6).

Further proof that some of the towns mentioned in the Chimalpopoca in the Huemac story were in Oaxaca, rather than in the Valley of Mexico, is also provided by the same document. For example, the personage Cuauhtli, who replaced Huemac as priest of Quetzalcoatl, was the guardian of Atzompan, one of the towns connected with Zaachila in which Mixtec were installed (Paddock, 1966d, p. 375; Velázquez, 1945, par. 66). Although there may be some doubt that the Cuauhtli of paragraph 66 is the same person as the Quauhtli of paragraph 58, I have assumed here that they are one and the same.

In any event, what is most important to our argument is the fact that Cuauhtli is said to be the "guardian of Atzompan," and analysis of the following paragraph indicates that these "guardians" were natives of towns in Oaxaca rather than inhabitants of places in the Valley of Mexico. For example, in paragraph 67, it is said that in ancient Cuauhtitlan a personage named Ato-

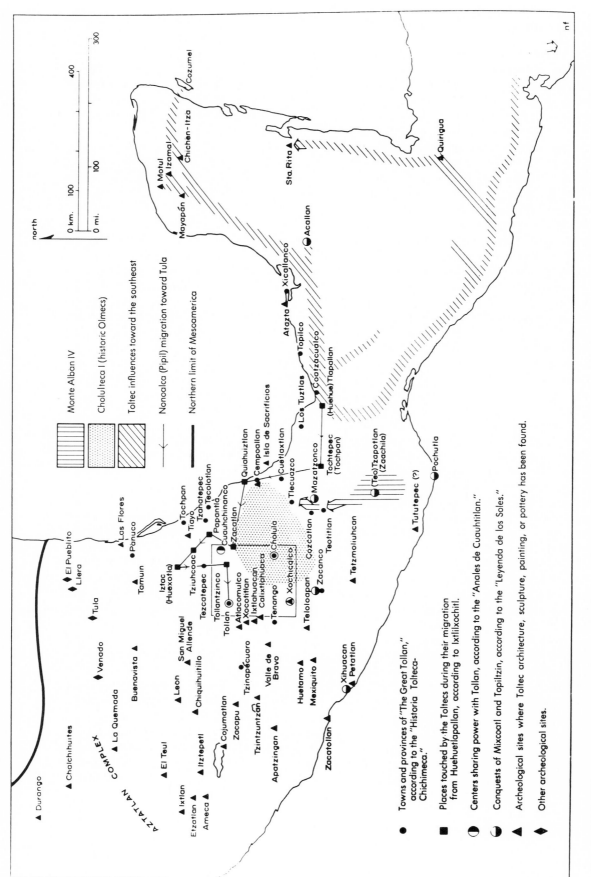

Fig. 4—MAP SHOWING CONQUESTS OF MIXCOATL. According to the *Leyenda de los Soles*, Mixcoatl conquered Teotzapotlan (Zaachila) in the Valley of Oaxaca. (After Jiménez Moreno, 1966, Map 4, p. 107.)

nal, a native of Tamaçólac, was the guardian there. Atonal or Atonaltzin ("The Lord of the Day Water") was a dynastic name in Mixtec Coixtlahuaca in Oaxaca (Art. 29; Caso, 1960b, p. 69, note 45). Further, in the same paragraph, the town Tamaçólac is listed after Teotitlan and Coixtlahuaca, thus indicating that the place in question was in Oaxaca. Whether or not the personages mentioned actually were "guardians" of towns near Tula is uncertain. We know that it was the native tendency to focus attention on one's home town; therefore, it seems likely that this was the procedure followed here by the Indian scribes. (See note 15.)

The fact that the Relación of Cuilapan mentions a Chapoltepec (in the Chimalpopoca, Huemac is said to have killed himself in the cave of Chapultepec, generally considered to be in the Valley of Mexico), a league and a half from Cuilapan, probably strengthens our case (Barlow, 1945c). This could be the present-day barrio of San Juan Chapultepec at the foot of Monte Alban (John Paddock, personal communication, March 6, 1969). Since we know that the native authors of the Chimalpopoca had codices at their disposal, and since we know that the meaning of some of the names of Aztec barrios in Oaxaca was the same in Aztec and Mixtec (e.g., Xochimilco), it would have been plausible to read a Yucutica (Hill of the Grasshopper, i.e., Chapultepec) glyph in Aztec with the same meaning that it would probably have had in Mixtec (Jiménez Moreno, 1962a, p. 93; M. E. Smith, 1966, p. 153). In other words, the place glyphs in the Mixtec codices seem to have been so drawn that they could be read in several languages, a situation not dissimilar to Chinese script.

Caso, however, has provided evidence that 8 Deer was sacrificed in Cuilapan, and, although it is possible that he could have been buried in San Juan Chapultepec, I believe that another hypothesis is the more likely. The 16th-century Relación of Cuilapan states that it was called Ynchaca in

Mixtec. It further states that when the Mixtec settled at this site, "it was not called Ynchaca as it is today, but Sayucu, which means 'at the foot of the hill' " (Butterworth and Paddock, 1962, pp. 38–39). Sayucu is the Mixtec name, given by Fr. Antonio de los Reyes in his "Arte en Lengua Mixteca," for Cuilapan (Caso, 1962b, p. 131).

Some of the confusion here can be resolved when it is noted that Ynchaca is a barrio of Cuilapan (Butterworth and Paddock, 1962, p. 55). The importance of this is readily seen when it is pointed out that Ynchaca is said to be a contraction of two words: "yncha, which is river, and tica, which is either a bell or the quacuyol (sic, grasshopper); but instead of saying Ynchatica, they say Ynchaca. Thus the town was named as it was either because of the river which runs through it, making a sound like the tinkling of a bell, or because of the quacuyoles. The latter seems more probable because of the name of the town in Mexican" (ibid., p. 38). I am unable to account for the linguistic confusion here, but tica means "grasshopper" on the south coast, according to Smith (1966). Therefore, apparently the barrio of Ynchaca in Cuilapan can be translated to mean Chapultepec.

If this is correct, then Caso's designation of the glyph of Cuilapan as the place where 8 Deer met his death is undoubtedly correct, and I suggest that the tomb of the great conqueror, 8 Deer, should be searched for in the barrio of Ynchaca. The fact that Stela 4 at Monte Alban depicts a man named 8 Deer standing on a place glyph and thrusting a lance into it (Paddock, 1966e, p. 202, note 11, fig. 149) may indicate that 8 Deer probably conquered some of the towns in Oaxaca.

This type of suggestion is now possible for the historical anthropologist since Caso has shown that the tombs of Zaachila contain the bodies of rulers who are depicted in Codex Nuttall with the "Culhuacan" glyph (Caso, 1964a, p. 87; 1964c; Codex Nuttall, p. 33, which shows the lord 5 Flow-

FIG. 5—PROBABLE GLYPH FOR CULHUACAN-YANHUITLAN, OAXACA. The Lord 5 Flower (left of temple) probably was buried in Tomb 1 in Zaachila. The royal family of Zaachila originally came from Yanhuitlan. (Codex Nuttall, pl. 33; Caso, 1966b, p. 319.)

er with the Culhaucan-Yanhuitlan glyph; he probably was buried in Tomb 1 in Zaachila; see fig. 5).

Further evidence in the codices supports the idea that 8 Deer conquered in this region. Codex Bodley, for example, states that in 1053, 8 Deer married a princess from the town of Skull-Grecas (Caso, 1960b, p. 40). The death of 8 Deer comes about as the result of his attacking part of the domain of his second wife (from Skull or Mictlan, i.e., place of the dead); his funeral is presided over by his brother-in-law, also from Skull. Further, he is succeeded by the son of his second wife, thus bypassing the rightful heir, the son of his first wife (Caso, 1960b, pp. 40–42). Caso has stated that Skull probably is Mictlantongo (*ibid.*). I believe that is possible therefore that Skull-Grecas (the

only appearance of Skull in which the stepped-fret motif is prominent is in connection with 8 Deer's second wife) probably is the glyph for Mitla. Caso (1965a, p. 870, fig. 32), in describing the mural paintings in Mitla, has pointed out that one mural depicts "the deer with two heads which, according to legend preserved by the Mexicans, was the god Mixcoatl," the personage who has been equated by Jiménez Moreno with 8 Deer. If our hypothesis that Skull-Grecas is Mitla is correct, then Caso's idea that 8 Deer met his death in Cuilapan probably is strengthened, and is further verified by our translation of the barrio of Ynchaca in Cuilapan as Chapultepec, the name of the cave in which Huemac is said to have hanged himself.

In this context, we note again that a "Cul-

TABLE 3

TOLLAN	MIXTECA
Huemac, 994–1063 (reign)	5 Alligator, 994–1030 (reign)
Topiltzin, 1031–1063 (reign)	8 Deer, 1031–1063 (reign)
(Clavijero, Ixtlilxochitl)	
Tecpancaltzin, 983–1031	5 Alligator, 983–1030 (see text)
(Ixtlilxochitl)	
Interregnum, 983–1031 (Clavijero)	
A "Quetzalcoatl" co-regent	12 Movement, regent in Tilantongo, 1030–1051
with Huemac 1029–1051	10 Cuauhtli defeats 2 Rain, heir to the throne,
(Chimalpahin)	1029 (see text); 8 Deer's first marriage, 1051
	(see text)

huacan" is mentioned in several versions with Totepeuh prior to the establishment of his son, called both Topiltzin and Huemac, in Tollan (see note 6). The importance of this is seen when it is pointed out that 9 Wind "Flint" (of the "Tezcatlipoca dynasty") is shown as the main personage in Nuttall 19a (the page immediately preceding the Quetzalcoatl-Tezcatlipoca battle) and that the most important glyph on this page is also a "Culhuacan" (see fig. 3). Nuttall (1902, p. 31) mentioned previously that a woman in Nuttall 19a held "a curious curved symbol, resembling the hieroglyph of the town of Colhuacan." Thus, we see that the "Tezcatlipoca dynasty" apparently ruled in Oaxaca for a considerable time.

Tecpancaltzin and Topiltzin in Ixtlilxochitl

There is evidence also that the Huemac story is that of Topiltzin and his father "Tecpancaltzin," in Alva Ixtlilxochitl (1952) and Veytia (1944). The proof of this allows further correlations with the codical version of 8 Deer. (Note the similarity between the names "Tecpancaltzin" and Atecpanecatl.)[8]

The idea that the story of Huemac in the Chimalpopoca is the same as that of Tecpancaltzin and his son Topiltzin in Ixtlilxochitl and Veytia is seen to be valid when it is pointed out that two personages appearing in connection with Huemac, Maxtla and Cuauhtli, also are characters in Ixtlilxochitl and Veytia. They appear as the two rulers who remain faithful to Topiltzin in his last battle. They are also the ones who swear him in when his father decides to relinquish the throne to his natural son (Kirchhoff, 1955, pp. 174, 188–89).

In the Chimalpopoca, Huemac is said to

[8] The fact that Ixtlilxochitl has a version similar to that of the Chimalpopoca is because this codex was in the possession of Alva Ixtlilxochitl! It seems to have passed from his family to Carlos de Sigüenza, who bequeathed it to the Colegio de Jesuitas in Mexico City, where it was discovered by Boturini (Velázquez, 1945, p. xi). Apparently Ixtlilxochitl's handwriting appears on the document, for Boturini considered him the author. Garibay (1953–54, 2: 279–80) states that if the marginalia were those of Ixtlilxochitl, he did not write the document but simply used it in compiling his own work. It is known that Sigüenza inherited some of the works of Torquemada also, and that Boturini had access to both collections. Veytia, too, made use of these documents (Jiménez Moreno, 1962b, p. 82). We know that Clavijero read the Relación of Valeriano, which had once been owned by Ixtlilxochitl (Cuevas, 1964, p. xii); he also used Boturini's manuscripts. I am unable to explain why he omitted the name Tecpancaltzin from his king list, for it appears in both Ixtlilxochitl and Veytia.

We thus make the following correlations: Huemac–Tecpancaltzin–Interregnum–5 Alligator; Topiltzin–8 Deer; Tecpancaltzin–Xochitl–5 Alligator–9 Eagle "Garland of Cocoa *Flowers*," i.e., *Xochitl*; and Queen Xiuhtzaltzin–1 Buzzard. Queen Xiuhtzaltzin was the mother of Tecpancaltzin, and grandmother of Topiltzin; 1 Buzzard "Tlaloc Skirt" was the mother of 5 Alligator, and grandmother of 8 Deer. She is the only person who possibly could have been considered the Queen Mother during the time of the change in dynasty because it was through her that her son established his right to rule. See Tables 2 and 3.

have killed himself in the cave of Chapulte-pec. This story can be equated with the Ixtlilxochitl version of Topiltzin's final days which also occur in a cave called Xicco (Velázquez, 1945, par. 69; Ixtlilxochitl, 1952, 1: 54). Thus, it seems fairly obvious that the tale of Huemac of Tollan in the Códice Chimalpopoca is the story of Topiltzin in Ixtlilxochitl and Veytia.

The evidence also points to the fact that Huemac in the Códice Chimalpopoca may be identified with both 5 Alligator and his son 8 Deer in the codices. Since the same king list, which appears in Ixtlilxochitl and Veytia also appears in another source, that of Clavijero (1964), with one important difference, we may assume that Clavijero's story of "Topiltzin" also is connected (see note 8). The dates of Huemac's reign, as well as other dates connected with personages during this time in the Chimalpopoca and other chronicles, when compared with dates in the lives of 5 Alligator and 8 Deer bear this out (Table 3).

First of all, we know that Huemac ruled from 994 to 1063, leaving Tollan when war broke out, but he did not die until 1070 (Acosta, 1956–57). The rights of 5 Alligator, on the other hand, to the throne of Tilantongo were recognized only in 994, although he had received new insignia in 983, and royal insignia in 987 (Caso, 1960b, p. 79). Although 8 Deer apparently never ruled in Tilantongo (as will be explained below), he did receive the domain of "Eagle Warrior of Stone," now identified as Tututepec, in 1031, and he died in 1063 (Caso, 1960b, p. 39; M. E. Smith, 1966). Thus we note again the actual reign of Huemac in Tollan covers the exact time span of the reigns of 5 Alligator and his son 8 Deer. Perhaps this explains Torquemada's statement (1964, p. 10) that Topiltzin and Tecpancaltzin were the same person.

The dates assigned here to "Topiltzin" must also be explained because Ixtlilxochitl gives many sets of dates that are often contradictory and confusing.[9] In the first place,

[9] For example, Ixtlilxochitl gives as one of the dates for the destruction of the Toltec and thus the probable date for the death of Topiltzin, the year 959, which is exactly one calendar round of 52 years earlier than the birth of 8 Deer in the Bodley (Ixtlilxochitl, 1952, 1: 72; Caso, 1960b, p. 37). In another place, Ixtlilxochitl (1: 54) dates the destruction of the Toltec in 1011, the date of the birth of 8 Deer. It is hardly coincidental that the dates of the life of 8 Deer span exactly one calendar round of 52 years. It is possible that Ixtlilxochitl followed a dating system which in some cases was two calendar rounds earlier than that which Caso has established for the Bodley.

With respect to the dates of Queen Xiuhtzaltzin's reign, 979–983 (taken from Clavijero), one should note that although we do not have the dates of 1 Buzzard's life, we know that she was a niece of 12 Lizard, the third king of Tilantongo, who was born in 939. She was also a cousin of 5 Movement, who began to reign in 972. Therefore, we may assume that 1 Buzzard lived during the time asisgned by Clavijero to Queen Xiuhtzaltzin's reign. According to Clavijero's dates, she died in 983. It therefore seems significant that 1 Buzzard's son, 5 Alligator, received new insignia in the same year.

Ixtlilxochitl gives two names for some of the rulers, beginning with Mitl or Tlacomihua. For example, he calls Topiltzin by the name of Meconetzin also (1952, 1: 46); Vaillant (1966, p. 95) has

Ixtlilxochitl (Vaillant, 1966)		Clavijero (1964)	
Chalchiuhtlanetzin	510–562	Chalchiuhtlanetzin	667–719
Ixtlilcuechahuac	562–614	Ixtlilcuechahuac	719–771
Huetzin	614–666	Huetzin	771–823
Totepeuh	666–718	. . .	. . .
Nacoxoc	718–770	Totepeuh	823–875
Tlacomihua	770–826 (829)	Nacaxoc	875–927
Queen Xiuhquentzin	826–830	Mitl	927–979
Iztaccaltzin	830–875 (885)	Queen Xiuhtzaltzin	979–983
Meconetzin	875–959	Interregnum	983–1031
Mitl	927–979	Topiltzin	1031–1063
Queen Xiuhtzaltzin	979–983		
Tecpancaltzin	983–1031		
Topiltzin	1031–1063		

I have chosen the date 1031 from Clavijero for the beginning of the reign of "Topiltzin" not just because it "fits" with the codical chronology, but because Clavijero is the only chronicler to infer that the period between 983 and 1031 was an interregnum, and the reasons for this can be explained from the codices (Clavijero, 1964, p. 49). Although I may be accused of "rigging the evidence," I believe the reasons for choosing these dates are valid. The date of "Topiltzin's" death is taken from Ixtlilxochitl, and is the date when the ruler following "Topiltzin" (i.e., Xolotl) parcels out land to his vassals (Ixtlilxochitl, 1952, 1: 93). The same objection may be applied here, but I feel that this is a valid procedure in view of all the similarities between the codical and chronicle versions (see note 9).

The dates of the interregnum, 983–1031 (taken from Clavijero), seem appropriate since 5 Alligator's reign could, in fact, be considered an "interregnum." For example, we know that 5 Alligator was actively attempting to gain the throne of Tilantongo, beginning as early as possibly 969, but that he received insignia in 979, new insignia in 983, royal insignia in 987, and had his rights finally recognized in 994 (Caso, 1960b, pp. 36, 79). Because 5 Alligator was a usurper king, and because we have evidence that a regent ruled in Tilantongo following his death, it is highly possible that his "reign" was considered an "interregnum" (Caso, 1950b, p. 26; 1966a, p. 139), at least by the "Quetzalcoatl" side of the family.

Other evidence supports this idea. For example, 5 Alligator appears in Codex Nuttall 26 married to 9 Eagle "Garland of Cocoa Flowers" (Caso, 1966a, p. 119); on the same page his second wife, 11 Water, appears. The glyph for Tilantongo does not appear on this page. In Codex Bodley (7-III to 7- 8-V), the usual glyph for Tilanton-

---

reconstructed the dates of his reign as 885–959. I believe the beginning date should be 875. In any event, when one compares the Ixtlilxochitl list (as reconstructed by Vaillant) with the Clavijero list, it becomes apparent that we are dealing with two sets of rulers.

I have placed the Ixtlilxochitl list (with some changes in dates which will be explained) alongside the Clavijero list, putting the Clavijero rulers opposite rulers with the equivalent time span in the Ixtlilxochitl list. In addition, four rulers—those for whom two names are given in Ixtlilxochitl—have been added to the Ixtlilxochitl list with their dates, which will be explained below. As an indication that Ixtlilxochitl did "compress" two lists into one, we note that he (1952, 1: 35), in the earlier chronology, states that Iztaccaltzin was the father of Topiltzin; it is noted by the editor of the Ixtlilxochitl edition that Iztaccaltzin is called Tecpancaltzin elsewhere.

From the lists it is apparent that Iztaccaltzin and Totepeuh are the same person, both being considered fathers of a "Quetzalcoatl" in several versions. Here, in the Ixtlilxochitl list, Iztaccaltzin (Mixcoatl, Quetzalcoatl's father, is called Iztacmixcoatl in some sources) is seen as the father of a "Quetzalcoatl," called Meconetzin, who is also called Topiltzin. The list also indicates that we have an earlier and later "Quetzalcoatl," i.e., Meconetzin (875–959, who can be equated with 9 Wind "Stone Skull") and Topiltzin (1031–1063, who can be equated with 8 Deer).

I have followed Vaillant's dates for the first five rulers; for the sixth, however, Tlacomihua, I have used the date 826 for the end of his reign rather than Vaillant's 829 because there is a conflict in Ixtlilxochitl's dates which I believe may be reconciled by using the date 826. Ixtlilxochitl (1952, 1: 35) states that Tlacomihua ruled 59 years rather than the traditional 52, and died in 826; elsewhere (1:37) he says that Tlacomihua died in 822. After Tlacomihua, I have adjusted Vaillant's dates accordingly, e.g., giving four years to the first queen's reign (1: 35, 38, 46) etc., ending the chronology, like Vaillant, in the year 959 (1: 72). The earliest of the three dates Ixtlilxochitl gives for the destruction of the Toltec is 959, the others being 1004 and 1011 (1: 70, 54). He also indicates (1: 81, 93) that Xolotl parcelled out land to his vassals in 1063, immediately following Topiltzin's death, which shows that his chronology actually is the same as that established by Caso in Codex Bodley and other works. I have used the Clavijero dates for the double-named rulers I added to the Ixtlilxochitl list.

I feel that this is the correct procedure because it seems that Ixtlilxochitl confused the two dates for the death of Tlacomihua, 822 and 826, and somehow converted this discrepancy into the extra seven years of his reign, i.e., $770 + 59 = 829 - 7 = 822$; $826 - 822 = 4$; $829 - 826 = 3$; $4 + 3 = 7$. Further, since Totepeuh ended his reign in 875, according to Clavijero, I judge that this date, which is ten years earlier than that given by Vaillant, is correct. Obviously a complete explanation must await treatment in a book-length exposition.

go does not appear with 5 Alligator; also the Bodley considers his second wife to be his first (Caso, 1966a, p. 120). An analogous scene does not appear in Codex Colombino, although it is possible that it may have been painted on one of the two missing pages of that document (M. E. Smith, 1966, p. 167). The two marriages are mentioned in the Vindobonensis (reverse) with certain discrepancies; again, 5 Alligator does not appear with the usual glyph for Tilantongo but with the glyph Caso calls House of Heaven, represented by a temple whose door is closed by a curtain with a sky band above (Caso, 1966a, p. 120; 1950b, p. 28). The only instance in which 5 Alligator appears on the same page with the usual glyph for Tilantongo, to the best of my knowledge, is in Codex Nuttall 42, but here 9 Wind "Flint" is seated over the Tilantongo glyph. Further, since the next appearance of the Tilantongo glyph is on Nuttall 53d above 8 Deer, but in suspect circumstances (see below), it seems highly possible that 5 Alligator may never have been fully recognized as king of Tilantongo (Smith, 1966). The fact that his son 12 Movement seems to have been only the regent of Tilantongo, according to Caso (1966a, p. 139), points to the probable validity of my interpretation of 5 Alligator's reign as an "interregnum."

If this interpretation is correct, then it is highly possible that 5 Alligator's mother may be Queen Xiuhtzaltzin (the mother of Tecpancaltzin) of the chronicles, the only queen mentioned (Ixtlilxochitl gives her two names) in any of the king lists extant (see note 9). This would be logical because Caso (1960b, p. 33) has said of 5 Alligator's mother: there was a princess of Tilantongo, 1 Buzzard "Tlaloc Skirt," "the aunt of 5 Movement (the last king of the first Dynasty) . . . upon whom the rights of succession must have been considered to fall" (see Table 2).

It can hardly be coincidental that Tecpancaltzin's wife was called Xochitl, and

that 5 Alligator's second wife (the mother of 8 Deer) is also nicknamed "Xochitl" or "Flower" (i.e., the aforementioned "Garland of Cocoa Flowers"). The fact that she is regarded as the second wife of 5 Alligator is analogous to the situation of "Xochitl" in the chronicles as the common-law wife or concubine of Tecpancaltzin (Ixtlilxochitl, 1952, 1: 44, 71). It is due to this, I believe, that 8 Deer's half-brother was the one who became regent of Tilantongo (see Tables 1 and 2).

Further correspondences between the chronicled and codical versions exist. For example, according to Chimalpahin, a "Quetzalcoatl" ruled as co-regent with Huemac from 1029 to 1051 (Kirchhoff, 1964, p. 88). This can be directly correlated with the Chimalpopoca version of Huemac as well as with the history of 8 Deer in the codices. We have stated previously that Huemac in the Chimalpopoca was first a priest of "Quetzalcoatl," but that he was replaced in this position by one Cuauhtli, also mentioned with Topiltzin in Ixtlilxochitl.

In Selden 3135 (A.2) there is a Cuauhtli or Eagle who appears in 1029 (the year in which a "Quetzalcoatl" became co-regent with Huemac). He attacks the defender of 2 Rain "Oconaña" (Caso, 1964a, p. 80). Since this man 10 Eagle (the brother of the third king, 12 Lizard, and "the only male descendant of the *Tilantongo* kings") was married to a woman with the calendrical name of Quetzalcoatl, 9 Wind, and also had a son with the other calendrical name of Quetzalcoatl, 1 Reed, it seems quite likely that he is the Cuauhtli of the chronicles (Caso, 1960b, p. 32; 1964a, pp. 80–81; see Table 2). This man was the king of Belching Mountain, which we believe is Atzompan in the Valley of Oaxaca.[10]

[10] Although Codex Bodley indicates that 2 Rain died in 992, the Selden chronology established by Caso shows that he was still alive in 1029. It is for this reason that I believe the Selden chronology is incorrect by one cycle of 52 years in certain instances.

I have given the years 1030–51 as the period of a probable regency in Tilantongo. Since 8 Deer first took a wife in 1051, prior to that time, he could not have produced a legitimate pretender to that throne (Caso, 1960b, p. 40). Also, this date provides another direct correlation with the Topiltzin story in the chronicles because 8 Deer was 40 years old when he first married (*ibid.*).

In Veytia (1944, p. 192) Topiltzin is said to have been 40 years old when he first married, and 40 when he began to reign. Ixtlilxochitl (1952, 1: 46–47) states that Topiltzin was more than 40 years old when he succeeded to the throne; also, that he had governed 40 years when signs presaging the fall of Tollan began. I believe these statements probably can be correlated with those in the Leyenda de los soles (Yáñez, 1964, p. 18) which say that 1 Reed was 40 years old (plus 15, plus 1, according to the indigenous author's reading of the codices) when he left Tollan.

The evidence again points to the fact that not only is the story of Huemac in the Códice Chimalpopoca that of both 5 Alligator and his son 8 Deer; it also indicates that the story of Tecpancaltzin and his son Topiltzin in Ixtlilxochitl, Veytia, and Clavijero is just another version. Further evidence confirms this.

Although none of the aforementioned chronicles indicate that Huemac was a great conqueror, as were 5 Alligator and 8 Deer, Torquemada states (1964, p. 13) that Huemac left Tollan to conquer and win lands throughout his reign. Owing to his continuous absence, another person was chosen to reign in his stead. This probably confirms the idea of an interregnum in Tilantongo during 5 Alligator's "reign." If it be provisionally accepted that 8 Deer and Ixtlilxochitl's "Topiltzin" are one and the same, further weight may be added to this hypothesis by comparing Ixtlilxochitl's text further with the codical life of 8 Deer. For example, in Ixtlilxochitl, Topiltzin sends his three principal enemies a *tlachtli* or ball

court during a peaceful three-year period just prior to the final battle in which he is defeated. Since there is evidence that these enemies were lords of an area which 8 Deer is now known to have ruled, this adds considerable strength to the validity of our argument.

The enemy lords ruled the nation of the Hueytlapancecas (Veytia, 1944, p. 189). Tlapanec was spoken in an extensive area of Guerrero just north of Mixtec- and Amuzgo-speaking regions in pre-Hispanic times (Marino Flores, 1958–59, map). Two of Mixcoatl's conquests were Pochutla and Xihuacan on the coasts of Oaxaca and Guerrero, respectively (Jiménez Moreno, 1966, map 7; fig. 4). According to Ixtlilxochitl (1952, 1: 54), one of the places of importance during Topiltzin's last battle was Totolopan; today there is a municipio of San Miguel Totolapan in Guerrero (Marino Flores, 1958–59, p. 98). Since 8 Deer ruled the province of Tututepec on the south coast of Oaxaca, and is shown in Codex Nuttall 80 undertaking an ocean voyage, this indicates that the battles of 8 Deer and Topiltzin could have occurred in the same area (cf. Jiménez Moreno citation in Dahlgren de Jordán, 1954).

The ball court that Topiltzin sent to his enemies, mentioned above, has a bearing on our argument. The only representation of a ball court as a purely architectural feature occurs in the Bodley with 8 Deer just prior to his becoming king of "Eagle Warrior of Stone," now identified as Tututepec (Caso, 1960b, pp. 38–39; 1966a). Further, in Nuttall 45, 8 Deer appears with a ball court immediately preceding the Tututepec glyph, and the glyph there has the added element of a ball court (Codex Nuttall, p. 45d). Smith (1966, p. 166) believes that 8 Deer won Tututepec as a result of this ball game. The foregoing indicates further that Topiltzin could be the same person as 8 Deer. Garibay (1964a, p. 89, note 6) states that the ball court (a place glyph associated with 8 Deer) shown in Nuttall 74 has the same colors as that described by Ixtlilxochitl.

Other similarities between the chronicles and codices exist. Codex Bodley states that a war began in which 8 Deer participated in 1046, and that he conquered a place called Xipe Bundle three years later (Caso, 1960b, p. 40). The chronicles, on the other hand, relate that the last war of Topiltzin took place after a 10-year truce, and lasted three years (Veytia, 1944, p. 205). Since no further mention of war appears in the Bodley until 1063, we believe that the coincidences are too many not to have meaning.[11]

[11] There is one other date and event in the chronicles which may be correlated with the codical account. Veytia states that in the year 13 Rabbit, Topiltzin sends ambassadors who give presents to his three enemies and thus wins the 10-year truce. If Veytia (1944, p. 199) is using a count which is 52 years later than the codical correlation, the date would be 1050. It seems especially significant then that the Bodley states that in a year 12 Rabbit (1050) 8 Deer "makes an offering to the lord 13 Rabbit 'War Eagle' which consists of a bowl of pulque" (Caso, 1960b, p. 40). In connection with 8 Deer's Guerrero enemies, it is noteworthy that in the Tlacotepec region of that state, which shares a migration legend with the vanishing Cuitlatec of Totolapan, a story has been recorded about how "there had once been a king (*sic*) named Camolutla in the Costa Grande, near Tixtlanzingo, and how he emigrated along the same route because of lack of water" (Barlow, 1945d, pp. 72–73). Although we cannot definitely connect this king with 8 Deer, such a conjecture seems plausible. This becomes clearer when we note that in the Tlacotepec migration legend, one of the leaders, Hueytlacatl, also found an egg with a hole in a rock and devoured it alone. That is why the hill is called Totoltepec (*ibid.*, p. 71). According to Ixtlilxochitl (1952, 1: 55), one of the places where Topiltzin's subjects fled was a town called Tototepec. Chimalpahin (Lehmann, 1958, p. 8) includes mention of a Tototepec in connection with Huemac, thus indicating again connections between that person and Ixtlilxochitl's Tecpancaltzin. Another of the migration leaders in the Tlacotepec legend changed himself into a serpent and made a lake, "which he had not been allowed to form on the plain of Ixtlahuacan. This is the Lake of Tuxpan" (Barlow, 1945d, p. 72). Although we cannot definitely connect this lake with 8 Deer, it is nonetheless interesting that during the battle for Xipe Bundle, 8 Deer is seen in Codex Nuttall 75 as a member of an expedition "against a hill which rises from a river or lake" (Caso note in Wicke, 1966, p. 342, fig. 11). This might be the Lake of Tuxpan mentioned in the Tlacotepec migration legend.

8 DEER, RULER OF TILANTONGO?

As stated earlier, I believe there is some doubt that 8 Deer ever ruled in Tilantongo, based on the fact that in Codex Nuttall 53, 8 Deer makes his first appearance with the usual Tilantongo glyph. This appearance is suspect because the figure of 8 Deer was painted over an erased place glyph (Donald Robertson, personal communication, 1968; Robertson and Chadwick, in preparation). Even though no erasures were apparent to Robertson on page 68 where the Tilantongo glyph and 8 Deer also appear, it should be noted that the Tilantongo glyph there rests on another hill glyph, and 8 Deer stands on a glyph which may be read in part as 5 House. We are unable to read the determinant (cf. Smith, 1966, pp. 167–68).

The appearance of 8 Deer in suspect circumstances with the Tilantongo glyph occurs on the page following the one in which he is made a *tecuhtli*. This place is usually referred to as Tula by Caso; the *tule* glyph appears with that place in the Bodley and Colombino codices. The Nuttall scene does not have a place glyph, but it gives other indications of where this ceremony took place.

According to Caso (1966a, p. 129), Nuttall 52 "says that two other individuals were present at this ceremony—both of whom wear the white bezote of the Puebla-Tlaxcala region. . . ." The Relación of Cholula (*ibid.*) states that ". . . the priests of Quetzalcoatl who governed that city were the ones who confirmed the authority of governors and rulers, who came to Cholula once they had inherited a domain, to acknowledge their submission to Quetzalcoatl and make their offerings." If 8 Deer was made a tecuhtli in Cholula, there is another story in Ixtlilxochitl and Veytia which can be explained in terms of his life, and which also allows us to identify provisionally several other glyphs in the codices.

We are told that Topiltzin soon began to

live a dissolute life, hiding his sins behind the veil of a religion which was in the hands of two priests named Tlatauhqui and Tezcatlipuca (Veytia, 1944, p. 193). Ixtlilxochitl (1952, 1: 47) calls these priests Tezcatlipuca and Tlallauhquitezcatlipuca (i.e., Tezcatlipoca). Torquemada (1964, p. 15) states that when Tezcatlipoca Huemac was in Tollan, many lords committed adultery there, especially that one.

These statements may refer to the fact that 8 Deer married five times between 1051 and 1063 (Caso, 1960b, pp. 40–43). Further, Caso has pointed out (1950b, p. 33; 1960b, p. 22) that although incestuous marriages were rare among Mixtec royalty, they nonetheless occurred several times among the descendants of 8 Deer.

Both Veytia (1944, p. 194) and Ixtlilxochitl (1952, 1: 47) tell of a prominent woman of Tollan who was seduced by priests in Cholula. A similar situation seems to have occurred with two of 8 Deer's granddaughters.

The Bodley version states that two of 8 Deer's children were taken to the "Tule-Glyph Place" where they made an offering at the "Temple of the White Dots." This brother and sister were married to each other (Caso, 1960b, pp. 41–42). Since the daughters of this couple married persons named 7 Flint *Mixcoatl* and 8 Deer *Quetzalcoatl*, lords of the cities of *Tula* (Tule-Glyph Place) and *Temazcal*, I believe that this is the same story mentioned in Ixtlilxochitl and Veytia. In the first place, the nicknames Quetzalcoatl and Mixcoatl are uncommon and could be priest names. Second, evidence supporting the idea that the "Temple of the White Dots" (where the incestuous marriage of the parents of these children took place) is Cholula strengthens the validity of our idea.

I believe "White Dots" should be identified with Cholula because: (1) 21 white dots form the roof of the former place; there is a place glyph in the "Mapa de Cuauhtinchan No. 2" with 23 white dots, which is

next the identified glyph for Cholula (Simons, 1968, p. 59, pls. 3–5). (2) a "Temple of White Dots" appears in Bodley I-IV, and possibly in Vindobonensis (obverse) 39 (cf. Caso, 1960b, p. 25). That this glyph in Bodley appears next to a staircase glyph—the name for Cholula in Mixtec means "Town of Stairs"—suggests that the place in question could be Cholula.[12] Simons (in press) also identifies white dots with Cholula. She believes it may be a barrio or calpulli. She notes that it appears next to another glyph with the attributes of Tezcatlipoca.

If my arguments are correct, then the place where 8 Deer became a tecuhtli was Cholula, and the place where two of his children made offerings also was Cholula. This indicates that many of the glyphs read by the 16th-century authors as Tollan, and interpreted in this century as Tula, refer not to that place but to Tollan Chollolan.

There is now one other problem to be explored regarding the Tollan of the chronicles: in which Tollan did the Tezcatlipoca (9 Wind "Flint")-Quetzalcoatl (9 Wind "Stone Skull") battle take place?[13]

THE FIRST TOLLAN

The first Tollan, where the Quetzalcoatl-

[12] On the same page in the Vindobonensis (p. 39), there appears a staircase glyph under which are two human feet. One of the glyphs for Cholula in the Codex Mendoza is a hill glyph on which a human foot is seen (Barlow and McAfee, 1949, p. 19). Another glyph for Cholula is a deer's foot (cf. Nicholson, 1967, fig. 11). Choloa in Nahuatl means *to flee* (Caso, 1960b, p. 28).

[13] Both the Relación de la Genealogía and the Origen de los Mexicanos state that between the reigns of Topiltzin and Huemac in Tula, that city lacked a ruler for 97 years (García Icazbalceta, 1891, reprinted 1942, pp. 243, 262). They both state that the Atecpanecatl killing of Totepeuh, Topiltzin's father, took place in a "Culhuacan." I believe the "Culhuacan" is Zaachila for reasons I have explored above. In the Origen de los Mexicanos (p. 259) the Atecpanecatl battle takes place in a "Culhuacan" only 17 years after the people had migrated from "*Eutivaca, cerca de Tezcuco*." The toponym *Neteotiloyan* (San Martín de las Pirámides) still exists today (Garibay, 1961, p. 308). The Origen statement indicates that the causes of the battle had their beginning in Teotihuacan.

Tezcatlipoca battle took place, is generally believed to be Tula in the present state of Hidalgo. Even if this were true, it would not render untenable our hypothesis that the rest of the Tollan dynasty in Codex Chimalpopoca ruled in Tilantongo. It is my opinion that the first Tollan is Teotihuacan, but the mater is so complex that it requires book-length treatment, although a preliminary argument can be stated here.

The Jiménez Moreno argument (1941) that the Tollan of the chronicles (he does not distinguish between a Tollan of Quetzalcoatl and a Tollan of Huemac; for him, both refer to Tula, Hidalgo) is based mainly on evidence contained in an 18th-century map in the Archivo General de la Nación of Mexico which lists certain place names around Tula, Hidalgo. These names are mentioned also in such 16th-century sources as the Códice Chimalpopoca and Sahagún in connection with the Quetzalcoatl-Tezcatlipoca struggle in Tollan. Were it not for the evidence presented in this article, and the fact that archaeology, to a degree, backs up a Teotihuacan-Tollan (i.e., first Tollan) correlation, the Jiménez Moreno argument would be unassailable.[14]

Sahagún, for example, calls the Tollan of Quetzalcoatl "Tollan Xicocotitlan" or "Tula next to Xicococ." Today there exists a hill called Jicuco near Tula, Hidalgo (Jiménez Moreno, 1941, p. 80). Sahagún also mentions a "Xippacoyan," which is the present-day town of San Lorenzo in the same area (*ibid.*). He names the river which flows through Tollan "Texcalapan"; this is the name of the river appearing on the map utilized by Jiménez Moreno. Other names of importance to the Jiménez Moreno thesis are Xochitla to the west of Tula and Cincoc, a hill north of Huehuetoca, visible from Tula. There are still others, but Jiménez does not mention them in his brief but classic article (*ibid.*).

Since the exposition above should have put considerable doubt on a one-to-one correlation of Tollan with Tula, Hidalgo,

there must be some explanation regarding the place names. They can be explained, I believe, by the fact that the Chimalpopoca contains information about some 15 other places besides Cuauhtitlan. Garibay has stated (Garibay, 1953–54, 2: p. 279, complete argument, pp. 276–81) that it was the tendency *"a centrar en la población nativa la historia de toda el país del Anahuac...."* This is a logical explanation for what may have happened. The fact that the native authors of the Anales de Cuauhtitlan use the adverb *nican* (here) several times with the name of their city has been cited by Garibay as one indication of this native tendency.[15]

The first reason for believing that the Tollan of the Quetzalcoatl-Tezcatlipoca battle

[14] Other authorities are beginning to note that a one-to-one Tula (Hidalgo)–Tollan correlation is untenable. Carmack (1968, p. 67) has suggested that Chichen Itza might be the Tulan "referred to in the highland Guatemala sources." Smith (1966, pp. 168–96) believes the Tula where 8 Deer became a tecuhtli in the Códice Colombino refers to Tulixtlahuaca on the south coast of Oaxaca. As she points out, in the Lienzo de Coixtlahuaca, "a glyph consisting of a temple base and the *tule* plant is drawn near the large central glyph of Coixtlahuaca. Because this lienzo is a cartographic document, we know from the context of the map that the *tule* glyph here represents San Miguel Tulancingo, a town west of Coixtlahuaca." Sejourné has pointed out repeatedly that Teotihuacan is the Tollan of the chronicles, but because "her writings on Teotihuacan reflect the European movement called *Strukturanlyse* in classical archaeology, which is devoted to discussing the central psychic metaphors of cultural history, represented in Europe by Friedrich Matz and Guido von Kaschnitz-Weinberg, and in America by the writings of Mircea Eliade" (Kubler, 1967, p. 3, note 1), this may be one reason why her arguments have been largely ignored by anthropologists. We accept Sejourné's thesis, but not her "proof." Wolf too has voiced the opinion (1959, p. 275) that a Tula-Tollan one-to-one correlation must be re-examined.

[15] Garibay has pointed out that the Códice Chimalpopoca contains some 15 local histories of places such as Cuauhtitlan (where the document was apparently composed), Culhuacan, Tenochtitlan, Cuitlahuac, Tula (Hidalgo), Azcapotzalco, Xochimilco, Huexotla, and even Tepeyacac (Garibay, 1953–54, 2: 229–30). There are more than a hundred entries about Cuauhtitlan, but only 23 about Tula, Hidalgo.

F<small>IG</small>. 6—QUETZALCOATL IN TEOTIHUACAN. The frame surrounding the portrait of "Quetzalcoatl" spells out his name. From a mural painting in a palace discovered by Eduardo Contreras in the north patio of the Plaza of the Pyramid of the Sun. (After Sejourné, 1965.)

refers to Teotihuacan rather than to any other Tollan is that we now know that a "Quetzalcoatl dynasty" seems to have been of importance there. A mural painting in the north patio of the plaza of the Pyramid of the Sun depicts a human "Quetzalcoatl" with his name written in symbolic fashion as the framing device. The frame is composed of a serpent (*coatl*) with the head of a quetzal; hence, we may read it as Quetzalcoatl (fig. 6; cf. Kubler, 1967, p. 9, figs. 11, 12). Since this palace has some architectural features which are analogous to monks' cells, I feel that it is highly likely that the Pyramid of the Sun itself may have functioned as the "lineage mountain" of the priesthood of Quetzalcoatl (cf. Coe, 1965d, pp. 110–11; Holland, 1964; Vogt, 1964, p. 402).

The Ciudadela has been compared by Armillas (1964a, p. 307) to the *tecpan* or royal palace of Tenochtitlan in Aztec times,

and he has suggested that it may have been the headquarters of the secular ruler of Teotihuacan. Since it is now known that the river directly north of the Ciudadela was part of a planned canal system (Millon, 1967, p. 42), it seems likely that the Ciudadela itself may have housed the lineage of Tezcatlipoca-Huemac-Atecpanecatl.

My reason for believing this is that this canal is apparently the largest canal in Teotihuacan, or at least it appears at the main transportation artery, and therefore is of great importance. Since the name Atecpanecatl may be translated as "Lord of the Irrigation Canal" (Rendón, 1965, pp. 298–99), I suspect that the Ciudadela housed the dynasty of Tezcatlipoca. According to Velázquez (1945, p. 79), Atecpanecatl was the title of the first king of Teotihuacan.

There is other evidence that the Palacio del Quetzalpapalotl near the Pyramid of the Moon may have been that in which the

497

FIG. 7—AN EARLY VERSION OF THE WAR OF THE STONE MEN. 7 Movement "Xolotl" sacrifices one of the "stone men." Personages bearing two of the calendrical names of the fifth sun, 4 Movement and 7 Flower, appear as death bundles on the following page. (Codex Nuttall, pl. 3.)

dynasty of Xochiquetzal lived. This could indicate that the Pyramid of the Moon may have been the "lineage mountain" of the lunar goddess, Xochiquetzal.[16]

Since archaeology points to the existence of Quetzalcoatl and Tezcatlipoca "dynasties" in Teotihuacan, the fact that there is little or no archaeological evidence for these dynasties in Tula, Hidalgo, leads

[16] Sejourné (1966, pp. 183–92) has pointed out that the iconographic device, *xochiquetzalpapalotl* (flower-quetzal-butterfly) is that of Xochipilli. Since Xochipilli is the husband of Xochiquetzal in the Histoire du Mechique (Garibay, 1965a, p. 109), and this couple become the parents of the personage who should have become the fifth sun in Teotihuacan, but became the moon when the former post was usurped by Topiltzin, we believe that the Pyramid of the Moon is the "lineage mountain" of that dynasty.

again to the conclusion that the Tollan of the chronicles is not that Tula.

Acosta has stated (1956–57, p. 107) that "the chronicles tell us about the defeat of Quetzalcoatl and the supremacy of Tezcatlipoca in Tula. Up to the present, not a single representation of the latter god has been found there." There are, however, sculptured representations of personages with feathered serpents (i.e., "quetzalcoatls") known to be from Tula, Hidalgo. This indicates the existence of a "Quetzalcoatl" dynasty there. But we know that the cult of Quetzalcoatl flourished in Xochicalco; the principal monument apparently depicts the calendrical name 9 "Reptile's Eye," which has been interpreted by Caso (1961b, p. 82) as 9 Wind, one of Quetzalcoatl's calendrical names. Thus, archaeologically, the two dynasties seem to have their roots in Tollan Teotihuacan, but appear in other centers throughout Mesoamerican history. Both dynasties also appear in Cholula at different time periods. (See Chadwick, 1970.)

But where did the first Quetzalcoatl-Tezcatlipoca battle of the chronicles take place? A partial answer may be given now, but I emphasize that what follows is simply a hypothesis. My previously published reasons (Chadwick, 1967, pp. 23–24) for believing the battle described in the Chimalpopoca refers to Teotihuacan, not Tula, Hidalgo, are in need of revision to cover what has become a more complex problem than first appeared. We know, for example, that the Myth of the Fifth Sun has its setting in Teotihuacan (see Yáñez, 1964, p. 16). I have shown (Chadwick, 1967, pp. 22-23) that the two candidates for this "office" were a "Quetzalcoatl" and a "Tezcatlipoca." However, the Leyenda de los soles distinguishes between a Teotihuacan and a Tollan: ". . . the name of this sun is Nahui Ollin (4 Movement); it is the one in which we live today . . . because the sun fell into the fires, in the divine oven of Teotihuacan . . . (and) it was the same sun of Topiltzin of Tollan . . . of Quetzalcoatl. Before this sun, his name was Nanahuatl, and he came from Tamoanchan" (Bernal, Piña Chan, and Cámara Barbachano, 1968, p. 64). I have identified Tamoanchan as Xochicalco (Chadwick, 1970), an opinion which probably is shared by Jiménez Moreno (1942; 1966, p. 60).[17]

The Nahuatl text published in the Velázquez edition of the Códice Chimalpopoca (Anales de Cuauhtitlan y Leyenda de los Soles) uses the words "Teotihuacan" and "Tollan," thus indicating that they may not have been the same place (Velázquez, 1945, pl. 77 according to my numbering).

Thus, the evidence suggests that the creation of the Fifth Sun (the election of the King of Teotihuacan?) took place in Teoti-

huacan, but that the ruler may have changed his place of residence to another Tollan. Since the only glyph contained in the Chimalpopoca original with the gloss "Tollan" is the *tule* or reed glyph, Tollan could be one of many places: Tula, Hidalgo (Tollan Xicocotitlan), Tollan Chollolan, Toluca, or even Tollan Teotihuacan (Velázquez, 1945, pl. 78 according to my numbering). In the Mapa Quinatzin the glyph for Tollan stands for Teotihuacan (Wolf, 1959, p. 275).

But we must remember that the Myth of the Fifth Sun is an allegorical story. I agree with Wolf's interpretation of this event, although he mistakenly places it during the final days of Tula. He states (1959, p. 122) that "a sacred ruler tried to impose his natural son, Quetzalcoatl, in contravention of legitimate succession. The opposition drove Quetzalcoatl into exile, at the same time splitting the loyalties which had hitherto cemented the structure of the empire." Wolf bases his interpretation on the version of the Fifth Sun Myth, which is related in the Historia de los mexicanos por sus pinturas.

In this source, Xochiquetzal is said to have died in a war just before the creation of the Fifth Sun. This is important to our

[17] The Sahagún story of the wise men probably is related. "The chronicler Fray Bernardino de Sahagún refers to people who settled in Tamoanchan, 'the place of the bird-serpent,' where they composed the count of the days, of the nights, and of the years, which continued in use until the times of the Aztecs or Mexicas. Sahagún also relates how from Tamoanchan some groups went to Xomiltepec and then to the city of Teotihuacan, where they elected their respective rulers" (Bernal et al., 1968, p. 63). The same authors state that Tamoanchan probably refers to Xochicalco, and point out that there is a site called Xomiltepec or Jumiltepec between Xochicalco and Teotihuacan. I believe the election referred to is the one recounted in the Myth of the Fifth Sun. We note also that Torquemada (1964, p. 10) recorded that the "Toltecs" had lived under the tyranny of certain kings for 500 years and that a meeting was held in Teotihuacan to decide the future of the nation. This meeting took place prior to the founding of Tula in 700 (p. 13).

499

FIG. 8—TEZCATLIPOCA IN CODEX VATICANUS B 19. Compare the appearance of the Tezcatlipoca here with that of 9 Wind "Flint" in fig. 1.

argument because a decapitated personage with the attributes of that goddess appears in Nuttall 3 in an earlier version of the "war with the stone men" (Seler, 1963, 2: 233; Caso, 1964a, p. 72; see fig. 7). Caso places the events depicted in Nuttall 3 in the years 5 House, 12 Flint, and 5 Reed, or 809, 816, and 835, respectively.[18] This indicates that

[18] The year 12 Flint (816) could be the same date as the one which appears in Nuttall 21, following the war with the "stone men" on page 20; but in Nuttall 21 it probably is 52 years later, 868, the date of the "war that comes from heaven," which takes place on the day 4 Movement, in the Bodley. This is logical because the "war with the stone men" takes place on Nuttall 20 in the year 859. Caso (1960b, pp. 28–29) has been unable to explain the different dates for this war.

the Myth of the Fifth Sun (personages bearing the two calendrical names of the fifth sun, 7 Flower and 4 Movement, appear in Nuttall 4) refers to an ongoing struggle between two dynasties since a later version of the "stone-men" war appears in Nuttall 20 (the Quetzalcoatl-Tezcatlipoca battle), with the date 3 Reed, or 859 (Caso, 1960b, p. 28; see fig. 1).

Finally, there is a poem in the collection known as the Cantares Mexicanos, which not only alludes to the fifth sun but also mentions one Tlacahuepan (one of the partisans of Tezcatlipoca in the Sahagún story of Quetzalcoatl). Since this statement is repeated in the Códice Chimalpopoca version of Quetzalcoatl, I feel that this indicates that the original battle took place

Fig. 9—1 DEATH "SUN HEADDRESS" SHOWN WITH PROBABLE GLYPH OF TEOTI-HUACAN, "HILL OF THE SUN." Glyph is at lower left. (Codex Nuttall, pl. 21.)

in Teotihuacan (Garibay, 1953–54, 1: 137; 1962, pp. 107–08; 1964b, 1: 80, 140; 1965b, 2: 11–12, LXXVI, XCVIII; Chadwick, 1967, pp. 23–24; Sahagún, 1950–69, bk. 3, p. 15).

Other evidence confirms this. The poem seems to place all these events in Teotihuacan. It states that it took place ". . . allí donde se hacen los dioses" (Garibay, 1953–54, 1: 137). This is one of the usual translations for Teotihuacan (cf. Sahagún, 1950–69, bk. 10, p. 191, note 84, which gives the translation of "teutioaca" [i.e., Teotihuacan] as "the place where lords are made." Garibay elsewhere (1962, p. 108; p. 160, note 21) translates the cited phrase as Teotihuacan.

It is for these reasons, as well as many others beyond the space of this article, that I believe the Tollan of the chronicles, when it refers to the Quetzalcoatl-Tezcatlipoca battle, means Teotihuacan in the sense that *the origins of a continuing battle between the two dynasties began there*. It is for this reason also that we believe that the glyph "Hill of the Sun" on Nuttall 21 probably is the main glyph for Teotihuacan in that codex (cf. Dibble, 1951, p. 138, *c-l*, where the glyph for Teotihuacan is a stepped pyramid over which is a sun disk; see fig. 9).

Because the "war with the stone men" in Nuttall, involving a struggle between "Quetzalcoatl" and "Tezcatlipoca" forces, seems to be the version from which Torquemada took his story of Tezcatlipoca Huemac and Quetzalcoatl (in which the seat of power of Quetzalcoatl is Tollan Chollolan whence he is routed by Tezcatlipoca),

501

it appears likely that the second Tollan, i.e., where Nanhauatl Topiltzin (Quetzalcoatl) ruled following his election as "fifth sun" in Teotihuacan, is Tollan Chollolan.[19] Thus, I believe that the staircase glyph on Nuttall 22 refers to the latter place (see fig. 10).

This reconstruction probably is corroborated by another poem in the Cantares Mexicanos which speaks of Quetzalcoatl (here called Nacxitl Topiltzin) and his successor, 10 Flower, mentioned previously as the second ruler of the First Dynasty of Tilantongo. The poem refers to a "Tollan" only in the sense that a Quetzalcoatl had once lived there. However, the poem states (in speaking of Quetzalcoatl and 10 Flower) that "allá en Cholula, salíamos," which again seems to indicate that the second Tollan refers not to Tula, Hidalgo, but to Tollan Chollolan (Garibay, 1961, p. 235).

I should like to point out again that in the Origen de los mexicanos version, the Atecpanecatl-Totepeuh battle is related as the first event which takes place in a "Culhuacan" (García Icazbalceta, 1891; 1942). Prior to being in Culhuacan, the people are said to have lived in a town called "Eutivaca" near Texcoco (ibid., p. 259). This strongly indicates once more that the dynastic struggle between the "Tezcatlipoca" and "Quetzalcoatl" forces began in Tollan Teotihuacan, and in no other Tollan.

CONCLUSION

From the foregoing discussion, we see that the dynasty of Tollan in the Códice Chimalpopoca seems to be the story of the First and Second Dynasties of Tilantongo, whose histories are related in the Mixtec codices. The history of Topiltzin in Ixtlilxochitl, Veytia, and Clavijero is that of 8 Deer in the codices. It seems likely that the story of Mixcoatl and his son 1 Reed in the Leyenda de los Soles also is the same history. The evidence further suggests that the "Culhuacan" in the chronicles, previously believed to be in the Valley of Mexico, probably is Zaachila in Oaxaca.

502

The problem of Tollan finds an answer in the likelihood that the first Quetzalcoatl-Tezcatlipoca battle took place in Teotihuacan and is the story related in the Myth of the Fifth Sun. This story is connected with "the war that comes from heaven" in Codex Bodley and "the war with the stone men" in Codex Nuttall. This war apparently refers to a continuing version of struggles between Quetzalcoatl and Tezcatlipoca, and is best related by Torquemada. Thus, as we reconstruct these events at the end of the Classic period, following the change of dynasties in Teotihuacan (first Tollan), the struggle continued in Cholula where Tezca-

[19] Torquemada (1964, pp. 13–17) states that Tezcatlipuca Huemac left a Tollan and went to Tollan Chollolan where he defeated Quetzalcoatl, becoming lord not only of Cholula but also of a province which included the cities of Quauhquechulan, Itzyucan, Atlixco, Tepeyacac, Tecamachalco, Quecholac, and Tehuacan. Quetzalcoatl, on the other hand, is said to have conquered or "populated" the provinces of Oaxaca, and all of the lower as well as upper Mixteca and the lands of the Zapotecs (ibid., p. 15). In Nuttall 21, the woman 1 Death "Sun Headdress" is seen as the ruler of "Hill of the Sun," which could be the glyph for Teotihuacan (cf. Dibble, 1951). In the Bodley, 1 Death is born from a tree; thus she is one of the people who conquered the Mixtec region, the overlords mentioned by Torquemada (cf. Caso, 1960b, pp. 23–24; see fig. 9).

The husband of the lady 1 Death, 4 Alligator "Bloody Eagle," was the son of a pair who had the names of Fifth Sun and Fifth Moon, respectively, 7 Flower and 4 Flint (Caso, 1960b, p. 25; 1961b, pp. 94, 96). The mother of 4 Alligator came from the "Temple of White Dots"; the father, from "Staircase"; and I have shown previously in this article that these places probably are both connected with Cholula. Since 4 Alligator is shown with 9 Wind "Flint" in Nuttall 21, fighting persons with the body paint of a huahuantin (that is, a Mixcoatl), and since the dead princes in the "war with the stone men" (Nuttall 20) also wear the face paint of Mixcoatl, we see that this war apparently was between the forces of Mixcoatl (Quetzalcoatl's father) and Tezcatlipoca. (9 Wind "Flint" is identical in appearance to Tezcatlipoca in the Codex Vaticanus B 19; cf. figs. 1, 8, 9.)

The date in Nuttall 21 is a Year 12 Flint, which is the date when the "war that comes from heaven" occurs in the Bodley, or A.D. 868 (Caso, 1960b, p. 28). In view of the fact that this war occurs on a day 4 Movement in the Bodley, the day and name of the Fifth Sun, we believe the two events are connected.

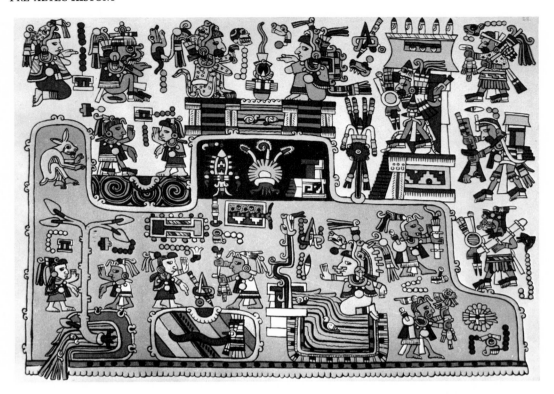

FIG. 10—STAIRCASE GLYPH, POSSIBLY THE GLYPH FOR CHOLULA. 9 Wind "Flint" is seen as the patron of the couple seated on the "Cholula" glyph (top, center). (Codex Nuttall, pl. 22.)

tlipoca finally routed Quetzalcoatl (second Tollan). From this city Quetzalcoatl (9 Wind "Stone Skull") went on to conquer the Mixteca, thus becoming the first overlord of Tilantongo. However, after three successors, the Tezcatlipoca dynasty, which had been ruling elsewhere, defeated the Quetzalcoatl forces in Tilantongo. The events here are not entirely clear, but it seems likely that the Tezcatlipoca forces (as represented by 5 Alligator and 8 Deer) first ruled the south coast of Oaxaca (perhaps with Cholula as their capital) and then subjugated the region in which Tilantongo is located. We know also that a higher authority ruled during much of the Postclassic, an omnipotent king to whom both the king of Tula (Tollan Chollolan?) and 8 Deer rendered homage (cf. Caso, 1960c;

Jiménez Moreno, 1962a, pp. 53–54; 1966, pp. 55, 62). Evidence shows that the seat of power of this personage was Teotitlan del Camino. This ruler seems to have been the patron of the Tezcatlipoca dynasty (his calendrical name was 1 Death, the most important name of Tezcatlipoca). I believe he is the Huematzin of Ixtlilxochitl, who acted as the "Toltec" kingmaker (Caso, 1961b, p. 85; Ixtlilxochitl, 1952, 1: 24, 29, 47).

This reconstruction, I am aware, is contrary to that generally accepted and related in most books with respect to Tula-Toltec history, but I am sure that mine are not the final words on the subject. It is at least now clear that the prehistory of the central valleys is much more complex than was previously supposed.

REFERENCES

Acosta, 1956–57
Alva Ixtlilxochitl, 1952
Alvarado, 1593
Armillas, 1964a
Barlow, 1945c, 1945d
—— and McAfee, 1949
Bernal, 1958a, 1968b
——, Piña Chan, and Cámara Barbachano, 1968
Butterworth and Paddock, 1962
Byers, 1967
Carmack, 1968
Caso, 1949, 1950b, 1951, 1954b, 1955a, 1955b, 1956b, 1958a, 1958b, 1958c, 1958d, 1960b, 1960c, 1960d, 1961a, 1961b, 1962b, 1963, 1964a, 1964b, 1964c, 1965a, 1965b, 1966a, 1966b, 1966c, 1967b, 1969
Chadwick, 1963, 1966, 1967, 1968, 1970, in press *a, b*
Chimalpahin, 1958
Clavijero, 1964
Codices: Becker, Bodley, Chimalpopoca, Colombino, Mendoza, Nuttall, Selden, Vaticanus B, Vindobonensis
Coe, 1965d
Covarrubias, 1957
Cuevas, 1964
Dahlgren de Jordán, 1954
DeCicco, 1969
Dibble, 1951
Fernández de Miranda, 1961
García Icazbalceta, 1886–92
Garibay K., 1940a, 1953–54, 1961, 1962, 1964a, 1964b, 1965a, 1965b
Holland, 1964

Jiménez Moreno, 1941, 1942, 1953a, 1953b, 1954–55, 1962a, 1962b, 1966
—— and Mateos Higuera, 1940
Kirchhoff, 1955, 1964
Kubler, 1967
Leach, 1966
Lehmann, 1938, 1958
Marino Flores, 1958–59
Mendieta, 1945
Millon, 1967
Nader, 1969
Nicholson, 1967, 1968
Paddock, 1966c, 1966d, 1966e
Paso y Troncoso, 1903
Peñafiel, 1967
Preuss and Mengin, 1937–38
Rendón, 1965
Robertson, 1959
Ruz Lhuillier, 1945
Sahagún, 1950–69
Sejourné, 1965, 1966
Seler, 1963
Simons, 1968, in press
Smith, M. E., 1963, 1966
Spinden, 1935
Torquemada, 1943–44, 1964
Vaillant, 1966
Velázquez, 1945
Veytia, 1944
Vogt, 1964
Wicke, 1966
Wolf, 1959
Yáñez, 1964

21. Archaeology of Central Veracruz

JOSÉ GARCÍA PAYÓN

RIO TABUCO or Tuxpan is the northern limit in this discussion of central Veracruz. The southern is Rio Papaloapan and the town of Tlacotalpan, excepting Cosamaloapan. From there the boundary extends west to San Pedro de Acatlan, today Perez Figueroa, in Oaxaca. It then penetrates the state of Puebla, passing near Chalchicomula and Tehuacan to Metaltoyuca, then drops to the upper Pantepec to follow the river to its mouth at Tuxpan in the Gulf of Mexico. Figure 2 shows 562 archaeological zones identified within Veracruz and 37 in the mountains of Puebla.

In this territory of both cold and hot climates, population centers flourished up to 2700 m. elevation at Cantona (fig. 2, no. 400) and Napatecutlan (no. 399), as well as on the slopes of Naucampatepetl (Cofre de Perote, 4,282 m.) and on those of Citlaltepetl or Pico de Orizaba (5700 m.). More settlements are on the spurs of the large mountains of the Sierra Madre Oriental: Teziutlan, Zacatlan (no. 16), and Metaltoyuca (no. 1) in Puebla; Chiconquiaco (no. 237), Cerro de la Morena (no. 215), Cerro de la Botella (no. 214), and on the coastal plains. Mists and rain prevail; temperatures, although moderate in certain times of the year, are high on the coastal plains, where there are salt flats and large rivers for navigation and fishing. There is also a semiarid area of temperate and warm savannas covered by thin humus. It has a long dry season and rickety vegetation with much cactus. Elsewhere, in both mountains and plains, the vegetation is tropical and semitropical except at the highest elevations, where cold climate and conifers predominate. The central area embraces the municipios of Apazapan, Jalcomulco, Emiliano Zapata, Actopan, Puente Nacional, Tenampa, Tlacotepec, Comapa, La Antigua, Manlio Fabio Altamirano, Manuel Gonzalez, Villa Cardel, Soledad de Doblado, Paso del Macho, Jamapa, Cotaxtla, and Carrillo Puerto. The southern area includes the northern parts of the municipios of Cuitlahuac, Tierra Blanca, Tlalixcoyan, and in the west it reaches the boundary of Jalapa.

505

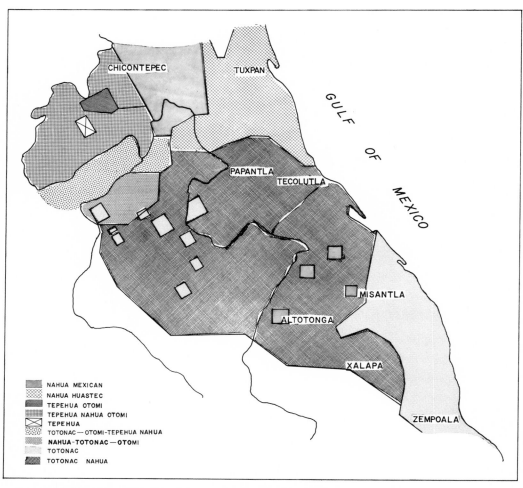

Fɪɢ. 1—DISTRIBUTION OF LANGUAGES IN VERACRUZ IN 1565

Fɪɢ. 2—ARCHAEOLOGICAL ZONES OF CENTRAL VERACRUZ AND ADJACENT PARTS
OF PUEBLA (ᴍᴀᴘs ᴀʀᴇ ᴏɴ ᴘᴀɢᴇs 510–511)

1. Benito Juarez (formerly Santa Ana de Juarez)	15. Ixhuatlan de Madero	29. Huilozintla
	16. Pisa Flores	30. Juanamosa
2. Tamaaolan	17. Nolanco	31. Tumilco
3. La Comunidad	18. Mohuillo	32. Tuxpilla
4. Tamazolingo	19. Poyecaco	33. Miahuatlan
5. Sececapa	20. Huexolitla	34. Zacate Colorado
6. Coacoaco	21. Tizatal	35. Congregacion Teayo
7. Zococapa	22. Huey Ixtlahuac	36. Castillo de Teayo
8. Embocadero	23. Jonotal	37. La Concepción
9. Cerro de Huehuetepec	24. La Jabonera	38. La Antigua
10. La Mata	25. Cerro Tlachichilco	39. Las Piedras
11. Llano Largo	26. Potrero de Don Mariano	40. Tabuco
12. Zapote	27. Pueblo Zacualpan	41. Xuchil
13. Ahuacapan	28. Mesa de Cacahuatengo or Piramide Cacahuatengo	42. Tihuatlan
14. Encinal		43. Lote 40

506

44. Miahuapan	111. Coxquihui
45. Lomas de Castillo	112. Zozocolco de Guerrero
46. Chichinantla	113. Aldama
47. Congregacion El Pital	114. Casitas
48. Paso de Cazones	115. Chumanco
49. Santo Cristo	116. El Cocal
50. Kilometer 31 or Cobos	117. Nautla
51. La Victoria or Kilometer 47	118. Barra de Palmas
52. La Curva, Kilometer 46	119. Puntilla
53. La Encantada	120. San Rafael
54. Barra de Cazones	121. Jicaltepec
55. Volador	122. Paso Telaya
56. Cerro Grande	123. Mentidero
57. Santa Agueda	124. Potrero Nuevo
58. Poza Verde	125. Tulapan
59. Puente de Piedra	126. Paso Largo
60. Tenixtepec	127. La Ceiba
61. Escolin	128. La Esperanza
62. Polutla	129. Perseverancia
63. Arroyo de Arco	130. Martinez de la Torre
64. Boca de Lima	131. Ojite
65. La Concha	132. San Marcos
66. Maria Andrea, Kilometer 292	133. La Chihuisa
67. Palmasola	134. Tres Encinos
68. Tuzapan	135. El Jobo
69. Chicualoque	136. Arroyo Negro
70. Ojital	137. Tlapacoyan
71. Congregacion Tajin	138. Vega de la Peña
71A. Lagunilla	139. Plan de la Vega
72. Rancho Tremari	140. San Juan Ahuatlan
73. Papantla	141. Pompeya or Tajin
74. Aguacate	142. El Refugio
75. La Noria	143. Paso Viejo
76. Monte Gordo	144. Martinica
77. La Ladrillera	145. El Pato
78. San Andres	146. Cerro del Tordo
79. Santa Rosa	147. Pila de Agua
80. Santa Luisa	148. Santa Cruz Hidalgo
81. Poza Larga	149. Potingo
82. Cacahuatal	150. Pachaca
83. Ispayat	151. Las Piñas
84. Tulapilla	152. Brazo Seco
85. Cornezuelo	153. Cerro de San Pedro
86. El Calalco	154. Cerro de los Muñecos
87. Miahuapa	155. Arroyo Hondo
88. Cañada Rica	156. Espaldilla
89. Pueblo Viejo	157. Corregidor
90. El Carmen	158. Pontitlan
91. Cerro Grande	159. Chapachapa
92. Espinal	160. Santa Catarina
93. Paso de Correo	161. Las Lajas
94. Las Acamallas	162. Arroyo de Fierro
95. Pueblillo	163. Quauhzapotitlan
96. Cuyusquihui	164. San Pedro Altepepan
97. San Antonio	165. Tapapulum I
98. La Magdalena	166. Paxilitla or Palpoala Ixcan
99. Tecolutla	167. Misantla
100. Etiopia	168. Plan de la Vieja
101. Malpica	169. Plan de la Vega
102. Huitepec	170. Colipa
103. Hueytepec	171. Guerrero
104. Playa Paraiso	172. Cerro del Cojolite
105. Marta Ruiz	173. Yecuatla
106. Las Ruinas	174. Chalahuite or Los Idolos
107. Coyutla	175. La Lima
108. Chichilintla	176. Cerro del Español, Locohxipec
109. Chumatlan	177. El Pozon
110. Santa Emilia	178. Cerro del Astillero

179. Cuauhtemoc
180. Tapapulum 2
181. Gentiles
182. San Isidro
183. La Cuchilla
184. Tepeican
185. El Rincon
186. San Salvador
187. Tatzallamala
188. Escalonar Atzatlan
189. Oxtoteno
190. Mexcalteco
191. El Palacio
192. Camaron
193. Pilopa
194. Tenoxtitlan
195. Plan Grande
196. Pueblo Viejo
197. Cihuacoatlan
198. Cruz Blanca
199. Pilon de Azucar
200. Cerro de la Campana
201. La Concordia
202. Aparicio
203. La Aurora
204. El Huanal
205. Tacahuite
206. Las Higueras
207. M. S. Juan
208. Soyacuautla
209. Emilio Carranza
210. Paso de la Palma
211. Rincon de Montezuma
212. Juan Martin
213. Tetela
214. Cerro de la Botella
215. Sierra de la Morena
216. Santa Ana
217. Yeitzcuinco
218. Xihuitlan
219. San Luis de los Reyes
220. El Morro
221. Boca de Loma
222. Palma Sola
223. Boca Andrea
224. Los Atlixcos
225. El Colorado
226. Cerro de Juchique or Laguna de Farfan
227. La Pahuita
228. Plan de las Hayas
229. Peña Colorada
230. Cerro Sombreros
231. Alto de Tizar
232. Cerro del Palmar
233. Plan del Pie
234. Plan de la Flor
235. San Isidro
236. Paredones
237. Chiconquiaco
238. Quinla
239. Landero y Coss
240. Miahuatlan
241. Tonayan
242. Monte Real (Pulpinab)
243. Xoxotla
244. La Concordia
245. Ermitaño
246. Temimilco

247.	Iztacapa	312.	Idolos (Acatomaltepec)	377.	Chiztla
248.	Mecalcalco	313.	Atexac	378.	Zacuapan
248.	Tularcillo	314.	Cacalotlan	379.	Zentla
249.	Alcececa	314A.	San Antonio Barranco	380.	Matlaluca
250.	Santa Cruz	315.	Coatepec	381.	Huatusco
251.	Cerro del Brujo	316.	San Tosa	382.	Cotlamanes
252.	Buena Vista	317.	San Isidro (Virgilio Uribe)	383.	Capulapa
253.	Los Muertos	318.	Casa de la Malinche	384.	Ixtla
254.	Guadalupe Victoria	319.	Chalahuite	385.	Calcahualco
255.	Huapala	320.	Monte Grande	386.	Tlapala
256.	Las Torrecillas	321.	Las Charcas	387.	Tuzamapa
257.	Omeapan	322.	Zempoala	388.	Alborada
258.	Atlapa Chico	323.	Mata Verde or Trapiche	389.	Jalapa
259.	Huichila	324.	El Limoncito	389A.	Macuiltepec
260.	Tlacolulan Viejo	325.	Cerro Piedras Negras	390.	Zoncuantla
261.	Chapultepec	326.	Porvenir	391.	Chapictla
262.	La Reforma	327.	Naranjillo	392.	Jesus
263.	Noalinco	328.	El Palmar	393.	Rio de Jorge V
264.	Jilotepec	329.	La Gloria	394.	Minillas
265.	Banderilla	330.	Arenal	395.	Las Palmillas
267.	Tenampa	331.	Chachalacas	396.	Ahuatepec
269.	Cerro Cercado	332.	Ursulo Galvan	397.	Agua de la India
270.	La Campana	333.	El Ciruelo	398.	La Gloria
271.	Coatepec	334.	San Jose de los Idolos	399.	Napatecutlan
272.	Brazo Fuerte	335.	Carretas	400.	Cantona
273.	Almolonga	336.	La Posta	401.	Pueblo Viejo
274.	Chiltoyac	337.	La Antigua	401A.	Hueyaltepetl (Pueblo Viejo)
275.	Loma Rogel	338.	El Hato	402.	Hacienda Tepiolo Tenexte-
275A.	Maxtlalan	339.	Remudadero		pec
276.	Ayotlan	340.	Tolome	402A.	Tenextepec
277.	Rincon de Negros	341.	Paso de Ovejas, El Faisan	403.	Xaltepec (San Isidro)
278.	Platanar	342.	Conquista	404.	Xaltepec
279.	Topiltepec	343.	Vargas	405.	Quauhtotolapan
280.	Rancho de Niño	344.	Tierra Colorada	406.	Coatitlan
281.	Collolillo	345.	El Retiro	407.	Cuatlatlan
282.	Bajo de Cantaros	346.	San Diego	408.	Coatepec Viejo
283.	Paso del Cedro	347.	Santa Fe	409.	San Marcos
283A.	El Cedro	348.	Buenavista	410.	Xico Viejo
284.	A Mariano	349.	Espinal	411.	Xicochimalco
285.	Texuc	350.	Mata Loma	412.	Ixhuacan
286.	La Cañada	351.	La Polvareda	413.	Texolo
287.	Tepetzala	352.	San Martin	414.	La Orduña
288.	El Viejon	353.	El Sauce	415.	Teocelo
289.	Villa Rica	354.	Portezuelo	416.	Tatatila
290.	Bernalillo	355.	Remojadas	417.	Pinillo
291.	Quiahuixtlan	356.	Teteles	418.	Tlaltetela
292.	Poza Jacinto	357.	Tenenexpan	419.	Poxtla
293.	Palmas de Arriba	358.	Palmaritos	420.	Xicuintla
294.	Palmas de Abajo	359.	Buenavista	421.	Atliaca
295.	Barra de la Mancha	360.	Pachuquilla	422.	La Pedrera
296.	Cerro de la Mancha	361.	Oceloapan	423.	Tatetla
297.	Cerro Marin	362.	Cantarranas	424.	Tetlalpan
298.	Tres Picos	363.	Amelco	425.	Chicuacentepetl
299.	La Luz	364.	Rinconada	426.	Comapa
300.	Mozomboa	365.	Palo Gacho	427.	Coscomatepec
301.	Llano de Zarate	366.	Plan del Rio	428.	Teteltzingo
302.	Cerro Montoso	367.	Carrizal	429.	Iztiuca
303.	Gallegos	368.	Apazapan	430.	Camaron
304.	Medina	369.	Otlaquiquiztlan	431.	Mata de Agua
305.	Chicuasen	370.	El Campo de las Moras	432.	Soledad de Doblado
306.	Las Animas	371.	Jalcomulco	433.	La Cantera
307.	Otates	372.	Tepetlapa	434.	San Juan Estancia
308.	Tinajitas	373.	Santa Maria Tatela	435.	Hacienda de la Esperanza
309.	Tonalmil	374.	La Palmilla	436.	Xicalango
310.	Ixtlahuaslu	375.	Conzoquitla	437.	Chalchicueyecan
311.	Actopan Viejo	376.	Tlacotepec	438.	Isla de Sacrificios

439. Tlapamicitlan	485. El Plan	530. La Esperanza
440. San Jose Novillero	486. Tepetipac	531. San Francisco
440A. Novillero	487. El Calvario	532. Dicha Tuerta
441. Joya de Martin Garabato	488. Las Balsaminas	533. Cerro de los Tiestos
442. Mictlancuauhtlan	489. Buena Vista	534. Cerro de Agua Dulce
443. Dos Bocas	490. Amellales, Amecalco	535. Nopiloa
444. El Tejar	491. San Jose de Abajo	536. Cerro de la Fraternidad
445. El Buzon	492. Tres Encinos	537. Cerro de la Gallina
446. La Venta	493. Santo Tomas	538. Cerro de los Pitos
447. Naranjal	494. Matanaranjo	539. Alvarado
448. La Palma	495. Palmar	540. Casa de Piedra
449. El Mangal	496. La Leona	541. Pueblo Nuevo
450. Medellin	497. Quauhtochco	542. Nueva Vida
451. Juan de Afaro	498. Loma de Enmedio	543. Cerro de Santa Getrudis
452. Paso del Toro	500. Copalillo	544. La Galera
453. Estacion Laguna	500A. Los Negritos	545. Tlacotalpan
454. La Campana	501. Vainilla	546. Palmilla
455. Xalisco	502. Corral de Piedra	547. La Chorrera
456. Vacas Gordas	503. Tlalnamacoyan	548. La Barranca
457. Quiebracha	504. Mata Espino	549. Paso Ancho
458. Paso del Macho	505. Nexpolo	550. San Jose del Cacao
459. Paso Caballo	506. Cueva Pintada	551. Nomaltepec
460. Atoyac	507. Rancho Viejo	552. El Moste
461. San Francisco Toxpan	508. Cotaxtla	553. Los Changos
461A. San Francisco	508A. Pueblo Viejo	554. San Cristobal
462. Cordoba, Palmilla	509. Buenos Aires	555. Colonia San Pablo
463. Joya de Ayotzin	510. San Luis	556. Paraiso Novillero
464. Cuauhtlalpan	511. Mata Espino	557. Ixmatlahuacan
465. Ahuilizapan	512. Capulines	558. Buena Esperanza
466. Escamela	513. Mecayucan	559. Amatlan
467. Cruz Verde	514. La Capilla	560. El Corte
468. Rio Blanco	515. Plata	561. Amates
469. Terango	516. Pozuelos	562. Cosamaloapan
470. El Xuchil	517. La Encantada	563. Vista Hermosa
471. Tlachichilco	518. La Tuna	564. Putalcingo
472. Maltrata	519. Cerro del Gallo	565. Cerro Gordo
473. Nogales	519A. Comapan	566. Paso Perritos
474. Huiloapan	520. Cerro Grande	567. Santa Cruz
475. Tecamamalucan	521. Cerro del Pastor	568. Rancho Nuevo
476. Acultzingo	522. Tlalixcoyan	569. El Pedregal
477. Puerto de Guadalupe	522A. Los Cerros	570. Paso de Limon
478. Xuchitiotla	523. Cerro del Gallo	571. Tejas
479. Amatlan de los Reyes	524. Salitral	572. Crucero
480. Atempa	525. Tuzales	573. Otatitlan
481. Tehuipango	526. Mata de Caña	574. Playa Maria
482. Tecuapa	527. Cerro de la Gallina	575. Tlacojalpan
483. Carrizo	528. Cerro de las Mesas	576. Las Piñas
484. Cerro de Temapa	529. Cocuite	577. Tuxtilla

Archaeological Zones of the state of Puebla

1. Metlaltoyuca	14. Tlacuiloloztoc	27. Libres
2. Zanatepec	15. Mecapalco	28. Coyotepec
3. San Rafael	16. Zacatlan	29. Quimixtlan
4. Peña Colorada	17. Ayotochco	30. Tepetitlan
5. Mesa de Coroneles	18. Hueytamalco	31. Aljojuca
6. Tenampulco	19. Apulco	32. Jalapaxco
7. Matlatlan	20. Yohualichan	33. Los Arcos
8. Amixtlan	21. Tetela	34. Atzizintla
9. Zacapoaxtla	22. Chignautla	35. Cuauhtemoc
10. Macuilquila	23. Xiuhtetelco	36. Paso Nacional
11. Acateno	24. Contla	37. Chalchicomula
12. Poza Larga	25. Taxtitlan	
13. Mesonate	26. Colhua	

(FIG. 2 MAPS ARE ON PP. 510–511)

Fig. 2—*Legend on pp. 506–509*

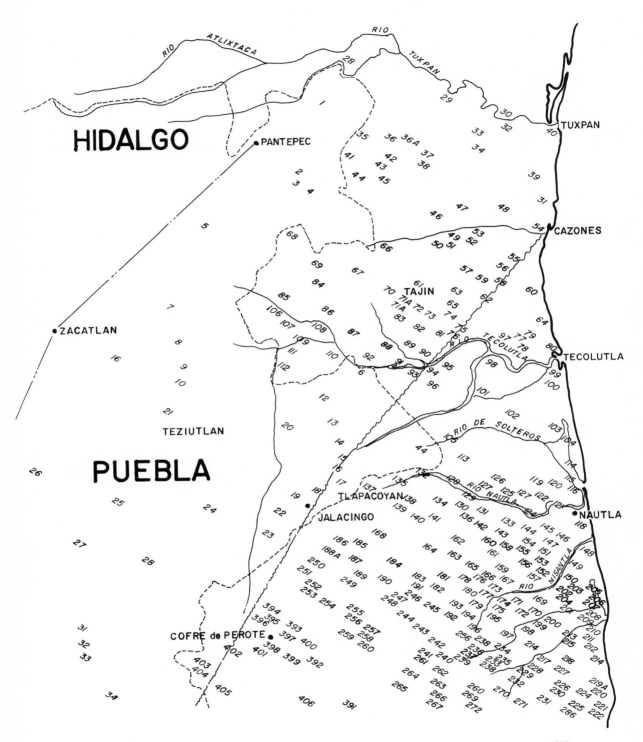

RIO ATLIXTACA
RIO TUXPAN

HIDALGO

TUXPAN

• PANTEPEC

28

29

30
32

40

33
34

35 36 36A 37
41 42 43 38
44 45

2
3 4

47 48
46

31

39

CAZONES

5

68

66

49 53
50 51 52
57 59 56
63

54

55
56

ZACATLAN

69 67

84

85
106 107 86
108
109
111
112 110

6/ TAJIN
70 71A 72 73 65
71A 83 82 81

88 89 90
92
9
6 93 94 95
96

60

62

64

97 79
78
80
TECOLUTLA
98
99
100

TECOLUTLA

7

8

9

10

21

20

13

14
15
16
17
18
19

12

44
0

102

RIO DE SOLTEROS
113 114

103
104

116

TEZIUTLAN

26

PUEBLA

25

24

27

28

31
32
33

34

22

23

137
135
139 140

TLAPACOYAN 138
JALACINGO

75
72
129 RIO NAUTLA
134 130 131 136 142
141

168
186 185
188A 187
189
184
190

250
251
252
249
253 254 255
256 257

164
163 165
162
160 159
161 156
155
154
157
181
178 176 173
182
167 159
166
RIO
179
191
246 245
247
248
244 243 242

126
127 125
129 127 122
124

119 120
118

145 146
144 147
153
152
150

148

149
MISANTLA
151

169
170

203
204
205
206
207
208
209

394
395 393
396 397 400
402 401
398 399 392
403
404
405

COFRE de PEROTE •

259 258
260

406

391

264
265

256 238
236
241 240 239
261 262 238
263
266
267

196
256 234
235
230
239 237
238
272

197
269
270

198
199
214
228
227
222

213
210
200 213
212
214
217 216
229 228
232
226
225
231

219A 220
230 218
224 220
226 225 221
286 222

271

511

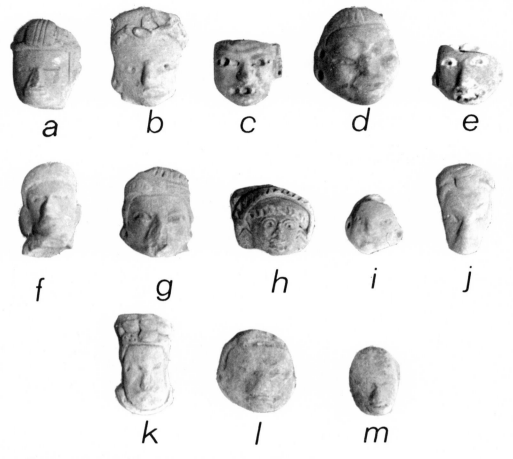

FIG. 3—FIGURINES FROM SANTA LUISA, TECOLUTLA

PRECERAMIC PERIOD

Pleistocene pachyderms have been found from the Gulf Coast to the mountains, at Atzalan (no. 188), Santa Elena at Kilometer 305 of the highway from Mexico to Tuxpan, between Papantla and Poza Rica, and many other sites. It has not been possible to corroborate their association with man. Evidence of possible pre-agricultural peoples in central Veracruz is limited to certain preceramic remains of Trapiche (no. 323) and El Viejon (no. 289). The Tehuacan region, the western boundary of Gulf cultural expansion where MacNeish (1961b) and associates carried on intensive excavations, has provided much useful information in interpreting the earliest ceramics of the central Veracruz area.

PRECLASSIC PERIOD

Preclassic remains have been found throughout central Veracruz, but are most abundant on the better-known coastal plains. In the basin and on the right bank of Rio Tuxpan, in the archaeological zones of Tabuco (no. 40) and Tumilco (no. 31), are many mounds lacking any trace of stone construction. The oldest pottery, according to Ekholm (1953, p. 415), who made brief explorations in 1946, is "Chila white" and "Chila black." They belong to Periods I and II of his sequence at Panuco.

512

In the drainage of Rio Cazones (no. 54) are potsherds with fluting parallel to the rim Medellín, 1952a; 1960a, p. 16), incising after firing, and a white slip (García Payón, 1945a). All these correspond to ceramics of the upper Trapiche-Chalahuite and Remojadas.

A small collection of Preclassic vessels comes from the Rio Tecolutla drainage, in the archaeological zone of Santa Luisa (no. 80) between the mouth of the river and the town of Gutierrez Zamora. There is also an interesting collection of figurines (García Payón, 1944a) that are not typologically directly related to any other known specimens, but which show influences from northern and southern Veracruz. In general they are of reddish clay with white temper and are hand modeled. Two of these figurines were found in El Tajin (fig. 3). I assign them to the Late Preclassic.

In 1952, in the archaeological zone of Tecolutla (no. 99) at the mouth and on the right bank of Rio Tecolutla, Medellín (1952a) found vessels that he classified "Lower Remojadas." They are brown with a polished cherry-red wash, brown with black wash, brown with reddish wash and black incised, and are related to Trapiche-Chalahuite types.

At several towns in the Rio Nautla drainage—Perseverancia (no. 129), Martinez de la Torre (no. 130), Potrero Nuevo (no. 124), San Rafael (no. 120), Mentidero (no. 123), and Hueytepec (no. 102)—archaeologists of the Instituto de Antropología of the Universidad Veracruzana collected Preclassic pottery. According to Medellín (1952a), most of it is related to Lower Remojadas and the white types to "Chila white" of Panuco. During these investigations, they found Huastec Panuco II figurines.

Among the hundreds of mounds in the Chachalacas drainage and the adjacent extensive coastal plains, the best-known ruins are Zempoala (no. 322), famous in conquest annals, and Chachalacas (no. 331),

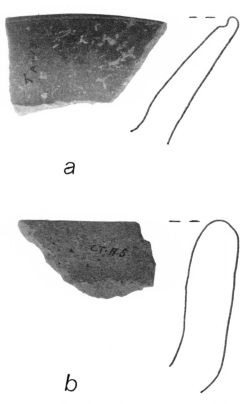

a

b

FIG. 4—STONE VESSELS. Scale of profiles, ⅓.

Trapiche (no. 323), Chalahuite (no. 319), Limoncito (no. 324), and El Viejon (no. 289), known also as Villa Rica de la Veracruz.

In 1942, after a flooding of Rio Chachalacas that destroyed a mound in the Zempoala region, a small exploration was carried out (García Payón, 1950c), followed, in 1951 and 1959, by explorations (García Payón, 1966) in the archaeological zone of Chalahuite (no. 319). Ceramic types found in these investigations included: buff or orange; comales; bowls with composite silhouette; negative painted; fluted; scraped; stick-polished; postfired incised or striated; black; white; bichrome; covered with rubber or asphalt; coarse brown; red-on-brown or bay; brown or bay; rocker-stamped; and impressed, with or without punctations. At Trapiche and Chalahuite two trenches were

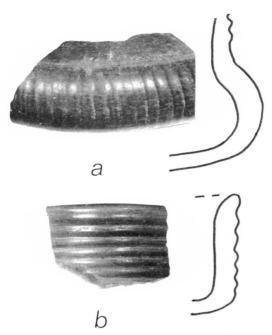

a

b

FIG. 5—FLUTED POTTERY. Scale of profiles, ⅓.

dug, one in the center of the mound and the other in flat land.

The oldest artifacts are vessel fragments of lead gray basalt, flat-bottomed plates with walls sloping outward, well polished, and with a small indentation around the rim interior. They are similar in form and decoration to the potsherds we found in the lower level (fig. 4). The most important types are listed below.

Vessels

NEGATIVE. *Apaxtles* (wide-mouthed jars), *cajetes*, and flat-bottomed plates have walls 9–12 mm. thick and are decorated with wide undulating stripes of bay or black on a micaceous red background. Those in Pavon II differ in paste and decoration (Ekholm, 1944, pp. 357, 428, figs. 8, K, *1*, M). Medellín (1950) found examples at Remojadas in Offering 4, approximating specimens of El Tajin "ivory" ceramics. Drucker (1943a, pp. 75, 89, 116; 1943b, pp. 38, 81, figs. 139, 140) mentions the sporadic presence of this

pottery at Tres Zapotes and Cerro de las Mesas and considers it most closely related to the El Tajin type.

FLUTED (fig. 5). Exterior grooves may be horizontal or vertical or both. On vessels with horizontal grooves, scratched geometric motifs sometimes were added after the application of the slip. Vessels with this type of ornamentation (except the Trapiche-Chalahuite large bottles) have been found on the Gulf Coast at Cerro de las Mesas, Tres Zapotes, and La Venta (Drucker, 1943a, figs. 23,*f*; 25,*b,c*; 28,*m*; 1943b, figs. 12,*r*; 26; 44; Weiant, 1943, pp. 16, 21, 123; Drucker, 1952). Ekholm illustrates two specimens similar to his "Prisco black," which R. E. Smith considers to be like a Uaxactun Mamom type. The other two examples from Trapiche-Chalahuite have finer paste and are more evolved (Ekholm, 1944, p. 351, figs. 7,*u,v*, 21).

BLACK (fig. 6). This ware is usually either undecorated or has one or two shallow grooves around the interior of the rim. It is one of the most important groups in the lowest levels and has a frequency of 12.75 per cent. Incised vessels have a frequency of only 1.28 per cent. This ware is similar in paste and form to specimens from Tres Zapotes, Cerro de las Mesas, and La Venta; as in La Venta, some examples were covered with a wash of liquid clay similar to that of which the vessel was made (Drucker, 1943b, pp. 81–82, figs. 91–99).

Domestic wares include large and small plates, saucers, basins or pans, vases with straight sloping walls, bowls with restricted orifice, *coscomates* (storage vessels) with rims reinforced by a rounded molding similar to examples found by Drucker (1943a, fig. 26) at Tres Zapotes, and jars without handles. In general, all are thick walled, at times with an everted flaring rim. They differ from the ceramics of Tres Zapotes, La Venta, and Cerro de las Mesas (Drucker, 1943a, figs. 21, 31, 36; 1943b, figs. 82–144; 1952, pp. 90, 92, 102, fig. 34; Weiant, 1943, figs. 1,*p,v*; 2; 4; 11,*a-d*) in that some are

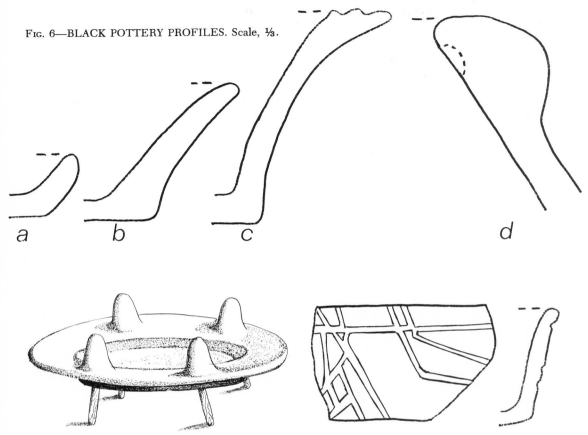

Fig. 6—BLACK POTTERY PROFILES. Scale, ⅓.

a *b* *c* *d*

Fig. 7—RECONSTRUCTION OF BLACK POT-
TERY CENSER

Fig. 8—INCISED POTTERY. Scale, ⅓.

incised and have thinner walls, as is true of the examples discovered by Medellín (1950) in Remojadas. Drucker mentions fragments with punctate decoration, and rocker-stamping.

A foreign form (fig. 7) is a black censer or goblet 3.8 cm. tall and 34.5 cm. in diameter, with walls 16 mm. thick. It has an indented base and on its rim are four hollow conical attachments to support some object. It is of coarse brittle clay with much white sand temper; imprints show that when being made it rested on a maguey fabric.

STRIATED (fig. 8). Weiant, who found these at Tres Zapotes, called them "incised sherds, general Ranchito collection." He differentiated them from others on the basis of their being "deep incised" (Weiant, 1943, p. 122; figs. 4; 45,*b,c*). Drucker (1943a, pp. 48–50, figs. 20,*b,e,g,h*; 1952, pp. 92–94, figs. 1,*a-d*; 32) calls them "incised coarse brown ware." Deep lines were cut to decorate pottery of various forms, clay, and finish. Over the decorated area was a wide band of thin red, cinnabar, or white paint. Surface texture is rough, for the pottery was not burnished or slipped.

INCISED. This ware, typical of Preclassic ceramics in central Veracruz, occurs abundantly from the Rio Tecolutla drainage to southern Veracruz. Weiant and Drucker found it in their excavations at Tres Zapotes, and Drucker found it at La Venta and

515

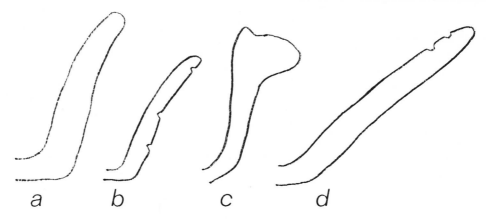

FIG. 9—WHITE POTTERY PROFILES. Scale, ⅓.

Cerro de las Mesas. It was abundant in Medellín's excavations at Remojadas (no. 355), Torres Guzmán's at Tlalixcoyan (no. 522), Bertha Cuevas' at Carrizal (no. 367), Waltraut Hangert's at El Faisan (no. 341), and mine at Santa Luisa, Chachalacas, Chalahuite, and Trapiche.

One of its peculiarities at Trapiche is a wide, sometimes thick, flaring, and at times undulating rim. On these vessels is a great range of engraved friezes and complicated geometric drawings and symbols of Olmec type, although some decorations are merely a series of oblique and interlacing lines.

In 55 per cent of the specimens the decoration was applied after firing. The incised lines were usually filled with cinnabar paint.

WHITE (fig. 9). This pottery was covered with white paint or lacquer, at times applied directly to the vessel without prior slipping. Because of the great variety of wares on which this finish was used, it forms one of the most interesting ceramic complexes of central, northern, and southern Veracruz.

Drucker called his Tres Zapotes specimens "coarse brown ware," color ranging from dark buff to reddish brown, plus variations due to bad firing. One variety is heavily tempered, others show scarcely any temper. Surface texture ranges from smooth to scaly, walls from thin to thick in the same stratigraphic levels (Drucker, 1943a, pp. 47, 48, 57, 58, 98, 108).

Weiant reports that unslipped specimens have a gray to dark-gray core paste. They are homogeneous, compact, and light. His "Middle Period" types A and B, called "normal white," have homogeneous gray to bay paste, fired to tile or black. This is true also of his Upper Tres Zapotes specimens. The colors change here from white to pale cream; deterioration of the slip may bring about delicate pink colors (Weiant, 1943, pp. 17, 19, 20, 65, 66, 69, 112).

In La Venta, Drucker found few examples which he could assign to this group, possibly because of the bad condition of the specimens. On many potsherds only small traces of the slip remained (Drucker, 1952, pp. 96–104). At Remojadas, Medellín (1950) found two vessels of this ware with true handles; they were brown with a polished white wash.

Ekholm reports that in the Huasteca "Chila white" paste has abundant sand temper, is coarse, granular, and gray to brown and reddish; the surface color is bay, and may have been polished, giving it a soapy texture (Ekholm, 1944, p. 341).

In the explorations at Trapiche-Chala-

516

huite I found three types of paste that, according to the firing temperature, showed a range of colors at the core, from clear bay or almost clear buff to dark bay, clear gray to black, and tile to reddish tile. This last corresponds to MacNeish's (1954a) "Progreso white."

Vessel walls are up to 15 mm. thick. Some are from cylindrical vases; others are convex, some with a wide protuberance at the base. Some have postfiring incised Olmec motifs, tetrapod mammiform and rectangular hollow supports, and fragments of appliqué decorative elements. One is rocker-stamped, and one has geometric decoration.

SCRAPED (fig. 10). A sharp object was used to scrape away parts of the vessel's exterior before firing, leaving the decorative motif in relief (champlevé); the remaining areas were then painted with cinnabar. The designs are highly complex and difficult to reconstruct in detail for lack of complete vessels. Besides geometric motifs there are symbols, hieroglyphs, and fragments of Olmecoid frets.

This type has not been found at Tres Zapotes and only sporadically at Cerro de las Mesas. Drucker assigns it to his Lower II period (Drucker, 1943b, pp. 38, 39, 82; figs. 115, 119, 120; pls. 19,*a*, 192). Medellín (1950) discovered an example that he calls "*de decoración recortada.*" It is a flat-bottomed bowl with vertical incised lines and a wavy stripe between two parallel lines around the rim. He places it chronologically in Lower Remojadas.

STICK-POLISHED (fig. 11). The paste is similar to that of black ware, having white sand temper and at times thick porous particles. Walls are 9–13 mm. thick. According to firing and slip, the core color ranges from dark gray to black and from reddish tile to dark bay.

The flat-bottomed vessels are similar in form to black and brown-bay specimens. Among them are plates and apaxtles with straight or curved, and vertical walls, at

FIG. 10—INCISED POTTERY. Scale, ⅓.

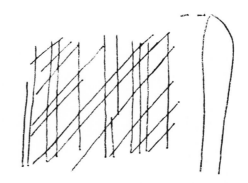

FIG. 11—STICK-POLISHED POTTERY. Scale, ⅓.

times reinforced with a molding at the rim. There are *tecomates* (rounded bowls with restricted orifice) with a wide reinforcement around the rim, and jars, some large with a tall neck, all lacking handles. The decoration is exclusively on the exterior, usually on the midportion of the vessel, especially on the shoulders, or on the neck of high-collared specimens.

Until now this ware has not been mentioned in reports on explorations in the Huasteca, or in reports by Medellín and Strebel on other sites of central Veracruz. It was apparently not found at Cerro de las Mesas or La Venta to the south. Only Weiant (1943, fig. 51) notes its sporadic occurrence at Ranchito in Tres Zapotes, where it was of coarse yellow clay with the texture and color of rust. There vessel interiors were occasionally covered with buff-colored slip

517

FIG. 12—BICHROME VESSEL

and subsequently polished. The decorative designs are somewhat similar to those found in Trapiche-Chalahuite.

NATURAL BICHROME (fig. 12). The vessels are either white and black or red and black. By controlled firing, the potters apparently attempted to make the upper portion, including the interior, white, and the bottom black. In many cases the colors did not come out well divided; or spots and other discolorations resulted; or the colors were reversed, the bases white and the upper parts black.

One can follow the development of this technique step by step by studying the potsherds of Trapiche-Chalahuite. There are examples in which the black extends over almost all the vessel surface, or occurs only in large spots; sometimes the reverse is true. The "white" may be clear gray, but always has black spots. If the vessel has remained entirely black, it may be typologically confused with the black ware; but they can be distinguished—in noneroded fragments—by the fact that bichrome ware has a bright luster and is well smoothed and burnished before firing. Forms are usually the same as in the black, brown, or bay wares. All are apodal and generally flat bottomed.

This ceramic group is characteristic of

518

Tres Zapotes, where it was found by Weiant and Drucker, and later by Drucker at Cerro de las Mesas and La Venta. Each man gave it a different nomenclature and expressed diverse opinions about its technology and, to a certain point, its chronology (Weiant, 1943, pp. 16, 17, 19, 20, 22, 25, 56, figs. 1,c-f, 8, 25,e; Drucker, 1943a, pp. 59–60, 114–15, fig. 21,g,h; 1943b, pp. 44, 81, fig. 20,c; 1952, pp. 92, 147–48).

In Alvarado, Veracruz, Medellín encountered this pottery (white and black) associated with the figurines type A and "Uaxactun" of Weiant. Later he found it at El Viejon and Tlalixcoyan associated with Lower Remojadas materials. For this reason he considers it to be one of the most ancient wares of the Preclassic in central Veracruz (Medellín, 1952a, pp. 11–12).

According to data supplied by Drucker, it is inferred that the two types were found only at La Venta and that their antiquity and origin continue to be in doubt. It seems to me that the larger variety of forms—their abundance, and above all, the fact that their evolution can be followed, indicate that it originated in central Veracruz.

BROWN OR BAY (fig. 13). In pastes and temper of grayish and white sand particles, these are similar to pottery found by Weiant and Drucker at Tres Zapotes, and by Drucker at Cerro de las Mesas and La Venta. Owing to their distinctive surface hues,

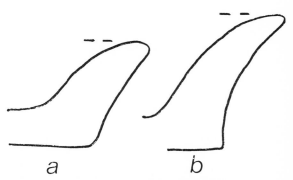

a   b

FIG. 13—BUFF OR BLACK POTTERY PROFILES. Scale, ⅓.

some could be designated—as Drucker (1952, p. 92) did upon comparing the "coarse brown ware" of La Venta and Tres Zapotes—as maroon-buff or simply maroon. They may also range, as at Cerro de las Mesas, from bright orange-brown to dark brick-red to dark chocolate (Drucker, 1943b, p. 34), or, as Weiant (1943, pp. 18, 21, 28) says, from varnished wood, dead-leaf brown, maroon or reddish maroon. They may also have black or gray spots.

I consider that this is a very old ceramic group and that the diverse hues are due to regional customs of manufacture and firing. I have no doubt, as Drucker (1943b, p. 48) states, that the specimens with less temper tend to be the oldest. Those with thick walls are more abundant in the lower levels than in the intermediate ones.

In clay and temper all are similar to the black ware, except for the presence of thick particles like small pebbles. This leads me to surmise that they utilized the sands on the Gulf Coast found around certain ant-hills. The thick-walled vessels, some up to 20 mm., are soft and fragile, perhaps because of bad firing. In some cases, in spite of the polish, aggregates of pores and long horizontal lines produced by the lack of fusion appear on the exterior surface. One can suppose that they employed the coiling method of manufacture, but the paste core gives no evidence.

Some pieces were covered with a wash of argil. Others show a slip on the interior and exterior and sometimes on the bottom. With the slip they formed grains as if they might have been trying to imitate wood (Weiant, 1943, p. 18, describes it as a ware having the appearance of varnished wood). Particles of mica are noted in some examples that have only a polished wash of diluted clay.

Forms in general repeat those of black ware vessels: large and small plates, apaxtles, cylindrical vases, vases with slightly slanted straight walls, tetrapod vessels with solid hemispherical supports, recep-

tacles with reinforced rims and one or two grooves, composite silhouettes, smooth lids, spoons, and jars. The greater number of the latter have no handles or have a simple elongated tongue-shaped piece of clay attached to the middle of the neck. Circular and irregular-shaped comals are coarse and vary from 9.7 to 43.7 cm. in diameter, with walls 12–20 mm. thick. A few examples have a thickened rim on the exterior.

This ware is the most abundant in Trapiche-Chalahuite (frequency 33.55 per cent). It was found in all levels, but the largest percentage was in the lower levels.

If we compare morphologically the vessels found by Weiant (1943, figs. 3; 15; 17, b,e,g; 25,b) and by Drucker (1943a, figs. 20,$a–j$; 21,$a–e,j$; 22,$a–h$; 23,a,e,j,p,h; 25,$a–c$) we will see many similarities, but they lack the simpler forms with thick walls. In addition they present more evolved forms such as rectangular supports, spouted vessels, effigy vessels, much incised decoration, handles, and incised composite-silhouette vessels. None of these have been found at Trapiche-Chalahuite. Nor is there a single mention of simple vessels at Cerro de las Mesas. For La Venta, Drucker (1952, figs. 26–28) shows only potsherds that are incised-before firing, rocker-stamped, and punctated. We therefore believe that this ceramic group originated in central Veracruz.

ROCKER-STAMPED OR PUNCTATE (fig. 14). Almost all the examples are of medium-compact clay and have generally thick walls, with abundant black, white, and gray sand temper, at times with pebble fragments up to 5 mm. long by 1 mm. thick. There are a few smaller vessels with thin walls.

The four basic vessel shapes are: (1) flat-bottomed plates with vertical or straight diverging walls, 9.5–13.0 mm. thick, 20.0–29.8 cm. in diameter; (2) flat-bottomed hemispherical bowls, sometimes with an exterior groove at the rim; (3) tecomates 7.7 cm. in diameter at the rim, at times with an in-

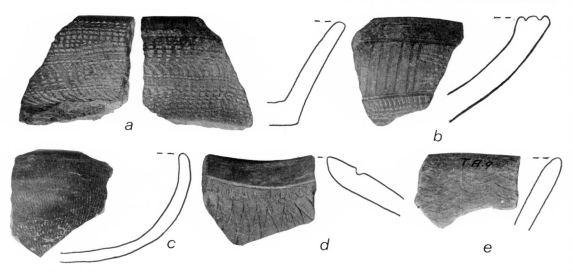

FIG. 14—ROCKER-STAMPED AND DENTATE-STAMPED POTTERY. Scale of profiles, ½.

cised (before firing) line around the top; and (4) jars with flaring necks, 20 cm. in diameter at the mouth and with walls 15 mm. thick.

Because the variety of stamped decoration is too great to describe completely, I shall summarize the main types (fig. 14). Some are oblong punctations, in the form of spines or twisted horns, symmetrical or asymmetrical, or possibly part of some decorative motif. Others depict tears, fish scales, and swirling water. There are plain lines and straight, broken, or curved microlines, such as those found by Drucker (1952, fig. 28,a–d). There are oblong punctations within and without a series of arcs that surround the bottom of the vessels (*ibid.*, fig. 33) or fill the background of larger incised designs (*ibid.*, fig. 34,f). Others show imprints of a mussel shell, or a row of circles similar to those found by MacNeish at Panuco, in his Progreso Metallic ware of the Pavon period.

LINE-IMPRESSED, WITH OR WITHOUT PUNCTATIONS. Figure 15 shows a photograph and profile of a vessel fragment with a series of lines impressed on the interior of the base when it was still soft. This was done with a blunt stick that left only some shallow impressions without cutting the clay. In only one example were the lines made with a sharp instrument. A series of coarse, deep punctations were sometimes applied.

Because of their clay and surface finish characteristics, this ware corresponds to the brown or bay ware, but has little white and gray sand temper. Shapes are the same as those of the thick-walled brown or bay and likewise have a soft, fragile core which ranges in color, according to the firing temperature, from dark gray and brown-bay to maroon and brick. In general, these vessels do not appear to have been slipped. Although some pieces were burnished and polished after receiving a wash of liquid micaceous clay, some are rough.

This group was not encountered in southern Veracruz in spite of its paste similarity with "coarse buff, coarse black and coarse brown" of Tres Zapotes and La Venta. I have the impression that the only near-comparable specimens are those found by MacNeish near Panuco in northern Veracruz. These he calls "Progreso white" and assigns them to the Ponce period (MacNeish, 1954a, fig. 12, nos. 7–10).

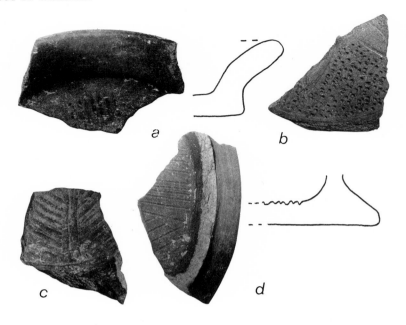

F_IG. 15—INCISED AND PUNCTATE-INCISED POTTERY. Scale of profiles, ½.

Figurines

The figurine types (fig. 16) found at Trapiche-Chalahuite have been described elsewhere (García Payón, 1966). Briefly, they are: Trapiche type (corresponding to the so-called "Morelos" of Weiant), named for the site where they were first found in 1942 (García Payón, 1950a, pl. 13, nos. 1–5, 7, 9, 10), Tres Zapotes type, Uaxactun type of Weiant, C-IV of Vaillant, Lower Remojadas, Type A, Baby Face, Prognathous, C-III of Vaillant or Prognathous with full cheeks, Blind, Triangular Face, Chubby-cheeks type, and another small unclassified group.

These figurines represent artistic idealizations of personages or deities with definite characteristics. Sometimes, as in the Trapiche and Tres Zapotes types, the style attains a rigid standardization.

Trapiche type is a regional one, typical of some sites in central Veracruz where Preclassic remains are found. One was found by Strebel (1885–89, 2: pl. 12, no. 167) in Misantla, three by Batres (1908, figs. 1, 2; pl. 1) at Alvarado; others occurred at Santa Luisa (no. 80) near Tecolutla, El Tejar (no. 441), Medellín (no. 167), and Rinconada (no. 364). Tres Zapotes figurine types have been found at Alvarado, Misantla, Ranchito de las Animas (no. 306), El Tejar, Rinconada, and Santa Luisa.

Other Artifacts

Stone artifacts include a smooth yoke in the mound at Trapiche, an incised jade tube, crude metates (one tetrapod), a mano worn by use, burins, pestles, mortars, polishers, bark beaters, ball-hammer, receptacle fragments, and a crude sculpture of amygdalin stone. Among the clay objects are small pellets for blowguns, and earplugs of various sizes and forms.

Habitations

One of the most interesting results of the

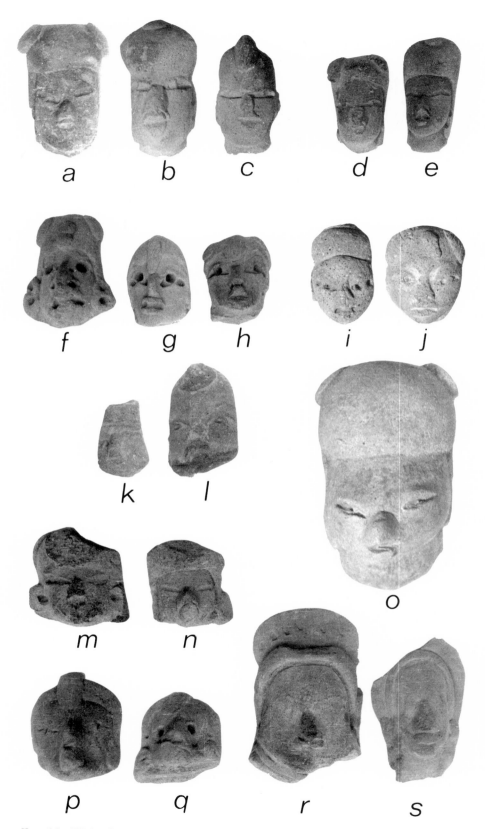

FIG. 16—TRAPICHE-CHALAHUITE FIGURINES. *a-e,* Trapiche type (Weiant's Morelos type). *f-h,* Tres Zapotes type. *i,j,* Weiant's Uaxactun type. *k,l,* Vaillant's Type C-IV. *m,n,* Hay's Type A. *o,* Chubby-cheeked hollow type. *p,q,* Prognathous type. *r,s,* Blind type.

FIG. 17—REMAINS OF SUBTERRANEAN HABITATIONS, CHALAHUITE

Trapiche-Chalahuite explorations during the 1959 season was verification that in the interior of the Preclassic mounds of central Veracruz are remains of rectangular and circular houses. These are either subterranean (pit houses) or semisubterranean (fig. 17). The walls are of rounded stones footed in earth fill. The houses were built on artificial mounds to protect them from flooding, as the Zempoalans did in the historic period. In one of these mounds in Chalahuite we found three superimposed structures. These habitations with stone floors must be of the type found by James A. Ford (1954, pp. 28–34) in the Guañape period of the Chicama Valley in Peru.

In the semiarid zone important remains have been found in Las Animas, but of much greater importance is the site known as Remojadas. Here 12 mounds are grouped in an area of 4 hectares, situated 5 km. northeast of Soledad de Doblado. Medellín Zenil found at Remojadas a number of offerings, including many ceramic objects in a very good state of preservation. Medellín

recognized two periods, which he called Lower Remojadas and Upper Remojadas.

The first is Preclassic and is characterized by the simplicity of the pottery forms, by modeling, appliqué, incising, nude figurines, tattooing, monochrome wares, near-absence of vessel supports, negative decoration, and postfired incising. There are brown vessels with black polished wash, brown with black wash and incised decoration, brown with a polished cherry-red wash, negative decoration, brown with a polished reddish wash, polished brown, clear polished brown, grayish polished, brown with polished cream wash, brown with polished white wash, and jars made of brown and creamy-red paste. The figurines included specimens with incised eyes and rudimentary limbs, "coffee-bean" eyes, flattened with rectangular eyes, flattened with a U-shaped base, and engraved eyelids with pupil in black paint. There are also hollow anthropomorphic sculptures with mammiform legs and handle, hollow zoomorphic sculptures with handles, and

523

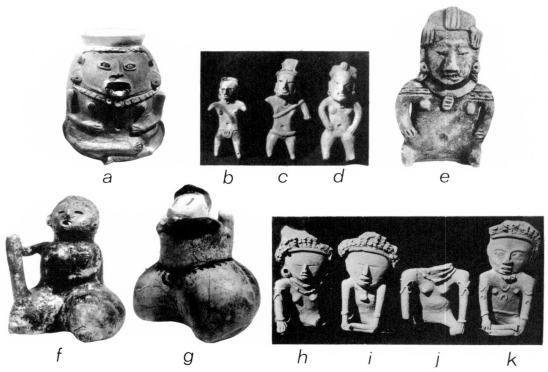

a   b   c   d   e

f   g   h   i   j   k

FIG. 18—POTTERY EFFIGY VESSELS AND FIGURINES, REMOJADAS AND CHICUASE

effigy jars. Medellín also mentions the use of cinnabar, *tizatl*, asphalt, and earth mounds, floors and walls of burned earth (*tierra quemada*).

Some of these traits, such as postfired incising, are found in Trapiche-Chalahuite, but for the most part are more evolved. This is seen in the flat bowls and tripod vases, effigy jars, spouts, large and small anthropomorphic sculptures, polished vessels, and even the negative type characterized by dots and circles with bands. All of these are distinct from the archaeological material of Trapiche-Chalahuite.

Medellín (1950, 1960b) considers all the aforementioned materials to be contemporary with El Arbolillo, Zacatenco-Copilco, Tlatilco I-II, Gualupita I, Monte Alban I, Lower Tres Zapotes, and Pavon I, in the 10th to 6th centuries B.C.

Preclassic elements have been found in other regions. In Orizaba *campesinos* brought in brown and black vessels with incised triangles crossed by parallel lines as at Trapiche, Remojadas, and Cerro de las Mesas. Oceloapan (no. 361), with Trapiche-type figurines (García Payón, 1949g, p. 504), has similar materials. At Carrizal in 1961 a secondary burial was found in a jar, and immediately north and south of it, "killed" yokes with representations of the earth monster. Both were associated with Late Preclassic material; one piece of yoke lay inside a jar (Bertha Cuevas, personal communication). At Chachalacas were found large Remojadas-type figurines as well as Tres Zapotes, Trapiche, and Lower Remojadas figurines, and brown-bay ware like that of the upper levels of Trapiche-Chalahuite (García Payón, 1951c).

There are also sites at El Mangal (no. 449), El Corte (no. 560), El Recreo, and

Alvarado. According to Medellín (1960a, p. 14), Alvarado yielded figurine types A of Vaillant and Uaxactun of Weiant. Cocuite (no. 529), near Tlalixcoyan, in 1961 contained a secondary burial in an apaxtle, similar to the brown-bay ware of the upper levels of Trapiche-Chalahuite. Wheeled figurines of jaguars, from the Classic period, were found with the skeleton. They are somewhat different in detail from the Period III specimen found by Ekholm (1944, pp. 472–74, fig. 49) at the Pavon site.

Drucker's Cerro de las Mesas pottery, especially polished brown ware, red ware, black ware, white ware, and negative painted (Drucker, 1943b, fig. 12,*a–c,e,f,j,l–n*), is similar to that in Lower Remojadas. Although vessel supports are abundant in Cerro de las Mesas and scarce at Trapiche and Remojadas, in both Cerro de las Mesas and Trapiche, Tres Zapotes and Trapiche subtype A figurines were discovered, but were not found at Remojadas. Facts such as these show the need for further investigations to determine whether there actually was a homogeneity among these archaeological regions such as Medellín and Melgarejo propose. They feel that the western limits of the Lower Remojadas culture reach from Acatlan de Perez Figueroa in Oaxaca to Metaltoyuca in Puebla (no. 1), via Chalchicomula, Puebla, and Tenextepec and Nepatecutlan[1] in the municipio of Perote. They also believe that this culture extended throughout central Veracruz (Medellín, 1952a).

Conclusions

In spite of many explorations these data demonstrate that we have not yet defined a regional nomenclature of ceramics, or summarized their typological correlations, or determined the distribution and evolution of the Preclassic period of central Veracruz.

[1] This site, now called Pueblo Viejo, was identified by Melgarejo. Palacios (1923a,b) had previously identified it as Hueyaltepec (Medellín, 1952a).

Fig. 19—APARICIO STELA

The Preclassic occupation extended throughout the Gulf Coast, where life was easier, but we lack exact information on most of the sites. The same is true of the mountainous regions, especially in the territory of Puebla.

It seems certain that the plain stone yokes appear in the Middle Preclassic and that the yokes carved with a representation of the earth monster appear in the Late Preclassic. It also seems certain that many

525

prototypes of Teotihuacan ceramics appear in the Preclassic of the Gulf (García Payón, 1952, pp. 35–36).

Because of the distribution and great variety of Preclassic ceramics and sculpture of this long period, we cannot apply to Veracruz the threefold chronology of Lower, Middle, and Upper Preclassic used in the Valley of Mexico. Instead, we have first a preceramic period, with stone receptacles later copied in pottery. They had temper of varying amounts, and thick walls. They appear to be associated with subterranean houses. A second period is represented by heavily tempered bay, brown, and black wares. There is possibly a third period with stamped or imprinted pottery of natural bichrome type. This is a good horizon-marker. A fourth period has Lower Remojadas traits that extend throughout the coast. A fifth sees the arrival of Olmec materials or influence and plain yokes. This corresponds to the Middle Preclassic of the Valley of Mexico. A sixth, corresponding to Late Preclassic, had stone yokes carved with representations of the earth monster, and saw the appearance of the Remojadas and Chachalacas figurines.

CLASSIC PERIOD

What Medellín (1960a, p. 55) calls "the violent change of forms and styles of the ceramics of this epoch" is astonishing. Very few Preclassic sites continued to be occupied. It is therefore natural to ask what happened to the Preclassic population of the central Veracruz Gulf Coast.

Beginning in Middle Preclassic times, people began to emigrate toward southern Veracruz and central America. Others took refuge in the Central Plateau, where we find some of their figurines, pottery, and other cultural traits in the valleys of Puebla, Mexico, and Toluca (García Payón, 1938, 1941b, 1950b; Covarrubias, 1950; Porter, 1953; Piña Chan, 1955b, 1958). Subsequently, during the first and third centuries A.D., because of climatic change and problems

of overpopulation, they returned again to the coast, carrying Teotihuacanoid cultural baggage. They founded such population centers as Tajin (no. 71), Lagunilla (no. 71a), Yohualichan, Puebla (no. 20), Malpica (no. 101), and Xiuhetelco, Puebla (no. 23), best known for their architectural monuments. Meanwhile the few groups that remained in the southern region underwent a cultural decadence and were subsequently influenced by peoples coming down from the Central Plateau. Their pottery changed radically, few of the older types surviving.

This period is characterized by regional diversity. The main archaeological complexes are: (1) stone yokes, palmate stones (*palmas*), and votive axes; (2) architecture of Tajin, Yohualichan, Lagunilla, etc., and ivory-colored kaolin pottery; (3) the smiling-face figures of the Tlalixcoyan–Remojadas–Tierra Blanca area. To these may be added large pottery sculptures and buff ware (not described here).

Tajin and Xiuhtetelco are the best-known archaeological centers so far as pottery is concerned (Du Solier, 1945a; García Payón, 1950d). Their oldest occupations correlate with the Teotihuacan Miccaotli and Xolalpan phases. Chief among the pottery remains is an ivory type, made of kaolin with negative-painted ornamentation or reliefs depicting esoteric scenes. It lasts until the Postclassic period, when we find Culhuacan-like flat-bottomed bowls. Some have cylindrical supports with iridescent black decoration painted with lead oxide on a reddish-brown base. This ware has also been found at Isla de Sacrificios and in Xiuhtetelco (Du Solier, 1943; Medellín, 1955, pp. 53, 56), continuing until the appearance of Isla de Sacrificios I and II ceramics.

El Tajin is also famous for its architectural style, involving the use of niches (fig. 37), friezes of frets, flying cornices, false arches, and flat roofs, forming a compact mass without interior reinforcement (García Payón, 1943, 1949a, 1949h, 1951a, 1951b,

TABLE 1—CHRONOLOGY OF EL TAJIN ARCHITECTURE

POSTCLASSIC	1100		Abandonment of El Tajin
	1000	Tajin XII	Building of the Columns. Monument V. Ceramics: Culhuacan, Tres Picos I, Isla de Sacrificios I
		Tajin XI	Monument D. Construction of tunnels
	900	Tajin X	South Ball Court with six sculptured panels
	800	Tajin IX	Monuments A, B, C
		Tajin VIII	Substructure of Monument A of Tajin Chico
	700	Tajin VII	Construction of the Tajin Chico promontory
	600	Tajin VI	North Ball Court with sculptured panels
		Tajin V	Pyramid of the Niches. Palmas
CLASSIC	500	Tajin IV	Monument III with panels. First ball courts with worked stones. Kaolin ceramics
	400	Tajin III	Substructures below Tajin Chico without cornices and with friezes of
	300		frets made with ashlar masonry. Carved yokes. Votive axes
	200	Tajin II	Pyramids with talud. Substructure of the Pyramid of the Niches. Ceramics: Teotihuacan I, II
	100	Tajin I	Small constructions; talud with unworked stones. Coarse ceramics
A.D.	0		
B.C.	100		
LATE PRECLASSIC	200		
	300		Yokes with representations of the earth monster
	400		
	500		
	600		
	700		
	800		Santa Luisa figurines and Late Preclassic ceramics
MIDDLE PRE-CLASSIC	900		
	1000		Plain yokes
	1100		

1954, 1938–62 field notes). The potsherds in the fill of these structures will eventually help to trace the evolution of this style (see Table 1).

Other salient sculptural motifs are the reliefs of interlaces (Proskouriakoff, 1953, 1954) mixed with sophisticated zoomorphic and anthropomorphic elements. Also one finds great realism in the presentation of esoteric scenes, some showing persons of distinct social classes. The chiefs wear breeches (Nahuatl, *maxtlatl*) and long trains (García Payón, 1959–61; 1963); the slaves are nude. One also sees cranial deformation of a child, human sacrifices, and dances. Beginning in Period VII the inhabitants began to emigrate south of Rio Nautla, where they constructed monuments like those of the last epoch at Tajin (García Payón, 1942; 1951b).

We know little about Classic period remains in the coastal region from Rio Nautla to the banks of Rio Pantepec. The most important is the archaeological zone of Kilometer 47 (no. 51) on the highway to Cazones. It consists of a mound with remains of a talud-tablero profile between two flat moldings, a pure Teotihuacan-type of con-

527

FIG. 20—NORTHEAST PANEL, SOUTH BALL COURT, TAJIN

struction. Yokes, palmas, and votive axes have turned up at some sites. The archaeological scene changes, however, when we reach the slopes of the Sierra Madre Oriental in the state of Puebla, ancient and present home of various Totonac groups. Here we find such archaeological centers as Xiuhtetelco (García Payón, 1950d), Macuilquila (no. 10), Ayotochco (no. 17), Tuzamapan, Ecatlan (Lombardo Toledano, 1931; García Payón, 1964), and Huachinango. There are ceramic and architectural similarities to Tajin, as at Yohualichan and Lagunilla, but there has been little exploration.

Well known in the Tajin region is the yoke–palmate stone–votive axe complex. The three traits (fig. 20) appear as ornamental motifs in the elaborate dress of persons depicted on the shafts of columns, and

on the four panels of the South Ball Court (García Payón, 1959–61), carved between A.D. 800 and 900. Two plain yokes and others with the earth-monster motif and symbolic elements have been found at Tajin itself. Many yokes, palmas, and votive axes have been found within a radius of 30 km. of Tajin, but so far not associated with tombs and offerings. Many yokes come from the Nautla–Tlapacoyan–Tlacolula–Zempoala region (Fewkes, 1907, 1919; García Payón, 1947b; Strebel, 1885–89, pls. 13–15), probably the region to which the inhabitants of Tajin emigrated after the destruction of the city. In this area are many architectural and ceramic correlations with the last epoch of Tajin.

Yokes have been found as far away as Copan (Honduras), Palenque (Chiapas),

528

FIG. 21—STONE STATUE, LOS IDOLOS

Oaxaca, Teotihuacan, Tulancingo, Metalto-yuca, and the southern Huasteca. They occur with much greater frequency in central Veracruz between Rio Papaloapan and Rio Pantepec.

Palmate stones are not so widely distributed as yokes. In the Espinal–Comalteco region, and at El Tajin and Yohualichan, many clay figurines have a palma springing from the abdomen. Most of these have been destroyed by prudes who mistook the palma for a phallus. Votive axes are found as far away as Palenque.

Farther south, there are several Late Classic monumental sculptures (fig. 21) in the archaeological zone of Los Idolos (no. 174) in the vicinity of Misantla. Sites occur from the mouth of Rio Chachalacas into the semiarid region: Ranchito de las Animas (no. 306), Chicuase (no. 305), Tolome (no. 340), Remojadas (no. 355). In the lower Papaloapan drainage, are Cerro de las Mesas (no. 528), Nopiloa, Tlalixcoyan, Dicha Tuerta, and Los Cerros. In Maltrata (no. 472) there is a monolith with interesting low relief bar-and-dot numbers and depicting a pyramid with niches or tableros. These resemble the numerals and the architecture shown on Monument 1 of Tajin. The pyramid has a thatched roof.

At Ranchito de las Animas, Talome, Chachalacas, and elsewhere, vessels of Late Preclassic type continued: cylindrical vases with or without supports, at times incised and finished in white, red, or brown. There

a

b

c

d

FIG. 22—CHACHALACAS POTTERY. *a,b*, Chachalacas Decorated. *c,d*, Chachalacas Incised.

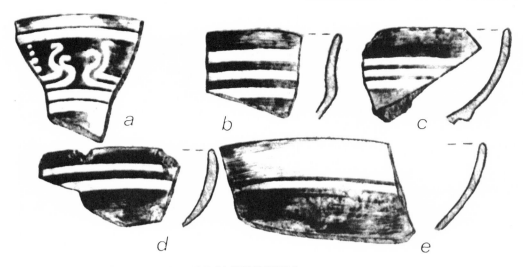

FIG. 23—POTTERY OF ISLA DE SACRIFICIOS 1

are also apaxtles, plates, and large dishes that resemble materials from the upper levels of Trapiche-Chalahuite. Among ceramics of Teotihuacan type are cylindrical vases with or without supports, cajetes with nipple supports, and flat-bottomed wide-mouthed jars (García Payón, 1951c; Strebel, 1885–89, pl. 5, nos. 1, 18). These occur also at Cerro de las Mesas (Drucker, 1943b, pp. 58–59, 82–84) and Remojadas. Medellín (1960b) has noted that the Upper Remojadas specimens may be pre-Teotihuacan, for they are not as well developed and they follow the Archaic remains of Lower Remojadas. The beginning of this period is characterized by two types of ceramics with red-on-white decoration: "Chachalacas decorated" (fig. 22,a,b) and "Chachalacas lined and scraped" (fig. 22,c,d; García Payón, 1951c, pls. 3,4). Both are thin walled. Medellín found a great variety of forms of the first type in Upper Remojadas. Shapes include cajetes, large apaxtles, zoomorphic forms with spouts, and Teotihuacan-type cylindrical tripod vases. Decoration depicts very stylized spider monkeys, at times represented by only the tail, and geometric motifs Medellín, 1960b). These vessels extend along the Gulf Coast to Rio Nautla

and the Papaloapan drainage. The second type is covered with white paint and finished in orange. The artists then scraped through the orange to make decorations by exposing the white underneath, outlining their features with incised lines (Medellín, 1960b; García Payón, 1951c). This type extended north to the Misantla region and El Tajin (García Payón, 1947b; 1938–64 field notes). There is also an orange ware without temper, called Isla de Sacrificios I (fig. 23), found in Zempoala and in the region of Misantla and El Tajin (Du Solier, 1945a, pl. 12, nos. 2, 3, 5; García Payón, 1947b, pl. 16). The color of the bottom varies; the linear decoration can be red or white.

The rattle-figurines (fig. 24) of Los Cerros and Nopiloa have a regional flavor. They remind us of specimens from Jaina and of the wheeled zoomorphic figurines from Tlalixcoyan.

Classic period masculine and feminine figures of various sizes have been found in Chachalacas, Chicuase (García Payón, 1951c, figs. 20–23; Strebel, 1885–89, nos. 7, 10, 25–30, 37–38), Remojadas (Medellín, 1960a, pls. 37–41, 52–54, 58–62), and Cerro de las Mesas (Drucker, 1943b, pls. 45, 46; Weyerstall, 1932, pls. 1, 2, 4–11) and appear

FIG. 24—POTTERY FIGURES, LOS CERROS AND NOPILOA

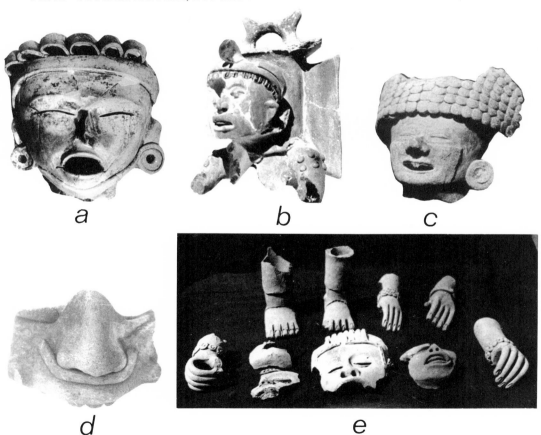

FIG. 25—POTTERY FIGURES. *a,c*, Remojadas. *b,e*, Chachalacas. *d*, Tajin.

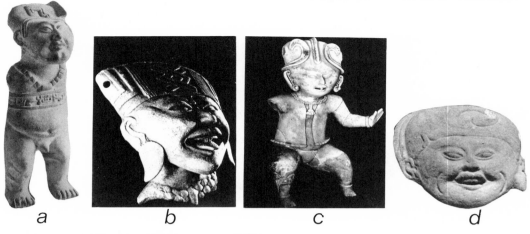

a   b   c   d

FIG. 26—SONRIENTES (SMILING) FIGURINES

to extend along all the coast from the bank of the Papaloapan to El Tajin (fig. 25), where so far we have been able to put together fragments of only their noses and bodies. The most surprising artifacts, unique in their style, are pottery figures of women and men with smiling faces (fig. 26). These *sonrientes* are found in only a part of the Papaloapan drainage.

According to Medellín, the smiling-face figurines developed through four phases. The oldest phase, which he calls "Loma de Carmona," is Early Classic. Whistles with small smiling figures appear here and in Remojadas, Los Cerros, Dicha Tuerta (no. 536), Apachital, Nopiloa (Medellín, 1960a, 1960b, 1962, 1953), and Chachalacas (García Payón, 1951c, fig. 17a). There followed "Los Cerros I" phase with smiling figures, "plain flat noses," and adornment between the eyebrows. The Late Classic period, "Los Cerros II," is characterized by saurian, heron, monkey, serpent, or human representations, serpent-in-panel motif, central and lateral geometric decoration, *xicalcoliuhqui* (stepped fret) and thin-line decoration, cranial deformation, and polished orange surface. The final phase, "Dicha Tuerta," features two types called "indented arcs" and "small rectangular" (Medellín, 1960a, p. 44).

Recapitulating the Classic period of central Veracruz, we see two paradoxical features and a third local one. The first, El Tajin, has a distinctively decorated and constructed architecture and a special kaolin pottery. The latter did not stay on the coast, but is found also in the Sierra de Puebla, Yohualichan, Xiuhtetelco, and elsewhere. The second is the great art of the smiling-face statuettes, which are contemporary with the pottery sculpture of Upper Remojadas, developing in a very limited region during five centuries (Medellín, 1960a). Yokes, palmas, and votive axes occur from Rio Tuxpan to Coatzacoalcos. The third are the Maya-like Los Cerros figures, found as far away as Los Tuxtlas.

The paucity of Classic period structures, perhaps 20 per cent as many as those of Preclassic times, is puzzling.

POSTCLASSIC PERIOD

In the Sierra de Puebla region, habitat par excellence of the Totonac, and extending to the lower spurs of the Sierra Madre Oriental and the El Tajin and Malpica (no. 103) archaeological zones, are remains of the Postclassic period. Both archaeology and 16th-century historical records reveal the invasion of the Toltec (García Payón, 1964). The Toltec constructed fortified towns such as Tenampulco, Puebla (no. 6), Tuzapan (no. 68), Castillo de Teayo (no. 36), and Cachuatenco (no. 28). This resulted in a slow but constant exodus of the Totonac over several centuries, toward the mountainous regions and the coasts from the Sierra de Misantla and Aparicio (no. 202), Tlapacoyan, Vega de la Peña (no. 138) to Tlacolula (no. 260), Zempoala (no. 322), and Oceloapan (no. 361). Here for a long time they reconcentrated their forces and established towns. Utilizing for construction the local stone slabs or boulders, they erected their temples in Tajinoid architectural style: platforms with lateral revetments of inverted taluds, communication tunnels, and columns and friezes with frets in high relief. All these are characteristic of the two last construction periods of El Tajin (García Payón, 1963).

At this great site, the period is characterized by a florescence of construction, producing the South Ball Court with its low-relief panels; Monument 5 with friezes of frets in high relief; and the civil buildings A, B, C, F, G. Toward the end of the period, architectural innovations were possibly introduced by the Toltec living in the vicinity, or Toltec intermixed with the local population of the city. They covered the niches and large friezes with rubblework in order to transform all into plain surfaces and superimposed staircases with smooth balustrades climbing directly to the second level of the buildings. New deities appear (García Payón, 1943, 1949a, 1949h, 1951a, 1951b, 1954, 1938–62 field notes).

One of the principal Toltec centers was Tuzapan (no. 68), investigated by Palacios (1945) and Du Solier (1939a). They consider Tuzapan to be Nahua-Totonac, from the fact that in conquest times it was a bilingual town. I believe that this center was founded by the Toltec, to judge from its location, fortifications, architecture, relief sculptures, and its earliest ceramics that are related to Mazapa, Coyotlatelco, and Culhuacan types.

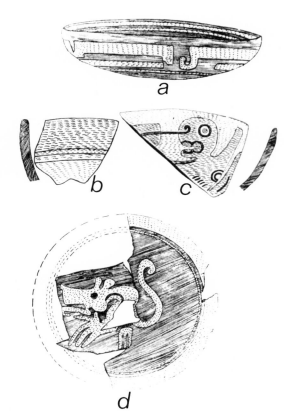

FIG. 27—TRES PICOS I POTTERY. Note representations of coyotes like those of Tajin bas-reliefs (cf. fig. 28).

Castillo de Teayo was probably founded in A.D. 815 (García Payón, 1950c, 1952). Its pyramid is in Tula and Calixtlahuaca style but different form, covering 576 sq. m., at the base, is 13 m. high, and consists of three superimposed units, with a *perron* to the west, oriented 17 degrees west, like other monuments of this culture. In the region are sporadic jaguar and Coyotlatelco relief, Mazapa ceramics, and Mazapa figures. In the lower levels of this largely unexplored zone are Huastec elements from Ekholm's (1944) Periods III and IV, overlain by Toltec remains; above these are Huastec elements of Ekholm's Period VI. Features of this archaeological center are sculptures preponderantly in the round, stelae and panels depicting Nahua-Huastec deities such as

F<small>IG.</small> 28—COYOTES DEPICTED ON BAS-RE-LIEF, TAJIN

Mixcoatl, Xipe, Tlazolteotl, Centeocihuatl, Tlaloc, and Quetzalcoatl. The sculptures are roughly executed, with beveled borders —completely different from the angular sculpture of El Tajin. The Castillo de Teayo stela depicts Atl-Tlachinolli, in contrast to Aztec monuments commemorating conquests, as at Xochimilco, Cuauhquechula, and Cuauhnahuac, which always show a war shield sometimes with crossed arrows (García Payón, 1952).

Toltec remains are found in Chachalacas in the first construction period of Zempoala, associated with sporadic Mazapa and Coyotlatelco ceramics (García Payón, 1951c, pl. 3), a chacmool made of stucco with a stone center (Paso y Troncoso, 1891, 1893), and two *tlachtemalacatl* from a ball court

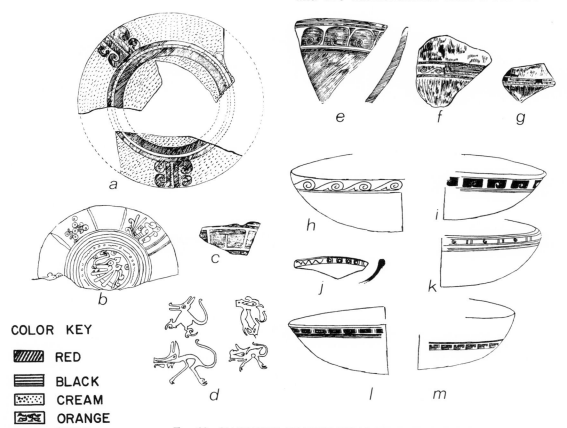

COLOR KEY

/////	RED
≡≡≡	BLACK
:::::	CREAM
〰〰	ORANGE
⊟⊟⊟	DARK BROWN
⩘⩘⩘	YELLOW

F<small>IG.</small> 29—VARIANTS OF TRES PICOS TYPE OF POTTERY

534

of which today not even a trace remains. The Postclassic Columns Group marks the apogee of plastic arts and bold architectural achievement. The associated Tres Picos I polychrome pottery (fig. 27) is Tajinoid (fig. 28). It is made of fine clay. The bottoms of the vessels carry painted monkey or dancing coyote figures. On the wall exteriors are panels decorated with symbolic motifs, or a narrow band incised before firing. This polychrome pottery comes from south of Rio Nautla (García Payón, 1947b, pls. 11–13). With Monument 5 were Culhuacan ceramics painted, sometimes in Tajinoid style, in iridescent black on a red background; forms include tripod cajetes and plates with cylindrical supports. Their geographical distribution reaches Tzicoac and Tabuco near Tuxpan, where there was a Toltec garrison (García Payón, 1946). Medellín (1955, pp. 53, 56) and Melgarejo believe, correctly I think, that this pottery originated in the Huasteca, in Ekholm's Panuco V period.

Also Postclassic are the archaeological zones of Paxil (no. 166), Aparicio (no. 202), Cerro de la Morena (no. 215), Tapapulum (no. 125), and Vega de la Peña (no. 138). The last two have ball courts, and at Vega de la Peña there is a frieze of frets in relief. Arroyo Fierro (no. 162), Escalonar (no. 188), Pompeya (no. 141), and Paxil have platforms, communication tunnels, and other features like those of Tajin Chico (García Payón, 1947b, 1949b, 1952, 1963). Their principal ceramics are Tres Picos I (García Payón, 1947b, where I called it Paxil I) and Isla de Sacrificios I and II types.

In the south, the most representative Postclassic sites are Cerro Montoso (Strebel, 1885–89, 1: pls. vii,*15,18,19*; viii,*21*; x, *1,2,4–14*; xi,*28,29*) and Isla de Sacrificios (Nepean, 1844, 1857; Nuttal, 1910; Joyce, 1912; 1920, pl. 18; Du Solier, 1943; Medellín, 1955). Isla de Sacrificios pottery has been interpreted as marking the beginning of the Totonac renaissance (Melgarejo,

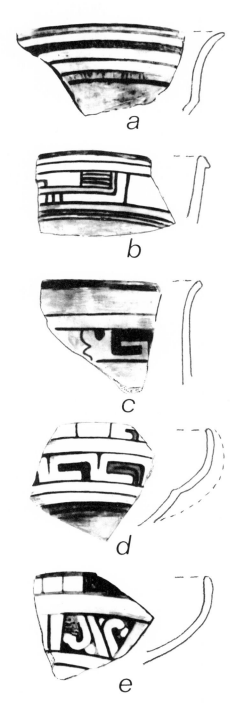

Fig. 30—ISLA DE SACRIFICIOS II POTTERY. *e*, Black and white bichrome.

535

a

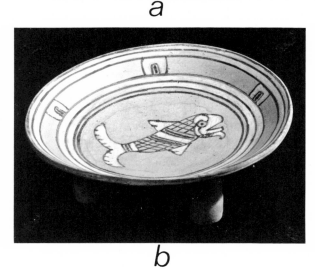

b

FIG. 31—ISLA DE SACRIFICIOS III AND IV POLYCHROME POTTERY. *a*, Period III. *b*, Period IV.

1943, 1950; Medellín, 1955, 1960a). To these two centers may be added the first construction period at Zempoala, Zoncuantla (no. 390), the last period at Xiuhtetelco, Cuetlaxtlan, Upper Cerro de las Mesas, and many other sites where isolated potsherds of this period have been found. The geographical distribution reaches the slopes of the Peak of Orizaba and the Sierra de Puebla.

FINE ORANGE. This Gulf Coast pottery, which may or may not have temper, extends from Rio Pantepec to southern Veracruz. In addition, in some sites such as Tajin, Yohualichan, Xiuhtetelco, and Upper Remojadas, it appears in the Classic period. There are various subgroups, but I shall describe only the Fine Orange of Isla de Sacrificios. Here we find little "flower vases" (*floreros*) with pedestal base, and little effigy jars, which are rare at Zempoala and Cerro Montoso and do not reach the Misantla–Xiuhtetelco–Tajin region. There are also "Isla de Sacrificios" vessels of three types (figs. 30, 31).

PLUMBATE. Although this is abundant at Isla de Sacrificios and is found sporadically in central Veracruz, I did not find it at Zempoala. In Chachalacas there was only one fragment. It does not occur in the Xiuhtetelco–Misantla–Tajin region.

BLACK-ON-RED. Du Solier and I found this at El Tajin and Xiuhtetelco and considered it to be a variety of the Culhuacan type that, as mentioned earlier, carries an iridescent decoration produced by oxidation of lead. Medellín and Melgarejo consider this to be of Huastec origin. It is not found in the region of Misantla.

TRES PICOS I. As already mentioned, its two subtypes were found in El Tajin and extend through all of Totonacapan with another contemporaneous type that has large incised motifs.

QUIAHUIXTLAN I. This has red linear decoration. It is found at Isla de Sacrificios, but is not abundant along the coast. It begins in the Zempoala Chachalacas region with fine-clay vessels with stamped bottoms. In the following period it spread throughout Totonacapan (García Payón, 1951d).

METALLIC. This ware, with its Fine Orange paste, was intended, according to Medellín, to imitate Plumbate. It occurs as vases and effigy jars. Although abundant at Isla de Sacrificios, it has not been found in Cerro Montoso, Zempoala, or Misantla.

HISTORIC PERIOD

The number of archaeological zones of this period is enormous, compared with the preceding. Toward the middle of the 16th century Yaohualichan was abandoned and was followed a little later by Xiuhtetelco, Malpica, and Tajin. The first two regions were occupied by Nahua people, but Tajin reverted to forest and was forgotten until discovered by the engineer Diego Ruíz (1785). Not far away were such Nahua towns as Tenampulco, Tuzapan, and Tabuco, on the banks and at the mouth of Rio Pantepec.

This period saw an increasing influx of peoples. First the Toltec and subsequently the Chichimec invasions forced an emigration of Totonac from the Sierra de Puebla toward the Gulf Coast, between Rio Nautla and Rio La Antigua or Huitzilapan, on the one hand, and the mountains of Tlapacoyan–Misantla–Tlacolula on the other. They later moved into the Rio Tecolutla drainage, where, with the mixing of Totonac and Nahua elements, Tenampulco, Tuzapan and Tabuco became bilingual towns. They founded other towns—Papantla, La Concha, Coatzintla, Xalpantepec—until, after the 16th century, the Papantla–San Andres–Coyusquihui–Gutierrez Zamora region became the most important nucleus of Totonac speech in Veracruz (García Payón, 1964). In the Sierra de Puebla, large and small Totonac nuclei are intermixed with Nahua people to this day and Totonac-speakers continue to come down to the Papantla region (see fig. 1).

Other people, whom Medellín calls the historic Olmec or Popoloca, occupy the Orizaba–Cordoba–Rio Blanco–Papaloapan regions of southern Veracruz. Their principal centers are Quauhtochco (no. 497), Cuetlaxtlan (no. 508), Mictlancuahtlan (no. 442), Comapa, Tlacotepec (no. 376), Zentla (no. 379), Cerro Grande (no. 520), and Tlalixcoyan (no. 522). Medellín says that they show little influence from the Totonac who occupy the southern region north of Rio La Antigua. He states that the pottery of this extensive region forms part of the Mixtec–Puebla ceramic complex. Wares include a stamped-bottom type, polychrome lacquer, compact polychrome —also found in Cerro de las Mesas (Drucker, 1943b)—gray slipped, reddish sandy coarse, fine thin gray, black on cherry-red and derivatives, censers, Aztec III and Aztecoid types that show influence from the Mixtec region and the Valley of Mexico (Medellín, 1960a, p. 138). They occur also in the archaeological zone of La Palmilla (no. 462) near Cordoba.

Among these archaeological zones, Quauhtochco is outstanding for its well-preserved, four-stack pyramid in talud, rising from a small platform. At the summit is a sanctuary. Nail-shaped stones were inserted into its façade, to represent the starred sky; this shows clear Aztec influence. Its location, walls, and breastworks caused Medellín (1952b) to believe it was a "city fort" in much the same style as that of the fortified Toltec cities of Tuzapan, Tenampulco, and Cacahuatenco. At the ruins of Comapan were found pyramids, palaces, tombs, patios, temples, standard-bearers, and walls. Tlacotepec and Zental, too, though still not explored, were fortified cities (Medellín, 1960b, pp. 150–51).

In Totonacapan there is a great conglomerate of cities in the area of the Sierra de Misantla–Atzalan, Tlacolula–Oceloapan, and on the coastal plains. From its size and technological development, Zempoala was probably the capital of the Totonac, and in 1519 it represented the apogee of Totonac culture. It had an elaborate canal irrigation system and extensive aqueducts (fig. 32), branching out through subterranean masonry passages and distributing water for daily use (García Payón, 1949e) in the ten-temple compound and principal houses of the town. The early chroniclers called this *"agua de pie"* (Torquemada, 1943–44, 1:

FIG. 32—SUBTERRANEAN AQUEDUCTS. *a-c*, Zempoala. *d*, Subterranean aqueduct (at right), Recinto de las Caritas, emptied into an irrigation canal northeast of the entrance through the wall surrounding the site. (Photographed by F. del Paso y Troncoso in 1891.)

538

396; López de Gómara, 1852, p. 317). Archaeological explorations have confirmed that by means of gradual inclines these aqueducts emptied into house- or enclosure-cisterns and from them, through another passageway, to other cisterns, until they finally discharged into an irrigation canal.

The Historic period architecture, abundant in Totonacapan, especially on the coast and the lower spurs of the Sierra Madre Oriental, follows the norm of Zempoala. The flat stuccoed walls are made of different materials, according to region. They differ from those of Zempoala and Oceloapan (García Payón, 1949g) in not enclosing temple areas or being surmounted by merlons. They represent the last period of construction in both cities.

The architectural styles of Totonacapan can be divided into two groups: those beginning between the middle and the end of the Postclassic, and those of the Historic period. The first tend to show some degree of Tajin influence: platforms of inverted taluds, tunnels, frets, and columns. The latter reflects the ascendancy of Zempoala, which, in its last two periods dating from the 15th century onward, shows great Mexican influence, although in the distribution and function of its rooms it was either largely independent or subject to a certain Maya influence (García Payón (1944b, 1947a, 1949c,d,e,f,i).

We find three types of tomb burials. The first, which seems to be the oldest, is a square, oval, cylindrical, or conical pit; parallelogram outlines predominate. It is situated on top of structures, in front of stairs, or in the center of the building. Interior veneers are slabs or small rounded stones covered with stucco. The majority are collective. The second type, apparently Postclassic, is cruciform, located in the center of the building, or below the level at the foot of the stairway. The third type may have originated before the conquest; it had a limited geographical distribution (García Payón, 1945b, 1950e). It is an individual or a

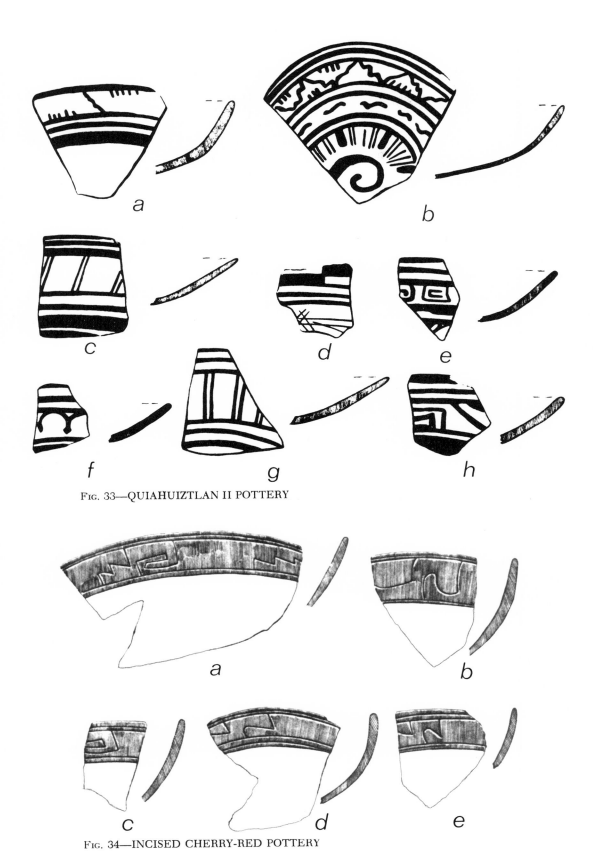

a

b

c

d

e

f

g

h

FIG. 33—QUIAHUIZTLAN II POTTERY

a

b

c

d

e

FIG. 34—INCISED CHERRY-RED POTTERY

FIG. 35—TRES PICOS II (ABOVE) AND TOTONAC POLYCHROME (BELOW) POTTERY

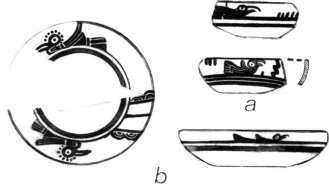

FIG. 36—TRICHROME POTTERY, ZEMPOALA. *a*, Interior above, exterior below. *b*, Interior at left, exterior at right.

540

collective mausoleum similar in form to a temple or house. It has a rectangular base, rising in one, two, or three stepped terraces with vertical walls, and has a balustraded stairway up the front. The roof is carved to imitate the palm-thatched roof of a house; sometimes it is flat, surrounded by merlons on three sides. Medellín considers these to be of pre-Spanish origin. He says (1960b, pp. 160–61) that they extend from Nautla on the north to the Rio Comapa on the south, in the Popoloca or Historic Olmec region, and to Tlacolula in the Jalapa region on the west and Monte Real near Misantla, but I consider that the center of diffusion was in Quihuiztlan, at Villa Rica.

The ceramics of this last period show a great range of forms, ornamentation, and paste clay. We may consider them in two groups which, however, overlap in some cases. The first may be assigned to the coast or Totonac culture that extended throughout Totonacapan; the second is related to the intrusion of Mixteco-Puebla and Aztec cultures of more limited distribution. The latter is abundant in Zempoala, sporadic in the Misantla region, and not present in Tlapacoyan, Gutierrez Zamora, Papantla, and Ayotocho.

The first type is usually of fine clay with little or no temper. Important horizon-markers are the types known as Isla de Sacrificios II and III, Quihuiztlan II and III (fig. 33), Tres Picos II (fig. 35,*a*) and III, Totonac polychrome (fig. 35,*b*), and Zempoala trichrome with its painted series of birds and other motifs that resemble the Fine Orange ware of Chichen Itza (fig. 36; Brainerd, 1941; 1958, pls. 77, 78). There is also undecorated Fine Orange, and modeled zoomorphic and anthropomorphic figurines with representations of Nahua deities, found as far away as Cerro de las Mesas (Drucker, 1943b, pls. 30–36; García Payón, n.d.,*c*), braziers, and cream-colored bottles with handles and cap. All Zempoala polychrome lacquer and compact polychrome are abundant. Their diversity of

a

b

Fig. 37—PYRAMID OF THE NICHES, TAJIN

form and design, and the vigor of the brushwork contrast with the opacity and timidity of Cholula (Noguera, 1954) and Quauhtochco (Medellín, 1952b) ceramic art.

Pottery with or without stamped bottom, with interior red rim, with or without horizontal white and black lines, and other decorative motifs, at times polychrome, also surpass the corresponding wares of the Central Plateau in their diversity of modeling and ornamentation (García Payón, 1951d). There is a black, bay or gray ware, so compact that when one breaks it, it resembles slate. The forms include plates, fruit-dish or cup with bell-shaped supports or tripodal conical or nipple supports. Pottery with black linear decoration on a yellow background is of Aztec II and III origin, or Aztecoid of regional manufacture. Another type has a vivid red slip with black or white decoration or both; it occurs as

perfumers (*tlemaitl*), plates, vases, and tripod cajetes, all forms typical of Aztec III.

There are also vessels with perforated walls and appliqué decoration; censers with two handles, common also in the valleys of Mexico and Toluca; stamps with geometric, zoomorphic, and symbolic motifs; models of circular and rectangular temples; and *omichicahuaxtli* with incised designs. These reveal at Zempoala the profound influence of the culture of the Central Plateau. If the Spanish conquest had come 50 years later, the Totonac culture would probably have been extinguished.

Metallurgy occurs late in central Veracruz. Specimens found in Chachalacas and Zempoala date from the 16th–19th centuries. They had so little copper that they imitated metal bells in pottery, but there are some very interesting small copper figures representing birds and other creatures.

REFERENCES

Batres, 1905, 1908
Brainerd, 1941, 1958
Covarrubias, 1950
Drucker, 1943a, 1943b, 1952
Du Solier, 1939a, 1943, 1945a
Ekholm, 1944, 1953
Fewkes, 1907, 1919
Ford, 1954
García Payón, n.d., *a,b*, 1938, 1939, 1941b, 1942, 1943, 1944a, 1944b, 1945a, 1945b, 1946, 1947a, 1947b, 1949a-i, 1950b-f, 1951a-d, 1952, 1954, 1959–61, 1963, 1964, 1965, 1966
Joyce, 1912, 1920
Lombardo Toledano, 1931
López de Gómara, 1852
MacNeish, 1954a, 1961b
Medellín Zenil, 1950, 1952a, 1952b, 1953, 1955, 1960a, 1960b, 1962

———, Paz, and Beveride, 1962
Melgarejo V., 1943, 1950
Nepean, 1844, 1857
Noguera, 1936, 1954
Nuttall, 1910
Palacios, 1923a, 1923b, 1945
Paso y Troncoso, 1891, 1893
Piña Chan, 1955b, 1958
Porter, 1953
Proskouriakoff, 1953, 1954
Ruiz, D., 1785
Strebel, 1885–89
Torquemada, 1943–44
Valenzuela, 1945
Weiant, 1943
Weyerstall, 1932

22. Cultural Ecology and Settlement Patterns of the Gulf Coast

WILLIAM T. SANDERS

Running from a few miles north of Tampico southward and eastward to the border between Campeche and Tabasco is the stretch of lowland plain known as the Gulf Coast. The term "lowland" refers to all land lying below 800 m. above sea level. This contour line is the traditional border between *tierra templada* and *tierra caliente*. The area has a fundamental ecological unity in several characteristics: (1) frosts are absent, permitting all-year cropping where precipitation cycles permit; (2) crops classed as tropical may be grown; (3) rainfall, with a few exceptions, exceeds 1000 mm. a year and averages from 1500 to 2000; (4) natural plant coverage is exuberant and tends to be tropical forest; (5) there are abundant permanent streams in addition to several major river systems with large basins and extensive flood plains.

Judged by size of the drainage area and volume of water flow, four of the largest river systems of Mesoamerica are in this region—the Panuco-Tamesi, Papaloapan, Coatzacoalcos, Grijalva-Usumcinta. These systems occur in northern Veracruz–southern Tamaulipas, southern Veracruz, and Tabasco. Central Veracruz is crossed by a series of permanent rivers with smaller basins and water volume and flood plains, but they are still major streams as Mesoamerican rivers are rated. From north to south they are the Tuxpan, Cazones, Tecolutla, Nautla, Actopan, Antigua, and Cotaxtla.

Although this great arc of low-lying territory is called a plain, there is considerable variation in topography. The four major basins have nearly flat terrain and extensive flood plain. A large part of the lower sections of these basins consists of drowned savannas, swamps, and lagoons. The entire stretch of plain, however, from the Panuco to the Papaloapan, is one of rolling hills and well-drained topography. Between the Nautla and Actopan rivers an eastward-running spur of the Sierra Madre, called the Sierra de Chiconquiac, extends nearly to the coast and breaks the monotony of the area. Between the great basins of the Papaloapan and Coatzacoalcos rivers in southern Veracruz is an isolated range of hills, with maximum elevation of some 600 m., called the Sierra de San Martin.

With a few exceptions, rainfall is heavy in this huge region but varies considerably from place to place. The maximal readings occur more often in the *tierra templada* belt just above the coastal plain in steep slope escarpment, than in the *tierra caliente* itself. Elevations within the plain also affect total precipitation. With the exception of such local interruptions, rainfall increases from north to south. In the Panuco basin, stations average about 1000 mm. Just south in the rolling terrain of the northern Totonacapan, precipitation increases to 1250–1500 mm.; on the northern slopes of the Sierra de Chiconquiac to 2500 mm. The latter range acts as a rain shadow so that precipitation in central Veracruz just south of it is greatly reduced. In this area rainfall varies from 674 to 1250 mm., a climax of aridity occurring at Rinconada. To the south the Papaloapan basin and the Sierra de San Martin stations record an average of 2000 mm.; farther south, in the Coatzacoalcos basin, this increases to 3000 mm. Over most of the Tabascan plain rainfall varies from 2000 to 2500 mm., but just behind the plain in the Chiapas-Tabasco border area it reaches a maximum for Mesoamerica of 4000–5000 mm. a year. This area is exceptional in that maximal rainfall occurs not in the *tierra templada* but still within the *tierra caliente* belt.

Vegetation follows these rainfall patterns. Most of the region south of the Rio Cotaxtla is covered by dense tropical forest. Exceptions are drowned flood plains in the Coatzacoalcos and Papaloapan basins with swamp-savannas and large stretches of inland savannas in Tabasco on elevated flat terrain. In most of central Veracruz, where precipitation is markedly reduced, the vegetation consists of scrubby bush, cactus, and grassy savanna interrupted by gallery forests along the rivers. The hilly plains of the northern Totonacapan are covered with tropical forests. The vegetation of the Pa-

nuco basin is difficult to reconstruct because plow agriculture and cattle raising have completely altered it. The rainfall suggests primarily savanna cover, but I suspect it was, in part, tropical forest.

Little is known about the soil of the Gulf Coast plain. In the better-drained hilly area soils tends to be red and yellow lateritic. They are moderately fertile and, under careful cultivation (combined with high rainfall), tend to be productive for maize. Relatively flat terrain out of reach of annual floods seems to be the least fertile of all lands, presumably owing to excessive leaching. Prize lands are those which are flooded annually by rivers where the flood is relatively brief and which receive annual deposits of alluvium. There are large tracts of lagoons, swampy savannas, and perpetually water-logged areas that are unusable agriculturally. In central Veracruz and in the Panuco basin, where rainfall is low, are soils classified as *pradera*, black prairie soil similar to chernozems in northern latitudes.

In summary, several major ecological features affect occupation by man. (1) Vegetation is exuberant and has great regenerative power, producing a serious obstacle to farmers with neolithic tools and a basic crop which requires annual preparation of the land, planting, and harvesting. (2) With the exception of the dry zone in central Veracruz, the area is relatively free from drought and benefits from all-year cropping, although droughts do affect winter crops. (3) Complete freedom from frost likewise permits all-year cropping under the proper conditions of precipitation. (4) There is a high percentage of agriculturally marginal land because of savanna cover, permanently inundated terrain, and barren or low-fertility soils. (5) With the exception of riverside strips of alluvium, soils are of low to moderate fertility in the areas of high precipitation. In the Panuco-Tamesi basin and in central Veracruz the prairie soils are of high fertility and, unfortunately, are combined in central Veracruz with savanna

544

vegetation and drought conditions. (6) The prize agricultural lands occur in well-drained flood plains or hilly terrain. (7) The area has abundant surface drainage from numerous major rivers and permanent streams, and in some parts lagoons provide transportation and aquatic food resources.

Factors Affecting Settlement
Agricultural Systems

In Article 1 of this volume, I postulated two sets of factors operative in determining settlement patterns of an area: primary, those directly related to the environment and its utilization, and secondary, the social, religious, and political institutions. Under primary factors I listed (a) direct geographical features such as water resources, local topography, and drainage; (b) agricultural systems, and (c) geographical complexity.

In this region today are practiced three basic systems of agriculture: (a) slash-and-burn, (b) barbecho or plow with annual cropping, and (c) commercial plantation agriculture with primarily slow-growing tree crops. These systems correlate closely in distribution with the ecological variations noted in the introductory section.

Slash-and-burn agriculture with maize as the staple plus an extraordinarily great variety of secondary crops is the primary agricultural pattern all over the Gulf Coast where the vegetal cover is tropical forest, and rainfall exceeds 1200 mm. and soils fall into the lateritic category. This system in general is linked with only moderate soil fertility and extremely vigorous natural vegetation. In the Gulf Coast the forest is cleared with steel machetes and axes, and the trash burned off. The crop is planted without working the soil, by using the digging stick to punch small holes in which the seed or cutting is dropped. The major agricultural activity is weeding; studies by Kelly and Palerm (1952, pp. 113–14) in the Totonacapan and by the Carnegie Institution staff (Morley, 1947, pp. 148–49) in Yucatan indicate that the task of weeding is more laborious and time-consuming than the primary clearing of the forest.

If high forest has been cleared, the soil is relatively fertile and weed growth is relatively slow so that labor need not be excessive and yields are very high. The main crop (*milpa*) is planted during the summer when rains are heaviest. Frequently a second winter harvest (*tonamil*) is planted. With each successive year of cultivation a combination of increasing weed competition and reduction of soil fertility makes it more economical, in terms of declining production and increasing labor requirements, to clear fresh forests and abandon previously cultivated fields. The land is rested until the woody trees grow high enough to kill off the weeds and grasses, then it may be cultivated again. In an area of relatively heavy population, one finds a patchwork of high forest, *acahual* or secondary forest, and milpa. Where population is heavy there may be no high forest, only acahual and milpa. The precise ratio of the three elements and the ratio of years of cultivation to years of rest vary enormously with local conditions of rainfall, soil, drainage, vegetation, and demographic pressure. In Mesoamerica, where the soil is not worked before planting, probably weed competition is a more important reason for reducing the period of cultivation than loss in soil fertility. The cycle of cultivation is therefore comparatively short, from one to three years, and the period of rest relatively long, from six to 12 years. In alluvial riverside lands, the cycle of rest is considerably shorter; ratios of periods of cultivation to rest are from one to three, one to two, and in some cases even one to one.

Barbecho or plow agriculture is found only in the Panuco basin and central Veracruz, where there is a combination of moderate rainfall, prairie soils, and (in central Veracruz and parts of the Panuco-Tamesi basin) savanna vegetation. Maize is the staple crop, and the variety of crops is

545

greatly reduced. Most of the land is used for cattle raising.

Plantation agriculture occurs primarily in river flood plains in the more humid parts of the area, sugarcane, bananas, and cacao being the three primary crops. This is perhaps the most successful kind of agriculture of all because it involves primarily a replacement of the natural forest by an artificial, productive one, and it is therefore best adapted to local ecological conditions. Unfortunately, however, none of the plantation crops provide a suitable staple for subsistence agriculture, a condition even more true in pre-Hispanic times when the banana was absent.

A number of significant agricultural features should be stressed. (1) The use of slash-and-burn agriculture means a drastic limitation on the growth of population and therefore on population density, because only a fraction of the land is kept in cultivation in any one year. (2) The system tends to produce either a dispersed rural settlement pattern of the ranchería type or one of small hamlets. (3) The system does not require cooperative labor beyond the nuclear or extended family, and furthermore one sees in it centripetal tendency that reduces large group integration. (4) A much greater variety of crops may be grown than in any other ecological segment of Mesoamerica. (5) Under conditions of light-to-moderate population density, the productivity of maize agriculture is very high in spite of the moderate-to-low fertility of the soils due to the abundant precipitation and prolonged rest. (6) Double-cropping is possible over much of the area, thus giving the economy a further boost and a marked advantage over the neighboring highlands by reason of the off-season. Theoretically maize may be planted throughout the year. In actual fact, flood cycles, short dry spells, and precise maximal precipitation tend to require rather definite timing and limitation of specific ag-

ricultural activities to a specific seasonal routine. In some areas the winter crop is planted on riverside land that is normally flooded in the rainy season, so that it is not double-cropping in the strict sense. Tonamil production tends to be much lower, and loss from drought much greater. (7) Crop security due to abundant precipitation is very high. The only serious menace to crops is insect pests. (8) Various plantation crops are well suited to the area and these have a high cash value as commercial crops on a national and international market. (9) A low population density today and the possibility of cattle ranching on a grand scale make economic opportunities for an agricultural population seem almost limitless. All these considerations are responsible for the fame of the Gulf Coast region in modern Mexico as a land of promise and opportunity.

Documentary data referring specifically to agricultural technology for the Gulf Coast area are extremely scarce for the pre-Hispanic period. Demographic and settlement-pattern data would suggest that the basic relationship of rural population to land did not differ strikingly from that of today. One major difference between modern and pre-Hispanic agriculture would be the use of polished stone rather than steel cutting tools for clearing the forest. I suspect that for much of the clearing of the land, the pre-Hispanic farmer relied more heavily on burning rather than on cutting. A crucial problem is that of weeding. Today it is done by slicing down to the ground with machetes. If the pre-Hispanic population uprooted the weeds, then grass invasion must have been a much more serious problem and the ratio of land under cultivation to land in fallow even lower than today. (See Kelly and Palerm, 1952, p. 114, on the Totonac and their summary of the Carnegie Institution experiments in northern Yucatan.)

It seems probable that the basic system

of slash-and-burn agriculture was characteristic for annual crops during the pre-Hispanic period. Descriptions by the conquistadors (Cortés; López de Gómara, 1943; Montejo [Chamberlain, 1948]; and Peter Martyr d' Anghiera, 1912) for the immediate conquest period give the impression that most of the land was forested (probably mostly secondary bush in terms of the population figures), with a great abundance of wild life, a picture which could only be true if the system of agriculture was similar to the modern one. The Relaciones Geográficas (PNE, 5: 1–11, 99–123, 189–201) provide more data on the general appearance of the land and its resources, but deal with the period when the population had declined to 9 per cent of the 1519 figure, and most of this population resided in the *tierra templada–tierra fría* escarpment. Of interest is the fact that the tiny population surviving the demographic disaster contracted to the prize agricultural areas such as riverside lands (see the Relación de Tacotlalpa, PNE, 5: 1–11) and rolling hilly terrain (Papantla, Los Tuxtlas). The elaborate irrigation system at Zempoala apparently collapsed along with most of the population, an indication of the costliness of maintaining a system of intensive agriculture in this region.

For the Peninsula of Yucatan, an area of similar agricultural exploitation, we do have specific references to slash-and-burn agriculture during the 16th century; this is the only part of lowland Mesoamerica that appears to have suffered no more population loss than the Mexican highlands. A quarter of a million people were still residing there in the late 16th century. In 1588 Fray Alonso Ponce (1932) described the situation.

It seems impossible that this maize, of which we speak, is able to yield in that province because the Indians sow it among rocks, where it seems there is no moisture whatever, and nevertheless the land is so good and fertile, that without any other tillage, plowing or spading, but with only the timely burning of the bush the land is left so well cultivated by the fire and so well prepared for sowing that, sown thus, it produces very tall and stout stalks and on each of them one, two and even three ears: and the more and better burned the milpa is, the more and better corn it produces because the fire and the ashes from it serve as dung that burns the insects and roots of the weeds, and when the milpa has been recently burned and the maize sown thus and the rains approach (of which the Indians keep careful count), it sprouts quickly and grows with the showers and when the weeds start to grow, they find the maize already up, so that they can not grow well before they are crushed and smothered, and the maize prospers and grows very fast till it reaches full size.

Several Relaciones Geográficas for Yucatan also mention the techniques of slash-and-burn agriculture.

For the Gulf Coast proper, the only specific reference I have found is that of López de Gómara (1943, 1: 90–91) who, referring to Tabasco, mentioned *barbechos* and *tierra labrada*.

According to the Relaciones Geográficas, the same features noted for modern agriculture apply to the 16th century and probably to pre-Hispanic periods: double-cropping, high yields, a great deal of crop security, and a rich variety of crop assemblage. One crop, for which we have no information on techniques of cultivation and which was extremely important in pre-Hispanic times and one of the major exports of the neighboring highlands, was cotton. Centers of its cultivation seem to have been in the drier parts of the lowland Maya region, such as northern Yucatan, the Huasteca, and the Totonacapan. Permanent orchard crops were all over the area and undoubtedly had an important effect on the settlement patterns. According to Roys (1943, 1957), most of the central communities apparently had a nearby zone of intensive commercial cultivation; the peripheral area was under slash-and-burn subsistence cultivation. In Yucatan and Tabasco, the central orchards were apparently owned by the upper class and the balance of the tributary zone used for slash-and-burn agriculture held in common by the lower class. Roys (1943, p. 104) describes cacao cultivation in Tabasco.

The most important product of Tabasco is cacao, for which the soil and climate are especially favorable. The trees require hot damp atmosphere and are planted in groves shaded by other taller trees. The kernel was so highly esteemed as an article of food that it served as a medium of exchange in many parts of Middle America. It was grown everywhere in Tabasco except in the Zoque towns, where the weather is said to have been too cool. The cacao groves took much attention. In addition to the work of planting, caring for the trees, and gathering the crop, the grove needed continual watching, while the fruit was maturing, to protect it from the menace of monkeys, squirrels, parrots, and other animals and birds. The crop was an abundant one. In 1579, we are told, "he who gathers least gets ten or fifteen *cargas* or more, and others as many as fifty or more." The carga, or load, was probably about 42 kilos.

In Tabasco, cacao was so extensively cultivated in the Grijalva flood plain that some districts apparently imported maize and other basic foodstuffs from the Zoque towns in the hilly headwater country on the Chiapas-Tabasco border. Apparently local rulers, and possibly an elite class of merchants and craftsmen, owned large groves and exported cacao to Yucatan and the neighboring highlands (Roys, 1943, p. 106). Such areas were probably more densely populated than most of the lowland region. Sahagún's description (1950–69, bks. 9 and 10) of the mercantile activities of the Pochteca in this area is extremely significant with respect to this pattern of regional trade.

Intensive agriculture involving subsistence crops apparently was limited to one and possibly two small areas. Palerm (1953, p. 165) cites documentary evidence for an extensive development of irrigation around Zempoala and nearby communities in the subhumid central Veracruz area. Archaeo-

logical evidence confirms this for Zempoala. From the scanty data available, it was late and spotty in its distribution. For example, for the neighboring Cotaxla basin, no irrigation is reported (see the Relación de Tlacotlapan). Possibly in many cases it was used only for the tonamil crop, as the Relación de Jalapa indicates (PNE, 5: 99–123). Another possible area of intensive agriculture is in the Panuco plain. Here rainfall averages approximately 1000 mm. a year, about the same as around Zempoala, and the extent of elevated terrain free from annual floods is very limited. Today such lands are plowed and planted every year. The soil is rich black pradera, extremely fertile. Archaeological evidence of occupation on these limited elevated strips shows that it was very heavy.

Geographical Diversity

There is a virtual absence of rural community specialization for the modern period in the Gulf Coast and Yucatan Peninsula in spite of the fact that northern Yucatan is well populated and has one of the highest percentages of Indians in Mesoamerica. There are few references to such patterns for the conquest period in those areas. In the eastern lowlands of Mesoamerica there is only slight internal zoning of natural resources and agricultural products, in contrast to the adjacent highlands. The Yucatan Peninsula, for example, including the states of Campeche and Yucatan, the territory of Quintana Roo, British Honduras and the Department of Peten, covers nearly 85,000 sq. miles over which the same crops and techniques were practiced. (Some zoning existed in that cotton was an important plant in the drier northwest, and cacao was cultivated on a minor scale in the more humid south.) The little zoning of natural resources that undoubtedly occurs did not approach the intensity of the physically more complex highlands. Furthermore, slash-and-burn agriculture tends to preserve many resources—materials for fuel, hous-

548

ing, wild plant artifacts, woodworking—in contrast to intensive agriculture which depletes all these resources and thus requires intercommunity trade and specialization to obtain them.

Secondary Factors

Ethnographic data are generally scant for the Gulf Coast area. Roys's study of Tabasco (1943) and Palerm's summary of the Totonacapan (1953) provide useful but brief references. More specific are the eyewitness accounts of the conquest period, and the Relaciones Geográficas (PNE, vol. 5) give a relatively clear picture of the significant factors in settlement-pattern studies. All over the region the socio-economic system included several major elements. (1) Society was stratified into two major classes: a small dominant minority, and a large tributary majority with corresponding differences in economic wealth, control of resources and labor, and exercise of authority. There is no evidence of a military class as in the highlands or the mayeque serf class, but slavery was apparently important. (2) The population was organized into small states ruled over by the dominant minority with hereditary rulers (see Article 1 in this volume). This same basic political unit as described for the Central Plateau has some significant differences. (a) A tendency toward the formation of large states based on conquest is lacking. (b) Evidence of localized kin groups larger than the extended family, such as the calpulli, is absent. This difference may be connected with the agriculture system, for cooperative labor beyond the extended family is not needed as in the Central Plateau. The data from Yucatan and Tabasco indicate that the extended family was a characteristic residential unit in that area. (c) There is no function of the state in terms of increasing agricultural potential. In central Mexico the state was an entrepreneur of agriculture, a builder of irrigation and terrace systems; not so in the Gulf Coast. (3) Cultural interest focused

in religion with a professional priestly class, temples, calendar, and elaborate formalized ritual. (4) There were no large urban congregations of craftsmen in true towns and cities. The craftsmanship of the elite class was exceptionally high in quality and there was undoubtedly a class of full-time professionals producing goods for the religious cult and the dominant minority, but the sources record scant evidence of large urban centers of the highland type. Markets are rarely mentioned (Zempoala is the only center noted for the Totonacapan; see Palerm, 1953, p. 167), so the present-day pattern of slight community specialization undoubtedly goes back to pre-Hispanic times. We have previously noted the ecological factors in this aborted development. Generally lacking in the Gulf Coast is the extreme economic symbiosis of rural communities to rural communities, lineage to lineage, and rural to urban population noted for the Central Plateau. (5) A great deal of international trade with the Central Plateau involved an exchange of surplus luxury goods for the respective ruling classes of both areas. With a near-monopoly of certain key luxury raw materials (cacao, cotton, feathers), the Gulf Coast was a symbol of wealth to the plateau peoples. (6) The demographic pattern called for a more evenly distributed population with much lower overall density than in the plateau.

PRE-HISPANIC SETTLEMENT PATTERNS

Comparative Data from the Maya Lowlands

Slash-and-burn agriculture tends to produce a relatively dispersed rural population. Merely as convenience, it is always advantageous for any rural people, regardless of the system of agriculture, to reside on their holdings—the ranchería settlement pattern. The modern inhabitants of the Gulf Coast follow this pattern. Slash-and-burn agriculture favors such a pattern, because the size of the holdings required for a balanced system is markedly greater and even small nucleated communities would acquire considerable tracts of land for their sustenance. Other factors, of course, nearly always operate besides this primary one. A simple desire for socialization could be another major determinant on a par with convenience.

Looking at the settlement patterns of other areas of the world where this system is practiced, we find that complete dispersion of population, as in the modern rancherías of Tabasco and Veracruz, is rare. The most common pattern is the small nucleated hamlet of less than 100 people but usually over 20. This kind of settlement might be considered a compromise in response to the principles stated above. Usually it has a kin-like structure, the basic membership being an extended family, a clan, or a small deme.

Secondary factors might also produce large nucleated villages. (1) State policy, as in Yucatan, directed the Spanish priesthood and the government to cluster the population of hamlets into true villages and towns to facilitate conversion and tax collection. Conceivably the pre-Hispanic ruling class might have attempted the same thing to assume a tighter control over labor resources. (2) Two responses might be expected as a result of warfare: complete seclusion within the small hamlet and even construction of stockades around it, as in many groups in New Guinea; or nucleation into large walled communities as among the Tupinamba of Brazil. (3) Part-time specialization could be based on specific localized resources. (4) Permanent orchard cultivation, such as cacao, could be tied in with the national economy.

In assessing the settlement pattern of any given segment of the Gulf Coast region, all these factors must be considered. With this theoretical orientation we will now examine the documentary data for the Gulf Coast, as well as comparative data from Yucatan, where the basic ecological system was similar.

With respect to the formation of towns

and cities, I am doubtful of any substantial development in the slash-and-burn agricultural area of the Gulf Coast and Yucatan Peninsula. A combination of circumstances —distance from fields to house, general dispersion of the population, distance of rural communities to the consumers' market, primitiveness of transportation, limited surplus food production possible with neolithic tools—would make the maintenance of a large urban community extremely difficult. Furthermore, the general self-sufficiency of the rural population combined with distance between markets of major centers and general lack of internal regional specialization would seem to deter the evolution of towns and cities. The factor which promotes modern urbanization in the area—efficient transportation and a national-international market for tropical produce—would not apply to the preconquest situation. Some urbanization based on markets linked with the highland trading system certainly occurred (Roys, 1943, pp. 46–56), but was primarily concerned with luxury products of elite craftsmen for the use of elite clientele, or products of peasant technologies and activities which do not require urban processing (cotton cloth, raw cotton, cacao, feathers, fruit).

The ecclesiastic and tax data for the mid- and late 16th century are practically worthless for establishing settlement patterns because of the drastic decline in population following the conquest. With the reduction of the population in the state of Veracruz to 9 per cent of its conquest period figure, the settlement pattern stated for the period 1560–80 is obviously very difficult to use. I have also pointed out a series of other impediments in utilizing this data, and the reader is referred to Article 1 for further discussion. One of the major problems is that of the centralization policy of the Spanish government by which small villages, hamlets, and scattered rural peoples were gathered into large nucleated villages and towns to facilitate conversion. Our earliest good descriptive data for the Gulf Coast are for the period 1579–80 (the Relaciones Geográficas, PNE, 5: 1–11, 99–123, 184–201) and by that time, most of the efforts toward centralization had been completed. Before presenting the scant data on the Gulf Coast, I refer the reader first to the relatively abundant documentary information for the Maya lowlands (*Handbook*, Volume 6, Article 4), where the cultural ecology is so similar to that of the Gulf Coast, that the data are pertinent to our area.

Gulf Coast Patterns: Documentary and General Archaeological Data

Documentary data that refer specifically to the Gulf Coast are scant. The conquistadors' descriptions are brief and vague in contrast to the detailed accounts of Central Plateau communities. Information provided by Torquemada for the Totonacapan suggests that the pattern typical of the Maya area applied here as well. In his fairly detailed description (1943–44, 1: 248–49) of conquest period communities he stresses that (1) in some areas of Mesoamerica planned nucleated centers were not possible because of the nature of the terrain; (2) in areas of broken topography, heavy forest cover, or general humidity the population was more dispersed (he compares the pattern with 17th-century Galicia in Spain); (3) instead of a city or town as an administrative center there were "congregaciones" where the temples and houses of the noble class were located—this congregación had a more formal plan than the dependent rural community but lacked the dense residential units with orderly street grids so characteristic of plateau Mexican and Spanish towns; (4) the rest of the population were scattered over hills, valleys, and ravines without order or plan; (5) the pattern was especially characteristic of the "Reino de Guatemala," Totonacapan and Metztitlan areas.

Cortés, Díaz del Castillo, Peter Martyr, and López de Gómara wrote brief descriptions of Tabascan communities, agreeing generally with Torquemada's statement about the Totonacapan. One gets the impression that some ceremonial centers in Tabasco had a relatively larger and denser population in their vicinity than did the average Maya center. Willey's analysis (1956b) of the settlement pattern of the Belize Valley in the Maya area showed a striking difference from the patterns in the Peten in the size of house-mound clusters and their density. His survey area was a narrow, flat alluvial terrace along the river. Probably the terrace was planted almost entirely in cacao groves, as were riverine flood plains in Tabasco, and probably the neighboring hills were used for slash-and-burn maize cultivation, either by the riverine population or by separate settlements of the standard Yucatecan type. If such was the case, the riverine population would probably have exchanged cacao for maize, which would explain the heavier density and larger size of the house clusters.

Data from the Relaciones Geográficas are much less useful in reconstructing settlement patterns in the Gulf Coast than in the Central Plateau. In the Suma de Visitas (PNE, vol. 1, a document predating the centralization policy) there is a description of the Papantla area that seems to suggest, although rather vaguely, the type of settlement. It states that the "*pueblo*" of Papantla had a total population of 210 "*casas*" occupied by 421 "*hombres casados*." The "pueblo," however, consisted of a "*cabecera*" and 14 "estancias" or dependent communities so that the population was scattered through 15 communities.

The Relación de Papantla by Juan de Carrión states that in 1581 it was the administrative center of a *partido*, and that at the time of the conquest the population was 64,000. The description gives the impression that the settlement pattern was similar to the modern one. The partido, approximately 2200 sq. km., in 1940 had a population

551

of 62,771. According to the census over the past 30 years, the rural population apparently has been relatively stable, which, along with the conquest population data, suggests that this is the maximal population with a stable slash-and-burn agricultural system, for this area.

Archaeological data on settlement patterns for the Gulf Coast are detailed only in the Chontalpa survey, which will be summarized in the next section. There is a marked paucity of house remains, potsherds, and refuse material in coastal sites with ceremonial architecture, in contrast to the Central Plateau sites, where such ceremonial complexes were part of a large urban center. A string of such ceremonial complexes lies along the Cotaxtla River, some 30 of them, each a few kilometers apart (Sanders, 1953). Most of these sites consisted of a single plaza, with a large 10–15-m.-high pyramid, a smaller pyramid, and one large low rectangular platform with an open end to the plaza on one side. Some of the larger sites had several such complexes. The correlation of settlement with river plain is significant in terms of slash-and-burn agriculture as the riverine strip is covered by a gallery forest in the area of generally savanna vegetation. Most of the people probably lived in Yucatecan-style hamlets, leaving only a small resident group of priests and rulers at the ceremonial complexes. Sites in the wetter, more forested area between the Rio Papaloapan and the Sierra de San Martin show the same pattern. Large numbers of house remains and heavy extensive refuse deposits are apparently lacking in such sites as Tajin, Tres Zapotes, and La Venta. Of the last site, Drucker (1952, pp. 19–20) says:

It is probably legitimate to regard the areas of deposit as the rubbish heaps of individual dwellings, or small clusters of dwellings, and these must have been scattered and few in number. The logical explanation is that the site was most likely never a "town" or independent subsistence unit in ancient times, but rather a ceremonial center occupied regularly only by a relatively small number of priests and perhaps nobles, and their households, except during brief periods of construction and monument moving. The manpower for all the major constructions must have been brought in from the scattered habitable areas for some distance around La Venta.

The one dissenting piece of evidence in this analysis of settlement patterns on the Gulf Coast is presented by MacNeish (1956) for the Huasteca. He describes a hierarchy of sites running from hamlet to village to town to city; with the exception of the first, this is the same hierarchy in size, population, and community densities and functions as I described for the Central Plateau of Mexico. Unfortunately, he has included in his analysis a huge area with a great variety of ecological zones. To understand the settlement pattern of the Huastec region, a breakdown into four ecological zones is imperative: (1) the Tamesi basin, a dry, nonforested, pradera-soil, plow-agriculture region; (2) the Sierra de Tantoyuca-middle Panuco basin, an area of rolling hills with tropical forest cover, higher rainfall, and slash-and-burn agriculture; (3) the arid mountain valleys to the west in the highlands of Tamaulipas and San Luis Potosi; (4) the lower Panuco plain, a region mostly under water part of the year and having small strips of elevated land with fertile pradera soil—today used for plow agriculture.

I have surveyed part of Zone 4 and agree that here agriculture was probably intensive in pre-Hispanic times and that settlements were generally compact and relatively large, although really large sites are lacking. In Zone 2 there are huge ceremonial complexes—for example, Tamuin and Tantoc, which are among the largest sites in Mesoamerica—but MacNeish does not demonstrate that they were true urban communities. His characterization of Tamuin as a city of 5 sq. miles is completely inaccurate. The site actually consists of several clusters of ceremonial and civic buildings on hilltops; there is no evidence of dense compact urban population in between these ceremonial precincts or around them. His measurement of 5 sq. miles is based apparently on the fact that within this whole area there are a number of ceremonial complexes, but they are not all even of the same age. The one site where he does give evidence of an urban congregation was Nuevo Morelos; he states that it covers 6 sq. miles and that he counted 900 house platforms in an area only one-quarter the size of the whole site. However, this site is in the arid mountain area of Tamaulipas (Zone 3), which corresponds more to the environmental conditions and probably agricultural system of the Central Plateau.

Most of MacNeish's data are drawn from the hilly, dry Sierra de Tamaulipas zone where apparently there is a settlement pattern like that in the Central Plateau. Even the largest sites, however, are much smaller in population and less compact than in the latter area.

The one site in the Gulf Coast area that might justifiably be called a city is Zempoala. The description by the conquistadors is vague but suggests a very large concentrated population, and my brief visits to the site convinced me that it had a much denser population than was usual in a Gulf Coast center. There is both documentary and archaeological evidence of irrigation and documentary evidence of a market system, the latter being the only reference to markets in a Totonac site at the time of the conquest.

Chontalpa Survey

In 1953 I participated in the first field season of the New World Archaeological Foundation in Mexico. Most of the fieldwork was conducted within a strip of territory 10 km. wide and 30 km. long, bordering the west bank of the Grijalva River between Huimanguillo and Cardenas. The area today is part of a larger region known as the

Chontalpa. The fieldwork, specifically directed toward settlement patterns, included survey and description of some 50–60 sites, extensive excavation of two of them, and small test-trenching of a half-dozen others. As the full report is not yet published, the analysis below is taken from the field and laboratory notes. This study has considerable significance for the topic of this article because it is the only settlement-pattern study in the Gulf Coast area and provides the primary test data. Besides this primary area, excavation and survey were carried out along some of the tributaries of the Tonala drainage to the west at the two rancherías of San Fernando and San Miguel. Within this large territory there are striking differences in ecology. Major ecological components of the overall survey area are: (1) Grijalva flood plain—the prize agriculture zone where all the plantation cultivation occurs, the best land for slash-and-burn maize cultivation, and the section where most of the population resides; (2) forested land lying outside the Grijalva flood plain; and (3) savannas. A surprising percentage of land is covered by savannas, which, from a description by Cortés and from a lack of sites, would appear to be ancient.

The Chontalpa offers exceedingly troublesome problems for large-scale, temporally economic techniques of settlement-pattern analysis. Exuberant vegetation makes site survey difficult; the lack of plowing plus the heavy vegetation makes surface sampling almost impossible. Complicating the latter situation is the fact that the settlement pattern is apparently one of small scattered hamlets and ceremonial centers, without large associated populations (as I shall demonstrate shortly). All formal civic architecture—pyramid bases, house platforms, ball courts—is of earth construction, preventing dating by architectural style. The only method of dating is test-trenching. Site survey would be aided by the presence of milpas, artificial pastures for cattle, and

553

orchards. Most of the sites found are therefore not dated, so we can not trace settlement-pattern changes in time but can only discuss them in atemporal terms.

Most sites are small and count as hamlets. They may be classified as (1) one or two isolated earth pyramids, 3–6 m. high, with no house mounds in the vicinity; (2) small clusters of 3–12 house platforms with no associated ceremonial architecture; (3) the same as Type 2 but with a pyramid or two and with a large high platform which might have been a residential platform of a local religious or political leader. Most people of the Chontalpa, from the beginnings of agriculture, probably resided in Types 2 and 3, which may be considered the standard rural settlement. It corresponds rather closely to the modern Valladolid hamlet in eastern Yucatan (see Volume 6, Article 4). One is tempted to equate such settlements with an extended family or lineage pattern of social organization, which Roys noted as characteristic of the area in the conquest period.

The site of Sigero, completely surveyed and intensively excavated, is a good example of the second major community type which we may call a small ceremonial center. Sigero was a Postclassic site, consisting of a central, formally oriented plaza with a pyramid on the north side 7 m. high; a large residential platform to the west, which was probably the residence of the local cacique; a ball court on the east; and two low platforms to the south. Three small pyramids are isolated from the main plaza. Some 15–20 low oval mounds, all less than 1 m. high and probably all house structures, complete the surface architecture. The main group occupies 2 hectares; the entire area surveyed covers some 15 hectares. One of the low mounds was excavated and identified as a house structure with a floor level. The mounding of the structure is apparently the debris of the collapsed house rather than a true basal platform. The average house mound is approximately 10 m. in diameter

so the occupants were probably a single nuclear family. These house mounds occur in small loosely planned clusters of two to four that may represent extended family aggregations. Heavy refuse deposits are exceedingly rare, and occupation, on the basis of the 17 trenches excavated across the noted surface area, was exceedingly sparse. The site is a ceremonial center in the classic Maya sense, with only a small nucleation at the center, certainly less than 150 or 200 people. The residents could well have consisted wholly of retainers and the family of the cacique and his household. Sigero was undoubtedly a center for a much larger population scattered over several square kilometers of neighboring territory and residing in small extended-family hamlet clusters of the type noted. The settlement pattern resembles the vague civic center one finds today in many modern Tabascan rancherías or in a congregación of the Tajin type. The survey was not complete enough to resolve the possibility that Sigero itself was probably dependent on a larger territorial state center. Such larger centers did exist in the preceding Classic period. Sites of the character and size of Sigero are probably, next to the noted hamlets, the most abundant settlement-pattern type in the Chontalpa. Occupation apparently was extremely short as heavy sherd deposits were not found, even in the house mound.

In size and number of public buildings, indications of occupation, size of residential population, and complexity and richness of technology the largest kind of site in the survey area is represented by some five sites, of which Tierra Nueva is typical. These may be called large ceremonial centers. Tierra Nueva is a Late Classic site and, during the 1953 season, was the scene of intensive excavations conducted specifically to ascertain its settlement patterns. In order to facilitate survey, a 20-m. grid was superimposed over the area by cutting trails through the secondary forests and high grass pastures. The main survey area cov-

554

ered by the grid is 500 by 500 m. A separate group of mounds was mapped 150 m. north of the primary survey area, and another separate group approximately 1 km. to the west.

The site includes a large central plaza measuring 120 m. east and west by 180 m. north and south. These are overall measurements, made along the outside of the surrounding structures. The latter include three pyramids 8–9 m. high, four pyramids 3–4 m. high, and one pyramid 5 m. high, a small ball court, and a large 3-m.-high rectangular platform that was probably the substructure of the local cacique's palace.

In the northwest corner of the grid area is a separate cluster of mounds that includes a ball court and two pyramids 4–5 m. high. Just north of the main plaza are two pyramids 3–4 m. high. West of the plaza is a pyramid 4 m. high. Southeast of the plaza are two isolated pyramids each 3 m. high. On the south edge of the site is another pyramid 3 m. high.

The isolated northern group, outside the grid area, consists of a pyramid 6 m. high, a mound 2 m. high, and a ball court. There are no associated house mounds. The west group, 1 km. from the main grid area, has a pyramid 7 m. high and three house mounds. All these constructions are of earth.

Within the 500-m. grid were mapped 80 house mounds. All but seven are under 1 m. in height, generally average about 50 cm., and are oval earth mounds. They occur in definite clusters rather than evenly throughout the survey area. Adjoining the east side of the plaza is the densest concentration of them, 24 in an area only 120 by 100 m., or a little over 1 hectare. There are four small clusters of two to four house mounds in various places over the grid. A great arc of nearly continuous platforms runs southwest of the plaza and includes three clusters of 8–12 mounds in each. The separate clusters of house mounds around the site are generally associated with one of the isolated pyramids. The house mounds range in size from 10 to 30 m. long. Individual mounds probably represent occupation by nuclear families, clusters by extended families or possibly some larger kin group.

If the total population of the site is calculated from the house mounds alone, it could not have exceeded 400–500 people, with an internal population density of 1600–2000 people per square kilometer, or about that of a modern Yucatecan village. Surprising, from the number and size of the civic and religious structures, is the relatively small size of the population. Tierra Nueva was undoubtedly the capital of a state as large as a central Mexican city state, and we would expect a community of several thousand people if the settlement pattern of the two areas were the same. It would seem to fit very well with Torquemada's description of the central community of the territorial state. The site is comparable in many ways to a site in Quintana Roo called Tancah (Sanders, 1960).

Besides survey, one complete house mound was excavated to determine its function more definitely. The nature of the deposits and the cultural debris identified it as a house structure.

In order to test the hypothesis that a count of the house mounds alone would give a maximal population estimate for the site, we excavated 157 trenches over the grid area at intervals of 40 m. All these trenches are 1 by 2 m. in surface area and all were excavated to the base of the archaeological deposits. The results of this testing tend to confirm our estimate of the population size and density, making the site very similar to Tancah. Heavy sherd deposits occur in and around mound clusters, especially in the small densely settled zone east of the plaza. Heavy deposits also occur sporadically and in a limited area rather than in dense continuous zones, even in the small urbanized area mentioned. These deposits are completely absent from the isolated north group. The data therefore tend to support the population reconstruction above. Of the trenches 84 produced less than 51 sherds, 29 from 51 to 100 sherds, 19 from 101 to 200 sherds, and 25 over 200 sherds. Of the last-mentioned trenches, eight were in the 1-hectare area of heavy house mound clusters, or one-third in an area of only 1/25 of the central grid area.

We have, then, a relatively large plaza, in terms of Mesoamerican centers as a whole, with 21 substructures of civic and religious buildings and a very small resident population, one-fourth of which appears to have resided in a small 1-hectare cluster adjoining the plaza, and the balance scattered over an area of 24 hectares with a total maximum population of 400–500 people. The entire population fits into one relatively short phase of the Mesoamerican sequence, the Late Classic, and probably does not completely span that period, for little internal chronology can be detected in the ceramics. I doubt that the site was occupied more than a century or two.

Trenches were excavated in two of the ceremonial structures. The house mound, completely excavated, provided some clues to the socio-economic functions of the center. Excavation around the pyramid structures revealed a great number and variety of specialized clay and stone cult objects in the form of incense burners, offering jars, sacrificial daggers, and large hollow figurines of the generic Late Classic Maya style which indicate a highly developed regional variant of the general Mesoamerican ceremonial complex. These objects were undoubtedly made by and used by full-time specialists for the formal ritual based on the calendar. Excavation in the areas of settlement reveal the presence of an elite residential group with such imported luxuries as Fine Orange and Fine Gray pottery, obsidian, and jade. The sample also included a locally made, polished black, serving ware of exceptionally high quality for Mesoamerican ceramics as a whole. Figurines and molds were found in one of the house mounds, plus numerous pottery polishing

556

stones, along with clay whistles and spindle whorls, perhaps indicating a house of the craftsman.

This picture of the pre-Hispanic community tallies very closely with Torquemada's description of the "Cabeceras de Provincias." Tierra Nueva was probably a ceremonial and elite residential center for a territory within which were a number of Sigero-like secondary centers and a large number of small dependent rural hamlets. Lack of chronological data for other sites of similar size, and presumably similar political rank and power, makes it difficult even to roughly delimit the size of the territory tributary to the site, but there is a site of comparable size 7 km. to the north and another 7 km. to the northwest so that the dependent district was probably not very large.

Of interest in the socio-political relationships of communities is the relationship of a site like Tierra Nueva, all earth construction and of relatively small size, to the huge site of Comalcalco with brick architecture, dated monuments, stucco modeling on the walls, and vastly greater size and number of civic buildings. The occupation of Comalcalco apparently is Late Classic. The site has all the attributes of Maya civilization. Tierra Nueva has only one specific relationship to Classic Maya culture—the figurine style—but the ceramics of the two sites are nearly identical. One is struck with the general paucity of house structures. Until a more detailed survey is made, however, all that can be said about the settlement pattern of Comalcalco is that it was probably similar to such Maya centers as Tikal and Uaxactun. Comalcalco may have been the capital of a relatively large compact state which included much of the region known today as the Chontalpa. The immediate area, roughly the present municipio of Comalcalco, is the prize cacao-banana area for Tabasco, and it could have supported, demographically, a site the size of Comalcalco without additional territory. The municipio of Comalcalco, for example, has a surface area 420 sq. km. and in 1950 had a population of nearly 34,000 people with a density of 80 per sq. km. of which only 4000 or 5000 were urban. This dense population is made possible today by the fact that most of the area is in cacao orchards and little land is used for slash-and-burn agriculture. A similar situation may well have been the case in Late Classic times. Roys's map (1943) of the distribution of communities in Tabasco at the time of the conquest shows that at that time, as well as in the Late Classic period, the part of the Chontalpa around Comalcalco seems to have been the major population center.

REFERENCES

Acosta, 1956–57
Alva Ixtlilxochitl, 1952
Alvarado Tezozomoc, 1944
Anghiera, 1912
Armillas, 1949, 1950
——, Palerm, and Wolf, 1956
Arzobispado de México, 1897
Barlow, 1949c
Brainerd, 1956
Buck, 1930
Bullard, 1960
Carnegie Inst. Washington, 1951–54
Carrasco Pizana, 1950
Cervantes de Salazar, 1936
Chamberlain, 1948
Chapple and Coon, 1942
Codices: Franciscano, 1941; Osuna, 1947
Conquistador Anónimo, 1941
Cook, 1949
—— and Simpson, 1948
Coon, 1931
Cortés, 1908
Díaz del Castillo, 1927
Drucker, 1952
Durán, 1951
Gamio, 1922a
Hester, 1953
Kelly and Palerm, 1952
Lewis, 1951
Linné, 1934, 1942
López de Gómara, 1943
McBryde, 1945
MacNeish, 1956
Mayer-Oakes, 1959
Maza, 1959

Mendieta, 1945
Millon, 1957a, 1960
Molina, 1944
Morley, 1947
Motolinia, 1914
Nuevos documentos . . . Cortés, 1946
Palerm, 1953, 1954, 1955
—— and Wolf, 1956
Papeles de Nueva España (PNE)
Parsons, 1936
Paso y Troncoso, 1905–06, 1939–42
Piña Chan, R., 1955b
PNE, see Papeles de la Nueva España
Ponce, A., 1932
Redfield, 1930
Ricketson and Ricketson, 1937
Rojas, 1927
Roys, 1943, 1957
Sahagún, 1946, 1950–69
Sanders, 1953, 1956, 1960
Sears, 1951
Stadelman, 1940
Suma de visitas, see PNE, vol. 1
Tamayo, 1949
Tax, 1952
Tolstoy, 1958
Torquemada, 1943–44
Toussaint, Gómez de Orozco, and Fernández, 1938
Vaillant, 1941
Vivó, 1949
West, 1948
—— and Armillas, 1950
Willey, 1956b
Wolf and Palerm, 1955
Zorita, 1941

23. Classic Art of Central Veracruz

TATIANA PROSKOURIAKOFF

THE SIERRA MADRE ORIENTAL rises at the eastern edge of the Mexican plateau and falls off sharply to the coastal plain of the Gulf of Mexico, forming a natural boundary between aboriginal cultures and delimiting distinct archaeological zones. Frontiers perpendicular to the coast are more difficult to draw, since there are no clear geographical divisions, and more particularly because we distinguish the three principal coastal regions by remains that are not contemporaneous and that overlap in their distribution to an indefinite extent.

In the north, the Huaxtec culture, extending southward to Tuxpan, is best represented by its latest period of architecture, ceramics, and sculpture, linked in part to the Aztec styles of the interior. The southern region, on the other hand, is usually defined by its "Olmec" culture, exemplified at the sites of La Venta, Tres Zapotes, and San Lorenzo, which were towns that flourished approximately at the same time as Tlatilco and Zacatenco on the Mexican plateau. At the time of the conquest, much of the intervening area was occupied by the Totonac

people, to whom a number of distinct ancient ceramic and sculptural styles have been ascribed. It is unwise, however, to credit modern ethnic groups with ancient remains unless there is solid historical and archaeological evidence of the unbroken continuity of their traditions. The style of carving formerly called "Totonac" is predominantly of the Classic period, that is, roughly of the first millennium A.D.; it is now more often called the "Tajin," the "Tajinoid," or the "Classic Veracruz" style.

I prefer the last designation because the late low-relief architectural carvings of Tajin are by no means characteristic of the style. Actually, its most spectacular manifestation is in small portable sculptures of definite shapes that suggest that they were made with some specific use in mind. The three most common forms are known as "yokes"; "hachas," "thin stone heads," or "axe-heads"; and "palmas," "palmate stones," or "paddle-stones." Evidence has been accumulating that all three are in some way associated with the aboriginal ball game, and Ekholm (1946, 1949) has shown

558

that they were worn by ball-players, if not actually in the game itself, at any rate in its accompanying ceremonies.

Not all such objects are carved in the Classic Veracruz style, and many in museums are probably mislabeled as coming from the Totonac region. Even those known to come from central Veracruz sometimes diverge sharply from the Classic style and indicate that there were diverse traditions in this area about which little is known. There are, however, a number of typical forms associated with distinct human types and with definite modes of symbolic expression, which can be grouped together as representative of the Classic style. The most characteristic feature of this style is the frequent use of intricate patterns of interlacing or interlocking scrolls interspersed with detached elements abstracted from zoomorphic grotesques.

The richness of this ornament and the exquisite quality of the carvings have made them highly prized among connoisseurs, and the dispersal of many pieces in private and museum collections without record of their provenience has added to the difficulties of distinguishing regional types and of associating them with other remains. As a result, we are still ignorant of the cultural background and the history of this style, and a recovery of pertinent data becomes more difficult with every passing year.

ANTIQUITY OF THE STYLE

The best data we have on the antiquity of ornamental scroll patterns such as were used in Veracruz are afforded by small carved bone objects found apparently as trade pieces among remains of widely separated regions. Two carved human bones from Chiapa de Corzo described by Dixon (1958, 1959) and Agrinier (1960) and attributed by them to Period VI of that site, show a scroll pattern very similar to some from Veracruz combined with grotesque figures of strongly Olmecoid character. Another piece of carved bone with entwined scroll

forms comes from Mound E-III-3 at Kaminaljuyu (Shook and Kidder, 1952, fig. 53) and is associated with objects of the Miraflores phase of the site. Such designs have not been reported from La Venta, and apparently originate in the later phases of what is called the "Preclassic" period, phases referred to by some as "Protoclassic."

Yokes and hachas may originate at about the same time, though we do not have a firm association of either of these forms with Preclassic or Protoclassic ceramics. García Payón (1947a, p. 327) reports a plain yoke that apparently came from a late Preclassic deposit at El Trapiche, Veracruz, but he expresses doubt of the validity of this association. There is certainly no evidence yet of the application of patterned scroll designs to yokes in this early period.

For the Early Classic period, the presence of decorated yokes and hachas in Veracruz, though largely inferential, is fairly well established, and the pattern of scroll ornament associated with the dominant forms is reflected outside the area in paintings and sculpture at Teotihuacan dating from its second period, and in a number of carved mirror backs such as that found with Esperanza remains at Kaminaljuyu (Kidder, Jennings, and Shook, 1946, fig. 156). The diffusion of regionally modified forms of yokes and hachas through Oaxaca and across the isthmus to the Pacific slope of Guatemala probably took place later, at some time during the Late Classic period, and though many of the pieces suggest a derivation from Gulf Coast styles, the patterned scroll decoration of the Veracruz yokes was not transmitted with them. In Veracruz the style probably underwent certain modifications at this time on Late Classic palmas, and persisted into the period of Toltec expansion in low-relief carvings at Tajin and in the Misantla region. It did not long survive the fall of Tula, however, and the numerous crude stone idols that fill local collections suggest a total degradation of the regional tradition in Aztec times.

559

FIG. 1—OPEN OVAL YOKE FOUND AT EL TRAPICHE, NEAR ZEMPOALA, VERACRUZ. (Courtesy, Dr. José García Payón.)

In its general configuration, the history of the Classic Veracruz style recalls that of the lowland Maya. Both are primarily graphic styles, composing even their high-relief sculpture on definite planes. The high development of both is marked by an elaboration of scroll designs and grotesques, contrasting with a strong naturalism in the representation of the human figure. Preoccupation with the niceties and regularities of forms, delight in ornament and in pure artistry, sets these two styles apart from all others in Middle America as having achieved a measure of emancipation from the solemnity of the ritual purpose that usually dominates incipient stages of civilization.

Yokes

The yoke is an object of stone shaped like

560

an arch or a horseshoe, weighing between 20 and 30 kgm., and measuring about 40 by 36 by 11.5 cm. Some yokes are of basalt, diorite, or granite, but the finest are of serpentine, porphyry, and other highly prized and fine-grained stones capable of taking a high polish.

At one time it was believed that yokes were used in human sacrifice to hold down the victim, but this notion was later rejected and a number of other suggestions were made, among them that yokes were funerary objects (Genin, 1928) or emblems of nobility and rank (Ernst, 1892). Lothrop (1923) called attention to the similarity of yokes to certain belts portrayed on clay figurines and on figures carved in stone at Santa Lucia Cotzumalhuapa, Guatemala. J. E. S. Thompson (1941b) identified these belts as part of the standard accoutrement of ball-players, rejecting the idea that they were meant to be yokes. In 1946 Ekholm was able to reconcile the divergent views by suggesting that yokes were worn in connection with the ball game, or were stone replicas of belts made of other materials. The association of yokes with the ball game is now generally accepted, though some doubt remains that such heavy stone objects could function efficiently in an actual game.

Yokes are usually classed as open or closed, plain or carved. A more useful distinction may be one based on the shape of the arch and of the cross-section. Thus one might designate as "oval yokes" those in which the arms are curved and in which the section is rounded on the outer surface, with bands on the upper and under surfaces outlining the inner curve. This class can in turn be subdivided into "ring yokes" in which the inner surface makes a complete smooth ring, "closed yokes" in which the oval is incomplete but is closed by a straight piece, and "open oval yokes" in which the arms converge but are not united. The plain open yoke found at El Trapiche (fig. 1 and García Payón, 1950b, foto 7) is of the open oval form. This also may be the form repre-

Fig. 2—CARVING TYPICAL OF CLASSIC VERACRUZ PORTRAITURE. On end of "standard" yoke from Veracruz. (Courtesy, American Museum of Natural History.)

sented by carved fragments from the Ranchito site at Tres Zapotes which Weiant designates as "the decorated open type" (Weiant, 1943, p. 118, pl. 66, no. 2; pl. 68, no. 11). When a human figure is carved on such yokes, it is usually spread on the outer surface with its head at one end. On the standard form, the head appears at the bow of the arch and the two sides of the body are depicted on the arms. On one closed yoke, formerly of the Dehesa and now of the Arensberg collection (Kubler, 1954, no.

161), the facial features of the figure (the drooping mouth and the pointed beard) suggest a connection with the Olmec style of La Venta.

The oval form is probably regional, being most often found in the south. Its chronological significance is uncertain. Weiant noted that the closed plain variety was associated with upper Tres Zapotes remains, whereas the carved open yokes he places in Middle Tres Zapotes B, a phase of uncertain date which includes sherds of a

561

FIG. 4—STONE YOKE FROM SALAMA, GUA-TEMALA. Note narrow upper surface. Such yokes are more often plain. (Courtesy, Museum of the American Indian, Heye Foundation.)

FIG. 3—DETAIL OF CARVING ON A "FROG" YOKE FROM VERACRUZ. (Courtesy, American Museum of Natural History.)

"carved" ware that is probably Late Classic. Kubler characterized the Arensberg yoke as "late." Nevertheless, the design on this yoke and the early association of the El Trapiche specimen suggest to me that the oval form is early in origin.

The second general class, termed "standard yokes," is distinguished by straight arms and a trapezoidal section with a sharply flaring and slightly convex outer surface (fig. 2). The "frog yoke" is the most common variety of this class. It is deeply carved in relief in the form of a grotesque creature called "the saurian monster" or in Spanish "batricio," which is sometimes identified with the earth dragon of Mexican and Maya mythologies. On some yokes a human figure is substituted for the frog without essentially altering its shape. The human type represented on such yokes has the broad face, wide flat nose, and full lips characteristic of Gulf Coast figurines. A deformation of the upper lip is frequent in these representations. Characteristically, the lip is slit into three sections, but in some cases the upper lip ends in scrolls, like the mouth of Tlaloc but without its fangs.

On the finest examples of frog yokes, an intricate network of low-relief scrolls is

562

superimposed on the monster form, often with secondary ornament executed in fine incision (fig. 3). The craftsmanship of these yokes is superb and apparently derives from small carvings in bone, shell, and possibly wood, rather than from monumental sculpture. Highly naturalistic and idealized human heads are depicted on the ends of such yokes and have the character of portraits of actual individuals (fig. 2).

Although the oval and the standard yokes appear to be two distinct types, there are occasional examples in which the characteristics are mixed. One is a closed yoke now in the Museo Nacional de Antropología, Mexico City, which has a cross-section similar to that of standard yokes, and is decorated with the representation of an owl. Another, to which Ekholm has recently called my attention, is owned by the Baltimore Museum of Art. It is an open yoke, with Classic decoration and trapezoidal cross-section but with arms lightly curved to give it ovate form.

It is difficult to say what range of designs on standard yokes can be attributed to central Veracruz and to the Classic period. Some show dominant motifs and mannerisms derived from the art of Teotihuacan and may have been manufactured beyond the sierra. Others exhibit varying degrees of ineptitude in their carving that suggest archaic or derivative styles. The varieties are more fully discussed elsewhere (Proskouriakoff, 1954), but no firm conclusions have been reached about the distribution or chronology of specific types.

Yokes in Late Classic remains on the Pacific slope of Guatemala are narrower in section than the standard Veracruz form and are almost always plain (fig. 4). The outer surface is more nearly vertical and has very little convexity. It may be convenient to put this form in a separate category of "narrow-section yokes" because of its peculiar distribution. The yokes reported from Palenque are of this type, and among 26 fragments representing at least 12 yokes,

FIG. 5—HACHA OR THIN STONE HEAD FROM TLAXCALA, PUEBLA BORDER REGION. Typical Veracruz form. (Courtesy, American Museum of Natural History.)

only two were carved. All were found in circumstances that suggest deposition in the terminal years of the city (Ruz, 1953).

HACHAS (thin stone heads, axe-heads)

Hachas have a distribution similar to that of yokes, and use similar decorative devices in their scroll patterns. The same type of lip deformation as on yokes can be observed on them, and, like yokes, they are sometimes made of fine stone and beautifully polished. The typical central Veracruz hacha is wedge-shaped and about 30 cm. in height. When it is resting on its base, the back surface slopes forward toward the top, and the bottom corner is cut away by a deep, almost rectangular notch (fig. 5). The hacha is carved on the sides in the semblance of a human, bird, or animal head with a high crest or headdress that comes to a sharp edge in front. The crest is sometimes decorated with interlocking scrolls, but there are specimens depicting featherwork and other features that link them closely with the art style of Teotihuacan. This is particularly true of one very tall variety of hacha with a triangular or trapezoidal crest that rises to a height of 40 cm. or more above the base.

Another variety of the notched hacha is considerably thinner in section and is often perforated (fig. 6). It has a larger range of motifs and sometimes depicts full figures, among which is a human figure in acrobatic pose (fig. 7). Scroll designs, when they occur on such hachas, are less rigidly patterned than on heavier forms, and this suggests that they are later in date.

The use of hachas is still problematical. Ekholm (1949, fig. 6) points out a small figurine wearing an hacha projecting from its belt in front, and another hacha worn on the belt is cited by García Payón (1950a, foto 1), but it is difficult to imagine what device could hold the heavy notched hachas in place. Their silhouette seems better adapted to rest on a horizontal support with its back against some architectural feature. At least in one case, however, the back of such an hacha had been carved (Lothrop, Foshag, and Mahler, 1957, pl. 17, no. 25).

In the region of Los Tuxtlas and to the south, a lightly notched form, finished with an oblique cut of the back corner, is more common. This form does not feature scroll decoration but depicts animal and human heads. The death motif is frequently repre-

564

Fig. 6—HACHA OF THIN, PERFORATED TYPE FROM VERACRUZ. (Courtesy, Museum of the American Indian, Heye Foundation.)

Fig. 7—HACHA OF THIN, PERFORATED TYPE. (Robert Woods Bliss Collection; photo by Nickolas Muray.)

FIG. 8—HEAD WITH CREST, SAID TO COME FROM AZCAPOTZALCO, MEXICO. Style typical of southern Veracruz. (Courtesy, American Museum of Natural History.)

FIG. 9—STONE HACHA FROM GUATEMALA. (Courtesy, Museum of the American Indian, Heye Foundation.)

sented by a human head with closed eyes and drooping cheeks, which apparently derives from a broader form of crested head commonly found in this region (figs. 8; 13,*a*; 14,*b*). Very thin forms show a variety of treatments of the back corner (fig. 6), and one exceptionally fine specimen formerly owned by Miguel Covarrubias is akin to Guatemalan forms in its characteristic combination of the animal with the human motif (Covarrubias, 1957, pl. 40, upper left).

The Guatemalan hachas usually have no notch (fig. 9), though a few rare pieces have a downward-pointed tenon. The death motif is often represented by a skull, and the associations noted so far have been exclusively with Late Classic remains. The hachas found in surface deposits at Palenque are of this type also. Those of Oaxaca, on the other hand, usually have a horizontal tenon, though it is sometimes reduced to a vestigial slight projection (fig. 13,*b*).

PALMAS (palmate stones, paddle-stones)

As Ellen Spinden (1933, p. 243) has observed, palmas and hachas are probably derived from a single older form. Typically the palma is tall (50–80 cm.), broad and flat at the top and narrower and thicker at the base, where its mass projects forward (fig. 10). Some varieties, however, are no taller than hachas, and one which Covarrubias calls "stone feathers" is laterally flattened and swings forward at the top. What distinguishes the palma from the hacha is chiefly the form of the base, which in the palma has a curved under surface and a piece projecting forward and downward in front, making it usually impossible for the palma to stand upright without support. The back surface of the palma is often slightly curved from top to bottom and may be sculptured in low relief, though the carving always stops somewhat short of the base.

It is even more difficult than in the case of the hachas to imagine how such objects

565

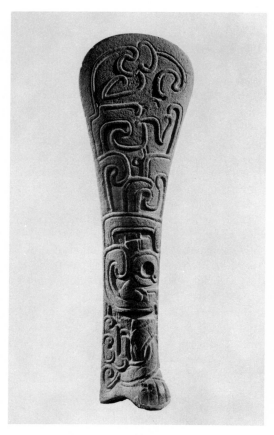

FIG. 10—TALL PALMA WITH TYPICAL SCROLL DECORATION, VERACRUZ. (Courtesy, American Museum of Natural History.)

FIG. 11—PALMA WITH UNUSUAL DESIGN OF BATS. (Property of Hugh A. Smith, Jr. Photo, courtesy of American Museum of Natural History.)

could have been attached to a belt, or how they could function in a ball game. Nevertheless, there is no question that palmas are represented as worn by figures on the ball courts of Tajin and on cornerstones from Sierra de Aparicio in the Misantla region (García Payón, 1949b, fig. 1). An Early Postclassic date is suggested for palmas by these carvings, though the ornamental scrollwork on some examples and their very fine rendering seem to imply an earlier origin in the Classic period.

The human type represented on palmas has a narrower face, a straighter nose, and thinner lips than that seen on yokes. Grotesque symbolism is expressed in detached

elements interspersed among scrolls, and the motif is presented more explicitly and realistically than on yokes, with the frequent help of simple animal symbolism. The predominant theme is death and human sacrifice represented by a figure with a gash in its breast. There are also examples of trophy heads held in the hand, skeleton figures, and skulls, which tend to link the symbolism on palmas with late Puuc and Toltec remains of Yucatan.

Palmas treat with a variety of subjects, and there are even attempts to present scenes of action, though they do not so much depict happenings as symbolize the nature of events. One such scene on a par-

566

Fig. 12—A VARIANT FORM OF HEAVY VERACRUZ HACHA OR PALMA. (Robert Woods Bliss Collection; photo by Nickolas Muray.)

ticularly beautiful palma (fig. 11), reproduced here with the permission of its owner, Hugh Smith, Jr., shows a man being pursued by bats, which in various mythologies of Mesoamerica are associated with death and the underworld. Scroll patterns are used alone or in conjunction with other motifs but are different in their forms and structures from those that appear on yokes and hachas, and are more akin to the patterns used on late ball-court sculptures at Tajin. Although the best of them show exquisite artistry and classic regard for regularity and refinement of forms, others are carelessly executed, and the style of many palmas suggests decadence or provincial origin. There is even on some a suggestion of central Mexican motifs and techniques that may indicate late survivals into the Aztec period.

The distribution of palmas appears to be somewhat more northerly and more remote from the coast than that of yokes and hachas, though a considerable number was found in the vicinity of Jalapa. Individual specimens have been reported from beyond the sierra (Hauswaldt, 1940) and even as far south as San Salvador (Lothrop, 1927, p. 32), but these appear to be exceptions, for there was no wide diffusion of the palma form comparable to that of hachas. It is even possible that the makers of palmas in

567

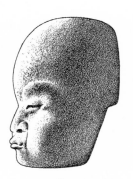
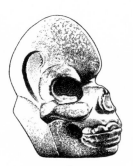

a b c

FIG. 13—REGIONAL HACHA FORMS. a, Southern Veracruz. b, Oaxaca. c, Pacific coast, Guatemala. (After Proskouriakoff, 1954, figs. 10,m; 11,j; 11,n.)

Veracruz pressed hard upon their neighbors and were responsible for the dispersal of the people who carried the hacha and the yoke across the isthmus into southern Guatemala.

VARIOUS OTHER FORMS

A small number of specific forms, particularly some that are carved in the semblance of birds (fig. 12), cannot be clearly classed as hachas or palmas although they belong in a larger category including both types of objects. Some have the notched base of hachas but are too broad in back, others have the palma base but are, like hachas, wedge-shaped. One bird form that is notched in back has a nearly globular body and a fan of tail feathers (fig. 14,c). Another form is characterized by a tenon ending in a triangular notch, and it is not clear whether such forms stand vertically, horizontally, or obliquely (fig. 14,b). Particularly deserving of notice are certain heads with closed eyes, drooping cheeks, and a high, apparently shaved, forehead with a light vertical ridge (fig. 14,a). These heads occur only in the southern part of the area, mostly in the region of Los Tuxtlas, and when they are laterally flattened they are generally classed as hachas. In Oaxaca there is a corresponding tenoned form with an exaggerated crest, which is also closely related to hachas, and

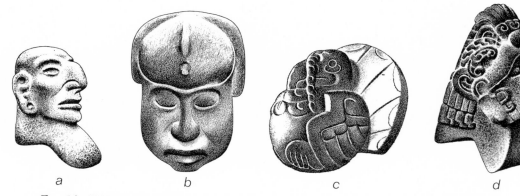

a b c d

FIG. 14—VARIANT FORMS. a, Low, portrait palma. b, Crested head, southern Veracruz. c, Turkey, notched form. d, Notched form, with influence from art of Teotihuacan. (After Proskouriakoff, 1954, figs. 12,a; 10,k; 10,h; and 10,j.)

in which the death motif takes the form of a skull.

Objects called "small yokes," or "curved stones" when the class includes various related forms, have a wide distribution, mainly outside of Veracruz. They have been found at Tlatilco with Preclassic remains, and Cook de Leonard (1953, pp. 435–36) reports a number from graves in southern Puebla together with Thin Orange pottery and with a black ware which she judges to be of the same period or later. Scattered specimens occur at sites as distant as Las Flores, Honduras. Most often there is no decoration, but a number of carved pieces resemble in varying degree the Olmec carvings of La Venta (Peterson and Horcasitas, 1957). None, to my knowledge, shows any relation to the style of central Veracruz.

So-called "padlock-stones" (Covarrubias, 1957, fig. 72) are usually unsculptured and tend to be classed with utilitarian objects. It is possible, however, that they correspond to the forms carried in the hand by some of the ball-players portrayed on the bench of the Great Ball Court at Chichen Itza, and that they have a sculptured prototype in wood or some other perishable material (see also Borhegyi, 1961a).

These marginal forms show the small sculptures of Classic Veracruz to be part of a widely spread and persistent complex which is still imperfectly understood in its various ramifications. In view of the distinct styles and varieties of the objects that occur even in Veracruz itself, such terms as "Totonac" and "Tajinoid" should be applied to them with caution and discrimination to avoid inappropriate connotations.

Mirror Backs

The earliest known examples of hematite mirrors are associated with the Olmec style of La Venta, but in Early Classic times, mirrors of hematite and pyrites were widely traded from central Veracruz. Kidder, Jennings, and Shook (1946, fig. 156) illustrate a slate mirror back decorated with typical

Fig. 15—CARVED MIRROR BACK. (Robert Woods Bliss Collection; photo by Nickolas Muray.)

Classic Veracruz tracery that was found in an Esperanza tomb, and Ekholm (1945) reports another of very similar design from Queretaro. The reflecting surface of the first is made in mosaic; the second is cut from a single piece of two naturally juxtaposed layers. Two other mirrors, at least one of which is of hematite (Lothrop, Foshag, and Mahler, 1957, pp. 235, 236) are reported to be from coastal Veracruz. These specimens are all similar in style, which is distinguished by the same somewhat irregular pattern of highly decorated interlocking scrolls that one finds on many Veracruz yokes (fig. 15). The compositions make no concession to the round shape of the discs, and the scrolls are used to form a rectangular field for the display of figures. Another specimen, now in the American Museum of Natural History (Covarrubias, 1957, pl. 44), is somewhat more sophisticated in style, being a portrait piece composed on curvilinear lines. I have conjectured that this piece may be somewhat later, but there is no definite evidence yet on which one can base a stylistic sequence.

ARCHITECTURAL RELIEFS

The bas-reliefs on the ball courts of Tajin and on its "Edifice of Columns" as well as the stones from Sierra de Aparicio are of that period which is usually called "Early Postclassic," but which in the Veracruz area might better be designated as "terminal Classic." In their motifs, in their general treatment and arrangement of figures, and in their symbolism, these reliefs are very much like the Toltec carvings of Chichen Itza. Specifically Toltec traits, however, are absent, and the scroll decoration, the forms of architecture portrayed, and the treatment of grotesque elements all show a continuity with the regional Classic tradition. The scrolls are like those on palmas, and palmas are actually depicted in the reliefs. The carving is done on masonry of large well-fitted slabs, a technique that can be observed at Santa Rosa Xtampak in Yucatan and at Chichen Itza. Columns are built of low cylindrical drums, and the sculptured figures on them are arranged in superimposed bands. We see on these reliefs, as on sporadic examples of palmas, the position of the figure typical of the Late Classic period in lowland Maya areas, where the figure stands with its body in full front view and its feet pointing outward. This position is also seen on a stone from Cerro de Moreno (García Payón, 1947b, fotos 2, 3), which, like the Aparicio stones, is carved on the front and on one side, suggesting that it may have been used as a cornerstone for some construction, possibly a ball court.

Very little is known of earlier forms of architectural decoration in Veracruz. It is very probable that there were stucco reliefs and painting, but except for a few bits of painted plaster no surviving example is known.

MONUMENTAL CARVING

The Classic style in Veracruz was not a monumental style, and there are only three monuments, all at Tajin, that can be properly ascribed to it. The earliest, associated with Period I of that site, is a panel depicting a ball-player, surrounded by a border of irregularly patterned scrolls (García Payón, 1950a, foto 1). The second is a block of columnar basalt, carved with a grotesque figure amid interlocked scrolls similar to those found on frog yokes. Although it was set into a structure of Period III (García Payón, 1949a, p. 300), it is completely different in style from the bas-reliefs of that period, and it is possible that it was salvaged from some earlier construction and reset in its final position. The third monument is the only one of the three that can be properly called a stela. It is carved in high relief and, though clearly related to the late sculptures of Tajin in style, suggests strongly an influence from the Maya area. This small and miscellaneous collection of monuments in a site the size of Tajin indicates that there was no consistent practice of stela erection, and that it is here an intrusive trait imperfectly assimilated in the ritual complex.

A few monuments are concentrated in the south on the fringes of the Olmec region. A large stela at El Meson (Covarrubias, 1957, fig. 68) and the monument from Alvarado (*ibid.*, fig. 29) clearly show their derivation from the Olmec style. The stela from Tepatlaxco (Kelemen, 1956, pl. 69,*a*), though identical in arrangement to the Alvarado monument, leans somewhat more toward the style of central Veracruz, and Kelemen rightly points out the resemblance of the head of the principal figure to that on the mirror back in the American Museum of Natural History. The only site in this general region which has a considerable series of monuments of Classic date is Cerro de Las Mesas, but, as Drucker points out (Drucker, 1943b, p. 85), the culture of this site was in a large measure a highland culture. Its particular importance lies in the role that it probably played in the movement of peoples and in the exchange of cultural traits between the Atlantic and the

Pacific coasts, as revealed in the startling similarity of some of its monuments to others at Tonala, Chiapas, and at Santa Lucia Cotzumalhuapa. The hacha and the yoke excavated by Drucker, though not identical to those of the Pacific coast, are closer to them than to the standard forms of the Classic Veracruz style.

CONCLUDING REMARKS

It is clear that our data are insufficient to define regional styles in Veracruz or to clarify temporal relationships between various forms, motifs, and types of ornament. The region south of the city of Veracruz, which touches on the area of Olmec culture, can be distinguished by the prevalence of oval yokes, of notched heads that express the death motif by closed eyes and drooping cheeks, and by hachas with a shallow notch or oblique cut in back. Whether or not any of these traits have also a chronological significance is still an open question.

Our inability to reconstruct the history of the Classic Veracruz style is particularly unfortunate because such a history would have a relevance beyond that of the region itself. Many observers have noted striking parallels between some of the Veracruz designs and those that were used on early Chinese bronzes. Not only are the two arts very similar in general conception, with their dragon forms almost lost amid intricate tracery, but there are specific and complex forms in the two styles so nearly alike that it is hard to believe that they were independently invented. Perhaps the most striking difference in the decorative forms is the avoidance in Veracruz tracery of the sharply pointed ends of curved forms that give lively accents to the Chinese scroll-

work. Whether the similarities are completely fortuitous or the result of convergence due to basically similar original formulations, whether they indicate repeated contact with the Orient, or whether they are rooted very deeply in the past and stem from early Asiatic migrations into America, are questions to which we cannot at present envisage even the possibility of an answer. Many serious scholars have considered them without reaching a satisfactory conclusion. If there is an answer, however, it lies in a slow and laborious reconstruction of the details of change and in a close comparison of the history of the two arts and their correlation in time. One can only hope that the dispersal of art objects from Veracruz will leave something for the future archaeologist who may command sufficient resources to investigate in detail the distribution and succession of forms and to clarify the sources and the course of development of its remarkably rich and varied style.

In spite of the many new specimens that have been added to private collections over a period of years, no large compendium representative of all varieties of carved objects from Veracruz is yet available, and little progress has been made in defining artistic schools in this area. Illustrations of individual pieces are scattered in many publications dealing with Mesoamerican arts, and short papers have appeared from time to time, notably: Galindo y Villa, 1921; Krickeberg, 1918; Beyer, 1924, 1927; Palacios, 1943; Kidder II, 1949; and Proskouriakoff, 1954. The best descriptive sources, however, remain those of the turn of the century: Strebel, 1890, 1893; Ernst, 1892; and Fewkes, 1907.

REFERENCES

Agrinier, 1960
Beyer, 1924, 1927
Borhegyi, 1961a
Cook de Leonard, 1953
Covarrubias, 1957
Dixon, 1958, 1959
Drucker, 1943b
Ekholm, 1945, 1946, 1949
Ernst, 1892
Fewkes, 1907
Galindo y Villa, 1921
García Payón, 1947a, 1947b, 1949a, 1949b, 1950a, 1950b
Genin, 1928
Hauswaldt, 1940
Kelemen, 1956

Kidder II, 1949
Kidder, Jennings, and Shook, 1946
Krickeberg, 1918
Kubler, 1954
Lothrop, 1923, 1927
——, Foshag, and Mahler, 1957
Palacios, 1943
Peterson and Horcasitas, 1957
Proskouriakoff, 1954
Ruz L., 1953
Shook and Kidder, 1952
Spinden, E. S., 1933
Strebel, 1890, 1893
Thompson, J. E. S., 1941b
Weiant, 1943

24. Archaeological Synthesis of the Sierra

RICHARD S. MAC NEISH

A REGIONAL SEQUENCE from southern Tamaulipas Sierra may be derived from two local sequences: one from the Sierra de Tamaulipas and the other from the Sierra Madre of southwest Tamaulipas. It is open to question as to whether this is within the bounds of the Huasteca subarea and even more questionable as to whether it fits into the Mesoamerica culture area at all time periods.

Much of this region is semidesert though fingers of tropical climate reach into it from the south. East along the Gulf of Mexico it is flat, then these coastal flats give way to the hills and canyon-cut mountains of the Sierra de Tamaulipas. Farther west are lower hills and the Guajeleyo valley which border the edge of the steeper Sierra Madre of southwest Tamaulipas.

During archaeological reconnaissance in the northern two-thirds of Tamaulipas (MacNeish, 1948), five excavations revealing stratigraphy were made in ruins in the Sierra de Tamaulipas. One ruin, Tm-r-86, on Cerro Guadalupe contained four occupation levels of the Laguna phase (then called

Pueblito I) under a floor of the Eslabones phase (then called Pueblito II). The other was at La Salta ruin (Tm-r-79), which had La Salta remains (then called Pueblito III) on the floor of a house platform over fill containing Eslabones sherds. Though some survey was undertaken along the Gulf coast and sites were ex-

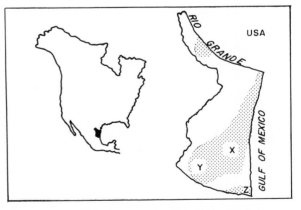

Fig. 1—STATE OF TAMAULIPAS, MEXICO, WITH THE AREA OF SURVEY AND EXCAVATION INDICATED. Stippling shows area surveyed. X, Canyon Diablo caves. Y, Canyon Infiernillo caves. Z, Tampico-Panuco region.

573

cavated in the Tampico-Panuco regions, most activities were in the Sierra de Tamaulipas (MacNeish, 1950). Three stratified caves were excavated. The first, Diablo Cave (Tm-c-81), contained a layer of Los Angeles remains over an ill-defined level of Eslabones phase materials, which were on top of Nogales artifacts in a poorly defined stratum. These were separated by sterile silts from a pure component with Lerma remains that in turn were over Diablo artifacts in high terrace gravels. Charcoal from a Lerma roasting pit yielded a carbon-14 date of 7314 B.C. ± 500 years (Crane and Griffin, 1958a, pp. 1103–04, M499). A second cave, Nogales (Tm-c-82), contained, in poorly defined strata, Los Angeles remains over Eslabones over Almagre over La Perra over Nogales. A third cave, La Perra (Tm-c-174), contained Los Angeles sherds and charcoal on the surface dated by carbon-14 A.D. 1292 ± 150 years (Libby, 1952, C201). Underneath these was a mixed layer of Laguna artifacts with a large amount of preserved foodstuffs and feces. These in turn were over floors containing La Perra remains which had even more preserved vegetal refuse. The top part of this occupation was dated by carbon-14 as 2492 B.C. ± 280 years (Libby, 1951, C687). Underneath these remains was a sterile dust deposit over two Lerma occupations.

In 1955 more archaeological reconnaissance was undertaken in the Sierra de Tamaulipas and two sites were excavated. Humada Cave (Tm-c-315) yielded strata with Almagre remains over a layer with La Perra artifacts; Armadillo Cave (Tm-c-314) had three floors of charcoal and perishable human remains of the Los Angeles culture over poorly defined patches containing La Salta tools. These in turn were over a thicker stratum with a thin layer of Almagre artifacts over a thick section with Nogales remains. Thus from the Sierra de Tamaulipas a sequence of nine cultural phases was obtained.

Further survey and excavation in south-

west Tamaulipas obtained a long stratigraphic sequence of cultures with preserved food remains in three stratified caves. In Romero Cave (Tm-c-274) 16 sequential occupations with food remains occurred over a few artifacts of the Infiernillo phase in the underlying gravels. Occupations 1–4 were of the Ocampo phase (Occupation 1 dated at 3244 B.C. ± 350, Occupation 4 dated 2604 B.C. ± 350; Crane and Griffin, 1958a, M502, M503). Occupations 5–8 were Guerra remains (Occupation 6 dated at 2700 B.C. ±300; ibid., M504, M567); Occupations 9 and 10 (dated 1486 and 1690 B.C. ± 200) were of the Mesa de Guaje phase (ibid., M505). Occupations 11 (dated A.D. 236 ± 200 years) and 12 were of the Palmillas phase (ibid., M506, M568). In the front of the cave were four thick stratified beds of vegetal materials and artifacts separated by sterile ash and/or dust layers. The lower two, Occupations 13 and 14, belonged to the San Lorenzo phase, 15 and 16 to the San Antonio phase.

Valenzuela Cave (Tm-c-248) confirmed the stratigraphy of Tm-c-247 and added considerably to our knowledge of the earlier phases. The earliest three lenses of refuse in Tm-c-248 contained artifacts and vegetal materials of the Infiernillo phase. The latest of these, Occupation 3, was dated at 6244 B.C. ± 450 years (ibid., M498). Occupations 4–6 were of the Ocampo phase (Occupation 6 dated at 3694 B.C. ± 350; ibid., M497). Occupation 7, which was relatively brief and was of a new phase called Flacco, was dated at 1991 B.C. ± 334 (Libby, personal communication). The next layer (Occupation 8), fairly extensive, was of the San Lorenzo culture. The thin top stratum, Occupation 9, contained San Antonio artifacts.

The final cave, Ojo de Agua (Tm-c-274), had 1.8 to 2.4 cm. of refuse but only the upper San Lorenzo Occupations 11 and 12 (dated A.D. 1436 ± 200) had preserved refuse (Crane and Griffin, 1958a, M501). Below this were three floors of the Palmillas phase, then a series of charcoal floors, Occupations 2–7, that belonged to the Flacco phase. A small charcoal area, Occupation 1, at the bottom of the deposit on top of gravels, yielded Infiernillo artifacts and a date of 6544 B.C. ± 450 (*ibid.*, M500).

Thus, the Sierra Madre shows a sequence of eight cultural phases extending from roughly 7000 B.C. to A.D. 1750. The only gaps in this sequence were before and after Palmillas and between Infiernillo and Ocampo.

Contemporary phases from the two locales are closely related. For this article I have telescoped the two sequences to form a general one for southern Tamaulipas, and thus reconstructed an unbroken sequence from 8000 B.C. to A.D. 1750, including 9000 years with preserved food remains. This combining of the two sequences has its limitations, and the cultures and environments are not exactly the same, but I believe they are sufficiently similar to give a fairly accurate general picture (Table 1).

I shall now briefly review the 13 sequential culture phases of prehistoric southern Tamaulipas, touching on subsistence, settlement patterns, and a few features of the material culture.

The Diablo complex, estimated to be older than 12,000 years, is very poorly defined and represented by only a few bifacial ovoid large knives, pebbles and bifacial choppers and large flaked, unifacial-side scrapers or knives. The few associated bones (including those of a horse) and the relatively small areas occupied suggest a primitive nomadic hunter group.

The Lerma phase, 8800–10,000 years old, represented by seven components, had a community pattern reflecting a society consisting of nomadic microbands. The proportion of bones to volume of refuse suggests that from 70 to 50 per cent of their subsistence was based on hunting, the rest on food gathering. The lenticular Lerma spear- or dartpoints, snub-nosed and stemmed end scrapers, large plano-convex end and side scrapers, gravers, pebble choppers, and ovoid or square-based bifacial knives can all be connected with the chase or meat and skin preparation.

It is with the Infiernillo horizons, 7000–9000 years old, that we obtain our first clear picture of ancient subsistence. Materials included abundant preserved vegetal matter. Some 50–70 per cent of the foodstuffs were obtained by plant collecting, from 45–25 per cent by hunting. The remainder (less than 5 per cent) are from incipient agriculture of pumpkins, peppers, and, in the latter stage, gourds. *Agave, Opuntia* and runner beans, all potentially capable of being domesticated, were collected along with other wild plant remains. The community pattern reflects a society of seasonal microbands, that is, bands from one to three families who were usually nomadic hunters but, during certain seasons when plants were ripe, settled down together in one spot to exploit these resources. Diagnostic tools include teardrop-shaped (Abasolo), diamond-shaped, or large contracting pointed-stem (Almagre) projectile points for attachment to spearshafts, or wooden dart foreshafts. Equally distinctive are large planes and flake choppers or scrapers. Other traits include Fuegian nets or baskets, Z-twisted hard yarn string with or without knots, simple coiled nets with or without a rod foundation, twilled and plaited mats, some peculiar wound-element coiled baskets (that superficially look like twined baskets), several shell beads, and awls with holes in their bases.

The next period,, 5000–3000 B.C., seems to have been filled by Nogales of the Sierra de Tamaulipas (without preserved remains) and the early part of Ocampo (with preserved vegetal remains) from the Sierra Madre. From 70 to 80 per cent of their subsistence was based on plant collection: *Panicum sonorum* (a millet), seteria, runner beans (*Phaseolus coccineus*), *Agave*, and *Opuntia*, all of which could be domesticated but were not. Domesticated plants,

575

TABLE 1—CULTURE SEQUENCE OF SOUTHERN TAMAULIPAS

	SIERRA DE TAMAULIPAS								SOUTHWEST SIERRA MADRE			
	Tm-c-81	Tm-c-174	Tm-c-82	Tm-c-314	Tm-c-315	Tm-r-86	Tm-r-79	Phase	Phase	Tm-c-247	Tm-c-248	Tm-c-274
1960 A.D.	Layer 1	Surface	Layer 1-2	Layer 1				Los Angeles	San Antonio	Occ. 15-16	Occ. 9	
									San Lorenzo	Occ. 13-14	Occ. 8	Occ. 11-12
1000 A.D.				Layer 2			Level 1-2	La Salta				
0	Layer 2	Layer 1	Layer 3			Level 1-3	Level 3-4	Eslabones	Palmillas	Occ. 11-12		Occ. 8-10
						Level 4-7		Laguna	La Florida			
1000 B.C.									Mesa de Guaje	Occ. 9-10		
									Guerra	Occ. 5-8		
2000 B.C.			Layer 4	Layer 3	Layer 1-7			Almagre	Flacco		Occ. 7	Occ. 2-7
3000 B.C.		Layer 2-3	Layer 5		Level 8-9			La Perra				
4000 B.C.				Layer 4					Ocampo	Occ. 1-4	Occ. 4-6	
5000 B.C.	Layer 3		Layer 6-7					Nogales				
		Layer 3										
6000 B.C.									Infiernillo	Occ. 1a	Occ. 1-3	Occ. 1
7000 B.C.												
8000 B.C.	Layer 5	Layer 5-6						Lerma				
9000 B.C.												
10,000 B.C.	Layer 6							Diablo				

5–8 per cent of the diet, were gourds, chili peppers, large and small varieties of pumpkin, and yellow seed varieties of *Phaseolus vulgaris*; other food came from hunting. Dartpoint shapes (for atlatl foreshafts) are subtriangular (Nogales), incipient stem (Almagre)—only in Ocampo—and teardrop (Abasolo). Other artifacts were large and small chipped bifacial disk choppers, mullers, disk scrapers, Clear Fork type of gouges, large flake end scrapers, full-turned coil nets, checker-woven and twilled mats and twilled baskets, and Fuegian baskets, as well as string often tied in a wide variety of knots. The community pattern seems to be that of seasonal macrobands.

The next period, 3000–2200 B.C., is represented by La Perra remains and late Ocampo components. About 15 per cent of their food came from animals, 70–76 per cent from wild plants: amaranths, *Panicium sonorum*, *Phaseolus coccineus*, *Opuntia*, tripiscum, and *Agave*. A fairly wide variety of domesticated plants composed 10–15 per cent of their diet: gourds, two varieties of pumpkins, peppers and long red and yellow seeded varieties of *Phaseolus vulgaris*. Present in La Perra were two varieties (A and B) of a corn race called Early *Nal-Tel*. The settlement pattern is much like that of the previous period. Dartpoint shapes are contracting stem (Almagre), subtriangular (Nogales), teardrop (Abasolo), and triangular with a concave base and a basal flute (Tortugas). Gouges, disk choppers, mullers, pebble manos, disk scrapers, simple coiled nets, twilled and checked mats and baskets, string, full-turned coiled nets, and multiple stitch-and-wrap baskets.

The Flacco and Almagre phases are the most similar in the two areas. It is estimated that they existed from 2200 to 1800 B.C. Subsistence was very much the same as in the previous phase, but with a little more agriculture (now 20 per cent). This is at the expense of plant collecting, 65 per cent. The only difference in crops is that the Bat Cave race of corn is found in Flacco. This occur-

rence of the *Bat Cave* race after Early *Nal-Tel* is somewhat peculiar in that the former is considered more primitive. The settlement pattern is also like that of the previous period, except for two sites of the Almagre phase: one contained wattle and daub, suggesting permanent houses; the other encompassed a large area, implying—if all the area was simultaneously occupied—a village. Thus we have classified these cultures as being of semisedentary macrobands. Artifacts included large stemmed, corner-notched (Palmillas), contracting stem with or without tanged shoulders (Almagre and Gary), teardrop (Abasolo) and triangular (Flacco and Tortugas) atlatl points; keeled and snub-nosed end scrapers; blades and polyhedral cores; coiled, twined, and twilled baskets; coiled nets; rabbit sticks; chipped gouges; twilled mats; string and ropes and a few pieces of string that might be cotton though most are agave. Mortars, boulders, metates, and pebble manos are still present.

Developing out of Flacco is the Guerra phase of the Sierra Madre which is represented by only six components though it contained abundant artifacts and food remains. Carbon-14 dates indicate it lasted from 1800 to 1400 B.C. The four open sites suggest that the people lived in small villages, and the cave occupations seem to have been of some duration, thus marking a community pattern of semipermanent villages. Domesticated gourds, peppers, pumpkins of two varieties, *Cucurbita moschata* (warty squash), yellow and red beans composed about 30 per cent of their diet; only a tenth came from meat, the rest were wild plants. There was also cotton. The changes in artifact types are not great. Corner-notched, contracting stem, and large or small triangular or leaf-shaped atlatl points occur along with choppers, disk scrapers, gouges and small plano-convex end scrapers. Simple coiled nets, twined blankets, twilled mats and baskets, half-hitch woven baskets and mainly coiled baskets were present. One difference is the greater variety of string than in the previous phase. Flexed skeletons buried under and on mats were uncovered.

The Guerra phase developed directly into Mesa de Guaje phase (estimated from carbon-14 tests at 1400–500 B.C.). It is represented by even fewer components, which, however, seem to show that people lived in semisedentary villages. Agricultural products were gourds, peppers, two varieties of pumpkins (*Cucurbita pepo*), yellow and red seeded beans, warty squash (*Cucurbita moschata*). Bat Cave and hybridized corn, teocenti, and sunflower composed about 40 per cent of the diet; hunting (10 per cent) and plant collecting (50 per cent) made up the rest. There was also cotton. Projectile points included straight and contracting stem, large and small triangular and leaf-shaped types; a number of foreshafts indicated these were used on darts. One of the distinctive features of this phase was the making of black, red, and plain flat-bottomed bowls and small-mouthed jars. No appendages such as feet, handles, or spouts occurred. There was a wide variety of twilled and checker-woven mats, usually with distinctive borders; split-stitch baskets in the form of pans or water bottles; coiled and laced nets; twilled two-over-two and one-over-one cotton loom-made cloth; string; choppers and scrapers.

Remains of the period developing out of Mesa de Guaje, La Florida, were found only in survey on the Sierra Madre, but they seem very similar to those of Laguna of the Sierra de Tamaulipas, which had domesticated plant remains. The people were basically agriculturists, 40 per cent of their subsistence coming from these activities, 51 per cent from plant collecting, and about 9 per cent from hunting or trapping of animals. Domesticated plants included gourds, pumpkins, manioc, peppers, beans (large red variety), cottons, three races of hybridized corn (*Breve de Padilla*, *Dzit-Bacal*, and *Nal-Tel*) and possibly earlier *Nal-Tel* (unhybridized) types. The other

plants found in Mesa de Guaje may have existed at this stage also, but the sample was too small to determine this. Habitations are fairly extensive, and I consider the community pattern to be that of sedentary temple-oriented village groups. That is, there were round platforms for wattle-and-daub houses associated with a plaza and larger pyramids to form ceremonial and village centers. These centers are surrounded by hamlets, camps, or villages. A wide variety of artifacts was manufactured, of which the most numerous was ceramic. Six monochrome wares predominate—fine cream, fine orange, polished black, polished red, brushed, and plain—in a diversity of forms including tripod, effigy, and flanged vessels. Also made of clay were modeled figurines, ladles, whistles, and clay discs. Twilled cotton cloth woven on a belt loom, twilled mats, twined bracelets, split-stitch coiled baskets, and several varieties of string were common. Ground stone artifacts included celts, adzes, mullers, cylindrical and rectangular manos, angled-back metates, bell-shaped pestles, mortars, and bark beaters. Chipped stone was relatively rare but appeared as prismatic flakes struck from cylindrical polyhedral cores; stemmed, side-notched, and corner-notched atlatl points; and large ovoid biface forms.

This late Formative phase is directly ancestral to Eslabones of the Sierra de Tamaulipas, which overlaps with early Palmillas of the Sierra Madre, roughly from 0 to A.D. 500. As only Palmillas had preserved vegetal remains, our reconstruction is based on these materials. Domesticated plants were several varieties of corn, pumpkin, moschata and mixta squash, gourds, chili peppers, probably tobacco, runner beans, sunflowers, panicium, amaranths, manihot, lima beans, six varieties of common beans, and cotton. Domesticated plants represented about 45 per cent of their diet, wild plant collecting 50 per cent; the remainder was from hunting or trapping of animals. This was the period of the greatest population concentration. At a number of sites many (up to 1400) house platforms are grouped around a rectangular plaza outlined by pyramids. Sometimes ball courts, tanques, and other architectural features are associated. These seem to be ceremonial centers or towns and often are on hilltops. Other smaller areas of habitations perhaps represent hamlets, villages, or camps. The basic community pattern is much like that in the former phase, but the centers are larger and more complex. This is also true of the rest of the material culture. Vessels of red, black, plain, and brushed wares are better made, more decorated (often by engraving), and more varied in form. Figurines are both moldmade and modeled. Elbow pipes, ladles, discoidal beads, and other objects are also made of clay. Mats, nets, cloth, and baskets are ornate and numerous. The few ground and chipped stone tools are much like those of the previous phase.

La Salta (A.D. 500–900) developed from Eslabones; and if we can judge from late Palmillas remains, which are very similar, these subsistence patterns were about the same. The settlement pattern differs in that many of the sites with stone house platforms are not associated with temples, and sites in general are smaller. The material culture also seems to be less complex. There are only four kinds of pottery: polished black, plain, smooth, and brushed utilitarian wares. Figurines, which are moldmade, are not numerous. Ground stone artifacts include celts, metates, manos, mortars and pestles. Of chipped stone, there were stemmed, side-notched, and corner-notched atlatl points as well as arrowpoints in the same forms but smaller. Scrapers, knives, prismatic blades, and cores still occur. If we can project from the late Palmillas remains, ornate mats, nets, woven cloth, and split-stitch baskets still continued as did clay elbow pipes. Cane cigarettes and arrowshafts are also present.

In the Sierra Madre, San Lorenzo devel-

oped from Palmillas but the regional equivalent has not been found in the Sierra de Tamaulipas. San Lorenzo (A.D. 900–1300) has most of the domesticated plants of Palmillas, but some of the varieties of *Zea mays* and *Cucurbita pepo* as well as panicium, teocenti, and sunflower are missing. Furthermore, agricultural foods represent only 40 per cent of their diet; 10 per cent is from meat. Perhaps the noticeable difference is that few stone architectural remains have been uncovered though wattle-and-daub houses were used. The few sites we have found are smaller and are not associated with pyramids or obvious ceremonial structures. The material culture is also simpler. Pottery is confined to a few types showing polishing, corrugating, engraving, smoothing, and brushing. These are relatively poorly fired and have few forms and no appendages. Figurines are absent but clay pipes and spindle whorls appear. Ground stone metates, cylindrical and rectangular manos, a possible adze, and coiled and laced netting appear as do twilled cloth, undecorated mats, skin belts and bags, split-stitch baskets, and cigarettes. It is in this period that various leaf-shaped, serrated, corner-notched, side-notched, and triangular arrowpoints outnumber atlatl points. Prismatic blades are rare but small end scrapers, biface tools, and choppers are fairly numerous.

The final period (A.D. 1300–1750) sees the Los Angeles phase in the Sierra de Tamaulipas and San Antonio in the Sierra Madre. Both last into historic times. Study of their food remains reveals that the people obtained 40 per cent of their food from agriculture, 42 per cent from wild food plants, and 18 per cent from animals they hunted or trapped. Domesticated plants are limited to one or two varieties of corn and beans, peppers, *Cucurbita pepo* and *C. moschata*, gourds, cotton, tobacco, indigo, and possibly canavalia beans. Sites are uniformly small though fairly numerous and seem to have been small rancheros with a few wattle-and-daub oval houses. Caves were again fairly extensively occupied. Pottery is more poorly made, less decorated, more limited in form, and is brushed, smoothed, or burnished black. Mats, nets, and split-stitch baskets still appear. Flat rectangular metates and manos, pestles of clay or stone and stone mortars occur. The bow and arrow are dominant over the atlatl and dart, and a whole series of small notched and triangular chipped points appear. Chipped stone choppers, knives, and scrapers again become common. Generally speaking, this phase seems to be much less complex and sophisticated than the previous three or four periods.

In conclusion, it seems relevant to attempt to relate this sequence to ones from adjacent regions or subareas. The relationships of the ill-defined Diablo complex can not be plotted, but with Lerma we are on slightly firmer footing. In the Diablo Dam region in the Big Bend of the Rio Grande River of Texas and in the rock shelter dug by C. Irwin in Queretaro, Mexico, Lerma points were found in the lowest layers. Also, the earliest materials from the Valley of Mexico and from the valley of Tehuacan contain Lerma points. Thus the Tamaulipas Lerma phase can be related to the earliest cultures in surrounding areas on the basis of this point type. Unfortunately, artifacts associated with these points from other areas are scarce, and it is impossible to assess just how firm are the relationships indicated by the points. Relationships to Infiernillo are equally vague. Teardrop-shaped points, boulder mullers and metates, Almagre points, slab and nodule choppers, large plano-convex end scrapers, domed scraping planes, and thick and thin side scrapers appear in the El Riego phase from the Tehuacan caves in the Santa Marta complex in Chiapas, with the Chalco industry of the Valley of Mexico and with Cochise-like remains in western Mexico, as well as with the contemporaneous Infiernillo complex. But does the pres-

ence of these generalized traits mean they are closely related? Relationships with the Nogales–Ocampo–La Perra part of the Tamaulipas sequence are only slightly easier to discern. Besides having the generalized traits mentioned above, gouges, pebble manos, blades (and inferentially polyhedral cores), Nogales triangular points, end-of-blade scrapers, and spokeshaves occur in Tehuacan caves, the Santa Marta complex, Chalco, perhaps Irwin's pre-ceramic material of Queretaro and Hidalgo, the Repelo and Falcon complexes as well as the Nogales–Ocampo–La Perra continuum. Perhaps they are more than casually related. Flacco and Almagre of Tamaulipas seem to be fairly closely related to Abasolo of northern Tamaulipas and the later pre-ceramic layers of the caves of Hidalgo and Queretaro excavated by Irwin in that they have not only many of the traits mentioned above but also such specialized point types as Langtry stemmed, Flacco indented base, Palmillas corner-notched, Kent or Markus stemmed, and Gary stemmed. Guerra of southwest Tamaulipas, though ancestral to Mesa de Guaje and probably contemporary with early ceramic remains farther south in Mexico, seems unrelated to anything so far found in Mesoamerica. Though most of its traits are distinctive, Mesa de Guaje does have relationships to the Ponce period or phase of the Panuco-Tampico region in that they have the Ponce Black pottery type in common. Laguna–La Florida materials of Tamaulipas again show many similarities to those of El Prisco (Period II) phase of Tampico-Panuco region. These similarities include: Panuco A, Panuco bulging eye, and Panuco coffee-bean-eye figurine types, bowls with a basal ridge, short solid conical tripod vessel feet, bowls with vertical recurved sides, bowls with incurved vertical sides, bowls with flaring sides bearing thickened or everted lips, hemispherical bowls, molcajetes with interior decorated by quadrants filled by parallel lines, pottery ladles, bark beaters, pottery discs, metates, flat oval manos, bell-shaped pestles, round stone house platforms, and truncated conical mounds.

Eslabones and early Palmillas are also very similar to Pithaya (Period III) of the Panuco-Tampico region in that both have jadeite beads, adzes, celts, lamellar obsidian flake knives, portrait-type figurines, flaring-sided carinate bowls, hollow conical vessel feet in conjunction with small conical solid vessel feet, Zaquil Red sherds as well as some of the traits mentioned in the previous paragraph.

La Salta–late Palmillas are even more closely related to Zaquil (Period IV) of the Panuco region. Zaquil Black Incised and Zaquil Red appear in both as well as a series of other specialized traits including moldmade figurines, clay cylindrical whis-

tles, sherd pendants, spindle whorls, hollow vessel feet, Palmillas points, Teotihuacan points, and clay pipes.

The last part of the Tamaulipas sequence —San Lorenzo, Los Angeles and San Antonio—do not seem connected with other nearby cultures. However, they have in common with many late cultures of Mexico and regions to the north a host of small specialized arrowpoint types.

It might appear that from southern Tamaulipas we have a very long and complete sequence. This is more apparent than real, for the total artifact complex of every phase and complex is inadequately known, relationships to other areas are poorly understood, and in both the local sequences there are gaps.

REFERENCES

Anderson, A. E., 1932
Borbolla and Aveleyra, 1953
Campbell, 1947
Cason, 1952
Crane and Griffin, 1958a
Du Solier, Krieger, and Griffin, 1947
Ekholm, 1944
Kaplan and MacNeish, 1960
Kelley, Campbell, and Lehmer, 1940
Krieger, 1951
Libby, 1951, 1952
MacNeish, 1947, 1948, 1950, 1954a, 1956

Mangelsdorf, MacNeish, and Galinat, 1956
Mason, 1935
Meade, 1942
Pearce and Jackson, 1933
Porter, 1948a
Prieto, 1873
Saldívar, 1943
Sayles, 1935
Stephenson, 1950, 1951
Suhm, Krieger, and Jelks, 1954
Whitaker, Cutler, and MacNeish, 1957

25. Ancient Sources on the Huasteca

GUY STRESSER-PÉAN

No AUTHOR OF THE 16th century has devoted to the civilization or the language of the Indians of the Huasteca any descriptive work which has come down to us. However, numerous bits of information can be gleaned in old writings which speak incidentally of the Huasteca or of the Huastec.

Sahagún devotes a special chapter and several isolated paragraphs to what the Aztec thought of their neighbors. Most of the other chroniclers of ancient Mexico mention the Huasteca in connection with the history of the people of the Central Plateau. Alvarado Tezozomoc (1878) and Alva Ixtlilxochitl (1891–92) are particularly important.

No pictographic Huastec codex is now known, but part of the post-Cortesian "lienzos" of the Totonac village of Tihuatlan portray the region of Tamiahua and Tuxpan. Moreover, manuscripts of central Mexico sometimes show events or things of the Huasteca.

Among the conquerors, Cortés and Bernal Díaz del Castillo describe campaigns in which they took part and furnish valuable information in this matter. To the "Anonymous Conqueror" we owe knowledge of some very crude details, which have often been cited. Less well known but not less interesting is a page of the "Primera relación anónima de la jornada que hizo Nuño de Guzmán a la Nuevo Galicia."

Religious authors have left us little. According to Mendieta, Fray Andrés de Olmos, the great Franciscan apostle of the Huasteca, wrote several accounts of the region and its language, but these works are apparently lost. Among the Augustinians, Fray Nicolas de Witte (1913) is the author of an extremely important letter.

The "Relaciones geográficas de Indias" of 1579–85 omit the greater part of the Huasteca. The only relación we have, that of Huejutla, gives detailed information of truly native origin, but describes only villages of the Nahuatl tongue.

Other administrative documents, entirely Spanish in origin, inform us about the ancient geography of the Huasteca. These are, particularly for the 16th century, the "Suma

582

de visitas de pueblos por orden alfabético" (PNE, vol. 1), the description of the bishopric of Tlaxcala (PNE, vol. 5), the description of the archbishopric of Mexico (PNE, vol. 3), and a remarkable map by Ortelius (1584; see fig. 1).

The 17th century furnishes geographic data of the same kind, with the Relaciones of Panuco, of Tampico, and of Huauchinango, to which one can add the notes of pastoral visits by Fray Alonso de la Mota y Escobar (1945). Important ethnological data are found in a short "Noticia sobre los Indios guastecos de la Provincia de Pánuco y su religión," as well as in archival documents. But these pieces of information, following the great concentrations of Indians brought about by the colonial administration, must be separated from the data of the 16th century. It is even more true for data of the 18th century, and especially for those in the very interesting "Noticia de la lengua huasteca" of Tapia Zenteno (1767). (See list of references at the end of this article.)

DISTRIBUTION OF POPULATION AND NATIVE LANGUAGES IN THE 16TH CENTURY

The Huastec Indians, linguistically allied to the Maya, have been established for at least 3000 years in the region of Tampico and Tuxpan. In pre-Columbian times, the Huastec seem to have occupied the whole extent of the Huasteca, and at certain periods, to have spread out to the mountains and the neighboring high plateaus. At the time of the conquest, however, they were practically reduced to their warm country domain, and had even lost a great part of that, on the south and the southwest, to Nahua-speakers. Yet these invaders, it seems, adopted in large measure the civilization of the Huastec people, whom they assimilated linguistically without suppressing them. We shall therefore discuss together the customs of these two groups, to whom the name Huastec (Cuextecatl) as inhabitants of the Huasteca (Cuextlan) was applied jointly.

We shall examine briefly the different parts of the 16th-century Huasteca, first the regions which still spoke the Huastec tongue, then those where Nahuatl took over. We shall note briefly the people who lived on the boundaries of the Huasteca: the Totonac, the Tepehua, the Otomi, and the Chichimec.

Regions of the Huastec Language

PLAINS AND HILLS OF THE PANUCO BASIN. We think that at the beginning of the 16th century the Huastec were primarily the people of the banks of the Panuco River and of its tributaries. The city of Panuco must have had a rather active river navigation, which doubtless favored regional cohesion and probably contributed to the maintenance of the Huastec tongue.

On the Panuco itself, or in its neighborhood, and toward the west on the Tamuin and the Tampaon rivers, Huastec villages followed each other as far as the foot of the mountains. In the dry plains of the north, the Huastec had, on the banks of the Tamesi River, a series of villages as far as Tanchipa, the last important outpost of Middle American civilization, near present-day Ciudad Mante. Away from the river, there were only little hamlets whose water supply seems to have been precarious. South of Panuco, several Huastec villages lay along the Moctezuma River, as far as the confluence of the Tancuilin River. Farther upstream, in spite of the predominance of the Nahua language, several Huastec place names persisted, among them Tamazunchale, the terminal point for boatmen coming from Panuco. Along the Tempoal River and its tributaries there were Huastec villages (or villages with Huastec names) as far as Tamoyon and Tanchel in one direction, and as far as the second Tamazunchale in the other (this last between Huejutla and Huautla). Away from the great permanent watercourses, the plains south of Panuco are exposed to drought, but in the 16th century little Huastec villages were scattered there.

The somewhat hilly regions of southern and southwestern Huasteca were better watered and more favorable for human population. But in the 16th century these regions were already partly taken over by Nahua-speakers. The Huastec hung on there precariously. In the sandstone hills of present-day Huasteca Potosina, they held no more than Huehuetlan and the heights north of the Tampamolon valley. Of the hills of Tantoyuca, they held only the northern part. Around the isolated volcanic massif of the Sierra de Tantima they were at home only in the northeast and in some isolated villages.

MOUNTAINS AND VALLEYS OF THE SIERRA MADRE. Outside the plains and hills, the Huastec language, at the beginning of the 16th century, held the remains of a domain formerly more important, being geographically part of the eastern Sierra Madre. There were first the three parallel synclines which gave Ciudad Valles its name. Farther west, people still spoke Huastec in some interior valleys, situated mostly in the present municipio of Tamasopo. To the south, the village of Oxitipa (Tanute) dominated the rainy mountains of the Sierra de Aquismon.

PLAINS AND HILLS OF THE TUXPAN BASIN. Here, in the 16th century, the Huastec language hardly survived, except around Tamiahua, a village bound to the north of the Huasteca by the navigable route of the coastal lagoons, and near Tuxpan.

Regions of the Nahua Language

At the time of the Spanish conquest, the Nahua language had about reached, in the Huasteca, the limits which it has today, except in some minor sectors, especially between the Temporal River and the Moctezuma River. Its expansion, at the expense of the Huastec language, seems to have increased slowly and to have still been active during the 16th century.

HILLS OF THE SOUTHWEST (COXCATLAN-HUEJUTLA). From this time on, in southwestern Huasteca, the densely populated hills at the foot of the eastern Sierra Madre were almost entirely conquered by Nahua-speakers. But their archaeology is essentially Huastec (as well as part of that of the Sierra de Metztitlan), and their toponymy has kept some Huastec names (Tampacan, Tamazunchale, Tancha) or Huastec-derived names.

In 1569 the priest of Coxcatlan, speaking of the inhabitants of Tanchinamol and Guauhtla (on the site of the present municipio of San Martin) says that the first "speak the Mexican and Huastec tongue," and that the second "are Huastec and speak the Mexican language."

THE TUXPAN BASIN. There must have existed, in pre-Columbian times, a Huasteca of the southeast, having its own physiognomy and perhaps a certain cultural peculiarity. The Sierra de Tantima and surrounding heights separated it from the basin of the Panuco. A limited network of navigable routes, formed by the Tuxpan River and its tributaries, converged there toward the town of Tuxpan.

Archaeology and native chronicles suggest that formerly the Huastec must have occupied this region, doubtless sharing it in the south with the Totonac, but from the 16th century on, Huastec toponomy was unusual there, except in the northeast. Spanish documents suggest a region early depopulated, where the Nahua tongue predominated, except, as we have said, around Tamiahua and Tuxpan.

Tezozomoc (1878) states that in the middle of the 15th century the "Huastec" of Xiuhcoac (or Tzicoac, near the present Ixhuatlan, Veracruz), of Tuxpan, and of Temapache had to use interpreters in order to speak with the Nahua warriors of the Valley of Mexico, but these data must be accepted with reservation. The ruins of Castillo de Teayo, considered by Seler as Aztec, are now attributed rather to the final Toltec period, which would imply that the Nahua tongue must have been known in the region of Tuxpan since the 13th century at least.

People of the Frontiers of the Huasteca

TOTONAC AND TEPEHUA. These peoples, who speak closely related languages, must have been in direct contact with the Huastec during many centuries, resulting in a certain community of civilization, as Sahagún's informants pointed out. But at the time of the conquest, the contact had become precarious because of depopulation and the interposition of Nahua villages in the region of Xiuhcoac and of Tuxpan. More to the west, Tepehua, submerged by Otomi, was no longer spoken except in isolated villages, but a narrative of 1580 seems to indicate its survival in the region of Huejutla (PNE, vol. 6).

OTOMI. About the 13th or 14th century the Otomi arrived at Tutotepec, Huayaco-cotla, and Xilitla, on the edge of the Huasteca. They do not seem to have established lasting relations with the Huastec.

CHICHIMEC. At the time of the Spanish conquest, the Huastec were in contact with the Chichimec to the north and west. These nomads or seminomads, of a rather low culture, lived then in regions which had once been Huastec, especially in the present state of San Luis Potosi. They gained more ground at the end of the 16th century and beginning of the 17th, occupying all northern Huasteca.

Although the Chichimec exerted, at least occasionally, a certain pressure on the Huastec, the civilizing influence of the Huastec must have spread among them. Sahagún speaks of acculturated Chichimec, called Cuextecachichimec, living in the vil-

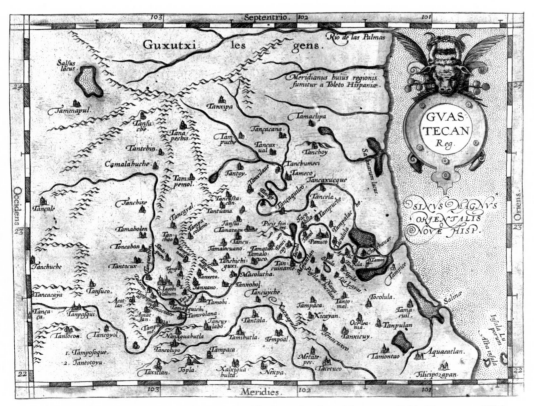

FIG. 1—MAP OF THE HUASTECA. From Abraham Ortelius, Theatrum Orbis Terrarum, 1584. Reproduced from the Collections of the Library of Congress.

lages, doing a little agriculture, and speaking the Huastec tongue in addition to their own. These groups in the process of becoming sedentary were found, it seems, in the eastern Sierra Madre (among the Pame) and in the Sierra de Tamaulipas (especially among the Olive).

Even in the poorest and most backward Chichimec areas there must have been a certain commerce, capable of carrying Huastec cultural elements to great distances. Postclassic Huastec ceramics have been found as far as the coast of Texas.

LEGENDARY HISTORY AND PRE-COLUMBIAN HISTORY

Legends of Origins

Sahagún (bk. 10, ch. 29), reporting the Aztec tradition, tells us that the first inhabitants of Mexico arrived by sea, coming apparently from the east, and that they landed in the Huasteca. This would explain the name Panuco, also called Pantlan or Panutla, 'the place of the crossing.'

These immigrants followed the coast of the Gulf of Mexico and pushed on as far as Guatemala. From there they returned, guided by their wise men, to establish themselves in a place called Tamoanchan, situated not far from Teotihuacan. Here the ritual calendar and the making of pulque were invented. A celebration was then organized on Mount Chichinauhya. Each participant was to drink only four bowls of pulque, but one of them went as far as five cups, got drunk, and let his loincloth fall, causing a scandal. This troublemaker was the chief of the Huastec. Having lost face, he had to flee with his people and went back to Panuco, where he settled and where his descendants still live. This is why these Indians, imitating their chief and ancestor, had kept up the tradition of drunkenness, masculine nudism, and abnormal behavior.

The idea that the first men came from the eastern ocean arises doubtless from the old belief that located the origin of all things in the direction of the rising sun. The voyage to Guatemala is seen by Jiménez-Moreno (1942) as a memory of the turning back of the Maya peoples who must formerly have occupied all the coast of the Gulf of Mexico. Tamoanchan and the mountain where pulque was invented were situated, according to all accounts, between the valleys of Mexico and of Morelos. Aztec traditions seem, therefore, to assume that the Huastec lived formerly on the Central Plateau, then withdrew into the warm lands of the region of Panuco. Lastly, the scandal and flight of the Huastec chief agree with what we know of the rites of drunkenness, nudity, and fertility practiced by the Huastec at the time of the Spanish conquest. This episode recalls, moreover, an adventure attributed to Quetzalcoatl in Codex Chimalpopoca, with the final departure toward the east, the suicide, and the apotheosis.

Toltec Period

The historical traditions of the Toltec period (10th–12th centuries) are doubtless less mythical than the preceding ones, but they are still full of legends and are difficult to interpret.

Ixtlilxochitl (1891–92) states that the Toltec, before settling down at Tula, accomplished a long migration which took them through different villages of southern Huasteca—Tuxpan, Tuzapan, Xiuhcoac, and Iztachuexuca (Huejutla)—arriving finally at Tulancingo. The last place is confirmed by other sources, but the earlier ones are doubtful. We may suppose a rather early penetration of elements of the Nahua language into southern Huasteca.

It is certain that the Toltec empire must have been in close contact with the Huastec, whose territory seems to have then stretched fairly far toward the west and the southwest. Paul Kirchhoff (1961a) even estimates that the Huastec occupied, at this time, the region of the Laja River, in the present state of Guanajuato, a region which probably was incorporated into the Toltec empire. Archaeology suggests that at the end of the Classic period and at the beginning of the Postclassic period a damper climate than the present one permitted agricultural people to occupy certain now arid zones, which were later reconquered by the nomads. Thus the present ruins of Huaxcama (near Guadalcazar) and those of the environs of the Verde River were probably, then, the work of the Huastec. But the Huastec occupation of the region of the Laja River has not yet been proved archaeologically.

Indigenous chronicles of the Toltec period, and even of more recent periods, often mention a place called Cuextecatlichocayan, "the place where the Huastec weeps." Kirchhoff (1961b) located it in the region of Celaya, Jiménez Moreno (1942) in the region of Pachuca, to mention only two possible interpretations. According to Codex Chimalpopoca, captive Huastec were led from this place to Tula, where female demons called Ixcuinanme sacrificed them by killing them with arrows. This episode is generally interpreted as the introduction at Tula, during the reign of Huemac, of a Huastec rite of the cult of the goddess of the earth, whom the Aztec called Tlazolteotl or Ixcuinan.

It was also during the reign of Huemac that Sahagún places the legend of the naked Huastec man, whom the daughter of the king of Tula saw in the marketplace and of whom she became so enamoured that she married him. The Toltec, and Huemac himself, angered at this alliance, sought to kill the intruder by abandoning him in the midst of a fight against the warriors of Coatepec. But the Huastec man, who was really the god-magician Titlacauan, was able to triumph in this unequal combat, and took his revenge for the treachery of the Toltec. He invited them to a feast and by his evil power, his music, and his songs, he drove them mad to the point that they threw themselves into the precipitous gorges of the Texcallauhco River, where they perished. The Huastec thus apparently contributed to the ruin of Tula.

The historical basis of this legend is obviously most doubtful, but it illustrates certain peculiarities attributed to the Huastec: masculine nudism, the practice of magic, and illusionism.

It is not certain that the Toltec empire extended to certain parts of the Huasteca, but Ixtlilxochitl (1891–92) assures us that after the fall of Tula, some of the Toltec settled at Tuzapan, Tuxpan, and Xiuhcoac. The ruins of Castillo de Teayo seem to confirm this tradition.

Chichimec, Otomi, and Acolhua Invasions

Ixtlilxochitl tells us how Xolotl, king of the Chichimec, settled his people in the devastated and depopulated Toltec country (among these halting-places is mentioned Cuextecatlichocayan). He was accompanied by his wife Tomiyauh, queen of Tomiyauh (Tamiahua?), of Panuco and of Tampico. Jiménez Moreno and Carrasco are of the opinion that the Chichimec of Xolotl must have been Pame, natives of the mountains near the Huasteca, which would explain the alliance of their chief with a Huastec princess. According to Ixtlilxochitl, Queen Tomiyauh wielded her authority in northern and southwestern Huasteca. This would assume a certain political unification of this region during the 13th century.

After the invasion by the Chichimec under Xolotl, other groups arrived in the Valley of Mexico from western regions. Among these newcomers some spoke Otomi, some Nahua.

The appearance of the Otomi in central Mexico occurs sometime in the 13th century. Shortly afterward an Otomi empire was founded, with Xaltocan as its capital. It seems that the Otomi spread out toward the north and the northeast, occupying particularly Ixmiquilpan, Metztitlan, and Tutotepec. A letter of Don Pablo Nazareo (1940) mentions Ojitipa as a dependency of Xaltocan, which would presuppose the conquest of part of the present-day Huasteca Potosina. Perhaps the arrival of Otomi elements at Xilitla dates from this time.

Also during the 13th and 14th centuries, Coatlinchan and later Tezcoco, towns in the eastern part of the Valley of Mexico, where the Nahua language predominated, expanded toward the northeast, in the direction of Tulancingo and Huauchinango. This thrust toward Tuxpan continued after the fall of Azcapotzalco, but its results were later misunderstood or overshadowed when the supremacy of Mexico was imposed in the Triple Alliance. This explains how Tezcoco claimed as her own the Aztec conquests in southeastern Huasteca, as given in the chronicles of Ixtlilxochitl.

Aztec Conquests

During the reign of Moctezuma Ilhuicamina, sometime between 1450 and 1460, the first campaign of the Triple Alliance took place in the Huasteca. It resulted in the conquest and pillage of Tuxpan, Xiuhcoac, and Temapache, towns guilty of the murder of certain merchants of the Valley of Mexico.

Axayacatl, about 1475, sent his armies into the same region which had just been conquered by his predecessor. It was probably a question of putting down a rebellion, but among the villages mentioned on this occasion, certain ones suggest an extension of the conquered territory, for example Tamomox (near Tamiahua), Miquetlan (near Castillo de Teayo), Tampatel (near Tantoyuca), and finally Quauhtlan (doubtless Huautla, Hidalgo). Tizoc also led a campaign in the same section of southeastern Huasteca, notably at Temapache and Miquetlan. About 1486–87, Ahuizotl again attacked and pillaged the same region, where the towns of Tuzapan, Tzapotlan (near Castillo de Teayo), Temapache, and Xiuhcoac became rebellious. During the reign of Moctezuma Xocoyotzin (1502–20), there were again some expeditions into southern Huasteca, especially against Miquetlan and Mollanco (near Xiuhcoac).

The Matrícula de Tributos mentions Oxitipa (near the present Aquismon, San Luis Potosi) among the tributaries of the Aztec confederation, but we have no information about its conquest. In order to reach it, the Mexicans would have had to get around the obstacle of the independent states of Metztitlan, Huayacocotla, and Tutotepec. It is not yet certain by what route they did so. We do not know, therefore, all the campaigns led by the Aztec against the Huastec. Those we do know of seem always to have taken the route of Huauchinango and to have been directed toward the regions of Tuxpan and Xiuhcoac-Chicontepec. They must have contributed to the depopulation of these areas.

The Aztec conquests were late and appear to have affected only a small part of the Huasteca. They cannot explain the Nahuatization of a great part of this region.

MATERIAL CULTURE

Agriculture

At the time of the Spanish conquest and for many centuries before, the natives of the Huasteca were primarily farmers, but the chronicles and ancient documents have little information about their agrarian techniques. Living in a tropical forested zone more or less damp, they practiced temporary cultivation on burned-over areas, without irrigation. Each village must have been surrounded by a forested area where the fields were shifted from year to year.

The Aztec applied to the Huasteca, as to other warm moist lands of the Gulf of Mexico, the name Tonacatlalpan, 'land of food,' doubtless being of the opinion that these regions were fertile and free from drought. They also thought that the name was justified by the great variety of plants cultivated in the warm parts of the Atlantic slope.

Certainly in the Huasteca, as in the rest

of Middle America, the plants were mainly maize, beans, squashes, pumpkins, and various peppers. To these can be added roots or tubers (sweet manioc, sweet potato, jícama, arum) and numerous fruits. Pulque agaves were important, in spite of the humidity. Cacao is mentioned only in the most southerly parts of the Huasteca, doubtless owing to climate. Among the nonedible plants were gourds (*Lagenaria*), cotton, and sisal hemp.

Gathering, Breeding, Hunting, and Fishing

Gathering had a special importance in the Huasteca. Certain vegetables were on the dividing line between gathering and cultivation, for example, arum (the *quequexquic* of Sahagún) and little peppers (*Capsicum frutescens*). Others were wild products: the fruit of *Brosimum alicastrum* (an important foodstuff in time of famine), rubber, and the bark used for making paper. Among animal products gathered were wild honey from the forests, oysters from the coastal lagoons, and shellfish which the sea left on the sandy shore. Minerals also were gathered, the most important being salt, which came particularly from the Chila lagoon.

Breeding was secondary in the life of the ancient natives of the Huasteca. They raised dogs and turkeys; they kept in captivity certain wild birds valued for their plumage, especially eagles, macaws, and parakeets. The *Axin* insect was more protected than truly domesticated.

Hunting must have been of considerable importance, although it is not detailed in the ancient documents. Besides animals hunted for food were others valued for the aesthetic and ritual use of their skins or plumage: jaguar, ocelot, eagle, macaw, and parakeets.

Fishing must have been most active near lagoons and great watercourses, but ancient documents are practically silent concerning its techniques. Aside from fish, shrimp, crayfish, water turtles, and mana-

tees were caught. We do not know if sea fishing was carried on.

Cooking

Ancient documents give scarce details on this subject, but some indications are furnished by Postclassic archaeological sites. *Metates*, *manos*, baking plates, and cooking vessels attest to the making of maize *tortillas*, *atoles*, and *tamales*. Pots must have served, as now, for the cooking of beans, pumpkin, manioc, sweet potatoes, and meat. Pepper was crushed with little pestles in terra cotta mortars.

Houses and Temples

In the Huasteca, a hot and wooded country, the natives seem to have constructed houses with wooden or wattle-and-daub walls and with roofs of thatch or leaves. The shapes of pre-Columbian houses are known from pottery models and from traces of excavated walls. Since before the conquest, Indians were familiar with circular, rectangular, and bi-apsidal oval house plans, which are still found in the region. The prominence of the round house in the Huasteca has often been associated with the fact that the Aztec constructed round temples in honor of the god Quetzalcoatl.

Vestiges of houses discovered in excavation have, generally, plaster floors, sometimes with traces of painted decoration. One finds also occasionally burnt clay floors, or asphalt-surfaced floors.

Furnishings were poor. The little low four-footed seats of the present-day Indians were then known, as shown by ceramic pieces.

Cortés (1866) and an anonymous companion of Nuño de Guzmán mention foundations or platforms, equipped with stairways, on which houses, palaces, or temples were built. Remains of these survive today in archaeological sites. In the region of Xiuhcoac and Tuxpan, the temples must have been built on true pyramids, high and

589

steep, for Tezozomoc says that they served as fortresses.

Villages

The mounds are distributed without order in most of the archaeological sites. Platforms arranged more or less regularly around a sort of court suggest the idea of ceremonial centers. Villages seem to have been located less for strategic reasons than for nearness to a water supply and safety from flooding. Certain important ruins are perched on hills, however, even on fairly steep outflows of lava.

In the relatively dry plains of northern Huasteca, archaeological sites generally include an artificial depression which must have served as a reservoir.

Craftsmanship and Techniques

What the ancient texts fail to say about techniques practiced by the Indians of the Huasteca is partly supplied by archaeology. Thus an incised shell shows the use of a fire-drill turned between the hands.

Work in stone seems to have been very active up to the Spanish conquest. Sahagún mentions only arrowpoints of flint or obsidian, but excavations show the perfection and the variety of stoneworking techniques which produced blades, scrapers, arrowpoints or spearpoints, and sacrificial knives. The hammering of hard volcanic rock furnished axes, adzes, bark beaters, pestles for pepper, manos and metates, these simple and footless. Statuary technique also used stone hammering and applied it selectively to the cutting of local rocks. Jadeite, fairly rare, was used parsimoniously.

Bernal Díaz (1950) states that Juan de Grijalva was attacked near Tuxpan by Indians armed with copper axes. Archaeological sites of the Huasteca have supplied a good number of bronze axes, adzes, and small bells. Gold was rare; silver has not been mentioned. Since the Huasteca was not rich in metals, perhaps the metal objects found there were imported.

590

Working in bone produced awls, spatulas, composite combs, and rattles. Marine shells, much used for adornment, supplied also some utilitarian objects, such as fishhooks. Basket making, favored by the abundance of palms and vines, furnished baskets and mats (*petates*), sometimes braided with strands of different colors. The use of gourds is evident from pottery vessels showing containers made from *Lagenaria* fruit. The Huasteca also produced lacquered bowls (*jícaras*), obtained from the fruit of the calabash (*Crescentia*). The wood industry produced dugout canoes, seats, drums, statues. The making of bark paper survived in southern Huasteca, but was formerly common throughout the region, as the discovery of stone beaters indicates.

Postclassic ceramics of the Huasteca are now fairly well known. Certain of the techniques have survived today in a few villages. A revolving plate and perhaps a simple furnace were apparently used. The most characteristic is a white pottery with black painted designs (or black and red), produced in a great variety of forms. The red pottery was less abundant and less varied. Pots, bowls, braziers, and cooking plates (*comales*) were coarse. Pottery was the principal material of such objects as figurines, seals, pipes, spindles, ear ornaments, bells, rattles, and whistles.

The Aztec, people of the high plateaus where cotton does not grow, admired the multicolored cloth of the Huasteca. The informants of Sahagún said that in the warm lands of Panuco different species of cotton were produced, probably corresponding to white cotton and brown cotton, still occasionally cultivated. The striking decoration of the cloth must have been achieved by brocading.

Clothing

Sahagún's informants insisted that male Huastec did not wear garments to cover the genitals. This exposure was then an old tradition, since it is one of the elements in the legend of the Huastec magician who married the daughter of Huemac, king of Tula. One must not conclude that this custom was general and constant, however, for men portrayed in painting, engraving, or sculpture by ancient Huastec artists are by no means always so represented. In the Huasteca, as in most of Middle America, normal masculine costume included a loincloth, a cape, and eventually sandals. The not wearing of a loincloth must have been related to certain circumstances or to certain persons, as in the legend of the Huastec prince who lost face because of being drunk and of having exposed his sexual parts.

The loincloth and the cape could have rich symbolic decoration, as can be seen from certain statues or manuscripts.

Most feminine statues of the Huasteca are clothed only in a skirt. This brief costume was formerly common in daily life, perhaps related to certain ritual ideas, but in public Huastec women covered their breasts with a *quechquemitl*.

Headdress

Sahagún's informants report that the ancient Huastec dyed their hair in different colors, especially red and yellow, and that they divided it into locks hanging on the nape and over the ear lobes. These differently colored locks must have reflected social distinctions or warlike exploits. Certain masculine statues show, on the head, bands in relief which appear to represent these locks.

Sahagún tells us that the women of the Huasteca braided their hair with feathers, the braids probably being arranged in a crown around the head.

Different types of conical or truncated head coverings (sometimes surmounting a sort of cubical or flattened form) seem to have had great ritual importance in the Huasteca. They appear on many statues of the region. One notices them, also, on the pictographic manuscripts of the Central Plateau, in the representation of Huastec armor, or on the heads of divinities which were thought to have connections with the Huasteca.

Jewelry

Tezozomoc and Sahagún speak of gold, turquoise, and jadeite jewels worn by the Huastec and allude especially to ear ornaments, bracelets, and lip plugs. Archaeology shows that the Huastec had few fine stones and little precious metal, so that their jewels were often of shell, calcite, or even pottery. But absence of the lip ornament makes one wonder if the documents are trustworthy, or if they refer to a short numbered aristocracy. We must, however, take into account the fact that the greater part of our archaeological information comes from northern Huasteca, whereas the Aztec knew especially the region of Tuxpan, Tamiahua, and Chicontepec.

Sahagún tells us that the Huastec inserted into a perforation of the nasal septum a gold tube or a reed from which protruded one or several macaw plumes.

Postclassic sites of the Huasteca have furnished numerous shell jewels in a great variety of forms: ear ornaments, pectorals, necklaces, bracelets, and rings. Some of these pieces are delicately worked and show remarkable engraving. Two types of pectorals merit special mention. One, in the form of a spiral, was obtained by sectioning transversely a Strombus shell. The Aztec called this jewel *ehecailacacozcatl*, 'the necklace of the whirlwind,' and considered it a symbol of Quetzalcoatl. Effigies of this god originating in the Central Plateau as well as in the Huasteca very often show him wearing this ornament. The other type of pectoral was shaped like an elongated triangle. It was cut longitudinally in the side of a Strombus shell and often showed a characteristic double curve. Certain examples are admirably engraved (fig. 2). Codex Borgia depicts this ornament worn by the goddess Tlazolteotl and by the gods of pulque, divinities who, like Quetzalcoatl, were thought to have connections with the Huasteca.

Ornaments

The bands of leather which the Huastec, according to Sahagún, wore around their arms or their calves must have been used to fasten plumes or stone beads.

Feathers must have played an important part in personal decoration, for Sahagún and Tezozomoc speak continually of yellow parakeet feathers and red macaw feathers. The Huastec, being at a great distance from Chiapas and Guatemala, must have had great difficulty in procuring the pliant green feathers of the quetzal.

Certain Huastec statues, especially of women, appear to be wearing behind their heads a sort of radiant aureola, reminiscent of a folded paper fan. These ritual accessories corresponded apparently to what Sahagún describes as circular ornaments of palm leaves or macaw plumes.

The Huastec used to file and color their teeth, to paint or tattoo their skin, and to deform the head of their infants.

Transport

Rivers and their tributaries of the Huasteca have been utilized by dugout canoes from pre-Columbian times to our own. In the mountains and in the plains distant from watercourses, hauling was done on men's backs with the help of a tumpline, baskets, and net bags. Liquids were carried either on the head, in globular-shaped pots, or on the back in elongated vessels provided with loop handles.

SOCIAL AND ECONOMIC ORGANIZATION

Family

We learn about Huastec family organization only through the confession manual of Tapia Zenteno (1767) and through modern ethnological inquiries, particularly those studied by Calixta Guiteras Holmes.

The old Huastec kinship system was probably Lowie's scheme of bifurcated fusion (Kirchhoff's Type D). This system equates father's brother with father, mother's sister with mother, parallel cousins with brothers, parallel nephews with sons. On the contrary, there are special terms for maternal uncle, father's sister, cross-cousins, and cross-nephews. Probably this system was formerly combined with marriage between cross-cousins and with sororal polygyny.

Tapia Zenteno tells us that even into the 18th century the Huastec took the name of both father and mother. Nicolas de Witte (1913) says that the eldest son received all the paternal heritage, at least of the land.

Social Classes

Nicolas de Witte, without distinguishing between the Huastec Indians who spoke Huastec and those who spoke Nahuatl, describes their social classes as homologous to those of central Mexico. He differentiates chiefs or kings, nobles, military dignitaries, and plebeians, among whom he classes merchants. He speaks incidentally of slaves, noting that chiefs possessed them. The existence of kings, nobles, and common people among the Huastec is confirmed by archival documents.

The greatest distinction seems to have been between the nobles and the plebeians. The latter formed the mass of the people and must have been chiefly peasants. They paid tribute and could be burdened with porterage.

Nobles were exempt from both these exactions. They probably had the privilege of polygamy and benefited from certain forced labor done by the common people. One might recognize them by facial tattoos, to which they alone had a right and also, doubtless, by other distinctions in dress and ornament. Nicolas de Witte distinguishes them by the Nahuatl name of Pipihuan, which is derived from pilli, 'son.' The name itself suggests that they constituted an hereditary caste. Kings and dignitaries were

592

part of the same caste, but were set off by special privileges.

The dignitaries whom Nicolas de Witte designates by the name *tiacham* (for *tiacahuan*, 'valiant') were apparently individuals whose warlike exploits gave them distinction (which was doubtless not hereditary in itself) and perhaps also access to the noble class, if they were not already a part of it by birth. These tiacham were probably the leaders of whom Tezozomoc tells us that they had the nasal septum perforated.

Those whom Nicolas de Witte indicates under the Nahuatl name *tlahuani* (for *tlatoani*, 'lords') were local chiefs or caciques of the little kingdoms of the Huasteca. Their position was hereditary. Bernal Díaz says specifically that the dignity of cacique, in the Huasteca, was transmitted by law to the sons or to the brothers of dead lords. The Relación de Uexutla (Huejutla) describes Cocotectli, the last pagan cacique of this village, as a true king-magician, controlling the rain and the fertility of the earth. Caciques collected tribute, exacted forced labor, dealt justice, and could evidently declare war.

Political Organization

Nicolas de Witte tells us that in the Huasteca each village (*lugarejo*) was independent and warred with its neighbors "as the Italian principalities do." One may then think that this region, which occupied a marginal position in the Middle American cultural area, had maintained an archaic political situation, comparable to that of the independent agricultural hamlets which we imagine to have existed in the Valley of Mexico in the Preclassic period.

The bellicose villages of pre-Columbian Huasteca, when they were spared by the conquest and its sequel, gave rise to local communities of which certain ones endeavor to survive today. These communities, where an endogamic tendency seems to have predominated, were able to sustain subdivisions, which colonial documents compare to the tlaxilacalli of the Indians of the Nahuatl language.

However, one should not accept literally Nicolas de Witte's statement about the basic political splintering of the Huasteca. Old colonial documents note subject-villages as dependencies of other villages apparently more important. It appears then that there was the beginning of the formation of political units greater than simple isolated villages.

This unifying tendency seems to have been more fully developed in southern and southwestern Huasteca, the areas nearer central Mexico, where the Nahuatl population had finally become predominant. The cacique of Huejutla, the only one about whom we have any data at all precise, ruled over a territory that must have been about 200 sq. km. Xiuhcoac or Tziuhcoac seems to have been the capital of a still more extensive province. Lastly, on the borders of the Huasteca, the kingdoms of Tutotepec and Metztitlan were important states, which had been able to resist the Aztec conquest.

We may conclude that, on an archaic Huastec tradition of political division, there was a centralizing action by conquerors from the more developed regions of central Mexico.

Land Tenure

It is difficult to get an idea of what could have been, in pre-Columbian times, the system of land tenure in the Huasteca. Nicolas de Witte mentions that the eldest son inherited all the paternal lands, to the exclusion of other members of the family, who were thus reduced to renting their fields. He adds that that was the inheritance system of the plebeians and that the eldest, in exchange for his privileges, was the one who owed forced labor and tribute to the cacique. Some ancient colonial documents of southern Huasteca show native nobles or caciques selling their lands to the Spaniards, as if they were private property. Other doc-

593

uments, confirmed by recent native tradition, suggest that formerly the land belonged to the community, and that it could be appropriated only during the temporary period when it was cultivated.

Nicolas de Witte insists that native society hardly tended to accumulate material possessions. The essential wealth of the nobles and of the chiefs was, he says, the forced labor of their vassals and the work of their slaves.

Commerce

We know through Tezozomoc that the villages of southeastern Huasteca, like Tuxpan and Xiuhcoac, had markets every 20 days. We do not know if this information should be applied to the more northerly regions, but there was certainly considerable commercial activity there.

In the territory of the Huasteca itself, trade must have gone on especially between the coast and the interior, salt being one of the principal items of barter.

There was also, surely, a regular commerce between southern Huasteca and the Central Plateau. But, at the time of the Aztec empire, this commerce with the Central Plateau was to a great extent solely in the form of tribute sent to Mexico or Tezcoco. From this tribute levied regularly and from the booty occasionally pillaged, we can see which of the numerous products of a warm humid region the people of the highlands judged worth carrying a long distance.

Cotton was the essential article, especially in the form of clothing more or less richly decorated, plus bark paper, mats (petates), and lacquered gourds. Tuxpan furnished some turquoise and jadeite, but perhaps had to purchase it from outside. Among foodstuffs, honey, dried peppers, and smoked fish were appreciated. Feathers were equally prized, and deer skins apparently were not considered negligible. We note the demand for living animals such as deer, eagles, and parakeets.

Aztec expeditions into the Huasteca had among their avowed purposes the rounding up of women and children whom they enslaved, and the capture of prisoners of whom they expected to make human sacrifices.

War

Nicolas de Witte says that the chieftaincies of the Huasteca were ceaselessly at war with each other, a matter confirmed for Huejutla. War therefore occupied a major place in the life of the region.

Military Organization

Cortés and Bernal Díaz speak of Huastec armies of great size. We can then assume that in the Huasteca war was the occupation of probably the majority of the men, not solely that of nobles or specialized warriors. There must have been military training, but we do not know to whom and how it was given.

The troops must have been officered by experienced warriors, those whom Tezozomoc designates in Spanish as *capitanes* and Nicolas de Witte in Nahuatl as *tiacham*. They probably had their faces tattooed and the nasal septum perforated. They were distinguishable in combat by special armor and feather ornaments.

The persistence among modern Indians of the Huasteca of eagle dances and jaguar dances shows that, in this region as in central Mexico, there must have existed military brotherhoods devoted to the cult of the sun.

Weapons

Ancient Huastec seem to have been primarily armed with bows and arrows. Sahagún describes their arrowpoints as somewhat broad, in flint or obsidian. Modern archaeology uncovers projectile points in great numbers.

Although old texts do not mention the throwing-stick, it was doubtless known and used, since it is shown on engraved shells of the region, as Hermann Beyer (1933)

594

has demonstrated. We can assume that the Huastec, in common with most other Middle American peoples, had been long accustomed to the use of the throwing-stick, but that contact with the nomad Chichimec had introduced among them the more recent bow.

Another Huastec weapon known only through engraving on shell is a sort of curved club, apparently of wood and with a cutting edge. Bronze axes with which the ships of Juan de Grijalva were attacked were perhaps rather tools than weapons. The use of wooden swords equipped with obsidian blades is not mentioned, except by the Relación de Uexutla.

Huastec of a certain rank, or at least those of the southeast, wore in combat armor of padded cotton (according to sketches in the Matrícula de Tributos and Codex Mendoza) and a very tall conical hat. The eagle or jaguar warriors had helmets and costumes suggestive of these animals. The complement of the armor was a round shield made of split and braided reeds. Tezozomoc mentions that Huastec warriors wore on their belts different sorts of rattles or bells.

Fortresses

Cortés states that he had to take by assault the principal Huastec villages of the region of Tampico because their inhabitants rejected his offers of peace, thinking that their position in the midst of the lagoons was almost an impenetrable natural defense.

Tezozomoc speaks, in unfortunately vague terms, of the preparations for defense which the Huastec Indians of Xiuhcoac and Tuxpan made in anticipation of the attack of the troops of Moctezuma. From this one can speculate that probably certain villages of the southeastern Huasteca had a defensive system including a central refuge consisting of the principal temple, a walled area in or around the village, and a fortified camp on a neighboring hill.

Conduct of War

The Huastec mode of warfare is learned through the story of the campaigns of conquest sent against them by the Aztec and later by the Spaniards.

Tezozomoc describes a battle fought in the time of Moctezuma Ilhuicamina. He pictures the Huastec warriors of Xiuhcoac and Tuxpan plumed and loaded with jewels, marching to the fight singing and defying the enemy. The nobles and the most renowned captains were in the first line. A military trick of the Aztec gave an opportunity to attack them from the rear by surprise and to take a great number of prisoners. It appears that this brought about the flight of the greater part of the Huastec army, which took refuge on the nearest hill, from where it offered its submission while watching from a distance the capture of the town.

Male and female captives of the ordinary sort were dragged away, groaning or singing sad songs. In contrast, the "captains" who were led away by a cord passing through the opening in the nasal septum, struck up songs of bravado, while uttering battle cries.

The campaigns of the conquering Spaniards, directed against northern Huasteca, encountered a bitter resistance, to the merits of which Cortés himself gave praise. Bernal Díaz shows that the Indians displayed a certain effort at strategic reflection, attempting to halt the army of Sandoval in deep gorges, then waging the decisive battle in three separate battalions. The Spanish campaigns are especially interesting because the Huastec won temporary successes in them and thus allow us to know something of their victory celebrations. Cortés and Bernal Díaz, who arrived in the region of Tampico after the extermination of the first Spaniards of Francisco de Garay, say that they found in the temples the skins of their compatriots' faces, tanned and prepared, with beard and hair, so that

FIG. 2—HUASTEC SHELL ORNAMENT. Middle American Research Institute, Tulane University.

one could still recognize them. Bernal Díaz, who speaks in detail of the last uprising of the Huastec, says that the captured Spaniards were sacrificed in order to be eaten. He mentions also, but without precise details, that 40 Spaniards were burned alive. Sahagún reports that when the Huastec had killed an enemy, they cut off his head and attached it, with others, to a pole.

Most of these details seem typically Middle American, including that of the prepared facial skins, which corresponded

probably to the masks of those sacrificed by flaying. The heads attached to a pole recall the *tzompantli* or ritual ossuary.

RELIGION

Data on the ancient Huastec religion are fragmentary and scattered, but can be placed and interpreted in the general cadre of Middle American religions. This was expressed, without his being aware of it, by an anonymous companion of Nuño de Guzmán when he wrote that the rites and ceremonies of the provinces of Ojitipa and of Panuco were similar to those of Mexico, and that they made sacrifices in the same manner, in spite of certain differences which could be expected from regions of different languages.

Divinities

No document of the 16th century gives a descriptive list of the divinities worshipped by the ancient Huastec, so we must reconstruct it. For this, we take as a starting point the Aztec religion, which honored certain gods and goddesses who had the reputation of being connected with the Huasteca, or who were shown with attributes of Huastec style.

One can put in the first rank the "goddess of impurity" Tlazolteotl, also called Toci "Our grandmother" or Ixcuina, an enigmatic name which students have tried to interpret through the Huastec language. In Mexico, Tlazolteotl was considered as the goddess of sexual love, of fecundity, of childbirth, of ritual medicine, and of divination. Under the name of Tlaelquani, 'eater of dirt,' she presided at the confession of sins. She was represented with spindles in her headdress and with the lower part of her face painted black around the mouth. Under the name Ixcuina, they said, she represented four women of different ages.

The ties of this Aztec goddess with Huasteca are not to be doubted. Sahagún says that the Huastec worshipped her. At her festival, called Ochpaniztli, 'sweeping,' her worshippers were called "her Huastecs." She wore on her head a conical hat of Huastec type and at her throat a shell pectoral equally characteristic.

In connection with the name Ixcuina, we recall legends of the female demons called Ixcuinanme who probably introduced the sacrifice by arrows at Tula by sacrificing their Huastec husbands there. We consider that these female demons symbolized the deified souls of women who had died in childbirth.

Hermann Beyer (1933) has described a Huastec shell pectoral, then at the Middle American Research Institute of Tulane University, on which was incised a typical representation of Tlazolteotl with the lower face painted black (fig. 2). A skull by way of helmet and a bundle of arrows in her hand make of this Huastec Tlazolteotl a goddess of war and death.

The Huasteca has yielded up a great number of feminine statues, having the appearance of youth and breasts uncovered. We think that these statues represent the same divinity as a young girl. It has to do with the goddess of the earth and the moon, whose memory persists in the region. She is supposed to pass, like the moon, through all the phases of the life of a woman and thus incarnates youth, fecundity, old age, and death.

Among the masculine statues of the Huasteca, the most frequent type represents a wrinkled and stooped old man, leaning on a sort of stick which sometimes takes the form of a serpent, sometimes that of a phallus pushing out of the earth. The Huasteca has also yielded up certain isolated stone heads, showing the wrinkled face, thin lips, and jutting chin which the Aztec gave to the old god of fire, Huehueteotl.

We think that these old men are none other than the old god of the earth and of thunder, lord of the year, ancestor of the Huastec, who was also the god of drunkenness and who was able, through alcoholic intoxication, to regain his youth. This is the drunken god who is mentioned by Sahagún in the legend of the invention of pulque, and to whom a myth of the Relación de Metztitlan alludes. One of his Huastec names, "Mam" (grandfather), shows that his origins go back to the most ancient common traditions of the Maya peoples.

This personage is doubtless the most original figure of the Huastec pantheon. His characteristics are dispersed among several Aztec divinities: Ome Tochtli, Tlaloc, Huehueteotl, and Quetzalcoatl. The Huasteca has furnished a certain number of representations of Quetzalcoatl decked with a mask or muzzle characteristic of Ehecatl, god of the wind. When these Huastec Quetzalcoatls are shown standing they usually have the sexual parts uncovered. Quetzalcoatl, whom certain myths show as a god of drunkenness or a victim of intoxication, is doubtless the Aztec god who shows the greatest number of connections with the Huasteca. He is often shown with a conical headdress and wearing at his throat the pectoral of the whirlwinds, that is, a transverse section of a Strombus shell.

Other masculine statues of the Huasteca show a young god, generally nude. He was probably the young god of the maize and of the morning star, the culture hero of the present-day Huastec legends. His personality had many points in common with that of Xochipilli. He must doubtless also have relationships with certain aspects of Mixcoatl. Hermann Beyer (1933, pp. 172–73, figs. 18, 20), in describing a young god of war shown on a Huastec shell pectoral, compares him to phallic representations of Mixcoatl, Huastec in appearance, from pages 26 and 41 of Codex Fejérváry-Mayer (fig. 3).

Huastec religion was based on a solar myth and included a cult of the sun, but figures of the sun are exceptional in the archaeology of the region. The Relación de Uexutla is insistent on the importance of the cult of Tezcatlipoca.

597

The deified or disembodied souls of the dead, especially the souls of women who died in childbirth, surely played an important role in the Huastec religion. Some of the most beautiful statues of the region are taken to be images of apotheosis, because they portray life on one face and death on the other.

Calendar

The Huasteca most certainly based its religion on the ritual and divinatory calendar common to all Middle American peoples. The fact that the region of Tuxpan held markets every 20 days is the proof of it. For the more northerly regions we have neither texts nor convincing archaeological material, but we can hardly doubt it.

Priesthood

There were certainly priests of Huastec paganism, but old texts do not speak of them, with the exception of the Relación de Uexutla, which deals with a region of the Nahua language. The priests of Huejutla painted themselves black. They were appointed for a year, during which they could not bathe or have sexual relations with their wives. They guarded and cleaned the temples, burned incense and pine wood there, and kept up fires in the court at night.

Human Sacrifice

The Huastec practiced human sacrifices similar to those of central Mexico, as an anonymous companion of Nuño de Guzmán wrote. Sacrifice by tearing out the heart is shown by a piece of earthenware from the Rayon region. Hermann Beyer (1933) has demonstrated that a young god, portrayed on a Huastec pectoral of incised shell, is engaged in squeezing a torn-out heart so as to make the blood run into a vase.

The skins of the faces which the Spaniards found in the temples of the Tampico region seem to have resulted from sacrifice by flaying. These sacrifices are shown also on statues of the Huasteca. We note that in Mexico the festival of Tlazolteotl included a sacrifice by flaying.

The Huastec, great archers, must have practiced arrow sacrifice. They may have introduced this practice at Tula.

The Relación de Uexutla tells us that, in this Nahua-speaking village, the children whom they sacrificed at the summit of the mountains while praying for rain had their heads cut off.

A text of Bernal Díaz speaks of Spaniards burned alive during the last revolt of the Huastec. The hypothesis of a regional practice of sacrifice by fire is likely, but the text is vague, and it is possible that these Spaniards perished in the burning of the houses where they were sleeping.

The bodies of those sacrificed were ritually eaten, and their skulls were evidently exposed on ossuaries similar to those of the Toltec or the Aztec, producing the numerous representations of human skulls in Huastec art.

Ritual Abstinences

The Indians of the Huasteca practiced the ritual fasts and penances of Middle American civilization. Their present-day descendants observe sexual abstinence before certain ceremonies.

Two famous bas-reliefs discovered at Huilocintla, near Tuxpan, show a Huastec Quetzalcoatl passing a stick with thorns through his tongue. The Relación de Uexutla speaks of scoring the tongue, the ears, and the calves.

Confession

The passing of sticks through the tongue was, in Mexico, one of the penances imposed by the priests of Tlazolteotl on sinners who came to confess to them. It is certain that the Huastec, followers of Tlazolteotl, practiced confession, though Sahagún assures us that they did not accuse themselves of lewdness because they did not consider it a sin.

598

Fɪɢ. 3—MIXCOATL. Codex Fejérváry-Mayer 41 and 26. (From Beyer, 1933, figs. 18, 20.)

Ritual Drunkenness

The cult of their principal god doubtless explains the Huastec practice of ritual drunkenness and ritual nudity.

Both the "Anonymous Conqueror" (1858) and another anonymous writer, a companion of Nuño de Guzmán, describe the Indians of the Huasteca having intestinal lavages of pulque by means of a tube. The second of these sources specifies that it was on the occasion of the festivals that they had recourse to this method of intoxication.

Music, Songs, and Dances

Singing, music, and dancing must have played a great part in the life of the Huasteca. In the myth of the Huastec prince who lost face for having been drunk and appeared nude, Sahagún adds that the Huastec, obliged to flee toward Panuco, took with them the tradition of their dances, with their accessories and with the songs by which they were accompanied.

The singers of the king of Mexico disguised themselves as Huastec to sing the song called *cuextecayotl*. The nobles of Mexico themselves, on the feast day of *ce xochitl*, did not disdain to sing this song, as well as the *tlauaca cuextecayotl*, the Huastec song of intoxicating drinking.

The musical instruments of the Huasteca were those common throughout Middle America: *teponaztli*, skin drum, conchs, flutes, whistles, rattles, bells, notched bones. They are attested by vague ancient texts, by modern ethnology, and by some archaeological discoveries.

Huastec dances are discoverable only from their present or recent survival. The dance called the "Volador," which was a short while ago widespread in the whole region, seems to have been in ancient times a ceremony of the warrior brotherhood of the eagles. A dance of the jaguars was its counterpart. There were also dances of the earth, of the rain, and of the maize.

Games

The two most important games of Middle America were played in the Huasteca, but we know them only through the testimony of archaeology. The existence of patolli is attested by paintings on stucco pointed out by John Muir (1926) on the plaster floors of certain old platforms of the Colonia Las Flores at Tampico. The Middle American ball game has left its traces in the Huasteca, in the form of numerous prepared fields, usually small and simple in form.

Cult Places

The ancient inhabitants of the Huasteca had natural sanctuaries, as do their present

599

descendants. We have cited the sacrifices of children at the summit of a mountain, mentioned by the Relación de Uexutla. Various caves of the region have kept evidences of the worship which was formerly paid there. Each family had to perform certain private rites in the house and in the fields.

The main part of public worship must have been carried on in the temples situated in the center of the villages, the existence of which is noted by several documents.

Bernal Díaz mentions idols in the temples. The Relación de Uexutla tells us that some were of stone and some of wood; archaeology confirms this. The statues discovered in the Huasteca vary in dimension, workmanship, and artistic quality, but their style is almost always distinct from that of neighboring regions. Almost all are provided with a sort of stalk which was thrust into the earth. Certain stelae, decorated in low relief or high relief, also seem to have been cult objects.

The Anonymous Conqueror tells us that, in the Huasteca, Indians worshipped the phallus and that they had representations of them in the temples and in the squares, with statues showing couples in the act of sexual union.

These fecundity rites do not seem at all incompatible with the worship which we can imagine for the pair of supreme deities of the Huastec. Codex Borbonicus, in the pages which show the feast of Tlazolteotl, as it was celebrated in Mexico, depicts the worshippers of this goddess, disguised as Huastec and equipped with enormous artificial phalli.

Archaeology has found only a very small number of phallic sculptures in the Huasteca. Portrayals of coitus are still more rare. We are thus led to ask if the Anonymous Conqueror exaggerated, unless the statues he described were almost all made of perishable material.

The walls of certain Huastec temples or the sides of their foundations, or of their altars, must have been decorated with frescoes. We know of two examples.

The material used in these temples included braziers and censers.

Funerary Rites

Ancient documents are almost silent about the ceremonies of the life cycle in the Huasteca. Only about the funeral rites do we possess certain facts, thanks to the discoveries of archaeology.

The dead seem to have been most often buried in the earth itself. Masonry tombs are rare. The bodies were frequently placed in a crouching position. It was thought proper to bury the dead, whom they feared, face down, in order to make them harmless. Some bodies have been found with masks over their faces.

Funeral furniture was very diverse. Certain of the dead were buried with their weapons or their tools. Most graves are furnished with pieces of pottery.

Magic and Divination

The ancient Huastec had a great reputation as magicians and illusionists. Sahagún says that they were capable of hypnotizing their listeners to the point of making them see an imaginary fire, or of making them believe that the magicians were being cut to pieces in their very sight.

Tezozomoc says that, at the time of the first Aztec campaign in the Huasteca, it was necessary to reassure the warriors of the Valley of Mexico by telling them that their adversaries were indeed men like themselves, and not demons, phantoms, or unreal beings.

The ancient Huastec practiced curative magic (notably by extracting the disease by sucking) and divination by crystal-gazing and by casting grains of maize. These practices have survived in different parts of the region. As with the Aztec, the patroness of these arts was Toci, homologous to the Huastec Tlazolteotl.

CONCLUSIONS

The Huastec Indians speak a language which belongs to the Maya family, but which seems to have been isolated for at least 3000 years. It may be supposed that about 1000 or 1500 B.C. the Maya peoples occupied for a time the coast of the Gulf of Mexico, from the mouth of the Panuco to that of the Usumacinta, as well as parts of Chiapas and Guatemala. Later, they seem to have been forced back to the southeast, leaving the Huastec behind. The latter remained until our times in their warm lands surrounded by mountains, with the exception of a small group which, much later, seems to have emigrated as far as Chicomucelo, in southern Chiapas.

Through the centuries, the Huastec seem to have lived in relative isolation, having perhaps as many contacts with the barbarous Chichimec of the north as with the civilized peoples of the south. They were separated from the other Maya before the latter began to develop their art and their great civilization. They received the influence of Teotihuacan, Tajin, Tula, Tezococo, and Mexico, without any of these contributions succeeding in overcoming their own cultural and artistic personality.

Insofar as we can offer an overall opinion about the ancient civilization of the Huasteca, we will say that it seems to be typically Middle American, but with a shade of archaism of which we find some elements in other regions, and which is perhaps a last reflection of pre-Toltec Mexico.

REFERENCES

Alva Ixtlilxochitl, 1891–92
Alvarado Tezozomoc, 1878
Armillas, 1964b
Barlow, 1946d
Beyer, 1933
Carrasco Pizana, 1950
Chilton, 1927
Codices: Borbonicus, Chimalpopoca, Mendoza, Telleriano-Remensis
Colección de documentos inéditos, 1864–84
Conquistador Anónimo, 1858
Cortés, 1866
Cruz, 1571
Descripciones: del Arzobispado de Mexico, de la villa de Panuco, de la villa de Tampico, de los pueblos de la provincia de Panuco, del pueblo de Guauchinango
Díaz del Castillo, 1950
Du Solier, 1945b, 1946, 1947b
——, Krieger, and Griffin, 1947
Ekholm, 1944, 1953
Epistolario de Nueva España, 1505–18
García, 1918
García Icazbalceta, 1858–66

Grijalva, 1624
Hakluyt, 1927
Huastecos, Totonacos . . ., 1953
Ixtlilxochitl, see Alva Ixtlilxochitl
Jiménez Moreno, 1942
Kelly and Palerm, 1952
Kirchhoff, 1961a, 1961b
Kroeber, 1939–44
Lienzo de Tlaxcala, 1892
MacNeish, 1954a
Mason, 1935
Matrícula de tributos, 1890
Meade, 1939, 1940, 1942, 1948, 1950, 1953
Melgarejo Vivanco, n.d. [1947]
Memorial . . . Tlacupan, 1939–42
Mendieta, 1870
Mota y Escobar, 1945
Motolinia, 1903
Muir, 1926
Nazareo, 1940
Norte de México, 1944
O'Gorman, 1941
Ortelius, 1584
Papeles de Nueva España, 1905–06

Paso y Troncoso, 1897
Primera relación anónima, 1855–66
Relaciones: Metztitlan, Tlaxcala, Uexutla
Sahagún, 1950–69, 1956
Schuller, 1923–24, 1925
Seler, 1904d
Spinden, 1937
Staub, 1923, 1924, 1926
Stresser-Péan, 1953a, 1953b, 1964
——, Ichon, and Guidon, 1963

Suma de visitas, 1905–06
Swadesh, 1953, 1961
Tapia Zenteno, 1767
Termer, 1930
Tezozomoc, *see* Alvarado Tezozomoc
Toussaint, 1948
Troike, 1962
Witte, 1913
Zimmermann, 1955

26. Ethnohistory of Guerrero

H. R. HARVEY

AT THE TIME of the Spanish conquest of Mexico, much of the area of the present state of Guerrero was under Mexican domination and paying rich tribute—copper, cacao, cotton cloth, gold, seashells, feathers, precious stones, and numerous other commodities (see fig. 2). The subjugation of Guerrero by the Mexicans began in the 1430's, after the formation of the Triple Alliance between Tenochtitlan, Texcoco, and Tlacopan, and continued until the advent of the Spaniards in 1519. During these years the conquest lists reveal steady gains by the Mexicans, and the rewards of victory are reflected in tribute as well as in the expanded array of goods traded in the market of Tlatelolco.

The subjugation of Guerrero was by no means easy, either for the Mexicans, as reflected in the number of towns which revolted from time to time, or for the natives, not a few of whom were taken back and sacrificed for special ceremonial occasions. The native population of Guerrero was greatly disrupted by 1519 as a result of many military campaigns against them, Mexican colonization in conquered areas and their occasional practice of relocating and dispersing conquered native peoples. Even under the Spaniards, Nahua-speaking peoples continued to expand, so that today many of the indigenous languages and cultures are extinct, and only brief mention in the earliest documents testifies to their former existence.

The first people in Guerrero to feel the effect of the invading armies of the Triple Alliance under Ixcoatl's command were the Chontal and Coixca (see fig. 3). After defeating the Tlahuica of Morelos in the late 1430's, his army entered Guerrero, proceeding south of Tetela del Rio,[1] east to Zacualpa, and west to Ixtepec. The towns of Tepetlacingo, Tepequaquilco, Iguala, and Cuezala were taken by force; Teloloapan

[1] The only conquest list which mentions Tetela among the conquests of Ixcoatl is Pablo Nazareo's letter to Felipe II, 1566 (Paso y Troncoso, 1939–42, 10: 118). Maps of the Mexican conquest of Guerrero (figs. 4–8) are based largely on Kelly and Palerm, 1952.

603

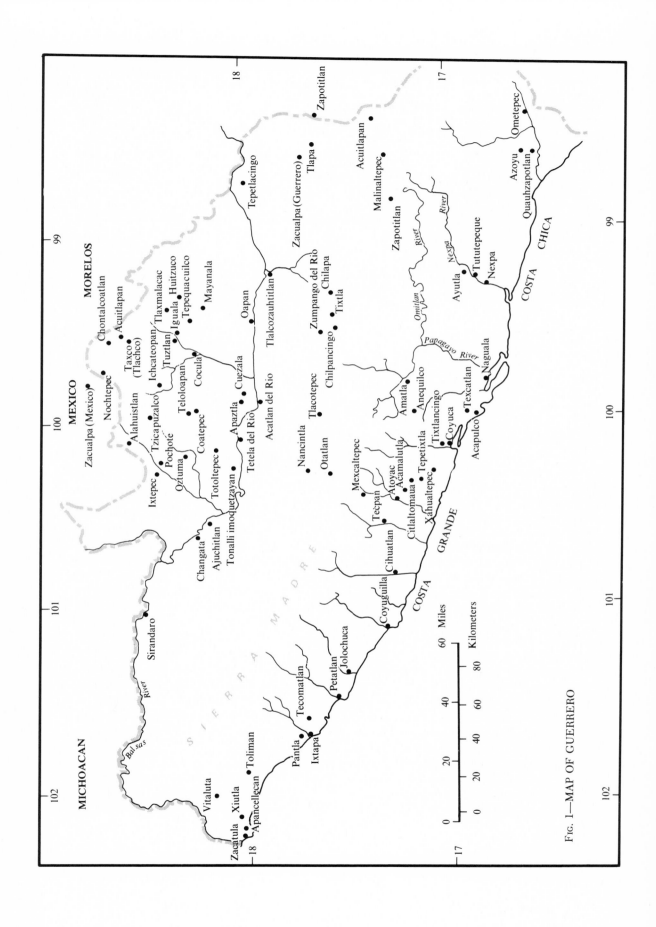

FIG. 1—MAP OF GUERRERO

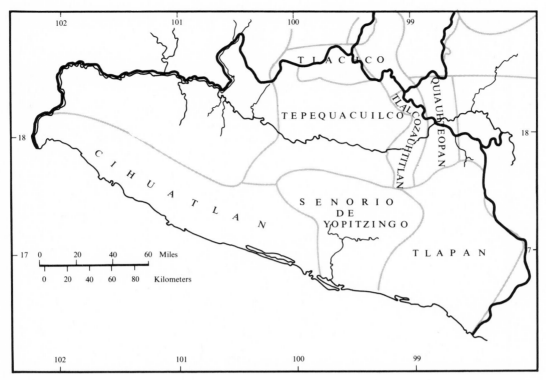

Fɪɢ. 2—TRIBUTE PROVINCES OF GUERRERO IN THE EMPIRE OF THE CULHUA—
MEXICA (After Barlow, 1949c)

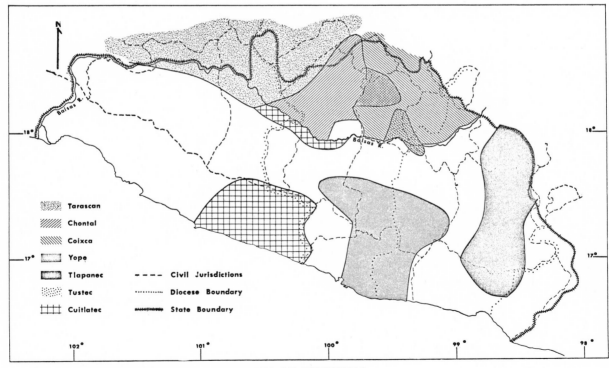

Fɪɢ. 3—MAJOR INDIGENOUS LANGUAGES OF GUERRERO

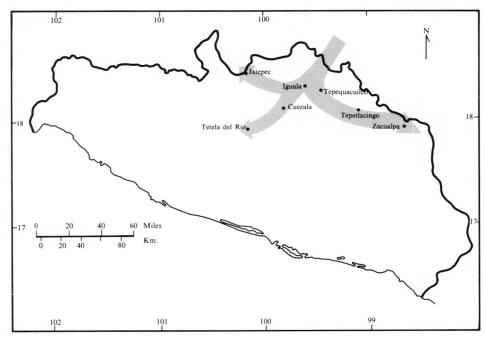

Fig. 4—MEXICAN CONQUEST OF GUERRERO: ITZCOATL, 1427–40

surrendered without a struggle (see fig. 4). In the next three decades, under Ixcoatl's successor Montezuma Ilhuicamina, the balance of Chontal and Coixca territory was subjugated, except for Alahuistlan in the extreme northwest, thus leaving the Mexicans in possession of most of north-central Guerrero. During the same period, they also broadened their foothold south of the Balsas and established a military garrison at Chilapa on the Yope frontier in 1458.[2]

According to the various Relaciones Geográficas, Chontal was spoken south to the Balsas River, west to the Alahuistlan River, north as far as the town of Zacualpa, and east into the province of the Coixca, where it was noted in the towns of Tepequaquilco, Iguala, and Cocula. In Tepequaquilco, for example, most of the population spoke Chontal; in Iguala, half; in Cocula, a third (Toussaint, 1931). For further discussion see Article 7 in volume 12 of this *Handbook*.

It would appear from distribution and other historical evidence that the Chontal-speaking peoples once held much of the

territory between the Tarascans on the west and the Tlapanec on the east, but had steadily lost ground to Nahua-speaking peoples since the latter first appeared in Guerrero in the 13th century.[3] These Nahua, known as Coixca, lived east of the Chontal, between them and the Tlapanec, and centered about Tlalcozauhtitlan at the junction of the Balsas and Amacuxcac rivers. According to Gaspar de Texera, vicar of the region, this land was called "Coyscatlalpa" and the language, "Coysca." He noted that, although the language was like Mexican, some words differed and that it was coarse compared to the refined speech of the Mexicans (Paso y Troncoso, 1905–06, 5: 249). The Relación de Iguala defines Coixca as meaning "land of lizards" (Toussaint, 1931). The later report from Tlalcozauhtitlan of 1777 describes the land as having

[2] The Relación of Chilapa of 1582 dates the establishment of the garrison as 124 years before (Paso y Troncoso, 1905–06, 5: 177).

[3] The date of this arrival is discussed by Barlow, 1948a, p. 183.

606

various kinds of poisonous snakes, spiders, scorpions, and lizards (Barlow, 1947a, p. 390).

Besides Tlalcozauhtitlan, which with its subject towns covered a large area both north and south of the Balsas, the Coixca province by the turn of the 16th century also included the towns of Iguala, Cocula, Huitzuco, Mayanala, Tepequaquilco, and Tlaxmalacac. The latter is the northernmost town specifically mentioned as Coixca. The presence of Chontal-speakers in such considerable number in the three easternmost towns as noted suggests that the Coixca were expanding westward at the expense of the Chontal.

South of Tlalcozauhtitlan, the towns of Chilapa, Tixtla, Chilpancingo, and Zumpango del Rio were Nahua-speaking, but again it was noted that the speech was not as "refined" as Mexican (Paso y Troncoso, 1905–06, 5: 176). From the description, there is little doubt that the dialect was similar, and that these Nahua were related to the Coixca linguistically, if not politically. To the northwest, beyond Tlaxmalacac, in the vicinities of Taxco and Nochtepec, Nahua-speakers had also heavily infiltrated the Chontal towns. Again the question arises as to whether these were Coixca, as the sources themselves do not refer to these people as Coixca.[4] There is little question, however, that the area had once been Chontal, which name is still preserved in the town name Chontalcoatlan.

Cuezala was another Nahua-speaking town, situated in the extreme southeast of the Chontal area, near the junction of the Balsas and Cocula rivers. According to the Relación de Cuezala, "their ancestors left the province of Michoacan in the company of the rest of the Mexicans who were to settle the city of Mexico, and they came by diverse routes and arrived in the land where they presently live" (Paso y Troncoso, 1905–06, 6: 138). This places their arrival in Guerrero at 1250 or earlier (see note 3). The Coixca were one of the tribes of the

peregrinación (Anales de Tlatelolco, 1948, p. 31), so it is not unlikely that the Cuezala people were related to them, perhaps being a splinter group.

The Chontal of Apaztla were engaged in a war with the Cuezala Nahua when the Spaniards arrived, and were still bitter about this event in 1579. According to the Chontal, the Cuezala Nahua were given land by them in good faith when they arrived in the area, but the latter rose up against the Chontal and became the lords of the land (Paso y Troncoso, 1905–06, 6: 144). The Cuezala Nahua claimed that when they arrived, they prevailed upon the Chontal for lands on which they might live, but were refused (*ibid.*, 6: 138). They then went to a nearby mountain and for a time lived there in the caves. During this period, they sustained themselves by hunting, supplemented by as much corn as could be obtained from the neighboring towns. Later, they built houses similar to those of the Chontal and raised crops, but meat remained an important dietary item. Their principal gods at this time were Huitzilopochtli and his sister (*ibid.*, 6: 139). The Cuezala Nahua did not cremate their dead, which lends support to the idea that the Mexicans, traveling by a different route during the peregrinación, had acquired this practice from the Otomi.

Between 1418 and 1428 the Coixca were defeated by the Tlahuica and became their tributaries.[5] When later subjugated by Ixcoatl and Ilhuicamina, they offered no resistance to Mexican domination until Tlalcozauhtitlan revolted during the reign of Montezuma II. The Chontal, on the other

[4] Orozco y Berra (1864, pp. 227–28) considered these people to be Coixca, and Barlow (1949d, p. 17) also felt that the province continued farther north than Tlaxmalacac "since the Coixca joined Malinalco in an attack upon the Cuauhnahuac (Cuernavaca) after the latter's surrender to Cortés."

[5] The Mexicans may have assisted the Tlahuica in the war with the Coixca, as they were allowed to share in the booty (Anales de Tlatelolco, 1948, p. 57).

hand, were not so apathetic about Mexican domination. Oztuma, for example, where the Mexicans maintained an important military outpost on the Tarascan frontier, was conquered by Ilhuicamina, but revolted under Ahuizotl, along with Teloloapan.[6] Alvarado Tezozomoc (1944, pp. 338–54) provides a vivid description of the revolt and the manner in which it was suppressed. After the coronation of Ahuizotl, Teloloapan closed its gates to the Mexicans and refused to continue paying tribute. Summoning his allies, Ahuizotl mustered an army and proceeded to Teloloapan, where after a short but bloody battle the leaders of the city sued for peace. Finding Oztuma also in rebellion, the army proceeded against them. Aided by the advice of the people of Teloloapan, the Mexicans were able to break through the defenses at Oztuma and "they began to kill them as if they were chickens," sparing only the young men and women who were to be taken back to Mexico. Following the slaughter at Oztuma, the Mexicans offered the people of Alahuistlan a chance to surrender; but they refused, saying that they would rather die than pay tribute. The Mexicans swept over the city annihilating men, women, and children. When the campaign ended, Ahuizotl ordered a count and found that 44,200 Chontal had been killed or captured. Their crops were harvested and sent back to Mexico. Afterwards, the towns were resettled by order of Ahuizotl with people drawn from all over the empire—altogether, 9000 married people, so divided that each town received 3000. With this campaign of Ahuizotl, Chontal resistance was crushed for all time.

Of the Chontal language the sources indicate only that "they speak in the throat" and that it is not written because it is not pronounced (Toussaint, 1931). Although Chontal is distinguished from other languages within the area—Tarascan, Nahua, Matlatzinca, Izcuca, and Mazatec[7]—the Relación de Iguala equates it with Tuztec (*ibid.*). Tuztec was spoken in Ichcateopan, Mayanala, Tlalcozauhtitlan, and Oapan, to the east of the Chontal; however, the difference between the two appears to have been more than geographical as they are clearly distinguished in the Relación de Ichcateopan (Paso y Troncoso, 1905–06, 6: 87). The implication is that they were dialects of the same language, with Chontal on the west and Tuztec on the east. Barlow (1948a, p. 182) points out that the term "Tuztec" could refer simply to speakers from Tuztlan, a town situated on the west side of the Cocula River opposite Iguala. The few and widely scattered pockets of Tuztec remaining in the late 16th century suggest it to have been the remnants of a pre-Coixca but Chontal-related population whose center of gravity lay to the east of the Cocula River.

Chontal subsistence was based on agriculture. Tezozomoc (1944, pp. 351, 342) describes Alahuistlan as having very fertile soils and a variety of water resources, producing cacao, honey, cotton, chile, and a wide variety of fruits. Other towns in the Chontal area were not so fortunately endowed with arable land, but the implica-

[6] Oztuma is also listed among the conquests of Axayacatl and Montezuma II. These do not appear to have been revolts, but rather Tarascan attempts to seize the town. The first conquest of Oztuma seems actually to have been made by Nezahualcoyotl in 1442 (Alva Ixtlilxochitl, 1952, 1: 257, 2: 201).

[7] Matlatzinca was spoken in Cocula and Tlalcozauhtitlan. Kirchhoff places these Matlatzinca or Matlame in an area between the Coixca and Chontal, south of Iguala. A portion of his manuscript map showing the Matlame distribution is published in Weitlaner, 1941. Izcuca was an unidentified language spoken in Teloloapan. We are told that "the yscucas and chontals are the most ancient natives, and thus each one has its own language and barrios" (Paso y Troncoso, 1905–06, 6: 146). Mazatec was reported spoken in Tzicaputzalco and Zacualpa. It is extinct and its relationship unknown, although it could well have been related to the Oaxaca Mazatec.

tion is that they planted where they could and with good results. In Teloloapan, for example, corn had to be sown around the rocks in the canyons, but its yield was high (Paso y Troncoso, 1905–06, 6: 147).

At least three types of settlement patterns are described. Teloloapan, Oztuma, and Alahuistlan were large towns "with a single broad street in each of them" (Tezozomoc, 1944, p. 340). In Ichcateopan the houses were widely scattered along the ravines (Paso y Troncoso, 1905–06, 6: 91). Around Acuitlapan the inhabitants were noted to have lived in "caves and ravines, like animals" (García Pimentel, 1897, p. 130). Typical of the general pattern in Middle America, each of the larger towns had numerous smaller settlements or estancias under its jurisdiction.

In this area houses are usually described as being very low, made of stone or adobe, having roofs of zacate and cane doors, and being surrounded by cane fences (Paso y Troncoso, 1905–06, 6: 93). In addition, some had small, low granaries, under which people slept (ibid., 6: 113). Chiefs' houses were described as being higher. The Chontal also constructed fortifications, many of which were adapted by the Mexicans as part of their system of defense along the Tarascan frontier. In warfare the Chontal used the bow and arrow, and spear. They carried shields and wore waist-length padded cotton armor. In time of peace, they wore a garment of loose cloth tied at the shoulder, and trousers; the women wore enaguas and huipils (ibid., 6: 91).

Chontal society was stratified into three classes: nobles, commoners, and slaves. The office of chief was hereditary, but of the manner of succession, the sources indicate only that when a chief died, he was succeeded by a relative. At Oztuma the lord of the town presided in all things, although he had two high-ranking assistants (ibid., 6: 108–09). The common people supported their chiefs by giving tribute equal to their

needs and were allowed to eat turkey and drink intoxicating beverages only on special occasions. The slave class was composed of war captives and thieves; the latter became the slaves of the person they had robbed, a practice shared by the neighboring Cuitlatec.

Almost nothing is known of Chontal religion except that stone temples with many steps were guarded by "old ones"; "when someone came to ask for something, he spoke to the old one and then the old one went before the stone idol and there pricked his tongue, ears and other parts. When he saw this, he left content" (ibid., 6: 118). Offerings of copal and cotton mantles were placed near the idol. Among some of the modern towns of the Chontal region, Weitlaner (1948b, p. 207) noticed a strong emphasis on the "cult of capillas," similar to the neighboring Matlatzinca and Otomi towns to the north. He has, moreover, observed that the people of this area tend to make their religious pilgrimages northward into the Matlatzinca-Ocuiltec region.

The dead were buried in a seated position, along with the individual's possessions, an abundant supply of food, and slaves if he had any. When a chief was buried, two slaves, one of each sex, were slain and buried with him. For Coatepec, it was reported that a person without relatives was not buried but simply thrown into a field (Paso y Troncoso, 1905–06, 6: 119).

The genetic relationship of Chontal to any other known linguistic group is a matter of speculation and may never be determined with certainty. It appears that there were not enough monolingual Chontal-speakers by 1579 to induce the clergy to learn the language. At this time, Antonio Martínez reported that there was no "minister in this New Spain who understands them" (García Pimentel, 1897, p. 125), but many of the Chontal could confess because they understood Nahua. It is therefore doubtful that linguistic evidence will come

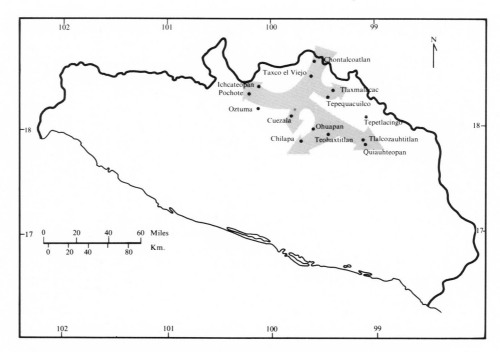

Fig. 5—MEXICAN CONQUEST OF GUERRERO: MONTEZUMA I, 1440–69

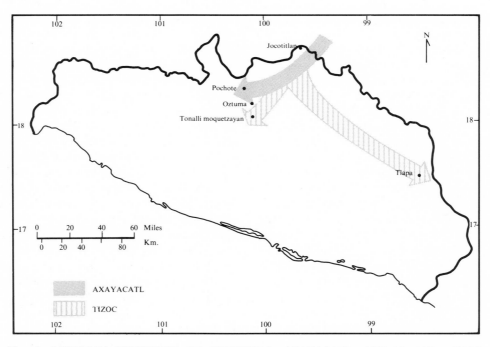

Fig. 6—MEXICAN CONQUEST OF GUERRERO: AXAYACATL, 1469–81, AND TIZOC, 1481–86

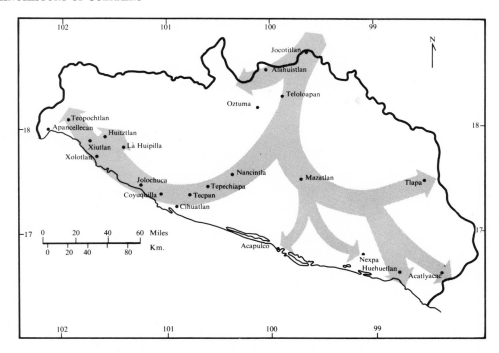

FIG. 7—MEXICAN CONQUEST OF GUERRERO: AHUITZOTL, 1486–1502

to light providing a basis for classifying the language.

After the extensive military campaigns of Ilhuicamina in the Chontal and Coixca areas of Guerrero (see fig. 5), the Mexicans seemed content with consolidating their gains, as only two or three new town names appear in the conquest lists of his immediate successors, Axayacatl and Tizoc (see fig. 6).[8] Ahuizotl, however, after quelling the Chontal insurrection, began the campaigns anew; and most of the balance of Guerrero fell under Mexican domination during his reign; only the Yope territory remained independent (see fig. 7).

The region inhabited by the Tlapanec was below the Balsas, south and east of Coixcatlalpan (see fig. 3). Their principal town was Tlapa, from which the tribute province took its name (see fig. 2). Within this province in 1571 there were many different languages: Mexican, Tlapanec, Mixtec, Amusgo, Cintec, Huehuetec, and Aya-

castec (García Pimentel, 1904, p. 107). To this list might be added Zapotec, which was reported for Quauhzopotlan, a town situated a little west of Azoyu (Barlow, 1944b, p. 359). The first Mexican ruler to invade the Tlapanec domain was Tizoc, in 1480 (see fig. 6). Six years later Ahuizotl made the definitive conquest (see fig. 7), and in 1487 the Tlapanec began paying tribute to the Mexicans.[9] In the same year a great feast was held to Huitzilopochtli in the Mexican capital, for which were sacrificed 80,000 war captives, 24,000 of whom were said to have been Tlapanec (Barlow, 1949d, p. 9; Ixtlilxochitl, 1952, 2: 273).

[8] Tonalliymoquetzayan and Otlappan [Tlapa] are among those listed in the Codex Chimalpopoca (1945, p. 67). In addition, Totoltepec is mentioned in the Relación of Ichcateopan as having been conquered by Axayacatl (Paso y Troncoso, 1905–06, 6: 149).

[9] Tlapa appears on the conquest lists; the Codices of Azoyu confirm these and provide the dates (Toscano, 1951).

611

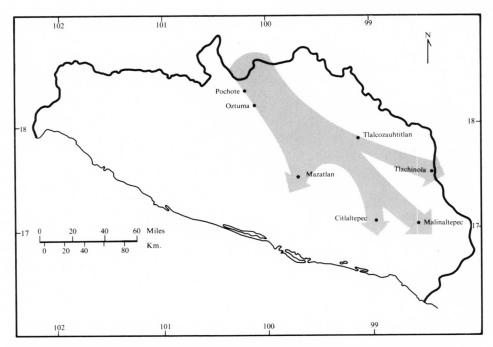

FIG. 8—MEXICAN CONQUEST OF GUERRERO: MONTEZUMA II, 1502–20

The province of Tlapa bordered the province of Quiauhteopan on the north and extended southward to the coast. Tlapanec-speaking towns were concentrated in the northern part. In the south the language reported was Yope, which appears to have been related to Tlapanec. According to Sahagún (1938, 3: 133), the "Yopimes and Tlapanecas are from the district of Yopitzingo; they call themselves Yopes because their land is called Yopitzingo, and they also call themselves Tlapanecs, which means 'ochre colored' men, because they paint themselves red. . . ." They also referred to themselves as tenime, pinome, chinquime, and chochonti. Until Yope linguistic materials come to light,[10] there is no possibility of confirming its relationship with Tlapanec. Radin, however, has reported (1933, p. 45) that Tlapanec was spoken

[10] There is an indication that catechisms were printed in Yope, but none of these has as yet been found (Paso y Troncoso, 1939–42, 14: 100–01).

30 years ago in two separate areas, and that the "differences between these two dialects is quite marked." One of the modern groups referred to their language as "Tlapaneca," whereas the other called theirs "Tlapaneco." The separate identity of the two may well reflect the old Yope-Tlapanec division, the southern group in Azoyu being descendants of the Yope. The nearest linguistic relative of Yope-Tlapanec is Subtiaba in Nicaragua, and Radin notes that they differ more from each other than either does from the latter.

The boundaries of Yope territory (see figs. 2, 3) or Yopitzingo have been defined by Ortega (1940, pp. 48–53). The boundary on the east was formed by the Rio de Nexpa or Ayutla, and along this frontier the Mexicans maintained a military garrison at Tutu-tepeque, a place which no longer exists but was near the modern town of Nexpa. The border on the north was formed by the Rio de Omitlan, a tributary of the Papagayo River; on this frontier the Mexicans maintained a garrison at Chilapa, established in 1458 by Ilhuicamina. The Papagayo River formed the western boundary, and the Pacific Ocean, the southern. The total area consisted of some 2000 sq. km. and is today composed of the municipios of San Marcos and Tecoanapa. The area adjoins the western boundary of the province of Tlapa and is a region characterized by steep mountains and hot climate.

The Yope were formidable warriors, who alone of the natives of Guerrero were able to preserve their independence in the face of Mexican expansion. In war they are described as "valiant men of the bow and arrow" (Gómez de Orozco, 1945, p. 60), who made wars and wanted to die in them in order to prove who they were (Paso y Troncoso, 1939–42, 2: 32). Although enemies of the Mexicans, they were nevertheless highly respected and were among those invited to witness the coronations of Mexican rulers. On these occasions, they were brought to the Mexican capital in secret to insure their safety, and when the festivities were over, they were safely escorted back to their border. The Yope were given many gifts when guests of the Mexicans and sent home so that they could "tell in their lands what they had seen" (Tezozomoc, 1944, p. 334). The Yope in turn showed their respect for the Mexican rulers, on one occasion bringing Montezuma rich gifts in the form of precious stones, gold dust, and jaguar, lion, and wolf pelts (ibid., p. 418).

The Yope were troublesome to the Spanish and before they were vanquished by Gutiérrez de Badajoz and Vasco Porcallo in 1531, they created considerable havoc among neighboring Indian settlements and their Spanish residents. Diego de Pardo, who went personally to view the destruction of the Nahua-speaking town of Cuscotitlan by the Yope, reported "the greatest cruelty and slaughter that I believe that Indians have done to one another in this land, as there was not a house that they left

unburned and they laid waste everywhere they went [leaving] the beheaded bodies of those they killed and sacrificing those they took alive along the way" (Paso y Troncoso, 1939–42, 2: 32).

All things considered, it is not surprising that the Mexican god Xipe Totec seems to have had his origin in the Yope-Tlapanec region. According to Sahagún (1938, 3: 133), in speaking of the Yope, "their idol was called Totec Tlatlauhqui Tezcatlipoca, which means red idol, because its clothing was red and its priests wore the same." Elsewhere, he says that its origin was in Zapotlan, but it seems more likely that it was Zapotitlan in the Tlapanec area (García Payón, 1941a, p. 344). Xipe's temple, called "Yopico," was in Tenochtitlan where the cathedral stands today on the Zocalo. He is often represented pictorially in a flayed human skin; his feast, called Tlacaxipehualiztli, means "man flaying." Not only was the victim's heart torn out and offered up to Xipe, but also his skin was flayed and worn by a person wishing to show special devotion to the god.

The sources are too meager in ethnographic detail to offer any real basis for comparison between the Yope and the Tlapanec. That there were cultural differences between them seems certain. Sahagún (1938, 3: 133) describes the Yope as "very clumsy, inept, and coarse; they were worse than the Otomi. . . ." Although the Yope knew agriculture, hunting played a dominant role in their subsistence and they were described as "great hunters." For example, a boy of seven years was given a bow and arrow by his parents and had to bring home some game if he wished to eat. Until marriage, neither sex wore clothing; afterwards "the women covered their parts with palm leaves" and the men, "with deerskins" (Gómez de Orozco, 1945, p. 60). Prominent among the gifts given to the Yope when guests of the Mexicans on the occasions described were articles of clothing.

The manner of marrying is described by

Gómez de Orozco (1945, p. 60). The only thing of special interest is that the girl's parents "summoned the betrothed and placed before him an ax, a coa, and a tumpline," symbols of the marriage. Divorce was permitted, but adultery was severely punished. For the first offense, the adulterers' noses were bitten off by the offended spouse, and for the second, the guilty were stoned to death.

To the west and northwest of Yopitzingo, and to the south of the Chontal, was a vast region inhabited by Cuitlatec, Tepuztec, and a host of smaller groups, most of whom have long since disappeared. This region, surrounded on three sides by water, embraced the Costa Grande and included the Balsas valley from Zacatula on the coast to Acatlan del Rio, a few miles east of Tetela. It is largely mountainous and much of it is unknown and unmapped today. The area was rich in raw materials, particularly copper, gold, seashells, and salt. It was also of strategic value to the Mexicans in checking the territorial expansion of their rivals, the Tarascans, who between 1370 and 1440[11] extended their control over the Balsas valley from Ajuchitlan to the Chumbia territory near the coast. The Tarascans remained in control of this region until defeated by the Spaniards.

Tetela was subjugated by Ixcoatl, but the rest of the region, with the exception of that dominated by the Tarascans, remained independent until Ahuizotl's time. After smashing the Chontal revolt, which culminated in the slaughter of the inhabitants of Alahuistlan, Ahuizotl's attention turned toward the Costa Grande (see fig. 1). None of the intervening towns between Tetela and the coast, except Nancintla, figure in the conquest list, suggesting strongly that his reputation had preceded him. The Tetela Cuitlatec stated that Ahuizotl threatened them "and since they saw that he was so powerful, they surrendered to him" (Paso y Troncoso, 1905–06, 6: 133). The Tepuztec of Otatlan did the same.

614

These and other bloodless victories paved the way and gave the Mexicans access to the coastal region, which they entered between 1497 and 1503.[12] Then followed a rapid series of conquests which included the towns of Jolochuca, Coyuca, Tecpan, Cihuatlan, Apancellecan, Xiutla, and Acapulco, placing most, if not all, of the Costa Grande, in Mexican hands. There are some doubts whether the Mexicans did in fact dominate the entire coast; Zacatula itself and many other prominent towns were not on the conquest list, and the Relación de Zacatula points out that Jolochuca was on the frontier (Barlow, 1947b, p. 264). The same document, however, states that the province paid tribute to Montezuma and this is supported by the Matrícula de Tributos. The Tarascans did not consider the people of Zacatula formidable enemies because in war "they always defeated them" (Relaciones geográficas . . . Michoacan, 1958, p. 113) so it is doubtful that they were much of a problem for the Mexicans. The absence of certain towns on the conquest list may only imply that they surrendered when they saw the strength of the Mexicans.[13]

The most numerous and geographically widespread people in this section of Guerrero were the Cuitlatec (see fig. 3). They were situated along the Balsas from Acatlan del Rio west to Changata, somewhat beyond Ajuchitlan, and in the coastal region. Leaving the Yope area, "the Cuitlatec begin farther on, almost at the edge of the Pacific, whose province runs from east to west more than eighty leagues and whose towns were numerous and heavily populated . . ." (Tor-

[11] Tarascan activity in Guerrero is discussed by Brand, 1943.
[12] The conquests of the Costa Grande towns follow in sequence after Amaxtlan, which the Anales of Tula say fell in 1497 (Barlow, 1949c, p. 10).
[13] Ixtlilxochitl records (1952, 2: 279–81) that a Texcocan noble, Teuhchimaltzin, with a handful of helpers posing as merchants entered Zacatula and were able to kill its king. Thereafter, its people were subject to Texcoco. Whether this account has any validity or not, it does indicate that Zacatula had lost its independence.

quemada, 1943–44, 1: 287). They extended up the coast to Petatlan or slightly beyond, and their principal town was Mexcaltepec, in the mountains above the modern town of Atoyac.[14]

The Cuitlatec language, of which a few speakers still remain, is as yet unclassified. The term "Cuitlatec" is thought to be derogatory, deriving from the Nahuatl "cuitlatl" meaning excrement. Brand, on the other hand, has suggested (1952, p. 58) that it may have derived from "teocuitlatl" meaning gold, which was abundant in their territory.

Subsistence was based on agriculture, and crops were planted along the riverbanks "when the river subsided" (Paso y Troncoso, 1905–06, 6: 135). Irrigation was practiced by carrying water to the fields. Crops included corn, chile, frijoles, cotton, cacao, pepitas, melons, and gourds. The latter were large, the size of "an average shield," and were used on the rivers for transport accompanying a swimmer (Relaciones geográficas . . . Michoacan, 1958, p. 77). As in the Chontal area, houses were small and low. Some were made of adobe, others of sticks, with thatched roofs. They were surrounded by fences of sticks covered with plaster. Chiefs' houses were painted.

Children were named after the day on which they were born, and the name was given seven days after birth. At age four or five, they were promised in marriage by their parents. As adults, they were taken before an idol; the parents of the bride gave the groom a mantle and the groom's parents gave the bride a huipil as symbols of the marriage. This marriage was expected to endure for life. Adultery was punished as severely as among the Yope, the adulterers' noses being cut off. Also, all the property and the sisters of the man involved were given to the husband of the adulteress

14 Villanseñor y Sánchez (1746–48, 2: 108) indicates that Atoyac was formerly called Mexcaltepec.

(Paso y Troncoso, 1905–06, 6: 135). The dead were buried in a temple and placed in a round hole in a seated position, accompanied by food, mantles, and all their clothes. A chief's slaves were killed and buried with him.

The Cuitlatec built stone temples to their principal gods in which they sacrificed prisoners of war and made offerings which included cotton mantles and incense. As among the Chontal, the temples were in the care of older priests, one of whom was the head priest. The latter spoke with the idol, remained by its side, and was expected to be chaste. To attain his respected position, he had to serve four years in the temple without ever leaving it (ibid., 6: 133). The Cuitlatec worshipped the sun, moon, and "idols of stone, clay, and wood, of various shapes and sizes" (Relaciones geográficas . . . Michoacan, 1958, p. 70). Their rites were said to be as diverse as their gods, among them being the usual bloodletting from tongue, ears, and other parts of the body. They were valiant in war and lent assistance to the Mexicans. To become brave warriors, they threw themselves into the river from which they emerged as "jaguars, others as lions or lizards or serpents and thus in effect they were transformed into these figures" (ibid., p. 70). They fought in squadrons and formed a line of attack against the enemy. Weapons of war included the bow and arrow, slings, and clubs; they protected themselves with shields and padded jackets (Paso y Troncoso, 1905–06, 6: 134).

Forming a wedge between, and perhaps isolating altogether, the coastal Cuitlatec and those along the Balsas were the Tepuztec or Tlacotepehua. Their principal towns were Tlacotepec, Otatlan, Anequilco, and Citlaltomaua. West of Citlaltomaua, their towns were interspersed with those of the Cuitlatec. The Tepuztec language is extinct and its linguistic relationship unknown. The only ethnographic descriptions of these people are in the Relaciones geo-

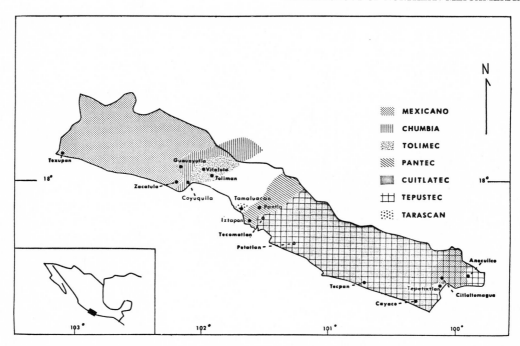

FIG. 9—LANGUAGE DISTRIBUTION, 1580: COSTA GRANDE OF GUERRERO

gráficas. These indicate a cultural similarity with the Balsas Cuitlatec in such things as house types, marriage patterns, medical practices, subsistence, and warfare. It is difficult to evaluate the differences, since they may be only a matter of emphasis, elaboration, or omission on the part of the reporters. For example, the Tepuztec worshipped "large trees and rocks and other things, such as animals and birds, and those who desired [something from the gods] climbed into the high mountains and sierras, and there they burned a resin-like white incense, and cut papers and other feathers, and there cut their tongues and other parts and offered all of this to the demon" (ibid., 6: 158). Burials were made in the floors of houses rather than in temples as the Cuitlatec did. Unfortunately, comparable descriptions are not available for the coastal Cuitlatec, to whom the Tepuztec may have been more closely related. According to legend, the Tepuztec of Tla-

cotepec originally lived on the Costa Grande, migrating from Tixtlancingo northward into the mountain area, where they were found at the turn of the 16th century.

The Costa Grande, as Barlow described it (1949c, p. 13), contained a "mosaic of vanished languages" (see fig. 9). The inhabitants of Acamalutla were reported to have spoken Tlacihuizteca, but several different languages were spoken in its estancias—Tistec, Coyutumatec, and Tlacotepehua or Tepuztec. In Amatla the language was Camotec; in Texcatlan, Texcatec; in Naguala, Tuztec. Above Tecomatlan, a town in which both Cuitlatec and Tepuztec were spoken, the language of Pantla and Ixtapa was Panteca. Tolimeca was spoken in Toliman and its subjects. North of Zacatula, in the mountains, still another unidentified language, Chumbia, was reported in Vitaluta and its subjects. Guayemeo, a barrio of Sirandaro in the middle Balsas region, spoke Apaneca; these Apaneca "in

616

times past came from the province of Zacatula" (Relaciones geográficas . . . Michoacan, 1958, 2: 40). Today, none of these languages remain, and many of the towns have also disappeared.

The implied language diversity would render the Costa Grande the most linguistically complex in Middle America, considering the limited extent of the area (see fig. 9). The sources are not adequate to permit a reduction of these languages by providing clues to their relationships, but they do suggest an explanation for the phenomenon. In 1580 it was observed that "there were in this province large towns and many people, and now there are few and each day less, because many die, and an Indian of this province never reaches age fifty" (Barlow, 1947b, p. 264). A census taken three decades before reveals that the population of 56. towns in the province had by then dropped to 13,753 (Borah and Cook, 1960, p. 110), so doubtlessly far fewer people were to be found in 1580 when the decline was still continuing. Torquemada (1943–44, 1: 287) reported a population of 150,000 for Mexcaltepec and its subjects alone, before it was moved by the Spaniards a few miles nearer the coast, after which the population declined to under 1000. Relocation was a common practice and "almost every town moved many times from one place to another" (Barlow, 1947b, p. 264). From the middle 1520's to the middle 1530's, the region north of Zacatula known as the Motines, was the most important gold-producing area in New Spain. For a time, Zacatula was an important shipbuilding center. These enterprises brought Spaniards and other native peoples into the area and, with them, disease. By 1580 Tepetixtla and Xahualtepec were almost depopulated by plagues, and the whole province was described as unhealthy because of smallpox and fevers. By this time, what was left of the native population was thoroughly uprooted and the lingua franca had become a

"corrupt Mexican" (*ibid.*, p. 260). It is in just such a situation that a report of such a potpourri of languages might be expected, and hence it need not be construed as a reflection of the pre-Hispanic linguistic heterogeneity, but rather the condition to which they had been reduced.

During the years of Montezuma's reign, the Mexicans maintained their position in Guerrero, defending Oztuma against attacks by the Tarascans, quieting a revolt in Tlalcozauhtitlan, and subjecting Malinaltepec. By this time the old ethnic boundaries had blurred, and Guerrero was divided into tribute-paying provinces (see fig. 2). Taxco and the Chontal towns north of it became the province of Tlachco. Tepequacuilco embraced the rest of the Chontal area, the western towns of the Coixca, and the northern Tepuztec and Cuitlatec. Old Coixcatlalpan became the province of Tlalcozauhtitlan, and was bounded by Quiauhteopan on the east and Tlapan on the south, the latter extending to the coast. The Costa Grande formed still another tribute province, Cihuatlan. A list of the tribute from these provinces can be found in Barlow (1949c), and this tribute pointedly reveals the strong economic interest the Mexicans had in Guerrero. It is interesting to note that shortly before they began their invasions of Guerrero, the Mexicans wore clothing made of henequen and ixtle. The conquest of Morelos and Guerrero provided a vast source of cotton, which they used from then on for clothing and armor.[15]

---

[15] Sahagún (1938, 2: 339) relates that "after the death of the above-mentioned lord (Quaquauhpitzauac), they elected another lord named Tlacateotl, and in his time . . . began the selling and buying . . . of mantas and maxtles of cotton, because previously they had only used mantas and maxtles of henequen and the women also used huipiles and enaguas of ixtle." This indicates that they did not shift to cotton clothing until the years 1418–28. Torquemada, on the other hand, reported (1943–44, 1: 104) that the Mexicans began to wear cotton clothing after the marriage of Huitzilihuitl to the daughter of the Tezcacohuatzin, the ruler of Cuernavaca, in 1396.

When the Spanish came, the tribute was continued (see fig. 2); but by the mid-16th century the population was a fraction of its former strength, and town after town reported its inability to maintain the rate of payment. The 17th and 18th centuries are dark ages in the history of Guerrero; by the 19th century most of the indigenous languages were extinct and their associated cultures with them. Today dialects of Nahua are spoken over most of the state, with some Tlapanec, Mixtec, and Amusgo remaining along the Oaxaca border.

REFERENCES

Alva Ixtlilxochitl, 1952
Alvarado Tezozomoc, 1944
Anales de Tlatelolco, 1948
Barlow, 1944b, 1947a, 1947b, 1948a, 1949c, 1949d
Borah and Cook, 1960
Brand, 1943, 1952
Codex Chimalpopoca, 1945
García Payón, 1941a
García Pimentel, 1897, 1904
Gómez de Orozco, 1945
Kelly and Palerm, 1952

Orozco y Berra, 1864
Ortega, 1940
Paso y Troncoso, 1905–06, 1939–42
Radin, 1933
Relaciones geográficas de Michoacan, 1958
Sahagún, 1938
Torquemada, 1943–44
Toscano, 1951
Toussaint, 1931
Villaseñor y Sánchez, 1746–48
Weitlaner, 1941, 1945a, 1948b

27. Archaeological Synthesis of Guerrero

ROBERT H. LISTER

APS OF THE MEXICAN state of Guerrero still designate an area in the west-central part as *Región Inexplorada.* From an archaeological point of view, many other sections of the state can also be referred to as "unexplored." It is true that many undocumented archaeological specimens, especially finely carved objects of stone and some items of metal, have been collected in Guerrero and have found their way into the hands of private collectors or museums. It also is true that since publication of the article (Spinden, 1911) describing the collections obtained in 1910 and 1911 by William Niven (a mining prospector) from Los Placeres del Oro, sporadic archaeological reconnaissance and limited excavations have continued to the present time.

Despite all this, we have only the barest outline of the state's culture history. Thorough digging of a major site, many of which exist, is yet to be undertaken. The few scientific excavations accomplished to date have been primarily stratigraphic, attempting to uncover remains in chronological sequence or of cultural significance. The results of some of these undertakings have not been published. If one may believe the stories associated with the well-fashioned stone objects from Guerrero, a great many burials and "tombs" have been looted for their grave furnishings. There is also reason to beware of the many fraudulent objects that have been made and sold to unwary collectors.

Considering the state as a whole and piecing together evidence from various areas, one may note a long cultural sequence generally similar to that of the rest of Middle America. Objects and data representative of the Preclassic, Classic, Toltec, and early historic horizons have been recovered under circumstances and in sufficient quantity to be unquestioned. Relationships with the well-known cultures which arose and expanded from the south-central Mexican plateau are obvious. Archaic, Teotihuacan, Toltec, Aztec, Tarascan, and Matlatzinca remains have been identified. Contacts with

619

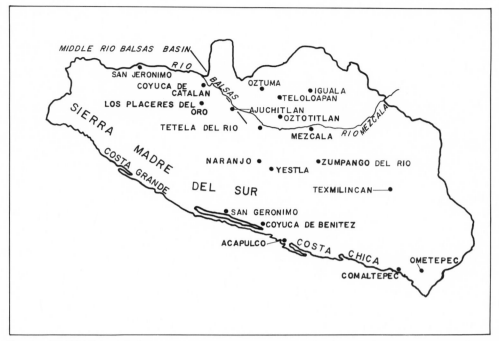

Fig. 1—ARCHAEOLOGICAL MAP OF GUERRERO. For ethnohistorical map, see Art. 26, fig. 1.

peoples to the east and south are demonstrated by numerous occurrences of items recognized as Olmec and Mixteca-Puebla, and occasionally Maya influences are reported. Covarrubias was even of the opinion that central and eastern Guerrero and adjacent parts of Oaxaca constituted the area where Olmec culture began. It also has been postulated that the Pacific coast served as a corridor for the spread of certain cultural elements originating as far south as Nicaragua and Costa Rica and extending north to the state of Sinaloa. Finally, local cultures sometimes imitate those which existed in adjoining areas or which, in some instances, appear to coincide with the distribution of certain historically recognized local groups.

The diversity of Guerrero cultures undoubtedly reflects the state's geographic complexity and its location peripheral to centers where important and distinctive cultural advances were achieved.

The northern section of the state is part of the dissected, volcano-marked, southern border of the central Mexican highlands. Most of its rugged surface is drained by the Rio Balsas and tributaries. The main stream of the Balsas has opened a deep east-west gorge well into the *tierra caliente*, and tributaries reach back into the higher country both south and north. Aside from the rare locations where valleys broaden out in small structural basins, there are few flat places in the Balsas region. South of the Rio Balsas a large mass of more resistant land has remained standing as an elongated block known as the Sierra Madre del Sur. It borders the Pacific and extends from southern Michoacan across Guerrero and into southern Oaxaca. In Guerrero its very steep slopes descend almost to water's edge, leaving only a narrow coast of sandy and generally hot, dry land. From north to south, therefore, Guerrero consists of a series of alternating highlands and lowlands: the

620

mountainous southern edge of the central plateau, the Rio Balsas basin, the Sierra Madre del Sur, and finally a narrow fringe of coast.

No areas are particularly deficient in moisture, but the rainfall is scarcely more than short, hard downpours during the summer months. Vegetation and crops are conditioned by altitude. Only in the higher elevations is plant cover fairly dense; elsewhere it is usually sparse. The Rio Balsas basin is truly *tierra caliente*, having the hottest year-around climate in Mexico. The rest of the area, aside from the higher mountain elevations, is *tierra templada*.

Population past and present has tended to concentrate in the lower lands and in the numerous valleys and canyons that penetrate all the highland areas. The Rio Balsas and the coastal strip are natural zones for east-west communication; the many tributaries flowing into the Balsas basin from the edge of the central highlands on the north and from the Sierra Madre del Sur on the south provide less convenient but quite satisfactory north-south routes. In addition, the terrain affords relative isolation within a few miles of the principal lines of travel. Even our present limited understanding of Guerrero archaeology demonstrates that both communication routes and isolated areas have influenced its culture history.

With the exception of Herbert Spinden's discussion (1911) of materials from Los Placeres del Oro and some references to archaeology in a general account of part of Guerrero by William Spratling (1932), published reports on the archaeology of Guerrero cluster in the 1940s, following field activities begun in the late 1930s and investigations conducted in the early 1940s. Donald D. Brand (1942) and Robert H. Lister (1947) reported on two seasons' archaeological survey and several small-scale excavations, as well as anthropogeographic investigations, conducted by the University of New Mexico in the middle Rio Balsas ba-

sin. Pedro R. Hendrichs Pérez included a section on the archaeology of the Rio Balsas basin, summarizing several short, earlier articles, in his general work on that region (1945). The Aztec fortress site of Oztuma was the subject of articles by Hendrichs Pérez (1940), Lister (1941), Hugo Moedano K. (1942), and Pedro Armillas (1942–44). Roberto J. Weitlaner and Robert Barlow (1944) described the results of reconnaissance and surface collecting in western Guerrero, and García Payón (1941a) did the same for eastern Guerrero.

Western Mexico was the theme of the fourth Round Table on Problems of Mexican and Central American Anthropology held at the National Museum of History in Mexico City in September, 1946. The proceedings of that meeting (*El Occidente de México*, 1948) contain the largest amount of information on the prehistory of Guerrero gathered together in a single volume. Gordon F. Ekholm described ceramic stratigraphy at Acapulco, and Barlow discussed some pottery types found north of the Rio Balsas; Miguel Covarrubias reported on the carved and polished stonework characteristic of the Rio Mezcala drainage; and the findings of regional surveys were described for western Guerrero by Armillas, for the Sierra Madre del Sur and the Costa Grande by Weitlaner, for Oztotitlan by Moedano, and for Teloloapan by Lister (see specific references at the end of this article).

Since 1950, a few articles dealing specifically with Guerrero have appeared (Bernal, 1951; Franco, 1960; Piña Chan, 1960a), but most recent discussions have been summary and have appeared as sections of publications considering other subjects in addition to archaeology or have included Guerrero in discussions of much wider geographic coverage (Marquina, 1951; Lister, 1955; Covarrubias, 1957; Peterson, 1959). The results of the recent survey and stratigraphic excavations made along the Pacific coast of Guerrero by Charles and Ellen Brush, of Columbia University, are recorded only as

621

preliminary field notes, which the Brushes kindly made available and from which I have extracted some information for this article.

Previous summaries of Guerrero archaeology have delimited several zones in which particular culture elements or complexes appeared to have been characteristic (Armillas, 1948; Lister, 1955). Although these zones are perhaps more illustrative of archaeological investigation than of the distribution of culture elements, a brief description of them may be useful to our present purpose.

The middle Rio Balsas basin, from about Tetela del Rio on the east to San Jeronimo on the west, possesses rich archaeological remains indicative of a long period of occupation, perhaps from Preclassic times. Examples of Olmec stone sculpture have been collected, and Maya-like stonework and a corbeled arch are reported. Aztec and Tarascan fortification and garrison sites are known to have existed prior to the conquest, revealing a quarrel over part of the zone by two major powers.

The Mezcala zone was proposed by Covarrubias to designate an area in which a peculiar style of stone objects occurs. It centers about the basin of the Rio Mezcala, a name sometimes applied to the eastern course of the Rio Balsas in Guerrero and Puebla, and the elevated lands to the north and south.

The Costa Grande, or the Pacific coast northwest of Acapulco, shows strong Preclassic and Classic (Teotihuacan) affiliations as well as contacts with southern Mexico and Central America as revealed by resemblances between local pottery and that of the Maya area, Nicaragua, and Costa Rica.

The Yestla-Naranjo zone in the Sierra Madre del Sur of central Guerrero contains late archaeological materials exhibiting similarities to Mixteca-Puebla and Aztec cultures.

Rather than repeat a detailed enumera-

tion of items occurring in each zone, many of which are of no value for outlining culture history at this time, I will note the distribution of elements that may be assigned to particular cultures or culture horizons or that coincide with established linguistic or tribal distribution. Later, some traits whose cultural relationships are not clear will be considered.

Although no sites earlier than Preclassic times have been reported, elements of cultures from the Preclassic horizon have been noted from several widely separated parts of the state.

Archaic-type, handmade clay figurines have come from the Rio Balsas basin southward across the Sierra Madre del Sur in central Guerrero to the Pacific coast, where they have been noted on both the Costa Grande and the Costa Chica. Correspondences between these and Archaic figurines from the Valley of Mexico and environs in style and technique have been noted by several investigators (Armillas, 1948, p. 75; Weitlaner, 1948a, p. 81; Ekholm, 1948, p. 101; Marquina, 1951, p. 30; Vaillant, 1934, p. 56). In stratigraphic excavations along the coast the presence of figurines of these styles below levels containing Classic horizon (Teotihuacan) and Toltec horizon (Mazapan) remains further supports their identification as Archaic. There is reason to believe that some handmade figurines of Archaic type continued to be made, at least along the Pacific coast of Guerrero, long after the practice of fashioning figurines in molds became commonplace elsewhere. The most common recognizable type of Preclassic figurine, found at Acapulco and northwest to the vicinity of San Geronimo, has gouged features, elaborate headdress, and a tendency toward an elongated face (Ekholm, 1948, p. 101).

Distributed widely over Guerrero, including sites where Archaic figurines resembling those of central Mexico occur, is a ceramic complex dominated by heavy red utility wares. Most are slipped but may be polished or unpolished. Shapes include bowls, jars, and ollas. At some sites these wares are in stratified deposits along with Archaic figurines, thus establishing their contemporaneity. In other localities such sherds occur as surface finds not always associated with Archaic figurines. Whether all these red wares are of the same type cannot be stated. They have been reported from almost everywhere archaeological investigations have been conducted. Some undoubtedly belong to the Preclassic horizon; some even may be related to well-established Archaic types found elsewhere. Ekholm (1948, p. 102) has noted similarities between red wares found at Acapulco in deposits beneath those containing Teotihuacan materials and Vaillant's Bay wares found in the Valley of Mexico, Puebla, and Morelos. It is evident that these wares are not limited solely to the Preclassic horizon in Guerrero, as revealed in a number of stratified sites, but continued to be made in later times, probably into the Historic horizon. Therefore, such sherds do not always serve as good horizon-markers, but a tradition of employing thick-walled red vessels for utility purposes appears to have been established in Preclassic times in many sections of Guerrero.

At most sites where red pottery occurs in Preclassic deposits, sherds of other types also are found. These vary from site to site and seem to represent wares which had limited distributions. Most are monochromes which sometimes carry incised or punctate designs. Vessel walls usually are thinner than those of the red utility wares, and their surfaces may be slipped or unslipped. Color varies greatly: black, gray, brown, red, orange, and white.

Another Preclassic trait noted along the Costa Grande of Guerrero is the clay earplug. These have been found at Acapulco by Ekholm, who mentions (1948, p. 101) their similarity to earplugs from late Ticoman levels in the Valley of Mexico, and at other sites on the Costa Grande (Weit-

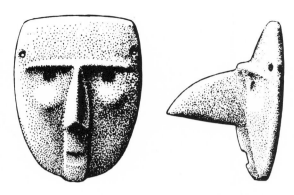

FIG. 2—"MEZCALA STYLE" STONE MASK. (From Covarrubias, 1957, fig. 43.)

laner, 1948a, p. 81). The most common type is a thin-walled cylinder with one end closed, the flat end being flared and carved or incised with naturalistic or geometric designs.

Although there is still considerable discussion over the position of the Olmec culture in the Middle American sequence, I consider the reported occurrence of Olmec culture elements in Guerrero to be assignable to the Preclassic horizon. Objects identified as Olmec have been noted or collected in the middle Rio Balsas and Rio Mezcala basins (Armillas, 1948, p. 75; Covarrubias, 1957, p. 110), on the Costa Grande (Covarrubias, 1948, p. 86) and Costa Chica (Piña Chan, 1960a, p. 74), and in the Yestla-Naranjo zone of the Sierra Madre del Sur (Covarrubias, 1948, p. 86). Figurines, masks, colossal axes, pendants, beads, and certain unique forms were finely carved from green or blue-gray jadeite. Covarrubias, who has plotted their distribution (1948, p. 86; 1957, p. 107), concludes that they are so frequent and important, particularly around Zumpango del Rio and near San Geronimo on the coast above Acapulco, that they cannot be considered trade objects. He believed the Olmec specimens in Guerrero marked the western frontier of an Olmec belt extending across Mexico from the Pacific to the Gulf of Mexico. Also, he noted that the Olmec objects from Gue-

623

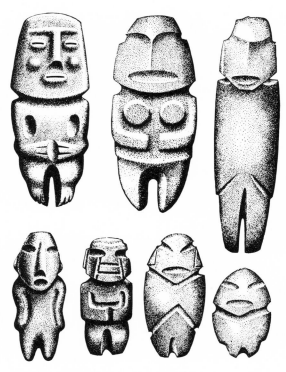

FIG. 3—"MEZCALA STYLE" STONE FIGU-
RINES. (From Covarrubias, 1957, fig. 46.)

rrero have a certain "archaistic" style and
do not include large monuments, whereas
those from the Gulf Coast seem more developed and elaborate and include monumental sculpture. To Covarrubias this suggested
that the Olmec occupation on the Pacific
coast may have been earlier than on the
coastal lowlands of the Gulf side.

Other students of Olmec culture recognize Covarrubias's contribution to our understanding of the nature of the Olmec
art complex, but question whether stylistic
analysis alone, unaccompanied by archaeological and stratigraphic evidence, is a reli-
able means of determining its origin and
development (Drucker, Heizer, and Squier,
1959, p. 254). Roman Piña Chan, after in-
vestigating a number of sites in the state
of Morelos, expressed the opinion that an
early center of Olmec culture is to be found
in that state, with a possible earlier focus
in the conjunction of the states of Puebla,

Morelos, and Guerrero (1955a, p. 26; 1955b,
p. 106). Most authorities, however, feel
that Olmec culture is of tropical origin and
was generated somewhere in the Veracruz-
Tabasco lowland area. They further believe
that instances of undoubted specimens of
portable Olmec carved stone art found outside the Veracruz-Tabasco heartland, such
as in Guerrero, represent collectors' items
"which may have been treasured heirlooms
and were ultimately lost or deliberately
buried as part of a grave offering or dedica-
tory cache by people far removed in distance and time from those who made the
specimens" (Drucker, Heizer, and Squier,
1959, pp. 253–59).

A scattering of traits identified as belonging to the Classic horizon has been recorded from Guerrero, especially along the coast
from Acapulco northwestward and to a lesser degree on the Costa Chica. Such traits
also have been found in the Rio Balsas and
Rio Mezcala basins, and in the Yestla-
Naranjo zone. A fairly important extension
of Teotihuacan culture into this area is postulated by Covarrubias (1957, p. 110), who
notes the frequent occurrence of stone
masks and figurines of Classic Teotihuacan
style in the Rio Mezcala region. Covarrubias collected carved stone objects from the
Mezcala area for 25 years and came to the
conclusion that a clear-cut cultural unit
could be distinguished along the Rio Mezcala basin, including territory as far south
as Zumpango del Rio and extending north
into the southern part of the state of Mexico
(pp. 106–11). In addition to the above-
mentioned Teotihuacan-like stone masks
and figurines and the previously considered
finely carved stone objects of Olmec style,
Covarrubias distinguished carvings of several transitional styles—"Olmec-Teotihua-
can," "Olmec-Guerrero (local style)," and
"Teotihuacan-Guerrero (local style)"—as
well as a purely local "Mezcala style" said
to resemble no other in Middle America except perhaps certain schematic stone objects from the Quezaltenango area in the

Guatemalan highlands and certain jade objects from Costa Rica (p. 110).

The chronological position of the items of "Mezcala style" is uncertain, but if Covarrubias is correct in identifying some of the transitional forms as fusions of local and Teotihuacan or Olmec and Teotihuacan styles, they may have belonged in the Classic horizon. Although nothing is known of the age or cultural affiliations of objects of the "Mezcala style," they do present an interesting stone complex. It contains figurines, masks, small effigies of animals and objects, beads, pendants, and earplug flares. They are carved from a variety of hard stones of green, gray-green, gray, and black color and display a highly stylized and schematic, vigorous character which readily identifies them.

The figurines have a basic form like a petaloid axe with symmetrically arranged cuts and planes that barely indicate the characteristics of the face and extremities. Individuals are shown standing or seated, with arms folded over the chest or extended alongside the body.

Masks are of all sizes and in many different styles. Features are indicated with raised welts, sharp edges, and concavities distributed in a square or trapezoidal face. A unique mask comes from the area between the Rio Mezcala and Sultepec to the north in the state of Mexico. It is made of marble, onyx, or obsidian, is flat and thin, and has a triangular face, with eyes and mouth absent or hardly indicated, and a large sharp, thin nose jutting out of a ridge that represents the eyebrows.

Mezcala-style effigies represent jaguars, frogs, snakes, monkeys, squirrels, and birds, as well as miniature stone vessels, and temple models with columns, cornices, and stairways, often with an effigy of a man in the central archway or lying on the roof (also see Franco, 1960).

Clay figurines of Teotihuacan style seem to be lacking in the Mezcala zone but are reported from the middle Rio Balsas by Ar-

Fig. 4—"MEZCALA STYLE" MODEL TEMPLE OF STONE. (From Covarrubias, 1957, fig. 47.)

millas (1948, p. 75) and from the Costa Grande and the vicinity of Acapulco by Piña Chan (1960a, p. 75), Weitlaner, and the Brushes. Those from the Costa Grande are described as moldmade with Teotihuacan-like headdresses (Weitlaner, 1948a, p. 81).

In Ekholm's stratigraphic excavation at Acapulco, pottery possessing Teotihuacan attributes was encountered in levels above those containing Archaic traits (1948, pp. 98–99). A type designated Acapulco Brown was fashioned into two distinctive vessel forms considered typical of Teotihuacan ceramics, the cylinder tripod and the tripod plate. The first is a vessel with flat bottom, vertical sides, and hollow rectangular legs. Some vessels also exhibit such distinctive Teotihuacan elements as molded figures and "coffee-bean" type of decoration appliquéd around the base of vessels, as well as typical Teotihuacan leg design molded on the surface of tripod supports. The tripod plates are usually rimmed and typically are supported by tall plano-convex legs whose

625

Fig. 5—EXCAVATIONS IN GUERRERO. *a*, Pyramid, Amuco. On left bank of Rio Balsas. Stairway and walls are stuccoed. *b-f*, Palos Altos, Arcelia.

flat exteriors are decorated with a molded and cut-out naturalistic or geometric design.

Another form common to Acapulco Brown, as well as to Acapulco Fine Paste, is a small hemispherical bowl with annular base. The base sometimes is cut out in a series of triangles. The shape is in general similar to a common form of Teotihuacan Thin Orange.

An extension of this Teotihuacan related ceramic complex has been found at several points to the northwest of Acapulco. Weitlaner and Barlow (1944) collected vessel legs of the types common to the cylinder tripods and the tripod plates at Coyuca de Benitez, and the Brushes report Teotihuacan-style ceramics in the vicinity of San Geronimo. The presence of clay *candeleros* of Teotihuacan type in this same area has been noted by Weitlaner (1948a, p. 81).

At sites in the vicinity of Ometepec and Comaltepec on the Costa Chica near the Oaxaca border, Piña Chan (1960a, pp. 73–76) has observed a variety of traits apparently belonging to the Classic horizon. A number of stone monuments, including plain and carved stelae and sculptures in the round, are associated with sites in these localities. They seem to have been placed in patios fronting mounds or pyramids. Carved stelae show stylistic similarities to both Teotihuacan and Monte Alban cultures. Some depict figures reminiscent of Tlaloc or Chalchiuitlicue in Teotihuacan style, others have elements described as classic Zapotec style. Stones sculptured in the round include a fragment representing a decapitated jaguar. Some stelae and sculptured stones have a glyph bearing a number. Pottery from these same sites includes gray incised, reddish orange, and polychrome lacquer types that are said to be related to ceramics from the Monte Alban II–IIIa stages.

A few references have been made to Maya or Mayoid traits in Guerrero. All lack detail and are difficult to evaluate. Moe-dano (1948, pp. 105–06), in a brief statement on archaeological remains near Oxtotitlan in the middle Rio Balsas basin, noted the presence there of tombs with corbel-arched roof construction and large carved stone monuments. He considered both as Mayoid. In the central Sierra Madre del Sur south of the Rio Balsas, Weitlaner found similar tombs with corbel-arched roofs (1948a, p. 77), and on the Costa Grande he obtained clay figurines said to have a decidedly Maya aspect (p. 81).

A number of culture traits diagnostic of the Toltec horizon have been identified in several parts of Guerrero, although such influences do not seem to have been as strong here as they were farther north.

Molded clay figurines referred to as Mazapan style are listed as present on the Costa Grande by Weitlaner (1948a, p. 81) and by Armillas (1948, p. 75), on the Costa Chica by the Brushes (n.d.), and in the basin of the middle Rio Balsas by Armillas (1948, p. 75).

Pottery said to be similar to that found by Linné at the site of Mazapan in the Valley of Mexico was recovered by Weitlaner on the Costa Grande (1948a, p. 82). In many parts of central and western Mexico red-on-brown wares are typical of the Toltec horizon. Such pottery occurs at Acapulco (Ekholm, 1948, p. 100), the Costa Chica (Brush, n.d.), and in the middle Rio Balsas (Lister, 1947, p. 73), and in the vicinity of Texmilincan in the eastern part of the state (García Payón, 1941a, p. 354); but whether any or all of it belongs in the Toltec horizon cannot be stated.

Plumbate and Fine Orange wares are hallmarks of the Toltec horizon. Both have been reported from Texmilincan (Caso, 1941, p. 90) and the Costa Grande (Weitlaner, 1948a, p. 81; Brush, n.d.). The Brushes recovered a considerable amount of Fine Orange pottery from one site near Acapulco and noted a scattered distribution of it along the entire Costa Grande.

Two traits which in all likelihood make

627

their first appearances in western Mexico in the Toltec horizon are present in Guerrero, *molcajetes* and objects of metal. Use of both continued into historic times, so their presence is significant only in dating deposits in which they occur as no earlier than Toltec horizon.

Molcajetes are bowls normally having tripod supports and a floor roughened by incisions to form a grinding surface. The form has been observed in northern Guerrero (Lister, 1948, p. 108), the middle Rio Balsas basin (Lister, 1947, p. 72), the Costa Grande (Weitlaner, 1948a, p. 82), and the Yestla-Naranjo zone (Weitlaner, 1948a, p. 80).

Because it is impossible to determine the chronological position of most metal objects from Guerrero at this time, their general distribution is summarized here; but it is realized that many such objects were fashioned in the following Historic horizon. Objects made of copper are fairly abundant, gold is much rarer. Copper was most frequently cast into small bells with elongated resonators which are slit at the bottom and have a ring for suspension at the top. Sometimes they were similarly shaped by a process of wire coiling. Oblong hatchet-like axe heads, semilunar knives, finger rings, tweezers, fishhooks, rings with small shell pendants which must have been elements of necklaces, beads, and needles also have been collected. The areas from which copper items have been recovered include the middle Rio Balsas (Lister, 1947, p. 75), the Yestla-Naranjo area (Weitlaner, 1948a, p. 78), Texmilincan (Caso, 1941, p. 90), and from Acapulco north up the Costa Grande (Brush, n.d.). Gold is present in the middle Rio Balsas (Brand, 1942, p. 146), at Texmilincan (Caso, 1941, p. 90), and on the Costa Grande (Brush and Brush, n.d.), and was made into bells, figurines, zoomorphic ornaments, and hammered into thin sheets with repoussé designs which probably were attached to the surfaces of wooden objects.

Archaeological objects attributed to the

Historic horizon have frequently been reported from Guerrero. Especially useful in establishing the presence of materials from this horizon are certain types of pottery or vessel shapes which have been identified with historic peoples or whose distribution coincides with that of small tribal entities in Guerrero.

Aztec conquests into Guerrero in the 15th century, some of which led to the establishment of colonies or garrison sites, are well documented (Barlow, 1949c). Itzcoatl (1428–40), Montezuma I (1440–68), and Axayacatl (1469–81) extended Aztec domination into northern Guerrero as far as the Rio Balsas basin. The garrison site of Oztuma was probably established during the reign of Axayacatl. Ahuitzotl (1486–1502) expanded the area under Aztec influence south across the central Sierra Madre del Sur to the vicinity of Acapulco and up the Costa Grande to the mouth of the Rio Balsas, and established control over the area along the eastern border of the state. Archaeological evidence for most of these Aztec penetrations has been obtained. In northern Guerrero, from the vicinity of Teloloapan northward, Aztec Black-on-Orange pottery is commonly found (Lister, 1948, p. 121). Most of it is classified type IIIa and may be correlated with the conquests of Montezuma I in that area. A scattering of Aztec Black-on-Orange sherds occurs at sites in the middle Rio Balsas basin and south into the Yestla-Naranjo zone (Weitlaner, 1948a, p. 83) as well as along the Costa Grande (Brush and Brush, n.d.). These appear to be a consequence of the later conquests of Ahuitzotl. Aztec sherds are most abundant in northern Guerrero, an area under longer Aztec domination than were localities to the south, where such sherds are found with less frequency.

Weitlaner states that Cholula Polychrome, a relatively late ware abundantly distributed throughout the Puebla area, Tlaxcala, and the Valley of Mexico, is associated with Aztec pottery in the middle Rio

628

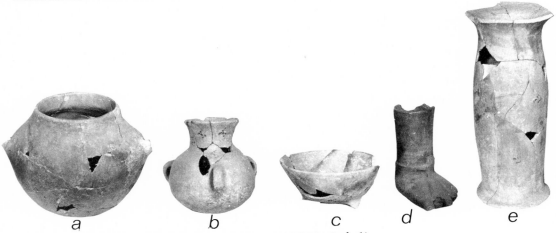

F<small>IG</small>. 6—POTTERY FROM PALOS ALTOS, GUERRERO. Scale ⅐.

Balsas basin and the Yestla-Naranjo zone (1948a, p. 83). He also mentions the finding of spindle whorls in the Yestla-Naranjo area which resemble Aztec forms typical of Aztec periods III–IV (p. 79). An Aztec period III clay figurine was collected at Teloloapan (Lister, 1948, p. 120).

Documentary materials tell of the conquest and colonization of regions along the Rio Balsas between Coyuca de Catalan and Ajuchitlan by Tarascans from 1370 to the time of the Spaniards (Brand, 1944). Archaeological excavations near Coyuca have produced evidence of this occupation in the form of pottery and clay pipes similar to those recovered from Tarascan sites in Michoacan to the northwest (Lister, 1947, p. 77).

The pottery complex furnishing evidence for Tarascan utilization of part of the Balsas basin includes Chandio White-on-Red, a type having simple, poorly executed designs in a chalky-white paint, vessels with teapot spouts, and vessels with hollow stirrup-shaped handles. Chandio White-on-Red and vessels with teapot spouts extend northward to the Tepalcatepec basin of Michoacan (Goggin, 1943, p. 51), and teapot spouts and stirrup handle appendages are present at the important Tarascan site of Tzintzuntzan (Moedano, 1941, p. 25).

Clay pipes found at Coyuca also are like specimens from Tzintzuntzan. They are elbow type with a flaring rimmed bowl, two nublike legs beneath the bowl, and either a thick cylindrical or a spirally twisted stem. White and red slips were applied to the stems, and some were decorated with incisions (Lister, 1947, p. 75; Moedano, 1941, p. 37).

Another type of pottery found in Guerrero may be attributed to the Matlatzinca. It occurs in the Valley of Toluca, Mexico (García Payón, 1941b, p. 277) and apparently extends into the mountainous area of northern Guerrero as far south as Iguala and Teloloapan (Barlow, 1948b, pp. 91–92; Lister, 1948, p. 108). Numerous whole vessels of this type have been collected. They usually are bowls or molcajetes supported by tall, hollow tripod legs resembling serpent heads. They are decorated with geometric, curvilinear, and occasionally naturalistic designs in maroon paint on a thick cream or white slip.

A polychrome pottery, with black added to the maroon-on-cream described above, has been collected near Teloloapan (Lister, 1948, p. 109). Vaillant (1934, p. 93) found similar sherds near Cuernavaca, and Noguera (1932, p. 17) identified it as Tlahuica pottery.

629

A black-on-white ware has been found in the eastern half of the middle Rio Balsas basin and southward into the Yestla-Naranjo zone. Its slip is so soft and weathers so easily that it appears to be fugitive, or unfired. Black geometric and curvilinear designs were painted on the white slip. Jars, bowls, and molcajetes frequently were placed on loop-shaped tripod supports (Lister, 1947, p. 73). The distribution of this ware is said to coincide with that of the old Tepuzteco area; the unusual loop- or ring-shaped legs are reported as similar to supports found on vessels in southern Veracruz, Nicaragua, and Costa Rica (Barlow, 1946c, p. 80). Several varieties of polychrome pottery from the Costa Grande, including some incised as well as painted, may belong to the Historic horizon.

An example of the tantalizing nature of many archaeological finds made in Guerrero is supplied by Bernal (1951), who examined a cave at Acapulco after it had been looted by treasure seekers. A few objects and fragmentary specimens overlooked by the diggers plus a small collection of objects recovered from the original finders illustrate the richness of the site. Objects from the cave, which Bernal believes to have been a repository for offerings rather than a burial place, included wooden masks with mosaic designs in turquoise and jade, a wooden shield with designs carved in low relief, over 100 copper bells, worked shell and stone, and a few potsherds. The only conclusion drawn after reviewing the scraps of evidence was that the materials are late and exhibit typological and stylistic similarities to items from the Mixteca (Bernal, 1951, p. 56).

To round out this synthesis, we note a variety of archaeological remains which either cannot be placed in any cultural or chronological framework with certainty or are of such generalized nature as to be nondiagnostic.

Archaeological sites are both numerous and diverse, ranging from sherd areas that mark the location of former villages whose habitations were built of perishable materials, to sites marked by mounds of stones or earth indicating more permanent houses, to localities featuring large complexes of stone-faced truncated pyramids which probably served as ceremonial centers, and to sites exhibiting groupings of both habitation and ceremonial structures. Hillsides adjacent to sites in or on the sides of narrow valleys and canyons sometimes are terraced, perhaps for agricultural purposes.

Ball courts and ball-court rings have been found in the middle Balsas basin and on the Costa Grande (Osborne, 1943, p. 62; Armillas, 1948, p. 75). Types of court are not identified.

Burial practices, according to limited excavation and local informants, were varied. Burials were placed in caves, in tombs (some masonry lined and supporting corbel-arched roofs), in simple graves adjacent to and within habitation and ceremonial centers, and beneath the floors of houses. Stone slabs, sometimes carved as at Placeres del Oro (Spinden, 1911, pp. 34–36), lay over and around burials at several localities. Inhumations were usually extended full length. Secondary urn burials and cremations are reported. Burial furnishings include pottery vessels, carved stone objects, and a variety of ornaments. Skulls from burials in the middle Balsas area reveal the practice of tooth mutilation by filing.

In addition to the complex of carved stone objects from the Mezcala area and other stone carvings previously discussed, sculptured stones have a widespread distribution in Guerrero. An interesting comparison has been made between the designs carved on slabs from Los Placeres del Oro and art motifs of the Chavin culture in Peru (Spinden, 1911, p. 34; Covarrubias, 1957, p. 113). Legless slab metates usually troughed but sometimes having flat grinding surfaces are common. Associated with them are small rectangular flat manos. Metates with tripod supports have been collected in the middle Rio Balsas basin. Mortars and pestles and stone bowls occur sporadically. Celts far outnumber axes, but both full-grooved and three-quarter-grooved axes occasionally are recovered. Stone ornaments such as beads, pendants, earspools, and labrets fashioned from various materials—obsidian, jadeite, alabaster, and onyx—are found. Among other items of stone from Guerrero are fiber beaters with grooves or crosshatched incisions on one or both sides, parallel-edged "prismatic" blades of obsidian, projectile points, leaf-shaped knives, and scrapers. Projectile points commonly were chipped from parallel-edged blades.

Identifiable pottery, fairly well described and of known distribution, has already been mentioned. I shall not attempt to list the numerous instances of other seemingly distinctive wares reported from various parts of the state. None are described in detail and most appear to have limited distributions. Other items of clay, which have a spotty distribution and which have not yet been discussed, include spindle whorls, miscellaneous figurines apparently rather important on the Costa Grande, masks, stamp seals, flutes, whistles, and rattles.

Shell bracelets and beads apparently are found throughout Guerrero. Needles, awls, and flaking tools of bone or antler are reported only in the coastal areas.

From the foregoing incomplete evidence a rough outline emerges, suggesting a long, complex culture history for Guerrero, but the synthesis is greatly oversimplified and full of gaps at the present writing. In an attempt to establish cultural relationships and the temporal positions of local developments it has been necessary to rely on diagnostic elements from surrounding better-known cultures said to be present in Guerrero.

REFERENCES

Armillas, 1942–44, 1948
Barlow, 1946c, 1948b, 1949c
Bernal, 1951
Brand, 1942, 1944
Brush and Brush, n.d.
Caso, 1941
Covarrubias, 1948, 1957
Drucker, Heizer, and Squier, 1959
Ekholm, 1948
Franco, 1960
García Payón, 1941a, 1941b
Goggin, 1943
Hendrichs Pérez, 1940, 1945

Lister, 1941, 1947, 1948, 1955
Marquina, 1951
Moedano K., 1941, 1942, 1948
Noguera, 1932
Osborne, 1943
Peterson, 1959
Piña Chan, R., 1955a, 1955b, 1960a
Spinden, H. J., 1911
Spratling, 1932
Vaillant and Vaillant, 1934
Weitlaner, 1948a
—— and Barlow, 1944

28. Ethnohistoric Synthesis of Western Mexico

DONALD D. BRAND

THE WESTERN MEXICO of "Mesoameri-can Culture," at the time that history may be said to have begun with the Spanish conquest, apparently was some-what less extensive than its archaeologic counterpart. The retraction of the frontier occurred in Sinaloa, Durango, Zacatecas, Aguascalientes, Jalisco, Guanajuato, and Queretaro. At the time of the conquest all of Queretaro, Guanajuato, and Aguascali-entes, as well as most of Zacatecas and Du-rango, and even parts of northern Michoa-can, were occupied by nonagricultural "Chichimec" and other non-Mesoamerican groups.

The beginning of the conquest period can be dated from the first Tarascan embassy to Cortés in the summer of 1521, but it is difficult to select a terminal date. The initial destructive contacts between Spaniards and Indians in our region took place between 1522 and 1531, but almost continuously thereafter until December of 1542 one area or another had to be "pacified," from the Motines of southern Michoacan to Sinaloa and Zacatecas. Even after the suppression of the Mixton or Great Rebellion in 1542, areas and pueblos "de guerra" continued to exist for some 10 to 30 years in western Jalisco and southern Sinaloa. Probably no great vio-lence will be done to reality if we consider that the conquest period in western Mexico terminated in 1565, which approximates the date of the reconquest of southern Sina-loa by Ibarra. We are not concerned with the Chichimec Wars (about 1550–90), or even with the revolts, pacifications, and con-quests that went on in the mountain and barranca country until the Acaxee were sub-dued in 1603, the Xixime in 1611, the Tepe-huán in 1618, and the Indians of Nayarit in 1724. Although these hostilities affected the Mesoamerican Indians of western Mexico somewhat, the Indian groups and the areas mainly involved were peripheral.

This ethnohistoric synthesis will attempt to identify, locate, and describe the more important ethnic groups or units as they were at the time of initial contact with Europeans, as they seem to have been short-ly before this contact and conquest, and as they were at the end of the conquest period.

For this it will be necessary to outline the routes and chronology of the conquest, and to describe briefly the location of some settlements and missions and the comprehension of certain civil-military-judicial and ecclesiastic administrative units. These items constitute the minimal bases or data points for the determination of the location of ethnic groups and their frontiers. Although many of the "facts" of such material are highly debatable, this brief article can be only summary and dogmatic.

Of the utmost importance are the evaluation and critical selection of the written sources that are available. No use is made of archaeological data. Reliance is placed primarily on approximately contemporary records: accounts by participants, dated documents, and historical summaries, all written within the period 1521–65. Some use is made of later materials of four categories: (1) written by participants but at some later time, e.g., some 20 or more years later as in Castañeda (in Winship, 1896) or Obregón (Hammond and Rey, 1928); (2) written or dictated by participants or witnesses who usually were mere children at the time, e.g., some of the *Relaciones Geográficas del Siglo Dieciseis* (Appendix A); (3) presumably written during the conquest period as defined, but available now only as quoted, abstracted, or reproduced in later works, e.g., most accounts of early missionary activity, and various items in the historical works by Tello (1891) and by Beaumont (1932); and (4) certain regional descriptions and *visitas* into the 17th century for supplementary data on place names and languages, e.g., Ponce (1872) and Ruiz Colmenero (in León, 1903a). The third kind of "late" source is the one that has been most used although at the same time the most erroneous. The inaccuracies and deficiencies of "folk memory" and the rapid acculturation by both European and extra-regional Amerindian influences have made suspect ethnographic data from either the second or the third "late" source. Perhaps most useful from such sources are linguistic data, but even these should be accepted only when they confirm or amplify contemporary data from the conquest period.

Most of the above-mentioned sources were written by Europeans or represent the European point of view, with the principal exceptions of parts of the *Relaciones Geográficas* and certain items reproduced in Tello and Beaumont. For other Indian accounts of the Spanish conquest there are the *Relación de Michoacán* and the *Lienzo de Tlaxcala*, and very little else. However, on the preconquest situation, especially in Michoacan, and relationships between the Tarascans and Mexicans there is a considerable and highly controversial literature (Appendix B).

Normally, whether for ethnology or history, the best approach is a positive and constructive one consisting of an exposition or narration of facts. Unfortunately, for the ethnohistory of western Mexico we are practically forced to begin in a negative and destructive fashion. This is due primarily to three factors: (1) The eastern or Tarascan part of western Mexico was conquered by the Spaniards out of a base in the Tlaxcalan highlands–Valley of Mexico region, with the consequent use of Nahuatlan-speaking allies, interpreters, and servants (who for the most part represented enemies of the Tarascans). (2) The western or Nueva Galician and Nueva Vizcayan part of western Mexico, as well as the southern and western parts of greater Michoacan, had such a great variety of languages that the religious made practically no attempt to learn the local languages but forced the Indians to learn the Mexicano (Nahuatl) which was the first and usually the only Indian language learned by the missionaries in the convents, colleges, and seminaries of the Mexico-Tlaxcala base area. (3) Although the Nahuatlans of the Valley of Mexico region had such 16th-century writers as Motolinia, Sahagún, Mendieta, Durán, and Torquemada who

633

were interested in the history and prehistory of these Indians, there was scarcely a single 16th-century historian of or protagonist for the Indians of western Mexico, with the exception of the anonymous Franciscan compiler of the Relación de Michoacán. Only with the 17th-century Tello for Nueva Galicia and the 18th-century Beaumont for Michoacan do we find chroniclers with a genuine interest in local Indian prehistory.

The historical consequences of these factors have been disastrous for our area. The Tarascan state and culture have been downgraded to an incredible extent as against the so-called "Aztec" state or Tripart Confederacy and its culture and might. This is somewhat understandable if we remember the picture painted of Carthage versus Rome by the historians of antiquity, and then further recall that there was no Carthaginian historian—only Romans and their Greek friends and servants. Even though the Tarascans had no publicized historian-defender, we can glean from the passing remarks of Spanish soldiers and missionaries that many considered the Tarascan monarch second in power and pomp only to Moctezuma of the Mexicans in all of New Spain, and a few ranked them as equals. Frequently these same persons went on to remark that the Lord of Michoacan was richer in gold and silver. Many of the missionaries who had served among both Nahuatlans and Tarascans considered that the Tarascans were superior to all other peoples in New Spain in appearance, intelligence, industry, and in beauty of language, which was likened to the Greek. Of possibly greater importance is that both Mexican and Tarascan sources seem to agree that whenever the Mexicans waged war against the Tarascans, the Mexicans were decisively defeated. This brings to mind the charge occasionally made that although the Tarascans fought well against the Mexicans, it was always defensively and in Tarascan territory. Several of the Relaciones Geográficas indicate that the Mexicans were on the defensive against the Tarascans along a considerable stretch of their frontier anchored on the fortress of Ostumba and that the Spanish conquest may have saved the Mexicans the embarrassment of a considerable loss of territory in that region.

One of the most aggravating items that one encounters in reading the historical and ethnological literature of the past 350 years is the assumption that the numerous and widespread Nahuatlan place names are native, and that most of the Indians of western Mexico (with the exception of the Tarascans and a few Otomi and Chichimec) spoke either Mexicano (Nahuatl) or a related language that was scarcely more than a regional dialect. Many authors, from the 17th century to the present, have attributed the Nahuatlan or pseudo-Nahuatlan names either to a great Mexican empire that extended without break into the northwest as far as Sinaloa and Zacatecas, or to the influence of various peoples of the Mexican migration myth in their supposed peregrinations across these lands, or to a combination of the two. It is saddening to think of the hundreds of hours spent by scholars such as Buelna (1892) in locating, identifying, and explaining "Aztec" or "Mexicano" place names and points along the legendary migration routes. It is even more depressing to discover that currently local historians, ethnologists, archaeologists, and geographers in Mexico are accepting the conclusions and work of Buelna and his kind as gospel truth to be applied in many connections. Apparently, from Colima and Jalisco to Sinaloa and Durango, if the local investigators go back earlier than Buelna and the Valley of Mexico school of interpreters of the Mexican migration myth, they go only to Tello and seldom or never examine the 16th century accounts. Later, in a discussion of languages and place names, these matters will be considered in some detail.

For reasons that are not clear, the most commonly used "primary" source for the history of western Mexico, from Jalisco to

ETHNOHISTORY OF WESTERN MEXICO

Sinaloa, has been the Spanish Franciscan Tello, who came to New Spain in 1619. Such 18th-century writers as Mota Padilla, Ornelas, Torres, and Beaumont followed Tello rather blindly for the history of the first century of Spanish occupation of the region. Then M. Orozco y Berra, J. H. Romero Gil, E. Mendoza, and I. Navarrete resurrected Tello in secondary forms which culminated in the publication of part of the original Tello in 1891. In the next 30-odd years, such writers as A. Santoscoy, L. Diguet, M. Galindo, and even the scholarly J. I. P. Dávila Garibi used the fuel in Tello to fire their imaginations. The net result, from Tello to J. López-Portillo y Weber, has been an authoritarian pyramiding, each writer contributing some new ornament until the resultant edifice is an historical monstrosity of almost pure fiction accepted as absolutely demonstrated fact. This influence of Tello has been so great that I have felt forced to discuss him and his work at some length in Appendix B.

One of these items that has developed from the Tello school has been an almost completely false native political geography, as of the time of the conquest, which is incorporated in nearly every textbook of the history or geography of western Mexico. This consists of a Chimalhuacan Confederacy (proposed first by I. Navarrete and A. Santoscoy, then developed by L. Diguet and others) comprising several large kingdoms or *hueytlatoanazgos* ruled by kings or great lords, together with a varying number of independent or quasi-independent lesser lordships or *tlatoanazgos*, each ruled by a *tlatoani*. This political system contradicts the records of the conquest. The contemporary accounts used such terms as *señor*, *cacique*, *principal*, *gobernador*, and *capitán* for the Indian "rulers" and leaders, but never *rey* (excepting occasionally for the Tarascan ruler) or the Mexican *tlatoani* in any form. It is most interesting, incidentally, that no matter what the local language may have been at the time of the conquest,

essentially all persons, places, and political entities are given Nahuatlan names. As will be brought out later, there were scores of little groups of villages termed *señoríos*, or *cacicazgos*, or *provincias*, but never a *tlatoanazgo* or *reino* (excepting Michoacan).

Now we are ready for a brief listing of the more important errors to be rectified and problems to be recognized and solved if possible. The empire of the Culhua Mexica or "Aztecs" did not reach Colima or even the lower Balsas-Zacatula river. Where was the Tarascan-Mexican marchland, and why did the Spaniards set up a greater province and diocese of Michoacan which included all of Zacatula and the Tierra Caliente of the Balsas? There were no kingdoms or advanced political structures west of the Tarascans. How far had Tarascan conquests extended west and south, and what were their relationships to the native political entities in the fringe lands that later constituted Colima, the Pueblos del Marques, and the Pueblos de Avalos? How did the insignificant village of Jalisco become converted into a presumably great lordship, and how did its name become attached to such a large area? The belief in an "Aztec Empire" and a long arm of Mexicano speech that reached northwest into Sinaloa grew out of an unquestioning acceptance of Clavijero and Orozco y Berra. What were the factors that led the missionaries and bishops to urge and accomplish a Mexicanization of western Mexico, the aftermath of which Nahuatlismo was the grafting of an alien mythology on the prehistory of the local peoples? What were the languages actually spoken at the time of the conquest, and what were their relationships? Finally, since so many of the details of ethnology come from accounts written between 60 and 120 years after the initiation of Spanish-Mexican contacts, how much of such material can be accepted?

CONQUEST

Western Mexico was conquered by the

635

Spaniards in three successive periods. Hernán Cortés, through his lieutenants, explored, conquered, and occupied essentially all southwest Mexico south of the Lerma–Rio Grande de Santiago between 1521 and 1528, most of this becoming part of New Spain proper. Under the personal direction of Nuño de Guzmán, between 1530 and 1536 the Spaniards conquered new lands north of the Rio Grande, and ultimately made good a claim to the reconquest of lands in what is today western Jalisco and southern Nayarit. These lands constituted Nueva Galicia. Under the first viceroy, Antonio de Mendoza, 1535–50, there were scattered rebellions and the ultimate definitive pacification of most of the southern portion of our region. The third period was that of the reconquest and pacification of parts of what are now the states of Sinaloa and Durango by Francisco de Ibarra in the 1560s, and these areas became parts of Nueva Vizcaya.

Cortés undoubtedly first heard of the Tarascan or Michoacan kingdom from the Mexicans. He received further information from a Tarascan embassy, apparently shortly after the fall of Tenochtitlan in August of 1521, and also from an exploring party led by Rodrigo Alvarez Chico which had reached the mouth of the Rio Zacatula (Balsas). Here we are plagued with vagueness and apparent contradiction in the few and brief available accounts, from the Third and Fourth Letters of Cortés (1877), through the Relación de Michoacán (1903), to the writings of the official chronicler Herrera y Tordesillas (1934), who used documents no longer available. The reconstruction of the exact chronology, routes, and personalities involved in the conquest has varied greatly according to personal loyalties, documents available, and the background and historical attitude of the writers. In general, I believe that Toussaint (1942, pp. 11–20, 221–22) and Sauer (1948, pp. 1–9) have made the best reconstructions of what took place. However, I must dis-

agree about many assumptions and details, such as the question of Mexican control of the Costa Grande from Acapulco to Zacatula, the routing of Alvarez Chico to Zacatula via Acapulco, etc. (See in part, Brand, 1944, pp. 39–48; 1960, pp. 54–66.)

Apparently the first Spaniard to reach the threshold of Michoacan proper arrived at Tajimaroa (Ciudad Hidalgo) in February, 1522. In the spring of 1522 a small group of Spaniards led by Francisco Montaño reached the capital city of Michoacan (Tzintzuntzan), and then, on instructions from Cortés to search for the reported land of the Amazons, proceeded with an army of Tarascan allies toward Colima. However, the native opposition was so strong (we do not know how far Montaño's party or the Tarascan vanguard reached) that the Spaniards returned shortly to the Valley of Mexico. Then came the definitive conquest or rather occupation of the lands of the Tarascan state by some 270 Spaniards led by Cristóbal de Olid, July to November, 1522. Essentially all sources, including Cortés (1877, p. 97), the piteous statement of the Tarascan king on his death pyre (Fourth Anonymous, p. 100), and the Relación de Michoacán (1903, pp. 93–103), are agreed that the Tarascan ruler submitted peacefully and that there were no battles or even scrimmages between the Tarascans and the Spaniards. Nevertheless, there has developed a literary tradition, enshrined in textbooks of Michoacan history, that there were several bloody battles beginning at Tajimaroa, and that the elder statesman and warrior, Timas, for some time carried on courageous warfare against the Spaniards. In Michoacan, cinemas, boats, streets, and even children have been named for the heroes of this synthetic Tarascan epic to which Eduardo Ruiz contributed so largely, and which shows up as recently as in Romero Flores (1946, 1: 73–84).

At the time of the Spanish conquest the Tarascan state had become a centralized kingdom to which were attached, by alliance or conquest, tributary and buffer areas on all the frontiers. It was necessary only to obtain the submission of the Tarascan king, and all the Tarascan lands surrendered peacefully. Overawed by the Spanish conquest of the Mexicans and the destruction of Tenochtitlan, the Tarascans yielded without a struggle. Actually, submission was volunteered, a fact noted by Spanish records, the Relación de Michoacán, and several of the Relaciones Geográficas. Unfortunately relaciones are lacking for several critical areas (e.g., Sayula, Colima, Jacona); some relaciones merely state that they paid allegiance to the Tarascan ruler and that they were conquered at the time of the general conquest of Nueva España by Cortés (e.g., Coalcoman), or that they were not conquered but submitted peacefully to Cortés (e.g., Tepalcatepec in Relación de Tancitaro, pp. 222–23); frequently there may be no specific statement on the subject.

Although Cristóbal de Olid is specifically mentioned in a number of relaciones (e.g., Jiquilpan, Periban, Chilchota, Tamazula), we cannot be certain that Olid in person received the submission. Furthermore, other individuals are mentioned specifically as having been sent out from the Tarascan capital by Cortés, as in the Relaciones de Zirandaro and Tancitaro. All this would seem to indicate that Olid and other Spaniards traveled widely over the Tarascan realm during July-November, 1522, and peacefully accepted submission of the principal villages and provinces in the names of the Spanish king and Hernán Cortés. It is indicated that individual Spaniards or parties fanned out from the Lake Patzcuaro area. We are not certain of the exact route followed by the Spaniards from Tajimaroa to Tzintzuntzan, whether it went circuitously around the Cerro de San Andres (the highest mountain in Michoacan) via Maravatio and Ucareo, or more directly to Zinape-cuaro via a line southwest of the mountain, and then on by way of Indaparapeo and Charo (Appendix C).

It would seem that the peacefully occupied Tarascan region extended from approximately the Rio Lerma on the north (in the vicinity of Puruandiro, Yuririapundaro, Acambaro, and Maravatio) into the Sierra Madre del Sur of Guerrero and Michoacan on the south. At the east the peaceful occupation presumably began with the marchlands protected by Tarascan forts and garrisons and by the settlements of allied Matlatzinca and Mazahua, and tributary Chontal and Cuitlatec, as in the areas of Tlalpujahua, Tuzantla, and Tlalchapa. So far as I know, there is no mention in a contemporary document or in any Relación Geográfica of any scrimmage or the slightest resistance to the Spaniards in this eastern march and buffer zone.

The picture is quite obscure on the western and southern fringes of the Tarascan realm. The lack of the Tlazazalca, Jacona-Zamora, and Sayula–Pueblos de Avalos relaciones is quite critical for the northwest and west. Whatever may have been the earlier and more westerly boundary of the Tarascan dominion, by 1522 the Tarascans apparently had lost control of part of the Lake Chapala area and all the lands west of a line drawn from Cocula through Tuxpan in Jalisco. The Poncitlan relación (p. 235) has the people of Cuitzeo fighting the Tarascans, and the people of Jamay at war with Ixtlan, north of Zamora. Because the Jiquilpan-Periban zone and the villages of the Tamazula-Tuxpan area (the erstwhile Pueblos del Marques) were tributary to the Tarascan ruler and surrendered to Olid without any recorded struggle, we assume that at least this far west the Pax Tarascana obtained. As the Cocula-Sayula area was conquered by the Tarascans one or more times, and as there is absolutely no contemporary record of armed Spanish conquest of this region, which in less than a decade became known as the Pueblos de Avalos from the name of the encomendero family, it is possible that this area also was part of the peacefully surrendered Tarascan realm.

South of the Sierra Madre del Sur, in the regions that became known as the Zacatula and Colima provinces, the Spaniards had to use force on several occasions. The Mexicans had briefly held part of eastern Zacatula in the Costa Grande of Guerrero (possibly from Coyuca as far west as Jolochuca and Petatlan), but they obviously had no dominion over these coastlands at the time of the Spanish conquest. The Tarascans, who also had briefly held part of the Zacatula coast, by 1521 had withdrawn into the Sierra Madre del Sur (the country south of Ajuchitlan, Guaymeo, Tumbiscatio, etc.) and apparently were exercising sovereignty over only that part of the coast of Michoacan south from Coalcoman.

There is no direct contemporary evidence as to how Alvarez Chico and his companion (the first Spaniards to reach the coast of western Guerrero and southern Michoacan) reached the sea at the Zacatula mouth. It was obviously neither through the land of the hostile Yope, who held Acapulco and the northern approaches to Acapulco, nor through Michoacan proper, since no Spanish contact was recorded until later. Sauer (1948, pp. 3–4, 9–10) proposes a route via Acapulco because the "Aztecs" controlled the Acapulco-Zacatula route—an assumption contrary to the evidence—and then supports this by having Cortés (1877, pp. 101–02) use the term "pacify" to imply an earlier conquest of or passage through the Acapulco-Zacatula region; actually Cortés says rather that war was waged and that the Spanish party "no pudo dejarla del todo conquistada" (speaking of the Yope area). Cortés goes on later to speak of pacifying, but the statement applies to the region between Zacatula and Colima (Cortés, 1877, p. 102; Brand, 1960, pp. 57–58). Here indeed Spaniards had been before.

The only safe assumption about the route of Alvarez Chico is that it lay somewhere between the Michoacan highlands and the Yope country. Most likely the route led down the basin of the Balsas-Zacatula River, possibly via Pilcaya, Ixcateopan, San Miguel Totolapan, Patambo or Guayameo, and on southwest over a relatively low sector of the Sierra Madre del Sur to Zacatula. I have been over most of this route by trails on foot and horseback, and I found it quite traversable. Another point to be considered in connection with the exploring party of Alvarez Chico is that they were supposed to reach the South Sea and to locate possible ports and areas for shipyards. If this party had actually been to or near Acapulco (which within some 10 years became a port and shipbuilding area), it does not seem reasonable that they would not have reported it to Cortés, who mentions nothing of the sort in his Letters.

In addition to the search for port sites on the South Sea, there was the lure of the gold and pearls and women of the legendary land of the Amazons which early made itself apparent. One of the Nahuatl names for the west was Cihuatlampa. No matter what this term may actually have meant to the Mexicans, it became Land of the Amazons for the Spaniards, as exemplified in the orders given Montaño in 1522 to push on westward from Michoacan in "busca de las amazonas" (Montaño in Toussaint, 1942, pp. 12–13). It is possible that there was some specific and important place or area known as "Place of Women" which the Nahuatlans called "Cihuatlan" directly or by translation from another language. Perhaps this was the general region from Colima and Jalisco into Sinaloa, where there seemed to be an unusually large number of cacicas or women rulers of villages, but the records would indicate that there were not more than five or six such cacicas encountered by the Spaniards. Nevertheless, although there were a number of places known as Cihuatlan elsewhere in Mexico (as in Guerrero and Michoacan), the Spanish search for Cihuatlan began with the lands west of Michoacan. The first one reached was on the border of modern Colima and Jalisco—the lower river Cihuatlan (Marabasco). The last and most disillusioning was in central Sinaloa—the lower river San Lorenzo.

The conquest of what is today Colima and southwestern Michoacan came partly from the search for seaports and Amazons and partly from reports of Indian communities with treasure of gold and silver. We need not consider the details here as the contradictory accounts of routes, personalities, and chronology in general agree that: (1) preparations for shipbuilding were begun near the mouth of the Zacatula in the spring of 1522 where a Spanish villa was founded in early 1523; and (2) Gonzalo de Sandoval pacified and conquered western Zacatula and Colima in the spring and summer of 1523 and founded a Spanish villa in Colima about September 22, 1523. Sauer has done an excellent job of outlining the events in this area (1948, pp. 9–17; also see Brand, 1960, pp. 56–63).

Despite the lack of 16th-century documentary backing or justification, a commonly accepted "history" of the conquest of the Colima area pictures a courageous prolonged defense of a Kingdom of Colima which involved several bloody defeats of the Spaniards at the hands of Teco Indians led by various named individuals. Apparently almost all this historical fabric is a tissue of inventions, chiefly of the 19th and 20th centuries. Lebrón de Quiñones (1945, pp. 118–19), only some 30 years after the conquest, insisted that not a single village in Colima and the adjacent provinces offered any resistance to the Spaniards with the exception of Tecoman on one or two occasions.

The idea of a great Colima state or kingdom apparently had its origin in a small unit in the southwest corner of the Tarascan "empire" of the 15th century which managed to become independent. Seemingly the local peoples or their chieftains had learned enough from the Tarascans to emulate the Tarascan military state on a small scale. This state or lordship occupied but a fraction of the modern tiny state of Colima. However, it did possess some of the best resources in the region, and here the Spaniards erected their march capital which became known as Colima. As the Spaniards explored and conquered out from this center, and as *vecinos* of Colima became encomenderos over a considerable region from the Rio Cachan in modern coastal Michoacan northwestward to the Rio Grande de Santiago in modern Jalisco and Nayarit, all the many little individual villages, and groups of villages, came under the jurisdiction of the Villa de Colima. Thus there came into being a "Greater Colima," which led later writers to assume a great native state or kingdom of Colima.

One further chapter in the conquest of "Colima" needs to be mentioned here. This is the nine-month *entrada* of exploration and conquest in 1524–25 led by Francisco Cortés at the command of his cousin, Hernán Cortés, to search northwest up the coast for good seaports and the land of the Amazons. The route out led through the more populous better-fed areas, from Cihuatlan (on the modern Colima-Jalisco border) north to Etzatlan and then northwest to Jalisco village and the Rio Grande de Santiago. The return trip was down the coast as ordered, to locate any usable ports.

Because no contemporary relación exists of this entrada, because of the obvious inventions of later writers, and because there is no record of encomiendas on the coast resulting from this entrada, a number of modern critical writers have assumed that Francisco Cortés probably turned inland at the Valle de Banderas (lower Ameca River valley). This is possible but not probable. When Nuño de Guzmán entered this region in 1530–36, there already existed such regional names as Tierra de los Frailes

639

ó Coronados (the warlike tonsured Indians of the region southeast of the Bahia de Banderas) and the river and village of Pascua (modern Tomatlan). Probably most of the conquistadores with Francisco Cortés believed that they could obtain encomiendas with more productive lands, not so warlike Indians, and not on the most distant frontier of New Spain. As it turned out later, although Nuño de Guzmán was able to claim western Jalisco and southern Nayarit for his Nueva Galicia through reconquest and occupation, parts of the Jaliscan coastlands remained "unpacified" into the 1550s. One of the most important byproducts of the Francisco Cortés conquest was what is almost certainly the earliest visita and census of a conquered area that we possess for New Spain which was made in 1525 (Visitación . . ., 1937, pp. 556–72).

The second period of conquest in our area was the highly publicized conquests of 1530–36 which resulted in the establishment of Nueva Galicia. This is perhaps the best documented of any of the entradas in Mexico because of (1) the letters that Nuño de Guzmán wrote to justify himself and his position as the conqueror of a new realm and government; (2) the investigation of Guzmán's execution of the Tarascan ruler and the disposition made of the *cazonci*'s presumptive wealth; and (3) the later investigation of his bloody conquest of Nueva Galicia, treatment of the Indians, and encroachment on the lands of Hernán Cortés and of the government of New Spain. Furthermore, most of this information is readily available in a few references (Carrera Stampa, 1955; Colección de documentos inéditos, 1864–84, vols. 13, 14, 15; García Icazbalceta, 1858–66, vol. 2). It is an interesting note that the highly informative letter of July 8, 1530, by Guzmán from Omitlan (Nayarit) was published as early as 1556 by Ramusio and as recently as in a Guadalajara series of Guzmán reprints beginning in 1960.

Most of the route and chronology of the Guzmán entrada can be traced quite accurately. An army of 300 Spaniards, 7000 or more Indian allies, and some 10,000 pigs and sheep for food left Mexico City near the end of December, 1529. After going via Ixtlahuaca to Tzintzuntzan, the invasion of new lands commenced with the fording of the Rio Lerma northwest of Puruandiro on February 2, 1530. Here begin the ethnographic notes, casual but so useful, that characterize the cartas and relaciones of the Guzmán expedition—such as that the Indians in the vicinity of the ford were peaceful but nonagricultural. Despite frequent modern routings of the expedition up to Guanajuato, Guzmán is explicit that they went six days through an unpopulated area, the first three days down along the river and then over to Cuinao. The route probably went through or near modern Ayo to Tototlan (without question the Cuinao of the conquest). Using Cuinao-Tototlan as camp headquarters, the main army went on as far as Cuinacuaro (Zapotlanejo), whence minor parties explored the right-bank valleys of the Rio Grande as far as near modern Cuquio. After reassembling at Cuinao, the entire force advanced on Cuitzeo, where one of the four great battles of the entire entrada was fought. After a few days of reconnaissance from Chapala to the La Barca area, the army went on to Tonala. Contrary to much loose writing, there is no evidence that any of Guzmán's parties went as far as the south side or the west side of Lake Chapala. Guzmán would not have bothered to do so since he was well aware that all that land was definitely conquered and already in encomiendas.

The second great battle of the entrada was fought in the vicinity of Tonala. Here the army stayed for about two weeks. The actual records show that Tonala was not the sumptuous capital of a great kingdom ruled by a glamorous queen, but rather the chief town of a small group of villages whose ruler was an old woman who pacified the Spaniards with a feast of turkeys and chickens. The presence of chickens in Tonala in 1530 is not surprising when we realize that Spaniards had been in possession of villages less than 25 miles away for more than six years.

On March 26, 1530, most of the army left Tonala and advanced by short marches (as all the *jornadas* were, perforce) across the barranca of the Rio Grande and via Tacotlan, Contla, and Yahualica to Nochistlan (in Zacatecas). Some three weeks, including Holy Week, were spent in Nochistlan, and in sending out scouting parties. Then the entire force moved on to Teul, whose sacrificial temple was imposing, but there was little food in the area. Here the army divided, and Chirinos led the group that made an almost incredible march pretty much due west to Tepic in 17 days. The Chirinos group lost some horses and most of their pigs, but they reached Tepic ahead of Guzmán, who had turned south across the Rio Grande with most of the army.

Immediately after crossing the river near Tequila, Guzmán was in country that had been conquered by Francisco Cortés. In fact, after Etzatlan, some of the villages were referred to as having submitted to Cortés peacefully. The route led through Ahuacatlan and Tetitlan and then through the volcanic "despoblado" to come out in the valley of Tepic.

Here it should be noted that when Francisco Cortés passed through this country, he reached Jalisco village before Tepic and as a consequence stayed in Jalisco. Presumably when his men returned to Colima and Mexico they referred to this Tepic valley area in terms of the Jalisco village. Chirinos arrived in this area before Guzmán, and his route brought him to Tepic before Jalisco. Consequently, Chirinos and later the entire army encamped in the vicinity of Tepic. The upshot was that Tepic was considered by Guzmán to be a superior place to Jalisco, and here was where ultimately Espiritu Santo–Compostela was founded. It should be added that

apparently both Tepic and Jalisco were independent villages, and that neither had a large tributary area. Furthermore, Tepic seemed to have had both a larger population and better lands and site than did Jalisco. All this is of interest because the earlier publicity given to the village of Jalisco had fastened the name of Jalisco on the valley of Tepic, and later the concept of a province of Jalisco became so widely accepted that the name Jalisco outlasted both Nueva Galicia and Guadalajara as the name for the largest political entity of the region today. In this connection it should be stated that no evidence shows that there was ever a Jaliscan state or lordship or native province which extended past the immediate vicinity of this village. It is doubtful that even nearby Tepic ever was subject to Jalisco.

Some three weeks were spent with Tepic as the headquarters. In this time the surrounding region was scouted to the sea, in the Zacualpan–San Blas sector, and to a ford of the Rio Grande in the wet lowlands of the Tierra Caliente to the north. On Pentecost Sunday the Rio Grande was forded, and the third great battle of the conquest was fought. Here again Guzmán was in new unconquered lands, north of the Rio Grande. The army advanced to a camp at Omitlan on the banks of the San Pedro River to recuperate and to await reinforcements from Mexico. Here in the lowland region of less physical diversity and more linguistic homogeneity than had obtained in so much of the country crossed previously, Guzmán encountered the first decent sizable province or political entity since leaving Michoacan. This province went by many names in the different languages of the natives, guides, and allies, but Guzmán called it Michoacan. It is today the Sentispac-Santiago–Ixcuintla-Tuxpan-Ruiz region of Nayarit.

Some six weeks were spent in the Omitlan-Sentispac region, during which time the rainy season got under way. It was de-

641

cided to move on to the Aztatlan-Tecuala area on the Acaponeta River to make "winter camp" over the rainy season. Here disaster struck in the form of a tropical cyclone in September. The resultant flood washed most of their food away, and the consequent famine and disease decimated Guzmán's forces and worse. As a consequence of this ill fortune, Guzmán and his aides embarked on the most appalling of their mistreatments of the natives—both allies (amigos) and recently conquered or submitted peoples. Slave workers and impressed allies were brought in from as far away as the Tuxpan to Lake Chapala country (Pueblos del Marques and Pueblos de Avalos), and more especially from Ahuacatlan, Jalisco, and Zacualpan in Nayarit. I mention these because most of the survivors (along with the few original Mexican and Tarascan "amigos" who survived the next 12 months) became the nuclei of the Otomi, Mexican, and other "foreign" settlements or colonies that became established in the state of Sinaloa.

Ultimately camp was transferred toward the end of the year 1530 to the banks of the Chametla (Baluarte) River. After about a two months' wait the labor reinforcements arrived, and the conquest was continued. The route consistently stayed away from the immediate coast and followed along what might be called a foothill route. After leaving Chametla the Spaniards had constant difficulty in finding even barely adequate interpreters, and most of the villages were unfriendly or abandoned. Because of unreliable interpretation and also some wishful thinking, briefly it was believed that they were finally at the land of the Amazons when they reached a village and valley whose name was interpreted to be Ciguatlan. Thence by a circuitous route the Valley of Culiacan was entered and conquered after several skirmishes and the fourth and last great battle of the entrada. Here effectively ended the Guzmán conquest of Nueva Galicia, although expeditions went north

into Sonora and east into the plains of Durango. However, in both directions quite barbarous peoples of inferior culture were encountered—to the north between the Mocorito and Sinaloa rivers, and eastward among the cannibals of the mountains and the nomadic Chichimec of the plains.

After founding the Villa de San Miguel on the San Lorenzo River in September, 1531, Guzmán turned back and founded other Spanish towns at Tepic-Compostela, Nochistlan-Guadalajara, Espiritu Santo–Chametla, and Purificacion in the next two or three years. Thus a Spanish dominance was implanted upon the land, but the native population had been reduced to a very large extent. It probably will be impossible to get much agreement among students of the matter as to the native population of Nueva Galicia in January, 1530, and how much it had been reduced by January, 1532. Without going into details, I would estimate the total 1530 population to have been considerably greater than the present rural population. Contrary to the general history elsewhere in the conquest of Mexico, the great reduction in population in Nueva Galicia was due not so much to diseases introduced by Europeans or induced by changes in manner of living (diet, clothing, and work), but rather to wanton destruction of houses, granaries, fields in cultivation, and the people themselves. The blame attaches primarily to the Spaniards who led the enterprise, but a large share must be placed on the native allies, especially the Mexicans (in the wide sense including the Tlaxcaltecans and all others of Nahuatl speech). This was in a sense, as has been said before, the last conquest made by the Mexicans and Tarascans.

The period of rebellions is neither one that should be considered a conquest period nor one that can be defined or limited precisely in time. There were individuals here, families there, and whole villages in another place who did not submit to the initial Spanish conquest or entrada. Some of these people took refuge in mountainous areas, and were not "pacified" until one or another of the congregations when some priest or civil officer would persuade them to come down into a valley or more accessible area. This took place on a minor scale in the Sierra Madre de Coalcoman in southern Michoacan, and on a very large scale in western Jalisco and in Nayarit and on the Durango-Sinaloa border. In addition there was a smoldering resentment linked with a refusal to accept the invulnerability of the Spaniards on the part of many of the Indians in those areas where they had not become accustomed to rather blind acceptance of authority. This meant that from the Sierra Madre del Sur in Michoacan and Guerrero to the mountains, barrancas and peñoles of Jalisco, Zacatecas, and Nayarit there were many pueblos "de guerra" or simply not providing the Crown or the encomendero with tribute and services.

Of course, it is suspected that in a number of instances Indians were provoked into the display of some kind of insubordination so as to give at least some slight justification for waging "war" and making slaves of the Indians. It is believed that the so-called pacification of the Motines in Colima and Zacatula was this sort of thing in the 1520s, and the same was probably true in parts of southern Nayarit in the 1530s. Although many history books would imply that the end of the Mixton or Great Rebellion in December, 1542, was the end of the last armed rebellion in New Spain, this was not so, as I mentioned at the outset of this article, because of the series of rebellions that had their foci among nominally settled agricultural peoples in the Sierra Madre Occidental. That, however, is not part of our account.

There remains to be mentioned the pacification or reconquest of southern Sinaloa by Francisco de Ibarra in 1564. Scarcely any of the mountain and foothill country from the Humaya to the Rio Grande had really been conquered as of 1563. This was

especially true where the mountains approached the sea and left very little coastal plain or lowlands in southern Sinaloa and northwestern Nayarit. This had become a sort of "gauntlet" which peaceful people ran when moving between Tepic in the south and Culiacan in the north. Ibarra came down out of Durango via Topia to Culiacan early in 1564. Then, after a sortie into the Sinaloa River country, he moved into the old Chametla-Quezala country and put a stop to the cannibal depredations of the coast. As a result the semicannibalistic people from the mountain country between the San Lorenzo and Piastla rivers also became quiet. With this we can consider that the Mesoamerican part of western Mexico had been conquered and pacified.

POLITICAL GEOGRAPHY

One of the most important elements in an ethnohistorical reconstruction is the nature and extent of the governmental units. The sources are essentially the same as for the history of the conquest. We start with the Tarascan kingdom or lordship which had a common boundary, or rather a march or frontier zone, with the lands of the Tripart Confederacy (Triple Alliance of Culhua Mexica, Aztec Empire, Mexicans) from about southern Queretaro into the Sierra Madre del Sur in Guerrero, to a point somewhat west of the Cerro de Teotepec (the highest in Guerrero) and approximately on a line between Ajuchitlan and Tecpan.

We cannot be certain of the location of the boundary or march in this area since there seems to be no relación extant for the corregimiento known by the Tarascan name Xanimeo and the Mexicano name Capulalcolulco (Suma de Visitas, 1905, p. 303; Papeles de Nueva España [PNE], 6: 127, 132; 7 Sup. Vargas Rea, 1946, pp. 23, 26). The available evidence indicates that Capulalcolulco (which was under Mexican control) was in the middle sector of the Arroyo or Rio Tehuehuetla, which flows into the Rio Balsas near Ajuchitlan. It is of considerable interest that Capulalcolulco is stated to be in Zacatula even though it bordered Ajuchitlan and Tetela del Rio and was in the middle Balsas valley and not on the coast. This was not unique, however, as several other Zacatula villages were in the Tepalcatepec drainage of southwestern Michoacan.

We can map and define the Tarascan-Mexican march fairly accurately, between the extremes indicated above (Brand, 1944, map facing p. 60, text pp. 77–78, 106–07). Tlalpujahua, Taximaroa, Tuzantla, Cutzamala, and Ajuchitlan were Tarascan administrative and military centers, and the Tarascan-controlled area extended a variable distance east of these points, e.g., up the Rio Balsas from Ajuchitlan to within 3 leagues of Tetela del Rio (Relación de Ajuchitlán, p. 23). On the Mexican side, garrison and administrative centers and forts included Jocotitlan, Tecaltitlan (3 leagues east from Sultepec), Tejupilco, Ostuma (above Acapetlahuaya near Teloloapan, and the strongest Mexican fortress on the Tarascan front), and Tetela del Rio.

The march area was occupied in part by local conquered peoples such as the Mazahua and Matlatzinca, in the Tlalpujahua-Tuzantla zone, and by Chontal, Cuitlatec, and Tepuztec to the south. In addition, the Tarascan rulers, beginning with Tariácure about 1400, commenced a policy of conquering or gaining as allies the peoples east of the Tarascans who were beginning to feel the force of the Mexicans. Many such peoples then were colonized in critical areas on the frontiers of the Tarascan state.

Tariácure is said to have colonized Otomi of Jilotepec and unspecified Chichimec on the northeastern frontier centering on Acambaro which marched with Queretaro and Jocotitlan (Acámbaro in Relación de Celaya, pp. 128–31, 134). The Matlatzinca especially (under such names as Otomi, Pirinda, and Matlatzinca), during the reign of Tzitzic Pandacuare about 1454–79, sought the protection of the Tarascan ruler

and were colonized around Taymeo and Tlalpujahua, in the Charo–Morelia–Santiago Undameo zone and the Huetamo area in the Tierra Caliente (Relación de Taymeo, pp. 101–03; Relación de Necotlan, pp. 109–10; Cutzio in Relación de Zirandaro, pp. 27–29). The Guayameo area just outside Zirandaro apparently was used as an entrepôt and recruiting center to supply and service the southeast frontier of the Tarascan dominion as Apaneca and many other peoples from Zacatula and Colima (chiefly conquered peoples) were colonized here and were required, along with the Huetamo Matlatzinca, to produce food and other necessities and transport them to the garrison of 10,000 Tarascans in Cutzamala and elsewhere (Relación de Zirandaro, pp. 12–13, 19, 20–21, 29). The size of the Tarascan garrison may be an exaggeration, but probably not by much since the Tarascans had the Mexicans on the run along the Pezuapa-Ostuma-Tejupilco line.

Next we should consider the hoary tradition that the Mexican empire extended to the mouth of the Zacatula River and that Moctezuma obtained tribute from this area. Unfortunately such careful scholars as Barlow and Sauer have perpetuated this idea, although Sauer merely relied on the work of Barlow. I have elsewhere briefly discussed this matter (Brand, 1944, pp. 39–44), but I shall here add further evidence.

Some reliance has been placed on the existence of a form of Nahuatl or Mexicano Corrupto in the western Zacatula area. I myself accepted such a "language" in that region until a few years ago (see statement under "Mexicano Corrupto" on back of map facing p. 60 in Brand, 1944). Now I am fully convinced that neither Nahuatl nor any Nahuatlan or Nahuatoid tongue was spoken in any part of Zacatula or even in the long coastal area extending west into Colima. All the Mexicano and Mexicano Corrupto was introduced during and after the Spanish conquest, unless the Tarascans colonized some Nahuatlana captives in a

644

few localities as they are known to have done in such places as Acahuato and Santa Ana Tetlama in the Tepalcatepec basin. Part of the evidence is in the very revealing statement made for Zacatula (Relación de Zacatula, p. 260) that there are many languages in the province, but that throughout the province the Mexicano is used for understanding (i.e., as a lingua franca), *especially by the men* (my italics), although in a corrupt form. Evidently the Mexicano was not the mother tongue in Zacatula province. The Relación de Motines of 1580 says much the same thing (Brand, 1960, pp. 124–28, especially p. 124).

Worthier of consideration is the claim that there was a Mexican conquest of part of Zacatula, and that Zacatulan villages appear on the Matrícula de Tributos. Scarcely a scholar today accepts the absurd story narrated by Alva Ixtlilxochitl (who was capable of inventing the lie that 5,000 Tezcocans accompanied Olid to Michoacan) that a Texcocan soldier in the company of a few merchants gained the submission of Zacatollan to Texcoco by killing the Zacatollan ruler. Barlow (1949c, pp. 8–22) has most plausibly argued for a Mexican conquest of all Zacatula to the mouth of the Zacatula River, but I do not agree with this conclusion.

We will accept the list of 45 pueblos conquered by Ahuitzotl between 1486 and 1502, but not all Barlow's identifications of the place names, which for the most part are descriptive and are found widely over the Mexican landscape, e.g., Coyuca, Ixtapa, and Cihuatlan, to cite a few that appear for the Costa Grande of Guerrero. Barlow writes that Ahuitzotl conquered the area of the modern port of Acapulco because he finds a pueblo of "Acapulco" was conquered by Ahuitzotl on his southern campaigns. However, Acapulco was Yope country, it is not known that the Mexicans ever were able to conquer the Yope, and "Acapulco" occupies a position on the conquest list that would indicate a location in the Balsas basin. Both the Relaciones Geográficas of Ichcateopan (pp. 123–24, 128–29) and of Zacatula (p. 264) provide data that make reasonable a conquest by Ahuitzotl out of the Balsas basin, over the Sierra Madre del Sur via Tlacotepec and probably Calpulalcolulco to the Joluchuca-Petatlan region on the coast and then east as far as Cayaco, which is near the Boca de Mita just west of the Rio de Coyuca. The conquest list has places along the coast from Xolochiuhyan (Joluchuca) to Coyucan (Coyuca de Benitez). There is no mention of a conquest of a Zacatula or Zacatollan, or of an Acapulco east of Coyuca. The Relación de Zacatula (p. 264) says specifically that in preconquest days the Mexican Moctezuma held subject in the province of Zacatula "the pueblos that are from Cayaco to Suluchuca where he had his frontier," and that these villages contributed food and weapons for the frontier, and that all the rest of the villages (in the province of Zacatula) were independent, each village having its own chief as there was no general ruler. In view of this positive statement in the relación, plus the lack of mention of Zacatula among the Mexican conquests, it seems unrealistic to insist that the empire of the Culhua Mexica extended to the mouth of the Zacatula River.

There remains the matter of the Tribute List which has in order, in the Hot Country, Ciuatlan, Colima, Panotlan, and on to Coyucac, Zacatulan, and Xolochiuhyan. This Tribute List, both in the Matrícula de Tributos form probably prepared in a hurry for the use of Cortés in 1521 and in the so-called Códice Mendocino prepared rather carelessly in the 1540s at the request of the Viceroy Mendoza, is not above suspicion as being an unreliable job which combined fact and fiction. I am rather convinced that the Cihuatlan and Colima on the Tribute List represent a concession to the rumors that had been reaching Cortés in the Valley of Mexico of a golden Colima and an Amazonian Cihuatlan which lay somewhere on

645

the shores of the South Sea to the southwest. At best, perhaps the Mexican scribes were like the Chinese of the Ming and early Manchu dynasties who did not distinguish among tribute, diplomatic gifts, and trade with foreigners, but lumped everything as tribute.

In any case, the juxtaposition of the provinces of Cihuatlan and Colima west of Michoacan, and this same juxtaposition in the Tribute List, plus the fact that no one has ever been able to find a Colima on the Guerrero coast, would seem to make the Guerrero identifications most doubtful. Such a situation and the absence of any recorded claim of Mexican conquest of Zacatula village (which terrain, Tarascan sources, and archaeology indicate was large, well endowed with resources, and widely known) indicate that a Mexican Zacatula never existed. Furthermore, the Ahuitzotl conquest area from Joluchuca to Coyuca was connected with the Mexican base by such a tenuous corridor across the lands of hostile Tepuztec and Cuitlatec that it must have reverted to its earlier city-state condition of many independent villages some years befor the coming of the Spaniards. The Tarascan conquests under Tzitzic Pandacuare must have been equally ephemeral, and there is little to show for them other than the reports in the relaciones of wars with Zacatula, and the moving of slaves and colonists from Zacatula into the middle Balsas valley.

The remainder of the boundary of the Tarascan state is of less concern and also less documentation. We are assured that Tarascan troops and governors once held areas into southwestern Michoacan and eastern and southeastern Jalisco. There is no evidence that any part of modern Colima actually was held by the Tarascans, although it might well have been. Past the area of definite occupation and control for at least a few years, there is a considerable zone or belt into which the Tarascans raided from time to time. This may have

reached to the vicinity of modern Guadalajara, Ameca, and Autlan, but the matter is both ephemeral and obscure.

The Tarascan state itself was perhaps the most efficient and powerful military entity in Mexico. This derived partly from the fact that the Tarascan ruler was an autocrat who shared his power with no one. Michoacan had become a centralized unitary state during the reign of Tangaxoan I, and his son Tzitzic Pandacuare reaped the benefits—much as Alexander reaped what his father Philip had sowed. Furthermore, the Tarascans stressed the use of the bow and arrow (as well as slings) more than did the Mexicans, and history shows that seldom can infantry hold it own against artillery. Finally, the Tarascan gods who accepted the perfume of constant fires, as well as human sacrifice, were not so bloodthirsty and demanding of human victims as were the Mexican deities. Consequently, as more of the peoples between the Mexicans and the Tarascans were attacked by the Mexicans seeking sacrificial victims, so more "nations" joined the Tarascan empire.

No other political entity in western Mexico deserved to be called a kingdom or state, either absolutely or in comparison with the Tarascan state. Nevertheless, writers seeking sensation, historians who placed local pride above pride of scholarship, and ignorant imitation and copying have bred a plethora of kingdoms and lordships in our area. All that is necessary, in order to bring sanity and proper perspective into the picture, is to go back to the original and contemporary documents. Here we find many villages and valleys, a few provinces, and no kingdoms.

At this point it should be pointed out that the word *provincia* was used in a number of senses by the conquering Spaniards, and there was a hierarchy among the provinces (Brand, 1960, pp. 54–56). As I have pointed out, for example, at one time the Pueblo de Pomaro was in the Provincia de Motin, which was in the Provincia de Colima, which was in the Provincia de Michoacan, and for a while it was also in a Franciscan Provincia de San Pedro y San Pablo de Michoacan which included much of southwestern Mexico. After examining scores of accounts by conquistadores and about entradas, I believe that it is possible to assume that, at the time of initial contact and for a varying but usually short time thereafter, the word *provincia* was usually applied to what the writer considered to be a political unit that was independent. But care must be taken to consider the context and the prior history, if any, of the regional term in question. Often the entity termed a provincia was made up of independent villages which seemed to be united merely because they were contiguous and spoke the same language.

Regarding the Provincia de Zacatula, we do not know what the native name was either for the village known as Zacatula or for any larger unit based on that village. It would seem that Nahuatlan interpreters gave the name Zacatula to a large village near the mouth of the river which became known by the same name. As soon as the Spaniards took cognizance of this area, developed plans for building ships here, and then established a Spanish town, an increasingly large zone that depended administratively on the only Spanish *villa* for many leagues became known as the Provincia de Zacatula. So, in less than 10 years, there developed a Provincia de Zacatula which included such discrete areas as part of the Motines and part of the Cuitlatecapan. It is possible that the Province of Zacatula was made to extend so far out of modern Michoacan into Guerrero because the Costa Grande was not first traversed by Spaniards out of Acapulco or the northeast, but by Juan Rodríguez de Villafuerte out of Zacatula. It is worth considering that Villafuerte, after founding the Villa de Zacatula in early 1523, may have returned to Mexico City via the Costa Grande as far as some point between Atoyac and Coyuca, after

which he followed the old trade and war trail through Tlacotepehua-Tepuzteca country (staying west of the Tlapanec Yope) to the Balsas-Mexcala and on to Mexico City. In any case, there is need for some explanation of the fact that the Provincia Mayor and Obispado of Michoacan included all of what is now western Guerrero until 1786, and the Obispado de Michoacan continued to include this region until about 1861. This means that in one way or another Zacatula was part of Michoacan during more than three centuries of European occupation.

Good examples of pristine provincias that probably were political units of a kind are provided by the Guzmán conquest. Beyond Michoacan there are such provincias as Cuinao, Cuinacuaro, Cuyula, and Coyutla north of the Rio Grande; Cuitzeo and Tonala along the left bank; Zacualpan, Jalisco, and Tepic—three provincias in what so many later writers have converted into the great state and province of Jalisco; Teimoac or Michoacan or Sentispac; Aztatlan or Acaponeta; and in what is modern Sinaloa, between the Cañas and Mocorito rivers, where the romantic school has the two great provinces and lordships of Chametla and Culiacan, Chametla, Quezala (Rio del Presidio country), Piaxtla, Pochotla (lower Rio de la Sal or Evora), Ciguatlan (lower Rio San Lorenzo), and Culiacan, and apparently several more.

In general, government was at a village level, with one larger "mother" village or *pueblo cabecera* commonly having several smaller and dependent *barrios* which today might be thought of as *ranchos* and *pueblos* subordinate to some larger pueblo which functions as the head of a *municipio*. There is a little evidence that in some villages or village groups the headship was inherited, but in others the cacique seemed to be selected by virtue of some special ability. The proper picture of western Mexican political geography, other than the Tarascan state, is one of scores of fighting and

647

feuding village groups, each of which seldom occupied more than a valley. Undoubtedly, on occasion two or more villages or village groups might band together against some temporary common enemy, but such groupings were opportunistic and ephemeral.

LINGUISTIC GEOGRAPHY

A few facts stand out in the linguistic geography and history of western Mexico. One is the block of Nahuatlan peoples along the eastern margin, as exemplified in the Mexicanos. Another, is the northwestern block of distantly related or "Sub-Nahuatoid" peoples including the Cahita-Tahue, Cora-Pinome, Tecual-Huichol, and comparable groups. A third is the presence of very diverse peoples, linguistically speaking, in the lands between, where we find Otomians, Tarascans, and unclassified and unclassifiable languages such as Cuitlateco and Cuauhcomeca.

A slight problem is presented by the presence of Nahuatlan Cazcan in the Jalisco-Zacatecas area. A much greater problem is presented by so-called Mexicano Corrupto. As I mentioned earlier, I do not believe that any of the Mexicano Corrupto previously mapped for parts of the coast from Guerrero up into Colima and Jalisco is preconquest. These are nothing but expressions of the exceedingly rapid spread of Mexicano (Nahuatl), which in from one to three generations was able to compete with and even eliminate the native languages of large areas. The priests were the most active in bringing about this Mexicanization, which obtained from the Costa Grande of Guerrero to the valleys of Sinaloa. A good example of what took place is to be found in southwestern Michoacan (Brand, 1960, pp. 124–30). Here one can trace through fairly consecutive documents the change from no Nahuatl at the conquest, through a bilingualism on the part of most people by 1580, to no retention of the native tongues by the early 1700s. Today the Indians of the Aquila municipio, for example, think of themselves as Náhual-speaking Mexicanos, and they were fascinated and delighted when I showed them that they were descended from an older people whose place names had been changed, warped, or translated into the Mexicano for the most part.

Such a process was repeated many times in "good Mexicano" Indian areas from Tecpan to Culiacan. However, many historical footnotes need to be added to the account, such as the slaves, servants, and allies that were moved around and colonized in many areas. These were not only Mexicans, but Tarascans, Otomi, and other peoples. Finally, there needs to be remembered the confusion that arose from the successive congregations, which sometimes resulted in three or four or more languages being spoken in one village alone.

APPENDIX A

As there is a general discussion of the *Relaciones Geográficas* in volume 12 of the *Handbook*, I here merely list the 35 known relaciones pertinent to western Mexico, of which 4 are lost. Elsewhere (Brand, 1944, pp. 75–81; 1952, pp. 108–18) I have commented on most of the relaciones pertaining to the Tarascan region and its borderlands. To these will be added the few from Nueva Galicia. Although Nueva España responded better to the 50-point questionnaire of 1577/78 than any other part of the Spanish Indies, this was mainly within the area of the audience of Mexico City. Consequently, of the 31 extant relaciones, 24 were prepared between 1579 and 1582 in *alcaldías mayores* and corregimientos of the jurisdiction of Mexico City, and but 7 were prepared in Nueva Galicia—all of these several years later in 1584 and 1585.

To speak of 31 available relaciones is being too precise, for frequently the same man would be alcalde mayor of one unit, corregidor of another unit, and possibly the responsible official of another unit, e.g., Celaya together with Yuririapundaro and Acambaro, or Coalcoman together with Motines. Also, commonly, within one alcaldía mayor or corregimiento by the time of this interrogation, there might be several clusters of villages, each having a cabecera in the name of each of which would be drawn up a partial or complete separate set of answers, as in Tancitaro to which had been added Tepalcatepec and Pinzandaro. This sort of thing has provided us with one of our few opportunities to check the reliability and consistency of the answers to the questionnaire provided by the natives of a given unit. There is a relación of 1579 for the corregimiento of Jiquilpan, which included separate statements for Jiquilpan, Chocandiran or Tingüindin, Tarecuato, and Periban. By 1581 apparently Tingüindin-Chocandiran was a separate corregimiento with another person as corregidor, and an entirely new relación was prepared. Although there is close agreement in many things, it is interesting that between 1579 and 1581, the Spanish conquest had changed from about 1519 through Olid sent out by Hernando Cortés to about 1533 through Olid sent out by Martín Cortés. Parenthetically, Barlow, in his edition of the Jiquilpan relación (Barlow, 1944a, p. 288) was wrong in supposing that there were two distinct entities known as Chocandiran since (among other things) they both had the same 11 subject villages by name. Today there is a ranchería of Chucandiran in the municipio of Tingüindin.

The relaciones described below have been grouped according to the modern Mexican state in which the area covered falls entirely or chiefly. Each relación or group of relaciones is identified by the key name in modern form (if such exists), followed in some instances by 16th-century names and the date of completion. Next is the present presumptive location of the original manuscript (AI = Archivo de Indias, Sevilla; AH = Real Academia de la Historia, Madrid; JGI = Joaquín García Icazbalceta collection in The University of Texas Library). Last is the status of publication. All but three have been published in essentially complete form. Over the years I have consulted the original manuscripts at The University of Texas and the Paso y Troncoso transcripts in the Museo Nacional in Mexico. For most of the relaciones I have paleographed typescript copies. For ease of reference, however, I will refer to the best published edition of each relación. For a considerable number there is but one available published form, that by Vargas Rea which is uniformly very poor.

MEXICO

Temascaltepec, 1580 (AI). Abstracted and paraphrased by Puente y Olea, 1889, 3: 203–14, Mexico, 1889. PNE, 7: 15–20.

Sultepec, 1582 (AI). PNE, 7: 8–14.

GUERRERO

Ixcateopan, 1579 (AI). PNE, 6: 87–152.

Citlaltomaua, 1580 (AI). PNE, 6: 153–66.

Zacatula, 1580 (JGI). Published nearly completely by Barlow, 1947b, pp. 258–68. The copy used by Barlow lacked the introduction of November 25, 1580, in Tecpan in which the alcalde mayor Hernando de Vascones explains that because there are no old settlers in the Tecpan area he is entrusting the preparation of the report to the officials and vicar in the town of Zacatula. Also, Barlow's copy lacked the covering letter dated February 25, 1581, in Tecpan, but all the essential text is presented.

Ajuchitlan, 1579 (AH). PNE, 7 Sup. Vargas Rea, (part 6) paged separately, Mexico, 1946; *Relaciones Geográficas de la Dió cesis de Michoacán 1579–1580*, 1: 61–82, Guadalajara, 1958.

Zirandaro, 1579 (AH). PNE, 7 Sup. Vargas Rea, (part 7) pp. 7–33, Mexico, 1946. *RGDM*, 2: 38–50.

GUANAJUATO

Celaya, 1580 (AH). PNE, 7 Sup. Vargas Rea, (part 4) pp. 113–57, Mexico, 1945. *RGDM*, 2: 50–70.

MICHOACAN

Cuitzeo, 1579 (AH). *Relaciones Geográficas de la Diócesis de Michoacán 1579–1580*, 1: 44–60, Guadalajara, 1958.

Taimeo, 1579 (AH). PNE, 7 Sup. Vargas Rea, (part 3) pp. 99–105, Mexico, 1945; *Relaciones Geográficas de la Diócesis de Michoacán 1579–1580*, 1: pp. 36–40, Guadalajara, 1958.

Tuzantla, 1580 (AI). Abstracted and paraphrased by Puente y Olea, 1889, 3: 211–13. *Tlalocan*, 5: 50–73, Mexico, 1965.

Sinagua (Cinguacingo), 1581 (AH). PNE, 7 Sup. Vargas Rea, (part 7) pp. 57–67, Mexico, 1946. *RGDM*, 2: 70–74.

Patzcuaro, 1581 (JGI). *Anales del Museo Michoacano*, 2: 41–48, Morelia, 1889; in Manuel Toussaint's *Pátzcuaro*, pp. 231–35, Mexico, 1942; PNE, 7 Sup. Vargas Rea, (part 7) pp. 35–55, Mexico, 1946. *RGDM*, 2: 107–17.

Tiripetio, 1580 (JGI). Not published. Although this relación concerns a relatively small corregimiento, it is one of the longest, most detailed, and informative.

Santiago Undameo (Necotlan), 1579 (AH). PNE, 7 Sup. Vargas Rea, (part 3) pp. 107–12, Mexico, 1945; *Relaciones Geográficas de la Diócesis de Michoacán 1579–1580*, 1: 40–44, Guadalajara, 1958.

Morelia (Valladolid de Michoacan), 1581. Lost. (López Velasco, 1583).

Capula. Lost. (López Velasco, 1583).

Tlazazalca. Lost. (López Velasco, 1583).

Chilchota, 1579 (AH). PNE, 7 Sup. Vargas Rea, (part 5) paged separately, Mexico, 1946. *RGDM*, 2:7–38.

Jiquilpan, 1579 (AH). Barlow, 1944a, pp. 278–306; PNE, 7 Sup. Vargas Rea, (parts 1, 2, 3) pp. 29–46, 65–84, 85–98, Mexico, 1944–1945; *Relaciones Geográficas de la*

Diócesis de Michoacán 1579–1580, 1: 7–36, Guadalajara, 1958.

Tingüindin (Chucandiran), 1581 (AH). PNE, 7 Sup. Vargas Rea, (part 8) pp. 71–90, Mexico, 1946. *RGDM*, 2:74–83.

Tancitaro, 1580 (JGI). *Tlalocan*, 3: 205–35, Mexico, 1952.

Coalcoman and Motines, 1580 (AH). Published in part by Vargas Rea as *Relación de Quacoman*, Mexico, 1952 (reprinted 1954 with slightly different title), and *Relación de Maquili, Alimanci, Cuxquaquautla y Epatlan*, Mexico, 1952 (reprinted 1953), which cover less than half the available relación. Furthermore, apparently Paso y Troncoso never located the portion of the relación dealing with Maquili and Aquila, which I have not seen anywhere.

JALISCO

Poncitlan and Cuitzeo, 1585 (AH). PNE, 8 (Vargas Rea), part 4, pp. 221–60, Mexico, 1947.

Sayula or Pueblos de Avalos, 1580. Lost. (López Velasco, 1583).

Tamazula, Tuxpan, and Zapotlan, 1580 (AH). PNE, 7 Sup. Vargas Rea, (part 8) pp. 91–130, Mexico, 1946. *RGDM*, 2: 83–107.

Provincia de Amula (Zapotitlan, Tuxcacuesco, Cuzalapa), 1579 (JGI). In *Noticias Varias de Nueva Galicia*, pp. 282–321, Guadalajara, 1878; Vargas Rea, *Relaciones de los Pueblos de Amula, Zapotitlan*, and *Tuscaquesco y Cusalapa*, paged separately, Mexico, 1952.

Purificación, 1585 (AH). PNE, 8 (Vargas Rea), part 2, pp. 78–130, Mexico, 1947.

Tenamaxtlan, 1579 (JGI). In *Noticias Varias de Nueva Galicia*, pp. 321–46, Guadalajara, 1878; Vargas Rea, *Relaciones de los Pueblos de Amula, Tenamaztlan*, paged separately, Mexico, 1952.

Ameca, 1579 (JGI). In *Boletin*, Soc. Mex. Geog. y Estad., 2 ep., 2: 464–78 (1870); reprinted in J. M. Pérez Hernández' *Dic-*

cionario Geográfico, Estadístico . . . de la República Mexicana, 1:381–95, Mexico, 1874; *Noticias Varias de Nueva Galicia*, pp. 233–82, Guadalajara, 1878; J. Amaya, 1951, pp. 23–76 (this is the most complete treatment to date of any relación); Vargas Rea, *Relaciones de los Pueblos de la Provincia de Amula, Ameca*, 2 parts paged separately, Mexico, 1951.

Teocaltiche, 1584 (JGI). In *Noticias Varias de Nueva Galicia*, pp. 346–60.

Hostotipaquillo (Xocotlan), 1584 (AH). PNE, 8 (Vargas Rea), part 1, pp. 33–57, Mexico, 1947.

ZACATECAS

Nochistlan, 1584 (AH). PNE, 8 (Vargas Rea), part 1, pp. 59–75, Mexico, 1947.

Jerez, 1584 (AH). PNE, 8 (Vargas Rea), part 4, pp. 193–219, Mexico, 1947.

NAYARIT

Compostela, 1584 (AH). PNE, 8 (Vargas Rea), part 1, pp. 11–32, Mexico, 1947.

APPENDIX B

As stated earlier in this article, the famous and interminably cited work by Fray Antonio Tello should not be used for the pre-conquest and conquest periods, either directly in the nominally complete edition (1891) which is plagued with gaps, or in the works of such as Mota Padilla (1870) and Beaumont (1932), who presumably had access to a more complete manuscript. In the first place, Tello was born in Spain, about 1593, and came to New Spain in 1619 at the age of 26 (Gómez Cañedo, 1959, pp. 118–20), instead of being a Guadalajara Creole or Mestizo, or possibly a Mexican Indian born as early as 1548 (Tello, 1891, p. v). Consequently, having first seen Nueva Galicia in 1620, Tello could not have known and talked with any of the conquer-

ors and Indians of the 1520–42 period for which he contributed so many details not found elsewhere.

Tello consistently gave erroneous dates, frequently confused the personalities in a given activity such as an entrada, and described actions and events that did not take place. A careful study of his extant works shows that in Guadalajara 1650–53 Tello apparently did not have at his command as good source material on the conquest of Nueva Galicia as exists today in available published form. Obviously he did not have access to the letters, relaciones, procesos, and residencias pertinent to the activities of Nuño de Guzmán, or he would not have made so many errors and he would not have so frequently cited distant and secondhand authorities such as Las Casas, Díaz del Castillo, Torquemada, and Herrera. It is quite likely that the Nueva Galicia archives from the Compostela days of government and audience (1531–60) already were missing in Tello's time, and no trace of these archives exists today (Páez Brotchie, 1940).

Among the fictions that Tello fathered or sponsored were such things as a conquest of Queretaro and Guanajuato by Nuño de Guzmán, an entrada by Guzmán's lieutenant, Chirinos, from the Cuitzeo area via Lagos and Zacatecas (area of the modern city) to Tepic, a pre-Spanish shipwreck of Christians on the Jalisco coast, an exaggerated concept of native kingdoms and feudal entities (by the use of such words as *king* and *vassals*), and a migration story. Because most modern historians of the area accept the Chirinos entrada as fact, it should be pointed out that the pertinent relaciones clearly state that the Chirinos party separated from the main Guzmán party at Teul (modern Teul de González in southwestern Zacatecas) and reached Tepic in 17 days, of which 14 were spent in the rough barranca land of the Rio Grande (de Santiago) where it was impossible to ride the horses. Since the Chirinos party con-

sisted of cavalry, infantry, hundreds of Indian allies on foot, and many hundreds of
pigs driven along for food, it could not
have taken the Zacatecas detour and
reached Tepic in 17 days. Furthermore, according to the Teul guide and informants,
the route they would follow would be a
nine-day route leading directly to Teimoac
or Mechuacan (the lower Rio Grande de
Santiago country just north of Tepic). As
Tello gives personal names to Indians and
quotes supposed conversations on this entrada to Zacatecas which did not take place,
we are forced to discredit all his other apparently precise factual information where
it is not supported by other earlier sources.
The shipwreck is an apparently confused
use of the wreck of one or two of Cortés's
ships on the Jalisco coast (*San Miguel* in
1532 and *San Lázaro* in 1535) in a ration-
alization of the tonsured heads of the Indians who were named by the Spaniards
"Frailes" and "Coronados." Parenthetically,
there is enough evidence for a return to
Colima from Tepic by Francisco de Cortés
along most of the intervening Nayarit-Jalisco coast so that we need not reject it on
account of the Tello version.

Probably Tello, who was a missionary
priest and not an historian, should be for-
given for his uncritical use of the garbled
native annals and other accounts to which
he refers occasionally. Our problem is to
determine where the truth lies in these ex-
tracts from accounts written by natives long
after the events described. In this connection it should be kept in mind that either
the native accounts were written down by
missionaries as they interpreted the narra-
tions, or else they were written by natives
after they had learned to write, and in
Castilian or Mexicano, both of which were
foreign tongues in Nueva Galicia.

We can check somewhat on the reliability
of the most-used native source in Tello's
Libro Segundo, that written from memory
by Don Francisco Pantecatl in 1565 which
included an origin legend (Tello, 1891, pp.

652

23, 599). In places (pp. 23, 27, 158) Pantecatl is referred to as the son of Xonacatl,
or Xonacatl-Tayorith, cacique of Acaponeta; elsewhere (p. 102) Pantecatl is the son
of Xonacatl-Tayorith, recently defunct lord
and king of Tzapotzingo at the time of
Guzmán's entrada in 1530. Again (p. 38)
we read that the Indians of Tzapotzingo,
led by Pantecatl, visited Francisco de
Cortés in Huaristemba (in 1525). From the
Guzmán relaciones we know that Zapotzingo was a large village about 2 leagues north
from Tepic on the margin of the Tierra
Caliente. Elsewhere in Tello (pp. 129, 137,
256, 359 and *passim*) we learn that Pantecatl's home villagers of Zapotzingo were
enemies of the people of Jalisco village, that
Pantecatl had been baptized in 1531 by
Fray Juan de Padilla, that he had been
briefly a prisoner of Nuño de Guzmán, and
that he had spent some 10 years in hiding in
the mountains and with his friends the
Tecuares. This does not add up to anything
that makes sense. The people of Jalisco
were Tecuares (Tecuales). Whether a native of Acaponeta or of Zapotzingo, Pantecatl probably was either a Pinome-Totora-
me or a Vigiteca-Tepehuan by language, or
possibly a Tecual. This would imply Cora
or Tepehuan or Huichol type of language,
none of which is Nahuatlan. Consequently,
the Nahuatlan names Xonacatl and Pantecatl, and Zapotzingo and Jalisco, and others
of the kind, either are translations into the
Mexicano or are pure inventions. It seems
strange that Pantecatl, a nobleman proud
of his ancestry, would have translated the
proper names into Mexicano rather than retaining the native form or using the Spanish
equivalent.

Two other items might be mentioned
about Pantecatl's account. He makes no
mention of one of the four greatest battles
that Guzmán's army fought in the entire
entrada, that at nearby Tecomatlan just past
the ford of the Rio Grande (de Santiago),
but instead (Tello, 1891, pp. 103–06) has
the reputedly very belligerent natives of

the area receive Guzmán with the greatest friendliness. The much-repeated and elaborated-upon origin and migration legend (*ibid.*, pp. 13–27) also includes a discussion of the local god and some elements of the theology. The entire thing is a patent mixture of Mexican migration myths with local adjustments, paganism, and Christianity. The Christian elements show up in the presumptive worship of a child-god who revealed himself and told about an all-powerful creator-god who lived in the sky where there also lived a sovereign virgin-mother lady who provided food for mankind, etc. In view of all this it would seem that we cannot rely on any ethnological data in Tello pertaining to the preconquest and conquest periods.

Finally, we are forced to question why there are no other origin and migration myths besides that of Pantecatl, a person from a peripheral area. Why are not Tonala-Tlajomulco, or the Gran Caxcana, or Jalisco-Tepic represented? We venture to guess that Tello (influenced by the migration accounts recorded by the religious in the Valley of Mexico) wanted a story by a person from the Aztatlan region—even though Pantecatl turned out to be from Tzapotzingo near Tepic and not from Aztatlan near Acaponeta.

APPENDIX C

The specific routes followed in the conquest of Michoacan are not important as there are no contemporary relaciones with significant ethnological data for places, areas, and peoples which have to be located and identified in terms of so many leagues or *jornadas* from some other place or people. However, in many later accounts and reports (such as for the conquest of Nueva Galicia, various inspection trips by bishops and *oidores*, and the *Relaciones Geográficas*), it is important

to realize that a number of the critical datum points have changed in one way or another. Quite frequently in the later accounts a distance will be given to the cathedral city of the diocese.

Prior to the summer of 1580 the bishop of Michoacan resided in Patzcuaro, but as a result of a cédula of 1579 the cathedral was moved to Valladolid-Guayangareo (Morelia). There is a shadowy period 1579–80, during which we cannot be certain to which city reference is being made. Frequently reference is made to the Ciudad de Michoacan, which term was used originally for the capital of the Tarascan state. For several years, perhaps until 1540, Tzintzuntzan was considered to be the heart of the capital city, and Patzcuaro was merely a barrio or ward. Then, with the erection of the diocese of Michoacan 1534–38 and the formal installation of Don Vasco de Quiroga as the first resident bishop, the barrio in which the bishop took residence and had his cathedral church became the center of the capital city. Shortly after installation in 1538 in Tzinztuntzan, Bishop Quiroga moved to Patzcuaro, possibly in 1538 and certainly by 1540. Consequently, between 1521 and the 1580s, we must be careful to decide whether Ciudad de Michoacan refers to Michoacan-Tzintzuntzan or Michoacan-Patzcuaro or Michoacan-Valladolid.

When the diocese of Nueva Galicia was organized in 1548–49 the cathedral was to be in the city of Compostela, which at that time was the seat of the royal audiencia for Nueva Galicia. However, the first bishop, after a brief visit to Compostela, refused to live there and made his residence and had his cathedral in Guadalajara, a much larger and richer city and more centrally located with reference to the European population. Nevertheless, the city of Guadalajara did not officially have approval as the cathedral city until the audencia was moved there in 1560. As a consequence, unless the context makes it clear, we cannot always be certain prior to 1560 which city is meant by a reference to the ecclesiastic or judicial cabecera of Nueva Galicia.

The matter of Compostela becomes more involved when we realize that the city of Compostela did not occupy its present site until the summer of 1540. The first capital of the government and kingdom of Nueva Galicia was founded by Nuño de Guzmán December 3, 1531, in the village of Tepic with the name of Villa del Espiritu Santo de la Mayor España. However, on royal order, the name was changed to Ciudad de Santiago de Compostela on January 17, 1532. Consequently, the city of Compostela was where is today the city of Tepic from 1532 to 1540, and when Coronado and his forces were reviewed by the viceroy before setting out for Cibola (New Mexico), the review took place on the site of the modern city of Tepic. This matter is important as it makes a difference of some 10 leagues in various distances measured from "Compostela."

There is a slight further complication about the early Compostela, for the name Espiritu Santo was a favorite with Guzmán, and also a number of events seemed to take place about the time of Pentecost. The present Rio Grande de Santiago was named the Rio del Espiritu Santo by Guzmán, but fortunately he founded no city along its lower course. However, the present Rio del Presidio or Mazatlan in southern Sinaloa was also the Rio del Espiritu Santo, and Guzmán had a town founded on its banks which was known as the Villa del Espiritu Santo de Quezala during its brief history, about 1532–35. Since this Espiritu Santo was the only Spanish town in or near a region or province known as Chametla, it also was known as the Villa de Chametla. This gave rise to a confusion among three places known as Chametla. The first was a large Indian village several leagues from the mouth of the Baluarte River, which is also known as Rio de Rosario and Rio de Chametla. The second Chametla was another large Indian village, fishing center, and port,

near the mouth of this same Chametla river. The third Chametla, of course, was the Villa de Chametla or Espiritu Santo.

There was at least one other Espiritu Santo to confuse the picture in Nueva Galicia, as Guzmán gave orders for a town to be founded at Nochistlan (in Zacatecas) with the name of Villa del Espiritu Santo, which was accomplished January 5, 1532. This was the first Guadalajara, as that name also was applied to this foundation. Because Guadalajara ultimately occupied four sites officially, the date must be considered whenever reference is made to Guadalajara. The Nochistlan site was occupied only from January, 1532, into August, 1533. The second move was intended for Tacotlan (in Jalisco, but on the north—right bank—side of the Rio Grande), but actually ended with most of the citizens or vecinos in Tonala and some in Tacotlan and some in Tetlan. The third move resulted from an order from Guzmán in March, 1535, for all to move to Tacotlan. Finally, as a result of the Indian rebellion, the fourth and last move of Guadalajara was made between October, 1541, and February, 1542, to the present site in the Valle de Atemajac.

Perhaps of greatest importance for us are the changes in location of the Spanish town or villa which became known ultimately as Culiacan. There was an Indian town of Culiacan on the banks of the river known today as the Rio de Culiacan. This important town and valley gave its name to a Spanish-created district or province known as the Provincia de Culiacan. When Guzmán decided to found a Spanish town in this general region, the best site was on the banks of the present Rio de San Lorenzo (also known as Lagunilla, Horaba, and Cihuatlan) about 7 leagues above the mouth. Here in the Valle de Horaba, near Oso and Quila, was founded on September 29, 1531, the Villa de San Miguel. Then, to get better farmland and food supply, the town was moved down the river 5 leagues at some date prior to December, 1533. Soon the town became known as the Villa de San Miguel de Culiacan. It was now in the old Cihuatlan area near modern Eldorado and old Navito, about 2 leagues from the mouth. Here the Villa de San Miguel or Villa de Culiacan remained for many years, as it was not moved away to its present site until some time between 1549 and 1564. Consequently, all statements of so many leagues from the Villa de Culiacan made in connection with such journeys and expeditions as those of Cabeza de Vaca in 1536, Fray Marcos de Niza, and Coronado, as well as the distances given in the *Suma de Visitas*, must be calculated in terms of the second Villa which commonly was considered to be 10 leagues from the Indian town of Culiacan.

There are many other instances of shifts of Spanish and Indian towns, such as Colima and Tecoman in the state of Colima, La Purificacion in Jalisco, and Huajicori and Guaynamota in Nayarit. However, almost as grave a source of error as change in location is the existence of one or more "Indian" homonyms. Among the more important in our area are such as Zapotlan, Tuxpan, Mazatlan, Coyuca, Jiquilpan, Amatlan, Panuco, Ocotlan, Cihuatlan, Chacala, Atengo, Copala, Ixtapan, Chapultepec, Tecomatlan, and Atotonilco. These usually were places with names in non-Nahuatlan form which were merely translated. For example, Tarascan Zirandaro becomes Nahuatlan Amatlan; Puruandiro is nearly the same as Atotonilco; Etucuaro turns into Ixtapan; and Ihuatzio becomes Coyuca. It is obvious that a very large percentage of names of places and areas are descriptive in origin. Such is the Nahuatl name Michoacan, which merely means "Place of Fish." The Nahuatlan allies and interpreters for the Spaniards referred to more than one place or area as "Michoacan." The best known of such, of course, is the Tarascan region, which got its Nahuatl name from the Lake Patzcuaro area. Less well known is the region between the Rio Grande de Santiago and the Rio de San Pedro in Nayarit, which the Nahuatl interpreters called Michoacan, although it was also known as Teimoac in Cazcan and Centiquipac (and many variants) in the Pinome. In this connection it should be noted that Nuño de Guzmán wrote his famous letter of July 8, 1530, from Omitlan in Michoacan. This brings up the point that a lot of nonsense has been written by various persons studying the Mexican origin and migration legends who assume that the remote and nonspecific Aztatlan, or Culiacan, or Michoacan encountered in these legends must refer to a specific place in Nayarit, or Sinaloa, or the state of Michoacan.

REFERENCES

Amaya, 1951
Barlow, 1944a, 1947b, 1949c
Beaumont, 1932
Brand, 1944, 1952, 1960
Buelna, 1892
Carrera Stampa, 1955
Castañeda, 1896
Colección de documentos inéditos, 1864–84
Cortés, 1877
Fourth Anonymous, 1955

García Icazbalceta, 1858–66
Gómez Cañedo, 1959
Hammond and Rey, 1928
Hernández y Dávalos, 1878
Herrera y Tordesillas, 1934
Lebrón de Quiñones, 1945
León, 1903a
Lienzo de Tlaxcala, 1892
Mota Padilla, 1870
Páez Brotchie, 1940

655

Papeles de Nueva España (PNE)
Ponce, 1872
Puente y Olea, 1889
Relación de Michoacán, 1903
Relaciones Geográficas de la Diócesis de Michoacán, 1958
Romero Flores, 1946
Ruiz, E., 1940

Ruiz Colmenero, 1903
Sauer, 1948
Suma de visitas, *see* PNE, vol. 1
Tello, 1891
Toussaint, 1942
Visitación . . ., 1937
Winship, 1896

29. Archaeological Synthesis of Michoacan and Adjacent Regions

ROBERT CHADWICK

MICHOACAN, like the rest of western Mexico, is characterized by the lack of any unifying cultural tradition through most of its history. Many of the diagnostic traits of Mesoamerica (Kirchhoff, 1943) are absent in the area.

Miramontes (1936) divides Michoacan into several physiographic regions. The northernmost is a *tierra templada* strip, then comes a belt of *tierra fría*, cold highlands, south of which is another narrow band of tierra templada. Except for the Sierra de Coalcoman in the southwest corner of the state, the southern remainder, almost one-half the entire state, is *tierra caliente*, or hot country. Tierra caliente is an inland extension of the coastal plain physiographic region. The Rio Balsas and its tributaries drain much of the area (West, 1948; 1964, fig. 6).

Michoacan presents a somewhat complex linguistic picture. At contact, the Tarascan Indians occupied much of the plateau region, and had brought some of the tierra

caliente under their control. Tarasco place names are known not only in Michoacan, but also in Guerrero, Guanajuato, San Luis Potosi, Jalisco, and Colima (Velásquez Gallardo, 1948, p. 125). In the 16th century, the Balsas River seems to have been a boundary line, dividing Tarasco-speakers in Michoacan from Nahuatl-speakers in Guerrero. In addition, Cuitlatec, Apanec, and Matlatzinca were spoken in the middle Balsas basin. Nahuatl was spoken near Zacatula in the delta, and this language has also been reported from the western coastal region. Nahuatl-speaking "Tecos" are said to have lived near the town of Tepalcatepec at the western end of the tierra caliente trough (Goggin, 1943, p. 45; Armillas, 1948, p. 76; Weitlaner, 1946).

MICHOACAN ARCHAEOLOGY

Excavations in Michoacan have been scattered and random. In 1852 the priest Ignacio Trespeña destroyed one of the *yácatas* near Tzintzuntzan in an attempt at excavation. In 1886 Hartford excavated another

657

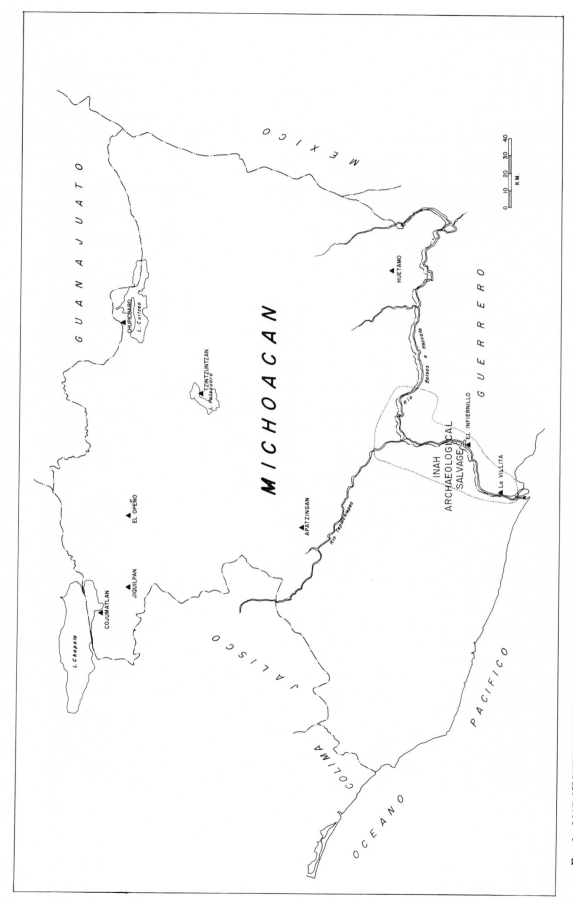

FIG. 1—MAP SHOWING MAIN ARCHAEOLOGICAL SITES IN MICHOACAN

building there. The oldest reference to archaeological remains in Michoacan (1565) appears to be in Beaumont's Crónica de Michoacan (1932). Plancarte (1893) mentioned archaeological remains in the state; and Lumholtz (1902) described a yacata at Paricutin, giving its measurements. León (1903b) described similar remains in such archaeological zones as Tingüimbato, Zirahuen, Ario, San Antonio, Corupo, and Coeneo. He also described monuments near Tzintzuntzan. Starr and Pepper, as well as Lumholtz, collected in the middle Balsas zone and in western tierra caliente around Taxco, Zumpango, Apatzingan, and Tepalcatepec in the 1880s and 1890s. In 1903 Pepper excavated two mounds at San Antonio and published (1916) a brief report.

The professional era dawned in 1930 with the work of Alfonso Caso and Eduardo Noguera in Zacapu, Zamora, and Patzcuaro (Caso, 1930b; Noguera, 1931). In 1937 and 1938 Caso continued work at Tzintzuntzan and Ihuatzio with the help of Acosta, Rubín de la Borbolla, and Moedano (Acosta, 1939; Rubín de la Borbolla, 1939, 1941; Moedano K., 1941). In 1938 Noguera excavated "shaft tombs" at El Opeño near Zamora; he obtained ceramic material at Cerro de Curutaran in the same area, and also excavated near Jacona (Noguera, 1942). Noguera's more recent work (1944) was in Jiquilpan in connection with salvage digging during the construction of the municipal airport. Further work in the highland region was carried out in the 1940s at Chupicuaro, Guanajuato, just across the Michoacan-Guanajuato border, by archaeologists of the Instituto Nacional de Antropología e Historia in connection with the construction of the Solís dam. These excavations have been fully reported (Estrada Balmori and Piña Chan, 1948a,b; Rubín de la Borbolla, 1948; Porter, 1948b, 1956). The University of New Mexico in the summers of 1939 and 1941 sent out a group to survey in the Tepalcatepec valley, and also in the middle Balsas zone, both in Guerrero and

in Michoacan (Brand, 1942; Goggin, 1943; Osborne, 1943). Part of this area, around Apatzingan, was later excavated and reported by Kelly (1947b). Lister, who had participated in the tierra caliente survey, also excavated and published his findings at Cojumatlan at the eastern end of Lake Chapala (Lister, 1949).

The little-known coastal region and the Rio Balsas delta have been surveyed briefly. In 1944 Armillas, with Hendrichs and Bernal, explored the middle Balsas as well as the lower zone and the delta region (Armillas, 1945). Lehmann (1948), Barlow (1947d), and Brand (1952, 1957–58, 1960) also visited and reported on the delta. In addition, Brand (1957–58) surveyed the south coast; Corona Núñez (1960b) summarized his survey of the north coast. More recently, two INAH salvage projects under the general direction of Lorenzo (1964) excavated and surveyed the lower Balsas as well as part of the middle Balsas basin in connection with the construction of the Morelos dam at El Infiernillo, and a second dam at La Villita (Litvak King, 1968; Paddock, 1968; Chadwick, field notes). Previously, Nicholson (1962, 1963) had made pits at Melchor Ocampo, and briefly surveyed the delta and part of the coastal region. I. W. Johnson (1964) has reported on textiles from Tzintzuntzan, and Mastache (1966) has recently analyzed textiles recovered in the El Infiernillo excavations. Schöndube (1968) has described petroglyphs from Michoacan, and has compiled information on figurines, including some from Michoacan, from many parts of western Mexico. Matos Moctezuma (1968) has described and illustrated pottery from Jerecuaro, Guanajuato, near Chupicuaro. Some further work was also done at Tzintzuntzan in the 1960s by Piña Chan.

General syntheses on the archaeology of Michoacan are nonexistent. Several preliminary summary articles were published as a result of the fourth Mesa Redonda of the Sociedad Mexicana de Antropología (El

Occidente de México, 1948). Brief résumés of Michoacan archaeology have been published by Marquina (1951), Lister (1955), Covarrubias (1957), Piña Chan (1960b), and Noguera (1965). The current task is further complicated by the fact that most of the work has been done on one-period sites by different groups over four decades. The random excavations have yielded a variety of styles of restricted distribution, which may be historically significant or may be due to inadequate reporting (Armillas, 1964a, p. 318). Thus the correlation of phases in the different chronological sequences presents a difficult, if not impossible, task with present knowledge. In some cases, isolated cultures have been arranged in chronological order to produce a sequence for a specific area. The scant data, however, preclude the establishment of developmental sequences for most of the state. Radiocarbon dates are lacking, and many of the cross-ties suggested by archaeologists with cultures in other regions are tenuous in some instances, questionable in others. No site has produced definite evidence of the existence of man prior to the Middle Formative. Only the historical data on the Tarascans permit sociological analysis. Therefore, a discussion of any regularities among the "evolutions" of the various regional sequences is premature (Steward, 1955). Further, we may not assume that Michoacan is typical with respect to cultural development in other areas. We seem to be dealing with short-lived and somewhat isolated cultures up to the advent of the Tarascans, and even their "empire" is essentially rural (Steward, 1955, p. 197; Armillas, 1964a, p. 318).

My approach has necessarily been limited to a description of the stylistic horizons in pottery and architecture, as well as burial customs. I have attempted to anchor the phases chronologically, but few absolute dates are proposed. I shall describe the archaeological cultures in order of their relative placement in time. Although the Willey

and Phillips (1962, pp. 61–201) historical-developmental stage names—Formative, Classic, and Postclassic—are used in this article, they are employed here as chronological dividers, i.e., periods. Future stratigraphic excavations may provide developmental sequences which will permit not only discussion of the evolution of specific cultures and the regularities observed among them (Steward, 1955), but also discussion of the evolution of Michoacan culture in more general terms (White, 1959; Sahlins and Service, 1960; see fig. 1).

Formative Cultures

To the best of my knowledge, signs of early man in Michoacan have not been published. The earliest culture found so far is possibly the Infiernillo phase in the lower Balsas basin, which is believed to date from the Middle Formative (Litvak King, 1968). Fluted points, probably Folsom, have been found in neighboring Jalisco (Lindsay, 1968, p. 122), and Pleistocene fauna were noted by Porter (1956) at Chupicuaro, and by Hewes at the northwest margin of Lake Cuitzeo (Noguera, 1965, p. 261).

El Opeño near Zamora and a probable early occupation of Jiquilpan are suggested by Jiménez Moreno (1966, p. 7) as dating also from the same period. The early dating of El Opeño is seriously questioned in this article. Jiménez Moreno suggests also that the Curutaran phase at Zamora and the Potrero de la Isla phase at Zacapu belong to the Upper Formative (1966, p. 25). The view taken here is that these "cultures" require further study before this dating can be accepted. There is little doubt that the Chupicuaro culture at the Michoacan-Guanajuato border dates from the Upper Formative, and continues into the Protoclassic (Willey, Ekholm, and Millon, 1964, Charts 1b and 2b). In addition, both Armillas (1948, cuadro correlativo) and Jiménez Moreno (1966, fig. 3) have suggested chronologies for the different Michoacan cultures (see Chart 1).

660

CHART 1—ARCHAEOLOGICAL PHASES IN MICHOACAN

	Highlands	Lower Balsas	Tierra Caliente
900 B.C.			
		Infiernillo	
	El Opeño		
500 B.C.			
	Early Chupicuaro		
200 B.C.			
	Late Chupicuaro		Chumbicuaro
	Jiquilpan?	Ojo de Agua?	Delicias
			Apatzingan
700 A.D.	Chapala	El Romanse	"El Infiernillo" Tepetate Mexiquito-Huetamo
1100 A.D.	Cojumatlan	El Poche	Chila
	Tzintzuntzan		

Both highland and coastal Michoacan were occupied perhaps as early as the Middle Formative. Whether or not the intervening tierra caliente trough contains formative cultures is unknown.

LA VILLITA. The Rio Balsas flows out of Tlaxcala and Puebla, crosses Guerrero, and empties into the Pacific Ocean between Guerrero and Michoacan. It is the largest river in southwestern Mexico, and ranks second in length among Mexican rivers (Brand, 1942). The Balsas and its western tributary, the Rio Grande de Tepalcatepec, lie in an east-west structural depression between the Mexican plateau and the Sierra Madre del Sur. Cross-faulting has been common, and the river, below the big bend at Hacienda Las Balsas near the inner limit of the coastal plain, occupies such a structural depression. Elevations range from about 105 m. at Hacienda Las Balsas to more than 3000 m. in the higher peaks of the Sierra Madre del Sur. The bulk of the middle Balsas valley lands lie between 105 and 450 m. above sea level, being entirely within the inhospitable, hotter, drier segments of the tierra caliente. Below Pinzandaran, beyond the sierra—in the zone in which the La Villita excavations were conducted—the flora becomes completely tropical.

Aside from Nicholson's excavations at Melchor Ocampo in 1962, the area surveyed and excavated in 1966–67 by the INAH La Villita group, in connection with the construction of a dam 13 km. from the mouth of the Balsas, was almost completely unknown to archaeology. The flooded area reaches 50 km. inland to about 2 km. below the Morelos dam at El Infiernillo.

It is emphasized at the outset that the suggestions put forth here are largely im-

FIG. 2—LA VILLITA. *a*, Stratigraphy at Site V-42. *b-f*, Formative pottery, Site V-42. *g,h*, Site V-6. *i-l*, Late Postclassic pottery. Scales in centimeters.

pressionistic, for collections are in storage and field notes are not at hand as this is written (summer, 1969).

Of the 68 sites located in the La Villita excavations, only one, designated as V-42, yielded evidence of a Formative occupation (Chadwick, field notes). One of a series of four low house mounds around a rectangular plaza was found to contain some 30 stratified burials with associated artifacts, which date from Middle or Upper Formative. The house mounds were built in Postclassic times (fig. 2). It is impossible to estimate what percentage of this "cemetery"

was left unexcavated, although 60 per cent would appear to be on the conservative side (cf. Paddock, 1968, pp. 126–27).

Litvak King (1968) dates the Infiernillo phase burials as Middle Formative on the basis of such diagnostic ceramic decorative techniques as fingernail impression, rocker-stamping, zoned crosshatching, and incising. According to him, the significant vessel forms were hemispherical bowls, gray bottle-like vessels, and globular ollas with short straight necks. Although Litvak King has had access to the V-42 ceramics since I excavated them three years ago, I recently

FIG. 3—RIO BALSAS, PRESA DEL INFIERNILLO. *a,b*, Site B-11. *c,d*, Site B-44. *e*, Site B-41. *f*, Site B-10.

Fig. 4—POTTERY FROM RIO BALSAS, PRESA DEL INFIERNILLO. Sites: *a*, B-73. *b*, B-5. *c-g*, B-10. *h*, B-44. *i-k*, B-54. *l*, B-68. Scales in centimeters.

examined the complete pots in a storeroom in the Department of Prehistory, Instituto Nacional de Antropología e Historia, in Mexico City. To the best of my knowledge, all but one were globular ollas with slightly outflaring necks (fig. 2, c-f). None was decorated with rocker-stamping or with fingernail impression. What Litvak King calls "incising" would probably be termed "deep grooving" by other archaeologists. The grooved motifs were in all cases geometrical. All these vessels were red or brown. Lorenzo, who examined them with me, saw no connections with other Middle Formative ceramics, although he did point out (personal communication, 1969) that one vessel, also decorated with frogs around the body, seemed to him to have Central and/or South American connections (fig. 2,e). A gray, highly polished, globular vessel with short, incurving neck could date from Middle Formative (fig. 2,b). Such vessels are said to have been found in Tlatilco (Cabrera Castro, personal communication, 1969). These vessels are called *bules* in Guerrero. All ceramics from this period are probably monochrome.

The earliest burials were found in Zones IX–X and were those associated with the vessels I have discussed above. It is to be noted, however, that five lower stratified levels were dug. Although sherds from these pits have been analyzed only in the field, preliminary observations indicate that the two lowest zones, some 6.5 m. deep, contained poorly fired, very crumbly, black and brownish sand-tempered sherds. Vessel form could not be determined exactly, but the sherds probably once composed *tecomates*. Charcoal samples were obtained from these levels, but so far no radiocarbon determinations have been processed. Quite early ceramics, dating from approximately 2800 B.C., were excavated by the Brushes at San Jeronimo, about 200 km. east of the delta. These ceramics are said to resemble those from the Purron phase in the Tehuacan valley, which MacNeish believes are

the earliest ceramics yet found in Mesoamerica. Recently, however, archaeologists under the direction of Lorenzo found a clay figurine at Tlapacoya, dating from about 3200 B.C. according to radiocarbon dates (Lorenzo, personal communication, 1969). Lorenzo has remarked to me on its similarity to figurines from Anatolia, which he believes is simply a coincidence.

All of the earliest burials lay extended on the back. Pits had not been dug; the individuals had been laid on the beach surface and then covered with sand. One burial contained three individuals. The most important person, to judge from the funerary costume and offerings, was a woman. Dental mutilation had been performed, and perhaps cranial deformation. A small polished greenstone ritual metate with nubbin supports had been placed at the xiphoid process of the sternum. In addition, a highly polished conch-shell trumpet with perforations had been placed (tied?) over the left parietal region. Besides identical sets of shell bracelets, decorated with incised parrots with inlaid turquoise eyes, a chain of shell ornaments crossed the region of the stomach. Jade, shell, and turquoise beads and plaques, numbering in the hundreds, were combined with jade pendants and small "ducks" of highly polished, finely carved reddish bone to form a complex necklace. The "ducks" also featured eyes of turquoise inlay. Similar objects, said to be from Guerrero, exist in private collections in Mexico City (Litvak King, personal communication, 1967). Two other persons (males?) were buried with this richly attired woman. One lay to her left and was extended in the same east-west orientation. The heads faced west. A third person lay east of the other two and was extended in a north-south direction (fig. 4). The skeleton next to the principal corpse had the right leg doubled up in a vertical position; the femur of the left leg was raised also in a vertical position with the knee slightly bent and with the tibia and fibula outstretched horizontally.

665

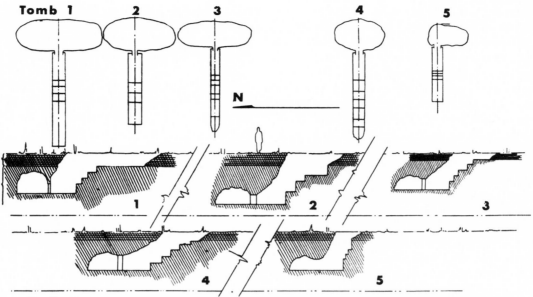

FIG. 5—PLANS AND SECTIONS OF TOMBS, EL OPEÑO, JACONA, MICHOACAN. (After Noguera, 1942, fig. 14.)

The burial had not been disturbed. The bule-like gray vessel lay to the left of the woman's face (fig. 2,*b*). No offerings were found with the other corpses.

This multiple burial may indicate a matrilineal system, since Kirchhoff (1948, p. 219) has given evidence that women in western Mexico were often *caciques* in late periods. Certain 16th- or 17th-century documents have been published in a Guadalajara newspaper which relate the history of a ruling female dynasty at Tonala, Jalisco.

No remnants of houses or other structures were found. From the abundance of projectile points and the near-absence of fishbones, hunting seems to have been more important than fishing.

EL OPEÑO. Noguera excavated three tombs which had been carved in the *tepetate* at El Opeño in the La Cañada subzone (see below) near Zamora (Noguera, 1942). The shape of the tombs—elliptical burial chambers reached by an entrance passageway with three or four steps—is similar to that of later shaft tombs in Jalisco, Colima, and Nayarit (fig. 5). The

Jalisco tombs have been dated by radiocarbon from the 2d century B.C. to the 3d or 4th centuries A.D. (Long and Taylor, 1966a, p. 652). In size, however, the El Opeño tombs compare more favorably with the Postclassic *sótanos* in the Mixtec region and in northeast Guerrero. In the latter area they tend to be bottle-shaped. A generic connection between these groups and with similar tombs in Colombia and Ecuador certainly should be investigated.

The dating of El Opeño as Middle Formative is based on the finding of figurines similar to Vaillant's D and C types in the Valley of Mexico, in addition to a greenstone Olmec-like figure. Although the similarity of the clay figurines to Vaillant's types is generally conceded, and although Coe (1965b) accepts as Olmec the greenstone figure, there are several reasons why I challenge this dating. First, neither the clay figurines nor the Olmec-like figure were recovered in Noguera's excavations. They had been obtained by local people and had been turned over to Noguera. All are said to have come from the same tomb.

666

Second, the so-called Olmec figurine was made of green stone, not the blue-green stone so prized by the Olmec. If indeed it is an Olmec object, one wonders why blue-green jade was not used in its manufacture since the apparent source of this jade seems to have been in the middle Balsas region (Coe, 1967, p. 94). Third, the jade figure was badly carved, and the so-called "jaguar" mouth was executed in very rudimentary form (Noguera, 1942, p. 583). Fourth, the clay figurines are said by Noguera to be of local manufacture. Although they are somewhat similar to the Valley of Mexico types, the El Opeño people adopted these foreign ideas only after coloring them with their own traditions. Fifth, if one considers the tombs to be contemporaneous in construction—a logical conclusion in view of the similarity of their plans and measurements—the finding of a negative-painted olla in Tomb 5 would tend to place all of them in the Upper Formative (Noguera, 1965, p. 71; 1942, fig. 7a; Coe, 1963, p. 35; Ford, 1969, p. 135). Sixth, since skull burials were found in Tomb 4, this again leads to the conclusion that the dating must be reconsidered. Skull burials occur in Monte Alban II, and sculptures in stone showing trophy heads apparently date from that period also at Dain-zu, Oaxaca. Skull burials are typical of the late phase at Chupicuaro and of Teotihuacan II (Porter, 1956, p. 534; Noguera, 1942, p. 580). They are not, to the best of my knowledge, diagnostic Middle Formative traits. Finally, a tetrapod pot, albeit zoomorphic, said to be from looted Tomb 1, could tend to place the tombs in the Protoclassic.[1]

Although the matter can not be definitely decided here, this object, if it is Olmec, might be an heirloom, and therefore a Late Formative or Protoclassic date should be considered. In this connection, we note that an Olmec heirloom was found in a Protoclassic burial at Cerro de las Mesas in association with skull burials in urns.

The El Opeño tombs each consisted of a long passageway dug in the tepetate to a depth of about 1.10 m. below the surface. Each shaft passageway differed in width but all approximated 0.75 m. Three or four steps were carved in the tepetate to facilitate descent. The passageway continued horizontally for 1 or 2 m. to a point where a narrow curved nichelike entranceway was encountered. The "niches" were covered by large stones. The burial chambers varied in size (fig. 5); they are elliptical in ground plan and have domed roofs. The dead in most cases were placed on platforms carved from tepetate (Noguera, 1942, p. 577). Burial position also varied: some skeletons were extended on the back; other burials consisted only of skulls; one individual may have been in a flexed sitting position. All the tombs contained multiple burials. Some of the bones had been painted with red ochre, a substance occasionally found in the ceramic vessels.

Besides the pottery vessels, a clay whistle was found. Other artifacts include painted jade earplugs, jade beads, laurel leaf-shaped atlatl points, and Schumla-like projectile points of obsidian. Schumla points in the Valley of Mexico date from A.D. 1 to 1100 (García Cook, 1967, pp. 154–55). A unique arc-shaped stone object, which

[1] In discussing the Tlatilco Olmec ceramics, Bernal (1969, p. 132) points out that negative painting, which is found much later in other sites, occurs as "otra novedad" at Tlatilco. He mentions (p. 135) that decapitation was also practiced at Tlatilco. Neither of these traits, however, appear as major customs but as occasional occurrences. In discussing the famed El Opeño "Olmec" object, Bernal (p. 143) says: "I find no Olmec evidence in the rest of western Mexico (aside from Guerrero), which means that these people did not reach that area. It has been said that the famous little sculpture of El Opeño, near Jacona, Michoacan, indicates that Olmec influence penetrated as far north as this region, so distant from the metropolitan center, but it seems to me that the figure is Olmec only in the most vague way, if it is at all. It has a semicircular mouth with the corners turned down, but outside of this detail it does not appear to be in the least Olmec." Cf. Ford, 1969, p. 135. Lorenzo (personal communication, 1969) believes the El Opeño tombs belong to the Classic period.

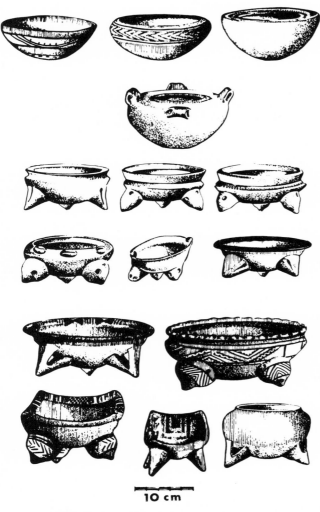

10 cm

FIG. 6—POTTERY FROM JERECUARO, GUANAJUA-
TO. (From Matos Moctezuma, 1968, fig. 6.)

at Chupicuaro and on figurines in shaft tombs in Jalisco (Furst, 1965a, fig. 1).

CHUPICUARO. The site of Chupicuaro, Guanajuato, is probably forever lost to archaeology, having been submerged under a lake in connection with the Solís Dam. Remains of this culture are widespread throughout Michoacan and extend eastward to the Valley of Mexico. This distinctive culture has been found at the following sites: Zinapecuaro, Zacapu, Purepero, and Jacona, all in the state of Michoacan; and at Tepeji del Rio, Cerro del Tepalcate, Cuanalan, Teotihuacan, Tulancingo, and Jerecuaro, Guanajuato (Jiménez Moreno, 1966, p. 25; Porter, 1956; Kelly,.1948, p. 45). Chupicuaro is in the highland geographical region called Middle Lerma by Armillas (1948, p. 211; see also West, 1948).

The archaeology of Chupicuaro is known mainly from the 390 human burials and associated pottery which were excavated by INAH archaeologists in the 1940s. Several preliminary articles have been published (Estrada Balmori and Piña Chan, 1948b; Porter, 1948b). One of three monographs published on Michoacan archaeology is based on the Chupicuaro excavations (Porter, 1956).

Chupicuaro is placed by Willey, Ekholm, and Millon (1964, Charts 2a and 2b) in the Upper Formative. Porter (1956, pp. 569–75) divided the culture into two phases, early and late. Her early phase is believed to be contemporaneous with such phases in the Valley of Mexico as Ticoman III, Cerro del Tepalcate, Cuicuilco, and Teotihuacan I. The second phase is equated with Teotihuacan II (Chart 1).

The division of the burial groups into two phases was based on the fact that the two major figurine types, the slant-eyed H-4 type in Vaillant's classification and a so-called "choker" type, were not found together in graves. H-types accompanied only black polychrome or black-on-red pottery, whereas "choker" figurines occurred almost exclusively with brown polychrome and

may have been a weapon, had carved on it the figure of a serpent, part of which had been painted red (Noguera, 1942, fig. 11). In addition to Types D and C, other clay figurines, said to be from one of the looted tombs, were different stylistically in that they wore long skirts over which polychrome designs had been painted. This polychrome technique is not characteristic of Middle Formative figurines in the Valley of Mexico, but is similar to that on figurines

668

brown-on-red pottery. The former group was considered to be early; the second, late. Graves yielding both types were considered as transitional (Porter, 1956, p. 536).

Chupicuaro pottery has been characterized as being heavy, thick-walled, and very durable. Paste is uniform, brown, and very coarse. The ceramics were fired at a very moderate temperature. Temper consisted of rhyolitic or dactic volcanic ash. Porter (1956, pp. 538–39) notes the absence of basaltic and andesitic ash, both of which are abundant in the area, as tempering material. The pottery clay is homogeneous; the same mixtures of clay and tempering materials were used for both black and painted pottery. Design is wholly geometric in both painted and incised varieties.

Chupicuaro pottery, at first glance, seems alien to Mesoamerica. The vessels—monochrome, dichrome, and polychrome—have many different forms: *patojos*, ollas, *tecomates*, plain bowls, pedestal-base bowls, effigy vessels, *tapaplato*-like bowls (plate lids with three looped handles), tripod dishes with tall supports, bowls in the form of a squash, vessels with basket handles, goblets, containers with human faces near the rim, bowls with looplike handles set around the rim, several cylindrical types, including one vessel composed of two cylindrical jars joined together at the base and mouth by thin ribbons of clay, and rectangular boxlike forms with an opening in the center (Matos Moctezuma, 1968, figs. 6, 7, 8; our figs. 6–8).

The early phase included: unpainted black types, including a ring-stand bowl, and such painted types as red-rimmed, red ware, red-on-buff, black and red, and black polychrome. Only the red, red-on-buff, and black polychrome continued into the second phase. Black wares characterize the first period; brown, the second. Incising, filleting, fluting, and engraving were the main modes of decoration. Black ware was usually smoothed and had a dull polish. Some specimens, however, were highly polished,

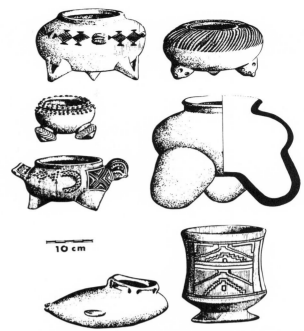

FIG. 7—POTTERY FROM JERECUARO, GUANAJUATO. (From Matos Moctezuma, 1968, fig. 7.)

FIG. 8—POTTERY FROM JERECUARO, GUANAJUATO. (From Matos Moctezuma, 1968, fig. 8.)

669

Fig. 9—BLACK WARE, CHUPICUARO, GUANAJUA-TO. (From Porter, 1956, fig. 6.)

Fig. 10—RED-ON-BUFF AND BLACK POLYCHROME POTTERY, CHUPICUARO, GUANAJUATO. (From Porter, 1956, fig. 12.)

but lacked the lustrous finish of the painted ware. Color varied from black to brown. Fire-clouds were common.

On other types, paint was black, brown, and red. A thin, yellowish slip, at times whitish, was usually applied first. Vessels were evenly fired, clouded areas were rare. Sometimes a high glossy polish was achieved. Burnishing strokes on the painted wares were much less apparent than on un-painted specimens. Most of the painted vessels were slipped, except for the red-rimmed types (Porter, 1956, pp. 544–45). Classification was based on the color combinations, and seven painted types were defined.

Black polychrome assumed many of the same forms as those previously mentioned. In addition, black polychrome tetrapods, a

Protoclassic diagnostic, were in vogue in the second phase. Vessels polychromed in black and white on red were decorated with diamonds, crosses, chevrons, zigzags, and xiconellis. The designs may have been copied from textiles (Porter, 1956, figs. 6, 12, 14; our figs. 9–11).

Chupicuaro polychromes used the base as a third color. This technique elsewhere has been called pseudo-trichrome (Wauchope, 1950, p. 234) and trichromatic (Vaillant, 1931, p. 281). Polychrome motifs, in addition to those mentioned above, were scrolls, diamond chain, checkerboard, interlocking teeth, diagonal lines bordered by steps, crosshatching, dot-filled diamond, stepped triangle, cross, and vertical stripes (Porter, 1956, p. 555).

In addition to the H-type figurines and

670

"choker" variety previously mentioned, there were several other types. Porter recovered four figurines of reddish clay with a white slip whose headgear was similar to that found on Teotihuacan II jadeite figurines from the Quetzalcoatl temple (Porter, 1956, p. 573).[2] The ubiquitous figures-tied-to-a-couch were also fashionable at Chupicuaro, as were large polychromed hollow figurines in black and red on cream (Bernal and others, 1968, fig. 132). All these types show connections with other areas.

Other Chupicuaro manufactures include clay beads, miniature vessels, pendants, stamps, worked sherds, balls, and earplugs, which are solid disks with concave sides. Rattles, clay ocarinas, bone rasps, and turtle shells were used as musical instruments (Porter, 1956, p. 560). Bone awls, punches, needles, and pendants were also found. Lithic objects of both obsidian and gray flint include knives, fine long blades, scrapers, and projectile points. Ten metates, both legged and plain, were found in graves.

Some 390 human burials were excavated, in addition to 46 dog skeletons and a group of charred remains from an "ossuary." Early-phase interments were from 0.25 to 2.50 m. deep, the tepetate often determining the depth. Many of the burials were scattered around firepits (*tlecuils*) which were often filled with fine ash and bits of charcoal. The bodies in both phases were usually extended on the back (fig. 12). Skull burials were especially popular in the second phase; only two trophy skulls were found in the first period graves. Artificial head deformation was practiced by occipital flattening and perhaps fronto-occipital deformation. One burial yielded a skeleton

[2] Bennyhoff (1967, p. 24) has stated that "there is no longer any evidence for the persistence of Chupicuaro until Teotihuacan II, and . . . Porter's seriation of burials is incorrect. The correct sequence, early to late as found at Ticoman, would be E2–H2–H4 and not H4–E2–H2 as used by Porter. Unfortunately, this reseriation cannot be done from the publication because the grave lots were omitted." Bennyhoff's basis for this statement does not seem convincing to me.

FIG. 11—BLACK POLYCHROME POTTERY, CHUPICUARO, GUANAJUATO. (From Porter, 1956, fig. 14.)

whose skull had been horizontally severed above the ears, with only the lower part of the cranium remaining intact. Other methods of skull-cutting were also practiced. Four cut skulls were found on the knees of a skeleton in another burial. Some of the skulls had been painted red. In the second phase the custom of extending the dead was less rigidly adhered to and positions were more varied. The number of ventrally extended skeletons increased. In most, offerings were concentrated at the feet, but they also occurred at other positions. Several of the cut skulls have been compared by Porter to the burial at Cerro de las Mesas mentioned above in connection with the El Opeño tombs.

Covarrubias (1957, pp. 42–43) considered the Chupicuaro culture to be without

671

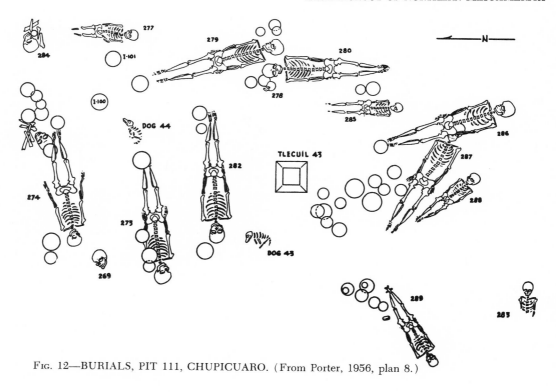

FIG. 12—BURIALS, PIT 111, CHUPICUARO. (From Porter, 1956, plan 8.)

antecedents; he believed it to be foreign and intrusive. The finding of shoe-shaped vessels, usually called *patojos,* corroborates Covarrubias's opinion (Chadwick, 1968). I have commented elsewhere in this volume (Art. 8) about a phenomenon which several other authors have also noted with respect to the tendency of patojos to appear at one site, then to disappear, only to reappear at a later period. For example, the patojo appears as a resident ware at Monte Alban only in the first and last periods. In the Guatemalan highlands, it appears in the Las Charcas A phase, then reappears in the Postclassic. In highland Peru at the Kotosh site, patojos appear in the Kotosh Kotosh phase (Middle Formative), disappear, and appear again in the Kotosh Higueras period —probably Protoclassic in Mesoamerican terms (Izumi and Sono, 1963, pp. 157–58; Caso, Bernal, and Acosta, 1967). Patojos appear in an intrusive context at Tres Zapotes

in the Postclassic "Soncautla" complex along with other vessel forms which Coe (1965c) suggests are "revivals" of Formative types. A temporal distribution of patojos occurs in Michoacan similar to that noted at Monte Alban: after Chupicuaro, patojos disappear from the area, but come into vogue again, along with such forms as stirrup-spouted vessels and "teapots," in the late Tarascan florescence. In other cultures during this period such as Monte Alban V, "Soncautla," Tairona in Colombia, and even the Southern Ceremonial Cult in the United States, both patojos and "teapots" appear. The stirrup-spouted vessel also shows up in the southeastern United States (Chadwick, 1968).

Rands and Smith (1965, p. 143) have mentioned the irregular occurrence through time of the patojo, and note that "specific cultural continuity is indicated."

Patojos, as well as shaft tombs and figures-tied-to-a-couch, have been cited by various authors as being indicative of connections between Mesoamerica and South America. The fact that patojos have been found in shaft tombs in the Late Postclassic Seca Quebrada complex in Colombia (Ford, 1944, pp. 40, 65, figs. 10, 18), and that "couch" figures in Mesoamerica also come from the shaft tomb area in western Mexico (Jalisco-Colima-Nayarit region), indicates that these traits may be related (Kelly, 1948, p. 66). "Couch" figures and patojos, along with a costume—*the xicolli*—which will later be the special garb of the Mixtec, appear at Teotihuacan only in the second period (Sejourné, 1959, fig. 18,*p,q,r*).

Of interest in this context is the fact that one Chupicuaro patojo was decorated with a figure having six-fingered hands (Porter, 1956, p. 454). Such a drawing could indicate that the users of this type of vessel were a rigidly endogamous group. Persons with six-fingered hands, caused by inbreeding, are common among the Old Order Amish in the United States and among the Veddoid Kadar in Kerala State in India (Coon, 1966, p. 196).

We shall return to this subject below. It seems logical to suppose that the Chupicuaro people may have been an endogamous group who were not native to the middle Lerma region.

After the late Chupicuaro occupation, the site seems to have been abandoned. There is no evidence that the Chupicuaro people were overrun by other groups (Porter, 1956, pp. 574–75). During the Toltec-Mazapan period, however, the area was again occupied. Toltec remains were particularly abundant at nearby Zinapecuaro.

Michoacan in the Classic Period

While the rest of Mesoamerica reached new heights in the attainment of civilization, Michoacan and the rest of western Mexico lagged behind. In many respects some of the Preclassic cultures of Michoacan seem more sophisticated than those which appeared in the Classic period. Certain elements of high culture did penetrate the area, particularly in the middle Balsas region. Moedano K. (1948) has mentioned a Mayoid tomb in this region, and Rubín de la Borbolla has commented on similar influences which appear to be manifested in the Huetamo stelae. It seems likely, however, that some of the suspected Mayoid infiltration goes back to the Protoclassic; the stelae appear to belong to the Early Postclassic. Teotihuacan penetrations were felt in parts of Guerrero, in the eastern tierra caliente of Michoacan at Huetamo, and perhaps at Apatzingan in the west. Slight evidence of Teotihuacan influence has been noted in the lower Balsas basin (Litvak King, 1968, p. 28). Apparently lapidary work at Tzintzuntzan in the Lower Lacustrine phase exhibits Teotihuacan traits. Moedano K. (1946) has postulated that Tzintzuntzan derived a large part of its earliest ceramic style from the "Antigua" phase at Zinapecuaro, which is contemporaneous with Teotihuacan III. Teotihuacanoid figurines and stone masks are known from Patzcuaro (Jiménez Moreno, 1966, p. 47). The same influences seem to have also reached Jiquilpan (Noguera, 1944). As mentioned, the Teotihuacan connections in the middle Lerma region disappear after the demise of the Chupicuaro culture.

APATZINGAN. Apatzingan lies in the western tierra caliente, the great low, east-west depression which crosses the state into neighboring Guerrero. The Tepalcatepec basin, in which Apatzingan lies, is bounded on the north, east, and west by mountains. On the west, the Sierra Madre del Sur forms a wall-like barrier along the Michoacan-Jalisco-Colima coast, thus dividing tierra caliente from the Pacific coastal area. The northern limit of the Tepalcatepec basin is approximately the 700-m. contour where the foothills rise abruptly to the Sierras. The lowest land in the area, however, some 200

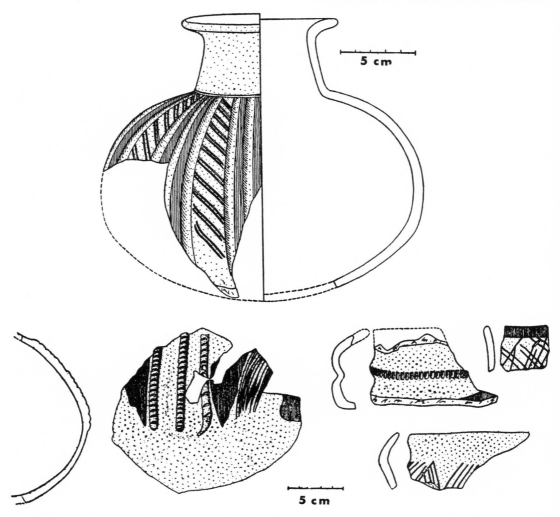

FIG. 13—APATZINGAN RED-ON-BROWN, INCISED WARE. (After Kelly, 1947b, figs. 22, 23.)

m. above sea level, lies along the Rio Tepalcatepec to the south. Although this is tierra caliente, the seasonal nature of the rainfall, very wet summers and dry winters, puts the area into the Koeppen Aw category of tropical savanna. The typical flora consists of low, spiney xerophytic legumes with a few forests of large tropical trees and some lush swamps (Kelly, 1947b; Goggin, 1943).

Willey, Ekholm, and Millon (1964, Chart 1b) place the Delicias and Apatzingan phases in the early classic. Kelly (1948, p.

68) has dated the Delicias phase as contemporaneous with Ortices in Colima, which in turn is thought to be of the same time period as Teotihuacan III. Long and Taylor (1966b, p. 1459) believe that Ortices, hence Delicias, should be pushed back to about A.D. 50. We have included Kelly's first three phases—Chumbicuaro, Delicias, and Apatzingan—in the Classic time period (see Chart 1). This would appear to be correct since both *molcajetes* and *malacates*, diagnostic Postclassic traits, appear at Apa-

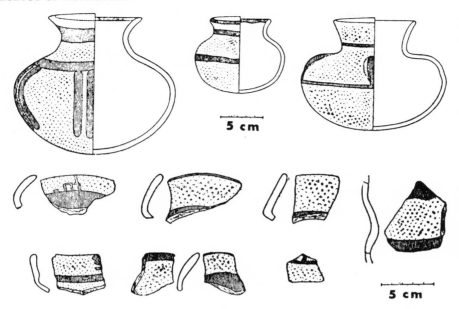

FIG. 14—DELICIAS RED-ON-BROWN WARE, APATZINGAN, MICHOACAN. (After Kelly, 1947b, figs. 24, 25.)

tzingan only in the succeeding Tepetate phase.

Kelly's strategy at Apatzingan was to pool the data from surface collections, test pits, and burials, from which five ceramic phases were defined. In one low mound at the Delicias site, misnamed a yácata, four of the five phases were found in stratigraphic position. The mound itself is presumably a Delicias phase construction (Kelly, 1947b, pp. 154–55).

The Chumbicuaro phase is known only from a small cache of sherds. It is characterized by two monochrome wares, one plain, the other incised. Wares were reddish and gray. Annular bases and supports were absent. The sherds were unslipped, and decoration was by incision. Forms include both ollas and bowls (*cajetes*).

The Delicias phase was defined on the basis of four "types": red-on-brown, red-on-buff, polished, and plain. Again supports and annular bases were absent. Delicias plain ware varies from cream, through dun, to dark gray, and has a fine satiny, some-

what dull polish. The typical vessel form is an olla with a slightly pointed base. A fairly sharp angle occurs on the shoulder just below the base of a slightly flaring neck. Other Delicias manufactures include composite ornaments of shell and pyrite, and pyrite mirrors.

The next phase, Apatzingan, possibly is contemporaneous with Delicias. Its two distinctive pottery types are an incised red-on-brown type, which occurs as flaring-necked ollas and deep bowls without rims, and a plain ware, which usually has such forms as large cajetes with flaring walls. Some short-necked ollas are also made in the same ware (Kelly, 1947b, figs. 22, 23, Apatzingan red-on-brown incised ware; figs. 24, 25, Delicias red-on-brown ware; our figs. 13, 14).

No figurines nor burials are known from the earliest horizon. Two figurines have been assigned to the Delicias phase, one to Apatzingan. Burials in the Delicias and Apatzingan phases were extended on the back with large stone slabs or boulders

675

covering the body. In some cases, legless metates (*tequiiches*) formed the covering (Goggin, 1943, p. 48; see text below for a description of the Postclassic phases).

So little is known about a possible Classic phase in southeastern Michoacan, around Huetamo in the middle Balsas zone, that we shall ignore it here except to mention again that both Teotihuacan and Mayoid influences have been noted there. No diagnostic classic pottery has been recovered, so far as I know. As noted, it seems likely that the stelae in the region more properly belong to a transitional Classic-Postclassic phase, which is somewhat analogous to the main occupation at Xochicalco in the central valleys.

VALLEY OF ZAMORA. The Valley of Zamora is also called La Cañada. It is a unique valley, about 2 km. wide and 10 km. long, through which runs the Patzcuaro-Zacapu-Zamora highway. Elevation ranges from 1,785 to 1,939 m. It includes the area from Jiquilpan to Zacapu (Beals, 1969; Armillas, 1948, p. 211). Sequences of isolated cultures from both Zamora and Zacapu have been defined chronologically by Jiménez Moreno (1966, fig. 3). He suggests that a phase called Curutaran, a Formative or perhaps Protoclassic culture, succeeded El Opeño. A Postclassic phase has been called Los Gatos. Similarly, Early Classic (Potrero de la Isla), Early Postclassic (Potrero de la Aldea), and Late Postclassic (Malpais) phases have been proposed for the Zacapu region. At Jiquilpan only a possible Classic period culture has been recognized.

The El Otero site near Jiquilpan was investigated briefly by Noguera (1944). On the basis of an oversized globular olla, decorated with the same cloisonné lacquer technique used in Uruapan today, Noguera proposed that the Jiquilpan occupation is contemporaneous with Teotihuacan III. The polychrome olla was decorated by horizontal bands, each containing rows of "priests" and "warriors," said to have been costumed in characteristic Teotihuacan style (Marquina, 1951, p. 264).

Spinden (1948, pp. 34–35) suggested that west Mexico was perhaps the center of diffusion for lacquer techniques which are found from Arizona to Argentina. Brand (1943, p. 60) believes that Mexican lacquer work may have originated in tierra caliente on the Gulf coast, and that it diffused across Oaxaca to the Balsas basin, whence it spread to the Tarascan highlands. Probably the earliest archaeological evidence of gourd-painting in Mesoamerica comes from Tikal, where two lacquered gourds have been dated to about 25 B.C. (Jenkins, 1967, p. 136).

A tetrapod alabaster vase was recovered at Jiquilpan, in addition to many complex necklaces of shell, turquoise, rock crystal, jade, and pyrite bars with turquoise inlay. Stone "pineapple" maceheads were also found there. The excavated burials were all extended on the back. Some buildings were also the object of a brief exploration. Construction techniques were more similar to those in the Valley of Mexico than to the techniques employed in building the Tarascan yácatas (Marquina, 1951, p. 264). A probable ball court was briefly investigated.

LA VILLITA. A possible Classic phase called Ojo de Agua was found in the stratified V-42 site. A double burial could perhaps represent a phase which is transitional between Preclassic and Postclassic. An extended burial (the Preclassic mortuary posture) was found in stratigraphic association with another, apparently a "montón de huesos" type. The montón de huesos burial is thought to be characteristic of one of the earliest Postclassic phases (Litvak King, 1968, pp. 28–29). In another site a surface find of a Teotihuacan-like vessel (Litvak King, 1968, pp. 28–29), described as being decorated by polishing and champlevé technique, is said to be evidence of a Teotihuacan infiltration in this area. I recently examined this vessel (Litvak King is correct in saying it is cylindical-hemispherical and without supports), and find it is decorated by negative painting, not champlevé. I could see no similarity between the Ojo de Agua vessel motifs and those from Teotihuacan (fig. 2,k).

Postclassic Cultures

Michoacan is famous as the homeland of the Tarascan empire. The origin of the Tarascan nation begins historically with the fall of Tollan, dated here at about A.D. 1063 (see Article 20, this volume). Prior to Tarascan domination, a red-on-buff ceramic horizon, corresponding to the Tula-Mazapan style of central Mexico, appeared in several areas. Also, the Mixteca-Puebla horizon style appears in at least one highland site. In Early Postclassic times, however, the entire state seems to have been characterized by a series of somewhat isolated local cultures, showing few relationships to other areas with the exception of possible Xochicalco influence in the middle Balsas. The absence of transitional ceramic styles at Apatzingan argues against an indigenous development, and could be indicative of shifting populations. On the other hand, one suspects a more stable situation in the lower Balsas basin.

A definite South American intrusion appears to exist in the middle Balsas region in Late Postclassic times. An adobe structure of perhaps three stories with a trapezoidal doorway of Inca form has been discovered not far from Arcelia, Guerrero (Paddock, 1967, p. 425). Lorenzo (personal communication, 1969) reports that several more buildings of the same general type have also been found recently. Ancient reports indicate that large trading-canoe expeditions, perhaps from the Pearl Islands of Panama or the coast of Ecuador, reached the mouth of the Rio Balsas in pre-Hispanic times (West, 1961, pp. 133–35).

Although the late Tarascan influence reached as far as the middle Balsas, other late groups also were important there. The province of the Cuitlatec at its western terminus overlapped with the area of Tarascan domination (Drucker, Escalante, and Weitlaner, 1969, fig. 1). According to Brand, Cuitlatec in Nahuatl means "bastard people" or "people of the place of gold" (cited *ibid.*, p. 565). The region was noted for its gold, copper, and silver. In addition, both Apanec and Matlatzinca were spoken in the same region (Beals, 1969, fig. 2). It is important to note that Tarasco is related to both Quechua and Aymara; the closest affinity between Tarasco and Macro-Maya languages is that of Tarasco-Matlatzinca. Cuitlatec is reported to be related to both Uto-Nahuan and to Chibchan (Swadesh, 1967, pp. 84, 92).

The apparent "Inca" intrusion in Postclassic times may be an example of a continuing tradition in this region. The sculptures reported by Spinden at Placeres del Oro have been called "Chavinoid" by Covarrubias, and other authorities have noted similarities between middle Balsas carvings and some in South America.

THE HUETAMO REGION (middle Balsas valley). Huetamo, in southeastern Michoacan, is in tierra caliente. The Huetamo region, however, contrasts somewhat with the western area. Wide and open valleys characterize the area, separated by high mesas running north and south. Owing to the height of the mesas, there is greater rainfall in this region. This factor and the rich limestone soil create a good jungle or a tropical rain forest vegetation. The open-patterned savanna vegetation, composed of thorny, leguminous shrubs, mimosa, semitropical deciduous hardwoods, and several types of cactus, prevails in the more arid valleys (Osborne, 1943).

Aside from the probable Teotihuacan infiltration, mentioned above, at Huetamo, Armillas (1945, pp. 79–81) has noted the presence at Mexiquito of a building constructed with the Teotihuacan panel-slope

677

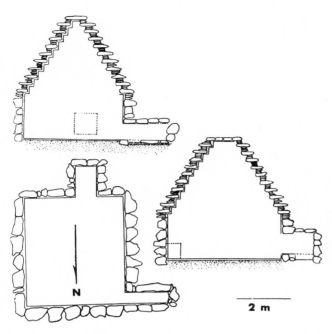

Fig. 15—VAULTED TOMB, OZTOTITLAN, GUERRE-RO. (From Moedano Koer, 1948, fig. 1.)

style. The building seems to belong, however, to an Early Postclassic phase since the relative proportions of tablero and talud are similar to those found on the main monument at Xochicalco. This dating may be corroborated by the fact that figurines in Mazapan style have also been found at Mexiquito (Noguera, 1965, p. 281). Still other possible influences from Postclassic Xochicalco may be indicated by the practice of erecting sculptured stelae in the region. Rubín de la Borbolla considered the stelae to be of Maya derivation. Phallic carvings have been noted also.

The Maya influence noted by Moedano K. (1948) in a tomb with a corbeled arch near Oztotitlan, Guerrero, is apparently believed by Jiménez Moreno (1966, map 3) to be the same influence which also reached Xochicalco during the Protoclassic. The influence alluded to presumably is connected to Vaillant's Q-complex. The "Maya" tomb explored by Moedano could date to the

Protoclassic: it shares some similarities with Monte Alban II tombs (fig. 15). The stelae at Huetamo, Mexiquito, and Santiago (Osborne, 1943, plate) in some respects appear similar to those recently found at Xochicalco. One suspects, therefore, that the stelae belong to the 700–900 period, which is called epiclassic in the central valleys. The eclecticism seen in this region seems analogous to the situation at Xochicalco in the Early Postclassic. A logical explanation for the importance of the area is that it was from here that the Olmec probably obtained the blue-green jade so characteristic of their portable art in the Formative period. As noted, the same zone was one of the most important for metal-mining in later times.

Osborne (1943, pp. 62–66) noted many different kinds of monuments in the area. He reports sites some 25 acres in area; one pyramid, he says, was approximately 30 m. high. Brand (1942, p. 144) mentions that the largest and highest "pyramids" are to be found in the river valley between El Cubo and Santiago, "where many artificial mounds more than sixty feet high" exist. A few pyramids, perhaps built upon and concealing a natural hill, according to Brand, exceeded 60 m. above the seeming natural level. The most common shape was that of a truncated wedge, with stages on one or more sides. The ramps and stages were frequently on the north and south, as well as on the west and east sides. Occasionally a group of platforms and other mounds would enclose courts, for example, some near El Puente de Campuzano and at Mexiquito. The buildings were commonly of rubble, were faced with uncut stone, and covered with stucco.

Two preferred modes of burial have been noted in the former Cuitlatec region. In some cases, the dead apparently were often buried under room floors. Urn burials of uncalcined bones were characteristic chiefly of the Huetamo area (Brand, 1942, p. 145).

A pottery type called Huetamo Coarse

Red was the most common ware in the region. The paste of this ware is reddish to grayish, and was usually tempered with quartz sand. Most examples were roughly slipped and smoothed or rubbed. Vessel forms include ollas, handled jars, bowls, tripod vessels, pitchers, and molcajetes. Loop handles were predominant; supports were long and short conical legs. Lister, covering much of the same region, reported that looped supports were also quite frequent; he suggests that a black-on-white type with looped supports may have been made by the Cuitlatec (Noguera, 1965, p. 279; Lister, 1948). Brand (1942, p. 147), too, notes the presence of a type called "looplegged maroon on cream." This ware is still made today at Zumpango and Tuliman in Guerrero.

Vessels with looped supports are commonly called *tapaplatos* (plate lids) in central Mexico. We have noted above a variant in the Chupicuaro culture. The tapaplato also appears in the following archaeological cultures (Chadwick, 1968): Teotihuacan II (along with patojos and "figures-tied-to-a-couch"); Monte Alban II-IIIa (along with patojos and Teotihuacan influence); Esperanza phase tombs at Kaminaljuyu; Mazapan period in the Valley of Mexico (along with patojos and molcajetes); Early Postclassic Costa Rica; Veraguas, Panama (various periods; tapaplatos are found in early shaft tombs there, and are said to be characteristic Veraguas vessel forms); "Soncautla" complex at Tres Zapotes (along with patojos; some of the tapaplatos were molcajetes); and in Ecuador after A.D. 700 (along with shaft tombs and patojos). We believe that these vessels are indicative of far-reaching connections, and that they belong to a ceramic complex whose most important member is the patojo.

Aside from the abundance of stucco-coated buildings, mainly platforms and "pyramids" in the Zindaro-Mexiquito-Santiago region, most of the sites were potsherd areas covered by stone outlines (Brand, 1942, p. 144). Armillas (1945, p. 77) noted similar groupings of *cimientos* as far east as Santo Tomas and Tetela in Guerrero. Similar rectangular outlines are typical of the Postclassic occupations in the lower Balsas and in the delta; they are reported also from Apatzingan, and Porter mentions stone outlines at Chupicuaro, probably dating from the Postclassic. The similarity of house-construction techniques over a large area could argue for a common cultural substratum, although it should be noted that several subtypes can be distinguished. For example, in the far eastern region of the middle Balsas, the house outlines were in the form of parallelograms with rounded corners; in the lower Balsas, they were generally rectangles, although some circular outlines were also recorded. Similar cimientos outline wattle-and-daub houses at Zacatula today.

Other artifacts found by Brand include flattened, spheroid malacates, as well as copper bells. Still others are legless, scoop, and trough metates; grooved and three-quarter grooved axes; effigy axes; greenstone celts; beads; pendants; whistles; clay stamps; hematite mirrors; earplugs; vessels of soapstone, onyx and alabaster; and club bark beaters (Brand, 1942, p. 146). Both rectangular grooved bark beaters with racket-shaped wooden handles and club bark beaters were found in Tehuacan (MacNeish, Nelken-Terner, and Johnson, 1967, pp. 130, 157, figs. 110, 111, 135). The racket type is identical to the Java-Celebes type in the Old World. MacNeish and associates note that ". . . the resemblance between this bark beater (racket type) from Tehuacan and those of the Celebes is truly remarkable. It is extremely difficult to believe that this complex tool was invented independently in both areas." Armillas (1945, p. 85) reported copper axe money only from Placeres del Oro.

EL INFIERNILLO. Extensive salvage operations were conducted in 1963 and 1964 by the INAH. The area covered was from San

679

Jeronimo in the east, in the vicinity of Santiago and Mexiquito, to the Hacienda de las Balsas where the river turns south. Some work was done toward the northwest, following the Rio Tepalcatepec; and in a southerly direction, past Pinzandaran to the dam site (fig. 1; Lorenzo, 1964, map), 104 sites were located on which were found 120 structures. A total of 251 burials were excavated, containing 191 offerings. Some 300 complete vessels were recovered in addition to approximately 600,000 to 750,000 sherds from test pits and surface. Lorenzo (personal communication, 1969) estimates that 98 per cent of the sherds were from monochrome wares. Also, approximately 3000 shell and 1000 lithic artifacts were found, plus some 60 metal objects. Other finds were fragments of 10 lacquered gourds, and numerous pieces of textiles.

According to a preliminary analysis, Lorenzo sees a late occupation in the area, beginning about A.D. 700, at which time metallurgy seems to have been introduced. Somewhat later, there is a Tula-Mazapan infiltration, and still later, a Tarascan intrusion. Connections are also seen with northwest Jalisco, southwest Zacatecas, and perhaps Nayarit and Colima. Mezcala traits are surprisingly absent. Connections in the earliest occupations are believed to have been with the southwest United States. Metallurgy is estimated to have been introduced somewhat earlier than is usually conceived.

Published artifacts include silver earplugs, copper fishhooks similar in form to Peruvian ones, tripod alabaster vases with globular bodies and straight necks, stone effigy palettes, and oversized globular ollas. According to the illustrations in the preliminary report, burials were extended, and architectural types seem to be similar to those found in the lower cuenca. Pareyón (Anonymous, 1960) has reported the finding of sótano tombs excavated in the tepetate at the Cancita site, as well as formative ceramics at the La Goleta site. Vessels

with looped legs, discussed elsewhere in this article, were also found in the El Infiernillo excavations.

LA VILLITA. Two Postclassic phases were defined in the lower Balsas project: an early period called El Romanse, and a later one named El Poche (Litvak King, 1968, chart 1). The El Romanse phase is characterized by reddish and brownish pottery (usually hemispherical bowls and globular ollas), plates with curved borders, and tripod vessels. Supports generally were zoomorphic. Figurines showed similarities to Mazapan types. Absence of El Infiernillo types of figurines which also appear in the Costa Grande region of Guerrero suggests a lack of contact between the La Villita and El Infiernillo peoples. Metal was present although in small quantities. Bark beaters were found.

Several modes of burial were in vogue in the Postclassic. One mortuary mound, faced with stucco-covered stones, yielded 61 burials in stratigraphic position. Only one-fourth of the mound was excavated. Burials in the earliest level consisted of piles of disarticulated bones (montón de huesos type), which were usually accompanied by a hemispherical bowl. Immediately above were burials whose offering was often one spindle whorl; at times jade beads and Mezcala figurines were included. Burials with similar offerings (limited, however, to the lone malacate, plus a copper fishhook in one case) at the V-42 site were usually seated over an ash area. In the Poche phase, typical burials were disarticulated bones, at times cut into rectangular sections, which were placed in globular red ollas, often being capped by small hemispherical bowls of the same clay. One olla burial contained a metal (silver?) plaque. At one site 18 urn burials were placed around some sort of low structure, perhaps an altar, located in front of a pyramidal structure, which also was associated with a complex layout of stone retaining walls.

House outlines or cimientos, as stated,

generally were rectangular stone enclosures which were flush with the surface. At other times excavation of a low-lying mound revealed similar stone outlines near the surface. At the V-42 site, a substructure, made of stones shaped differently from the usual Postclassic variety, was found in zone V. Possibly this structure dates from the Classic period. In many cases, groups of structures were built on slopes, and uncut stone retaining walls were used in constructing terraces. Only at a few sites was the typical Mesoamerican pattern of four mounds built around a central patio observed.

Clay "ovens" were excavated in several sites in association with cimientos. The "ovens" had flat bottoms and sides which tapered inward to form a dome-shaped roof. The interior of one of these constructions was covered with a limelike white substance. Their use is unknown, but Litvak King (1968, p. 29) has suggested that these clay constructions may have been ovens used in making ceramics.

Groups of dispersed cimientos line both banks of the river. The impression one receives of a fairly dense population may be misleading. To judge from the custom today of moving from place to place in connection with slash-and-burn agriculture, it is pos-

sible that this was an ancient practice. The presence of projectile points and the absence of fishbones is noticeable in all periods. Presumably the ancient peoples ignored fishing as do their "descendents" today. It has been suggested that residences of a more permanent kind were those situated around plazas. Most of these are on sites near the confluence of smaller streams with Rio Balsas. Buildings other than cimientos in the El Romanse phase were earth- and cobble-filled platforms; these were faced with uncut stones. A later custom was the addition of a central stairway; also, low platforms or banquetas were often connected to the main building. Stucco was used in some cases.

The delta region presents different characteristics. Sites are larger, and contain numerous mounds. Nicholson (1963, p. 45) estimates that the Melchor Ocampo site covered an area approximately 2 km. from north to south, and about 0.5 km. from east to west. Some 200 house mounds were located in the northern section of this site. A few mounds, perhaps 9 m. high, are thought to have been temple substructures. In one mound Nicholson excavated seven extended burials whose funerary offerings included seven poorly fired monochrome pottery ves-

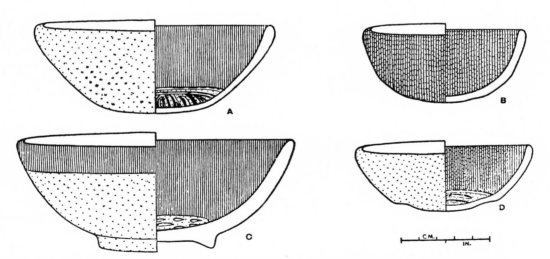

Fig. 16—SAN VICENTE MOLCAJETES, APATZINGAN, MICHOACAN. (From Kelly, 1947b, fig. 44.)

681

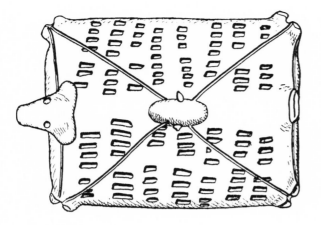

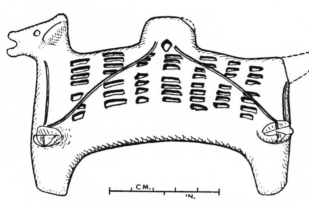

FIG. 17—CAPIRAL TAPADERA, APATZINGAN, MICHOACAN. (From Kelly, 1947b, fig. 30.)

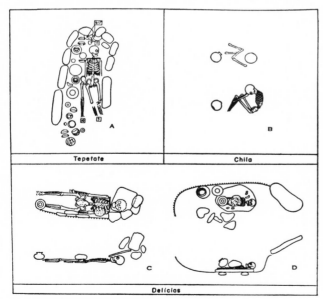

FIG. 18—TYPICAL INTERMENTS, APATZINGAN, MICHOACAN. (From Kelly, 1947b, fig. 92.)

sels. Moldmade figurines and malacates found in the same excavation would place these burials in the Postclassic. In view of the differing burial customs in the coastal area, one suspects that the lower Balsas basin, including the delta, formed two subcultural areas, which in turn differed from those of the inhabitants up the coast. The finding of red-on-buff, white-on-buff, and incised pottery would appear to corroborate this supposition since most of the La Villita ceramics were monochrome.

Armillas (1945, p. 84) surveyed what may have been the ancient site of Zacatula. The site was an immense area with many large and small mounds, one of which was 20 m. long, 5 m. wide, and 2 m. high. Olla burials from these mounds perhaps indicate a more urban delta aspect of a generalized Rio Balsas culture. Large numbers of stone-row, enclosed house platforms, plus larger mounds, perhaps ceremonial, were also encountered. Zacatula was the Tollan (metropolis) of the delta at contact.

No evidence of South or Central American connections was uncovered in the La Villita excavations with the possible exception of some copper axe money. Nicholson (1963) notes that "pineapple" maceheads, considered by some authorities as indicative of southern connections, have been found along the coast just north of the delta. "Pineapple" maceheads are widely distributed in a zone just west of the Tarascan heartland, from Sayula, Jalisco, to Apatzingan, Michoacan (Lister, 1955, p. 151; Kelly, 1947b, pp. 136, 140). Star-shaped maceheads have been reported from early shaft tombs.

APATZINGAN. The earliest Postclassic phase, Tepetate, marks the appearance of a number of widespread ceramic traits such as the ring-base; small, solid, tripod supports; resist painting; and the molcajete whose floor may be grooved or punched, but never incised. The introduction of the molcajete in the Postclassic period occurs throughout much of Mesoamerica. It appears in a Classic context in shaft tombs in Jalisco, and in the Formative at Tlatilco and the Ajalpan phase at Tehuacan (termed pseudo-molcajete at the latter place). At Tehuacan in this period an Olmecoid influence was noted; Morelos-like hollow figurines were found in bell-shaped burial pits.

One typical Tepetate phase molcajete (Kelly, 1947b, fig. 44) utilized the low ring-stand base; its profile is identical to one of the most common vessel forms of thin orange, the trade ware par excellence in classic times (fig. 16). Other distinctive artifacts, called *capiral tapaderas*, are *sahumadore* covers (incense-burner covers). They may be visualized (fig. 17) as inverted bowls, with four legs and a handle on the top. Decoration is always applied, incised, or punched, never painted. These seemingly intrusive objects have a distribution similar to that of the "pineapple" macehead, mentioned above (Lister, 1948, p. 90). A variant type from Gualupita, Cuernavaca, Morelos, has been reported; and others in a private collection at San Miguel Allende, Guanajuato, whose exact provenience is unknown, have been published (Bernal and others, 1968, fig. 124). Burial customs in the Tepetate phase (Kelly, 1947b, fig. 92) were similar to those in previous periods (fig. 18).

The final phase, Chila, is characterized by the introduction of two polychrome wares, a distinctive brazier style, and three red wares (Kelly, 1947b, pp. 35–41). One polychrome type, Llano polychrome (*ibid.*, fig. 4; our fig. 19), utilized red and white designs over a brownish background. In addition, negative painting was used. The most typical vessel form is a tripod cajete or open bowl with slightly outflaring sides and striations on the bottom for grinding chiles. Legless molcajetes in this ware were also popular. The legs in other wares usually are small prolongations or nubbins, although some types include anthropomorphic supports which are usually hollow with clay rattles inside; solid supports also occur.

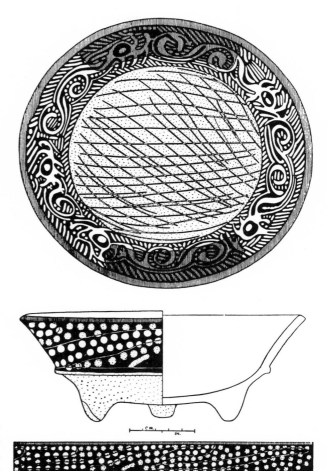

FIG. 19—LLANO POLYCHROME WARE, APATZINGAN, MICHOACAN. (From Kelly, 1947b, fig. 4.)

Another pottery type, Chila polychrome, utilized black and white motifs over the natural color of the clay, as well as resist painting. The form was usually an unsupported open bowl.

A new type of burial posture was introduced in the Chila phase. Instead of the extended position, used previously, in Chila times the flexed seated position came into vogue. Textiles with copper bells were found in one Chila interment. Copper bells were strung by several techniques such as the use of a six-ply thread run through the objects, multiple-strand cordage in the ring of the bell, and two-strand basketry twining, holding the bells together (Kelly, 1947b, p. 144). An imprint of a petate or mat was found in an ash deposit; the fragment was woven of multiple warps and wefts.

Other typical artifacts in the Postclassic at Apatzingan are worked sherds, rattles, pottery drums, and clay pipes (fig. 20). The pipe bowl is relatively tall, and the stem is cylindrical and slightly tapering. Two small lugs appear at the bowl-stem junction. Discoidal, cylindrical, and spool-shaped malacates with bifacial decoration are confined to the Tepetate phase (Kelly, 1947b, p. 111). Chipped stone artifacts include black obsidian cylindrical cores, fine blades, and several types of projectile points. Ground stone artifacts—maceheads, palettes, axes, and hammerstones—appear throughout the Postclassic sequence. Club bark beaters, similar to those mentioned above, appear in the Chila horizon (Kelly, 1947b, fig. 76,E-G, obsidian and ground stone). Other ground stone artifacts are pestles, and *manos de metate*, the latter appearing in several subtypes: plano, plano-convex, convex, squared and unsquared. Metates include both footed and unfooted varieties. The ubiquitous *tiqüiche* was the only type found by Goggin (1943, p. 54) in his surface survey in the same area. Metalwork, made by casting and hammering techniques but not repoussé, was abundant, and included such objects as bells, rattles, tweezers, beads, buttons, hooks, eyed needles, awls, and wire. No copper axes were found at Apatzingan. Goggin (1943, p. 54)

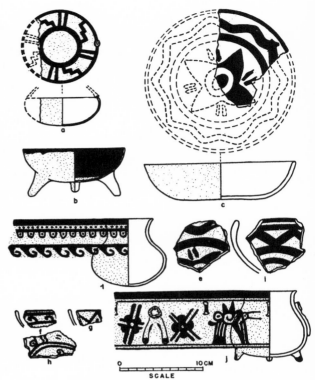

reports finding bola-like copper blades called *tarequas*, whose distribution includes Huetamo, Uruapan, and sites in Colima. A unique copper bowl, 18 cm. in diameter, 8 cm. deep, and 1 cm. thick, was also found by Goggin. The exterior surface was covered with small, punched holes. Artifacts of bone include awls, tubular beads, bracelets, pendants, round beads, and earrings.

Goggin (1943, p. 46) recorded the presence of cobble yácatas, earth yácatas, village sites, terraced hillsides, caves, burial sites, and others, which combined several of these characteristics. The popular type of house foundation, the rectangular cimiento, was commonly found in sherd areas. Yácatas presumably served as both mortuary and habitation structures. Kelly (1947b, p. 143) notes another type of mound which might have been connected with a local copperworking industry. At the El Llano site, numerous low mounds, from 10 to 20

FIG. 20—PIPES FROM APATZINGAN, MICHOACAN. (From Kelly, 1947b, fig. 56.)

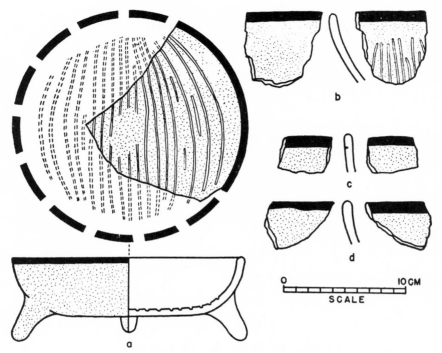

FIG. 22—COJUMATLAN TAN, RED-RIMMED WARE. (From Lister, 1949, fig. 14.)

FIG. 23—COJUMATLAN INCISED POLYCHROME WARE. (From Lister, 1949, fig. 7.)

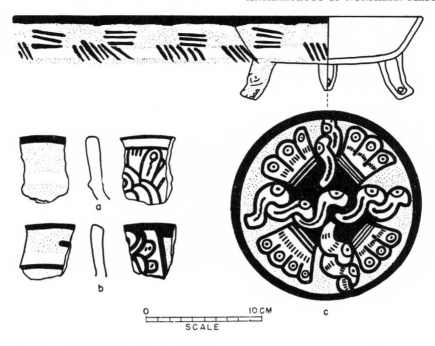

FIG. 24—COJUMATLAN POLYCHROME WARE. (From Lister, 1949, fig. 4.)

m. in diameter, and about a meter in height, were found. One mound was composed, first, of a layer some 1.25 m. thick of stone and black ash, which was followed by a zone of light gray ash. The bulk of the mound contained vast quantities of stone which had been deliberately broken. Most stones had been subjected to severe heat, and several fragments were partially vitrified.

Tarascan contacts were negligible. Both Kelly and Goggin believe that the area as a whole was somewhat culturally isolated. Whether the cultural isolation in western tierra caliente, which contrasts so strongly with its eastern counterpart, is more apparent than real must necessarily await further excavation analyses.

COJUMATLAN. Lister's (1949) excavations were carried out along the shores of the Bay of Cojumatlan at the southeastern end of Lake Chapala. In some respects, Cojumatlan seems to have participated in the central Mexican mainstream of cultural development more than other areas of Michoacan. On the basis of two stratigraphic trenches, Lister defined two Postclassic phases: (1) an earlier period called Chapala with affinities to the Tula-Mazapan style in central Mexico, and (2) a later culture, Cojumatlan, characterized by traits of the Mixteca-Puebla horizon style (see Article 8, this volume).

The earlier phase is characterized by a Mazapan-like red-on-brown ware, figurines of the Mazapan type, plumbate ware, and molcajetes (Lister, 1949, p. 26). Two other important wares also appeared in this phase: Chapala Polished Red and Chapala Brown Ware. The second phase saw the introduction of two polychrome types: Cojumatlan Polychrome and Cojumatlan Incised Polychrome. In addition, the phase was characterized by polychrome pottery with designs employing such motifs as feathered serpents, feathers, and headdresses. Many

686

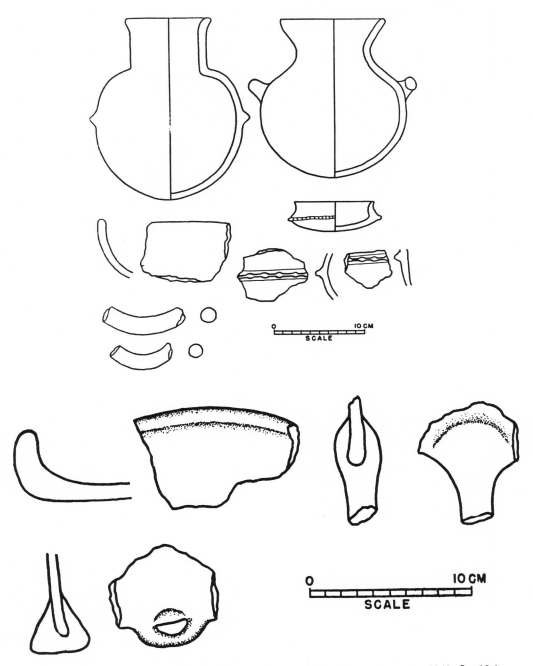

FIG. 25—COMALES, CHAPALA BROWN UTILITY WARE. (From Lister, 1949, fig. 19.)

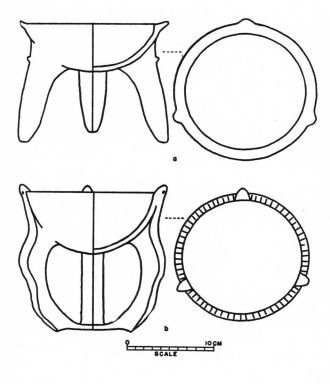

FIG. 26—CHAPALA BROWN UTILITY WARE. (From Lister, 1949, figs. 19, 20.)

of these designs are quite similar in execution to some in the "Soncautla" phase at Tres Zapotes, Veracruz. Tlaloc censers also made an appearance, and tripod legs in the form of human and animal effigies were innovations (Lister, 1949; our figs. 21–24).

Chapala Brown Utility ware (Lister, 1949, figs. 19, 20; our figs. 25, 26) made up from 73 to 90 per cent of the sherds in all levels throughout the sequence. Forms included a large jar-shaped vessel with heavy crenelated shoulders. Heavy semicircular loop rugs occurred often in this ware. Fragments of flat comal-like utensils with raised rims and loop handles were popular. Temper was primarily of sand, and a slip color of brick-red to dark brown was added to the exposed surfaces. A single loop-handled jar occurred in Chapala Brown ware, as did open bowls with split legs, somewhat similar to the loop legs of tapaplatos (Lister, 1949, figs. 17, 18; our figs. 27, 28). Vessel forms of other types in both phases include shallow open bowls without supports, tripod molcajetes, open bowls with incurving rim and basket handle, tripod cajetes with conical legs, flaring-necked ollas, olla-like vessels with small conical supports, cajetes with hollow supports with clay pellets inside, and vessels supported by slightly bulbous legs or large bulbous legs that come to a point at the bottom, stepped slab feet, and effigy supports. Tall tripods also occurred as well as a unique type with tripod

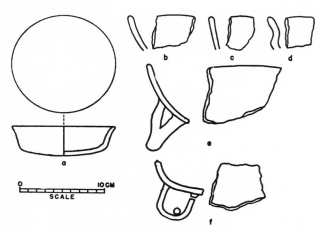

FIG. 27—CHAPALA BROWN WARE. (From Lister, 1949, fig. 17.)

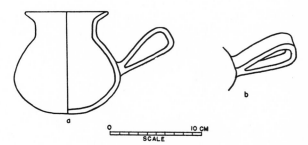

FIG. 28—CHAPALA BROWN WARE. (From Lister, 1949, fig. 18.)

legs, which were convex and joined to a triangular platform on which the vessel rested. The four plumbate sherds recovered appear to be of the San Juan variety, but this can not be determined definitely. Decoration was both naturalistic and geometric, the latter being confined to such motifs as red and white circles flanked by red and white horizontal lines, flower-like elements, oblongs, hooks, and combinations of these.

Of the 17 human burials excavated, 13 were infants and children. The skeleton was usually flexed and in the common sitting position, most often facing west. Burials were placed in hurriedly made pits or underneath earthen house floors. No difference in burial type was noticed throughout the sequence. One specimen showed fronto-occipital flattening; three individuals had mutilated teeth similar to those found at Tzintzuntzan. In one burial, pottery vessels had been placed around the body, and a bowl had been put upside down over the head of the deceased. Lister noticed no similarity between his finds and those excavated by Noguera 20 miles away at Jiquilpan. No Tarascan influence was found.

In addition to ceramics, many artifacts of copper, bone, obsidian, flint, stone, and shell were recovered. Clay malacates appeared as truncated cones, cylindrical (straight-sided), cylindrical (convex-sided), conical, jar-shaped, and effigy-shaped. Design was by incising. Clay musical instruments, flutes and whistles, were found, as were several fragments of clay pipes. Copper artifacts were bells, beads, needles, and awls. A necklace of 79 discoidal iron oxide beads was found with one of the burials. Metates were both legless and legged, with the former type predominating. Shell bracelets, pendants, and appliqué sets similar to those at Apatzingan were found, as were bone awls, spatulas, needles, and a harpoon-like tool. Perishable material included fragments of cord preserved in the rings of several small bells; textile impressions in clay were recovered.

TARASCAN ARCHAEOLOGY

At contact Tarascan speech extended from Lake Chapala to south of the Rio Balsas and from slightly west of the Tepalcatepec River into part of Guanajuato (Beals, 1969, p. 725). Tarascan architecture terminates with a fairly sharp boundary along the south shore of Lake Chapala. The historical nucleus of the Tarascan nation was the basin of Lake Patzcuaro, situated near the western edge of the Central Plateau. There is no archaeological evidence to indicate that the central Michoacan region had played any important role prior to the rise of the Tarascans. Even with a high population density and a strongly integrated polity, the Tarascan "empire" seems to have been overwhelmingly rural. The historical capitals, Tzintzuntzan and Ihuatzio, apparently were not towns of any great consequence (Armillas, 1964a, p. 320).

The region around Tzintzuntzan lies in the so-called sierra region, and in several adjacent valley and lake basin areas, the main ones being the basin of Lake Patzcuaro and the smaller lake Zirahuen to the south. Although closely surrounded by the sierra type of domain, the lake communities are actually at higher elevations than some of the sierra regions. Most Tarascans lived within or near the region of coniferous forests of pine and fir trees (Beals, 1969).

The archaeological zone at Tzintzuntzan, the ancient capital, has been explored more than any other aboriginal settlement. Sites such as Ihuatzio, Jacona, Quiroga, Patzcuaro, Tangancicuaro, and Huetamo contain apparent Tarascan ruins, which have scarcely been touched by the spade of the archaeologist. At Tzintzuntzan, five yácatas were discovered which shared a large common platform, some 260 m. wide and 440 m. long (Piña Chan, 1960b, p. 151). Three of the four sides of the platform were built up of taludes; the fourth side featured a ramp or staircase (Marquina, 1951, pl. 74; our fig. 29). Five yácatas were built on this plat-

689

FIG. 29—YÁCATA AT IHUATZIO, MICHOACAN. (From Acosta, 1939, fig. 5.)

form facing east, having been placed close to the west end of the platform, thus leaving a large open area for ritual activities. Yácatas are typically Tarascan; identical buildings have not been found elsewhere in Mesoamerica.

Yácatas are composed of three parts: (1) a rectangular stepped pyramid, (2) a round stepped pyramid, and (3) a stepped passageway which joins the round body to the rectangular platform. The round structure (Acosta, 1939, fig. 5) is placed at the midpoint of the platform, opposite the stairway, and thus, with the passageway, all three building units form a T-shaped edifice in ground plan (fig. 29 and Article 2, fig. 2). *Lajas* without mortar formed the nucleus of the buildings, which were faced with cut volcanic stone called *xanamu*. The xanamus are joined by a mud mortar, and in some instances show low-relief carving. Covarrubias (1957) remarked on the similarity in construction techniques to those employed in Inca buildings. Burials have been found in the nucleus of the large yácata substructure, at the sides of the yáca-

690

tas, and in a common cremation area. Yácata V, the only one completely explored, has the following measurements: total length 65.75 m., total width 42.60 m., width of the rectangular section 22.10 m., maximum diameter of the round structure 28.90 m., and approximate height 13 m. (Marquina, 1951, p. 257).

Several modes of burial were popular. In addition to cremation, there were skull burials, primary and secondary single and multiple burials, radial burials, and burials of individuals flexed in a fetal position. Many of the longbones (femurs) had grooves cut on them to make a rasping musical device. A type of cranial deformation described as occipital-parietal was common, and dental mutilation was often observed. Of interest is the fact that the population seems to have been composed of two physical types: dolichocephalic and brachycephalic.

Offerings of ceramic vessels commonly were placed with the dead, including such vessel forms as gourd-shaped "teapot" vessels, some with stirrup spouts, others with basket handles; patojos with basket handles; fluted vases; and miniature vessels, such as patojos, and pots with looped supports (Piña Chan, 1960b, p. 155). Most of the funerary forms were decorated in black, red, cream, and gray; both naturalistic and geometric motifs were utilized. Rubín de la Borbolla (1948, p. 30) has commented that one Tarascan characteristic is the use of foreign vessel forms, which were often decorated in the negative-painting technique. The funerary vessels contrast with domestic wares, which generally were ollas, open bowls, plates, and comals. Most of these were roughly finished, and were black, brown, and reddish due to variations in firing.

Aside from the characteristic funerary ceramics, other diagnostic Tarascan traits include advanced techniques in metallurgy such as cold hammering, the lost-wax process, filigree and soldering techniques, and gold-plating. Such virtuoso productions as fish with gold bodies and silver fins are known, as well as other items such as copper bells modeled as turtles, files with human and animal heads, and labrets with floral designs made of gold leaf. Other metal artifacts include copper tweezers, axes, chisels, arm ornaments, and masks of Xipe Totec, the patron of lapidaries and smiths. Lapidary work in jade, obsidian, rock crystal, and pyrite was also characteristic of the Tarascans. They made such luxury items as translucent obsidian earplugs, which were often partly covered with turquoise mosaics, and labrets of obsidian or rock crystal, which were covered with turquoise mosaics or gold leaf. Featherwork was a notable Tarascan manufacture. They also excelled in stone sculpture, and examples of the chacmool have been found in the heartland. Other artifacts include fragments of textiles with copper bells, malacates, obsidian knives and projectile points, and manos de metates and metates of volcanic rock.

Tarascan archaeology has long been an enigma to Mesoamericanists. Not only have the linguistic connections to South American languages constituted a problem, but the exotic ceramic assemblage also has prompted much speculation regarding origin. Rubín de la Borbolla has remarked (1948, p. 33) that Tarascan archaeology has a unique personality because of its singular development in architecture, ceramic manufacture, and lapidary and metalworking techniques. Nevertheless, the Tarascans seem to have invented little, seeming to have borrowed their exotic traits and transformed them with the stamp of their own cultural tradition. It is important to note that, according to the Relación de Michoacan, the Tarascan invaders of the lake area spoke a dialect of the language spoken by the indigenous inhabitants of the region (Jiménez Moreno, 1948, p. 148). The invaders were recognized as kinfolk.

A post-contact document, the Lienzo de Jucutacato (Jiménez Moreno, 1948, pp. 146–57), contains clues, we believe, with respect to the introduction of some of the alien elements in Tarascan culture. There is general agreement among students of Michoacan archaeology that the document depicts persons who came to the Tarascan area in search of mines. After establishing themselves at Xiuhquillan, four expeditions set forth: one toward Coalcoman, two toward the Cuitlatec region, and the fourth toward Patzcuaro, where Jiménez Moreno (1948, p. 154) suggests a barrio of orfebres was established. The ethnic identity of these persons has been proposed as Tarascan by Caso (discussion in Jiménez Moreno, 1948), Nahua by others, and even such names as Teco and Teco-Tarascan have been mentioned. Jiménez Moreno, we believe, has come closest to the identity of the protagonists in the painting. He proposes that they were the Nonoalcas, but wrongly identifies them as Mazatec (ibid., p. 156). Sahagún (1950–69, bk. 10, p. 256) identifies the Nonoalca as Mixtec.

The document, however, offers several other clues which tend to identify the persons in the lienzo as Mixtec or Chocho. One of the immigrants appears with the gloss "Atonal." Atonal was a dynastic name in Mixtec-Chocho Coixtlahuaca in the 16th century (Caso, 1960b). The supposition that the immigrants were Mixtec or Chocho is corroborated by the fact that they wear the ubiquitous Mixtec xicolli. Although the xicolli was also worn by the Tarascans, it differed from the Mixtec variety in that it covered only as far as the navel; no maxtlatl was worn. The garb shown in the lienzo, however, apparently was the Mixtec type (Mateos Higuera, 1948, pp. 161–62).

If it be granted that the persons depicted in the lienzo were Mixtec metalworkers (they are seen climbing out of shafts in hills), the question resolves itself as: Is there evidence which connects any of the alien traits noted in Tarascan culture not only to the Mixtec, but more specifically to metalworkers or miners?

Patojos are generally considered to be

characteristic Mixtec vessel forms in the Postclassic (Bernal, 1966). There is also evidence which points to a connection between the patojo and metalworking cultures. To the best of my knowledge, no previous author has pointed out this connection. For example, patojos have been found in shaft tombs in Colombia in association with copper sheets (Ford, 1944, pp. 40, 65, figs. 10, 18). The best proof of a connection, however, appears in Peru: patojos are introduced with the first copper in the Kotosh Higueras phase in the highlands and in the Gallinazo III phase of the same period on the coast (Bennett, 1950, pp. 93, 117; Izumi and Sono, 1963, pp. 157–58, fig. 46). Lest these examples be thought indicative of coincidence—and nothing more—let me hasten to point out that a parallel situation has been noted by Childe (1941) in Macedonia where an intrusive complex from Anatolia arrives, introducing the first copper plus the patojo. It seems likely that the European occurrence is best thought of at this time as an example of cultural convergence. Although I can not connect the two traits functionally (certainly there is no reason to believe that the patojo was used in connection with metallurgy per se), Arden R. King (personal communication, 1968) has suggested what appears to be a likely solution. He notes that traveling "tinkers" may have used the patojo because

it would have been convenient in campfire cooking, for a patojo is made so that one end may be placed over a fire, allowing a person to lift the other end without being burned. We note also that the tapaplato (the plate-lid with looped feet or handles) is considered a characteristic vessel in the Veraguas region of Panama, one of the regions where metallurgy was proliferated. We have mentioned above that this type of vessel seems to have been characteristic of the Cuitlatec metalworking zone in the middle Balsas and in Guerrero.

Caso has proposed (1965b) that the Mixtec Tlailotlaque were those who introduced metallurgy to Mesoamerica from Central America. We propose, therefore, as an hypothesis, that many of the alien elements in Tarascan culture may have been introduced by Mixtec miners. This hypothesis perhaps gains in validity when it is pointed out that only three linguistic groups in Mesoamerica share certain "sub-Andean" traits: the Mixtec, Tarascans, and Zapotec (Dahlgren de Jordán, 1954, pp. 382–83). This points to a connection between the three cultures which warrants further investigation.[3]

[3] I express my gratitude to Professor José Luis Lorenzo, head of the Department of Prehistory, Instituto Nacional de Antropología e Historia, for giving me the opportunity of participating in the La Villita excavations and for providing me with unpublished information and photographs.

692

REFERENCES

Acosta, 1939
Anonymous, 1960
Armillas, 1945, 1948, 1964a
Barlow, 1945d, 1947d
Beals, 1969
Beaumont, 1932
Bennett, 1950
Bennyhoff, 1967
Bernal, 1966, 1969
—— and others, 1968
Brand, 1942, 1943, 1952, 1957–58, 1960
Caso, 1930b, 1960b, 1965b
——, Bernal, and Acosta, 1967
Chadwick, 1968
Childe, 1941
Coe, 1963, 1965b, 1965c, 1967
Coon, 1966
Corona Núñez, 1960b
Covarrubias, 1957
Dahlgren de Jordán, 1954
Drucker, Escalante, and Weitlaner, 1969
Estrada Balmori and Piña Chan, 1948a, 1948b
Ford, 1944, 1969
Furst, 1965a
García Cook, 1967
Goggin, 1943
Izumi and Sono, 1963
Jenkins, 1967
Jiménez Moreno, 1948, 1966
Johnson, I. W., 1964
Kelly, 1947b, 1948
Kirchhoff, 1943, 1948
Lehmann, 1948
León, 1903b
Lindsay, 1968
Lister, 1948, 1949, 1955
Litvak King, 1968

Long, S. V., and Taylor, 1966a, 1966b
Lorenzo, 1964
Lumholtz, 1902
MacNeish, Nelken-Terner, and Johnson, 1967
Marquina, 1951
Mastache, 1966
Mateos Higuera, 1948
Matos Moctezuma, 1968
Miramontes, 1936
Moedano Koer, 1941, 1946, 1948
Nicholson, 1962, 1963
Noguera, 1931, 1942, 1944, 1965
Occidente de México, 1948
Osborne, 1943
Paddock, 1967, 1968
Pepper, 1916
Piña Chan, 1960b
Plancarte y Navarrete, 1893
Porter, 1948b, 1956
Rands and Smith, 1965
Rubín de la Borbolla, 1939, 1941, 1948
Sahagún, 1950–69
Sahlins and Service, 1960
Schöndube, 1968
Sejourné, 1959
Spinden, 1948
Steward, 1955
Swadesh, 1967
Vaillant, 1931
Velásquez Gallardo, 1948
Wauchope, 1950
Weitlaner, 1946
West, 1948, 1961, 1964
White, 1959
Willey, Ekholm, and Millon, 1964
—— and Phillips, 1962

30. Archaeology of Nayarit, Jalisco, and Colima

BETTY BELL

THE AREA OF WEST Mexico which now comprises the states of Nayarit, Colima, and Jalisco was added to the New World empire of Spain within the first few years after the conquest of central Mexico, part of it to the Audiencia de Nueva España and part to the newly formed Audiencia de Nueva Galicia. Although its importance had declined by early in the 17th century, it was at least briefly an important source of mineral wealth, and a base for land and sea expeditions to the north and for voyages to the Orient.

By 1522, expeditions under Parillas, Montaño, and Olid had pushed into the Tarascan empire as far as Tajimaroa and then on to Tzintzuntzan, the Tarascan capital at Lake Patzcuaro. From this point parties were sent down to the coast at Zacatula, at the mouth of the Rio Balsas, to establish a port and begin shipbuilding operations as a preliminary to sea-borne exploration of the western coast and seas. The first entry into present-day Colima seems to have been made by a party under Rodríguez de Villa-

fuerte, whose group, bound for Zacatula, heard reports in the Tarascan capital of the wealth of gold and silver in Colima, and made a brief and unscheduled investigation. Leaving the Zacatula trail, the Villafuerte party pushed westward across the mountains to Coahuayana and on to Tecoman, where they raided and looted the town before withdrawing and continuing on their way to Zacatula. The following year, Cortés instructed Gonzalo de Sandoval to secure the submission of the entire coastal area. Sandoval journeyed up the rugged coast, now one of the most isolated areas in Mexico, from Yopelcingo (near Acapulco) to Sihuatlan (south coastal Jalisco), subjugating the Indian populations and founding the Villa de Colima.

The Spaniards who had remained in the Lake Patzcuaro area were not content for long with a country which promised little except good land, and they decided to find the source of the gold and silver which they had been extorting from the Tarascans. Accordingly, plans for a permanent settle-

694

ment were abandoned, and the Spaniards pushed west to Tamazula and Zapotlan (now southern Jalisco), where they were established in 1524 when Francisco Cortés arrived to administer the Province of Colima. It is said that his party journeyed from Zapotlan to the coast at Villa de Colima by way of a trail down through the barranca country, and thus were the first Spaniards to use what was later to become a main route from the west coast to Mexico City.

Francisco Cortés had been sent not only to administer the Province of Colima, but also to explore northward in search of the fabled Amazons, whose land was reputed to lie somewhere on the coast to the north. With this object in mind, he set out with an expedition late in 1524 from the Valle de Sihuatlan. Documentary sources permit his route to be traced through Autlan and the Valle de Milpa, Ayutla, and Etzatlan (all in Jalisco), thence around the Volcán Ceboruco and on to Tepic (Nayarit). The party seems to have remained in the area for some time, exploring the coastal and lowland pueblos; some accounts indicate that these explorations extended as far as the Rio Santiago, others that they reached only to the tropical lowlands south of San Blas. Land in lowland and plateau alike was parceled out among members of the party. There is no clear account of Francisco Cortés's return route to Sihuatlan. Historians of a later date believed that he returned by way of the coast, and there is definite record of his entry into coastal pueblos south of San Blas. If he did traverse this area, he made no grants of land in it, such as he made elsewhere on his expedition, but fact and tradition are so intermingled that the return route cannot be traced.

By 1530 Colima and much of southern Jalisco were under Spanish control and incorporated into the Audiencia de Nueva España, and in this year an expedition under Beltrán Nuño de Guzmán left Tepic to explore the northern coastal areas of present-day Nayarit and Sinaloa. Moving down

off the plateau, the Guzmán expedition crossed the Rio Santiago and proceeded northward up the coastal lowlands, meeting little resistance but burning the towns and effectively devastating the countryside. The party reached the area of the Rio Sinaloa before turning back. Late in 1530 complaints from settlers on the western frontier about the difficulties of being administered from Mexico City led to separation of the Tepic plateau area from the Audiencia de Nueva España and its incorporation into the Audiencia de Nueva Galicia, which also included most of what is now Jalisco and the remainder of Nayarit.

Conquest-period accounts describe a dense and rather prosperous aboriginal population for Nayarit, Jalisco, and parts of Colima. Guzmán's chroniclers noted that the Nayarit lowlands were thickly dotted with settlements from the coast to the Sierra; Kelly (1945b), comparing *visita* records with archaeological sites, postulates a greater and denser population for the Autlan-Mylpa area of Jalisco than it bears today. There were a number of sizable towns throughout the area, and material culture was apparently rich and varied, though lacking the glittering treasure coveted by the Spaniards (cf. Beals, 1932; Sauer, 1948; Sauer and Brand, 1932). Land was apportioned to the Spanish conquerors in grants varying from a few hectares to one sizable enough to be designated as the Provincia de Avalos—the holding of a single family. On numerous grants made in the mountain-and-barranca country of Colima the Spaniards established mines and maintained them successfully for some years. In contrast, many of the encomiendas in Nayarit were being abandoned by the early 1540s, as the encomenderos, dissatisfied with a land which promised no mineral wealth, began to leave for Peru. Aboriginal life was disrupted, and within a few years after the Spanish conquest the Indian population had declined sharply, owing largely to newly introduced diseases. Moreover,

695

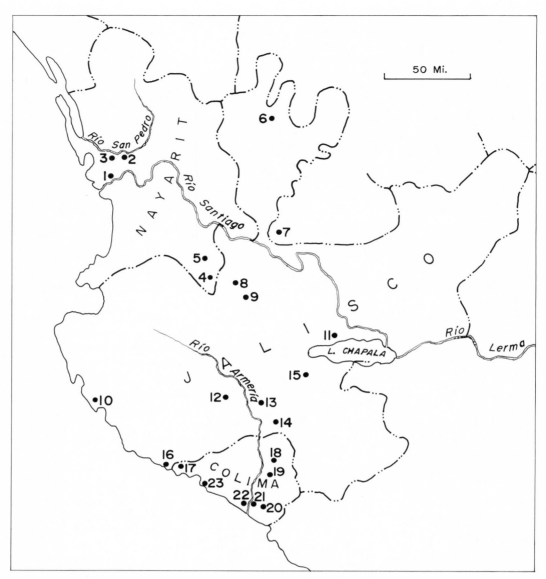

Fig. 1—ARCHAEOLOGICAL SITES AND AREAS IN NAYARIT, JALISCO, AND COLIMA

Nayarit
1. Amapa
2. Peñitas
3. Coamiles
4. Tequilita (Las Cebollas)
5. Ixtlan del Rio

Jalisco
6. Totoate; upper Rio Bolaños
7. Caxcana (Jalisco-Zacatecas)
8. Magdalena Lake Basin (Etzatlan, El Arnal, San Sebastian, Huistla, Las Cuevas)
9. Ameca
10. Coastal Jalisco
11. Lake Chapala Basin

12. Autlan
13. Tuxcacuesco
14. Zapotitlan
15. Sayula-Zacoalco
16. Barra de Navidad

Colima
17. Morett
18. El Chanal
19. Los Ortices
20. Tecoman (Chanchopa)
21. Periquillo
22. Armeria
23. Playa del Tesoro

696

many Indians abandoned their settlements and fled into the mountains of northern and eastern Jalisco, and into the Sierra de Nayarit. These areas remained unsubjugated for many years after the conquest, and later the Indians of at least one of them were almost able, in the Mixtón War (1540–41), to overthrow the Spanish authorities.

A considerable portion of the state of Jalisco lies at the western edge of the central plateau of Mexico, and forms the lowermost of a series of basins which descend to the northwest from the Toluca basin. The central portion of the state is a lake-dotted plateau, bounded on the north and east by mountains, and on the west falling away steeply to a narrow coastal plain. To the southeast, the plateau area extends into northern Michoacan; to the southwest, the adjoining state of Colima lies largely within the rough mountain-and-barranca country which forms the western escarpment of the plateau. Most of coastal Nayarit consists of a fairly wide plain, although the mountains extend out to the coast in the southern part of the state. To the east, Nayarit is bordered by the Sierra de Nayarit, which forms part of the Sierra Madre Occidental; to the southeast, the Nayarit highlands are part of the rough mountainous country which extends across northern and eastern Jalisco.

Parts of all three states lie within the volcanic zone which extends in an arc along this western and southern portion of the escarpment of the central plateau. Apart from the coastal plains and the basins of Jalisco, much of the country is rough and deeply cut by barrancas. The Rio Lerma flows into the eastern end of Lake Chapala, and the Rio Santiago flows out of it to the northwest, draining through a system of gorges which form an impassable barrier to modern transportation. The Rio Santiago flows into the Pacific Ocean about midway along the Nayarit coast, which in this area is a wide alluvial plain, crisscrossed by numerous old river channels. Throughout most of the area the average annual temperature is quite high, and the rainfall abundant. Because of the rugged terrain and the contrasts in altitude, the pattern of vegetation is irregular. In general, however, the parts of the coastal plain not brought under agriculture are covered with a dense and thorny scrub growth characterized by such plants as the thorn acacia; some of the warmer and moister parts of southern coastal Nayarit, the southern Jalisco coast, and the Colima coast have a plant assemblage much like that of the tropical forest. On the lower slopes throughout the area there is a dense scrub forest, which gives way at higher altitudes to oak forests and then to conifers. Conquest-period accounts note that the area was rich in a variety of large and small game; the rivers and coastal waters abound in many kinds of fish and shellfish.

Climatic conditions throughout the area seem to have been such that the aboriginal population had a dependable supply of wild plants for food, and were able to raise a variety of crops. Maize was apparently the principal crop, but documentary sources for the postconquest period (cf. Arregui, 1946; Mota y Escobar, 1940; Ponce, 1873) describe many other crops such as beans, squash, chile, cotton, yucca, sweet potatoes, tomatoes, pineapple, cacao, tobacco, and maguey in various parts of Nayarit, Jalisco, and Colima. Palerm (1954), drawing extensively on Lebrón y Quiñones and the Suma de Visitas de Pueblos, notes the prevalence of irrigation in southern Nayarit, south-central Jalisco, and northern Colima during the years immediately following the conquest, and offers this extensive use as evidence that the technique was aboriginal in these areas.

The archaeological art of perhaps no other area of Mexico is as well known as that of the modern states of Nayarit, Colima, and Jalisco, but in perhaps no other area has there been so little controlled excavation. Countless fine figurines and other artifacts are in private collections, lacking secure provenience, assignable to regions only on stylistic grounds, and thus of limited use in culture-historical reconstructions. Earlier travelers through the area, such as Lumholtz (1902), Starr (1897), and Hrdlička (1903), gave detailed descriptions of the archaeological material they saw, but their collections too were largely purchased and thus cannot be fitted neatly into reconstructions based on controlled scientific work. (Much of this material is reported on in Ross, 1939.)

In 1956 the University of California, Los Angeles, excavated sites at Peñitas, Nayarit (Bordaz, 1964) and at Coamiles, Nayarit (a single test pit at a petroglyph site; unpublished), and in 1959 UCLA excavated extensively at a large site at Amapa, Nayarit (Bell, 1960; Clune, 1963; Grosscup, 1961, 1964; Meighan, 1959, 1960; Pendergast, 1960). During three field seasons (1960, 1961, 1962), UCLA conducted its Project A, an archaeological survey of the central and south Pacific coast of Mexico, in the course of which test pits were dug at Santa Cruz and Chacala, Nayarit (Meighan, 1961). (Project A comprised one section of the project on the Interrelationships of New World Cultures, conducted under the auspices of the Institute for Andean Research.)

In Jalisco, Kelly excavated sites in the Tuxcacuesco-Zapotitlan area in the southwestern part of the state (Kelly, 1949), and Project A excavated at Barra de Navidad, a coastal site only a few kilometers from the Colima border (Long and Wire, 1966; Meighan, 1961). In 1963–64 UCLA archaeologists excavated the small site of Huistla, on the outskirts of Etzatlan, as part of a larger project involving a survey of the Magdalena Lake basin (Glassow, 1967); and in 1963, J. Charles Kelley (personal communication) excavated at Totoate in extreme northern Jalisco, a site originally dug by Hrdlička (1903, pp. 392–95) in 1902. There are some brief reports (Corona Núñez, 1960a; Piña Chan, 1963a; Sáenz, 1966a, b) on the excavation of a mound at Ixtepete, on the outskirts of Guadalajara. In Colima,

Project A excavated the site of Playa del Tesoro on Manzanillo Bay (Crabtree and Fitzwater, n.d.; Meighan, 1961), and the inland Morett site, about 25 km. to the northwest (Meighan, 1961; Nicholson, 1963; Susia, 1961); both are close to the Jalisco-Colima border. Kelly (personal communication) excavated in Colima during 1966, but the monograph on her work is still in preparation.

Surface collections are reported by Fay (1959) for northern coastal Nayarit; by Gifford (1950) for Ixtlan del Rio, Nayarit; by Corona Núñez (n.d.) for the southern Nayarit highlands; and by Kelly (1945b) for Autlan, Jalisco. Kelly also has made surface collections along the coasts of all three states; and in the Ameca and Sayula-Zacoalco area of south-central Jalisco, in the Caxcana area along the Jalisco-Zacatecas border, and in several parts of Colima (Kelly, 1944, 1945c, 1947a, 1948). Unfortunately, none of this material has been published in the kind of detail which would permit close comparisons with material from other areas. Project A archaeologists made surface collections at roughly four dozen sites along the coasts of southern Nayarit, Jalisco, and Colima, and also reported the existence of petroglyph sites. Brief preliminary studies of a small part of the ceramic material are incorporated into a series of seminar reports on file in the Department of Anthropology at UCLA, but none of it has been published. In 1965, geographer William Byron (California State College at Los Angeles) made an extensive archaeological-geographical survey to locate and map sites in the southern Nayarit lowlands between the Rio Santiago and San Blas; he reports (personal communication) numerous large sites with mounds, and several petroglyph sites. Furst (1965a,c, 1966) and Long (1965) have studied material excavated personally from partially looted shaft tombs and collections which can be tied securely to particular tombs in southern Nayarit and northern Jalisco (see fig. 1 for locations of sites). There are a few brief descriptions of archaeological sites and artifacts in largely unknown areas (cf. Galindo, 1922; Medina de la Torre, 1934), but usually these are the work of local *aficionados* of archaeology and are too imprecise to be of use.

It is this oddly assorted mass of material, uneven in quality and coverage and much of it unpublished, which must be fitted together in a report on the archaeology of Nayarit, Jalisco, and Colima. It is hoped that further study and publication, together with a more extensive series of radiocarbon dates (cf. Berger, Fergusson, and Libby, 1965; Berger and Libby, 1966, 1967; Berger, Taylor, and Libby, 1966; Long and Taylor, 1966a,b), will help to fill many of the present blanks in the archaeological picture of west Mexico.

The archaeology of this part of west Mexico cannot be discussed without reference to the Aztatlan complex, which now seems almost to have become the Aztatlan culture. As originally described by Sauer and Brand (1932) on the basis of surface collections in coastal Sinaloa and Nayarit, the Aztatlan complex consisted of related pottery types unlike any previously found in the area, and their widespread distribution along the west Mexican coast made them seem promising as a time-marker in the areas of their occurrence. The basic pottery of the Aztatlan complex appears to be red-on-brown or red-on-buff, with red rim and an exterior band of small geometric design elements in red. The pottery which Sauer and Brand designate as Aztatlan ware has in addition a white band with incised decoration; in the simpler Aztatlan ware (Chametla, Culiacan) this decoration usually consists of small geometric elements, whereas in the more elaborate variety (Guasave) the incised designs may be quite complex. The Guasave Aztatlan ware may also include decoration in black paint. Red-and-black-on-cream (or red-and-black-on-buff) polychromes and a variety of incised

wares are associated with the Aztatlan complex.

As more work was done in west Mexico, a variety of other pottery types associated with the Aztatlan wares, and eventually other kinds of artifacts as well, came to be included in the Aztatlan complex (cf. Ekholm, 1942; Kelly, 1938, 1945a; Kelley and Winters, 1960). Kelley and Winters have separated this expanded Aztatlan complex into three largely sequential assemblages and have assigned to it a considerable time span, while postulating varying relationships among areas at various points during that time; clearly, the areas of its occurrence seem to be linked by the invariable presence of certain wares and by considerable overlap in others during the Aztatlan horizon (cf. Kelley and Winters, 1960, fig. 7), and at the same time by a great diversity in associated pottery types and other artifacts. At some sites its content is quite meager and simple, at others varied and elaborate, and in no case is there complete certainty about its duration. Aztatlan-related ceramics are reported in surface collections for some parts of Jalisco, but are not described; they are so far unreported for Colima. At Ixtlan del Rio, Nayarit, the pottery designated as Aztatlan seems to be largely of the simpler sort described by Sauer and Brand, and by Kelly for Chametla. At Amapa, Nayarit, the Aztatlan-related pottery and associated artifacts more closely resemble those from the Aztatlan complex at Guasave, which was marked by strong influences from central Mexico.

For present purposes, the Aztatlan complex may be loosely defined as a series of distinctive and related pottery types which appear to have spread along much of the coast and into part of the highlands of west Mexico during the early Postclassic. The exact content of the complex at the various sites will not be described here, since it has been analyzed primarily for the sites in Sinaloa. Inasmuch as reference must be made to it, however, a brief summary may be in order. Kelley and Winters have eliminated Kelly's Early, Middle, and Late designations for the sequences at Chametla and Culiacan (Kelly, 1938, 1945a), and have substituted a series of phase names which they use in their discussion of the Aztatlan-related materials. The Baluarte phase (Middle Chametla) at Chametla is thought to show a kind of developmental Aztatlan complex. The Acaponeta phase, present at both Chametla (Late Chametla II) and Culiacan (Early Culiacan II), marks the appearance of a more fully developed Aztatlan complex; it reaches its peak of elaboration and complexity in the Guasave phase, which includes a large part of the material excavated at that site (Ekholm, 1942). Kelley and Winters present impressive evidence for their hypothesis, largely on the basis of crossties between Durango and Sinaloa. Much more work is needed, however, to answer questions regarding the extent, duration, and internal and external relationships of the Aztatlan complex.

Much of the recently excavated material is still being analyzed, but even preliminary studies indicate that some parts of this area of west Mexico were occupied during the Preclassic. Many of the traits listed as diagnostic of the Valley of Mexico Preclassic (cf. Piña Chan, 1952; Wauchope, 1950) have not been found thus far, although they are present in Michoacan and Guerrero. There is increasing evidence of Preclassic cultures both on the coast and in the inland regions—cultures which may have shared some traits with those of the Valley of Mexico, may have lacked others, and may have had certain distinctive characteristics of their own. Although the Preclassic evidence is still fragmentary, stratigraphic excavation has demonstrated occupation extending at least from the Early Classic until the time of European contact. The total picture of west Mexican archaeology is far from clear as yet, but recent work has wrought a considerable change in earlier reconstructions of west Mexican culture history.

tory. The data on excavations and surveys are presented here under state-name headings, but this is a purely arbitrary choice, based in large part on the difficulty of finding another way in which to present comprehensibly the scattered and uneven data for a wide area. A concluding section will offer a tentative chronology, and examine the distinctive traits, the temporal and subareal differences, and internal and external relationships at various points in time.

NAYARIT
Southern Lowlands and Coast

Early in 1956 the University of California, Los Angeles, excavated two areas at Peñitas, on the plain of the Rio San Pedro about 8 km. east of Tuxpan. Excavations in Peñitas A, in an area roughly 100 by 125 m., revealed a cobblestone temple-platform mound, two looted burial mounds, two habitation mounds, and three permanent pit kilns. Peñitas B, roughly 1.5 km. distant, is on the bank about 10 m. above the Rio San Pedro; it had been partially eroded away, but test pits and trenches were dug in three mounds and in the areas between them. Although the report on Peñitas deals largely with the cultural implications which can be drawn from the kilns and their associated material (Bordaz, 1964), some general statements can be made about chronology and relationships.

Bordaz believes that Peñitas was occupied between ca. A.D. 400 and 1300. Analysis of his material in terms of Sequence Placement Groups 1–7 (from early to late) established three occupation phases: Tamarindo, Chala, and Mitlan. Two radiocarbon dates for SPG 7—ca. A.D. 1270 (T-218; Trondheim, Norway) and ca. A.D. 1255 (UCLA-974; Berger and Libby, 1967)— date the end of the Mitlan phase, and a radiocarbon date of ca. A.D. 1080 (T-219; Trondheim, Norway) for SPG 3 dates the beginning of the same phase. Material from the earliest level of SPG 1 gave a radio-

FIG. 2—BICHROME AND POLYCHROME POTTERY FROM PEÑITAS, NAYARIT. *a,b*, Red-on-orange. *c-f*, Red, black, and white on orange. (*a-d,f*, Southwest Museum, Los Angeles. *e*, University of California, Los Angeles.)

carbon date of ca. A.D. 180 (UCLA-973; Berger and Libby, 1967).

The earliest levels at Peñitas (Tamarindo phase) included sherds of vertically ribbed red vessels similar to those found in Colima associated with the hollow, polished red-ware dog effigies which Kelly (1948) correlated with Teotihuacan III on the basis of a thin orange vessel found in a Colima tomb. These sherds form the basis for Bordaz's postulated starting date of A.D. 400, well within most presently accepted dates for Teotihuacan III but inconsistent with the radiocarbon date of ca. A.D. 180. Bernal (1965a) believes that recent radiocarbon

dates from Teotihuacan (see Berger, Fergusson, and Libby, 1965) indicate that the time span of Teotihuacan III is ca. A.D. 150–300, but even if his hypothesis is rejected, the radiocarbon date may still be acceptable inasmuch as thin orange, once thought to appear in Teotihuacan III, is now known to occur in Teotihuacan II. At Peñitas A there is definite evidence for a cultural and occupational break following the Tamarindo phase. The Chala phase is related to the Early Chametla complex (Tierra del Padre phase) at Chametla, Sinaloa (Kelly, 1938); shared traits include Early Chametla Polychrome, red-rimmed utility ware, and black-

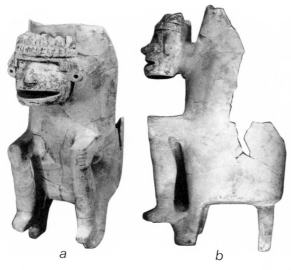

a   b

FIG. 3—ALABASTER EFFIGY JAR FROM PEÑI-
TAS, NAYARIT. Height 13 inches. Traces of blue
paint are still visible on the face. *a*, Front. *b*, Side.
(Southwest Museum, Los Angeles.)

banded ware. Material from the Mitlan
phase seems related to the early Postclassic
material from central Mexico; within west
Mexico, it has similarities to the Late Chametla I and II (Lolandis, Acaponeta, and
El Taste phases), Early Culiacan I and III
(Acaponeta and La Divisa phases), and
Guasave. The occupation seems to have terminated at a period coeval with the start of
Middle Culiacan (Yebalito phase) and the
middle of the Ixcuintla phase at Amapa
(see below).

In addition to Bordaz's report on Peñitas,
there is a brief published report (von Winning, 1956) on a museum collection which
was removed from the site by private excavation. The pottery includes several monochromes, both undecorated and incised
with geometric designs in broad exterior
bands; a number of bichromes; and several
elaborate polychromes, some of them incised; the latter are predominantly red,
black, and white on orange (fig. 2). Painted
designs run largely to intricate combinations of geometric and curvilinear motifs,

but at least one is apparently a variation of
the stylized feathered-serpent motif found
in central Mexico. The collection also includes a number of copper bells, a clay
plaque with geometric designs incised on
both sides, an effigy jar, several clay conch
shells strikingly similar to those of Classic
Teotihuacan, and a badly damaged alabaster tripod effigy vessel, which still bears
traces of blue and gold paint (fig. 3). Although it was claimed that this entire collection was obtained from Peñitas, there is
reason to believe that some items may have
come from elsewhere, and thus no attempt
was made to integrate it with the excavated
material.

During the course of the work at Peñitas
a test pit was dug at Coamiles, on the south
side of a low range of hills approximately
16 km. to the southwest. Coamiles is notable
chiefly for its huge monolithic slabs, decorated primarily with carved geometric and
curvilinear motifs (fig. 4). The small collection of sherds from the test pit showed that
the pottery is quite unlike that from either
Peñitas or Amapa, which is a short distance
to the southwest. Subsequent to the work
there, Coamiles was badly damaged by dy-
namite in the course of pothunting activities, and there is little chance of finding another undisturbed deposit. The petroglyph
sites reported by Project A for coastal Nayarit have not been described, but none of
the petroglyphs located and sketched by
William Byron in the Nayarit lowlands
south of the Rio Santiago bears any resemblance to those at Coamiles (Byron, personal communication).

In 1959 the site of Amapa, Nayarit, was
excavated by the University of California,
Los Angeles. Amapa lies near the southern
end of the coastal plain which forms the
Pacific margin of Sinaloa and Nayarit, and
is located on a flood plain approximately
midway between the Rio San Pedro and the
Rio Santiago; it is about 15 km. from the
coast, and roughly 250 km. south of Mazatlan. The area is known to have been quite

702

FIG. 4—PETROGLYPHS AT COAMI-LES, NAYARIT. Approximate size: *a*, height 6 feet; *b*, width 8 feet; *c*, width 6 feet.

densely populated at the time of European contact (1530); Grosscup (1964, pp. 15–31) made a careful study of the early documentary materials in an effort to determine whether the site was one of the settlements noted in the contact-period accounts. He was unable to tie Amapa conclusively to any named population center, however, and concluded that it had probably been abandoned by the time of the Guzmán *entrada*.

The site of Amapa is about 1.5 km. square and contains a total of perhaps 200 mounds of various sizes and shapes; all the mounds excavated consisted entirely of dirt fill with a scattering of river cobbles. The four areas excavated, which comprise only a small portion of the total site, included a habitation area, a small ceremonial complex, a ball court, and a large cemetery. The house mounds in the habitation area yielded a large collection of sherd material, a number of artifacts, and some evidence as to domes-

FIG. 5—VARIOUS TYPES OF FIGURINE FRAGMENTS FROM AMAPA, NAYA-
RIT. *a-g*, Late period. *h-n*, Early period. (See Grosscup, 1961, for discussion of types.)

tic house types; wattle-and-daub construction was apparently common, and there was
also some use of adobe-brick and adobe-cell
construction. In the ceremonial complex,
two large mounds had borne cut-stone stair-

cases with balustrades. The temples which
topped these mounds were presumably
made of perishable material and had disappeared, but a clue to their form is available in a pottery temple model recovered

704

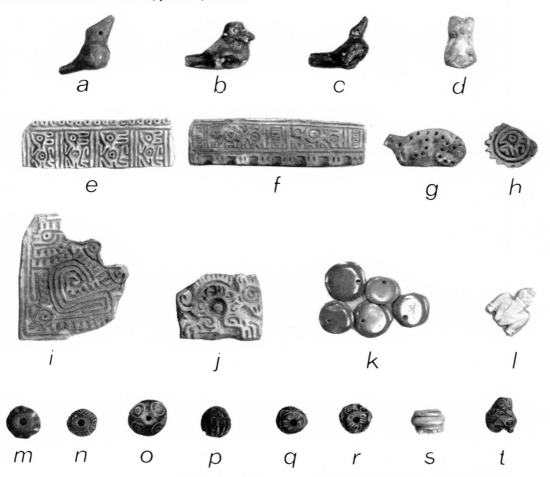

FIG. 6—SMALL ARTIFACTS FROM AMAPA, NAYARIT; WHISTLES, STAMPS, ORNA-
MENTS, SPINDLE WHORLS. *a-d*, Pottery whistles. *e-j*, Clay stamps. *k*, Pierced and polished
greenstone discs. *l*, Carved greenstone frog. *m-r,t*, Pottery spindle whorls. *s*, Polished stone
spindle whorl.

from one of the cemetery pits. The ceremonial complex yielded an unusually large
number of figurine fragments (fig. 5) and
some of its sherd material was quite unlike
that from elsewhere in the site. The ball
court, which is several hundred kilometers
from the nearest one known previously,
showed three distinct phases of occupation;
only a little sherd material and very few artifacts were recovered from it. Altogether
86 pits were dug in the cemetery area, from
which was obtained virtually all the large
collection of whole pottery and a great va-

riety of artifacts. A number of burials were
exposed, each accompanied by a variety of
grave goods; a substantial portion of the
skulls showed fronto-lambdoid flattening, of
the sort described by Stewart (1948) for
elsewhere in Mexico.

The artifact assemblage from Amapa included nearly 800 whole or reconstructible
pottery vessels (including 90 annular-base
molcajetes) and two stone vessels; several
hundred figurine fragments; a number of
clay whistles, elaborate stamps, and spindle
whorls; bone tools and ornaments; shell

705

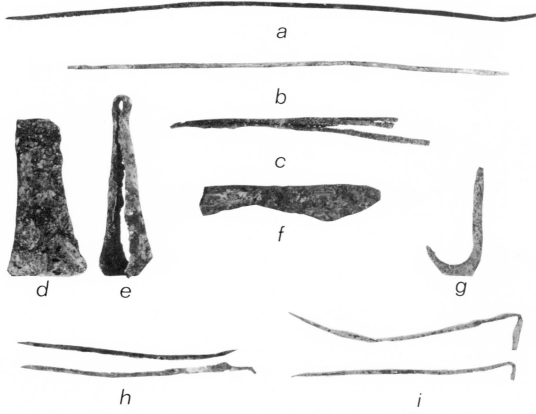

FIG. 7—COPPER ARTIFACTS FROM AMAPA, NAYARIT. *a-c*, Needles. *d-e*, Tweezers. *f*, Knife. *g*, Fishhook. *h,i*, Pins. (From Pendergast, 1960.)

FIG. 8—CARVED STONE SLAB FROM AMAPA, NAYARIT. Dimensions approximately 23 by 19 inches.

bracelets and beads; carved stone beads and pendants; clay earspools and labrets (fig. 6); and small ovoid clay objects with iron pyrites set in one end, which may have been used as strike-a-lights. Annular bases substantially outnumber tripods, negative painting occurs, and two sherds of plumbate were recovered. The collection, however, did not include any of the large, hollow figurines for which other parts of west Mexico are famous, or any fragments which could be attributed to them. Copper objects included a number of bells of various shapes and sizes; needles, awls, tweezers (fig. 7), small rectangular slugs, and a finely wrought ring. Stone artifacts included obsidian scrapers, obsidian and chert points of many sizes, obsidian cores, three-quarter grooved axes, and metates either legless or with two or four legs. Several cenotaph

FIG. 9—MONOCHROME POTTERY FROM AMAPA, NAYARIT. *a*, Gadrooned tripod jar, slipped and polished buff. *b*, Ring-base jar, slipped and polished brown. *c*, Tripod jar, slipped orange. *d*, Ring-base goblet, unslipped brown. *e*, Wide-mouthed jar, slipped dark red. *f*, Bowl, slipped and polished buff with stick-polished design on exterior.

markers, stone slabs decorated with graffiti or with relief carving, were also found in the cemetery area (fig. 8).

The collection of whole pottery included nine monochromes, one of them decorated with appliqué; nine bichrome types; six incised types, some of them decorated with paint; and seven polychrome types ranging from three to six colors; one polychrome was also incised, and one decorated with stucco paint (figs. 9–12). Stylistically, the Amapa incised pottery is much like that from Peñitas; some of the bichromes are similar, but there is little resemblance between the Peñitas and Amapa polychromes.

In general, the Amapa painted pottery is notable for its stylistic variety and intricacy, and perhaps its most outstanding characteristics are the number and diversity of animal designs (fig. 13) and the high degree of asymmetry in layout (cf. Bell, 1960).

The cemetery obviously represents a fairly late occupation. Design analysis of the whole vessels showed stylistic similarities among the Amapa polychromes, the ceramics of the Mixteca-Puebla area (Noguera, 1954), and the Aztatlan polychrome at Guasave (Ekholm, 1942); also present at Amapa were frying-pan censers and appliquéd plainware censers of a type which

707

FIG. 10—BICHROME POTTERY FROM AMAPA, NAYARIT. *a*, Bowl, black-on-buff. *b*, Jar, red-on-buff. *c,d*, Bowls, red-on-orange. *e*, Deep spherical bowl, red-on-orange. *f*, Shallow bowl, red-rimmed white.

FIG. 11—POLYCHROME POTTERY FROM AMAPA, NAYARIT. *a,b*, Bowls with white-on-red design on exterior, red-and-white-rimmed orange interior. *c,d*, Bowls with interior design, black-and-white-on-red. *e*, Bowl with interior design, red-and-white-on-orange. *f*, Ring-base bowl, red-and-white-on-orange. *g*, Stepped tripod bowl, red-and-white-on-orange. *h*, Ring-base bowl, exterior dark red, black, white, and pinkish-red on buff, interior red-on-orange animal design.

708

FIG. 12—INCISED POTTERY FROM AMAPA, NAYARIT. *a*, Dark brown ring-base jar, with stick-grooving on body. *b*, Red-rimmed orange double jar with design incised through medallions of red slip. *c*, Slipped orange bowl. *d*, Design incised through band of red slip on orange bowl. *e*, Buff tripod bowl. *f*, Polished black tripod bowl with imitation gadrooning.

date from the Postclassic in the Valley of Mexico. This placement is further substantiated by the presence in the cemetery of a large number of copper artifacts (cf. Meighan, 1960; Pendergast, 1960). Moreover, fronto-lambdoid skull deformation is also present at Guasave, and is noted by Stewart (1948) as occurring in Mixteca-Puebla sites and on the Gulf Coast in periods which equate with the Mexican period at Chichen Itza. Some resemblances to materials from Costa Rica and from the Southwestern United States have also been noted (Meighan, 1959) but not placed chronologically. In this connection, it might be added that Pendergast (personal communication) suspects that metalworking may have reached the Amapa area via sea routes from Central America, and that the area may thus have served as a corridor for the diffusion of metallurgical techniques to other parts of western and northern Mesoamerica. There is still no certainty regarding the introduction and development of metallurgy, but other suggestions of water-borne contact, in the Amapa area and elsewhere in west Mexico, lend some weight to the possibility.

More than 40 different pottery types or wares were defined for Group B, the ceremonial complex, which represents a much longer span of occupation than does the cemetery. Through analysis of this sherd material, Grosscup (1964) established six phases: Gavilan, Amapa, Tuxpan, Cerritos, Ixcuintla, and Santiago (from early to late). The first two phases, Gavilan and Amapa, constitute the Early period at Amapa; there are indications of some probable relationships to Early Ixtlan del Rio, but much clearer indications of relationships between the Gavilan and Amapa phases and their

709

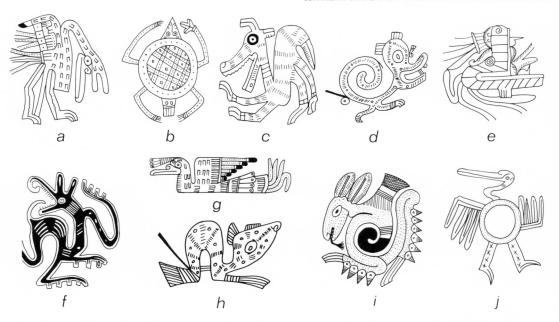

F$_{IG}$. 13—SOME ANIMAL DESIGNS FROM THE POTTERY OF AMAPA, NAYARIT. (From Bell, 1960.)

temporal equivalents at Chametla—the Tierra del Padre and Baluarte phases (Early and Middle Chametla). The Cerritos, Ixcuintla, and Santiago phases constitute the Late period. The Cerritos phase is equated with the Acaponeta phase at Chametla (Late Chametla II) and at Culiacan (Early Culiacan II), and with Middle Ixtlan del Rio. This phase marks the appearance of Aztatlan pottery at Amapa, but much of it shows such strong resemblances to the elaborate Aztatlan material from Guasave that Grosscup believes the Cerritos phase overlaps the Guasave phase, and thus postulates an earlier date for the latter than do Kelley and Winters (Grosscup, 1964, fig. 45; Kelley and Winters, 1960, fig. 8). The Ixcuintla and Santiago phases are equated roughly with Late Ixtlan del Rio, and cover the time span filled by the La Divisa, Yebalito, and La Quinta phases (Early I, Middle, and Late) at Culiacan and partially filled by the terminal El Taste phase (Late I) at Chametla. Grosscup believes the Santiago

phase to have been very short, and to have overlapped with the Ixcuintla phase. Both show the very strong influence of pottery from late Ixtlan, and Grosscup (personal communication) thinks it is possible that the Santiago phase may not be a separate and distinct phase, but may simply reflect greater trade with the Ixtlan region. The Tuxpan phase, intermediate between the Early and Late periods, is in a sense a hypothetical phase, for the pottery gives clear evidence of an occupation break. Grosscup (1964, pp. 184–85) notes that, "With the exception of a scattering of Early sherds in Late deposits and vice versa, whose presence may be explained as the result of mixture or intrusion, no Early Period ceramic persists into the Late Period and no Late Period ceramic begins its development in the Early Period. No clear relationship exists between any Late Period ceramic type and a presumed Early Period type or types," although there are "a number of modes or traits which bridge the gap between the Early and Late Periods." Among these are use of red paint, particularly on the rim of buff or orange pottery; use of white paint or slip; and use of incising. There is also a marked decline in the number of sherds; the levels representing the Tuxpan phase yielded only a handful of sherds, in comparison to large yields for the phases of the Early and Late periods. Grosscup believes that, for some still-unknown reason, Amapa probably was abandoned during the Tuxpan phase; there is some suggestion that Chametla may also have been abandoned during the temporally equivalent Lolandis phase (the early part of Late Chametla II), but the evidence there is far from clear.

The Early period is thought to start at about A.D. 250 and last until ca. 650–700; the Late period covers the time span between A.D. 900 and ca. 1520 (see Grosscup, 1964, fig. 45). A radiocarbon date of ca. A.D. 1260 (Deevey, Flint, and Rouse, 1963, pp. 245–46) for material which should date the end of the Gavilan Phase is rejected by Grosscup (1964, pp. 250–51) as "one datum which is contradicted by many data," but he finds acceptable (personal communication) a more recent date of ca. A.D. 1305 (UCLA-956; Berger and Libby, 1967) for approximately the end of the Ixcuintla phase. An additional bit of evidence for dating is the existence of the plumbate sherds in one level of a pit in Group A, the habitation area. Analysis of the other sherds from the same level placed it in the early part of the Ixcuintla phase. Dating of plumbate in the Maya area (Wauchope, 1948, pp. 143–45; Brainerd, 1958, pp. 64–65) places it in the Toltec-Chichen substage, which is dated approximately A.D. 980–1200 according to the Goodman-Thompson-Martínez correlation.

On the basis of the sherd analysis, the Gavilan Phase (Amapa) and Tierra del Padre phase (Chametla) are regarded as regional variations of the same basic phase, with local styles developing to form the Amapa phase (Amapa) and the Baluarte phase (Chametla). The Cerritos phase, following reoccupation of the site, includes the widespread Aztatlan ceramics, but their similarity to the Aztatlan pottery of Guasave indicates influences from central Mexico at this time. These influences are still discernible in the Ixcuintla phase, but local styles again develop and show an increasingly close relationship to the southern Nayarit highlands until the end of the Amapa occupation (Santiago phase). The relationships, dating, and occupation break are also reflected in Grosscup's study of the figurine fragments from the ceremonial complex (Grosscup, 1961). The figurines showed a clear division into two periods, with no Early type directly ancestral to any Late type. In general, the Early figurines show definite relationships to those placed by Kelly (1938) in Early and Middle Chametla (Tierra del Padre and Baluarte phases); with the Late period, resemblances shift more toward the south and east. The Late material includes a number of Mazapan figurines, dated approximately A.D. 900–1200 in the Valley of Mexico, as well as some which are obviously local variations of the Mazapan type.

Excavation of the vertical-walled, I-shaped ball court (Clune, 1963) showed two construction phases, with five renovations within the first phase and one in the second, and its later use as a habitation site. Stone center-markers, topped with cups, were discovered for both phases, but there appear to have been no rings; ball court center-markers of stone are described in the conquest-period literature, but the cup-shaped top is unique. A stone-lined drain, associated with the later construction phase, is similar to ball court drains at Toltec-period Chichen Itza and at Tula. The basic construction was mud plaster over dirt fill, or, in the case of the benches along the playing ranges, over cobble walls; this construction technique is unknown elsewhere. In the final renovation, coursed cut stone

711

a   b   c   d

Fig. 14—LARGE, HOLLOW POLYCHROME FIGURINES FROM IXTLAN DEL RIO, NA-
YARIT. Decoration in black, white, red, and yellow on red slip. *a*, 14½ inches. *b*, 24½ inches.
c, 15 inches. *d*, 13 inches. (*a*, collection of Dr. and Mrs. Ernest Fantel; *b*, Stendahl Collection;
c,d, collection of Dr. George C. Kennedy.)

was used in place of the mud-plastered cobbles, but there is no evidence for the use of lime plaster at any time. Clune believes that the earliest possible date for the court is early in the Late period, probably during the Cerritos phase. With the exception of a few sherds from what is obviously fill, all pottery from both construction phases and the habitation debris is comparable to that from the cemetery area. On the basis of structural similarities between the Amapa court and those of the Toltec period in central Mexico and Yucatan, Clune feels that the influences from central Mexico provided the impetus for construction of the Amapa court.

Little is known about other parts of the Nayarit coastal plain. Illustrations in Fay's report (1959) on his surface survey in the northern area suggest similarities between

his sherd material and some of the pottery from Amapa and Peñitas, but the type collection available for study was too small to permit firm crossties. Kelly reports (1947a, p. 75) of the Acaponeta area that "archaeological remains are plentiful and conspicuous, and large artificial mounds are clustered on the flood plain; from this valley alone collections were made from over seventy mounds." Her collections are said to represent all the Chametla time periods and wares, but as they are not described they cannot be related to material from elsewhere in Nayarit. The valleys of the Rio San Pedro and Rio Santiago "form a distinct unit, although they likewise affiliate with Sinaloa. The relationship is, however, confined to a certain cluster of wares which has been designated as the Aztatlán complex." The Project A survey of the Nayarit coast (Meighan, 1961) sampled 28 sites between the mouth of the Rio Santiago and the Jalisco border; both this survey and that made by Byron in the interior indicate a fairly dense population, but the collections have not been analyzed. Three test pits dug by Project A at Santa Cruz revealed, in addition to ceramic material, some architectural remains, two urn burials, and copper rings. Preliminary study of the ceramics, plus the presence of copper, suggests a Postclassic occupation. Corona Núñez (1954, p. 46) describes two bottle-shaped tombs found at El Llano, roughly 10 km. south of Santa Cruz; he regards this as the earliest of the three types of tombs which he describes ("botella," "tiro y bóveda," and "fosa simple"). The four pottery jars said to have come from one of these tombs are regarded by Corona Núñez as "un tipo arcaico"; they are not clearly described or illustrated, but one of them, a nubbin ware, is of a type regarded by Furst (1966) as early in the southern Nayarit highlands (see following section). Two test pits dug by Project A at Chacala, a short distance south of El Llano, yielded several thousand sherds; most were plainware, but the decorated types could not readily be related to other types of pottery known for this part of Mexico (Meighan, 1961).

Southern Highlands

Unquestionably the most striking archaeological materials from the Ixtlan del Rio area of southern Nayarit are the large hollow figurines, both monochrome and polychrome, which are said to come from tombs. Lumholtz, who collected a number of them, reports (1902, 2: 307) that some were found in "a subterranean vault divided

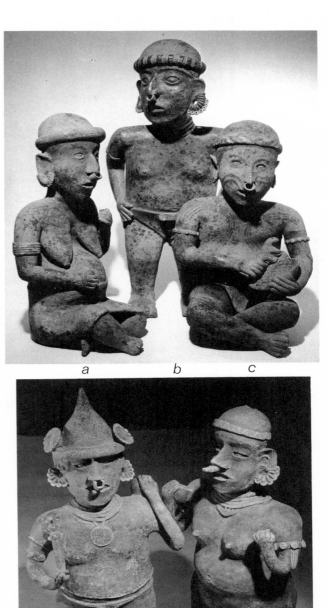

a   b   c

d   e

Fig. 15—LARGE, HOLLOW POLYCHROME FIGURINES FROM IXTLAN DEL RIO, NAYARIT. Decoration in black and white on red slip. *a*, 16 inches. *b*, 21 inches. *c*, 15½ inches. *d*, 34 inches. *e*, 31¼ inches. (*a-c*, collection of Mr. and Mrs. Edgar Dorsey Taylor; *d,e*, Stendahl Collection.)

a *b*

FIG. 16—RED-AND-CREAM FIGURINES FROM IXTLAN DEL RIO, NAYARIT. *a*, 9¼ inches. *b*, 11¼ inches. (Stendahl Collection.)

into sections, and in the vault they perceived twenty-seven figures, together with many beautifully made vessels. According to my informants the larger figures were all in one room and the smaller ones in the other." Corona Núñez (1954, pp. 47–48) describes a shaft tomb at Corral Falso, roughly 35 km. northwest of Ixtlan del Rio. Two rectangular chambers, one smaller than the other, were found at the bottom of a 4-m. shaft; both chambers contained burials, apparently accompanied by a variety of grave goods. Relatively shallow one-chamber shaft tombs occur virtually on the outskirts of Ixtlan del Rio.

Many of the large Ixtlan figurines are almost caricatures, with grossly thickened legs, matchstick arms, and long, sharp noses; some, in addition, appear to depict various diseases and pathological conditions. They are, however, a valuable record of the dress and ornament of the people, and exhibit a variety of patterned shirts and skirts, loincloths, elaborate headdresses, nose rings, earrings, bracelets, and face and body paint (fig. 14). The figurines may be seated or standing, idle or engaged in a wide range of activities (cf. Lumholtz, 1902, vol. 2, pls. 1–5; Gifford, 1950, pls. 7–10). Another type of large figurine is often simpler in details of dress and ornamentation, but it is marked by greater naturalism in the treatment of the body and especially the face (fig. 15). A slightly smaller type, invariably red-and-white or red-and-cream (occasionally with black decoration), is rather stylized in treatment and gives only a sketchy indication of clothing or adornment (fig. 16). Innumerable small, solid figurines, stylistically akin to the large cari-

714

FIG. 17—VILLAGE GROUPS FROM SOUTHERN NAYARIT. Decorated in various combinations of black, white, and orange paint on red slip. *a*, Village scene; diameter 17 inches. *b*, Battle scene; height 9¾ inches. *c*, Game or ritual resembling the *voladores*; height 14½ inches. *d*, House model; height 15½ inches. (*a*, collection of Mr. and Mrs. Alan Schwartz; *b,c*, collection of Dr. George C. Kennedy; *d*, Stendahl Collection.)

FIG. 18—POLYCHROME AND BICHROME POTTERY FROM IXTLAN DEL RIO, NAYA-RIT. *a*, Black, white, and orange on dark red. *b*, Exterior red-on-buff, interior black-on-buff. *c-e*, Orange-and-white on dark red. *f*, Black-on-buff. (Stendahl Collection.)

cature-like figures, portray a great diversity of physical types and activities. Gifford (1950, pl. 5,*b*) illustrates the bottom half of a two-part effigy vessel, which he assigns to Early Ixtlan. The ware and decoration are consistent with known types of Nayarit shaft-tomb pottery, but the two-part effigy is very rare in west Mexico. It is found, however, in Teotihuacan, Kaminaljuyu, and in the Maya area in Early Classic contexts. There are also house or temple models, which show small structures on earth platforms; they are topped by peaked thatch roofs and decorated with geometric designs. The so-called Tarascan villages allegedly come from the southern Nayarit highlands, but their exact source is unknown. These action scenes occur in a variety of sizes and shapes; each includes a number of figures, both human and animal, usually several structures, and often a small terraced mound in the center. The activities depicted range from ceremonial processions and ball games to portrayals of the multitudi-

nous pursuits of an entire small village (fig. 17; see also von Winning, 1959).

Unfortunately, no figurine or "village" had come from a controlled excavation, and their chronological placement was uncertain. In an attempt to associate the figurines owned by the University of California with other ceramic material, Gifford in 1946 made sherd collections from the surfaces and exposed cuts of 16 sites in the Ixtlan area, and tentatively defined Early, Middle and Late periods there (Gifford, 1950). The figurines, Gifford believes, are associated with Early Ixtlan pottery, which includes several monochromes, incised wares, a variety of bichromes, and some fine and distinctive uniface and biface polychromes (fig. 18). Pottery belonging to the Aztatlan complex (Gifford, 1950, p. 225; Kelly, 1938, p. 19) is assigned to the Middle period, which includes an abundance of red-on-buff as well as several other bichromes and incised wares; Middle period polychrome is very sparsely represented and much less distinctive. Little of the sherd material assigned to Middle Ixtlan resembles the Guasave Aztatlan pottery, but it must be emphasized that no stratigraphic work has been done at Ixtlan. Annular-base molcajetes and three-quarter grooved axes appear in this period; the objects which Gifford designates as plaques (Gifford, 1950, pl. 28) and assigns to the Middle period are clearly fragments of Mazapan-type figurines. Plain wares and bichromes are present in the Late period, which seems to lack incised wares and polychromes. The characteristic painted pottery of this period is a white-on-red, very similar to the Autlan (Jalisco) white-on-red which is late at that site (Kelly, 1945b, p. 42); it also strongly resembles the Ixcuintla phase white-on-red from Amapa. Gifford equates Early Ixtlan and Early Chametla (Tierra del Padre) on the basis of stylistic similarities between Early Chametla polychrome and Early Ixtlan biface polychrome. Middle Ixtlan is equated with late Chametla II (Lolandis-Acaponeta) and Early Culiacan II (Acaponeta), the Aztatlan horizon at those sites, and with the Aztatlan complex at Guasave. Late Ixtlan "may correspond to Late, Middle and (or) Early Culiacán I" (Gifford, 1950, p. 237), but it is equated specifically only with the Autlan complex, on the basis of the resemblances noted above.

The large site south of the town of Ixtlan del Rio has been the object of intermittent excavation and much speculation (cf. Gifford, 1950, pp. 193–97; Corona Núñez, 1952), but the only report on recent work there (Contreras S., 1966) deals entirely with reconstruction of some of the architectural features. The mounds which have been excavated so far show the use of cut stone slabs mortared with adobe, and two large petroglyph slabs were imbedded in the wall of one structure. Gifford found no Early Ixtlan pottery at this site, and assigned it to Middle and Late Ixtlan, roughly equivalent in time to the construction and use of the Amapa ball court. Gifford's

Site 4 at Jala, a few kilometers to the northwest, gave special promise of contributing to the dating of the Ixtlan area, but a recent (1966) attempt to locate it was unsuccessful. Site 4 consisted of a deep cut in which a thick layer of pumice separated two strata of differing cultural horizons. Below the pumice Gifford (1950, p. 188) found only sherds attributable to the Early period, whereas the stratum above the pumice layer yielded sherds of the Middle and Late periods. Should the site be relocated, dating of the volcanic debris might give a definite end-date for Early Ixtlan.

In 1965 the area around the little town of Tequilita, southeast of Compostela and approximately 50 km. south of Tepic, became known as the site of numerous shaft-tomb cemeteries. Furst's investigations there revealed the existence of 24 such cemeteries, with the staggering total of 390 looted tombs. The tomb explored by Furst (1966) at Las Cebollas, near Tequilita, had been looted only of its large figurines. Remaining in it were 83 pottery vessels, 125 complete or fragmentary conch shells, eight complete small figurines and fragments of six others, two intact slate "mirror" backs and the fragments of many more, slate pendants and beads, shell bracelets and beads, and several pottery flutes.

For several years, the Mexican antiquities market has offered a new style of large pottery figurine characterized as "Chinesca." The name, which was bestowed by collectors of antiquities, carries no diffusionist implications. Rather, it reflects a feeling that the style is vaguely Oriental in appearance (fig. 19; see also Furst, 1966, pls. 4–12). In Furst's words, "One of the major identifying characteristics of the style is a remarkable majesty of pose and serenity of expression in a rather naturalistically treated face with high cheekbones and slanted almond eyes. These combined with other, admittedly rather impressionistic details, convey a vaguely Oriental feeling. . . . *Chinesca*, as now understood, is a collective heading for

717

a

b

FIG. 19—CHINESCA FIGURINES ATTRIB-
UTED TO THE AREA OF TEQUILITA,
SOUTHERN NAYARIT. Red-slipped and dec-
orated with positive and negative painting. *a*, 30
inches. *b*, 31½ inches. (Nayarit State Museum,
Tepic.)

a

b

FIG. 20—SMALL, SOLID, UNSLIPPED CHI-
NESCA FIGURINES FOUND IN THE VICIN-
ITY OF AMAPA, NAYARIT. Both approximate-
ly 8 inches. (From photographs on file at the
University of California, Los Angeles.)

a number of previously unknown or unrecognized ceramics of diverse but vaguely related styles whose principal common denominator seems to be, on the one hand, their origin in shaft-and-chamber tombs, and on the other, their remarkable aesthetic appeal and quality of execution, which causes them to stand out unmistakably amid West Mexican tomb art. . . ." (Furst, 1966, pp. 15, 34). The Chinesca figurines were said to come primarily from southern Nayarit, and to occur occasionally as far north as Rosamorada in the central part of the state. Three of the complete figurines from Las Cebollas were of the small, solid trichrome-decorated type found in the Ixtlan area (Furst, 1966, pl. 30,a,b; Gifford, 1950, pls. 5,c; 8,c); four were complete in themselves but had been broken off at the base, suggesting attachment to a village model (Furst, 1966, pl. 32,d–g); and one was in the style of the small Chinesca figurines, a style far less delicate and naturalistic than that of the large figurines, but nevertheless distinctive (Furst, 1966, pls. 50, 51, a–c). The fragments included the head of a large Chinesca figurine and portions of another, and the concave base of a "Martian" Chinesca, so named because of its peculiar head form (Furst, 1966, pls. 31,a,b; 33). Small Chinesca figurines also appear in the Gavilan phase at Amapa (fig. 5,k; see also Grosscup, 1961, figs. 3,n; 4,s,t); although no complete Chinesca figurine was recovered from the excavations there, people in nearby villages had many which they had found in areas around the site (fig. 20). A radiocarbon date of ca A.D. 100 (UCLA-1012; Berger and Libby, 1966) was obtained for Las Cebollas; Grosscup places the start of the Gavilan phase at A.D. 250. However, Grosscup (personal communication) now feels that the Amapa deposits may not have shown the start of the Gavilan phase, and that it may be slightly earlier than he first believed. The "Martian" Chinesca figurines are relatively rare, and most complete specimens known to date are in private collec-

FIG. 21—"MARTIAN" CHINESCA FIGURINE FROM SOUTHERN NAYARIT. Red-slipped and decorated with positive and negative painting. Height 11¼ inches. (Collection of Mr. and Mrs. Vincent Price.)

tions (fig. 21; see also Furst, 1966, pls. 53–55); one, however, is included in the Ixtlan collection studied by Gifford (1950, pl. 3,a), who places it in Early Ixtlan.

Relationships between the pottery vessels from Las Cebollas and those from Early Ixtlan del Rio are so strong as to suggest very close contact or even a common source of manufacture. Similarities include numerous composite silhouettes, abundant negative painting, the unusual blue-slipped ware, nubbin ware, and almost identical colors, layouts, and design elements in the bichrome and polychrome pottery (Gifford, 1950, pls. 11–19; Furst, 1966, pls. 21–29). Further, both the Ixtlan and Las Cebollas collections include pieces which are strongly suggestive of Chupicuaro pottery (Gifford, 1950, pl. 15; Furst, 1966, pl. 25,*d,f*). Gifford (1950, p. 212) believes that the Ixtlan piece represents trade ware, and Furst is inclined to agree with regard to the Las Cebollas specimens. He remarks that, "The general appearance and careless decoration of the Ixtlán and Las Cebollas examples places them in the middle to upper range of Chupícuaro ceramic evolution, perhaps around 100–200 A.D." (Furst, 1966, p. 266). Grosscup (personal communication) adds that he feels there are some "general resemblances" between the Chupicuaro material and some of Amapa's Gavilan phase material.

The pyrites which had encrusted the mirror-backs had disintegrated, but traces discernible on one indicated that it had been covered with neatly fitted polygonal pieces of pyrite, having from four to nine sides, much in the manner of a well-preserved piece from the Lake Chapala area of Michoacan (Furst, 1966, pl. 46). Furst summarizes the data on construction techniques used in the manufacture of pyrite mirrors, which form the basis for chronological ordering, and concludes that the specimens from Las Cebollas equate in time with those from the Esperanza phase (Early Classic) at Kaminaljuyu, Guatemala. Despite their wide spatial distribution (from Panama to the Southwestern United States) the "close technical correspondences between all of these mirrors and the identity of chronological characteristics" suggest a single pyrite-mosaic industry, although the number or location of the manufacturing centers cannot as yet be determined (Furst, 1966, pp. 171–98).

Of the 125 conch shells in the Las Cebollas tomb, 120 belonged to a single species, *Turbinella angulatus* Solander; this is the common West Indian chank, native to the Caribbean and found from Florida to the northern coast of South America. Four were

Strombus gigas Linné or Queen conch, also a Caribbean shell, and only one, a *Strombus peruvianus*, was of Pacific coast origin. Of these shells 111 were end-blown trumpets. A comparison of the Las Cebollas specimens with the numerous representations of conch shells at Teotihuacan shows that the same shell (*Turbinella angulatus* Solander), apparently having the same function, predominated at both places. The decorations on the Las Cebollas shell trumpets are very similar to those shown on the Teotihuacan conch shells, and on a shell trumpet from Kaminaljuyu, although the Kaminaljuyu specimen is a *Fasciolaria princeps* (another Caribbean shell). Although the prevalence in west Mexico of a shell native to the Caribbean may simply reflect widespread trade, Furst notes that it may equally well indicate that some well-defined meaning, possibly related to ritual, was attached to a particular species. If this is true, he suggests, there may have been an ideological link between the west Mexican shaft-tomb cultures, Early Classic Teotihuacan, and, if the design motifs are taken into consideration, possibly Early Classic Kaminaljuyu (see Furst, 1966, pp. 153–70). The radiocarbon date of ca A.D. 100, obtained from a *Turbinella* shell trumpet, places the tomb at about the beginning of the Early Classic.

The tomb at Las Cebollas was on a slope above a milpa, and local informants maintained that shaft tombs are always found at elevations somewhat above the habitation sites. It was long surmised that the depth of the shaft might be related to the importance of the tomb's occupants, but it now appears that depth may instead be a function of the location of the *tepetate*, a hard, impermeable layer of varying thickness which underlies the less consolidated soil at varying depths. (Tepetate may be composed of various materials, but in this part of west Mexico it is said to be a water-deposited volcanic tuff.) In this area, the tomb chambers are carved out of the tepetate and apparently always have at least 2 m. of it above their ceilings. The tomb investigated by Furst consisted of two chambers roughly 4 m. square, with inward-sloping sides and slightly vaulted roofs, located at the bottom of a 5.25-m. shaft; the floors of the chambers were almost a meter lower than the base of the shaft. The top 2.2 m. of the shaft were circular, about 2 m. in diameter, and lined with a stone retaining wall; seemingly this formed an entry to the square shaft, 1 m. on each side, which descended to the short, connecting tunnels that led to the chambers. This construction is typical of shaft tombs in the Tequilita area, as are the so-called *claraboyas*, narrow, tube-like openings which connect the chambers of several tombs. Occasionally, also, a vertical claraboya extends from the ceiling of a tomb to the surface of the ground above. It was reported that at nearby Cuatro Albillas, four retainer burials, accompanied by offerings, were found arranged in a square around the circular opening of a shaft tomb; a similar retainer burial, but vertical instead of horizontal, is reported for an area near Guadalajara, and another near Comala, Colima (Furst, 1966, pp. 62–63).

Using informants' statements regarding the average number of burials per chamber, Furst (1966, p. 229) estimates that approximately 3500 individuals were buried in the 390 tombs located so far in this one municipio, and he believes that perhaps no more than 30 per cent of the tombs have yet been discovered. On the basis of tentative population estimates he concludes that the occupants of a shaft tomb represent a single generation of one family, and offers two interpretations of the stylistic variation in the shaft-tomb offerings of Nayarit and elsewhere in west Mexico: (1) they may reflect some form of exogamy, in which "persons buried in these tombs brought into the common archaeological context objects conforming to their own local traditions"; or (2) "the area in which shaft tombs occur might have been sufficiently unified culturally, if not politically, so that some pot-

tery-making centers or individual ceramic sculptors might have been able to supply the needs of different communities scattered over a relatively large geographical region, because their work found a greater response among the population" (Furst, 1966, pp. 236–37, 267–68). Long, working with the shaft tombs of the Magdalena Lake basin in Jalisco, a short distance to the south, comes to a different conclusion (see following section).

There are a few other data, largely fragmentary, about the southern Nayarit highlands in the reports by Corona Núñez (n.d.) and Ross (1939), but the material described lacks both stratigraphic placement and indisputable provenience. A large part of the material studied by Ross was purchased by Lumholtz, and the collection is drawn from an area extending from Tepic and extreme northern Jalisco to central Michoacan. From Tepic comes the famous plumbate turkey effigy collected by Lumholtz (1902, 2: 295), who also noted the existence there of gold and turquoise ornaments; another plumbate vessel is said to come from Terrero, south of Ixtlan del Rio. A handsome cloisonné vessel purchased in Tepic is included in the Lumholtz collection, but the evident concentration of this ware around Totoate and Estanzuela (both in Jalisco) suggests that it is an import. Ross and Corona Núñez describe annular bases and a variety of tripods, but, as noted, their material cannot be firmly placed either temporally or spatially. "Tripod vessels are early in Colima, but die out" (Kelly, 1944, p. 208) and were generally assumed to be fairly late elsewhere in the west Mexican sequence, although they occur early in the Valley of Mexico and as far west as Chupicuaro. Much of the material ascribed to the southern Nayarit highlands lacks either annual bases or tripods. Gifford's sherd collection, however, included fragments of annular-base and tripod molcajetes; he assigns the former to Middle Ixtlan and the latter to Late Ixtlan, but, curiously, assigns to Early Ixtlan a bichrome tripod bowl in the University of California collection which he studied (Gifford, 1950, pp. 231–32; pl. 13,*d*).

JALISCO

Northern Jalisco

The shaft-tomb complex present in the southern Nayarit highlands extends into north-central Jalisco, where, in fact, some of the first shaft-tomb discoveries were made. Tombs are particularly abundant in the Magdalena-Tequila-Etzatlan area and around the shores of the Magdalena Lake basin (the lake was drained artificially about 60 years ago). They are reported virtually on the outskirts of Guadalajara and are known as far south as Acatlan de Juarez, about 35 km. south of Guadalajara, where there is a looted shaft tomb in the town cemetery. The first published report of a shaft tomb was that on the looted three-chambered tomb found in 1954 at El Arenal, near Etzatlan (Corona Núñez, 1955; Covarrubias, 1957, fig. 38).

In 1963 the Los Angeles County Museum of Natural History was given the complete contents of a tomb discovered at San Sebastian, about 8 km. northeast of Etzatlan and only 2 km. from the El Arenal tomb. The collection, which was purchased at the site and kept intact, included 17 large, hollow figurines, 40 polychrome vessels, several pottery boxes with covers, and various shell and obsidian ornaments and artifacts, including "mirrors" and shell trumpets. The University of California, Los Angeles, had surveyed the Magdalena Lake basin in 1962, and more intensive work was done there during 1963–64; the hope of finding an unlooted tomb was not fulfilled, but the investigations yielded much information about the shaft-tomb complex in this area. Data were obtained from about nine tombs in four cemeteries within a small area: El Arenal (3), Mary Perez (3), Santa Maria (2), and Las Cuevas (1), in addition to the tomb at San Sebastian (see Long, 1965, pp.

44–60; figs. 4–13). Some of the information was obtained from Long's firsthand investigation of the tombs and study of material left behind by the looters, and some from informants in whose hands much of the tomb material remained.

The Magdalena Lake basin tombs had from one to three chambers, at the bottom of rectangular shafts which ranged from 3.5 to 11 m. in depth. There was no indication of the circular entry described for Las Cebollas, or of retainer burials on the surface. In general, the chambers were 3 or 4 m. square, with inward-sloping walls and slightly vaulted roofs, although some of the smaller chambers were roughly oval; this form is also described for southern Nayarit, apparently for a tomb at Corral Falso (Corona Núñez, 1954, p. 47). One single-chambered tomb (Mary Perez, Tomb One) was barely large enough for one interment, whereas the San Sebastian tomb contained nine burials; the chambers of other tombs were said to have contained two, three, or four burials. Tomb One at El Arenal was aberrant in having one chamber, with a separate entrance shaft, at a level 2 m. above the other two chambers; this chamber was also connected, however, with the main entrance shaft (Long, 1965, fig. 6); Corona Núñez (1954, p. 48) notes this as "un subtipo" in Nayarit, but does not locate it. The three tombs at Mary Perez fall outside the usual pattern of constructing the chambers within the stratum of tepetate; here the tombs, all single chambered and of relatively shallow depth, had merely been cut into the soil. It is possible, though not likely, that either there is no stratum of tepetate in this location or it lies at a depth unattainable by the existing technology. It seems more probable that, for whatever reason, no effort was made to reach it, as the chamber of the nearby San Sebastian tomb is cut into tepetate at a depth of 5 m., and the three chambers of Tomb Two at El Arenal, about 3 km. to the northeast, were in tepetate at a depth of 11 m. (None of the

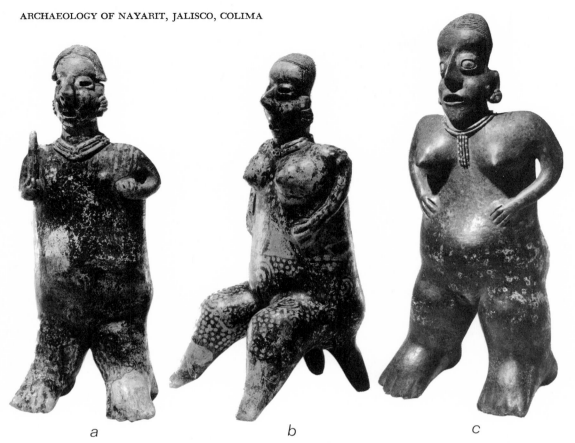

a   b   c

FIG. 22—LARGE, HOLLOW FIGURINES ("SAN SEBASTIAN RED") FROM SOUTHERN NAYARIT AND NORTHERN JALISCO. a,b, From the San Sebastian tomb in northern Jalisco, red-slipped with decoration in black, cream, and negative-painting, 19 and 18 inches respectively. c, Southern Nayarit, red-slipped with decoration in black and cream, 20 inches. (a,b, Los Ángeles County Museum of Natural History, photographs by Armando Solís; c, Stendahl Collection.)

El Arenal tombs reported here is the one discovered in 1954.)

In an effort to give provenience and chronological placement to the many figurines long known from this general area, and to reconstruct at least a partial culture history, Long studied the material from the San Sebastian tomb, the material (pottery vessels, figurine fragments, obsidian artifacts, shell, and bone) he obtained from various looted tombs and that in the hands of his informants. In addition to a stylistic analysis (Long, 1965, pp. 64–75 and appendix), he brought to bear on it a variety of dating techniques. The San Sebastian tomb

material, which seems to have an indisputable provenience (a figurine arm found by Long in the tomb proved to fit a figurine in the Los Angeles County Museum collection), forms the core of the analysis, but the other material considerably enlarged the scope of the results.

The San Sebastian tomb contained figurines of two distinct types, which Long has named San Sebastian Red and El Arenal Brown and assigns to different time periods. Intermediate between them he places the fine monochrome figurines—Ameca Grey, in Long's terminology—so popular with collectors, which are said to come from the

723

FIG. 23—LARGE, HOLLOW FIGURINES ("AMECA GREY") FROM THE AMECA AREA OF NORTHERN JALISCO. Decorated in red and black on buff. *a*, 22½ inches. *b*, 19 inches. *c*, 14¼ inches. (*a*, private collection; *b*, collection of Dr. and Mrs. William Kaiser; *c*, Stendahl Collection.)

FIG. 24—LARGE, HOLLOW FIGURINES ("AMECA GREY") FROM THE AMECA AREA OF NORTHERN JALISCO, GENERALLY INTERPRETED AS WARRIORS. Decorated in red and black on buff. *a*, 14¾ inches. *b*, 18 inches. (Collection of Mr. William P. Palmer.)

Ameca area south of the Magdalena Lake basin. The San Sebastian Red figurines are of the type characterized by Kirchhoff (1946, pp. 51–54) as "Los Desnudos," and heretofore known to occur only in Early Ixtlan (fig. 22; see also Gifford, 1950, pls. 4, 6). They are thick bodied and thick legged, with very thin arms (often both hands are placed on the upper abdomen); the heads are rather rounded but elongated, and the eyes and mouth may be mere horizontal slits. The figurines are red slipped; they may be decorated with black paint (occasionally black and white), and negative painting is common. They may be nude, decorated with body paint, or be depicted wearing a brief skirt, shirt, or a waistband; simple band headdresses, simple necklaces, and ear ornaments are usually present. Some figurines wear what is usually described as armor and a helmet. The Ameca Grey figurines have elongated faces, often finely molded, with large, thin noses, and frequently wear high crossband turbans; some are also adorned with pellets on the shoul-

a b

FIG. 25—LARGE, HOLLOW FIGURINES ("EL ARENAL BROWN") FROM THE SAN SEBASTIAN TOMB, NORTHERN JALISCO. Red-slipped with red, black, and white paint. a, 14 inches. b, 18 inches. (Los Angeles County Museum of Natural History.)

ders. The forms are ample and smoothly rounded; many figurines depict seated women, holding a jar or a baby, and some represent what are thought to be warriors armed with clubs. The figurines are unslipped but burnished, and range from buff to gray to brown. Ornaments other than earrings are seldom depicted, and painted decoration is rare except for resist-painted scrolls on the breasts of the female figurines (figs. 23, 24; see also Arte Precolombino . . ., 1946, pls. 45–52, 54). The El Arenal Brown figurines (so named for the color of the paste) are known so far only for the cemeteries of the Magdalena Lake basin. They have chunky bodies, thick, rounded legs, and short, stubby arms, sometimes decorated with shoulder pellets. The head is elongated and decorated with a

headband which sometimes resembles hair combed outward or downward from a center part; the face is a trifle less elongated than in the other two types, and the eyes and mouth are appliquéd. The figurines are red slipped; earrings and nose rings are indicated by appliqué, but other ornamentation (and often clothing) is rendered in white, black, or red paint (fig. 25). Some large figurines so far found only around Antonio Escobedo, a short distance east of Etzatlan, seem to be a distinctive and highly localized style. They show some characteristics of Long's named types, but cannot be fitted neatly into any of them (fig. 26; see also Parres Arias, 1962).

On the basis of his stylistic analysis, Long postulates different time periods for each of his three figurine types; pottery vessels of

725

FIG. 26—LARGE, HOLLOW FIGURINE FROM ANTONIO ESCOBEDO, NORTHERN JALISCO. Red, black and buff paint on cream. Height 20 inches. (Stendahl Collection.)

similar wares, also found in the tombs, are correlated with the figurines. In an effort to substantiate the admittedly tentative, style-based chronology, Long submitted other types of tomb material to the analysis. All bones from the San Sebastian tomb were examined under ultraviolet short-wave and long-wave light, and six bones (each a left tibia) were measured for nitrogen content. The fluorescent color-range and the nitrogen measurements were consistent in suggesting interments over a considerable peri-

od, but the results of the subsequent bone-collagen analysis were equivocal (Berger and Libby, 1966, 1967). One bone sample (UCLA-966) from a presumed late interment gave a radiocarbon date of ca. A.D. 220, but the second sample (UCLA-1032), which should have dated an early interment, gave a date of ca A.D. 335 (Long, 1965, pp. 90–92). Obsidian from the San Sebastian tomb and from one chamber of Tomb One at El Arenal was analyzed by the obsidian-hydration technique. The samples from El Arenal fell within a range which indicated a single period of use; those from San Sebastian fell into two groups which suggested separate periods of tomb use (Long, 1965, pp. 84–86). Three shell samples from the San Sebastian tomb were submitted for radiocarbon dating (Berger, Fergusson, and Libby, 1965; Furst, 1965a); they gave dates of ca. 140 B.C. (UCLA-593A), ca. 280 B.C. (UCLA-593B), and ca A.D. 240 (UCLA-593C). The first date was obtained from a Caribbean shell (*Strombus gigas* Linné), the second from an unnamed Pacific shell, and the third from another Pacific shell (*Murex nigritus* Philippi). Subsequently, research on local upwelling and on the carbonate content of contemporary Pacific coast marine shells obtained prior to the atomic bomb tests has resulted in a revision of these dates (Berger, Taylor, and Libby, 1966; Long and Taylor, 1966b), and the date sequence now is: 140 B.C., 120 B.C., and A.D. 400. The first date has not been revised, owing to lack of comparable data from the Caribbean area; it is possible that considerable time may have elapsed before the shell found its way along the trade routes to west Mexico, and that it was placed in the tomb at a somewhat later date. Nevertheless, the Pacific shell dates seem to reflect two different periods of tomb use, starting in the late Preclassic, whereas the bone-collagen dates suggest yet another period between them.

Obsidian-hydration analysis of material from a habitation site excavated at Las

Cuevas showed a chronological overlap between the early habitation period and the period of tomb use, and a radiocarbon date of ca. A.D. 1110 for charcoal from Las Cuevas (UCLA-1017; Berger and Libby, 1966) indicates occupation in the Early Postclassic. Analysis of the pottery excavated from a habitation site at Huistla, on the outskirts of Etzatlan, showed that "Huistla's ceramics bear no relation to the known ceramic types found in the tombs" (Glassow, 1967, p. 80); rather, they resemble the Aztatlan pottery of Nayarit and southern Sinaloa, with a few specific stylistic similarities to the Guasave ceramics. Thus, Glassow concludes that Huistla was occupied at a period coeval with the Cerritos phase at Amapa and with Middle Ixtlan del Rio. Long (1965, pp. 102–06) offers a culture-historical reconstruction for the Magdalena Lake basin, starting with the earliest period of tomb use and extending to the time of European contact, but the scarcity of habitation-site excavation in the area makes it highly speculative.

Kelly's surface collections from the Ameca area, a short distance to the south, contain a number of monochrome sherds of gray, buff, and cream, which she believes are related to the Ameca figurines; she regards this material as "fairly early" (Kelly, 1948, pp. 59–61). A later horizon, characterized by red-on-buff and red-on-brown wares, shows only vague resemblances to late wares in the Sayula-Zacoalco and Autlan-Tuxcacuesco areas farther south; there are also a few generalized similarities to Autlan polychrome. Thirty of the cloisonné vessels in the collection studied by Ross (1939, pp. 30–34, 77–78; see also Lumholtz, 1902, 2: 460–61, pls. 13–15) are said to have come from Estanzuela, a few kilometers west of Ameca. The cloisonné technique, which is distinct from fresco painting, is thought to be approximately coeval with the Mazapan materials from central Mexico, i.e., Early Postclassic.

The only archaeological site reported for the vicinity of Guadalajara is Ixtepete, on the southwestern outskirts of the city (Corona Núñez, 1960a; Piña Chan, 1963a; Sáenz, 1966a,b). Work there has been concentrated on excavation and reconstruction of a low pyramidal structure with stone staircases (Sáenz, 1966b, fotos 21–23); the single strata-pit yielded pottery which is probably Postclassic. The figurine fragments illustrated by Sáenz (1966a, figs. k,l) seem to resemble some described by Ross (1939, pp. 61–62) for Michoacan; they are also identical to a number of figurines recently obtained from illegal excavations at Querendaro, Michoacan, where they are reported to come from shallow burials which also contained copper. The material said to come from Tlajomulco, south of Guadalajara (Parres Arias, 1963), suggests a rather earlier period, but it cannot be placed stratigraphically.

Lake Chapala Basin

The Lake Chapala region is known largely through Lumholtz's descriptions of material purchased in the area, and through Ross's paper on the collection in which the Lumholtz purchases figure prominently. Ross describes effigy vessels, pot covers apparently similar to those from Tuxcacuesco (Kelly, 1949, p. 78), red-on-buff, red-on-brown, and red-on-brown utility wares, black-on-red pottery which also seems to resemble that from Tuxcacuesco (Kelly, 1949, p. 65), nubbin ware, and a quantity of plumbate. The pottery which Ross (1939, pp. 30, 76–77) characterizes as Atoyac Wavy Line seems to resemble the Coyotlatelco pottery of the Valley of Mexico, but unfortunately the lack of illustrations in her report precludes the possibility of close comparisons with material from other areas. She also notes the presence of several types of small, solid, handmade figurines (now known to derive from various areas), and of a hollow Nayarit-type monochrome figurine; the figurines which she regards as characteristic of the Chapala area (Ross,

1939, pp. 55–56) appear to be the well-known Ameca figurines. The impression given by the variety of material described is that the Lake Chapala area was in Lumholtz's time a marketplace for archaeological material from a wide area, as it is today; the lack of controlled excavation around Lake Chapala makes it impossible to ascertain what part of the material described is truly representative of the Lake Chapala basin. The miniature vessels described by Ross and by Starr (1897) were taken from the waters of the lake along the northern shore, and are regarded as votive offerings; similar miniature vessels were found in the excavations at Huistla (Glassow, 1967, p. 80), also a lakeshore site, which is thought to be Early Postclassic.

A suggestion of early occupation is given by a shell trumpet (*Fasciolaria princeps* Sowerby, a Caribbean shell) in the possession of the Instituto Jalisciense de Antropología e Historia, in Guadalajara (Furst, 1966, p. 168, pl. 45). It is reported to come from the Lake Chapala area, and its decoration is closely similar to that on shell trumpets from the Las Cebollas tomb and from Teotihuacan and Kaminaljuyu. Feldman (1967) notes that seven species of Caribbean shells have been obtained from the region around the eastern end of Lake Chapala; their exact provenience is unknown, but probably they have come from burials. It is possible that they originated in the tombs with inclined, stepped shafts which Noguera (1942) describes for El Opeño, and which Furst (1966, p. 53) believes are approximately coeval with Middle Chupicuaro. In 1966 Meighan and Foote excavated a site at Tizapan el Alto, on the southern shore of Lake Chapala, and a monograph on this work is now in preparation. Radiocarbon tests of four charcoal samples gave dates of A.D. 950, 2100 B.C., A.D. 1105, and A.D. 995 (UCLA-1073A,E,K, G; Berger and Libby, 1967). Berger notes that "the radiocarbon ages for UCLA-

1073A-K have been compared to the secular variations of the atmospheric C-14 level . . . resulting in somewhat more recent dates." The extremely early date would appear to be open to some question, in view of the stratigraphic placement of the samples, but none of them can be evaluated until all the material from the site is analyzed. The demonstrable existence of early occupation in areas fairly close to the Lake Chapala basin emphasizes the need for more stratigraphic excavation to establish a sequence for it.

Southern Jalisco

In 1939, 1940, and 1942 Isabel Kelly (1945b, 1949) made extensive surface surveys in the Autlan and Tuxcacuesco areas of southern Jalisco, and in addition made a number of test excavations near Tuxcacuesco. On the basis of this work she was able to construct chronologies for the areas, to crosstie them, and to establish at least tentative relationships to material from Colima. Both these areas are noted in conquest-period documents as having a dense aboriginal population, and this is borne out by archaeological evidence. There is considerable diversity in the archaeological remains throughout this part of Jalisco (Kelly, 1949, p. 44), but also sufficient similarity between quite localized areas to permit their being placed in a chronological framework.

At Autlan, Kelly defined three ceramic complexes—Cofradia, Mylpa, and Autlan—the last two of which she believes to have been largely contemporaneous. The Cofradia complex is characterized by a variety of red-on-buff and red-on-brown wares; most of them are too diverse to be classified (Kelly, 1945b, p. 27), but two are distinctive: Cofradia Red-on-brown, and Autlan Red-on-brown potstands. The major diagnostic of the Mylpa complex is Autlan polychrome, an orange-and-white-on-red ware, which is sometimes incised as well as painted (fig. 27). This continues into the Autlan

FIG. 27—AUTLAN POLYCHROME, FROM THE TOLIMAN COMPLEX AT TUXCACUES-CO, SOUTHERN JALISCO. (Reprinted from Kelly, 1949, pls. 11 and 12, by permission of the University of California Press.)

complex, which, however, is dominated by Autlan White-on-red; the distinctive utility ware of the Autlan complex is Altillos Red. Autlan Polychrome is found throughout a fairly wide area of southern and south-central Jalisco, and generically similar wares occur in both interior and coastal Colima. In contrast, Kelly found Autlan White-on-red to be confined to the Autlan and Mezquitan valleys, and thus believed that the polychrome ware has a considerable time depth, whereas the white-on-red ware represents a geographically localized specialty which began too late in the Autlan-Mylpa period to achieve wide distribution. However, the subsequent finding of very similar white-on-red wares at Ixtlan and Amapa indicates that it may have had a wider distribution than did the polychrome. The miscellaneous artifacts said to come from Autlan are often hard to place, for many of them were purchased. The figurine fragments, classified into four types, cluster largely in the Cofradia and Mylpa complexes; there are a few very slight resem-blances to figurines of the Tuxcacuesco complex at that site. (Fig. 28 shows figurines obtained at Autlan subsequent to Kelly's work there.) Spindle whorls are apparently represented in all three periods. Pottery bracelets appear with the Mylpa and Autlan complexes; one fragment each of a clay whistle and a cylinder seal are assigned to the Mylpa complex, as are three fragments of shell bracelets. Single-flake obsidian blades are associated with all three complexes; one fragment of a three-quarter-grooved axe is placed with the Mylpa complex, and a fragment of a fully grooved axe is related to the Autlan complex. No metal was obtained at Autlan.

Work in the Tuxcacuesco-Zapotitlan area, which included excavation of a number of trenches, yielded a larger and more varied artifact collection. Here, too, Kelly was able to define three ceramic complexes—Tuxcacuesco, Coralillo, and Toliman—which could be related to those of Autlan. There was little evidence for a complex earlier than the Cofradia at Autlan, but the

a   b

FIG. 28—SOLID, UNSLIPPED BUFF FIGURINES FROM THE AUTLAN AREA OF
SOUTHERN JALISCO. *a*, 10 inches. *b*, 9½ inches. (Collection of Dr. and Mrs. William
Kaiser.)

Tuxcacuesco complex at the site of that name clearly antedates Autlan's Cofradia. The Tuxcacuesco complex is characterized by two red wares, one of them incised; the only painted ware is a black-on-red, which is of very minor occurrence but confined to sites of this horizon. The Coralillo complex which follows is equated with the Cofradia at Autlan because of the predominance in both of red-on-buff and red-on-brown wares; sherds of Autlan Polished Orange and Autlan Red-on-Brown potstands, associated with the Cofradia complex, also appear in Coralillo period sites at Tuxcacuesco. The major diagnostics of the Toliman complex, the latest at Tuxcacuesco, are Autlan Polychrome and the related Toliman Red-on-brown; Altillos Red is the dominant utility ware, as it is in the latest horizon at Autlan. Kelly equates Toliman with the Autlan-Mylpa complex at Autlan, but finds some evidence (Kelly, 1949, pp. 39–41) for believing that eventually it, too, should be subdivided into two largely contemporaneous assemblages.

Figurines tend largely to be associated with the Tuxcacuesco complex, and are very sparsely represented in the two later complexes (fig. 29). As Kelly notes, they present a problem, for most excavated fragments were too small to be classified, and with one exception all of the whole figurines were purchased and can be assigned to complexes only on the basis of their alleged provenience. One of the several types of small solid figurines (the Tuxcacuesco-Ortices type) assigned to the Tuxcacuesco complex is strikingly similar to those from the Ortices complex, which is regarded as the earliest in Colima (fig. 30; see also Disselhoff, 1932; Kelly, 1949, figs. 79, 80). The hollow, polished dog effigy illustrated by Kelly (1949, pl. 28,*d*) and assigned to the Tuxcacuesco complex is apparently identical to those placed in the Ortices complex in Colima, but its provenience, too, is uncertain. The Coralillo moldmade figurines of

a *b* *c*

Fig. 29—SMALL, SOLID FIGURINES FROM THE TUXCACUESCO COMPLEX AT TUXCACUESCO, SOUTHERN JALISCO. *a*, 6½ inches. *b*, 4¼ inches. *c*, 7½ inches. (Reprinted from Kelly, 1949, Pl. 23, by permission of the University of California Press.)

the Coralillo complex appear to resemble Mazapan figurines, but they are extremely rare at Tuxcacuesco and seemingly not found at any other site in the southern Jalisco-Colima area.

As at Autlan, spindle whorls occur throughout all phases. Clay whistles occur with all three complexes; rattles, cylinder seals, and stamps are associated only with the Toliman complex. A purchased effigy flute is placed in the Tuxcacuesco complex on the basis of its similarity to specimens from the synchronous Ortices complex in Colima. Pottery earspools and pendants, lacking at Autlan, appear with the Tuxcacuesco complex; pottery bracelets are assigned to the Toliman complex. Shell and stone ornaments are represented at Tuxcacuesco although lacking at Autlan, save for the three shell fragments assigned to the Mylpa complex; shell ornaments are associated with all three complexes, and stone with Tuxcacuesco and Coralillo. There is

731

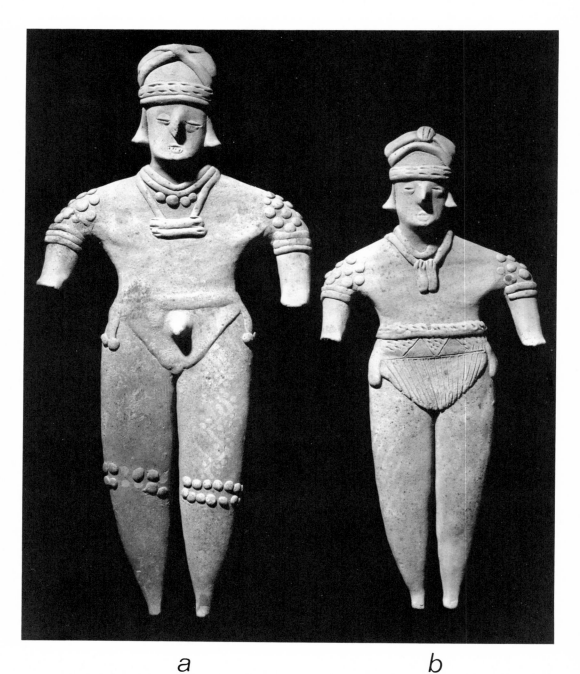

a   b

F<small>IG</small>. 30—UNSLIPPED BUFF SLAB FIGURINES FROM COLIMA. Of the Tuxcacuesco-
Ortices style also found in Southern Jalisco. *a*, 14¾ inches. *b*, 12½ inches. (Stendahl Collection.)

an abundance of single-flake obsidian blades at all levels, but scrapers of obsidian and other stone are assigned to the Coralillo and Toliman complexes. Ground-stone mace heads—globular, star-shaped, and pineapple type—occur with the Toliman complex, as do small stone palettes; celts are associated with all three complexes. Copper, which is assigned to the Toliman complex, occurs largely in the form of small spherical bells; a few bear stylized Tlaloc-like faces in relief, and two are constructed of simulated wirework. Circlets of copper wire occur, and there is one copper earspool. A purchased fragment of a mosaic plaque is assigned to the Tuxcacuesco complex because of the occurrence in an excavated Tuxcacuesco Incised Red bowl of flakes of pigment similar to that which fills the areas between the inlaid units on the plaque.

The Sayula-Zacoalco area, northeast of Autlan-Tuxcacuesco and centered around the Sayula basin (Kelly, 1945c; 1948, pp. 63–64), is thickly dotted with sites. On the basis of sherd collections there, Kelly tentatively established three ceramic complexes—Verdia, Sayula, and Amacueca—which she related to the sequence at Tuxcacuesco. The Verdia complex has very little resemblance to the Tuxcacuesco complex; the Sayula complex, characterized by red-on-buff and red-on-brown wares, seems quite closely related to the Coralillo; the Amacueca, characterized by Autlan polychrome and certain distinctive vessel forms, is related very closely to the Toliman complex of Tuxcacuesco. Fragments of a restorable Teotihuacan thin orange vessel were found at one of the Sayula basin sites (Kelly, 1945c, pp. 211–12). South of the Sayula basin proper, in the neighborhood of Ciudad Guzman, surface collections were varied and without clear relationships elsewhere, save for the sporadic occurrence of Autlan Polychrome. There are also suggestions of relationships to Colima's early Ortices complex, and of Tarascan influence at a late period (Kelly, 1948, p. 64). Some

of the vessels described by Ross are said to have come from Zacoalco, Atoyac, Sayula, and from as far south as Zapotiltic, near Ciudad Guzman; their provenience is uncertain, but they seem in general to conform to the pottery types in Kelly's sherd collections.

Northwest of Autlan-Tuxcacuesco, the region which Kelly (1948, pp. 61–62) designates as Martin Monje comprises the western slopes of the Jalisco plateau from the Nayarit-Jalisco border southeast through the upper Purificacion drainage, and into northwestern Colima. This area is said to have supported a sparse aboriginal population, and archaeological exploration to date seems to bear this out. The few sites from which collections were made yielded poorly, and the material could not be related to that from elsewhere in west Mexico.

Peripheral Areas: Northeast, Extreme North, and Coastal Margin

Northeastern Jalisco—the area known as Los Altos—is another of the many parts of west Mexico in which there has been little or no formal archaeological work. Recent work there by the author (December, 1968) was the first done in this area, and more extensive excavation is planned. Los Altos is the source of a distinctive type of large, hollow figurine—the horned figurines—which earlier were thought to originate somewhere in Zacatecas. These are found in pairs, readily identifiable by similarities in their polychrome decoration, and, unlike most of the figurines from elsewhere in west Mexico, the poses are invariably the same. The males, who have small, flat-topped horns projecting at angles from each side of the head, are seated with knees drawn up and arms resting on them; rarely, there is a cylindrical drum between the knees. The females, who do not have horns, are seated with the legs thrust straight out in front, and the hands are placed on the hips.

Looted collections from this area show

733

an assemblage virtually identical to the contents of the shaft tombs, but there appear to be no shaft tombs in northeastern Jalisco. The grave goods, which come from burials at 2–3 m. in depth, include the large, hollow figurines, conch-shell trumpets, pyrite mirrors, many bone and stone ornaments, large quantities of shell beads, and elaborate negative-painted pottery. Occasionally the negative decoration is applied to a plain, highly polished redware, but more often it appears on pottery which combines red, orange, and buff. Descriptions volunteered by pothunters assert that the burials are covered with a thick layer of fine ashes, topped with a slightly domed cap of clay which might suggest an imitation of the shape of the tomb chambers, but this has yet to be verified by excavation. Two unpublished radiocarbon dates obtained from looted shell material gave a date of approximately A.D. 100–200 for the burials.

More than a dozen strata pits were excavated at a site near Teocaltiche which is known to be the source of some of the looted material, and the sherd material obtained, which included several reconstructible vessels, can definitely be tied to the burial pottery. Preliminary study indicates that the site had but one occupation, possibly a fairly brief one, which was contemporaneous with the deep burials. The general impression given by material from the site suggests that it may be transitional between the shaft-tomb area to the west and the still unknown cultures to the north and east, and the work now being planned may help to verify this tentative suggestion. For the present, however, no attempt is made to integrate northeastern Jalisco into the discussions of chronology and relationships.

In the extreme north, Hrdlička in 1902 investigated approximately a dozen sites along the upper Rio Bolaños in extreme northernmost Jalisco. The river flows through a deep, narrow valley, and the escarpments on both sides are cut by deep barrancas which extend for some distance

back from the river valley; all sites known to date are on promontories overlooking the river. There are suggestions of cultural affiliations to Durango and Zacatecas, and at the same time much in the artifact assemblage which is related to material from more southerly parts of the state. The mesa-top sites, constructed largely of cut-stone masonry, appear to have been fortified, as they tend to be in Durango and Zacatecas, but there is also terracing and the construction of mounds over quadrangular masonry enclosures, such as Kelly (1949, p. 188) reports for Tuxcacuesco. Many sites were extensive and complex, and Hrdlička believed some of them to have been major ceremonial centers. In 1963, J. Charles Kelley (personal communication) excavated the site of Totoate first dug by Hrdlička in 1902. The portion excavated by Kelly consisted of a large circular area with one rectangular platform each on the north, east, and south sides, and two on the west side; at the center of this area is a structure which his site diagram indicates as a stepped, circular altar. Hrdlička appears to be speaking of this structure when he describes a mound which "consisted of a thick outer layer of stones (including some broken slabs with petroglyphs), beneath which was a large quantity of stones and earth, and of a central house of seven or eight rooms, a part of which was filled with stones and earth and a part with stone-covered cremation burials" (Hrdlička, 1903, pp. 393–94). He also found burials in the three platforms into which he dug. Kelley's work has not been published, but he has supplied two radiocarbon dates for Totoate: A.D. 460 and A.D. 505 (GX0609 and GX0610, Geochron Laboratories, Inc.). He regards both dates as acceptable for "the main Totoate occupation." Both are surprisingly early in the light of previous assumptions about the occupation of the area, but such assumptions were based largely on collections which included only demonstrably late materials.

The Bolaños drainage is the westernmost

boundary of the so-called Caxcana area, which includes two parallel north-south valleys to the east (Teul-Tlaltenango and Juchipila drainage, both in Zacatecas), the Jalisco-Zacatecas border area, and probably part of the northeastern area of Jalisco known as Los Altos. So little is known at present about the Caxcana that no statements can be made regarding its chronology or culture history, but fragmentary evidence suggests that Kelly (1948, pp. 59–60) is probably correct in regarding it as a distinct archaeological subarea.

The Totoate material described by Ross (much of it collected by Hrdlička) includes red-on-brown utility wares, black-on-red pottery, negative painting, and plumbate, all of which indicate ties to the southern Nayarit highlands, to the southern portions of Jalisco, and to Colima (Ross, 1939, pp. 28, 29, 78, 81; see also Lumholtz, 1902, vol. 2; Kelly, 1948, 1949; Corona Núñez, n.d.). Numerous cloisonné vessels are reported for Totoate (Ross, 1939; Hrdlička, 1903), and cloisonné is said also to occur in the Caxcana (Kelly, 1948). Ross notes that the two groups of cloisonné vessels ascribed to Totoate and to Estanzuela differ markedly in their ranges of vessel forms, and suggests two contemporaneous but quite separate centers of manufacture. Copper is reported for the Caxcana, but not for Totoate. Although such techniques as plumbate and paint cloisonné are no doubt sufficiently well defined in time and space to be useful time-makers and possible clues to culture contact, it must be emphasized that some of the resemblances noted here are based on apparent similarities between artifact assemblages which are briefly described but not illustrated, and which cannot be placed stratigraphically.

The coast of Jalisco is virtually unknown. UCLA Project A archaeologists located and sampled eight sites in the northern coastal area, extending from a short distance northeast of Puerto Vallarta to about half-way along the southern shore of the Bahia de Banderas; on the southern Jalisco coast, eight sites were located and sampled between the Bahia de Chamela and the Jalisco-Colima border, and one—Barra de Navidad—was more extensively excavated. The coastal margin between the Rio Cuixmala and the Rio Purificacion is said to be one of the most important archaeological areas on the Jalisco coast (Brand, 1957–58, part 2, p. 122), and two of the surface surveys were made in this general region. The area between the Bahia de Chamela and Cabo Corrientes (the southern promontory of the Bahia de Banderas) was traversed but not explored intensively. The entire coastal margin is rough and cut by numerous river drainages. The northern coast, along the shores of the Bahia de Banderas, resembles the southern Nayarit coast both in general environment and in showing evidence of a considerable aboriginal population. Between Cabo Corrientes and the Bahia de Chamela the country is more arid and covered with a dense, thorny brush, and although it was not investigated thoroughly, it gave little evidence of aboriginal occupation. The more tropical vegetation characteristic of the Colima and Michoacan coasts appears in the region of the Bahia de Chamela, and from there to the Colima border there was again evidence of a substantial population. With the exception of the material from the Barra de Navidad excavations, none of the collections has been analyzed.

Near Tomatlan, about half-way between Cabo Corrientes and the Bahia de Chamela, Kelly (1948, p. 62) noted the existence of "rather concrete" but unspecified resemblances to the Aztatlan complex of the Sinaloa coast, and also the strong resemblance between Tomatlan burial urns and those from Sinaloa. A red-and-black-on-brown polychrome is found in many places (Kelly, 1947a, p. 75); since copper artifacts occur in direct association with this, Kelly infers a late occupation. At Sihuatlan, at the extreme southern edge of the Jalisco coast, a few sherds appear related to late wares in the Sayula-Zacoalco, Autlan-Tuxcacuesco, and Colima areas (Kelly, 1948, p. 63). Here, too, is concentrated a polychrome ware closely related to Autlan Polychrome (Kelly, 1945b, Map 1).

Extensive excavations were carried out by Project A in a shell midden at Barra de Navidad, about 10 km. north of the Rio Marabasco, which forms the Jalisco-Colima border (Long and Wire, 1966). The site was in a mangrove swamp, near the head of a small salt-water lagoon; it consisted of a mound roughly 185 m. in diameter, and about 8 m. high. Much of the center down to a depth of 2.5 m. above ground level had been removed for road material, but two pits were dug on the rim, two in the slope, and one in the low portion in the center. A datum point was established at the top of the mound, and the stratigraphic column of 7.5 m. includes the combined levels of all pits except the one in the center. The existence of numerous downward-sloping strata within the large mound suggests that it was formed of several small mounds which were occupied at various times during the total occupation span, and the concentrations of sherd material tend to bear this out.

The predominant pottery, found in all levels, was Navidad Red, a heavy utility ware which is also found at Morett and Playa del Tesoro (Colima) but which otherwise has not been equated with any pottery known so far in west Mexico; Navidad Incised is basically the same ware, but its designs resemble those on sherds from El Revalcito (about 30 km. to the northwest) —where, however, the pottery was formed by paddle and anvil (Long and Wire, 1966, pp. 15–16). Barra de Navidad yielded what is clearly a variant of Autlan Polychrome, and another pottery type—Barra Red-on-buff, confined exclusively to molcajetes with solid or hollow conical tripod legs—is similar to Toliman Red-on-brown; both are late types in the Autlan-Tuxcacuesco area.

There may indeed be a generalized resemblance between Barra Red-on-buff and the late-period Toliman Red-on-brown, but the Barra Red-on-buff tripod molcajetes extend throughout the entire stratigraphic column (postulated starting date, A.D. 650). Kelly's assignment of tripods and molcajetes exclusively to the Postclassic in Jalisco (Kelly, 1944) was made at a time when few stratigraphic data were available, and it now appears that both traits may have a fairly long history in west Mexico. Long and Wire (1966, p. 16) suggest that their Navidad Red-on-buff could be related to the Terrero Red-on-buff of the Coralillo complex (the middle period) at Tuxcacuesco, but the sample was too small to make a definite comparison possible. Another type, Navidad Red-on-grey, could be similar to the undescribed Periquillo Red-on-grey (Kelly, 1948, p. 43) which is late in the Colima sequence postulated by Kelly. Some suggestion of an early occupation is given by Navidad Black-on-red, which may be related to the undescribed Los Ortices Black-on-red of the Ortices complex (the earliest) in Colima, and to the Tuxcacuesco Black-on-red which is found in the earliest complex at that site. Long and Wire point out, however, that black-on-red may be early, as in Tuxcacuesco and in Colima, or late, as in Guerrero (cf. Lister, 1955, p. 27). Two sherds of Tuxcacuesco Incised (early at that site) were also found at about the middle of the stratigraphic column. Spindle whorls (five) and whistle fragments (seven) were found to a depth of 400 cm. Chipped obsidian occurred throughout most of the stratigraphic column, but all the ground stone artifacts (eight manos and two celts) were salvage finds, as were the four figurine fragments. An anthropomorphic lug handle, very like those from Costa Rica, was found at 320 cm. in one pit (depth 600 cm. below the datum point), and the 0–20-cm. level of a mound-top pit yielded fragments of copper tweezers.

Two Barra de Navidad radiocarbon dates

—ca. A.D. 1190 (charcoal, UCLA-145; Fergusson and Libby, 1963) and ca. A.D. 1580 (bone collagen, UCLA-907; Berger and Libby, 1967)—were inconsistent with the stratigraphic placement of the samples, but the range of obsidian-hydration measurements did seem to conform to the stratigraphic data. Obsidian samples from 0–200 cm. yielded values equivalent to a date-range of A.D. 1200–1550, and samples from 280–440 cm. gave dates of A.D. 650–1100. Late Barra de Navidad falls within the former range, and Early and Middle Barra de Navidad (regarded, in a sense, as a single phase) within the latter. The postcontact end date is strengthened by the presence in the top levels of glazed sherds which Long and Wire believe to be Spanish colonial. The preliminary nature of the available Morett analysis (see following section) and the peculiarities of the Barra de Navidad site make it difficult to crosstie the two. Long and Wire regard Middle Morett, as defined by Susia (1961), as a transitional phase rather than a distinct and definable complex, and their tentative crosstie is at about A.D. 710—a little above midway in the Morett sequence and early in the first date-range for Barra de Navidad (see also Long and Taylor, 1966b). Navidad Red, the dominant Barra de Navidad pottery, also occurs in Early Morett, but Long and Wire regard it as nondiagnostic and therefore insufficient evidence for an overlap between Barra de Navidad and Early Morett.

It is not known definitely whether Barra de Navidad was occupied permanently or seasonally. "The site may have been a seasonal gathering ground used by inland people, or a village depending on shellfish for subsistence and trading salt, fish, and shellfish to the interior in exchange for other products" (Long and Wire, 1966, p. 47). There were numerous thick, tightly packed strata of shells, often interspersed with strata of sand; this, together with the evidence that the mound was composed of several smaller mounds occupied at various time periods, suggests seasonal occupation. The remains of nine burials were found, but none was accompanied by grave goods of any kind. Obviously, shellfish formed the main subsistence basis; fish bones were rare, as were the bones of birds or mammals. The presence of manos, molcajetes, spindle whorls, and net impressions on pottery indicates some reliance on plant resources for food and other purposes, but the relative importance of shellfish and plant foods cannot be determined. Although there was no archaeological evidence for salt collecting, shortly after Spanish contact (1548) the Barra de Navidad area was a salt-collecting center, and salt collecting is still an important summer activity. Long and Wire (1966, pp. 41–42) remark of Barra de Navidad that its "lagoon situation would be consistent with this activity, since salt water left by receding tides would yield salt on lagoon flats by the processes of evaporation and precipitation." The question of permanent versus seasonal occupation will have to await an answer until other sites of this type have been excavated. The nearest excavated coastal shell midden is at Puerto Marquez, Guerrero, where the earliest occupation is thought to be Preclassic (Nicholson, 1961b, p. 595); they are reported at various points along the Colima, Jalisco, Nayarit, and Sinaloa coasts, but have received little archaeological attention.

COLIMA

The uniformly fine archaeological ceramics of Colima are well known and widely represented in museums and private collections in both Mexico and the United States, but there has been little controlled excavation in the area. Kelly's unpublished work (referred to in Kelly, 1944, 1948) consisted of the investigation of several tombs in the Los Ortices district and one at Chanchopa, near Tecoman, and surface collections in several parts of the state. Disselhoff's work (Disselhoff, 1932) was confined largely to locating and exploring tombs. The artifacts

FIG. 31—LARGE, HOLLOW REDWARE FIGURINES FROM COLIMA. Some decorated
with black paint. *a*, 12½ inches. *b*, 16½ inches. *c*, Height 12½ inches, length 14¾ inches.
d, 13 inches. (*a*, collection of Mrs. Ellsworth LaBoyteaux; *b*, Stendahl Collection; *c*, collection
of Dr. George C. Kennedy; *d*, collection of Dr. and Mrs. William Kaiser.)

FIG. 32—LARGE, HOLLOW REDWARE FIGURINES FROM COLIMA. *a*, 10½ inches. *b*, 11¼ inches. *c*, 13 inches. *d*, 11½ inches. (All from Stavenhagen Collection.)

described and illustrated by Galindo (1922) were acquired incidentally in the course of plotting an "archaeological geography" for Colima, and the large number of Colima vessels and figurines reported on by Ross (1939) are part of the collection purchased by Lumholtz. There are now stratigraphic sequences for two sites, but statements about chronology still have a rather tenuous basis.

Southeast of the town of Colima, in the hilly country along river drainages, Disselhoff explored four types of tombs: vertical-walled, bottle-shaped, a domed chamber opening off the bottom of a vertical shaft, and two or more domed chambers at the bottom of a shaft (Disselhoff, 1932, fig. 1). From these he obtained a variety of ceramic objects: hollow dog effigies, flutes, bird figurines, human figurines bound to flat surfaces, flat figurines similar to those from Tuxcacuesco (see fig. 30) and a great variety of action figurines (Disselhoff, 1932, figs. 2, 8, 15).

Prior to 1940, Kelly made surface collections in various parts of Colima, and in 1940 investigated the tombs referred to above.

On the basis of her work, she established four ceramic complexes: Ortices, Colima, Armeria, and Periquillo. The middle two, she believes, are largely contemporaneous, with Armeria perhaps a little later. This sequence, however, is not derived from a single site; the Ortices complex is defined largely on the basis of tomb material from a limited area, and the Colima, Armeria, and Periquillo complexes are based on surface materials from several different areas.

The Ortices complex is characterized by finely executed, large, hollow figurines of almost infinite variety. Human representations include such diverse types as warriors, hunchbacks, and dwarfs, static or animated (figs. 31, 32). There are effigies of birds, turtles, snakes, fish, crabs, snails, and the famous Colima dogs portrayed in countless variations (fig. 33). There are bowls in the shape of fruits, vegetables, drums, human heads, and helmets; large vertically ribbed jars, much like flattened pumpkins, are supported by three parrots or small atlantean figures (fig. 34). This effigy pottery is highly polished and generally red slipped. Associated with the large human

739

FIG. 33—REDWARE ANIMAL FIGURINES FROM COLIMA. *a*, Iguana, length 15 inches. *b*, Armadillo, length 12 inches. *c*, Dog, length 13½ inches. *d*, Ducks, width 8¾ inches. (*a,d*, Stendahl Collection; *b,c*, Primus Collection.)

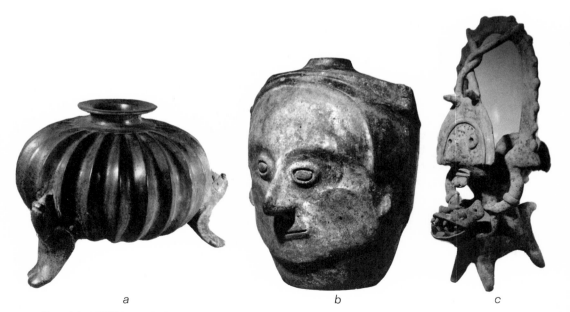

FIG. 34—VESSELS FROM COLIMA. *a*, Redware parrot-tripod bowl, diameter 12½ inches. *b*, Effigy vessel, redware with buff and black decoration; height 9½ inches. *c*, Basket-type figurine atop an animal, unslipped buff with red and black decoration; height 19¼ inches. (*a*, collection of Mr. and Mrs. Donald M. Jones; *b*, Stendahl Collection; *c*, collection of Dr. and Mrs. Melvin Silverman.)

a   b   c

FIG. 35—SMALL, SOLID FIGURINES FROM COLIMA. All unslipped buff. *a*, 9½ inches (has traces of white paint). *b*, 6 inches. *c*, 6½ inches. (*a*, collection of Morton D. May; *b*,*c*, Museum of West Mexican Archaeology, Instituto Jalisciense de Antropología e Historia, Guadalajara.)

figurines are a number of small, solid, unslipped figurines, often depicting various activities (fig. 35). The dominant noneffigy pottery in the tombs is Los Ortices Black-on-red and a polished red ware; there is some negative painting. Los Ortices Polychrome (red-and-black-on-brown) and red-on-cream ware, not found in the tombs, may be coeval with them (Kelly, 1948, pp. 65–66).

The Colima complex is apparently the most widespread, and is found throughout the area surveyed. It is characterized by red-on-orange pottery; also present in this complex are a red ware, a wiped red, and an incised red probably related to those of Tuxcacuesco and Sayula. Armeria is essentially a coastal complex, and often occurs in surface association with the Colima complex. Kelly believes that the two overlap considerably in time but that Armeria is a little later, as it includes annular bases and

the Colima complex lacks them. The principal wares are red, cream, and red-on-cream. The Periquillo complex is localized in a small area around Periquillo on the lower Rio Armeria. The characteristic pottery is obviously a variant of Autlan Polychrome, and Kelly believes the two are "genetically related." She notes that apparently there are many localized wares in various parts of Colima, but so far she has been unable to place these other materials.

By means of trade sherds found at Tuxcacuesco, Kelly (1949, pp. 74–75) gives tentative chronological placement to the Colima complexes. The presence of Los Ortices Polychrome, Los Ortices Black-on-red, and Colima Shadow-striped serves to equate the Ortices and Tuxcacuesco complexes, as does the presence in both of strikingly similar figurines; Colima Red-on-orange and the Armeria cream wares crosstie the Colima-Armeria complexes to Tuxcacuesco's

741

Coralillo complex; and the strong resemblance of Periquillo Red-on-grey to Autlan Polychrome is the basis for equating the Periquillo and Toliman complexes. A pottery strikingly similar to Colima Shadow-striped is abundant in Guanajuato, Queretaro, and Hidalgo (Tula), where it is known as Blanco Levantado or Tula Water-colored. Originally it was assigned to the central Mexico Postclassic, but recent work indicates that it has a long history in the area and that it had its beginnings in the Late Preclassic (Kelly and Braniff de Torres, 1966). A Teotihuacan thin orange vessel from the Chanchopa tomb, which is thought to be associated with the Ortices complex, provides the basis for Kelly's tentative equation of the earliest sequences in Colima and at Tuxcacuesco with Teotihuacan III. The plumbate vessels attributed to Colima which are described by Ross (1939) cannot be used to help date the sequences there because they lack provenience.

As noted earlier, at the time of Kelly's work it was generally assumed that thin orange did not appear before Teotihuacan III, whereas it is now known to be present in Teotihuacan II. A radiocarbon test has been made of bracelet fragments of *Glycimeris* shell (a Pacific species) found in the dirt removed by looters from a tomb near that which yielded the thin orange vessel. The date of ca. A.D. 10 (UCLA-1066; Berger and Libby, 1967) is consistent only with their placement in Late Teotihuacan I or early Teotihuacan II in most present interpretations of the date sequences for that site. In view of the uncertainties surrounding correlation of the Colima and Teotihuacan sequences, at present it can only be stated that there now appears to be evidence that the tombs in this area (near Tecoman) were in use during the Late Preclassic–Early Classic period.

After a lapse of 25 years, Kelly (personal communication) has resumed archaeological work in Colima, in the hope of checking and expanding the tentative and simplified

sequences which she published earlier (Kelly, 1944, 1948). A series of small test pits was dug: four in the general area of Comala, one at Chanal, two near Periquillo, and seven at various sites in the Amoles-Ortices area. As before, no stratigraphy resulted, but it is hoped that the chronology may eventually be established through radiocarbon dating. The recent tests, however, permit a much clearer definition of ceramic complexes than was possible heretofore, and those identified earlier have been subdivided. The monograph on her recent work which Kelly is now preparing should be of great help in defining and dating the Colima sequences.

In 1960 archaeologists of UCLA's Project A excavated the Morett site, on the eastern side of the Rio Marabasco, about 10 km. from the coast and approximately 15 km. east of Barra de Navidad. The site was a fairly extensive midden deposit (roughly 100 by 400 m.), which was more than 3 m. deep at some points (Nicholson, 1966). Two test pits were excavated (one to a depth of 320 cm., the other to 160 cm.), and the material from them was subsequently analyzed by Susia (1961). Her report, admittedly intended as a preliminary study, does not describe the named pottery types which form the basis for the analysis, but nevertheless the general outline of the postulated Morett sequence can be ascertained.

Only about 10 per cent of the Early Morett (below 200 cm.) sherds were decorated, but they consist largely of two types which appear to be local variations of Tuxcacuesco Incised and Colima Shadow-striped (see Kelly, 1949, pp. 74–75, 80–83). The plainware and monochrome pottery was dominated by Morett Orange, which may be a local variant of Tuxcacuesco Red-ware (Kelly, 1949, pp. 95–97); Banderas Plain and the Navidad Red of Barra de Navidad formed smaller portions of the collection from this phase. The figurines closely resemble Kelly's Tuxcacuesco-Ortices type (Kelly, 1949, pp. 115–19). The

742

same plainwares and monochromes continue through Middle Morett (140–200 cm.) and Tuxcacuesco Incised continues to be the dominant decorated pottery, but six new decorated types appear. Two of these —Morett Polychrome and Morett Red-on-orange, both confined exclusively to Middle Morett—form the basis for the Long and Wire crosstie to Barra de Navidad. The Tuxcacuesco-Ortices figurine type continues through Middle Morett. The once-dominant Morett Orange fades out of the plainware-and-monochrome pottery of Late Morett (above 140 cm.), to be replaced by four new types: a white, a buff, an orange, and a "miscellaneous orange-slipped." Morett Red-on-buff and Tesoro Polychrome comprise the bulk of the decorated pottery, and three new types appear: a black-on-white, a red-on-white, and a red-on-brown. Two distinctive figurine types, one moldmade, are virtually limited to this phase (see Susia, 1961, pp. 3–10). Tripod legs first appear in Early Morett, and molcajetes in Middle Morett. Earlier, Kelly (1944, p. 208, fig. 3) believed that tripods occurred in the Ortices complex, were absent from the Armeria-Colima complexes, and reappeared in the terminal Periquillo complex, but more stratigraphic work may fill the apparent gap; she assigned molcajetes to the Early Post-classic in Colima, roughly equivalent to the end of Late Morett (Kelly, 1944, fig. 2).

Susia (1961, pp. 18–21) concludes that Early Morett can be at least tentatively equated with the Tuxcacuesco (Jalisco) and Ortices (Colima) complexes established by Kelly. She does not specifically crosstie Middle Morett to any of Kelly's sites, but the continued prevalence of Tuxcacuesco Incised would indicate that it, too, could be placed within the Tuxcacuesco time period; this, together with the continuation of the same plainwares and monochromes, lends weight to the Long and Wire suggestion that Middle Morett is a transitional phase. Late Morett is equated tentatively with Kelly's Coralillo-Cofradia

complexes on the basis of the appearance of a variety of red-on-buff and red-rimmed wares, and the absence of the widespread Autlan Polychrome characteristic of the latest phases at Autlan-Tuxcacuesco. The precise relationship of Morett to Barra de Navidad cannot be determined at present; the sites are, as noted earlier, tentatively crosstied about midway in the Morett sequence. None of the pottery characteristic of Late Morett is found at Barra de Navidad, but the upper levels of the latter site contain material which clearly postdates the latest occupation at Morett. This would seem to indicate an occupation break of some length at Barra de Navidad, but Long and Wire believe that their obsidian-sample dates indicate only short, seasonal breaks in occupation, and not abandonment for any considerable time.

Subsequently, in the 1961–62 field season, more work was done at Morett. The shallower of the first two pits was deepened, and five more were excavated; the deepest of them reached 360 cm. Seven burials were found, and one—a multiple burial of at least nine individuals—contained numerous pottery vessels and figurines; its stratigraphic position (320 cm.) places it in Early Morett. The material from this season has not been published, but a monograph now in preparation may alter the tentative Morett sequence. A series of 16 radiocarbon tests gave approximate dates of: B.C. 750, 745, 525, 150 (two samples), 100, 50 (two samples); B.C.–A.D. 0; A.D. 250, 255, 345, 450, 560, 710, 1300 (see Fergusson and Libby, 1963, and Berger and Libby, 1967, for UCLA numbers, stratigraphic location, and information about material tested). Some of these dates have subsequently been revised and the following tentative sequence established: B.C. 150; A.D. 25 (two samples), 450, 650, and 710 (Berger, Taylor, and Libby, 1966; Long and Taylor, 1966b). The very earliest dates have not been revised, and a full evaluation of the series must await publication of the mongraph now under way, but there seems to be good evidence for occupation of Morett during at least the Late Preclassic. The date of A.D. 1300 cannot at present be accepted for the latest occupation of the site, since other material from the same pit and level yielded a much earlier date, but the stratigraphic context of the A.D. 710 date is fairly consistent with Susia's hypothesis regarding the placement of Late Morett in relation to other Jalisco-Colima sequences.

The Playa del Tesoro site is on a peninsula about midway along the inner shore of the Bahia de Manzanillo, and approximately 25 km. southeast of Morett; it had been badly damaged by construction activities and by the 1959 hurricane (Crabtree and Fitzwater, n.d.). Three pits were excavated to depths of 120, 180, and 240 cm. The 120-cm. pit was abandoned when "a stone feature" was encountered; it proved not to be part of a burial, but was otherwise not investigated. The material from the other two pits was analyzed by Crabtree and Fitzwater; sherds were classified first into four wares (brown, orange, red, buff) and then into a number of types and "eleven miscellaneous categories"; figurine fragments were grouped into four major categories with 17 major and minor groupings within them. In order to avoid a proliferation of terms, only types previously mentioned for other sites will be named here.

A very large proportion of the Playa del Tesoro pottery was Banderas Plain (Morett). Navidad Red (Barra de Navidad) accounted for the largest percentage of the "painted or otherwise decorated pottery"; various local types comprised smaller percentages, and Morett Orange also occurred between 40 and 160 cm. in one pit. Morett Red-on-buff, the dominant decorated pottery of Late Morett, was found throughout the Playa del Tesoro sequence. There were annular-base molcajetes, with four types of grinding surfaces: wide parallel grooves covering the entire floor; short, random gouged grooves; punched dots; and simple geometric patterns. (A similar variety of

surfaces is described for Morett.) Further, Crabtree and Fitzwater (n.d., p. 18) remark that some molcajete fragments "raise the possibility that some were pottery slabs with a grinding surface." A pot stand suggests some contemporaneity with Cofradia-Coralillo complexes (Kelly, 1944, p. 208, fig. 5). The presence of polychrome pottery at both Morett and Playa del Tesoro contradicts Kelly's assignment of polychrome exclusively to the terminal complexes in her Jalisco-Colima sequences, but again, the sequences were established at a time when only one stratigraphic excavation had been made in the area. One of the figurine types, Group Ib, is thought to resemble figurine fragments placed by Susia in Late Morett; another type, Group III, is tentatively equated with the Coralillo phase at Tuxcacuesco, by means of a rather tenuous crosstie via a surface collection from the nearby Las Colonias site (Crabtree and Fitzwater, n.d., p. 28). Group IV figurines "have many traits in common" with Kelly's Tuxcacuesco-Ortices type, which antedates the Coralillo material; Crabtree and Fitzwater point out, however, that Kelly believes this type continues into the Coralillo complex in reduced frequency. Some moldmade fragments (Group V) are similar to moldmade figurines assigned to Late Morett, but neither the Playa del Tesoro nor Morett specimens resemble Mazapan figurines.

Largely on the basis of the existence throughout the sequence of Morett Red-on-buff, the dominant late-period decorated pottery at that site, the entire Playa del Tesoro occupation is thought by Crabtree and Fitzwater to be approximately coeval with Late Morett. Banderas Plain and Navidad Red are not useful time-markers, inasmuch as they occur throughout the entire sequences at Morett and Barra de Navidad, respectively; however, Morett Orange, which dominates the Middle Morett monochromes and virtually disappears from Late Morett, also occurs at Playa del Tesoro. Charcoal from the 140–160-cm. level yielded a radio carbon date of ca. A.D. 520 (UCLA-148; Fergusson and Libby, 1963), which has not been revised as have the Morett dates of comparable age. As it stands, it indicates a very considerable overlap between Playa del Tesoro and the middle range of the Morett sequence, and even some revision upward would still show an overlap.

Very little other than ceramic material has so far been described for Colima. Kelly (1949, p. 132) reports that a private collection in Colima includes shell lunate ornaments of local origin. With regard to copper, the one reference (Kelly, 1944, p. 209) does not make it entirely clear whether the metal has yet been found there. Galindo's survey (1922) includes some generalized descriptions of the architecture of hilltop sites, and Rosado Ojeda (1948) published a brief note on a terraced pyramid at Chanal which bore a representation of what seems clearly to be Tlaloc (Rosado Ojeda, 1948, pl. X, 4); but Rosado Ojeda prefers to interpret it as Curiacaveri, a major Tarascan deity, and thus to date the structure to the "Tarascan" period. (The discussants of his paper disagreed with him.) In her discussion of his paper, Kelly remarked that El Chanal could not be fitted into the Colima ceramic series then known, and suggested that it might belong to a distinct culture centered around the area of the Volcan de Colima. Although this large and complex site is virtually on the outskirts of the capital city, it has not been carefully investigated and no definite statements can be made about it. (Fig. 36 shows a censer of a type now being found at El Chanal, which bears a Tlaloc-like face.)

Much earlier, Kelly (1948, p. 66) noted a possible relationship between Colima and southern Nayarit. In both areas there are prepared tombs and group burials; with the burials are large, hollow figurines, associated with a variety of small, solid figurines. Both areas, too, yield the curious small figurines bound to flat surfaces. Hollow dog

FIG. 36—INCENSARIO WITH TLALOC-LIKE FACE, FROM AREA OF EL CHANAL, COLIMA. Unslipped buff, height 24¾ inches. (Stendahl Collection.)

effigies are found in both Colima and southern Nayarit, although stylistically they differ considerably between the two areas. Perhaps one of the most striking resemblances resides in the concept underlying a large percentage of the figurines in each area: that of portraying action, either by single figures or by groups. The figurines from many other parts of Mesoamerica yield similarly detailed information about dress and ornament, but those from Colima and southern Nayarit are unique in their portrayal of a range of activities from the

745

simplest domestic tasks to games, dances, and rituals. Kelly further suggested that the contemporaneity of the Ortices and Nayarit tomb figures might be demonstrated by seeking a continuous distribution of the relevant traits. At the time of her writing, the only links in the chain were the similarities between Nayarit and Ameca figurines, in the north, between Tuxcacuesco and Ortices figurines, in the south, and between the looted tomb of El Arenal and those investigated in Colima, but subsequent work has borne out the usefulness of her suggestion. Shaft tombs are now known from north of Ixtlan del Rio, Nayarit, to south of Guadalajara, Jalisco. There are persistent reports of shaft tombs as far north as Sinaloa, but they cannot be verified. Material apparently related to the shaft tombs (for example, Chinesca figurines) does occur in central Nayarit, however. In Colima, shaft tombs are now known to extend as far north as Comala, near the Colima-Jalisco border. Similarities between Ortices material and material from Tuxcacuesco and the Ciudad Guzman area suggest that shaft tombs may ultimately be found in southern Jalisco as well. Continuing study and dating of the tombs and their contents is demonstrating the existence of a widespread shaft-tomb complex in west Mexico, and its probable contemporaneity in Nayarit, Jalisco, and Colima. The principal remaining gap in its distribution is still the western edge of the Jalisco plateau.

SUMMARY

The preceding sections have summarized the available data on the archaeological sites of Nayarit, Jalisco, and Colima, and the bases on which they are correlated to others. It remains to place them within a chronological framework (Chart 1; see also Long and Taylor, 1966b) and to relate it to the chronology established for other parts of Mesoamerica, and to summarize their relationships both to each other and to distant areas. The obvious gaps in the chrono-

logical chart reflect the very spotty distribution of data, and emphasize again the lack of excavation of the kinds of sites which would yield the stratigraphic sequences needed to fill them. The comparability of the data leaves much to be desired—they are both old and new, stratigraphic and stylistic, based on new dating techniques and on educated guesses—but the chronological framework attempts to fit them together as consistently as possible at present. A chart of this sort drawn even a few years hence may well arrange them differently, for the culture-historical outline of this part of Mexico is only now beginning to take shape.

Chronology

Two sites can with some assurance be placed in the Late Preclassic: Morett, Colima, a habitation site, and the shaft tomb at San Sebastian in northern Jalisco. The earliest Morett dates have not been revised, nor has the earliest San Sebastian date, but nevertheless the Preclassic evidence now available seems unequivocal. Similarities between Early Morett pottery and Tuxcacuesco-Ortices material raise some questions about the latter two complexes, usually assigned to the Early Classic, and make it difficult to assign them neatly to one or another time period. Although there is still only one firm Preclassic date for the shaft-tomb complex, to which many of the other materials are linked, the stylistic sophistication and technical mastery exhibited by the tomb contents suggest a fairly long period of development, as yet undiscovered, extending well back into the Preclassic. Not until an unlooted shaft tomb is discovered can there be a more definite answer to the questions of tomb dating and possible reuse over a period of several centuries, and further excavation of habitation sites is needed to demonstrate the cultural sequences which preceded the shaft-tomb complex.

Dates now available for Ortices (southern Colima), the Magdalena Lake basin (northern Jalisco), and Las Cebollas (southern Nayarit) place the shaft-tomb complex firmly within the Early Classic; although there are no radiocarbon dates for Ixtlan del Rio, the many close similarities in tomb structure and tomb contents justify placing Early Ixtlan in the Early Classic as well. Material excavated from the lowest levels of Amapa and Peñitas in the Nayarit lowlands shows some links to the shaft-tomb material, although no tombs have been discovered in this area. The occupation of at least one part of Amapa is thought to have started at about A.D. 250 or perhaps a little earlier (Gavilan phase); the starting date of ca. A.D. 180 for Peñitas seems the more acceptable of the two offered in view of the demonstrated occupation break at the end of the first phase (Tamarindo) and the relationship of the next phase (Chala) to Early Chametla, still in the Early Classic. The radiocarbon dates for Totoate show an Early Classic occupation in the mountains of extreme northern Jalisco; some of the excavated material from the habitation site of Las Cuevas (Magdalena Lake basin) can be crosstied chronologically to the nearby shaft tombs; and the similarities between Tuxcacuesco and Ortices material indicate occupation of southern Jalisco during the period of tomb use. Whether Middle Morett is a transitional phase or a distinct complex, it can tentatively be placed near the end of the Early Classic, as, apparently, can the early part of the Barra de Navidad occupation. The single radiocarbon date for Playa del Tesoro suggests an origin in the Early Classic, but it still cannot be evaluated properly.

The latter part of the Early Amapa occupation (Amapa phase) falls largely within the Late Classic, and seemingly the Chala phase occupation of Peñitas continues through this period, inasmuch as there is no indication of another occupation break there. At Amapa, however, the Tuxpan phase (ca. A.D. 700–900) represents an oc-

cupation break which bridges the Late Classic–Early Postclassic time period. The early half of the Barra de Navidad occupation extends through the Late Classic, as do the crosstied Late Morett and Playa del Tesoro, and the Tuxcacuesco complex. Presumably, the shaft-tomb areas of Nayarit, Jalisco, and Colima continued to be occupied during the Late Classic, but there is still no firm evidence. Gifford's sherd collections suggested to him that Early Ixtlan might extend through Middle Chametla (Late Classic), but he was far from certain about this. There are no habitation-site excavations which might demonstrate continuing occupation of the Ortices area, and the few habitation-site data for the Magdalena Lake basin have thus far yielded no information about a Late Classic occupation of that area.

There is stratigraphic evidence of the reoccupation of Amapa (Cerritos phase) in the Early Postclassic, for the continuing occupation of Peñitas (Mitlan phase), and for occupation of Huistla and Las Cuevas in the Magdalena Lake basin; it is not known, however, whether Las Cuevas had been occupied continuously since the Early Classic. Much of the collected material attributed to Totoate is generally regarded as distinctively Postclassic, but again, continuity of occupation has yet to be demonstrated. Similarities between Ixtlan ceramics of the Aztatlan complex and those from Late Chametla II are the basis for Gifford's placement of Middle Ixtlan in the Early Postclassic, and ceramic crossties also form the principal basis for Kelly's correlation of her Armeria-Colima, Cofradia, and Coralillo complexes. Crossties to Kelly's Jalisco-Colima sequences indicate that Late Morett extends into the Early Postclassic, as does Playa del Tesoro. The Early Postclassic also marks the end of the first obsidian-dated occupation period at Barra de Navidad, and the start of the second.

Both Amapa (Ixcuintla and Santiago phases) and Peñitas (Mitlan phase) con-

747

tinued to be occupied in the Late Post-classic; Peñitas was abandoned in the early part of the period, but Amapa was occupied until very close to the time of European contact. Kelly's excavated Toliman-complex material is Late Postclassic in date, and the surface-collected Autlan-Mylpa complexes are crosstied to this; and similarities between the white-on-red pottery from Late Ixtlan and Autlan, and between many of the terminal-period ceramics from Ixtlan and Amapa, assign Late Ixtlan del Rio to the Late Postclassic. It is not known definitely whether Ixtlan and the Jalisco sites were occupied at the contact period, but the latter may well have been. The highly localized Periquillo complex of Colima is placed in the Late Postclassic, again on the basis of ceramic crossties, and the second Barra de Navidad occupation extends on to the arrival of the Spaniards.

Relationships

There is still no substantial body of data for a Preclassic occupation of this part of west Mexico, but clues increasingly point to its existence. Geographers Brand (1957–58) and Moriarty (1964, 1965) discuss the morphology and natural resources of the coast of Nayarit, Jalisco, and Colima, and suggest its probable suitability as a setting for an early occupation based on utilization of fish, shellfish, and/or plant resources. Both also point out the large number of still-unexplored archaeological sites on the coastal margin, many of them middens, and emphasize the need for further investigation there. The shaft-tomb area, which extends almost unbroken from southern Colima to the southern Nayarit highlands, can now be placed firmly in the Early Classic, with a strong hint of Preclassic origin, but interest has centered largely on the tomb material to the neglect of possibly contemporaneous habitation sites. It is not illogical to assume, however, that the technological and conceptual complexity manifested by the shaft tombs presupposes the existence,

at the start of the Classic period, of well-developed cultures with some time depth.

The shaft tombs provide a strong suggestion of contact with distant areas on the Late Preclassic–Early Classic time level. In Mexico, shaft-and-chamber tombs are known only in the areas noted here (with the exception of the El Opeño tombs with inclined, stepped entries), but they are widespread in northern South America and extend south into Peru and north into southern Central America. Long (1967) and Furst (1966, 1967) summarize the data on shaft-tomb types and their distribution, and argue convincingly that the existence of such tombs in this single area of western Mexico is evidence of early, water-borne contact with northern coastal South America. Long, in particular, analyzes construction types and types of interments (insofar as these are known); he concludes that the west Mexican tombs show some variation but tend to be more similar as a group, whereas the South American tombs show a wide range of variation. There are, unfortunately, no dates available for the South American shaft tombs, but the numerical order of shaft-tomb occurrence is: Colombia, Ecuador, Mexico, Panama, and Peru (Long, 1967). This, together with the greater typological variation in the Colombian and Ecuadorian tombs, suggests northern South America as the center from which the shaft-tomb complex spread to the north and south. The exact duration of the shaft-tomb complex is still unknown; the radiocarbon dates for the tombs of northern Jalisco seem to favor Long's hypothesis that they were used over a period of several centuries after their initial construction, but comparable date-ranges are not yet available for any other area of the complex.

Within a more limited area, there is, as Furst (1966) points out, evidence of possible ideological links among the shaft-tomb complex of west Mexico, Teotihuacan II–III, and the Early Classic Maya of Guatemala, and the prevalence of Caribbean shells in the west Mexican tombs suggests that this area participated in a rather wide network of trade by at least the Early Classic.

Furst (1965c, 1966) expands the area of possible contact by making an interpretation of shaft-tomb figurines from Colima and a few from Jalisco and Nayarit in terms of shamanistic beliefs, ritual, and paraphernalia. He brings together a mass of ethnographic detail from both the New World and the Old World, and it can be said (without plunging into the overheated waters of the diffusionist argument) that he makes a persuasive case within certain limits. Given their undeniable context as mortuary offerings, it is as valid to interpret the figurines in terms of religious beliefs as to interpret them as "warriors" or "ballplayers." His case is most persuasive when he deals with Mesoamerican and northern South American ethnographic data, at least if one is willing to assume that the shamanistic beliefs, ritual, and paraphernalia have persisted virtually unchanged for two millennia, but it is clear that not all the shaft-tomb figurines can be interpreted in this way; those from Colima lend themselves readily, but the majority of those from Jalisco and Nayarit are not so amenable. The shaft-tomb users of Colima may have immortalized their religious beliefs in their grave goods,but those of Jalisco and Nayarit seem largely to have surrounded their dead with depictions of everyday activities.

Little can be said about the occupations presumably coeval with the shaft-tomb complex. Those of southern Jalisco (Tuxcacuesco) and Colima (Early and perhaps Middle Morett) appear to be related to each other and to the shaft-tomb manifestation at Ortices. On the basis of what she characterizes as "generic similarities," Kelly (1947b, pp. 186–88) relates the material from Colima and southern Jalisco to her Apatzingan (Michoacan) material; relationships are weakest on the early level, but there are some resemblances between the Tuxcacuesco and Ortices complexes and the Apatzingan-Delicias phases. The Magdalena Lake basin habitation site (Las Cuevas), which is linked to the shaft tombs by obsidian-hydration dating, showed no artifactual crossties to the tomb material, leading Long to conclude that the tomb contents represented artifacts made specifically and exclusively for use as offerings. The Early Classic occupations of Amapa and Peñitas, Nayarit, show weak links to the shaft-tomb complex farther south, but the bulk of their material is more closely related to that from southern Sinaloa. The shaft-tomb complex, as such, seems not to have existed in a uniform cultural matrix, but undeniably it gave some measure of unity to a wide area.

The shaft-tomb complex appears to have vanished by the Late Classic, and the data for this period, too, are few and scattered. The cultures of coastal and southern Jalisco (Barra de Navidad, Tuxcacuesco) and coastal Colima (Morett, Playa del Tesoro) can be related to each other, but so far show little relationship to other areas. In Nayarit, Amapa and Peñitas continue to show links to southern Sinaloa, but more distinctive local styles begin to develop. The Late Classic occupation of Ixtlan del Rio is a matter of question. Gifford felt that Early Ixtlan might extend through the Late Classic, but the disappearance of the shaft-tomb complex, characteristic of Early Ixtlan, from other parts of west Mexico by this time makes it doubtful. The site at Jala (the only Ixtlan-area site with a clear indication of stratigraphy), which showed a layer of volcanic debris separating Early and Middle Ixtlan deposits, suggests a possible occupation break during at least part of the Late Classic.

The Early Postclassic marks the appearance of both varieties of the Aztatlan complex, and of the widespread red-on-brown (or red-on-buff) pottery horizon, and these three threads again unite various parts of west Mexico in various ways. The red-on-brown/or -buff pottery is thought to be contemporaneous to the Coyotlatelco and Mazapan periods (the Toltec horizon) in the Valley of Mexico (cf. Kelly, 1941; Lister, 1955, pp. 25–27). The ware is found throughout Nayarit, Jalisco, and Colima on this time level, and in fact it is often a major consideration in aligning phases between one site and another and in establishing chronologies. Moreover, to the north it is found in Sinaloa, Zacatecas, and Durango, and it may be related to the red-on-brown pottery of the Hohokam region of southern Arizona; to the south it appears in Michoacan, Guerrero, and Oaxaca; and of course it is heavily represented in the Toltec horizon ceramics of central Mexico. Its place of origin, however, is still unknown; it has been suggested that the ware originated in the area between the Rio Lerma and the Rio Balsas or in the Lake Chapala basin (Lister, 1955, p. 26), and, alternatively, that it spread outward from the Valley of Mexico (Kelly, 1941). But whatever the origin of this pottery horizon, its existence can be documented throughout the area discussed here.

The Aztatlan complex per se is now known to extend down through southern Nayarit and into northern Jalisco, but southern Jalisco and Colima appear not to have shared in it. The Cofradia, Coralillo, and Armeria-Colima complexes, and perhaps the materials from the Sayula basin, are quite clearly related to each other and to the Tepetate phase at Apatzingan, but they show no Aztatlan influence. The only possible exception is the area around Tomatlan, where Kelly felt that there were similarities to the Aztatlan complex; this is well outside the area of the complex as it is known at present, and lack of excavation on this part of the Jalisco coast makes it impossible to evaluate her suggestion, but the two coastal or near-coastal sites excavated farther south—Barra de Navidad and Morett—had no Aztatlan material.

The traits which Ekholm associates with the Aztatlan complex at Guasave are obviously derived from southern sources, principally the Mixteca-Puebla area and the Valley of Mexico. He believes that the similarities are too close and specific for the traits to have been diffused from one culture to another through the hundreds of miles intervening, and postulates a migration of peoples from the Mixteca-Puebla area to Guasave. The route, he felt, might have been across the western plateau to the region of Guadalajara, then down past Ixtlan and Tepic, and north along the coast. In the Lake Chapala basin, Lister (1949) found evidence of strong influence of this sort at Cojumatlan, Michoacan; some of the collected materials attributed to the area seem to show central Mexican influences, and the forthcoming monograph on Tizapan el Alto may help to demonstrate them further. The conventionalized figures on some cloisonné vessels said to be from Estanzuela and Totoate resemble designs on Mixteca-Puebla ceramics. Ross's report does not indicate whether they are from both areas or only one, but the cloisonné vessels which Lumholtz purchased in Tepic, and which probably came from Estanzuela, fall into this category. The pottery of Huistla, in the Magdalena Lake basin, resembles the Sinaloa pottery of the original Aztatlan complex, but it also has a few stylistic similarities to the Guasave Aztatlan material. Some central Mexican influences can be detected at Ixtlan del Rio (Middle), which still lacks the stratigraphic excavation needed to define its cultural sequences more precisely; they appear strongly at Amapa (Cerritos phase) and are very evident at Peñitas (Mitlan phase). It is curious, however, that they are lacking at Chametla and Culiacan, which lie between the Amapa-Peñitas area and Guasave; the Aztatlan material at these sites is of the sort originally described by Sauer and Brand. At the end of the Early Postclassic, which marks approximately the end of the Aztatlan complex, Peñitas was nearing the close of its occupation span, but Amapa (Ixcuintla phase) continued to reflect influences from central Mexico and at the same time was developing close ties to Ixtlan del Rio.

In the Late Postclassic, again, the Colima-southern Jalisco complexes (Toliman, Autlan-Mylpa, Sayula basin, Late Barra de Navidad, Periquillo) form a unit, showing various relationships to each other but few to any other area save to the Chila phase at Apatzingan. Autlan and Tuxcacuesco, in particular, seem to have been (as Kelly suggests) a kind of enclave, closely linked to each other but having relatively few ties to distant areas. Tuxcacuesco shows clearer relationships to Colima than does Autlan, but the distinctive Autlan Polychrome is found in a fairly wide area of southern and coastal Jalisco. The Late Ixtlan white-on-red pottery which Gifford thought similar to Autlan White-on-red gives the only suggestion of contact with a more distant area. There are indications of Tarascan influence in the terminal-period material from Autlan and Tuxcacuesco, but little evidence of any contact with central Mexico. The presumed Late Postclassic occupation of northern Jalisco is poorly known. Long's tentative culture history for the Magdalena Lake basin postulates continuous occupation from the time of the shaft-tomb complex, but substantiation for it is still lacking. Totoate and the other sites of the upper Rio Bolaños were presumably occupied at this time, and their architecture suggests influences from Durango and Zacatecas. Peñitas was probably abandoned during most of the Late Postclassic, whereas Amapa continued to be occupied until a short time before the Spanish conquest. The Late Postclassic ceramics of Peñitas and Amapa show a few similarities to the pottery of Culiacan, but no close relationship. The terminal period at Amapa, however, continues to reflect strong central Mexican influence, together with an increasingly close relationship to Ixtlan and, in the use of adobe construction, possible contact with the Durango-Zacatecas area.

On the basis of present evidence, then, it can be said that the cultures of a wide area of west Mexico, extending from southern coastal Colima to southern Nayarit, were linked on the Late Preclassic–Early Classic level by the shaft-tomb complex, itself probably the result of contact with northern South America. The basic features of the complex—shaft-and-chamber tombs usually containing multiple burials accompanied by large and small figurines and a variety of other grave goods—were present throughout the area of its occurrence, but details differed from place to place, and, to the extent that they are now known, the cultures which manifested the complex also differed; those of Colima and southern Jalisco can be placed in one group, those of northern Jalisco and southern Nayarit in another. The Late Classic cultures fall into roughly the same two groups, but without the unifying element provided by the shaft-tomb complex. Not until the Early Postclassic, with the appearance of the Aztatlan complex and the red-on-buff/red-on-brown pottery horizon, can common threads again be traced. Whether the pottery horizon had its origin in some part of west Mexico itself or in central Mexico, it is manifest throughout the Early Postclassic cultures of Nayarit, Jalisco, and Colima. The Aztatlan complex as first described probably originated in southern Sinaloa, but it can be found as far south as northern Jalisco. Its most striking manifestation, however, is that which bears the unmistakable imprint of influences from central Mexico—influences which can now be traced from the Lake Chapala basin through northern Jalisco and into southern and south-central Nayarit in the Early Postclassic. Apart from their participation in the widespread red-on-buff/red-on-brown pottery horizon, the cultures of southern Jalisco and Colima continue to form the same interrelated group, apparently touched neither by the original Aztatlan complex nor by central Mexican influence. In the Late Postclassic, Colima and southern Jalisco

751

still form an enclave; their late sequences reflect some Tarascan influence, and a hint of possible contact with southern Nayarit. The two Late Postclassic cultures of Nayarit, Amapa and Ixtlan, are closely related, but Amapa continues to show stronger central Mexican influence than has so far been revealed at Ixtlan. Amapa, in fact, exhibits an unusually wide range of contacts throughout its occupation span, but its diversity and complexity may well be matched when other sites receive equally intensive excavation.

It is worth noting that Kelly (1947b, p. 188), 20 years ago, speculated that the cultures of west Mexico formed two groups: a southern group including southern Jalisco, Colima, and southwestern Michoacan, and a northern group which comprised northern Nayarit and Sinaloa. This was a very perceptive suggestion to have made on the basis of such fragmentary data as she then had at her disposal, and the work done since has altered it little except to expand the area of her northern group to include southern Nayarit and part of northern Jalisco.

This part of west Mexico was not the cultural outlier it was once thought to have been, virtually unpopulated until the Postclassic, and at best a backwater of the high cultures of central Mexico. It boasted distinctive and well-developed cultures of its own, which further work will illuminate more clearly. The gap in shaft-tomb distribution may be closed by archaeological investigation of the western edge of the Jalisco plateau, but even more urgently needed are the less spectacular excavations of habitation sites which yield the stratigraphic sequences on which chronologies and statements about relationships can be firmly based. Another problem awaiting clarification concerns the influences which reached west Mexico from central Mexico and seemingly from northern South America—their nature, extent, and duration, and the means by which they reached this area. More intensive archaeological work in Nayarit, Jalisco, and Colima might also contribute to the solution of another problem of diffusion: that of the route by which Mexican influence reached the Hohokam. It now seems probable that two waves of Mexican influence reached the American Southwest at different times and via different routes; there is increasing evidence that one of these routes may have passed through the highlands and along the coast of west Mexico (cf. Ekholm, 1942, pp. 134–36; Haury, 1954; Jennings and Reed, 1955). The problem of chronology remains troublesome, since the time allowed for this diffusion seems impossibly short; with reference to some traits, in fact, the chronologies of the two areas seem almost to suggest that the diffusion was from north to south. Stratigraphic excavation in central Jalisco and more work in highland and coastal Nayarit, coupled with re-examination of the existing chronologies and of the correlation problem, might provide the bases for some definite statements about Mexican-Southwestern culture contact.

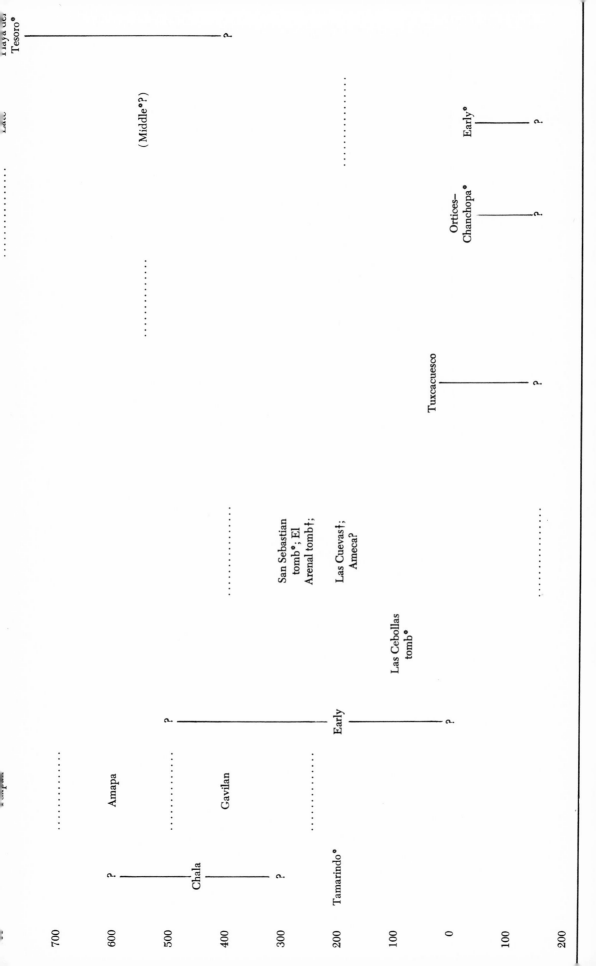

CHART 1—CHRONOLOGICAL CHART. Asterisks indicate the existence of radiocarbon dates; daggers, obsidian-hydration dates. Some of these dates are accepted, some are inconsistent with other excavated material, some are contradictory, some have been revised and others have not been; all, however, are discussed in the text, and the placement of the phase-names on this chart is not intended to indicate exact chronological placement of the dates. Horizontal dotted lines indicate phases established on the basis of radiocarbon or obsidian-hydration dating and/or artifact (largely ceramic) crossties; some of these crossties are to areas outside the geographical limits of this chart, but they are noted in the text. Vertical solid lines indicate unknown duration; it is not meant to imply that a given phase so marked covers a time span equivalent to the length of the line. (Note: There are radiocarbon dates for Totoate and Tizapan el Elto, but these sites have been omitted from the chart because the dates cannot be evaluated properly until the other excavated material has been analyzed.)

State	NAYARIT					JALISCO			COLIMA		
Area	Central		Southern		Northern	Southern		Coastal	General	Coastal	
Sites	Peñitas	Amapa	Ixtlan del Rio	Tequilita	Magdalena Lake Basin	Autlan	Tuxcacuesco	Barra de Navidad	Kelly sequences	Morett	Playa del Tesoro
1500											
1400		Santiago									
1300	Mitlan*	Ixcuintla*	Late			Autlan–Mylpa	Tolimán	Late*†	Periquillo		
1200					Las Cuevas*						
1100					Huistla						
1000	Cerritos		Middle			Cofradia	Coralillo	Early (and Middle)†	Armeria–Colima		
900											

REFERENCES

Arregui, 1946
Arte Precolombino, 1946
Beals, 1932
Bell, 1960
Berger, Fergusson, and Libby, 1965
—— and Libby, 1966, 1967
——, Taylor, and Libby, 1966
Bernal, 1965a
Bordaz, 1964
Brainerd, 1958
Brand, 1957–58
Clune, 1963
Contreras S., 1966
Cook and Simpson, 1948
Corona Núñez, n.d., 1952, 1954, 1955, 1960a
Covarrubias, 1957
Crabtree and Fitzwater, n.d.
Deevey, Flint, and Rouse, 1963
Disselhoff, 1932
Ekholm, 1942, 1958
Fay, 1959
Feldman, 1967
Fergusson and Libby, 1963
Furst, 1965a, 1965b, 1965c, 1966, 1967
Galindo, 1922
Gifford, 1950
Glassow, 1967
Grosscup, 1961, 1964
Haury, 1954
Hrdlička, 1903
Jennings and Reed, 1955
Kelley and Winters, 1960

Kelly, 1938, 1941, 1944, 1945a, 1945b, 1945c, 1947a, 1947b, 1948, 1949
—— and Braniff de Torres, 1966
Kirchhoff, 1946
Lister, 1949, 1955
Long, 1965, 1967
—— and Taylor, 1966a, 1966b
—— and Wire, 1966
Lumholtz, 1902
Medina de la Torre, 1934
Meighan, 1959, 1960, 1961
Moriarty, 1964, 1965
Mota y Escobar, 1940
Nicholson, 1961a, 1961b, 1963
—— and Smith, 1960
Noguera, 1942, 1944, 1954
Palerm, 1954
Parres Arias, 1962, 1963
Pendergast, 1960
Piña Chan, R., 1952, 1963a
Ponce, A., 1873
Ramírez Flores, 1935
Rosado Ojeda, 1948
Ross, 1939
Sáenz, 1966a, 1966b
Sauer, 1948
—— and Brand, 1932
Starr, 1897
Stewart, 1948
Susia, 1961
Wauchope, 1948, 1950
Winning, 1956, 1959

31. Archaeology of Sinaloa

CLEMENT W. MEIGHAN

SINALOA, one of the pioneer areas for investigation of west Mexico, is now in the anomalous position of being better known because of work in adjacent areas than because of current studies in Sinaloa itself. It has been 20 years since significant monographs on Sinaloa archaeology have appeared—a most fruitful 20 years for archaeology of other parts of Mesoamerica—with the consequence that much of the original work in Sinaloa can now be seen in clearer perspective than when it was done. Kelley's extensive program in Durango to the east (Kelley and Winters, 1960) and the work of the University of California at Los Angeles in Nayarit and Jalisco to the south (Meighan, 1959) now provide the data for reevaluation and clarification of Sinaloa archaeology. Kelley and Winters present a revision of the Sinaloa sequence, based on trade materials found in Durango.

Somewhere in Sinaloa (probably the drainage of Rio Fuerte) lies the boundary between cultures of the desert southwest and those of Mesoamerica. This extreme northward extension of Mesoamerica appears to have been by no means as diluted or late in time as was formerly believed. "Mazapan" figurines are reported as far north as Mazatlan, and a relatively full-blown Mesoamerican culture seems to have extended as far as southern Sinaloa by the early Postclassic, if not the full Classic, of Mesoamerica. Sinaloa therefore holds the answer to many important archaeological questions, including Mesoamerican-Southwestern relationships and the expansion and "colonial relationships" of Mesoamerican civilization.

ETHNOHISTORY

Sauer and Brand have reviewed the Spanish accounts and related them, as well as possible, to the archaeological remains they observed. They comment (1932, p. 41): "Our area was almost completely destroyed because it was overrun in 1530 and 1531 by about as hard a gang of killers as Spain let loose anywhere in the New World and because in those days there was no stay upon the killing propensities of conquerors. The very ferocity of Nuño de Guzmán's entrada however led later to a series of depositions and relations which give a fair insight, for the time, into the conditions of native life at the moment of conquest."

From these early documents emerges a picture of a heavy population and remarkable cultural elaboration and complexity. The wealth and civilization of the region in prehistoric times were largely discounted by scholars until archaeology verified the early accounts. A number of factors have contributed to our failure to appreciate and understand the ethnohistoric record.

1. The total destruction of native life by the Spaniards led to a depopulation of the coastal region only recently overcome. It is likely that the prehistoric population of Sinaloa was as great as it is today.

2. There was a natural tendency to discount the stories of conquerors, particularly accounts of their military exploits. The accounts mention in many places towns with thousands of people and "armies" counted in the thousands. For example, the cacique of Chametla is reported to have welcomed the Spaniards with 5000 warriors. These accounts are probably not as exaggerated as has been assumed.

3. The Sinaloa region lacked a central government or "empire" comparable to the Aztec region. It appears to have had no dominating capital, but rather a series of small city-states, each with tributary towns and villages. Chametla, for example, reportedly had 22 pueblos subject to its jurisdiction. If we accept this statement, it is not surprising that the cacique could assemble 5000 persons to greet the Spanish. This kind of political organization explains a feature of the region's archaeology—the fact that in delta, estuary, and flood-plain regions the sites sometimes appear to go on for miles with no apparent major centers. These remains represent many of the "pueblos" adjacent to one another and show a dense but rather evenly distributed population without major urban centers.

4. Coupled with the absence of major cities is a corresponding scarcity of stone architecture, monumental sculpture, and similar obvious evidences of civilization. This contributes to the picture of a marginal and simple region, corrected only by the evidence of other kinds of archaeological finds. To the degree that ceramics are an index of cultural elaboration, western Mexico shared in the complexities of Mesoamerican civilization. A comparison can be made with the Maya area, where some of the marginal regions did not erect stone buildings or dated stelae, yet shared in Maya culture in most other respects.

Sauer and Brand (1932, pp. 51 ff.) have analyzed the 16th-century documents for observations on material culture. Many of these observations are confirmed by archaeology, giving a general picture of great cultural elaboration. The people were prosperous farmers, and the Spaniards ordinarily had little difficulty in acquiring great quantities of supplies. The population wore cotton garments, often decorated in blue and white (embroidery?). Ornaments included shells, pearls, copper bells, gold, and silver. The last was used in considerable quantity, apparently more than in other parts of Mesoamerica.

In warfare the people used leather shields, bows and arrows, and the obsidian-edged wooden clubs best known for the Aztec region. Chiefs were carried in hammocks.

ARCHAEOLOGY

Table 1 summarizes the previous archaeological work in Sinaloa; figure 1 shows locations of principal sites.

The archaeological situation in Sinaloa can be compared in some respects to that of coastal Peru. Like Peru, Sinaloa has a number of short rivers draining into the Pacific Ocean out of a high and steep mountain scarp. The river-drainage systems pro-

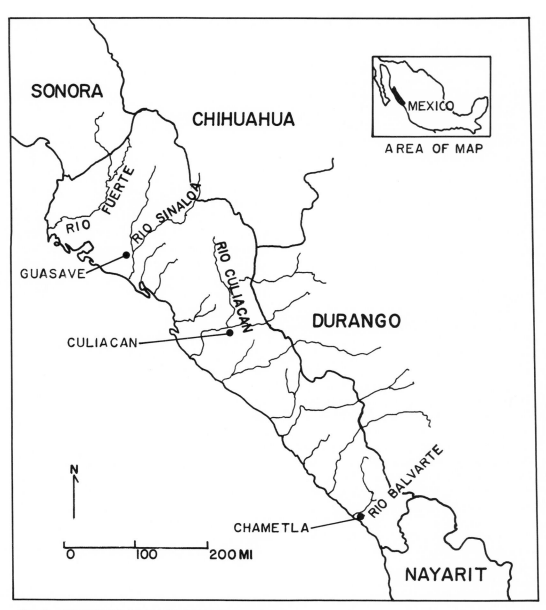

FIG. 1—PRINCIPAL SITES IN SINALOA, MEXICO

TABLE 1—SUMMARY OF ARCHAEOLOGICAL RESEARCH IN SINALOA

Date	Investigation	References
1930	Reconnaissance	Sauer and Brand, 1932[*]
1935	Excavations at Chametla and adjacent sites	Kelly, 1938
1935	Excavations at Culiacan	Kelly, 1945a
1937	Reconnaissance and excavations at Guasave	Ekholm, 1939
1939	Excavations at Culiacan	Kelly, 1945a
1939	Reconnaissance	Kelly, 1947a

[*] Sauer and Brand (1932) list 28 sites in Sinaloa. The Mexican "Atlas Arqueológica" lists 48 sites, 26 of which were recorded by Ekholm. Sites mentioned include a few shell middens, several petroglyph locations, and burial and habitation areas.

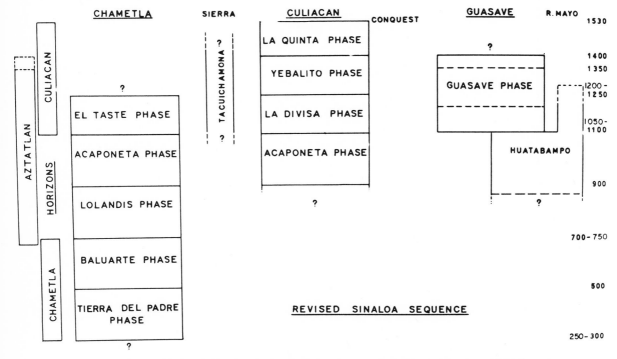

Fig. 2—SINALOA ARCHAEOLOGICAL SEQUENCE. (From Kelley and Winters, 1960, fig. 8.)

vided routes of travel and also agricultural land where relatively dense population centers could develop. Also as in Peru, archaeological remains are classifiable into generic "styles" found throughout the region, but local specialization and diversity are marked, and each drainage system has its own cultural flavor, particularly in details of ceramics and small artifacts. The analogy cannot be pushed too far, but it is worth mentioning, for this is not the usual Mesoamerican situation.

One of the principal problems for discussion has been the route by which Mesoamerican influences were transmitted to the Southwestern United States, an important question as no understanding of these southwestern cultures is complete without an appreciation of the role played by Mesoamerica in Southwestern development (see Article 5, volume 4). In the initial work done along the west coast of Mexico, pre-

vailing opinion saw the west coast as the corridor of diffusion through which Mesoamerican cultural influence was transmitted to the Southwestern United States. The subsequent work of Lister and Kelley in highland Durango raised the possibility of influences following the mountain ranges rather than the coast. Most recently, the question of a coastal diffusion corridor has again been raised (for general discussion see Jennings, 1956; Meighan, 1959). Further, as yet unpublished finds have shown the existence of a paddle-and-anvil, red-on-buff, pottery horizon in coastal Nayarit and Jalisco.

The answer to this important question of diffusion route will no doubt be shown to be much more complex than previously supposed; it looks as if both coast and highland played a role in transmission of cultural features northward. So far the Sinaloa region has not been particularly illuminating on this question, probably because the Sinaloa

757

FIG. 3—GUASAVE POTTERY. (From Ekholm, 1942, fig. 4.)

sites excavated are for the most part too late in time to be significant in formative southwestern cultures.

Questions of chronology in western Mexico remain extremely difficult. There are no radiocarbon dates for sites in Sinaloa, so we must depend on correlations with dated materials elsewhere. Such stylistic crossties are in large part rather tenuous, although the actual trade pieces recovered by Kelley and Winters (1960) provide a somewhat firmer chronology, at least in relating the sequence of Sinaloa to those in adjacent areas.

Without radiocarbon dates, there are two

758

major difficulties in estimating age for aspects of Sinaloa archaeology. The first is the question of marginality, the problem of persistence of older traits into more recent periods. At present, there is no systematic way of dealing with this problem, although we know that such elements as crude figurines of "archaic" appearance occur in relatively recent horizons.

The second problem is difficulty in estimating the duration of given cultural manifestations. The original fieldworkers in Sinaloa had a tendency to view the sequent cultural phases as quite limited in time span, and they accordingly considered all the known archaeology to be relatively late. However, during the past 15 years, several workers have come to realize that the original chronology, although correct in sequence, was somewhat too compressed in time. The best statement of this is made by Kelley and Winters (1960), who extend the Sinaloa sequence back to about A.D. 250 or early in the Classic period. I concur in these judgments of extended chronology.

A summary of Sinaloa archaeology, using the terminology used in the general Mesoamerican sequence, follows.

Preclassic

So far no remains of definite Preclassic origin have been found in Sinaloa. The term "archaic" has been used in the literature to refer to finds there, but must be understood to have only stylistic implications in Sinaloa. The term has been primarily applied to occurrence of certain figurine types and some simple ceramic types. However, these are likely to be attributed to marginality, as referred to above. The simplest pottery complexes, Huatabampo and Tacuichamona, are both considered Postclassic in date, although it must be admitted that the dating is unsure for either.

On present evidence, then, it appears that there was no settlement of Sinaloa by a Preclassic people who could be considered part of the Mesoamerican tradition. On the oth-

er hand, since no remains older than about 1500 to 2000 years can be demonstrated, and since the river systems of Sinaloa were probably inhabited in this earlier period, it would be premature to draw a conclusion about the presence or absence of Preclassic remains. Until remains earlier than the Christian Era are found in Sinaloa, it must remain an open question as to whether the Mesoamerican Preclassic extended this far north. No preceramic sites have been excavated in Sinaloa, and it is interesting that the earliest pottery horizons include a variety of pottery types, among which are relatively elaborate polychromes. Therefore, either there are earlier complexes in Sinaloa out of which the later ones developed, or the region was settled by colonists who brought with them a relatively advanced Mesoamerican civilization.

Classic

The only excavated site in Sinaloa that appears to belong principally to the Classic phase is Chametla (Kelly, 1938), from which the Classic horizon in west Mexico has been named. The site of Chametla also includes later material, but the phases called Early Chametla and Middle Chametla by Kelly and referred to as Tierra del Padre and Baluarte by J. C. Kelley seem definitely to be correlated in time with Classic horizons in Mesoamerica. The time placement was shown stratigraphically at Chametla, and has since been even more clearly demonstrated at the site of Amapa in Nayarit. The Chametla horizon includes relatively elaborate polychrome and engraved ceramics, spindle whorls, and small figurines. It apparently merges into the following Aztatlan horizon, and there is some overlap or mixture of cultures at the end of the Chametla occupation. The critical question of chronology is that of the beginning of the Chametla horizon. On the basis of the appearance of spindle whorls, Kelley and Winters (1960, p. 560) place the early Chametla material on a time level to be cor-

759

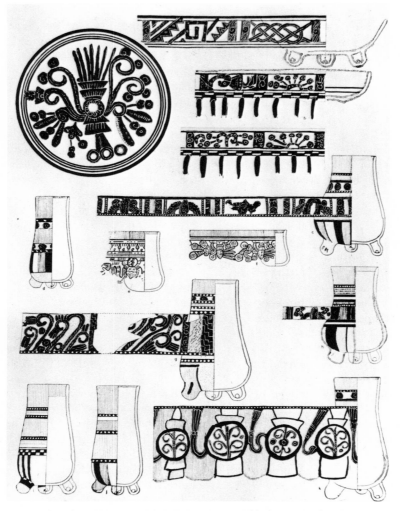

Fig. 4—GUASAVE POTTERY. (From Ekholm, 1942, fig. 7.)

related with Teotihuacan III. From the evidence of the Chametla site itself, the Chametla horizon does not appear to predate the introduction of spindle whorls by very much. However, spindle whorls are absent from the beginning of the Chametla phase, so the earliest Chametla manifestations must extend back in time an unknown distance prior to Teotihuacan III. On the basis of recent research in the Chametla horizon of Nayarit, it appears likely that the beginnings of the Chametla horizon will be shown to extend back to the beginnings of the Teotihuacan sequence.

Postclassic

Since the original survey work of Sauer and Brand, Postclassic remains in the Sinaloa area have been referred to a complex or horizon given the name of Aztatlan. This term has been used in different ways by different writers and is subject to some confusion. It has been applied to a time horizon, a ceramic style (never defined in detail), and sometimes to a geographic region (its original meaning in the Spanish accounts). In general, Aztatlan has come to mean a complex of elaborate polychrome ceramics, quite late in time, and restricted to Sinaloa and northern Nayarit. The principal contribution of Kelley and Winters' article is the more precise definition of an Aztatlan horizon, in which several phases are recognized within the broader Aztatlan term. Whether or not the individual phases are confirmed by future work, a significant advance is made in recognizing that the Aztatlan horizon spanned some 500 years. The earliest manifestation, Lolandis phase, would slightly predate the Tula-Toltec developments in the Valley of Mexico, and it seems that the Lolandis phase should be correlated with the terminal Classic and very early Postclassic Mesoamerican developments. The end of the Aztatlan horizon is usually set at about A.D. 1400, or just prior to the Spanish conquest.

Archaeological evidence of the Aztatlan horizon is most abundant in surface collections and survey work in west Mexico. In Sinaloa, it is known in all the major sites excavated, including Chametla, Culiacan, and Guasave. The horizon is characterized by some of the most elaborate prehistoric pottery known in the New World, including a tremendous diversity of engraved and polychrome varieties. The pottery is more variegated and more elaborate than the contemporaneous pottery in the Valley of Mexico. The Aztatlan horizon includes four-, five-, and six-color polychromes, engraved wares, negative painting, and some modeled ceramics. It also shows an abundance of metal artifacts, primarily copper, but includes objects of silver and gold. Owing to the general absence of stone architecture and sculptured monuments, Sinaloa, along with the rest of west Mexico, has long been considered a diluted backwash of Mesoameri-

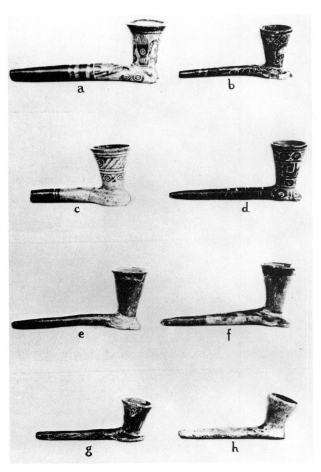

FIG. 5—GUASAVE PIPES. (From Ekholm, 1942, fig. 15.)

can culture. However, there can be little doubt that during the Aztatlan horizon Sinaloa was occupied by a dense, highly developed, and wealthy population.

Also, in the Postclassic period Kelley and Winters proposed a horizon called Culiacan, after the site for which it is primarily known. This horizon overlaps the Aztatlan horizon but extends to the period of the Spanish conquest. Three sequent phases are proposed, all correlated with Aztec manifestations in the Valley of Mexico. The Culiacan horizon continues to be relatively

FIG. 6—CHAMETLA FIGURINES. (From Kelly, 1938, pl. 18.)

simple in architecture and sculpture, but maintains a very elaborate ceramic tradition and shows no real signs of decline until terminated by the Spanish conquest.

Characteristic Artifacts

The published archaeology of Sinaloa reports surface surveys, a burial mound (Guasave), and stratigraphic tests which encountered some burials (Culiacan, Chametla). The purpose of the archaeology done so far was to discover chronological sequence and determine relationships with other regions. This approach yields abundant data on finds such as ceramics, but offers little for cultural reconstruction. So far the archaeology has not contributed direct evidence for house types and settlement patterns, although we know from 16th-century accounts that the region had thatched houses, some with adobe walls.

Lister (1955) has included the Sinaloa work in his distributional survey of west Mexico and has plotted on his maps all the distinctive artifacts recorded from Sinaloa. The present discussion describes some of the general classes of finds.

Ceramics

Sinaloa ceramics are distinctive and their relationships seem to be all to the south, particularly to the adjacent state of Nayarit. Sinaloa pottery is not at all like Hohokam pottery or any ceramic complex of the Southwestern United States. In the early period (Early Chametla or Tierra del Padre) it has simple vessel forms but a variety of decorative styles. Most distinctive is the type decorated with broad-line and crude red designs over a thick cream-colored slip. The same white-slipped pottery is often incised around the rims of vessels. There is also a rather crude but flamboyant polychrome: red, white, and black on a tan-to-orange slip. Engraved ware, black ware, and a variety of other types also occur. The dating of the assemblage is perhaps A.D. 200–600.

It is clear that this is hardly a formative ceramic assemblage and that it represents an evolved pottery tradition from some simpler antecedent, as yet not known to exist in Sinaloa. This oldest known ceramic assemblage suggests an influx of a fairly complex Mesoamerican people, from the coastal region to the south, in the early centuries of the Christian Era. It seems likely, however, that older ceramic assemblages will be found in Sinaloa and that the existing picture sets only a minimum date for the penetration of Mesoamerican culture into this region.

From this early beginning, the pottery of Sinaloa increases steadily in diversity of form and decoration and in elaboration of ceramic style. In the later periods, contemporaneous with Aztec developments in central Mexico, Sinaloa reveals a striking richness of decorated ceramics. Among the painted vessels such as El Taste Polychrome (Kelly, 1938, pl. 1) are six-color poly-

FIG. 7—LATE POLYCHROME POTTERY, CHAMETLA. (From Kelly, 1938, pl. 1.)

chromes using black, white, red, pink, gray, and yellow in complex designs of geometric, naturalistic, and symbolic or "glyphic" elements.

Although the later pottery of Sinaloa is distinctive in its overall style, the decoration has abundant elements specifically "Mexican," including motifs found in Aztec art, both ceramics and in the codices. These similarities, analyzed in detail by Ekholm (1942), are convincing evidence that Sinaloa, despite its distance from the heartland of Mexico, was fully involved in the Mexi-

763

FIG. 8—POLYCHROME POTTERY, CULIACAN. (From Kelly, 1945a, pl. 1.)

red ware. Ekholm reports that this kind of pottery occurs from the Mayo River in the north to Guasave in the south, is found on sites lacking the characteristic painted wares of Sinaloa, and may represent a mixing of Southwestern and Mesoamerican features. The age and affiliation of this complex are still conjectural, and it represents one of the more important unsolved problems of Sinaloa archaeology.

Other pottery artifacts in the Sinaloa collections are rather crude figurines, whistles, flat and cylindrical stamps or seals, spindle whorls, and elbow pipes (late periods only). The pipes are often elaborately decorated and are apparently more abundant in west Mexico than in central Mexico. In addition, two pottery masks are known (Ekholm, 1942, fig. 16).

Copper objects are absent in the earlier Sinaloa sites but relatively abundant in sites dating after A.D. 1000. The origin of copper working is not known, but copper objects were in common use by the time of the Guasave site, which yielded 134 copper objects from 183 complete and disturbed burials. Most copper objects from Sinaloa are bells, but Ekholm also reports rings, tubular beads, and an earspool of copper (1942, pp. 97–98).

Artifacts of other materials are not numerous in the Sinaloa collections, but a sprinkling of grinding tools, chipped obsidian objects (including the common Mesoamerican single-flake blade), and shell beads and ornaments is reported, as well as a very few nondescript bone artifacts. Some striking paint cloisonné gourds were found at Guasave. So far none of these kinds of objects appear widely enough to be of much temporal or cultural significance.

Burial patterns reported for Sinaloa include extended supine burial, secondary bundle burials, and secondary urn burial of individuals in large jars. The site of Guasave indicated a sequence of burial custom, the oldest being extended burials

can civilization of the immediate preconquest period.

A unique assemblage of pottery from Guasave is the collection of 42 vessels of Guasave Redware reported by Ekholm (1942, pp. 74–77). This has been taken to be representative of a Huatabampo complex; the distinctive nature of these vessels indicates a separate cultural unit of some kind. The vessels are bowls and narrownecked jars of hard, slipped, and polished with head to the south, succeeded by north-ward-oriented burials contemporaneous with secondary burial in jars. Bundle burials occurred in both periods. Urn burial appears to be late (after A.D. 800–1000?). No cremations have been reported from Sinaloa, although one was found at Amapa, Nayarit; they are common in the Arizona–Southern California desert regions.

A series of questions and their presently available answers may give us the best way of understanding our present knowledge of Sinaloa archaeology. Three major questions are:

1. What is the beginning of culture in the Sinaloa region? As already indicated, the answer to this question must be considered unknown. We can hypothesize a hunting-gathering phase perhaps comparable to the culture of the modern Seri Indians, but there is no archaeological reflection of this unless it is present in certain shell mounds reported to exist along the Sinaloa coast.

2. What general line of development was followed in this region? There are obvious strong Mesoamerican influences in the Post-classic period, which, however, appear to be grafted onto an indigenous civilization of some complexity, the origins of which are unknown.

3. What indications do we have for exterior relationships? Relationships to the north have been discussed. There seems to be little in the adjacent state of Sonora that shows specific similarity to the cultures described for Sinaloa. It is for this reason that the drainage of the Rio Fuerte is suggested as the northern boundary of Sinaloa culture and accordingly also the northern boundary of clearly Mesoamerican complexes. The broader question of relationship to the Southwestern United States remains unanswerable until older ceramic horizons are found and studied in Sinaloa.

Relationships to the east have been amply demonstrated by Kelley and Winters (1960). These long-lasting and relatively

FIG. 9—POLYCHROME POTTERY, CULIACAN. (From Kelly, 1945a, pl. 2.)

frequent trade relationships are significant because they show the coastal region to have been by no means isolated geographically. There must have been considerable travel and contact between the people of the coastal lowlands and those of the mountains to the east. Presumably it was the river-drainage systems that provided access to the interior.

Recent excavations in the states of Nayarit and Jalisco show extremely strong cross-ties between Sinaloa archaeology and regions to the south. If the known Sinaloa

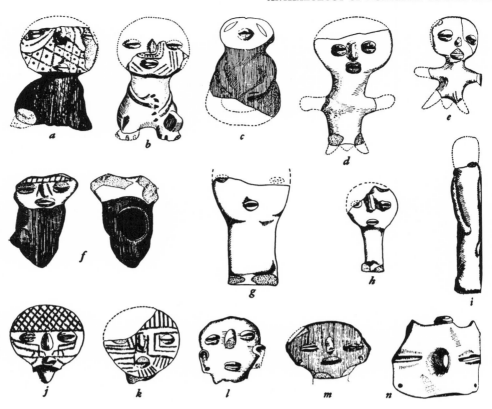

FIG. 10—CULIACAN FIGURINES. (From Kelly, 1945a, fig. 64.)

phases represent a kind of colonization or movement of peoples, such a movement must have originated from a southern direction, presumably from Nayarit. This raises a broader question as to the origin of the archaeological cultures of Nayarit. The beginnings of such culture are also unknown, but they do not seem to be directly derivable from any known complex in central Mexico.

The southern relationships along the coast have another significance as well. When the site of Guasave, in northern Sinaloa, was excavated by Ekholm, it seemed to be explainable as a colonial outpost very distant from the centers of Mesoamerica at that time. However, with the discovery of sites similar to Guasave along the coast to the south in intermediate locations, Guasave itself takes on a somewhat different significance. It can still be considered an outpost of Mesoamerican civilization, since it is the northwesternmost site of what might be called full-blown Mesoamerican appearance, but it no longer appears to be an isolated and detached Mesoamerican manifestation.

To conclude, it is worth noting that in Sinaloa, the northwestern corner of Mesoamerica, the "Florescent" or peak development (in both population and cultural elaboration) seems to belong to the Postclassic, after about A.D. 1000. In other parts of Mesoamerica, there often appears a decline in cultural complexity with the Postclassic, and particularly with the Late Post-

766

classic. But so far as present knowledge goes, Sinaloa was at its peak at the time of Spanish entry into the New World. This observation has two significant implications: first, the indication of a shift in Mesoamerican cultural vitality to marginal areas; second, the chronological alignment with the Southwestern United States, where the florescence of both Anasazi and Hohokam is closely coterminous with peak developments in western Mexico.

ADDENDUM: Although this article was completed some years ago, as of 1970 it has not been superseded by additional fieldwork since no additional published site reports have appeared. Some investigations are under way; the most important is the fieldwork at Teacapan, on the Sinaloa-Nayarit border, under the direction of Stuart Scott of the State University of New York, Buf-

falo. His preliminary reports indicate the archaeology of the region to be more like that of Nayarit than the Sinaloa sites discussed here.

One radiocarbon date has been obtained for the site of Guasave (UCLA 964, published in *Radiocarbon*, 9: 484). The date was obtained from carbonized pitch or gum adhering to remains of a coiled basket, from Ekholm's original excavations. The date was published as 830±130 years ago, or A.D. 1120. Reiner Protsch of the UCLA radiocarbon laboratory informs me that the published date is uncorrected and that the laboratory now applies a correction for the Suess effect; application of such a correction alters the date to A.D. 1220 (±130 years). The latter age is just about exactly what the archaeologist would estimate for the ceramic styles at Guasave.

REFERENCES

Ekholm, 1939, 1942, 1958
Jennings, 1956
Kelley and Winters, 1960
Kelly, 1938, 1945a, 1947a, 1948
Lister, 1955
—— and Howard, 1955
Meighan, 1959
Sauer and Brand, 1932
Willey, Vogt, and Palerm, 1958

32. Archaeology of the Northern Frontier: Zacatecas and Durango

J. CHARLES KELLEY

ETWEEN CIRCA 100 B.C. and A.D. 1000 Mesoamerican cultures expanded northward in Mexico until a relatively stable frontier with the Chichimec, the northern barbarians, was established. This north-central frontier extended northwestward from southwestern San Luis Potosi through Zacatecas and Durango, along the eastern flanks of the Sierra Madre Occidental, almost to the Chihuahua boundary, east of the Mesoamerican boundary on the west coast, near Guasave, Sinaloa. Between these Mesoamerican salients along the Sierra Madre Occidental and in its western barrancas, there are archaeological cultures, relatively unknown, whose Mesoamerican affiliation is dubious. This extreme northern frontier was not maintained into conquest times; by the early 16th century, Mesoamerican cultures no longer occupied the northern salient and the frontier ran southeastward from central Sinaloa through Nayarit, across southern Zacatecas, through eastern Jalisco and along the Michoacan Guanajuato frontier almost to the Valley of Mexico (Sauer, 1941, pp. 354–55 and gf. 1; Wolf, 1959, pp. 8–9). It is with the archaeology of the northern Mesoamerican salient in Durango and Zacatecas that this article is concerned. Potentially, the existence of this frontier, which survived into colonial and even modern times, and its fluctuations in space are of great anthropological interest.

The area includes southwestern Zacatecas, southwestern Durango paralleling the Sierra Madre Occidental, and the extreme northern tongue of Jalisco lying along the Rio Bolaños between Durango and Zacatecas. Significantly, the Mesoamerican cultural frontier in this area closely paralleled an ecological frontier, approximately delineating the southwestern peripheries of the Mesa del Norte in which agriculture without major irrigation constructions appears to have been normally practicable on the southwest and impossible or impracti-

768

cable on the northeast. This ecological boundary zone marks distinct changes in physiography, soils, vegetation, and climate.

Within the area concerned fieldwork has revealed scattered sites of an earlier preceramic occupation, essentially Desert culture (Archaic) in type, (Kelley, 1953) and even some evidence of a Paleo-Indian occupation (Lorenzo, 1953). Along the Sierra Madre Occidental and its eastern foothills and valleys, a rather simple ceramic and presumably agriculture occupance, the Loma San Gabriel culture, has been identified over an area from southern Durango into west-central Chihuahua. This culture is Mesoamerican only to the extent of having ceramics, presumably agriculture, and a simple hamlet-like clustering of houses. In Mesoamerican terms it would have to be classified as a simple and early Preclassic type of occupance; actually it resembles Southwestern United States cultures, especially the early Mogollon and the Pioneer Hohokam, much more than the nearest Mesoamerican equivalents.

The Mesoamerican occupance of the area includes at least three major regional cultures: the Bolaños-Juchipila cultures of southern Zacatecas and Jalisco; the Malpaso culture to the north, best represented at La Quemada; and the Chalchihuites culture of southwestern Zacatecas and western Durango.

Only for the Chalchihuites culture has a detailed cultural sequence been developed, and the general status of archaeological research in the region is such that only the broad outlines of its culture history are known. The following working hypothesis may be used, subject to modification as research continues. Probably agriculture, simple ceramics, and village life, in that order, diffused into a basic Desert culture occupance of the Sierra Madre Occidental and its eastern foothill region, almost certainly from a Preclassic source to the south. The Loma San Gabriel and related cultures may date back to such beginnings; in the refuge area of the high mountains they have survived almost unchanged into recent times.

With the development of late Preclassic cultures such as Chupicuaro in the region just south of Zacatecas, somewhat more specialized and advanced Mesoamerican cultural complexes were introduced into the region. Probably during the first three centuries of the Christian Era either colonization or diffusion or both established the nuclei for each of the three major regional cultures noted, through merging of a basic late Preclassic pattern with newly developed Classic concepts from central Mexico. These merging ideas, and possibly groups, must have moved northeastwardly from the valley of the Rio Grande de Santiago up the great parallel valleys of its northern tributary streams; from east to west those of the Rio Juchipila–Malpaso, the Rio Tlaltenago–Jerez (Rio Colotlan tributary of the Rio Bolaños), the Rio Bolaños–Mesquitic, and the Rio Chapalanga (Guaynamota). The local developments that then followed appear to have been overtaken by Postclassic ideas and traits and may have had their greatest development during the early part of that horizon. Perhaps the events that ended the early Postclassic in central Mexico also influenced the cultures of this region; alternatively, they may have been directly influenced by massive Chichimec movements or by shifting of the ecological frontier. Whatever the causes, the frontier retreated everywhere in the region, so that by about A.D. 1350, the local cultures seem to have disappeared, except in the extreme south in the Caxcana, where a strong group—probably derived from the older Bolaños-Juchipila culture—survived into the conquest period (Kelly, 1948, pp. 59–60, note 2).

BOLAÑOS-JUCHIPILA CULTURE

This is an archaeological area rather than a

unitary culture, and one which is almost unknown. Kelly (1948, pp. 59–60, note 2) has termed it the Caxcana archaeological zone, but it seems preferable to use this ethnic term strictly for the contact period. A number of archaeological sites are known from this area, especially Totoate, Banco de las Casas, Teul, Las Ventanas, and others, but the only excavations were those by Hrdlička in Rio Bolaños sites in 1898 and 1902 (Hrdlička, 1903, pp. 389–401, 425–34), until Kelley excavated briefly at Totoate in 1963. Otherwise available information has been derived from surface collections made by Hrdlička, Lumholtz (1902), Kelly (1948, pp. 59–60, note 2), Margain (1944), Kelley (field notes, 1960 session), and Señor Federico Sescosse of Zacatecas (in the Juchipila zone). Ceramic wares common to most of the major sites, except Banco de las Casas, are paint cloisonné, negative painted, red-on-buff or -brown, red-on-white, and some white-on-red polychrome, and engraved or incised wares. There is some time depth; observed intrusives range from Chupicuaro affiliated types through very late white-on-reds, and locally there were survivals into the contact period.

Sites of the Rio Bolaños Barranca

In the deep barranca of the Rio Mesquitic-Bolaños from Mesquitic southward to Bolaños, Hrdlička and Lumholtz, separately, made collections and recorded sites. Hrdlička collected, and excavated locally, at the sites of Mesitas, Nostic, La Escondida, Totoate, Cerro Prieto, Banco de las Casas, Ocata, La Pena, Mesa Encanta, Borego, and Cerro de Colotlan.

Totoate

This ruin occupies the northern point of a high mesa forming the east side of a canyon through which runs the Rio Mesquitic–Bolaños, some 5 km. south of Nostic,

below Mesquitic. An extensive ruin area of masonry platforms, courts, rocks with petroglyphs, and refuse covers most of the mesa. Of especial interest is a large masonry walled circular court, partly subterranean, with terraced platforms attached at the cardinal points. In the center of the court there is a multiple walled circular stone tower (fig. 1,*a*). In 1960 we observed two similar circular courts with attached structures across the river on the Mesa Prieta. Hrdlička excavated in the platform areas without recognizing their nature or that of the court. In the central tower he noted "rooms" packed with cremated burials, with paint cloisonné bowls in association. He illustrates two of these bowls (Hrdlička, 1903, pl. 39), and I have examined others in the collection in the American Museum of Natural History. Ekholm (1942, p. 94) describes the paint cloisonné ware: "Ten vessels in this Museum. Small hemispherical bowls with low ring base. Base colors green and black; colors: red, white, green; designs: horizontal lines, complex symbolic figures."

Aside from the paint cloisonné wares, the Totoate collections now in the American Museum of Natural History include much polished red and black ware, together with red-on-cream or -tan, negative-paint ware in black, red, and buff, white-on-red, and one red-filled engraved vessel. Decorations on the negative-paint wares are characterized especially by groups of large spirals in black, both inside and outside. Common vessel forms are small simple bowls on low annular bases (ring stands) or on small nubbin tripod feet, and small narrow-neck jars. Other artifacts are shell trumpets, shell nose ornaments, pyrite mirror backs of pottery, stone pendants, effigy grooved axes, obsidian knives, spindle whorls (principally biconical, one "collar-button" of Durango type; white or plain, one incised), and "woven cloth" (reported by Hrdlička).

The University Museum of Southern Illinois University made surface collections at Totoate in 1960, and in 1963 carried out minor excavations there as part of a general study of the northern frontier region, financed by the National Science Foundation. Hrdlička's old excavations (1903, pp. 392–95, fig. 9) were cleared out and enlarged (fig. 1,*a*, Str. 2) and an adjacent structure (fig. 1,*b*, Str. 1) was outlined by trenching around the walls. Although the trenches dug by Hrdlička were definitely identified, they did not conform precisely to his drawing, nor is his description at all correct except in a very general way. He described Mound A (the central structure in our excavations, fig. 1,*a*) as follows (p. 394): ". . . nearly 200 feet in circumference and over 11 feet in maximum height. It consisted of a thick outer layer of stones . . . beneath which was a large quantity of stones and earth, and of a central stone house of seven or eight rooms, a part of which was filled with stones and earth and a part with stone-covered cremation burials."

As we found it, the entire "mound," representing the stone structure and the fallen upper walls and fill, measured some 25 m. in diameter. The stone "house" inside it was actually a series of concentric stone walls representing a central platform or court altar which had been enlarged three times after its original construction. Hrdlička's trenches had been dug through all four stone walls and the fill to meet in the fill of the original platform. The "rooms" of his house must have been the small spaces between the concentric walls. We found no traces of cremated burials—no fragments of burned bone in his spoil heaps—but we did find part of an extended inhumation near the junction of his trenches in the central platform. Nor did we find any sherds of paint cloisonné pottery, which reportedly accompanied his cremated burials, among the many sherds in his spoil heaps and in the original fill. Hrdlička must have made

only the roughest of notes and much of his description must have been written from memory after his return from the field.

The second structure (Str. 1) which we excavated at Totoate (fig. 1,*b*) adjoined Hrdlička's structure on the southeast. This was a rectangular, nearly square, court surrounded by raised walkways and attached platforms, clearly the bases for houses made of perishable materials. The remnants of a rectangular platform altar were found in the center of the court. Portions of older platforms underlying the main structure were found in two places, and various stages of construction and remodeling of the structure were identified.

Our own collections from Totoate include polished red, black, and brown monochrome wares in quantity, together with plain, brushed, and "fingernail"-marked brown utility ware. The principal decorated ware recovered was a broad-line red-on-brown pottery, in association with smaller amounts of negative-painted ware in black, red, and buff, and some engraved black ware with red-filled designs. Only three sherds of paint cloisonné were found, and none of these came from Hrdlička's old excavations. A number of trade sherds have been identified, including sherds of Suchil Red-on-Brown and Refugio Red-on-Brown from the Chalchihuites culture, representing a range from the Alta Vista phase into the Las Joyas phase. A number of intrusive types from the west coast were found, ranging in age from the Gavilan–Early Ixtlan phases into the Lolandis-Acaponeta phases of the Aztatlan horizon. The indicated time range is from the first centuries A.D. to about A.D. 900, but the sequence may have begun earlier and lasted later. Radiocarbon dates of 51 B.C. and 82 B.C. were obtained from samples associated with the old platforms underlying the main rectangular court-platform assemblage, but the ceramic associations of these platforms are not clear. Two other radiocarbon dates of A.D. 460 and A.D.

771

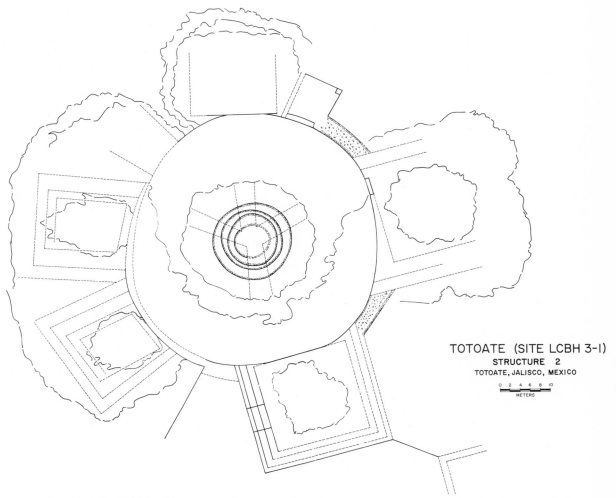

TOTOATE (SITE LCBH 3-1)
STRUCTURE 2
TOTOATE, JALISCO, MEXICO

0 2 4 6 8 10
METERS

FIG. 1a, TOTOATE, JALISCO. Plan of excavated Str. 2, in barranca of the Rio Bolaños, near Nostic. Trenches originally dug by Hrdlička are shown.

505 were associated with the main occupation of the site.

The Sescosse collection of finds made on the riverbank at sites along the Rio Juchipila in southern Zacatecas approximately duplicates the Rio Bolaños pottery, but also has numerous figurines, some resembling Late Chupicuaro types, and others Ixtlan del Rio figurines. Similar sherd associations are reported for Momax, Teul, and other sites of the area, although paint cloisonné rarely appears in surface collections. Margaín's

(1944, Table III) Teul collection adds to the list red-on-cream ware with geometric motifs in red outlined in white.

About 11 km. down the Rio Bolaños from Totoate, on the same mesa, lies the variant Banco de las Casas site. This ruin consists of scattered small rectangular masonry platforms, conical mounds, and one square masonry platform, some 20 m. on the sides and 2–3 m. high. Also noted were oblong conical stones standing upright in the ground, stones with petroglyphs, and a

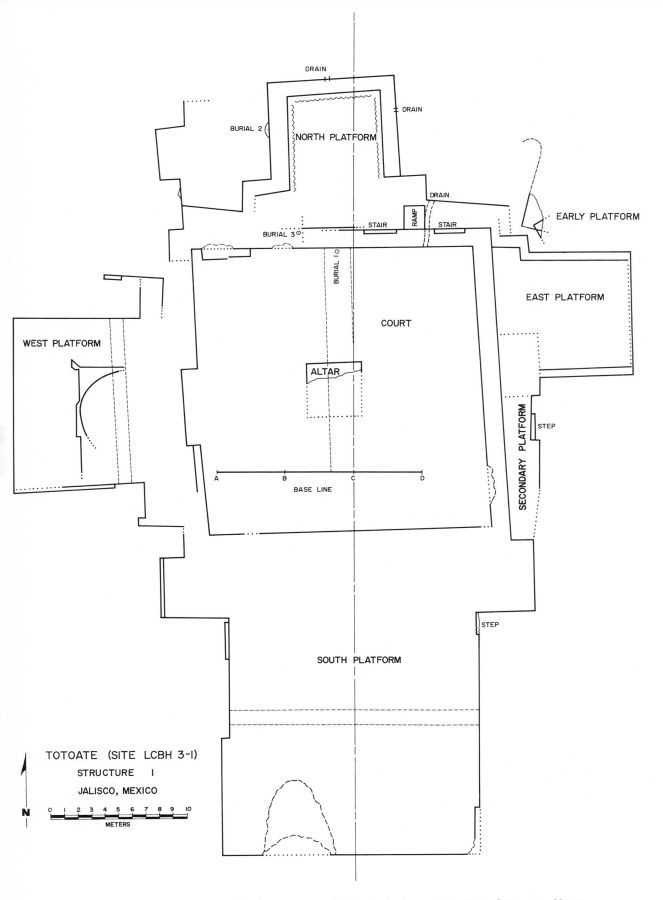

DRAIN

DRAIN

BURIAL 2

NORTH PLATFORM

DRAIN

EARLY PLATFORM

RAMP

STAIR

DRAIN

STAIR

BURIAL 3

BURIAL 1

EAST PLATFORM

COURT

WEST PLATFORM

ALTAR

SECONDARY PLATFORM

STEP

A   B   C   D

BASE LINE

STEP

SOUTH PLATFORM

TOTOATE (SITE LCBH 3-1)

STRUCTURE I

JALISCO, MEXICO

N

0 1 2 3 4 5 6 7 8 9 10

METERS

Fig. 1b, TOTOATE, JALISCO. Plan of excavated Sr. 1, in barranca of the Rio Bolaños, near Nostic.

large metate carried on the back of a turtle. The masonry walls were over 2 m. thick, and the center was filled with rubble (Hrdlička, 1903, pp. 396–97). The associated ceramic complex, based on our 1960 collections, is unfamiliar; red wares and red-on-brown are present but not in quantity. Notable is the preponderant gray utility ware together with a thick gray ware decorated with incised designs along the rim exterior, and a broad punctate zone below. Apparently the vessel form represented is a tall cylindrical one, perhaps with short nubbin feet. The ceramic complex is unfamiliar and the site may be very early in the area—or alternatively may represent protohistoric Tepecano remains.

One other unusual site should be mentioned. This is Las Ventanas, a cliff house some 40 feet long by 10 feet high, formed by a plastered masonry wall enclosing a small rock shelter in the Cerro de las Ventanas south of Juchipila (Hrdlička, 1903, pp. 431–32). The wall exterior is pierced by four doors or windows and is decorated with six broad vertical stripes contrasting with the earth color of the walls. The ceramics of associated sites apparently fit the general pattern for this broad area.

The culture history of the area is virtually unknown. Paint cloisonné (or alfresco) and negative-painted wares first appearing in Preclassic of the Valley of Mexico have been referred to a west Mexican source.

MALPASO CULTURE

This appears to have been a strong cultural development directly on the frontier. Certainly, it served as a buffer for the Mesoamerican cultures to the south, and in its latter phases it may actually have represented an imperium related to, if not actually part of, the Tarascan political domain. Although some of the archaeological remains of this culture are well known and documented, notably, the great site of La Quemada, the culture history of the area is practically unknown. La Quemada, already

a ruin, came to the attention of the Spaniards during the conquest period. There is a description of the site (called Tuitlan) in the history of Nueva Galicia written by Fray Antonio Tello in 1650 (Tello, quoted in Noguera, 1960a, p. 23). In the two decades following 1820 several parties visited and described La Quemada. Berghes' famous map of the Malpaso Valley, showing La Quemada and smaller sites and the network of connecting roadways, was made in 1833 and published in part with Nebel's description of the site in 1839 (Nebel, 1839, discussed in Noguera, 1960a, p. 23). A detailed scale map of La Quemada itself was made by Guillemin Tarayre in 1866 and published in 1869; this map has served as the basis for all later published maps of the site. Batres visited and described the site in 1903 as did Noguera and Agustin García Vega about 1926. García Vega supervised clearing of much of the ruin area and made some modifications in the Guillemin Tarayre map (Noguera, 1960a, p. 27). Carlos Margain and Hugo Moedano excavated at La Quemada and in smaller sites in the Malpaso valley, intensively at Pilarillos, in 1947; and Pedro Armillas excavated in La Quemada itself in late 1951 and early 1952. In 1955 José Corona Núñez reconstructed the stairway of the Piramide Votiva. In 1963 a Southern Illinois University field party, directed by Pedro Armillas and financed by the National Science Foundation, carried out an intensive program of field reconnaissance, and geological and botanical studies in the valley of the Rio Malpaso in the La Quemada area. Excavations were made at several sites, including La Quemada itself, outlying sites, and sections of the roads or causeways (Armillas, 1963). Specimens and data obtained are still being studied and specific findings are not available.

La Quemada is one of the great ruins of Mexico. It is smaller than Xochicalco, which it resembles in situation and general appearance. Detailed descriptions and illustra-

774

tions may be found in Marquina (1951, pp. 243–49). The site is veritably a fortress; most of it is built along the top of the cliffs of a high elongated hill. The northwest part of this hill is enclosed by a stone wall, and even the lower parts of the site lying on a relatively low terrace to the southeast are protected by walled structures. A broad roadway leads from the valley floor up to the southwest group of structures on this terrace, and other roadways radiate out from the site to smaller sites over the valley and pyramids on the hills to the east. The Berghes map shows 13 of these roadways extending out from La Quemada; others run between the smaller sites in the valley. Several of these roadways can still be identified; one exposed in cross section was constructed by building parallel masonry walls and filling between them with rubble to form a high, broad, stone paved roadway similar to the *sacbeob* of the Maya. The fortress-like nature of La Quemada itself, its situation directly on the ecological-ethnic frontier, together with its roadway and village network blocking the passage of the Chichimec down the open valley of the Rio Malpaso–Jerez, an avenue leading deep into Mesoamerica in the Tarascan area—all suggest that the city and the area were organized and constructed deliberately to defend the northern frontier.

La Quemada itself is a huge pile of stone masonry—walls of well-fitted tabular stones, with rare adobe brick construction—made up of courts, surrounded by halls and pyramids, or having small pyramids and altars within them. There is much variation in construction and plan from one part of the site to another; certain important structures are described below.

The low terrace to the southeast is occupied by a related group of structures. At the extreme southeast is a square walled courtyard. It is to the northwest side of this courtyard that the main roadway runs, entering it between two small guarding pyramids and, apparently, by means of a grand

stair. Along the west side of this court there is a broad walkway, serving as a terrace for the hall of columns, sometimes called La Catedral, paralleling it on the east. Inside this great hall are 11 round stone pillars, plus two pillars bounding the entryway, grouped around a rectangular open central area, which is paved with baked red plaster. A subterranean passage near its exterior northwest corner appears to have been roofed with a corbeled arch. Northwestward from this group of structures the terrace is relatively bare of construction until its northwest end is reached. There stands the Votive Pyramid, a small but high (more than 10 m.) pyramid with steeply sloping sides, without stages or terraces, long thought to be a true nontruncated pyramid. Actually, it was truncated, and remnants of a stair on the south have been uncovered and in part reconstructed. Between the pyramid and the hall of columns the terrace is occupied by a long parallel walled structure, considered by some to be a ceremonial way. Actually, it is almost certainly a long I-shaped ball court.

Above the northwest end of this terrace, on the west, the so-called Acropolis of La Quemada rises in a series of steps of massive masonry construction on the side of the cliff. Massive battered walls rise to incredible heights to bound building groups made up of courts surrounded by groups of halls, some of which must have been two stories in height. In the center of the principal courts there are stepped masonry altars, miniature pyramids in themselves; on the northeast there are small stepped pyramids. The west edge of this mass of masonry structures conforms to the edge of the cliffs, battered walls rising as if they were a continuation of the cliff itself. Higher up there are isolated groups of somewhat similar structures and continuing from them the great defensive wall which swings in a great bulging curve to include the entire hilltop, returning again to the cliffs adjoining the Votive Pyramid.

775

Regardless of its huge size and excellent preservation, La Quemada has produced very little in the way of specimens. Areas exposed by excavation show that the site was burned at the end of its occupation, and perhaps cleared of valuable goods and abandoned prior to that. This is highly reminiscent of the end of Teotihuacan and Tula, possibly a common end for great dominating ceremonial center–fortress cities in Mesoamerica.

Apparently there are many small sites in the Malpaso valley. Best known of these is Pilarillos, at the end of one of the La Quemada roadways southwest of the site. There, two or more large courts are surrounded by groups of isolated or joined rectangular platforms.

Collections are available from small sites and from debris at the base of the La Quemada cliffs. Plain and brushed brown utility ware; polished red and black; and a unique red-on-brown ware with small decorative unit figures, widely spaced, both life forms and geometric elements (cf. Noguera, 1930, p. 62, fig. 5, jar); a gray or black ware with decoration in shallow engraved lines (red-filled) forming simple geometric designs; rare polychromes—all these constitute the ceramic complex. Stone artifacts include full (and probably three-quarter) grooved polished axes, projectile points, stone scrapers, and balls. Armillas (field notes, 1951–52, unpublished) reported finding large numbers of axes, adzes, manos, and metates (troughed) in the rooms he excavated, together with smaller quantities of flint, obsidian, bone and antler artifacts. Moedano (personal communication, 1952) noted the presence of large numbers of stone snubnose end scrapers at La Quemada and speculated that they might be very late there. Older collections from La Quemada included bowls almost certainly of Chupicuaro culture origins, effigy stone axes, effigy pottery pipes and whistles, an alligator-effigy jar, clay figurines related to Chupicuaro and Patzcuaro types, side-notched arrow-

points, and other items (cf. Batres, 1903a; Noguera, 1930). Collections attributed to La Quemada on display in the Museo Nacional de Antropología e Historia in Mexico City include small red-on-brown bowls and jars, paint cloisonné vessels in annular-base forms resembling those from Alta Vista, Chalchihuites, and one small exterior-engraved bowl.

Practically nothing is known of the culture history or chronology of La Quemada. In a lecture to a Southern Illinois University field session in Durango in 1952, the late Hugo Moedano stated that, based on his excavations at La Quemada and related sites, two culture periods were represented: an early period characterized primarily by polished black and gray vessels in tripod form with some engraved designs, and a later period with red-on-brown ware like that of the Chalchihuites culture. Although nothing to this effect has appeared in print, a similar ceramic sequence has been discovered in the Chalchihuites area by Kelley and associates. The three radiocarbon dates currently available from La Quemada (Michigan 430, 890 ± 200, or between A.D. 867 and 1267; Michigan 431, 780 ± 200, or between A.D. 977 and 1377; Michigan 432, 1210 ± 200 or between A.D. 547 and 947; all B.P. dates from 1955, cf. Crane and Griffin, 1959) suggest an occupation span of around 1000 years, paralleling our estimates for the duration of the Chalchihuites culture. Armillas has a large new series of radiocarbon dates, as yet unpublished, for La Quemada and nearby sites. Reportedly, they show approximately the same time range as the earlier published dates, with a concentration of occupation around A.D. 900–1000.

La Quemada and related sites of the Rio Malpaso area lie within the zone of transition to the arid Mesa del Norte; within the 35-km. distance to the city of Zacatecas the transition is completed. The La Quemada–Malpaso valley probably represents the maximum advance of the Mesoamerican farming-based economy into the Mesa del

776

Norte, except locally where special ecological conditions existed. Truly, La Quemada was on the northern frontier, ecologically, archaeologically, and culturally.

CHALCHIHUITES CULTURE

Approximately 175 km. airline directly northwest of La Quemada lies the site of Cerro de Moctehuma, on the eastern branch of the Rio Suchil, some 8 km. above its junction with the Rio Colorado near Suchil, Durango. The site occupies the top of a long high mesa, bounding on the south the eastern end of a canyon through which flows the Rio Suchil. This is a miniature La Quemada, with masonry and general architectural patterns highly reminiscent of that site. Here are several courts surrounded by platforms with an altar in the center of each, and a small pyramid on one side. Near the north end of the site, overlooking the river, there is a moderately large pyramid. Below it on the south is a large court with an almost intact altar in its center, and adjacent to this court on the south is a high-walled room which may be a hall of columns. The court at the foot of the pyramid was partially excavated by Kelley and associates in 1962; buried in the central altar was a stone idol, probably a fire-god representation. Along the upper Rio Suchil above Moctehuma are many other archaeological sites of the Chalchihuites culture, representing primarily an earlier Canutillo phase (circa A.D. 200–500) and a later Vesuvio phase (circa A.D. 500–950). Excavations were carried out by Kelley and associates in 1962 at the sites of El Vesuvio and Loma de las Flores.

Across a dividing range of mountains and hills to the southwest is the western main branch of the Rio Suchil, known as the Rio Colorado. Here also are many sites of the Chalchihuites culture, including especially the ceremonial center of Alta Vista and the stronghold sites of El Chapin and Cerro Pedragoso. In this area the Canutillo phase already noted for the upper Suchil valley was present in the period circa A.D. 200–300. In the Rio Colorado valley the Canutillo phase sites apparently were overrun and replaced with components of the Alta Vista phase around A.D. 300. The site of Alta Vista itself, a ceremonial center located on the *potrero* west of the Rio Colorado and the town of Chalchihuites, was excavated in part by Gamio (1910; see also Noguera, 1930, 1960a). The site consists of a concentrated area of high mounds or mound groups surrounding court depressions and ruins of a number of contiguous structures (Gamio, 1910, Croquis no. 4). There Gamio excavated one principal structure and certain attached features at the northwest edge of the site. This excavated structure was a square court, approximately 20 by 20 m. on a side, having walls standing nearly 3 m. high and an entrance on the east. Inside the structure were 28 masonry columns in four rows of seven each, averaging about 0.5 m. in diameter at the base (but becoming smaller toward the top), oriented east to west. Eight of these columns subsequently were remodeled by the addition of extra stone or, in some cases, adobe brick courses around them, producing six large circular columns, one semicircular column, and one prismatic column two or three times the diameters of the original columns. All columns were plastered, as were the walls, and in the western wall of the court wooden posts had been set to aid in supporting the wall. Outside the court on the southwest was a terraced platform, probably a small pyramid, reached by a complex of stairs from the north. The doorway of the hall of columns on the east led to an ascending stairway; attached were other rooms and stairs. Materials used in construction included irregular stone blocks, small stone slabs, and red adobe bricks of a somewhat standardized size, averaging 10 cm. wide by 89 (19 cm.?) cm. long, perhaps made in forms. Some bricks appeared to Gamio to have been fired deliberately; these he termed tiles. Both adobe and sand-lime plasters

777

were used. Gamio believed that the site had been deliberately abandoned, with doorways walled up, and had subsequently been destroyed by fire.

Alta Vista is the type site of the Alta Vista focus (circa A.D. 300–500). There are many components of the focus in sites dispersed along the Rio Colorado, the Rio Chapalangana (Guaynamota) to the south, the Rio Graceros to the west, and the Rio Suchil below the junction of the Rio Colorado. Excavations carried out by the Southern Illinois University at the sites of Cerrito de la Cofradia (in 1961) and Potrero del Calichal (in 1963) produced evidence that the Canutillo phase of the Rio Suchil was present in the Rio Colorado valley as well, prior to the appearance of the Alta Vista phase. At the Calichal site evidence of post–Alta Vista phase occupation was found. There a Calichal phase grew out of the Alta Vista phase and appears to have existed from about A.D. 500–650. Subsequently there was a short-lived terminal occupation called the Retoño phase, dated very roughly at circa A.D. 650–750; actually the terminal date may have been as late as A.D. 950.

During the Calichal phase, Mesoamerican colonies were established in Durango to the north near Villa Union and Antonio Amaro, and to the northwest near the city of Durango in the Guadiana valley. Other colonies were established to the northeast in Zacatecas, at Atotonilco, and later on near Rio Grande. In the Durango area the Mesoamerican colonization had a long local development which we estimate to have lasted through four separate phases, from circa A.D. 550 to 1350. We refer to the Mesoamerican cultural developments in the Rio Colorado and the Rio Suchil valleys, and in the immediately adjacent areas, as the Suchil branch, while the related but somewhat later developments in Durango are referred to as the Guadiana branch. Together, these related cultural developments made up the Chalchihuites culture.

The term "Chalchihuites culture" was coined by J. Alden Mason, who carried out an archaeological survey of Durango and adjacent parts of Zacatecas in 1936. Mason (1937) noted that archaeological sites with basically similar assemblages occurred from La Quemada and Alta Vista northward as far as Zape in northern Durango, and concluded that this cultural development was essentially Mesoamerican in relationship. Brand (1939) investigated sites near Zape in 1936 and supported Mason's conclusions. Later Robert H. Lister and Agnes M. Howard studied Durango archaeological collections and published a detailed description of the Chalchihuites culture, again supporting Mason's conclusions (Lister and Howard, 1955). In 1952 the Southern Illinois University began archaeological survey and excavation in Durango, with summer field sessions in 1952, 1954, 1956, and 1958. This work was extended to western Zacatecas and extreme northern Jalisco with major field seasons in 1960, 1961, 1962, 1963, and 1964, and shorter periods of investigation thereafter. Several preliminary reports (Kelley, 1953, 1956, 1963; Kelley and Shackelford, 1954; Kelley and Winters, 1960; Kelley and Abbott, 1966; A. S. Johnson, 1958; Weigand, 1968) have resulted in the conceptualization of the Chalchihuites culture as presented here, and its separation from other Mesoamerican developments in the Zacatecas-Jalisco region.

Suchil Branch of the Chalchihuites Culture

SITES AND SETTLEMENT PATTERN. Five principal types of sites are known: (1) Sherd areas with occasional concentrations of boulders, suggesting the former presence of masonry platforms, in fields on river floodplains, or on adjacent low terraces. (2) Village sites on mesatops or potrero slopes, usually near the edge of river valleys. There are many of these sites; Vesuvio, Cofradia, and Calichal are examples. Such sites usually have one or several large depressions, representing courts, surrounded

778

by mounds which are platform remains. Often the courts have a small mound, certainly an altar or a shrine, in the center and a larger structure, perhaps a small pyramidal platform, at one end. There is evidence that perishable houses of dry masonry and, presumably, thatch once stood on the platforms. (3) Ceremonial centers on high mesatops or potrero slopes near the rivers, or at some distance. Characteristically, they have better stone and adobe masonry than do other sites, with architectural remains including pyramids, halls of columns, altars, and large masonry-walled courts. Such sites also occur in connection with the stronghold sites discussed below. Alta Vista, Cerro de Moctehuma, Cerro de los Viveras, and perhaps Cerro de Rancho Colorado are examples of this type of site. (4) Strongholds on high prominent hilltops or mountains, often located strategically with regard to the occupied terrain and far from any water source. Such sites usually include one or more large courts surrounded by high masonry platforms made of boulders, and associated features such as defensive walls, protected portals, and utilized cliffs. Dwelling platforms and ceremonial features such as pyramids sometimes occur. These sites include Cruz de la Boca, Cerro de Gualterio, Cerro Pedragoso, and El Chapin. (5) Mines or quarry sites on and in high alluvial terraces (mostly gravel, conglomerate, and caliche) at the edge of river valleys or arroyos. Extensive areas of such aboriginal mines are now known, including such sites as Ejido Cardenas, Gualterio, Alejandro, San Jose, La Escondida, Rancho Colorado, and Rancho Rafael. Although Gamio saw and described (1910) several of these mine areas, he considered them to be "refuse areas." Kelley and associates correctly identified them as mines in 1960–63; Weigand (1968) has published a study of them. Essentially, each mine area is made up of either (a) deep pits with a spoil heap on one side and a vertical face with one or more tunnels cut into it, or (b) working

faces exposed on sides of hills or in arroyo banks, with spoil heaps thrown out behind and tunnels entering the working face in front. In both instances, the entrance tunnels often branch out within the terrace, forming a succession of rooms and side passages, many of which still remain open. In these interior rooms, Weigand found sorting piles, discarded torch butts, and discarded maul handles. Large stone mauls and axes occur commonly around the mine entrances. Weigand believes that a number of materials were garnered from the mines, specifically a white "chalchihuitl" stone used locally for making jewelry, perhaps some actual turquoise, limonite and hematite, and perhaps other material as well. We do not as yet know what industrial or craft need led to the development of the incredibly vast mining activity reflected in these sites. These sites appear to belong especially to the late Canutillo phase, the Alta Vista phase, and perhaps the later Calichal and Vesuvio phases.

Clearly, the Chalchihuites culture, Suchil branch, was supported largely by farming, perhaps secondarily at some times by the mining industry. Maize and beans have been found, but as yet no identification as to type is available. Much of the farming in both Rio Colorado and Rio Suchil valleys must have been then, as it is today, *temporal* farming of the potrero slopes, made possible physically by the presence of a resistant "blanket" of secondary limestone or caliche underlying the local red and yellow alluvium which served to conserve and distribute subsurface water, maintaining a high water table. River-bottom farming by flood irrigation certainly was practiced also, especially in the Rio Suchil valley, but with more limited available area. The aboriginal population, like the modern *campesino* population, must have used the rivers and certain spring-fed side arroyos for their water supply. The relative paucity of bones of food animals in archaeological deposits, together with the scarcity of projectile points,

779

suggests a relatively minor dependence on hunting as a source of food.

Prevalent mortuary practice for the Suchil branch was flexed inhumation in circular or oval pit graves, with or without mortuary offerings. At Cofradia there were two extended inhumations, both child burials. At Calichal there was one very late burial of relict bones, apparently followed immediately by abandonment of the site. Burials were made beneath platform floors, beneath court floors, or, prevailingly, in ruins of abandoned structures. Pottery was the principal burial offering, followed by jewelry (including turquoise beads and shell beads), pottery bells, and pottery half-bells. Ocarinas were also included with burials. Data are not yet available on physical types. Lambdoidal deformation was common, and Gamio (1910) reported finding a trepaned skull at Alta Vista.

ARCHAEOLOGICAL PHASES OF THE SUCHIL BRANCH. *Canutillo Phase* (circa A.D. 200–300, Rio Colorado valley; A.D. 200–500, Rio Suchil valley). Principal diagnostics of the phase are the pottery types Canutillo Red-Filled Engraved and Gualterio Red-on-Cream in association. Gualterio Red-on-Cream, however, continues also as a diagnostic ware of the subsequent Vesuvio phase, and as yet valid distinctions between earlier and later Gualterio cannot be made.

Canutillo Red-Filled Engraved (exterior and interior). Single shallow line engraving, filled after firing with red pigment. Single, multiple, composite band decoration, exterior or interior; motifs repeated or continuously repeated; design bands framed above and below and separated by simple multiple lines.

Decoration exterior of bowls and interior of plates and rarely on flattened rim. Exterior decoration of geometric elements in single band of one or several strips including zigzags, steps, rectilinear and curvilinear scrolls. Interior decoration geometric elements similar to exterior decoration in single, multiple, or composite bands. Rare-

ly vessel center shows possible stylized life form, perhaps late.

Deep hemispherical bowl tripod; rounded shoulders; conical, squat, tapering legs, occasionally "kneed" or "hipped" slightly; rarely recurved to form "feet"; very rare paired, opposed, pierced rim tabs. Plate or shallow bowl, fairly large.

Gualterio Red-on-Cream (exterior and interior). Red paint on cream slipped or self-slipped background. Single, multiple, or composite band decoration, exterior or interior; motif repeated singly or continuously; design bands framed and separated above and below by multiple simple lines.

Decoration exterior of simple bowl in single band of one or more strips of geometric elements including four-lobed "plus" figure interlocking, linear scrolls, zigzags, triangles. Paneling with vertical lines known on water jar only. Interior decoration of plates similar to exterior decoration in single, multiple, or composite bands containing one or more strips of geometric elements. Red band usually covers rim extending to exterior, or rim may show geometric elements. Rarely vessel center shows possible stylized life form, probably late. Quadrate interior rare and late; shows quarters formed by intersecting vertical lines: two opposing quadrates of alternating bands of usually geometric elements and other two quadrants containing life forms ("alligator monster").

Simple hemispherical bowls; plates or shallow bowls; small narrow-neck water jars; wide-mouth, flaring-rim ollas.

Other ceramic types: Polished red ware, polished black ware, polished buff ware; plain brown, buff, and red utility ware, brushed brown and "fingernail"-incised brown utility ware. These wares occur throughout the Chalchihuites cultural sequence and as yet no phase distinctions are available for them. Also, Vista Paint Cloisonné and Negative A occur as presumed "trade" wares in *late* Canutillo phase components in the Rio Suchil valley as well as in the contemporary Alta Vista phase. These wares are described below in the section on the Alta Vista phase.

Other traits: Stone artifacts—scoop-type non-legged metates and two-hand manos, full and three-quarter grooved axes and mauls, stone bowls, stone balls, polishing stones, end scrapers, rare projectile points—occur in late Canutillo phase components in the Rio Suchil valley and presumably early in the phase also, although this has not been demonstrated. These types continue throughout the various phases of the Chalchihuites culture in both Suchil and Guadiana branches, as do bone awls, shell beads, and turquoise. A carved stone idol, presumably representing the fire god of the world below, was found in the altar excavated at Cerro de Moctehuma but may belong with the later Vesuvio phase. Characteristic seated figurines of clay begin with this phase and carry over into the Vesuvio phase. Worked potsherds, including pierced discs, occur in all phases. The architectural pattern involves construction of stone-walled walkways and platforms (presumably serving as bases for perishable houses) around central courts, in the center of which rectangular stone shrines or altars were constructed. Masonry walls were constructed by building dry walls of small stones placed horizontally and faced on the exterior with large stone slabs set vertically, but inclined inward; these were dressed with small stones in the interstices and then covered with either adobe or lime plaster. Occasionally, small narrow stone slabs were set horizontally in this plaster for decorative effect. Normally, small stairways of stone masonry, either set against or built into the wall, provided access to the platforms of the four cardinal sides of the court, and on the outside of platforms as well. Platforms were constructed by filling between masonry walls with caliche, dirt, rubble, refuse, or any combination of these. Platforms were then floored with cobbles which were plastered over. Shallow circular clay-lined hearths occur frequently near the center of main platforms. These architectural traits of the Canutillo phase continued to characterize village construction throughout the various phases of the Suchil branch, and appear in modified form in the Guadiana branch as well.

Alta Vista Phase (circa A.D. 300–500). Principal diagnostic traits for the phase are the pottery types Michilia Red-Filled Engraved and Suchil Red-on-Brown in constant association, together with small quantities of Vista Paint Cloisonné and Negative A pottery, especially in ceremonial centers. Monochrome and utility wares continue, as described for the Canutillo phase.

Michilia Red-Filled Engraved. Champlevé technique, filled after firing with red pigment; both negative and positive designs used. Single band decoration, exterior; sequence of motifs, usually repeated; serrate or multiple simple line borders to bands.

Geometric elements plus life forms: several birds; three quadrupeds; deer, coyote, jaguar (tiger-lion?); "alligator monster"; sinuous scaled two-horned serpents with anthropomorphic head, plumes, hands; others.

Shouldered tripod forms with slightly outflaring rims; small; specialized diagnostic leg-foot form; "hipped" or "kneed," broad but thin at foot, recurved, feet often vertically striated (toes); paired, opposed vertical, pierced, rim suspension tabs.

Bowl interiors, plain, polished black or tan.

Suchil Red-on-Brown. Red-on-orange-brown decoration, unslipped or self-slipped (?).

Decoration interior, exterior, or both. Basic decoration consists of circling repeated or continuously repeated elements below rim on interior or exterior or both, and on lip; framed and separated by one or several parallel circling lines; elements include dots, circles, circles with dots, S's, paired interlocking linear scrolls, single scrolls; continuous squiggled lines, vertical lines

781

(diagonal and single or in groups), vertical and diagonal squiggled staggered lines, singly or in groups; concentric squiggled triangles, continuous single and double or opposed terraces; others. Broad framing lines just below rim interior, exterior, and at base of design bands. Bowl and plate bottom interior plain or decorated; plates decorated; most common quadrate division of bottom circular area by broad straight-sided intersecting lines or bands bordered by several narrow lines; two of the opposed bottom segments thus formed filled with parallel straight bands of alternating lines, wavy lines, geometric elements as in circling bands; opposed pair of panels have one life form each, surrounded by dots; "alligator monster," turtle (?), birds (including hummingbird), two-faced masked "man" (priest), or isolated geometric elements. Life forms usually accompanied by one or two star or sun symbols. Some bowl interiors below circling bands filled with one centered life form: spiraling, scaled serpent, with hands, plumes, anthropomorphic head.

Shallow bowl or plates; simple hemispherical, shallow bowl; composite-silhouette bowls; small narrow-neck globular jars with flaring rims; larger narrow-neck olla; footed cup or goblet. Bowl rim forms direct, expanded, or beveled; square-cut lips of plates have decorative band. Flaring rim of jar and ollas painted red on exterior extending to interior.

Vista Paint Cloisonné (inadequately known). Broad zones and band of decoration around vessel exteriors and in interior of upper vessel compartment.

Decoration is appliquéd, postdrying, perhaps postfiring, in pigments of green, red, blue, white; elements separated by lines of black pigment, representing base color into which designs were cut and filled with other colors.

Decorative pattern includes circling bands of repeated simple elements and complex interlocking elements; geometric elements; curvilinear and rectilinear scrolls, simple and interlocking; triangles, terraced figures, zigzag diagonal lines; life forms, human and animal figures, flowers, fruits. Life form filling bottom interior of upper bowl occurs. Intricate many-color designs and sophisticated decorative technique highly suggestive of higher cultures of central Mesoamerica.

Common vessel form is high annular-base cup or goblet, some low annular-base forms; small globular jars with narrow neck and flaring rim known.

Occurs in late Canutillo phase and Alta Vista phase associations. Probably is a trade ware, with source unknown, or local product of traveling artisans.

Negative A. Interior decoration of buff negative circles and dots on dark slipped background; randomly dispersed small to large dots and circles, or arrangements of same into layout patterns of broad bands paralleling rim, others perpendicular to rim, possibly representing quadrate decoration but total layout pattern uncertain because ware known only from sherds. Rare line decoration. Lost-wax technique of decoration produces dots with blurred edges or "shadow circles."

Shallow bowls or plates are the only vessel forms known.

Ware is probably trade ware or nonlocal ware made by traveling artisans but geocultural source not identified. Especially well represented in late Canutillo phase but also occurs in Alta Vista phase.

Other traits: Stone artifact types as described for the Canutillo phase continue in use. In addition there are animal effigy-headed axes and small cut-stone figurines of animals were made. There are numerous beads and pendants of turquoise and other stone, including turquoise mosaics. Shell beads and ornaments, pottery whistles, flutes, and ocarinas are found. Pottery bells and "buttons" in the form of pottery half-bells occur, perhaps late in the phase. Pottery figurines like those of the Canutillo phase occur, perhaps as intrusives. Among notable artifact finds are those made at Alta Vista by Gamio (1910), including especially a conch-shell trumpet and two composite mosaics, the latter found in an offering placed beneath the floor of the hall of columns. One of these mosaics, called by Gamio a "joyel pectoral," was made of a central disc of yellowish pottery, 7 cm. in diameter and 9 mm. thick, encircled by a ring of wood, prismatic in cross-section and made up of several sections. Near two opposed edges of the front of the disc were two oblique holes that joined inside; in the edges of the disc also were two perforations. On one face of the disc were incrustations of a mixture of "clay and resin" with resin only on the wooden ring. The incrustations on the disc formed the picture of a human being, similar to those found on [paint cloisonné] vessels from Estanzuela. The incrustations on the wooden ring molded the shapes of the many small multifaceted pieces of turquoise, beryl, and steatite found loose nearby. Clearly, what Gamio found was a stone mirror with paint cloisonné decoration, within an encircling ring of mosaic, on the back; but he does not mention the presence of the iron pyrite cut pieces which should have formed the actual mirror.

In architecture, the court-altar-platform complex continues in the villages. New are ceremonial centers with cut-stone and adobe-brick architecture, halls of columns, pyramids, and stairs. It is believed that the stronghold sites and the mines belong to this period. This was also a time of great population expansion, as indicated by the large increase in number of sites actually occupied. Inferentially, there were hieratic lineages, seasonal corvée labor (certainly in the mines, and probably also in the strongholds and ceremonial centers), and exploitative economic system, and perhaps even a primi-

tive state organization (see Weigand, 1968). The presence of a well-organized and formalized Mesoamerican ceremonialism is indicated, with primary emphasis on cults related to the plumed serpent, the sun, the fire god, earth and water monsters, and undoubtedly Tlaloc worship. A priesthood, heart sacrifice, cloud beings, world quarters, astronomical (and probably calendrical) concepts, and the speech scroll are all present.

Vesuvio Phase (circa A.D. 500–950). In the Rio Colorado valley the Canutillo phase population, which had survived the "invasion" of the Rio Colorado valley by the Alta Vista phase occupance, was slowly acculturated by the latter. The potters who made Canutillo Red-Filled Engraved exterior-decorated tripod bowls began to borrow practices from the Michilia potters of the Alta Vista phase. Slowly, under this influence, Canutillo exterior-decorated evolved into Vesuvio Red-Filled Engraved, exterior-decorated, and Canutillo interior-decorated engraved plates were no longer made. Similarly, the potters who made Gualterio Red-on-Cream were influenced by the makers of Suchil Red-on-Brown, so that later Gualterio interior-decorated plates or shallow bowls often have quadrate interior decoration incorporating life forms in opposed quadrants, like those of Suchil. Essentially, the diagnostic ware of the Vesuvio phase is Vesuvio Red-Filled Engraved, in association with Gualterio Red-on-Cream.

Vesuvio Red-Filled Engraved. Shallow crosshatch engraving of large areas filled after firing with red pigment; both positive and negative designs used. Well-balanced red and black decorative layout and execution. Single band decoration, exterior; motifs continuous or repeated within panels; design band framed above and below by multiple simple lines or by lines and strips of small geometric elements.

Decoration of geometric elements and

783

life forms; birds, jaguar (tiger-lion?), other unidentified quadrupeds; common use of secondary elements. Designs large, flamboyant, often crowded into decorative band and into panels.

Highly diagnostic tripod bowl, larger than Michilia; large, paired, opposed, pierced rim tabs, flaring and decorated by red-filled engraving, emphasizing grossness; leg usually in effigy form with prominent "knees," recurves to form broad "feet," "toes" indicated by vertical striations, "stocking" design engraved between "knee" and "foot."

Bowl interiors plain polished black or gray.

Other traits: Sometime during this period a ceremonial center, previously described, was constructed at Cerro de Moctehuma. Even earlier, during the later Canutillo phase, mining operations had begun in the area, and it is probable that the Gualterio stronghold had already been built. There was no great expansion in the number of sites occupied, however, and after about A.D. 800 sites of the Vesuvio phase declined in number. It appears that from that time on the population slowly ebbed, with the last occupation concentrated in small mesa-top villages such as Loma de las Flores in the 10th century. Although some Vesuvio phase elements appear to have joined the migrations of people from the Rio Colorado valley to Atotonilco and the Villa Union area, they quickly became submerged in those developments, and there are no known direct cultural descendants of the phase.

Calichal Phase (circa A.D. 500–650). In the Rio Colorado valley there appears to have been a great population decline, beginning around A.D. 500, with the disappearance of the Alta Vista phase as a cultural entity. Throughout the area most sites, including the Alta Vista ceremonial center, seem to have been abandoned at this time. In a few sites, such as the farming village of Potrero del Calichal, an agricultural pop-

ulation continued in occupance for another two or three centuries. In these villages pottery such as Suchil Red-on-Brown and Michilia Red-Filled Engraved continued to be made, but in smaller quantities, while Vista Paint Cloisonné and Negative A wares disappeared. Evolving from a combination of Suchil and Michilia, with some influence from the Gualterio wares of the Rio Colorado, two related new wares appeared: Mercado Red-on-Cream and Amaro Red-on-Cream. These wares, in association with smaller quantities of Michilia and Suchil, are diagnostics of the Calichal phase.

Amaro Red-on-Cream (now recognized as probably Mercado Red-on-Cream component). Maroon decoration on creamy white slip; broad exterior band around rim exterior, continuous with similar line along and inside rim; latter band often broken into short segments by two or more cream panels bearing geometric design; below this band on interior is a narrow circling band of parallel lines or bands of geometric elements (linear scrolls, zigzags, squiggled lines) principally on vessel walls; flattened-bowl interior bottoms characteristically decorated. Decoration of bowl interior centers consists of: (a) One central life form surrounded by dots; "alligator monster," turtle. (b) A duplicate pattern (1) with zone divided in two opposed parts by broad band, expanded at ends, framed by several parallel lines; life forms (undulating two-horned serpents, with associated sun or star symbol; birds including roadrunner; "alligator monster") surrounded by outline of dots; or (2) formed by a pair of large scrolls, framed by concentric lines, interlocking in center; with life forms or geometric forms outlined by dots, in opposite panels. (c) A quadrate division into four panels formed by intersecting broad bands, expanded at ends and framed by parallel lines; panels filled with (1) four identical life forms, birds (including roadrunner), two-horned serpents, "alligator monsters," outlined by dots; (2) identical geometric

784

figures, scrolls, etc., surrounded by dots, perhaps conventionalized life forms; (3) two opposed panels filled with life forms as in (1), other two with geometric figures as in (2).

Shallow simple bowls with flattened bottoms, low gently curving walls.

Mercado Red-on-Cream. A ware or type cluster with several component types; considerable internal variability; apparently derived from varying combinations of preceding Michilia Red-Filled Engraved and Suchil Red-on-Brown.

Maroon decoration on creamy white slip. Exterior decoration only; also a maroon band runs along lip and adjacent rim interior. On footed cup and water jar a cream band with a procession of circling horned serpents encircles vessel interior just below rim (in reality this is on flare of rim and corresponds to lip decoration); below this is the interior bounding maroon band. Other vessels have exterior decoration in one or two circling bands separated and bounded by narrow and broad parallel framing lines. Bands may consist entirely of continuous or repeated geometric elements —scrolls, terraced figurines, parallel wavy or zigzag lines, line-and-dot combination— or may be broken into panels by vertical or diagonal dividers, consisting of a broad line or solid panel with bordering narrow straight or wavy-line groups, or by line combinations without the broad-line center; intervening panels usually filled with life forms that are outlined by dots or solid line; sinuous serpents with plume or horns, hands, human head, usually two on opposite sides of vessel; two-horned serpents; "alligator monsters"; elaborate conventionalized birds, usually in defensive-offensive position with claws extended and speech scroll (roadrunner); or very frequently rebus-like pairings of horned serpents, like those described or spiraling up from base of band, and birds; rarely scorpions. Upper framing line, occasionally lower framing line, or both, ticked or serrate on upper

side; entire band is a copy of the Michilia Red-Filled Engraved serrate band in painted design.

Hemispherical bowls with incurving walls, deep composite-silhouette bowls, deep tripod bowls, with paired opposed and unpierced vertical rim tabs (rim tabs, feet, and vessel shape copied from Michilia Red-Filled Engraved), rare high annular-base cups, small narrow-neck flaring-rim jars, and flaring-rim ollas.

Other traits: Principally, the Calichal phase was a time of cultural loss. In ceramics the engraving, champlevé, paint cloisonné, and negative-paint techniques of decoration were discontinued during the period. In ceremonialism there seems to have been a breakdown in formalism, great divergence in ceremonial practice (as inferred from pottery decoration), a loss of older concepts, and undoubtedly the rise of schismatic cults. The ceremonial centers disappeared, and there is no evidence that the mines were still worked. The strongholds continued in use throughout the period. Architecture deteriorated. During this period there clearly was continued migration out of the area to the north and east, and probably to the south, with new colonies founded especially in Durango.

Retoño Phase (circa A.D. 650–750). During the last century or so of occupation of the Calichal site there was continued degeneration of architecture and ceramics, and probably in other arts as well. A new pottery type, Refugio Red-on-Brown, evolved out of Mercado Red-on-Cream; Mercado and Amaro were reduced in popularity, and Michilia and Suchil were no longer made. Refugio Red-on-Brown, hence is the diagnostic ware of the phase.

Refugio Red-on-Brown. Vessel "self-slip" (?) brown rather than cream, painted designs in red rather than maroon; decoration as in Mercado Red-on-Cream, except: designs much simpler and cruder in execution; former ticked or serrate bounding line now is a line with dots above it, sometimes

785

touching it; interior rim band solid red or, on composite-silhouette bowls and water jars, the outflaring rim is design band of life forms; decorations usually consist of single band below rim exterior with framing lines above and below; band divided into panels by groups of diagonal straight or wavy lines, outer line dotted, center line usually broad; life forms in panels; life forms surrounded by fewer larger dots; life forms primarily birds (eagle or macaw); squirrels with furry tails; coyote or doglike quadrupeds executed in "shorthand" style (usually lacking tail); male and female dancing figures in front view (rarely in profile) with hands raised, flowing hair locks or wig, heart-shaped face, occasionally with serpent in one hand, rattle in other; rare "alligator monster."

Little variation in vessel form; primarily tripod bowls resembling those of Mercado but with shorter incurving upper walls, larger legs and feet, rim tabs large and unpierced and often flaring when present; rim tabs occasionally replaced by basket handle joining two opposed sides of bowl and representing arching double-headed serpent (such basket handles characteristically flat on top and bottom and have molded serpents heads on each end near rim); large composite-silhouette bowls with sharply angled shoulder; possibly small jars with narrow neck and outflaring rim, or small composite-silhouette bowl without angled shoulders; effigy bowls in form of turtle or duck with head, tail, and three zoomorphic legs and feet.

Other traits: Only a few components are known for this period, principally those at Calichal itself and at Cerro Pedragoso. Little is known of the cultural content of the phase, aside from ceramics. The ceramics show continued deterioration in workmanship, and there is a marked reduction in variability of vessel shapes and designs, including ceremonial depictions. Indeed, there is some evidence that in these last few straggling, dying villages of the Suchil

branch there was a "purification" of ceramic decorative concepts and of ceremonial concepts, with some instances of a return to the practices of the classic Alta Vista phase. Diffused to the Chalchihuites colonies in Durango, these new-old concepts appear to have had an electrifying effect, leading to a remarkable revivalist movement in the Las Joyas phase there.

GENERAL DISCUSSION OF THE SUCHIL BRANCH. Archaeologically, the Chalchihuites sites present serious interpretational problems. Refuse deposits rarely are found where they were originally deposited, because refuse was commonly used for filling platforms; hence most refuse occurs as secondary deposits, with the constant possibility and frequent occurrence of admixture of assemblages of different periods. The cultural habit of keeping house floors (hence platform surfaces) and courts clean of debris makes house-floor or court-floor associations rare or suspect. Early post-abandonment collapse of poorly constructed platform walls constantly produced tertiary admixtures of secondary deposits. Only careful comparison of associations from site to site, platform fill to platform fill, and in special situations such as mortuary furniture, fill of cache pits and drainage canals, plus rare incidents of occurrence of refuse deposits in stratified position, has enabled construction of a reasonably dependable sequence of ceramic types and assemblages, with pertinent associations of other artifact types, architectural features, etc. Two basic examples of actual stratification, one very tenuous, led to development of the present general stratigraphic sequence of phases and their relationship between river valleys, but the sequence once ascertained has been supported and amplified by many other types of evidence so that it may be regarded as fairly firm. Actual estimates of time are another matter, and it is assumed that the estimates given here are subject to considerable future modification as new evidence accumulates. Especially dubious are the beginning date for the Canutillo phase, estimated at circa A.D. 200 when it may have been a century or more earlier, and the estimated terminal date of A.D. 750 for the Retoño phase, which may have been a century or more later.

Radiocarbon dates available are of considerable help in establishing probable time spans for the various phases, and, significantly, they are for the most part consistent with other evidence derived both locally and from Mesoamerica in general. Again, the main problem is one of establishing firm relationships between dated radiocarbon samples and archaeological assemblages, in view of the peculiar nature of Chalchihuites refuse deposits. For the Canutillo phase in the Rio Colorado valley, in refuse in apparent original depositional location, underlying Alta Vista phase refuse, we have dates of A.D. 56 and A.D. 110; for reasonably pure Canutillo phase refuse in altar fill at Moctehuma in the Rio Suchil valley we have dates of A.D. 95 and A.D. 410. From somewhat mixed refuse deposits at Vesuvio in the Rio Suchil valley we have dates of A.D. 118 and A.D. 120. In the Rio Suchil valley there are probable Vesuvio phase dates of A.D. 530, 750, and 795 at Cerro de Moctehuma; A.D. 540, 740, and 811 at Vesuvio; and definite but late Vesuvio phase dates of A.D. 810 and 990 at Loma de las Flores. For the Alta Vista phase there is one fairly good association at Cofradia with a date of A.D. 557, which appears to be slightly late; and a sample dated at 330 tentatively associated with Alta Vista phase deposits at Calichal. There is no good Calichal phase date; for the roughly contemporaneous but slightly later Ayala phase in the Guadiana sequence there are dates of A.D. 400 (too early), 590, and 640. There is a possible Retoño phase date of 785 from Calichal; dates of 800, 920, and 1005 at the same site may refer to the Retoño phase there, but more probably apply at least in part to a post-Mesoamerican occupation, since two of them are from intrusive pits. Dates of 390 and 600 from the Cueva de Maria Lizardo in the Ejido Cardenas mining group almost certainly apply to the Canutillo phase occupation, but there is no direct association of diagnostic artifactual material. Dates of 484 B.C. and 2462 B.C. from the Vesuvio site are regarded as erroneous, for unknown reasons, inasmuch as they represent specimens in mixed Vesuvio-Canutillo phase association, and the actual dates are unbelievably early.

In summary, the earliest Mesoamerican occupation of the area, the Canutillo phase, apparently represents a simple agricultural population derived largely from a Preclassic cultural base. This simple agricultural adaptation continued in occupation for many centuries in the Rio Colorado valley, with some minor elaboration. The appearance of the Alta Vista phase in the Rio Colorado valley at circa A.D. 300 implanted a formalized Mesoamerican Classic cultural pattern in that area: almost certainly this was a primitive exploitative state inspired by and perhaps even controlled by Classic Teotihuacan, far to the south. With the decline of Teotihuacan after A.D. 500, its influence seems to have been withdrawn from the Chalchihuites area. For reasons as yet unknown, the Mesoamerican cultural occupance there continued to decline in cultural level and actual population for several centuries and finally disappeared entirely toward the end of the 10th century. But meanwhile, perhaps as early as A.D. 550, Mesoamerican colonies derived from the Suchil branch had been established to the northwest in Durango, where they continued in existence until about 1350, when Mesoamerican occupance of that area, the Guadiana branch of the Chalchihuites culture, also was terminated.

Guadiana Branch of the Chalchihuites Culture

In the Guadiana branch are classified the principally Mesoamerican archaeological sites of the Guadiana valley, near the capital city of Victoria de Durango, those lying

787

along the eastern foothills of the Sierra Madre Occidental as far to the northwest as Zape in northern Durango; and also sites such as La Atalaya, near Villa Union, and Antonio Amaro, which are intermediate in location and in culture between the Suchil and Guadiana areas. With rare exceptions, such as La Atalaya (on a low knoll in an open alluvial valley), Guadiana branch sites are situated either on high foothills or mesas, or clustered about their bases. Two major sites are known: the Schroeder site on the Cerro de Casa Colorado, lying within a curve of the Rio Tunal some 8 km. south of Victoria de Durango; and Navacoyan, on a hill on the same river about 8 km. east of the city. The Southern Illinois University, under the direction of Kelley and associates, excavated at the Schroeder site in 1954, 1956, and 1958. Navacoyan was largely destroyed through promiscuous excavation by local villagers, who found a ready market for their loot in nearby Victoria de Durango. Most of the incredibly rich spoils from this vandalism became part of the collection of the late Federico Schroeder of Durango; the collection has since been smuggled into the United States, but its disposition following Schroeder's death is unknown. The late Agnes M. Howard also made a large surface collection at the site (Howard, 1957). The Schroeder site appears to have been primarily a ceremonial center and residential area; Navacoyan, a tremendous burial ground and also perhaps a ceremonial center and priestly residential area. Notably lacking in the Guadiana valley are true farm sites. Whereas farm villages of the Suchil area belong to the same cultural phase as the ceremonial centers, those of the Guadiana area belong to the Loma San Gabriel culture, whose participants continued to reside in the region after the Chalchihuites colonization.

The Schroeder site occupies two east-west-trending hills, the intervening "saddle," and adjacent lowlands, south and east of the Rio Tunal, within a curve of the river. The alluvial lowlands of the narrow river valley probably were the principal fields used then as today. The eastern hilltop was crowned with a pyramid; the entire northern or occupational face of the higher western hill was terraced with such regularity that it must have resembled a tremendous pyramid. Scattered over hilltops, saddle, natural terraces, and nearby flats are the ruins of many masonry structures. Former roadways connecting them can be traced. On the lowland at the northeast edge of the site are large natural boulders, some partially shaped and polished. One has a petroglyph—a stick figure of a man with one arm up and one down—and others have mortar holes and grinding areas. Mortar holes occur elsewhere in the site on boulders and bedrock ledges.

A number of the structures have been partially excavated. Most of them pertain to the Chalchihuites culture, but there was occupation by the Loma San Gabriel culture also. Str. 20, on the topmost part of the high western hill, was a large rectangular masonry platform which had only Loma ceramics in its exposed fill and associated debris.

Aside from the pyramid, a ball court, and one circular platform with stairway, the Chalchihuites structures conform to a standard pattern. A central court was surrounded in whole or in part by platforms, on which presumably stood perishable houses. Some of these, such as the Central (South) Court of Str. 1, seem to have been constructed as units: the court, the surrounding platforms, stairs entering the court from the four cardinal directions, stairs descending the platforms to outside banquettes or to the ground, masonry drains beneath the platforms draining the courts. Others such as Str. 5 grew from simple alignments of platforms into L-shapes, or, by addition of an extra wing and enclosure of the court with a wall, into closed box shapes. Where structures rested on sloping ground the downhill side was brought to proper level

788

by offset stages of construction, giving a stepped effect. Open spaces between platforms were walled in and apparently served as rooms; these were later filled and used as burial areas and cache pits, and finally were surfaced and transformed into platform extensions. Parts of structures were often cut from bedrock, carefully shaped to form floor and walls as in the Central Court of Str. 1. In Str. 9 bedrock was cut to form most of one wall, complete with a bench, part of another wall, and a section of the floor.

Remodeling of structures occurred constantly. New wings were added, sometimes as in the Str. 1 entire new court-platform units; platforms were extended, raised, and refloored. Courtways became partially filled with debris, or were refloored after new drains were cut, or in some instances were filled in on one side and paved to form new platform areas.

Platforms were built by constructing masonry walls on four sides, faced on the exterior, and by filling the enclosure with site refuse and/or rubble, and by paving the fill at the level of the top of the walls with cobblestones or slabs which were then covered with adobe plaster. Often only the platform edges were stone-paved, with adobe plaster placed directly on the fill. Many of the platforms had adobe-lined basins, possibly hearths, in their centers. The late northwest platform of Str. 1 had a rectangular adobe block altar near one side, stone slab compartments on another. The platforms were repeatedly resurfaced; usually the clay basins were replastered at the same time. No trace of the perishable structures that once occupied the platforms was found. Platform walls were plastered in red.

The stone masonry ranged between two extremes. Popular early, but surviving late also, were walls made of horizontally placed stones, usually fairly regular, sometimes shaped in rectangular "pillow" blocks with rounded edges and corners. Beginning early but attaining great popularity late

was masonry utilizing large vertical stone slabs, sometimes partially shaped to fit with adjoining slabs, the platform surface, or the underlying bedrock. This masonry was occasionally finished off quite handsomely by placing carefully selected stones horizontally between the vertical slabs. Occasionally, as in Str. 12, horizontal block masonry was finished by carefully placed thin vertical stone slabs. Mortar and plaster appear to have been of the adobe type entirely, without use of lime. A few adobe bricks were found but no construction using them was identified. Hillside terraces were made by building masonry walls in semicircular plan on the downhill side and filling with earth and rubble behind. They were used for houses, for burials, and perhaps as garden terraces.

The pyramid, on top of the eastern hill, was constructed in part around a bedrock core. On three sides it had two stages; on the south side there may have been more inasmuch as the steep hillside below has much masonry rubble. Its form was essentially rectangular, measuring approximately 25 m. by 32 m., but this form had been modified on the northeast corner to produce two additional inside corners on each stage. A stairway, with a balustrade on the second stage, ascended the east side; there were traces of a stair on the south side as well. On the north side were elusive traces of a stair, but nothing definite. Here the pyramid edge had in part covered a series of earlier platforms; a ramp may have ascended the pyramid at this point. There was a sunken rectangular court in the top of the pyramid, entered by stairways on the cardinal directions, as well as traces of other construction.

Occupying the remaining area of the eastern hilltop and extending to the base of the pyramid is Str. 7, a large and heterogeneous collection of platforms, walkways, courts, and stairs. This structure and the pyramid were built during the earliest phase of the occupation of the site; the oldest pottery

789

comes from the pyramid fill. Thereafter, Str. 7 was abandoned, but the pyramid seems to have had some subsequent usage, including later repairs.

Lying almost at the foot of the pyramid in the eastern edge of the saddle was Str. 6, tentatively identified as a ball court. Here parallel platforms with taluded basal zones and banquettes formed a north-south-oriented rectangular court (4.2 m. by 10.4 m.) open at both ends. The surface of the hill outside each end of this court was cleared over a rectangular area roughly marked by occasional boulders. It appears to be a very small and crude ball court, probably constructed early in the site's occupation (Ayala or Las Joyas phase).

Burials occurred in the fill of rooms, platforms, courts, banquettes, and terraces, and were also intrusive into the fill or covering debris of abandoned structures. They were flexed, extended, or secondary, with no apparent consistent orientation or phase difference. One infant burial in an olla was associated with the final occupation of the site. Secondary burials often consisted only of a few bones, perhaps a mandible and a femur. Burial accompaniments varied but were never extremely rich.

The general ceramic complex of the Guadiana branch of the Chalchihuites culture consists of polished red, buff, and black wares; plain, "fingernail"-worked, brushed, and brown utility wares carrying on the general complex of the Suchil branch; plus red-on-brown, red-on-cream, red-on-white, white-on-red, and rare polychrome painted wares; as well as rare red-filled engraved black and tan wares; plus incised molcajetes and a red-on-brown ware with fluted zones on or below rim exteriors. Vessel forms were tripod bowls and jars, basket-handle tripod bowls, annular-base vessels (rare), flattened and hemispherical simple bowls, composite-silhouette and seed bowls, narrow-neck jars, wide-mouth jars or ollas, and effigy vessels.

The pecked, polished, and chipped stone

artifacts of the Suchil branch continued in use in the various phases of the Guadiana branch. In addition, there are new stone-artifact types, some of them confined to one or more phases only. Such new types include carved stone bowls, ring stones, cup stones, "medicine stones," paint palettes, small pestles, effigy pestles, incense burners on nested inverted cones, stalactite polishing stones, large stone discs (including one large ball-court style of stone ring), obsidian flake knives, composite-stone mirror backs (with mosaic mirror of fitted pyrite pieces), and turquoise mosaic pendants.

Copper bells, a finger ring, needles and awls or ornaments, hooks, and a chain (with long triangular shell pendants attached to side links and a rectangular turquoise mosaic pendant at the bottom) represent the Chalchihuites copper complex. Gold beads are reported in an amateur collection.

Artifacts of clay other than pottery include pipes of Guasave style, spindle whorls (small engraved flattened spherical, large spherical incised, biconical forms with notched edges, and conical "collar-button" types with white filled engraved designs), rare bird-effigy whistles and figurines in a variety of styles (apparently trade objects), cylindrical and "bird-wing" stamps, potsherd discs, tapered cylindrical beads, and miniature pots.

Shell work is plentiful, varied, and skillfully done. A variety of beads—pierced disc, tubular, tinklers, Hohokam-type bilobed, finger-ring style with notched edges—occur but pendants were the Chalchihuites specialty. Triangular and ellipsoidal pendants are common, but most interesting are the tabular pendants in conventionalized effigy form. Small human heads, turtles, birds, and other life forms were carved in the round with great skill (Howard, 1957, fig. 44). Bracelets were present but rare. Bone awls occur.

SEQUENCE OF PHASES AND CHRONOLOGY OF THE GUADIANA BRANCH. Refuse heaps as such are generally lacking at the Schroeder site. However, the custom of using refuse as platform fills, the superposition of platforms, the accumulation of refuse in courts, and the differential times of abandonment of structures have made possible the identification of four trait complexes, primarily ceramic, in the Guadiana branch, and their placement as sequential phases: from early to late, Ayala, Las Joyas, Rio Tunal, and Calera. The sequence of phases is further substantiated by the presence of intrusives from the previously established Sinaloa sequence and by the presence of Mesoamerican horizon-markers, including molcajetes, spindle whorls, pipes, and copper artifacts.

Thus, at the Schroeder site all four Guadiana ceramic associations occur in "pure" or unmixed assemblages. In Str. 5, platform fills of lower and older platforms contain Ayala materials; those from the fill of superimposed platforms and a later platform in the court contain Las Joyas phase types. The central court and associated platforms of Str. 1 rest upon leveling refuse containing Las Joyas specimens; similar types occur in the lower fill of the court, in associated ventilators, and in the fill of attached platforms.

The older (Las Joyas) fill of the court was leveled and sealed off by new floors, and new ventilators were constructed to drain the new high court. Fill in the upper court and ventilators contained Rio Tunal types; these also occurred in the fill of a new series of platforms constructed along the north side of the court and in refuse that accumulated over the north banquette and the terrace north of it. Ceramics of the subsequent Calera phase did not occur in any of the previous refuse deposits of Str. 1 but appeared in the surficial layers of refuse containing Rio Tunal materials and in the fill and on the floor of the Southwest Platform which was added to and partially superimposed on the earlier construction. Horizon-markers, as noted, which occur late in Mesoamerica, occur late in the phase sequence established on the evidence cited

above, plus many supplementary instances of segregation and superposition of assemblages.

The Guadiana branch sequence of ceramic phases is correlated with the Suchil branch sequence in the following ways: (1) Pottery types Amaro Red-on-Cream and Mercado Red-on-Cream, characteristic of the Calichal phase of the Suchil branch, clearly evolve there from preceding Michilia Red-Filled Engraved and Suchil Red-on-Brown, which continue to be made there in smaller numbers during this period. In the Guadiana branch, Amaro and Mercado occur as almost identical types, but with only rare associations of Michilia and Suchil, as diagnostic wares of the Ayala phase, the earliest period in the sequence. There are no local antecedents for Amaro and Mercado in the Guadiana sequence. On various grounds the Calichal phase is estimated to date at circa A.D. 500–650; the Ayala phase, at 550–700. It is clear that early in the Calichal phase in the Suchil branch at least some potters emigrated to the Guadiana valley in Durango, where they were the earliest Mesoamerican settlers, and continued to make there the pottery types Amaro and Mercado as they had made them earlier in their original homes. The later phases of the Guadiana sequence develop from the Ayala phase base, plus some external influences. (2) In the Suchil area the pottery type Refugio Red-on-Brown evolves through recognizable transitional stages from Mercado Red-on-Cream, and is there diagnostic of the Retoño phase between A.D. 650 and 750. The same Refugio Red-on-Brown pottery appears in the Guadiana sequence as an intrusive, without local developmental forms, at the very end of the Ayala phase, around 700. There it quickly evolves locally into Neveria Red-on-Brown, which becomes the diagnostic ware of the subsequent Las Joyas phase, dated circa 700–950. From these data it seems certain that the Guadiana phase sequence is an offshoot of the Suchil branch

791

during the Calichal phase of the Rio Colorado, in that sequence, and that while the culture of the hearth area survived there, it continued to affect the Durango developments, which otherwise took place locally.

A tentative chronology for the Guadiana branch sequence has been developed, based on stylistic correlation with Southwestern and Mesoamerican master sequences—and a compromise between their respective chronologies—plus the evidence of several radiocarbon dates. Detailed crossties with the phases of the Sinaloa sequence make it possible to apply reasoning regarding chronology there to the Durango sequence also (Kelley and Winters, 1960).

The Durango-Sinaloa sequences are correlated as follows: Alta Vista–Ayala phases equate with Tierra del Padre and Baluarte phases (Early and Middle Chametla); Las Joyas–Rio Tunal phases correlate with the Aztatlan stage and its divisions; Rio Tunal (late) and Calera phases equate with La Divisa and Yebalito phases (Early and Middle Culiacan). Ekholm places the Chametla culture as late Classic, the Aztatlan as early Postclassic, Culiacan as full (and late) Postclassic (Ekholm, 1958, p. 17), essentially the placement of the corresponding Durango phases.

The west Mexican white-on-red wares are generally placed as late Postclassic (Lister, 1955, p. 27); in Durango, Nayar White-on-Red is diagnostic of the Calera phase. Copper artifacts, pipes, and molcajetes are regarded as diagnostic of the Postclassic in Mesoamerica (Lister, 1955, pp. 19, 36–38, 46–48); in Durango these occur only in the Rio Tunal–Calera phases, except for molcajetes, which appear in late Las Joyas times. Spindle whorls first appear during the late Classic in Mesoamerica but are numerous and important only in the Postclassic (Lister, 1955, pp. 38–40); in Durango they appear as intrusives from the Chametla culture in the Ayala phase, but do not become important until the Las Joyas phase and later.

792

These data indicate that the Rio Tunal and Calera phases are full Postclassic in affiliation, and that the Las Joyas phase may in part be so. Accordingly, the Ayala phase and the preceding Alta Vista phase of the Suchil branch should be Classic in age and affiliation; probably Ayala should be equated with Teotihuacan IV, Alta Vista with all or part of Teotihuacan III. Inasmuch as the equivalent Chametla periods have also been assigned a Classic status, this correlation seems in line with the evidence. However, there are important implications here for Mesoamerican culture history in general. Paint cloisonné is one of the diagnostic wares of Alta Vista; the tendency has been to regard paint cloisonné as Postclassic in age, the related alfresco technique as Classic (Ekholm, 1942, pp. 91–96). However, the designs and the general appearance of the paint cloisonné of Alta Vista, Totoate, Estanzuela, and Jiquilpan are much closer to the alfresco wares of Classic Teotihuacan than to equivalent Postclassic paint cloisonné. At Jiquilpan paint cloisonné vessels were accompanied by an alabaster double cup and shell trumpet decorated alfresco; on this evidence both Noguera and Kidder accept the Jiquilpan finds as Classic (Noguera, 1948, p. 38; Kidder, in discussion section of same article, p. 39). Shell trumpets also occur with the paint cloisonné of Totoate and Alta Vista, but it is not known if they were decorated.

Actually, it would appear that paint cloisonné in northwest Mexico is the typological equivalent of alfresco ware in central and southern Mexico. Both must go back at least to Classic times, both probably, in their respective areas, to the Preclassic, with the alfresco technique largely disappearing with the fall of Teotihuacan. With this correlation, the red-filled engraved pottery is also aligned with the champlevé ware of Classic Teotihuacan, where it belongs in technology and style. Similarly, Suchil Red-on-Brown of the Alta Vista phase with its quadrate-design bowl interiors is probably to be derived from Chupicuaro red-on-brown wares rather than from the much later Coyotlatelco wares. Everything considered, Alta Vista looks full Classic—Xolalpan—in age and affiliation, whereas Ayala probably equates with the late Classic of Teotihuacan IV, or Azcapotzalco.

Space does not allow a detailed treatment of trait and stylistic relationships between the Chalchihuites development and that of the Southwestern Hohokam. In outline, however, there is strong evidence that Alta Vista began to influence the Hohokam in the late Pioneer period, before A.D. 500; there are firm correlations between the Calichal-Ayala phases and the Colonial Hohokam, and equally firm correlations between the Las Joyas phase and the terminal Colonial and early Sedentary Hohokam. Otinapa Red-on-White ware of the Rio Tunal phase is stylistically related to Three-Circle Red-on-White of the Mogollon, corresponding in time to the Sedentary Hohokam, and Nayar White-on-Red ware of the terminal, or Calera, phase of Chalchihuites is clearly related to (and almost certainly contemporaneous with) various Southwestern White-on-Red wares that are largely Classic Hohokam in age. A three-way correlation of the Durango–Sinaloa–Hohokam-Mogollon sequences supports the general sequential and temporal placement of the Durango sequence as given here, and by extension indicates that estimated dates for the beginning and end of the Classic in central Mexico may be slightly earlier than the currently orthodox dates applied by Mesoamericanists.

Radiocarbon dates available for the Schroeder site include five dated samples in association with Ayala phase ceramics: 550 B.C. (certainly erroneous), A.D. 400 (slightly too early), A.D. 485, A.D. 640, and A.D. 800 (too late, probably Las Joyas phase); four dates in excellent Las Joyas phase association: A.D. 660, A.D. 675, A.D. 700, and A.D. 730. The Las Joyas dates

appear to be too early, but within the probable error they are excellent and close-grouped dates. The two additional radiocarbon dates available for the Schroeder site, A.D. 730 and 1223, are not clearly associated with specific phases. Taken together, the radiocarbon determinations indicate Schroeder site dates ranging from A.D. 400 (discarding the obviously erroneous 550 B.C. date) to 1223; the estimated range of dates is from A.D. 550 to 1350, a reasonable correspondence.

Listed below are some of the principal phase diagnostics, plus new, unique, or otherwise significant traits. Some traits of the culture appear to have existed throughout the Guadiana sequence occupation: basic mortuary custom, masonry platforms, courts, stairs, polished red, buff, and black pottery (with some percentage variations), plain and brushed brown utility, basic pottery vessel forms, full and three-quarter grooved axes, scoop-type troughed metates, manos, chipped arrowpoints (increasing in percentage at end of occupation), side-notched end scrapers, rather elaborate work in shell, and others. A number of the traits listed below may extend throughout the sequence, but we have inadequate control of the position of "luxury" items, and we have very few data for the final Calera phase.

Ayala Phase (circa A.D. 550–700). Pyramid with one zigzag corner and sunken court with four directionally oriented stair-entries; small ball court(?), central alley with opposed stepped platforms, taluds, double open ends (perhaps very late in phase); first appearance of large vertical slab masonry. Clay-lined basins in platforms. Bedrock cut and ground to complete platform and room outlines.

Amaro Red-on-Cream (see Calichal phase, Suchil branch, for description).

Mercado Red-on-Cream (see Calichal phase, Suchil branch, for description).

West coast trade items (Kelley and Winters, 1960, figs. 3, 4) especially: Early Chametla-Middle Chametla (transitional) Polychrome, Middle Chametla Polychrome and Polychrome Engraved, Middle Chametla Black-Band Engraved, Chametla Red-Rim Ware and Red Rim Utility, Chametla Scalloped Rim, Marbelized Interior Ware and Mano Colorado Ware (Chametla), Chametla White-Filleted figurines. Rare small incised flattened spherical spindle whorls; stone balls, cup stones, ring stones; tapered tubular pottery beads.

Inferentially, strong emphasis in ceremonialism on "world quarters" with appropriate deities; repeated rebus-like pairing of bird and serpent; indication of duplicate Quetzalcoatl concept, one in each of two opposed world divisions, probably east and west, with associated astronomical symbols, star or sun signs; in ceremonial area (Str. 7) near base of pyramid life forms represented were overwhelmingly horned serpents, suggesting its dedication to a serpent cult.

Las Joyas Phase (circa A.D. 700–950). Extensive building and remodeling operations at Schroeder site; increased popularity of large vertical slab masonry and cut-bedrock features in architecture; oval-shaped "pithouse" with projecting slab-lined entryway on north and rectangular hearth in interior.

Refugio Red-on-Brown (see Retoño phase, Suchil branch, for description).

Neveria Red-on-Brown. Principal diagnostic of phase; locally survives into Rio Tunal phase, more frequently vessel form survives but with slip, paint, designs of Otinapa Red-on-White.

Decoration in reddish brown on yellowish brown "self-slip"(?); decoration entirely in exterior band below rim and on basket handles; decoration of bowl rim band characteristically framed by two lines above and below, plus one along lip extending to interior rim; decorative band divided into panels by characteristic diagonal dividers consisting of one broad central line, several parallel bounding lines on each side of it, external line ticked on outside each side;

occasionally central broad line is hourglass figure and narrow lines each side are in form of nested Vs pointing on each side toward waist of hourglass figure, with long ticking lines on inside of inside V on each side, giving it the appearance, significantly, of an open, toothed jaw on each side of dividers. Panels are filled with life forms, invariable procession of quadrupeds (usually with tails), squirrels, dogs or coyotes, portrayed as if marching in same direction around vessel, in case of hourglass dividers as if marching out of and into the toothed jaws; life forms large with no surrounding dots or with a few near the animal at one point.

Basket handles decorated on upper surface in geometric designs apparently representing serpent markings, with procession of birds or quadrupeds in alternating triangular or rectangular panels or in open series between two framing lines each side, or by procession of sun and star symbols; occasionally quadrupeds shown as if marching into toothed mouths like dividers on rim bands; triangular modeled serpent head with open mouth pointing to rim on each side of vessel, with features painted on some serpent heads modeled as knobs, with conventionalized painted features; great variety in decoration of basket handles.

Vessel forms invariably tripods, basket handled, or duck or turtle three-legged effigies; bowls large, upper vessel walls incurve rapidly, often rounded, belly of bowl hemispherical; tripod legs large and out-flaring, with abrupt hip, round in cross-section above changing to broad transverse wedge at foot; basket handles large usually oval or circular in cross-section, invariably with knob on outside a few centimeters above rim junction on each side, knob occasionally is a carefully modeled open head of serpent.

Interior-decorated bowls in Suchil-Amaro tradition disappear; replaced by imported interior-painted bowls from Sinaloa:

Lolandis Red Rim ("red-rim decorated"

794

of Kelly, 1938, pp. 18, 19; pl. 7,*a–f,j*; "Decorated Red-rimmed Red-on-buff" of Sauer and Brand, 1932). This appears suddenly at beginning of Las Joyas phase with no local developmental antecedents, but in such quantity that trade alone does not seem an adequate explanation of its presence; perhaps a migrant group is represented (as with the Rio Grande Tiwa group on the Hopi First Mesa). It is one of the principal decorated wares of the phase.

Decoration is in red on a buff or orange wash; a broad red band, continuous over the lip, encircles bowl interiors and exteriors at the rim; below this on interior or exterior walls is an encircling band framed by several parallel lines, with geometric elements: triangles, zigzags, stripes, scrolls, circles, rare conventionalized animals (?) used as fillers. Some bowl interiors below rim stripe and fringing parallel line have massive complicated design filling entire area; plumes common in such designs; one reconstructed bowl interior is filled with a "disassociated" bird: a line of bird heads along one side, a central body, two detached wings or plumes each side, and balancing heads across bowl a zigzag line, perhaps a serpent (Kelley and Winters, 1960, fig. 4,*w*).

Bowl forms only, deep hemispherical bowls with slightly incurving rims, direct or swollen, rounded or squared lips, no legs.

El Campo Buff. A new utility ware, probably derived from Loma plain ware; simple non-legged buff bowls with encircling deep modeled grooves below rim on exterior.

Small quantities of Sinaloa trade wares from the Acaponeta phase of the Aztatlan horizon; Aztatlan Ware, Cerro Izabal Incised, Aguaruto Exterior Incised, others. Also Acaponeta (Chametla-Aztatlan) type incised spherical spindle whorls (Kelley and Winters, 1960, fig. 4,*m,n,o*).

Terraced stone incense burners (late?).

"Medicine stones."

Iron pyrites mirrors on stone backs; py-

rites on central disc, rim area stuccoed, probably with design; back plain (?); two holes, not connected, near opposed edges of disc. May have been present throughout but not identified for Ayala phase.

Cylindrical and flat (bird-wing) clay stamps.

Effigies and pendants in stone and shell.

Conical spindle whorls with scalloped edges (late in phase, perhaps of Aztatlan derivation).

Inferentially, Neveria basket handle represents (a) double-headed serpent, possibly twin serpent deities (Quetzalcoatls) of east and west; (b) sun's path, along which move sun symbols, birds, quadrupeds. Quadrupeds on handle and on rim probably represent Xolotls, dog-twins of Quetzalcoatl (or squirrels, as substitutes for dogs, as in Huichol). Scenes in which quadrupeds, Xolotls, enter toothed jaws (dividers) on vessel rim and, rarely, on lower arcs or handles, almost certainly represent the Quetzalcoatl twin, ushering the sun deity, being swallowed by the earth monster, Tlalticuhtli. To judge by modern Huichol ceremonial symbolism this set of inferences may be mythologically correct, but the actual deities may be local counterparts of the central Mexican gods listed.

Rio Tunal Phase (circa A.D. 950–1150). There was very little building activity at the Schroeder site during this phase, although older structures were remodeled. Str. 9, built during this phase, was cut to a remarkable degree from bedrock; at its southeast corner a rectangular "altar" had been cut from bedrock, with a lipped basin on top and a human line-figure on its north face. Similarly, aside from the site of Navacoyan, where there is a rich representation of both Rio Tunal and Calera phases, there was only scattered occupation of the Guadiana valley during this phase. However, the Santa Ana site at Zape, in northern Durango, appears to have been occupied extensively during this period; representing the maximum known extension of the Chalchihuites-Mesoamerican frontier toward the north. Likewise, there was considerable Chalchihuites influence on Loma San Gabriel components at this time. In many ways the Rio Tunal occupance represents a profound break with earlier traditions in ceramics and architecture.

Otinapa Red-on-White. This is the principal diagnostic ware of the phase. Locally, Neveria Red-on-Brown survived into this phase; Morcillo Molcajetes lasted throughout; late in the phase Canatlan Red-Band became important. But at Santa Ana, apparently a one-phase (Rio Tunal) site, Otinapa is the only painted ware known. In background color, layout, design element and some vessel forms, it represents a ceramic innovation in the Chalchihuites culture, resembling in some ways the Three Circle Red-on-White of the Mogollon culture to the north. However, some designs and vessel forms carry over, and new elements may have been diffused into the area and grafted onto the local ceramic development. It is possible that very late Gualterio Red-on-Cream of the terminal Vesuvio phase of the Suchil branch may have influenced this development.

Decoration is in a strong red on a creamy to chalky-white slip; in the most common olla forms decoration was applied to a broad zone of one or more bands covering upper half to two-thirds of vessels as well as a decorative zone along inside of rim. In bowl forms usually one decorative band, often quite broad, runs along the vessel exterior below the rim; surviving basket-handle bowls have decoration on handles.

Decoration is almost entirely exterior, geometric, and rectilinear rather than curvilinear; and is bold, exuberant, large, in execution. Most common decoration consists of broad bands of opposed right-angle triangles with hypotenuse terraced, separated and connected by intervening parallel straight and zigzag lines; often in connection with rectilinear interlocking scrolls

with opposed ticked or terraced triangular bodies. Opposed triangles, concentric triangles and ∪ figures, negative panels, checkerboard are common. Small elements including sun and star symbols survive from earlier design, primarily on the surviving older basket handles, but life forms are entirely absent, save for one or two dubious figures and the modeled serpents of the rare basket handles.

Ollas (globular with broad neck and mouth and flaring rim; globular with medium neck and mouth and slightly flaring rim; and globular with no neck, broad mouth, slightly inturned rim) are most common forms, followed by large bowls with hemispherical bottoms, shoulder angles, and convex converging upper walls. Relatively rare are Neveria-type, basket-handle tripod bowls decorated in Otinapa designs, either on the Neveria brown slip (or self-slip) or the Otinapa white slip.

Morcillo Molcajetes. These tripod "chili grinders" appeared late in the Las Joyas phase and are common in Rio Tunal times.

Small, rather crudely made, brown ware bowls with stocky tripod legs bearing pronounced humps halfway down. Body of bowl is a shallow hemisphere broken near the top by a fairly sharp shoulder, above which the vessel walls curve abruptly inward producing an inward-slanted rim area, somewhat concave on the exterior.

Decoration is restricted, aside from an occasional red lip band, to the "chili grater" interior. A crudely drafted incised circle occupies the center of the vessel interior bottom. This is divided by transverse incised lines into four quadrants, which are filled with incised lines, usually running in opposed directions from quadrant to quadrant, or with incised lines forming nested triangles. These lines sometimes extend outside the circle, giving it a ticked effect.

Canatlan Red-Band. This ware appears in the Rio Tunal phase, perhaps late, and locally is very common during the phase; it accompanies Nayar and Madero wares in the subsequent Calera phase. It appears to derive from the preceding redwares, rather than from decorated types, but may represent an imported idea.

Vessel forms include large ollas with globular bodies and flaring rims, shallow bowls, and seed bowls. The sandy paste is slipped in bright orange, polished on the exterior and part of the interior of ollas, the interior of bowls. The olla exterior is often painted bright red except for a band of exposed slip along the rim exterior and interior. Sometimes the red paint is applied in a series of broad bands, horizontal and vertical, which contrast strongly with the slip. The shallow bowls have a broad red band around the interior or exterior of the rim, sometimes both. Seed bowls are decorated with a broad exterior red band extending from the lip to below the extreme curvature of the bowl. Canatlan vessels were polished after painting so that smudges of paint occur on the exposed areas of orange slip.

Spindle whorls: conical with expanded flattened tip, giving a "collar-button" appearance; black or buff, decorated with incised geometric designs, filled with white pigment, on upper surface. These may be late in the phase; they survive into the Calera phase.

Pottery smoking pipes: possible fragmentary pipe stems occur in late Las Joyas deposits, and appear also during the Rio Tunal phase and apparently survive through the Calera phase. These are basically elbow pipes, with bowls like miniature pots placed squarely or at angle on the platform base (Howard, 1957, fig. 45,c); some bases are footed. Stems are long and flattened; the base color is black or buff; most pipes have geometric incised decoration filled with white pigment. Pipes were not common at the Schroeder site, but a number were found at Navacoyan.

Stone pestles, small dumbbell-like; plain

slab rectangular paint palettes; large carefully shaped stone discs, perhaps column pediments or caps or bases for god statuettes (Huichol).

Copper bells, small globular and pear-shaped and large pear-shaped with upper "neck" portion in "wire technique." Also copper needle, awl, ring, hooks, pendant and chain (with associated shell pendants and turquoise mosaic). (Kelley and Winters, 1960, fig. 4). Copper artifacts also occur in Calera phase debris.

West coast trade wares, including Guasave and Sinaloa polychromes from the late Aztatlan Guasave phase; also many other trade sherds unidentified as to source.

Inferentially, either a pronounced drop-off in Mesoamerican ceremonial symbolism or its transference from pottery to a perishable medium (such as the Huichol votive baskets, which carry much ceremonial symbolism in their decoration).

Calera Phase (circa A.D. 1150–1350). Components found principally in central and southern Durango; no pure component known; the Calera phase existed at the Schroeder site literally "among the ruins." Str. 1 there was almost entirely in ruins when a new Calera phase platform was built on its southwest edge. This platform had a floor surfaced with red plaster, with many replacement layers present. There was an adobe basin with a small cuplike recess in bottom; the basin had been relined each time the floor was replastered. Near it was a plastered adobe rectangular block set on the floor, apparently an altar. Small vertical stone slabs formed a compartment on the south and a wall on the west. Piles of stone with hollow centers on the platform surface suggested placements for wooden post butts. Intrusive into the platform was a plain brown ware olla containing an infant burial. Str. 4, a circular platform with vertical slab walls and a stair on the northwest, may have been built at this time. In general the Schroeder site seems to

797

have been used only as a shrine area in Calera phase times, whereas Navacoyan was used as a burial ground. Calera phase marks the appearance of many foreign elements in the Chalchihuites culture; some of these, such as Nayar White-on-Red pottery and its component elements, show close relationships with similar types widespread in both western Mesoamerica and the Southwest United States.

Nayar White-on-Red. Diagnostic ware for the phase (Peithman, 1961). Thick white paint (which often flakes away) used for decoration on bright red slip, which was often not applied to vessel base, making the ware technically a polychrome; decoration applied in broad band above the vessel shoulder and on interior of flared rim.

Decorative pattern characterized by layout of alternating or repeated elements in encircling panel framed by lines or by narrow bands of checkerboard, repeated dumbbell figures. Elements often placed somewhat haphazardly around vessel with little effort at balance or overall planning. Elements varied, including especially nested "boxes" of concentric lines, or four groups of boxes in square arrangements; nested or concentric triangles; groups of parallel vertical zigzag lines; panels of checkerboard; dumbbell figures; large vertical V figures, with recurved ends. Most such figures have ticking along exterior lines (on interior of V figures), and ticked multiple or single lines placed diagonally in the panel or attached to corners of other figures are common. Star or sun symbols are placed here and there in the panels.

Vessel forms include, especially: small jars with fairly wide mouth, rim outwardly curved, hemispherical to flattened, with or without peg legs or feet; and deep-shouldered tripod bowls with incurving convex upper walls, bearing the decorative zone, and tripod legs. Tripod legs are either peg type or short triangular type resembling those on Morcillo Molcajetes. Many Nayar bowls have a molcajete bottom; usually a

circle, plain or ticked, incised, divided into four quadrants containing straight lines placed at right angles to each other in alternating quadrants or nested triangles similarly placed. Effigy forms with human faces on side occur.

Madero Fluted. This is a strange ware without local background or known associations elsewhere in Mexico or the Southwest United States. Together with Nayar and, to a lesser degree, Canatlan wares, it is diagnostic of the Calera phase.

Madero Fluted vessels are tripod bowls with low-set nearly triangular chunky legs like those of Morcillo and Nayar. The body of the bowl is nearly hemispherical, with the bottom almost reaching the surface on which the feet rest. High up on the body the vessel wall usually is sharply incurved to form a pronounced though slightly rounded shoulder. This upper shoulder is shallow and above it the low rim flares out abruptly; the vessel profile is a pronounced composite silhouette.

Characteristically, Madero bowls are decorated by an encircling band of deep parallel vertical flutes; the fluted band averages some 3 cm. or more in width; individual flutes appear to have been made by pressing a short cylindrical object of small diameter into the wet vessel wall, forcing the clay to form small vertical ridges between the depressions; the flutes and ridges were then wiped or scraped smooth, the ridges usually rounded. There is some variability in placement of the fluted bands: (a) one band encircles the rim, to the lip; in such cases the rim is usually a continuation of the incurved upper bowl wall or shoulder, without a flare; (b) the rim zone is left plain and smooth while the narrow incurving upper vessel wall is fluted; (c) fluted bands are placed in both locations with an intervening smooth surfaced band; or (d) a fluted band on the shoulder spirals upward to form a fluted band along the rim.

The interior of the vessel, the fluted bands, and the base of the bowl is customarily the smoothed brown or buff of the vessel; the remainder of the vessel exterior is painted a deep red, unevenly applied.

Smoking pipes, copper, and the collarbutton type of spindle whorl appear to be associated with the Calera phase but little evidence is available.

With the Calera phase, the Chalchihuites culture came to an end. The terminal date of A.D. 1350 is highly speculative; certainly there seems to have been no such occupation of the area in the conquest period. Especially during the Rio Tunal and Calera phases there was strong influence of the Chalchihuites culture on the Loma San Gabriel culture; certain Chalchihuites elements may have become incorporated in the latter and thereby have survived into modern times in the culture of the contemporary Huichol and Tepehuan (see Riley and Winters, 1963).

LOMA SAN GABRIEL CULTURE

The Rio Florida branch of the Rio Conchos flows in a short canyon through a long hill ridge about 8 km. above Villa O'Campo, almost on the Durango-Chihuahua border. The long high ridge extending south from the Rio Florida has masonry-walled terraces along its upper flanks; its narrow top is crowded with a series of crude masonry platforms, usually low with vertical slab or horizontal stone walls, and other features. This is the Loma (or Cerro) San Gabriel site, type site for the culture (Kelley, 1953; 1956, pp. 132–33). Other Loma sites are widely distributed throughout the eastern foothills of the Sierra Madre Occidental from southern Durango and northwestern Zacatecas through the upper Rio Conchos drainage in Chihuahua, almost halfway through the state of Chihuahua from north to south. The region around Zape in northern Durango is especially rich in Loma sites. Sites usually are situated on high rocky isolated hills or mesas, with farmland and some water source below. They also occur in the high mountains, situated on high natural terraces above the valley floors; typical of such sites is the Weicker site, some 50 km. west of Victoria de Durango on an upper branch of the Rio Tunal, partly excavated by the Southern Illinois University in 1952 (Kelley and Shackelford, 1954).

Architecturally, Loma sites are characterized by groups of small rectangular platforms and rooms, formed by placing small stone slabs vertically in the ground to form an enclosure, which was then usually paved with stones. Some structures are true platforms standing several feet high; others are mere paved areas, or adobe-floored enclosures. At the Weicker site there were two "compounds" or large rectangular living areas partly surrounded by low retaining walls of small vertical stone slabs. These two compounds occupied a natural terrace that had been further leveled by building a low stone wall on the downhill side. Within each compound there was a recognizable floor, apparently the tramped and hardened soil surface. Pairs of small, almost square, platforms, or platform-room combinations were set at intervals along the long axis of the compounds, running at right angles with it. Clay-lined hearths were placed in the floor between houses. It is not known whether the compounds were roofed and the platforms represent perhaps sleeping platforms, or whether the platforms were the bases for small perishable sleeping and storage houses and the open compound represented the group living area. The latter alternative seems more probable, and as such closely resembles modern Tepehuan hamlets. Circular platforms also occur in Loma sites, and on very high hill peaks such as the western hill at the Schroeder site or the hill above the village of Morcillo, large and fairly high rectangular masonry platforms occur, perhaps embryonic ceremonial centers. The upper hillslopes below Loma sites consistently are terraced.

Associated with the architecture described is a characteristic ceramic and stone artifact complex. The basic pottery (Loma

Plainware) is a plain brown ware, which ranges from a buff to almost a white (wash?) surface at Zape. Vessel forms range from small simple bowls through bowls with incurved rims and small jars and large ollas. Rare tripod bowl forms, and perhaps the brushed and "thumbnail"-marked utility that appears locally, are apparently borrowed from the Chalchihuites culture. There is also a crude red-on-brown ware (Chico Red-on-Brown), usually represented by small hemispherical bowls with slightly everted rims, with crude designs in broad red bands, straight and curving, in the vessel interior or along its rim. One such bowl intrusive into the Santa Ana site at Zape is decorated with one broad transverse red band. Near one rim this band curves to form a crude horned serpent head with open mouth. The design thus produced is very similar to modern Huichol serpent depictions. Some polished red pottery also occurs. The associated stone complex is very simple, consisting primarily of basin-shaped milling stones and associated one-hand manos, hammerstones, smoothing stones, the ground stone cross, and a limited roster of chipped flint implements: points, drills, knives, blades. Locally, Chalchihuites intrusives such as spindle whorls and vessel legs occur.

Loma San Gabriel sites apparently represent a considerable range in time. At Hervideros and Zape in northern Durango occasional sherds of Michilia Red-Filled Engraved ware, diagnostic of the Alta Vista phase, have been found associated on the surface with otherwise pure Loma ceramic assemblages. Similarly, pottery identified as Loma Plain has been found with Ayala and Las Joyas phase materials as platform fill at the Schroeder site. Spindle whorls of the Rio Tunal–Calera phase type have been found in several Loma sites; at the La Manga site, about 2 km. east of Schroeder, there was a very curious combination of Loma architecture and pottery with much Chalchihuites pottery and other traits. A Loma

burial, identified as such by the associated pots, had been intruded into Str. 9 (Rio Tunal phase) at the Schroeder site. Str. 20 on the high western hill at the Schroeder site had absolutely no Chalchihuites pottery in its fill or overlying debris and consequently must either antedate or postdate the Chalchihuites occupance there, probably the former. Also, there are Loma sites in the Durango area that look as if they had been abandoned yesterday; platforms intact and covered not at all with debris. As Riley and Winters (1963) have pointed out, there is strong evidence for deriving the modern Tepehuan, perhaps also some Huichol, from the Loma San Gabriel culture. It looks as if the Loma culture occupied western Durango before, during, and after the Chalchihuites occupance; during such long occupance there should be phase differences, but so little work has been done that no temporal cultural distinctions are known.

Loma culture in many ways closely resembles the late Desert culture occupance, the Caracoles culture of the region. The stone complex and characteristic location of sites is common to both Loma and Caracoles manifestations. In the field, what appears to be a Caracoles site often turns out to be a Loma site—after a few sherds of pottery and a house outline or two have been found. Loma ceramics and architecture are not specifically Mesoamerican; in fact, resemblances with the Southwest cultures, especially the Mogollon, are much greater than those with Mesoamerica. Significantly, northward along the Sierra Madre Occidental, Loma sites are replaced by Mogollon sites, with little if any break in continuity of distribution.

The following working hypothesis may be advanced for testing. Perhaps in the last few centuries B.C., early Preclassic Mesoamerican traits such as simple ceramics and basic platform architecture were diffused to Caracoles (Desert culture) groups in western Durango who had already begun to depend in part on simple farming for

800

subsistence, producing the Loma San Gabriel culture—and perhaps beyond its range the earliest Mogollon-Hohokam. Later, around A.D. 200 the Canutillo phase of the Chalchihuites culture developed in the Rio Suchil–Graceros area, probably out of the late Preclassic. Then about A.D. 300 a wave of full Classic traits from central Mexico appeared in the Suchil area, producing the Alta Vista phase. This culture began to influence the Loma development and, through trade along the Loma-Mogollan continuity, the developing Southwestern cultures as well. Then between A.D. 500 and 600 Chalchihuites colonies were established in central Durango, and there followed the development of the Guadiana branch previously described. In Durango, however, the Loma people continued in existence, constituting the peasant-farm population, whereas the Chalchihuites occupance remained concentrated in and near the ceremonial centers, its bearers serving as a religious-economic and perhaps military upper class superimposed on the peasantry. Over the centuries the Loma settlements closest to the Chalchihuites centers were strongly acculturated by the higher culture, and part of its way of life, particularly its ceremonialism, was accepted into the Loma pattern and was in turn transmitted to the Southwestern cultures. Following the disappearance of the Chalchihuites culture from the area, probably as a result of changing ecological or political factors, the Loma occupance continued, perhaps with some dilution and simplification of the borrowed Chalchihuites traits, culminating in the historic Tepehuan and, perhaps, Huichol cultures.

REFERENCES

Abbott, 1960
Armillas, 1963
Batres, 1903a
Brand, 1939
Crane and Griffin, 1958a, 1958b, 1959
Ekholm, 1942, 1958
Gamio, 1910
Guillemin Tarayre, 1869
Howard, 1957
Hrdlička, 1903
Johnson, A. S., 1958
Kelley, 1953, 1956, 1960, 1963, 1966
—— and Abbott, 1966
—— and Shackelford, 1954
—— and Winters, 1960
Kelly, 1938, 1948, 1949

Lister, 1955
—— and Howard, 1955
Lorenzo, 1953
Lumholtz, 1902
Margain, 1944
Marquina, 1951
Mason, 1937
Nebel, 1839
Noguera, 1930, 1948, 1960a
Peithman, 1961
Riley and Winters, 1963
Sauer, 1941
—— and Brand, 1932
Tello, 1650
Weigand, 1968
Wolf, 1959

REFERENCES AND INDEX

REFERENCES

ABBOTT, E.
1960 An analysis of Mercado Red-on-Cream: a diagnostic ceramic grouping of the Ayala phase of the Chalchihuites culture. Master's thesis, Southern Illinois Univ.

ACOSTA, J. DE
1604 The natural and moral history of the Indies. English trans. London. (Original ed. 1590.)

ACOSTA, J. R.
1939 Exploraciones arqueológicas realizadas en el estado de Michoacán durante los años de 1937 y 1938. *Rev. Mex. Estud. Antr.*, 3: 85–98.
1940 Exploraciones en Tula, Hidalgo, 1940. *Ibid.*, 4: 172–94.
1941 Los últimos descubrimientos arqueológicos en Tula, Hidalgo, 1941. *Ibid.*, 5: 239–48.
1945 Las cuarta y quinta temporadas de exploraciones arqueológicas en Tula, Hidalgo, 1943–1944. *Ibid.*, 7: 23–64.
1956a El enigma de los chacmooles de Tula. *In* Estudios Antropológicos, pp. 159–70.
1956b Resumen de los informes de las exploraciones arqueológicas en Tula, Hidalgo, durante las VI, VII y VIII temporadas, 1946–1950. *An. Inst. Nac. Antr. Hist.*, 8: 37–115.
1956–57 Interpretación de algunos de los datos obtenidos en Tula relativos a la época tolteca. *Rev. Mex. Estud. Antr.*, 14: 75–110.
1957 Resumen de los informes de las exploraciones arqueológicas en Tula, Hidalgo, durante las IX y X temporadas, 1953–54. *An. Inst. Nac. Antr. Hist.*, 9: 119–69.
1960 Las exploraciones en Tula, Hidalgo, durante la XI temporada, 1955. *Ibid.*, 11: 39–72.
1961a La doceava temporada de exploraciones en Tula, Hidalgo. *Ibid.*, 13: 29–58.
1961b La indumentaria de las cariátides de Tula. *In* Homenaje Martínez del Río, pp. 221–28.
1962 El Palacio de las Mariposas de Teotihuacán. *Bol. Inst. Nac. Antr. Hist.*, 9: 5–7.
1964a La decimotercera temporada de exploraciones en Tula, Hgo. *An. Inst. Nac. Antr. Hist.*, 16: 45–76.
1964b El Palacio del Quetzalpapalotl. *Mem. Inst. Nac. Antr. Hist.*, no. 10.
1965 Guía oficial de Teotihuacán. Inst. Nac. Antr. Hist. Mexico.
1966 Una clasificación tentativa de los monumentos arqueológicos de Teotihuacán. *In* Teotihuacán, pp. 45–56.

ACOSTA SAIGNES, M.
1946 Los Teopixque: organización sacerdotal entre los Mexica. *Rev. Mex. Estud. Antr.*, 8: 147–205.

AGRINIER, P.
1960 The carved human femurs from Tomb 1, Chiapa de Corzo, Chiapas, Mexico. *New World Archaeol. Found.*, Pub. 5.

AGUILAR P., C. H.
1946 La orfebrería en el México precortesiano. *Acta Anthr.*, vol. 2, no. 2.

ALCOCER, I.
1935 Apuntes sobre la antigua México-Tenochtitlan. *Inst. Panamer. Geog. Hist.*, Pub. 14.

ALEXANDER, H. B.
1920 Mexico. *In* The mythology of all races, L. H. Gray, ed., 10 (Latin American): 41–123. (2d ed. 1964.)

ALMARAZ, R.
1865 Apuntes sobre las pirámides de San Juan Teotihuacán. *In* Memorias y Trabajos ejecutados por la Comisión Científica de Pachuca en el año de 1864, pp. 349–58. Mexico.

ALVA, B. DE
1634 Confesionario mayor y menor en lengua mexicana. Mexico.

ALVA IXTLILXOCHITL, F. DE
1891–92 Obras históricas. A. Chavero, ed. Vol. 1: Relaciones. Vol. 2: Historia de la nación chichimeca. Mexico.
1952 *Idem*, reprinted.

ALVARADO, F. DE
1593 Vocabulario en lengua mixteca, hecha por los padres de la orden de predicadores, que residen en ella, y últimamente recopilado y acabado por el Padre . . . Vicario de Tamazulapa, de la misma orden. Facsimile ed., ed. by W. Jiménez Moreno. Inst. Nac. Indigenista and Inst. Nac. Antr. Hist. Mexico, 1962.

ALVARADO TEZOZOMOC, H.
1878 Crónica mexicana. Hacia el año 1598.
1944 *Idem*, reprinted. Mexico.
1949 Crónica mexicayotl. A. León, trans. *Univ. Nac. Autónoma Méx., Pub. Inst. Hist.*, 1st ser., no. 10.

AMAYA, J.
1951 Ameca, protofundación mexicana. Mexico.

ANALES:

Cakchiquels
1953 The Annals of the Cakchiquels. A. Recinos and D. Goetz, trans. Univ. Oklahoma Press.

Cuauhtitlan
1938 Die Geschichte der Königreiche von Colhuacan und Mexiko. W. Lehmann, ed. and trans. Quellenwerke zur alten Geschichte Amerikas Aufgezeichnet in den Sprachen der Eingeborenen. *Ibero-Amerikanischen Inst.*, I. Berlin.
1945 Códice Chimalpopoca: Anales de Cuauhtitlan y Leyenda de los Soles. P. F. Velázquez, ed. and trans. *Univ. Nac. Autónoma Méx., Pub. Inst. Hist.*, 1st ser, no. 1.

Mexicanos
1903 Anales del Museo Nacional, ép. 1, 7: 49–74. Mexico.

ANALES—*continued*

Tecamachalco
1903 A. Peñafiel, ed. *In* Col. doc. para la historia mexicana. Mexico.

Tlatelolco
1939–40 Unos annales históricos de la nación mexicana: Die Manuscrits mexicains nr. 22 und 22bis der Bibliothèque National de Paris. E. Mengin, ed. *Baessler-Archiv*, 22 (2–3): 73–168; 23 (4): 115–39. Berlin.
1945 Unos annales históricos de la nación mexicana: manuscrit mexicain nr. 22, nr. 22bis. E. Mengin, ed. *Corpus Codicum Americanorum Medii Aevi*, 2. Copenhagen.
1948 Anales de Tlatelolco: Unos annales históricos de la nación mexicana y códice de Tlatelolco. H. Berlin and R. H. Barlow, eds. *Fuentes para la historia de México*, 2. Mexico.

ANCIENT OAXACA
See Paddock, 1966c.

ANDERSON, A. E.
1932 Artifacts of the Rio Grande delta region. *Bull. Texas Archaeol. Paleontol. Soc.*, 4.

ANDERSON, A. J. O.
1963 Materiales colorantes prehispánicos. *Inst. Hist., Estud. Cultura Náhuatl*, no. 4. Mexico.

—— AND C. E. DIBBLE
1950–69 *See* Sahagún, 1950–69.

ANDERSON, E., AND R. H. BARLOW
1943 The maize tribute of Moctezuma's empire. *Ann. Missouri Botanical Garden*, 30: 413–20.

ANDREWS, E. W.
1961 Excavations at the Gruta de Balankanche, 1959. *Tulane Univ., Middle Amer. Research Inst., Misc. Ser.*, Pub. 11, pp. 28–40.
1965a Archaeology and prehistory in the northern Maya lowlands: an introduction. *In* Handbook of Middle American Indians, R. Wauchope, ed., vol. 2, art. 12.
1965b Progress report on the 1960–1964 field seasons, National Geographic Society—Tulane University Dzibilchaltun Project. *Tulane Univ., Middle*

Amer. Research Inst., Pub. 31, pp. 23–67.

ANGHIERA, P. M. D'
1912 De orbe novo, the eight decades of Peter Martyr d'Anghiera. Trans. with notes and introduction by F. A. MacNutt. New York.
1944 Décadas del nuevo mundo (1530). Buenos Aires.

ANNALS OF THE CAKCHIQUELS
See Anales: Cakchiquels.

ANONYMOUS
1933 Aztec sculpture. *Amer. Mag. Art,* 26: 485–94. New York.
1960 Investigaciones arqueológicas. *Bol. Inst. Nac. Antr. Hist.,* 2: 5–9. Mexico.

ANONYMOUS CONQUEROR
See Conquistador Anónimo, El.

ANTON, F.
1961 Mexiko, Indianerkunst aus präkolumbischer Zeit. Munich.
1965 Alt-Mexiko und seine Kunst. Leipzig.
—— AND F. DOCKSTADER
1968 Pre-Columbian art and later Indian tribal arts. New York.

ARAGÓN, J. O.
1931 Expansión territorial del imperio mexicano. *An. Mus. Nac. Arqueol. Hist. Etnog.,* ép. 4, 7 (1): 5–64.

ARAI, A. T.
1960 La arquitectura de Bonampak: ensayo de interpretación del arte maya; viaje a las ruinas de Bonampak. Mexico.

ARCHIVO GENERAL DE LA NACIÓN
1935a Licencia para buscar antiguos tesoros. (General de parte 1587, vol. 3, p. 181.) *Bol. Archivo General de la Nación,* vol. 6. Mexico.
1935b Las pirámides de San Juan Teotihuacán en 1760. (General de parte 1760, vol. 41, fs. 225.) *Ibid.,* vol. 6.

ARMILLAS, P.
1942–44 Oztuma, Guerrero, fortaleza de los mexicanos en la frontera de Michoacán. *Rev. Mex. Estud. Antr.,* 6: 165–75.
1944 Exploraciones recientes en Teotihuacán, México. *Cuad. Amer.,* 16 (4): 121–36. Mexico.

1945 Expediciones en el occidente de Guerrero. II: El grupo de Armillas, febrero–marzo, 1944. *Tlalocan,* 2: 73–85.
1948 Arqueología del occidente de Guerrero. *In* El Occidente de México, pp. 74–76.
1949 Notas sobre sistemas de cultivo en Mesoamérica. *An. Inst. Nac. Antr. Hist.,* 3: 85–113.
1950 Teotihuacán, Tula y los Toltecas: las culturas post-arcaicas y pre-aztecas del centro de México: excavaciones y estudios, 1922–1950. *Runa,* 3: 37–70. Buenos Aires.
1962 Volumen y forma en la plástica aborigen. *In* Cuarenta siglos de plástica mexicana. Mexico.
1963 Investigaciones arqueológicas en el estado de Zacatecas. *Bol. Inst. Nac. Antr. Hist.,* 14: 16–17.
1964a Northern Mesoamerica. *In* Jennings and Norbeck, 1964, pp. 291–329.
1964b Condiciones ambientales y movimientos de pueblos en la frontera septentrional de Mesoamérica. *In* Homenaje Márquez-Miranda, pp. 62–82.
——, A. PALERM, AND E. R. WOLF
1956 A small irrigation system in the valley of Teotihuacan. *Amer. Antiquity,* 21: 396–99.

ARREGUI, D. L. DE
1946 Descripción de la Nueva Galicia. F. Chevalier, ed. Seville.

ARREOLA, J. M.
1921 *See* Gamio, 1921b.
1922 Sellos, indumentaria, utensilios domésticos, utensilios industriales, objetos rituales, caracteres alfabéticos o numéricos. *In* Gamio, 1922a, 1: 212–20.

ARTE PRECOLOMBINO DEL OCCIDENTE DE MÉXICO
1946 Monografía que la Dirección General de Educación Estética publica con motivo de su exposición. Estudios de S. Toscano, P. Kirchhoff, y D. Rubín de la Borbolla. Mexico.

ARZOBISPADO DE MÉXICO
1897 *See* García Pimentel, 1897; Paso y Troncoso, 1905–06, vol. 3.

AUBIN, J. M. A.
1885 Mémoires sur la peinture didactique

et l'écriture figurative des anciens Mexicains. Paris.

1893 Histoire de la nation mexicaine depuis le départ d'Aztlan jusqu'à l'arrivée des conquérants Espagnols (et au delà 1607). Paris.

AVELEYRA ARROYO DE ANDA, L.

1959 Los cazadores del mamut, primeros habitantes de México. *In* Esplendor del México Antiguo, 1: 53–72.

1963 Le estela teotihuacana de La Ventilla. *Inst. Nac. Antr. Hist., Cuad. Mus. Nac. Antr.*, 1. Mexico.

1964 Obras selectas del arte prehispánico (adquisiciones recientes). Fotografías de I. Groth-Kimball. Consejo para la planeación e instalación del Museo Nacional de Antropología. Mexico.

—— AND M. MALDONADO-KOERDELL

1953 Association of artifacts with mammoth in the Valley of Mexico. *Amer. Antiquity*, 18: 332–40.

BANCROFT, H. H.

1875 The native races of the Pacific states of North America. 5 vols. New York.

BANDELIER, A. F.

1877 On the art of war and mode of warfare of the ancient Mexicans. *Peabody Mus., Harvard Univ.*, 10th ann. rept., 2: 95–161.

1878 On the distribution and tenure of lands, and the customs with respect to inheritance, among the ancient Mexicans. *Ibid.*, 11th ann. rept., 2: 385–448.

1880 On the social organization and mode of government of the ancient Mexicans. *Ibid.*, 12th ann. rept., 2: 557–699.

BARBA DE PIÑA CHAN, B.

1956 Tlapacoya: un sitio preclásico de transición. *Acta Anthr.*, ép. 2, vol. 1, no. 1. Mexico.

BARLOW, R. H.

1943 The periods of tribute collection in Moctezuma's empire. *Carnegie Inst. Wash., Notes Middle Amer. Archaeol. Ethnol.*, no. 23.

1944a Relación de Xiquilpan y su partido. *Tlalocan*, 1: 278–306.

1944b A western extension of Zapotec. *Ibid.*, 1: 267–68, 359–61.

1944c Los dioses del templo mayor de Tlatelolco. *Mem. Acad. Mex. Hist.*, 3: 530–40.

1945a Some remarks on the term "Aztec Empire." *The Americas*, 1: 344–49. Washington, D.C.

1945b Tlatelolco como tributario de la triple alianza. *Mem. Acad. Mex. Hist.*, 4: 200–15.

1945c Dos relaciones antiguas del pueblo de Cuilapa, estado de Oaxaca. *Tlalocan*, 2: 18–28.

1945d The Tlacotepec migration legend. *Ibid.*, 2: 70–73.

1946a Cerro de San Lorenzo, Coahuila: dos sitios arqueológicos. *Rev. Mex. Estud. Antr.*, 8: 266–67.

1946b Materiales para una cronología del imperio de los mexica. *Ibid.*, 8: 207–15.

1946c Some examples of Yeztla-Naranjo geometric ware. *Carnegie Inst. Wash., Notes Middle Amer. Archaeol. Ethnol.*, no. 73.

1946d The Tamiahua codices. *Ibid.*, no. 64.

1947a Relación de Tlalcozauhtitlan. *El México Antiguo*, 6: 383–91.

1947b Relación de Zacatula, 1580. *Tlalocan*, 2: 258–68.

1947c Conquistas de los antiguos mexicanos. *Jour. Soc. Amér. Paris*, 36: 215–22.

1947d Exploración en el occidente de Guerrero. III: Enero de 1948. *Tlalocan*, 2: 280–84.

1947–48 La fundación de la triple alianza (1427–1433). *An. Inst. Nac. Antr. Hist.*, 3: 147–55.

1948a Apuntes para la historia antigua de Guerrero. *In* El Occidente de México, pp. 181–90.

1948b Tres complejos de cerámica del norte del Rio Balsas. *Ibid.*, pp. 91–94.

1948c El derrumbe de Huexotzinco. *Cuad. Amer.*, 7: 147–60.

1949a El Códice Azcatitlan. *Jour. Soc. Amér. Paris*, 38: 101–35.

1949b Las conquistas de Moctezuma Xocoyotzin. *Mem. Acad. Mex. Hist.*, 8: 159–72.

1949c The extent of the empire of the Culhua Mexica. *Ibero-Amer.*, no. 28. Univ. California Press.

1949d Anales de Tula, Hidalgo. *Tlalocan*, 3: 2–13.

1950 Una nueva lámina del Mapa Quinatzin. *Jour. Soc. Amér. Paris*, 39: 111–24.

—— AND B. MCAFEE, eds.

1949 Diccionario de elementos fonéticos en escritura jeroglífica (Códice Mendocino). *Univ. Nac. Autónoma Mex., Pub. Inst. Hist.*, 1st ser., no. 9.

BARNES, A.

1947 The technique of blade production in Mesolithic and Neolithic times. *Proc. Prehist. Soc.*, 13: 101–113. Gloucester.

BARNETT, MADAME

1913 Quelques observations sur les petites têtes de Teotihuacan. *18th Int. Cong. Amer.* (London, 1912), Acta, p. 203.

BARRERA VÁSQUEZ, A.

1944 Canción de la danza del arquero flechador. *Tlalocan*, 1: 4.

1948 [ed.] El libro de los libros de Chilam Balam. Fondo de Cultura Económica. Mexico.

1949 The Maya chronicles. *Carnegie Inst. Wash.*, Pub. 585, Contrib. 48.

BASLER, A., AND E. BRUMMER

1928 L'art précolombien. Paris.

BATRES, L.

1887 Informe que rinde el inspector y conservador de los monumentos arqueológicos de la República, de los trabajos llevados a cabo de octubre 1885 a abril 1886. *In* J. Baranda, Memoria que rinde al Congreso de la Unión, pp. lv, 377–93. Mexico.

1889 Teotihuacán o la ciudad sagrada de los Toltecas. Mexico.

1902 Exploraciones arqueológicas en la Calle de Escalerillas. Mexico.

1903a Visita a los monumentos arqueológicos de la Quemada, Zacatecas, México. Mexico.

1903b ¿Tlaloc? Exploración arqueológica en el oriente del Valle de México. Sec. Justicia e Instrucción Pública. Mexico.

1905 La lápida arqueológica de Tepatlaxco-Orizaba. Mexico.

1907 Teotihuacán. *15th Int. Cong. Amer.* (Quebec, 1906).

1908 Civilización prehistórica de las riberas del Papaloapan y costa de Sotavento, estado de Veracruz. Mexico.

BAUTISTA, J. DE

1600 Advertencias para los confesores. Mexico.

BEALS, R. L.

1932 The comparative ethnology of northern Mexico before 1750. *Ibero-Amer.*, no. 2. Univ. California Press.

1969 The Tarascans. *In* Handbook of Middle American Indians, R. Wauchope, ed., vol. 8, art. 35.

BEAUMONT, P.

1932 Crónica de la Provincia de los Santos Apóstoles S. Pedro y S. Pablo de Michoacán (1565). Archivo General de la Nación, Pubs. 17, 18, 19. Mexico.

BELL, B.

1960 Analysis of ceramic style: a west Mexican collection. Doctoral dissertation, Univ. California, Los Angeles.

BENAVENTE, T. DE

1903 *See* Motolinia, 1903.

BENNETT, W. C.

1950 The Gallinazo group, Viru valley, Peru. *Yale Univ. Pub. Anthr.*, no. 43.

BENNYHOFF, J.

1966 Chronology and periodization: continuity and change in the Teotihuacan ceramic tradition. *In* Teotihuacán, 1966.

BENSON, E., ed.

1968 Dumbarton Oaks conference on the Olmec. Washington, D.C.

BERGER, R., G. J. FERGUSSON, AND W. F. LIBBY

1965 UCLA radiocarbon dates, IV. *Radiocarbon*, 7: 336–71.

——, J. A. GRAHAM, AND R. F. HEIZER

1967 A reconsideration of the age of the La Venta site. *Contrib. Univ. California Archaeol. Research Facility*, 3: 1–24. Berkeley.

—— AND W. F. LIBBY

1966 UCLA radiocarbon dates, V. *Radiocarbon*, 8: 467–97.

1967 UCLA radiocarbon dates, VI. *Ibid.*, 9: 477–504.

——, R. E. Taylor, and W. F. Libby

1966 Radiocarbon content of marine shells from the California and Mexican west coast. *Science*, 153 (3738): 864–66.

Bernal, I.

1950 Compendio de arte mesoamericano. *Enciclopedia Mex. Arte*, vol. 7. Mexico.

1951 Nuevos descubrimientos en Acapulco, México. *In* Tax, 1951, pp. 52–56.

1958a Archaeology of the Mixteca. *Bol. Estud. Oaxaqueños*, no. 7. Mexico City College.

1958b México: pinturas prehispánicas. New York Graphic Soc. Col. UNESCO de Arte Mundial.

1959 Tenochtitlan en una isla. *Inst. Nac. Antr. Hist., Hist. Ser.*, 2. Mexico.

1962 Bibliografía de arqueología y etnografía: Mesoamérica y norte de México, 1514–1960. *Mem. Inst. Nac. Antr. Hist.*, no. 7. Mexico.

1963 [ed.] Teotihuacán: descubrimientos, reconstrucciones. Inst. Nac. Antr. Hist. Mexico.

1965a Teotihuacán: nuevas fechas de radiocarbono y su posible significado. *An. Antr.*, 2: 27–35. Mexico.

1965b Archaeological synthesis of Oaxaca. *In* Handbook of Middle American Indians, R. Wauchope, ed., vol. 3, art. 31.

1966 The Mixtecs in the archeology of the Valley of Oaxaca. *In* Paddock, 1966c, pp. 345–66.

1967 Teotihuacán: su prehistórica historia. Conference, Mus. Nac. Antr. Mexico.

1968a Ancient Mexico in colour. Photographs by I. Groth-Kimball. London and New York.

1968b El mundo olmeca. Mexico.

1969 The Olmec world. D. Heyden and F. Horcasitas, trans. Berkeley and Los Angeles.

——, R. Piña Chan, and F. Cámara Barbachano

1968 3000 years of art and life in Mexico as seen in the National Museum of Anthropology, Mexico City. New York.

—— and B. Villaret

1962 Arts anciens du Mexique: architecture et sculpture. Paris.

Beyer, H.

1918 La piedra de sacrificios (techcatl) del Museo Nacional de Arqueología, Historia y Etnología de México. *Disertaciones Científicas de Autores Alemanes en México*, 3: 35–46. Mexico.

1920 Algo sobre los "signos chinos" de Teotihuacán. *El México Antiguo*, 1: 211–17.

1921a El llamado "calendario azteca." Mexico.

1921b Nota bibliográfica y crítica sobre el quinto tomo de las memorias científicas de Seler. *Mem. y Rev. Soc. Cien. Antonio Alzate*, 40: 57–64.

1921c La gigantesca cabeza de la diosa Coyolxauhqui-Chantico. *Rev. de Rev.*, 569: 27–28.

1922a Sobre una plaqueta con una deidad teotihuacana. *Mem. y Rev. Soc. Cien. Antonio Alzate*, 40: 549–58.

1922b Relaciones entre la civilización teotihuacana y la azteca. *In* Gamio, 1922a, 1: 273–93.

1924 Sobre algunas representaciones de los antiguos Totonacos. *Antropos*, 18: 253–57. Vienna.

1927 Algunos datos sobre los "yugos" de piedra prehispánicos. *El México Antiguo*, 2: 269–78.

1930 A deity common to Teotihuacan and Totonac cultures. *23d Int. Cong. Amer.* (New York, 1928), Acta, pp. 82–84.

1933 Shell ornament sets from the Huasteca, Mexico. *Tulane Univ., Middle Amer. Research Inst.*, Pub. 5, pp. 155–216.

1955 La "Procesión de los Señores," decoración del primer teocalli de piedra en Mexico-Tenochtitlan. *El México Antiguo*, 8: 8–42.

1965 Mito y simbología del México antiguo. Segundo tomo especial de homenaje consagrado a honrar la memoria del ilustre antropólogo Doctor Hermann Beyer. . . . Primer tomo de sus obras completas recopiladas, traducidas y arregladas por C. Cook de Leonard. *El México Antiguo*, vol. 10.

1969 Cien años de arqueología mexicana: Humboldt-Beyer. Tercer tomo especial de homenaje a Hermann Beyer y segundo tomo de sus obras completas recopiladas, traducidas y arregladas por C. Cook de Leonard. Con un suplemento en honor a Alejandro de Humboldt. *El México Antiguo*, vol. 11.

BEZINA, A.
1959 Der mexikanische Federschild aus Ambras. Archiv für Völkerkunde. Vienna.

BLAKE, W. W.
1891 The antiquities of Mexico as illustrated by the archaeological collections in its National Museum. New York.

BLISS COLLECTION
See Handbook of the Robert Woods Bliss Collection.

BOAS, F.
1911–12 Álbum de colecciones arqueológicas. Pub. Escuela Internac. Arqueol. Etnol. Amer. Mexico. (See Gamio, 1921a, for text.)

1913 Archaeological investigations in the Valley of Mexico by the International School, 1911–12. *18th Int. Cong. Amer.* (London, 1912), Acta, pp. 176–79.

BOBAN, E.
1891 Documents pour servir à l'histoire du Mexique. Catalogue raisonné de la collection de M. E. Eugène Goupil. 2 vols. Paris.

BOBAN CALENDAR WHEEL
1867 M. Doutrelaine, Rapport à son exc. M. le Ministre de l'Instruction publique sur un manuscrit mexicain de la collection Boban. *Archives Comm. Scientifique du Mexique*, 3: 120–33. Paris.

BORAH, W., AND S. F. COOK
1958 Price trends of some basic commodities in central Mexico, 1531–1570. *Ibero-Amer.*, no. 40. Univ. California Press.

1960 The population of central Mexico in 1548: an analysis of the Suma de Visitas de Pueblos. *Ibid.*, no. 43.

BORBOLLA, S. A. R. DE LA, AND L. AVELEYRA ARROYO DE ANDA
1953 A Plainview point from northern Tamaulipas. *Amer. Antiquity*, 18: 392–93.

BORDAZ, J.
1964 Pre-Columbian ceramic kilns at Peñitas, a post-classic site in coastal Nayarit, Mexico. Doctoral dissertation, Columbia Univ.

BORHEGYI, S. F.
1950 A group of jointed figurines in the Guatemala National Museum. *Carnegie Inst. Wash., Notes Middle Amer. Archaeol. Ethnol.*, no. 100.

1954 Jointed figurines in Mesoamerica and their cultural implication. *SW. Jour. Anthr.*, 10: 268–77.

1961a Ball-game handstones and ball-game gloves. *In* Lothrop and others, 1961, pp. 126–51.

1961b Shark teeth, stingray spines and shark fishing in ancient Mexico and Central America. *SW. Jour. Anthr.*, 17: 273–96.

BOSCH GARCÍA, C.
1944 La esclavitud prehispánica entre los aztecas. Fondo de Cultura Económica. Mexico.

BRAINERD, G. W.
1941 Fine Orange pottery in Yucatan. *Rev. Mex. Estud. Antr.*, 5: 163–83.

1956 Changing living patterns of the Yucatan Maya. *Amer. Antiquity*, 22: 162–64.

1958 The archaeological ceramics of Yucatan. *Univ. California, Anthr. Records*, no. 19.

BRAND, D. D.
1939 Notes on the geography and archaeology of Zape, Durango. *In* So live the works of men, D. D. Brand and F. E. Harvey, eds., pp. 75–105.

1942 Recent archaeologic and geographic investigations in the basin of the Rio Balsas, Guerrero and Michoacan. *27th Int. Cong. Amer.* (Mexico, 1939), Acta, 1: 140–47.

1943 An historical sketch of geography and anthropology in the Tarascan region. Part I. *New Mexico Anthr.*, 6–7: 37–108. Albuquerque.

1944 *Idem*, reprinted as a separate.

1952 Bosquejo histórico de la geografía y la antropología en la región tarasca. Part I. *An. Mus. Michoacano*, ép. 2, 5: 41–163.

1957–58 Coastal study of southwest Mexico. Part I, 1957; Part II, 1958. Univ. Texas, Dept. Geography.

1960 Coalcoman and Motines del Oro: an ex-distrito of Michoacan, Mexico. Univ. Texas, Inst. Latin Amer. Studies. The Hague.

BRASSEUR DE BOURBOURG, C. E.

1861 Popol Vuh: le livre sacré et les mythes de l'antiquité américaine avec les livres héroïques et historiques des Quichés. Paris.

BRETON, A. C.

1919 Some Mexican clay heads. *Man*, vol. 19, no. 3. London.

BRINTON, D. G.

1894 Nagualism: a study in native American folklore and history. *Proc. Amer. Phil. Soc.*, 33: 1–65.

BRUSH, C., AND E. BRUSH

n.d. Field notes on archaeological investigations on the Costa Grande and Costa Chica of Guerrero.

BUCK, J. L.

1930 Chinese farm economy. Univ. Chicago Press.

BUELNA, E.

1892 Peregrinación de los Aztecas y nombres geográficos indígenas de Sinaloa. 2d ed. Mexico.

BULLARD, W. R., JR.

1960 Maya settlement pattern in northeastern Peten, Guatemala. *Amer. Antiquity*, 25: 355–72.

BURGOA, F. DE

1934 Geográfica descripción de la parte septentrional y sitio astronómico de esta provincia de predicadores de Antequera, Valle de Oaxaca. (Mexico, *Nación*, vols. 25, 26. Mexico. 1674.) *Pub. Archivo General de la*

BURLAND, C. A.

1948 Art and life in ancient Mexico. Oxford.

1964 The bases of religion in Aztec Mexico. *Guild of Pastoral Psychology*, Guild Lecture 127. London.

1967 The gods of Mexico. London.

BUSHNELL, G. H. S.

1965 Ancient art of the Americas. London.

BUTTERWORTH, D., AND J. PADDOCK, eds.

1962 The Mixtec and Zapotec cultures: the Zapotecs. *Bol. Estud. Oaxaqueños*, no. 21. The Mixtec and Zapotec cultures: the Mixtecs. *Ibid.*, no. 22. Relaciones of Oaxaca of the 16th and 18th centuries: relaciones of Cuilapan, 14th chapter of the relación of Chichicapa, and description of the city of Antequera. *Ibid.*, no. 23. Mexico.

BYERS, D. S.

1967a [ed.] The prehistory of the Tehuacan Valley. Vol. 1: Environment and subsistence. Published for the Robert S. Peabody Foundation, Phillips Academy, Andover, Mass. Univ. Texas Press.

1967b Climate and hydrology. *In* his 1967a, 1: 48–65.

CABROL, A., AND L. COUTIER

1932 Contribution à l'étude de la taille de l'obsidienne au Mexique. *Bull. Soc. Préhist. Française*, 29: 579–82. Paris.

CAHILL, H.

1933 American sources of modern art. Mus. Modern Art. New York.

CALDERÓN DE LA BARCA, F.

1843 Life in Mexico. Boston.

CALENDARIO MEXICANO

1919 Calendario mexicano, latino y castellano. *Bol. Biblioteca Nacional*, vol. 12, no. 5. Mexico.

CALLEGARI, G. V.

1922–23 Scultura, lapidaria, oreficeria nel Messico precolombino. *Dedalo: Rassegna d'arte diretta de vgo ojetti*, 3: 541–66. Rome and Milan.

CAMPBELL, T. N.

1947 The Johnson site: type site of the Aransas focus of the Texas coast. *Bull. Texas Archaeol. Paleontol. Soc.*, 18: 40–76.

CANTARES MEXICANOS

1887 D. G. Brinton, Ancient Nahuatl poetry. *Library Aboriginal Amer. Lit.*, no. 7. Philadelphia.

1899   A. Peñafiel, Cantares mexicanos: cantares en idioma mexicano, impresos según el manuscrito original que existe en la Biblioteca Nacional. *In* Col. doc. para la historia mexicana, vol. 2. Mexico.

1904   A. Peñafiel, Cantares en idioma mexicano: reproducción facsimilar del manuscrito original existente en la Biblioteca Nacional. Mexico.

1957   L. S. Schultze-Jena, Alt-Aztekische Gesänge. Quellenwerke zur alten Geschichte Amerikas Auggezeichnet in den Sprachen der Eingeborenen. *Ibero-Amerikanischen Bibliothek*, 6. Berlin.

1965   A. M. Garibay K., Poesía Náhuatl, II: Cantares mexicanos, manuscrito de la Biblioteca Nacional de México. Part I. *Univ. Nac. Autónoma Méx., Inst. Invest. Hist., Fuentes Indígenas de la Cultura Náhuatl*, no. 5.

1968   A. M. Garibay K., Poesía Náhuatl, III: Cantares mexicanos, manuscrito de la Biblioteca Nacional de México. Part II. *Ibid.*, no. 6.

CARMACK, R. M.

1968   Toltec influence on the postclassic culture history of highland Guatemala. *Tulane Univ., Middle Amer. Research Inst.*, Pub. 26, pp. 49–92.

CARNEGIE INSTITUTION OF WASHINGTON

1951–54   Annual reports, Department of Archaeology. *Carnegie Inst. Wash.*, Year Books 50–53.

CARO BAROJA, J.

1957   Vasconiana. Madrid.

CARR, R. F., AND J. E. HAZZARD

1961   Map of the ruins of Tikal, El Peten, Guatemala. *Univ. Pennsylvania, Tikal Reports*, no. 11.

CARRASCO PIZANA, P.

1950   Los Otomies: cultura e historia prehispánicas de los pueblos mesoamericanos de habla otomiana. *Univ. Nac. Autónoma Méx., Pub. Inst. Hist.*, 1st ser., no. 15.

1961   El barrio y la regulación del matrimonio en un pueblo del Valle de México en el siglo XVI. *Rev. Mex. Estud. Antr.*, 17: 7–26.

1963   Las tierras de dos indios nobles de Tepeaca en el siglo XVI. *Tlalocan*, 4: 97–119.

1964a   Tres libros de tributos del Museo Nacional de México y su importancia para los estudios demográficos. *35th Int. Cong. Amer.* (Mexico, 1962), Acta, 3: 373–78.

1964b   Family structure of sixteenth century Tepoztlan. *In* Process and pattern in culture, R. A. Manners, ed., pp. 185–210.

1966a   Documentos sobre el rango de tecuhtli entre los nahuas tramontanos. *Tlalocan*, 5: 133–60.

1966b   Sobre algunos términos de parentesco en el náhuatl clásico. *Inst. Hist., Estud. Cultura Náhuatl*, 6: 149–66. Mexico.

1971   Social organization of ancient Mexico. *In* Handbook of Middle American Indians, R. Wauchope, ed., vol. 10, art. 14.

in press   Sucesión y alianzas matrimoniales en la dinastía teotihuacana. *Rev. Mex. Estud. Antr.*

CARRERA STAMPA, M., ed.

1955   Memoria de los servicios que habia hecho Nuño de Guzmán, desde que fue nombrado gobernador de Pánuco en 1525. Mexico. (See also Fourth Anonymous.)

CARRERI, G.

1927   Viaje a la Nueva España. 2 vols. (Other eds. 1697, 1700, 1955.)

CASO, A.

1927a   Las ruinas de Tizatlán, Tlax. *Rev. Mex. Estud. Hist.*, 1: 139–72.

1927b   El teocalli de la guerra sagrada. *Monogr. Mus. Nac. Arqueol. Hist. Etnog.*, no. 3. Mexico.

1928   Las estelas zapotecas. *Monogr. Mus. Nac. Arqueol. Hist. Etnog.*, no. 3. Mexico.

1930a   Un códice en Otomí. *23d Int. Cong. Amer.* (New York, 1928), Acta, pp. 130–35.

1930b   Informe preliminar de las exploraciones efectuadas en Michoacán. *An. Mus. Nac. Arqueol. Hist. Etnol.*, 6: 446–52. Mexico.

1932   El culto del dios de la lluvia en Tizapán. *Bol. Mus. Nac. Antr. Hist. Etnog.*, 1: 235–37. Mexico.

1934 Sobre una figurilla de hueso del antiguo imperio Maya. *An. Mus. Nac. Arqueol. Hist. Etnog.*, ep. 5, 1: 11–16. Mexico.

1935 Tenayuca. *In* Tenayuca, pp. 293–308.

1936 La religión de los Aztecas. *Enciclopedia Ilustrada Mex.*, 1.

1937 ¿Tenían los teotihuacanos conocimiento del Tonalpohualli? *El México Antiguo*, 4: 131–43. (Reprinted in his 1967a, pp. 143–53.)

1939 La correlación de los años azteca y cristiana. *Rev. Mex. Estud. Antr.*, 3: 11–45.

1940a El entierro del siglo. *Ibid.*, 4: 65–76. (Reprinted in his 1967a, pp. 129–40.)

1940b Pre-Spanish art. *In* Twenty centuries of Mexican art, pp. 26–66. Mus. Modern Art. New York.

1941 El complejo arqueológico de Tula y las grandes culturas indígenas de México. *Rev. Mex. Estud. Antr.*, 5: 85–95.

1942a El paraíso terrenal en Teotihuacán. *Cuad. Amer.*, 6: 127–36.

1942b Aztecas de México. *Ibid.*, 6: 155–60.

1942c Definición y extensión del complejo "Olmeca." *In* Mayas y Olmecas, pp. 43–46.

1946 El calendario Matlatzinca. *Rev. Mex. Estud. Antr.*, 8: 95–109.

1947 Calendario y escritura de las antiguas culturas de Monte Albán. *In* M. O. de Mendizábal, Obras Completas, 1: 5–102.

1949 El mapa de Teozacoalco. *Cuad. Amer.*, 8: 145–81.

1950a Una máscara azteca femenina. *México en el Arte*, 9: 2–9. Mexico.

1950b Explicación del reverso del códice Vindobonensis. *Mem. Colegio Nac.*, 5: 1–46. Mexico.

1951 Base para la sincronología mixteca y cristiana. *Ibid.*, 6: 49–66.

1953 El pueblo del sol. Fondo de Cultura Económica. Mexico. (English ed., The Aztecs: people of the sun. Univ.

Oklahoma Press, 1958. 2d ed. enlarged and corrected, Mexico, 1962.)

1954a Instituciones indígenas precortesianas. *In* Caso, ed., Métodos y resultados de la política indigenista en México. *Mem. Inst. Nac. Indigenista*, no. 6.

1954b Interpretación del códice Gómez de Orozco. Mexico.

1955a Vida y aventuras de 4 Viento "Serpiente de Fuego." *In* Misc. Estud. Fernando Ortiz, 1: 291–98. Havana.

1955b Der Jahresanfang bei den Mixteken. *Baessler Archiv*, n.s., 3: 47–53.

1956a Los barrios antiguos de Tenochtitlán y Tlatelolco. *Mem. Acad. Mex. Hist.*, 15: 7–63. Mexico.

1956b El calendario mixteco. *Hist. Mex.*, 5: 481–97. Mexico.

1958a El mapa de Xochitepec. *32d Int. Cong. Amer.* (Copenhagen, 1956), Acta, pp. 458–66.

1958b Lienzo de Yolotepec. *Mem. Colegio Nac.*, 3: 41–55. Mexico.

1958c El primer embajador conocido en América. *Cuad. Amer.*, 17: 285–93.

1958d Comentarios al códice Baranda. *In* Misc. Paul Rivet, 1: 373–93. Mexico.

1958e El calendario mexicano. *Mem. Acad. Mex. Hist.*, 17: 41–96. (Reprinted slightly revised in his 1967a, pp. 3–41.)

1958f *See* his 1953.

1959a Nombres calendáricos de los dioses. *El México Antiguo*, 9: 77–100.

1959b Nuevos datos para la correlación de los años aztecas y cristianos. *Inst. Hist., Estud. Cultura Náhuatl*, 1: 9–25.

1959c Glifos teotihuacanos. *Rev. Mex. Estud. Antr.*, 15: 51–70. (Reprinted in his 1967a, pp. 154–63.)

1959d La tenencia de la tierra entre los antiguos mexicanos. *Mem. Colegio Nac.*, 4: 29–54. Mexico.

1960a La pintura mural en Mesoamérica. Conference, El Colegio Nacional. Mexico.

1960b Interpretación del códice Bodley 2858. Soc. Mex. Antr. Mexico.

1960c El dios 1 Muerte. *Mitteilungen Mus.*

für Völkerkunde, 25: 40–43. Festband Franz Termer.

1960d Valor histórico de los códices mixtecos. *Cuad. Amer.*, 19: 130–47.

1961a Los lienzos mixtecos de Ihuitlán y Antonio de León. *In* Homenaje Martínez del Río, pp. 237–74.

1961b *See his* 1959a.

1962a Calendario y escritura en Xochicalco. *Rev. Mex. Estud. Antr.*, 18: 49–79. (Reprinted in his 1967a, pp. 166–86.)

1962b Vocabulario sacado del "Arte en lengua mixteca" de Fr. Antonio de los Reyes. *In* Vocabulario en lengua mixteca, W. Jiménez Moreno, ed., pp. 109–53.

1963 Representaciones de hongos en los códices. *Inst. Hist., Estud. Cultura Náhuatl*, 4: 27–38.

1964a Interpretación del códice Selden 3135 (A.2). Soc. Mex. Antr. Mexico.

1964b El lienzo de Filadelfia. *In* Homenaje Márquez Miranda, pp. 138–44. Madrid.

1964c Los señores de Yanhuitlán. *35th Int. Cong. Amer.* (Mexico, 1962), Acta, 1: 437–48.

1965a Sculpture and mural painting of Oaxaca. *In* Handbook of Middle American Indians, R. Wauchope, ed., vol. 3, art. 34.

1965b Lapidary work, goldwork, and copperwork from Oaxaca. *Ibid.*, vol. 3, art. 36.

1966a Interpretación del códice Colombino. Soc. Mex. Antr. Mexico.

1966b The lords of Yanhuitlan. *In* Paddock, 1966c, pp. 313–35.

1966c El culto al sol: notas a la interpretación de W. Lehmann. *Soc. Mex. Antr., Traducciones mesoamericanistas*, 1: 177–90.

1966d Dioses y signos teotihuacanos. *In* Teotihuacán, pp. 249–79.

1967a Los calendarios prehispánicos. *Univ. Nac. Autónoma Mex., Inst. Invest. Hist., Ser. Cultura Náhuatl*, Monogr. 6.

1967b Nombres calendáricos de los dioses. *In* his 1967a, pp. 189–99. (Originally published in his 1961b.)

1967c Un antiguo imperio mesoamericano. Conference, Mus. Nac. Antr. Mexico.

1969 El tesoro de Monte Alban. *Mem. Inst. Nac. Antr. Hist.*, no. 3. Mexico.

—— AND I. BERNAL

1952 Urnas de Oaxaca. *Mem. Inst. Nac. Antr. Hist.*, no. 2. Mexico.

1965 Ceramics of Oaxaca. *In* Handbook of Middle American Indians, R. Wauchope, ed., vol. 3, art. 35.

——, ——, AND J. R. ACOSTA

1967 La cerámica de Monte Albán. *Mem. Inst. Nac. Antr. Hist.*, no. 13. Mexico.

CASON, J. F.

1952 Report on archaeological salvage in Falcon Reservoir, season of 1952. *Bull. Texas Archaeol. Paleontol. Soc.*, 23: 218–59.

CASTAÑEDA, F. DE

1905a Relación de Tecciztlan y su partido. *In* Paso y Troncoso, 1905–06, 6: 209–30.

1905b Relación de Teutitlan del Camino. *Ibid.*, 4: 213–31.

CASTAÑEDA, P. DE

1896 Relación de la jornada de Cibola. *In* Winship, 1896, pp. 414–546.

CASTILLO, C. DEL

1908 Fragmentos de la obra general sobre historia de los mexicanos, escrita in lengua náhuatl . . . a fines del siglo XVI. *Biblioteca Náhuatl*, 5: Tradiciones migraciones, Cuad. 2, pp. 43–107. Florence.

CASTRO LEAL, A., ed.

1934 Escultura mexicana antigua. Exposición, Palacio de Bellas Artes. Mexico.

CEBALLOS NOVELO, R.

1926 Informe al director de arqueología. *Bol. Sec. Educación Pública*, 5: 154–69. Mexico.

CERVANTES, V.

1889 Ensayo de materia médica vegetal de México. Sec. de Fomento. Mexico.

CERVANTES DE SALAZAR, F.

1914 Crónica de la Nueva España. Madrid.

1936 Crónica de la Nueva España. *In* Paso

y Troncoso, Papeles de Nueva España, 3d ser.

CHADWICK, R.
1963 The god Malteutl in the "Histoire du Mechique." *Tlalocan*, vol. 4, no. 3.
1966 The "Olmeca-Xicallanca" of Teotihuacan: a preliminary study. *Mesoamerican Notes*, nos. 7–8. Mexico.
1967 Un posible glifo de Teotihuacán en el códice Nuttall. *Rev. Mex. Estud. Antr.*, 21: 17–41.
1968 The diffusion of a ceramic complex in the New World. MS.
1970 Un posible glifo de Xochicalco en los códices mixtecos. *Tlalocan*, vol. 6, no. 3.
in press, *a* La correlación de las historias de Quetzalcoatl en los códices mixtecos con la versión del Códice Chimalpopoca. *An. Inst. Nac. Antr. Hist.* Mexico.
in press, *b* Estudio de los toponímicos mixtecos. *Ibid.*

—— AND R. S. MacNEISH
1967 Codex Borgia and the Venta Salada phase. *In* Byers, 1967a, pp. 114–31.

CHAMBERLAIN, R. S.
1948 The conquest and colonization of Yucatan, 1517–1550. *Carnegie Inst. Wash.*, Pub. 582.

CHAPMAN, A. M.
1957 Port of trade enclaves in Aztec and Maya civilizations. *In* Trade and market in the early empires, K. Polanyi, C. M. Arensberg, and H. W. Pearson, eds., pp. 114–53.

CHAPPLE, E. D., AND C. S. COON
1942 Principles of anthropology. New York.

CHARDIN, P. TEILHARD DE
See Teilhard de Chardin, P.

CHARLOT, J.
1940 Twenty centuries of Mexican art. *Magazine of Art*, 33: 398–443. New York.

CHARNAY, D.
1884 Mis descubrimientos en México y en la América Central. *In* América pintoresca: descripción de viajes al nuevo continente. Barcelona.
1887 The ancient cities of the New World; being voyages and explorations in Mexico and Central America from 1857 to 1882. J. Gonino and H. S. Conant, trans. New York.

CHAVERO, A.
1877 La piedra del sol. Part 1. *An. Mus. Nac. Méx.*, 1: 353–86.
1882 *Idem*, part 2. *Ibid.*, 2: 3–46, 107–26, 233–36, 291–310, 403–30.
1886 *Idem*, part 3. *Ibid.*, 3: 3–26, 37–56, 100–14, 124–26.
1887 Historia antigua y de la conquista. *In* México a través de los siglos. Riva Palacio, ed., vol. 1. Mexico.
1901 Pinturas jeroglíficas de la Colección Chavero. 2 vols. Mexico.

CHÁVEZ, G. DE
1924 Relación de la provincia de Metztitlan. *Bol. Mus. Nac. Arqueol. Hist. Etnog.*, 4: 109–20. Mexico.

CHILDE, V. G.
1941 The dawn of European civilization. (6th ed. rev., 1957.)

CHILTON, J.
1927 A notable discourse of M. John Chilton touching the people, manners, mines, cities, forces and other memorable things of New Spain. . . . *In* Hakluyt, 1927, 8: 264–79.

CHIMALPAHIN QUAUHTLEHUANITZIN, D. F.
1889 Annales de Domingo Francisco de San Antón Muñon Chimalpahin Quauhtlehuanitzin. Sixième et septième relations (1258–1612). Rémi Siméon, ed. and trans. *Bibliothèque Linguistique Américaine*, 12. Paris.
1949–52 Diferentes historias originales de los reynos de Culhuacan, y México, y de otras provincias. . . . Manuscrit mexicain, nr. 74. E. Mengin, ed. *Corpus Codicum Americanorum Medii Aevi*, 3. Copenhagen.
1950 Diferentes historias originales de los reynos de Culhuacan y México, y de otras provincias. Das manuscrit mexicain nr. 74 der Bibliothèque Nationale de Paris. 5. Relación. Übersetzt und erläutert von Ernst Mengin. *Mitteilungen aus dem Museum für Völkerkunde in Hamburg*, XXII.
1958 Das Memórial Breve acerca de la fundación de la ciudad de Culhuacan

und weitere ausgewahlte teile aus den "Diferentes historias originales" (Manuscrit mexicain nr. 74, Paris). Aztec text, with German translation by W. Lehmann and G. Kutscher. *Quellenwerke zur alten Geschichte Amerikas*, 7. Stuttgart.

1963 Die Relationen Chimalpahin's zur Geschichte Mexiko's. Part 1: Die Zeit bis zur Conquista 1521. Text herausgegeben von G. Zimmermann. Univ. Hamburg, Abhandlungen aus dem Gebiet de Auslandskunde, Band 68, Reihe 8 (Völkerkunde, Kultur-geschichte und Sprachen), 38. Hamburg.

1965a *Idem.* Part 2: Das Jahrhundert nach der Conquista (1522–1615). Aztekischer Text herausgegeben von G. Zimmermann. *Ibid.*, Band 69, Reihe B (Völkerkunde, Kultur-geschichte und Sprachen), 39.

1965b Relaciones originales de Chalco Amaquemecan. Paleografiadas y traducidas del Náhuatl, con una introducción por S. Rendón. *Biblioteca Americana, Ser. Literatura Indígena.* Fondo de Cultura Económica. Mexico.

CHRISTENSEN, B.
1942 Notas sobre la fabricación del papel indígena y su empleo para "brujerías" en la Sierra Norte de Puebla, México. *Rev. Mex. Estud. Antr.*, 6: 109–24.

CIUDAD REAL, A. DE
See Ponce, A.

CLARK, J. COOPER
See Cooper-Clark, J.

CLAVIJERO, F. J.
1917 Historia antigua de México. Trans. from the Italian by J. Joaquín de la Mora. Mexico.
1964 *Idem*, reprinted.

CLINE, H. F.
1964 The Relaciones Geográficas of the Spanish Indies, 1577–1586. *Hisp. Amer. Hist. Rev.*, 46: 341–47.

CLUNE, F. J., JR.
1963 A functional and historical analysis of the ball game in Mesoamerica. Doctoral dissertation, Univ. of California, Los Angeles.

CODICES:

Aubin
1893 Histoire de la nation mexicaine. Reproduction du Codex de 1576. Paris.

Azcatitlan
1949 Códice Azcatitlan. *Jour. Soc. Amér. Paris*, n.s., vol. 38, appendix.

Azoyu 2 (reverse)
1893 *In* E. Seler, Die mexikanischen Bilderhandschriften Alexander von Humboldt's in der Königlichen Bibliothek zu Berlin (atlas). Berlin.
1943 S. Toscano, Los códices Tlapanecas de Azoyú, p. 136. *Cuad. Amer.*, 10: 127–36.
1964 J. B. Glass, Catálogo de la colección de códices, fig. 119. Inst. Nac. Antr. Hist. Mexico.

Becker I, II
1961 Facsimile edition. Mus. für Völkerkunde. Vienna.

Bodley
1960 Facsimile edition of a Mexican painting preserved in the collection of Sir Thomas Bodley, Bodleian Library, Oxford. Interpreted by A. Caso, translated by R. Morales, revised by J. Paddock. Soc. Mex. Antr. Mexico.

Borbonicus
1899 Codex Borbonicus. Manuscrit mexicain de la Bibliothèque du Palais Bourbon. E. T. Hamy, ed. Facsimile. Paris.

Borgia
1898 Il manoscritto Messicano Borgiano del Museo Etnografico. . . . Loubat ed. Rome.

Carolino
1967 Códice Carolino. Manuscrito anónimo del siglo XVI en forma de adiciones a la primera edición del vocabulario de Molina. *Inst. Hist., Estud. Cultura Náhuatl*, 7: 13–58.

Chimalpopoca
1945 Códice Chimalpopoca: Anales de Cuauhtitlán y Leyenda de los Soles. P. F. Velázquez, trans. *Univ. Nac. Autónoma Méx., Pub. Inst. Hist.*, 1st ser., no. 1. Mexico.

Colombino
1892 Códice Colombino. Pintura precolombina de la raza mixteca. *In* An-

CODICES—*continued*

    tigüedades mexicanas publicadas por la Junta Colombina. Mus. Nac. Mex.

Cospi (Bologna)

1898   Descripción del códice Cospiano. Manuscrito pictórico de los antiguos náhuas que se conserva en la biblioteca de la Universidad de Bolonia. Loubat reproduction. Rome.

Fejérváry-Mayer

1901   Codex Fejérváry-Mayer. Manuscrit mexicain précolombien du Free Public Museum de Liverpool (12014/M). Loubat reproduction. Paris. (See also Seler, 1901b.)

Florentine

1905–07   *See* Sahagún, 1905–07.

1926   Edición completa en facsímile colorido del códice Florentino que se conserva en la Biblioteca Laurenzio Medicea de Florencia, Italia. F. del Paso y Troncoso, ed. Mexico.

1950–69   *See* Sahagún, 1950–69.

Franciscano

1941   Códice Franciscano, siglo XVI. J. García Icazbalceta, ed. Mexico.

Ixtlilxochitl

1891   *In* Boban, 1891, 2: 116–31; atlas, pls. 65–71. Paris.

1951   *In* D. Durán, Historia de la Indias de Nueva España y islas de tierra firme (atlas). Mexico.

Kingsborough

1912   Memorial de los Indios de Tepetlaoztoc al monarca español contra los encomenderos del pueblo. F. del Paso y Troncoso, ed. Madrid.

Laud

1831   *In* Kingsborough, 1830–48, vol. 2, pt. 2.

1961   Códice Laud. C. Martínez Marín, ed. *Inst. Nac. Antr. Hist., Ser. Invest.*, 5. Mexico.

1966   Codex Laud (MS Laud Misc. 678, Bodleian Library). True-colour facsimile of the old Mexican manuscript. Intro. by C. A. Burland. Graz.

Magliabecchiano

1903   Z. Nuttall, ed., The book of life of the ancient Mexicans. . . . Part 1: Introduction and facsimile. Univ. California, Berkeley.

1904   Codex Magliabecchiano XIII, 3.

CODICES—*continued*

    Manuscrit mexicain postcolombien de la Bibliothèque Nationale de Florence. Loubat reproduction. Rome.

Matritense

1907   Códice Matritense de la Real Academia de la Historia. Textos en náhuatl de los indígenas informantes de Sahagún. F. del Paso y Troncoso, ed., vol. 8. Facsimile. Madrid.

Mendoza

1925   Colección de Mendoza o códice Mendocino, documento mexicano del siglo XVI que se conserva en la Biblioteca Bodleiana de Oxford, Inglaterra. F. del Paso y Troncoso [and J. Galindo y Villa], eds. Mexico.

1938   Codex Mendoza. The Mexican manuscript known as the Collection of Mendoza and preserved in the Bodleian Library, Oxford. James Cooper-Clark, ed. and trans. 3 vols. London.

Mexicanus

1952   Codex Mexicanus n. 23–24 de la Bibliothèque Nationale de Paris. E. Mengin, ed. *Jour. Soc. Amér. Paris*, n.s. 41: 387–498 (facsimile reproduction in album).

Nuttall

1902   Codex Nuttall. Facsimile of an ancient Mexican codex belonging to Lord Zouche of Harynworth, England. Intro. by Z. Nuttall. Peabody Mus., Harvard Univ. Cambridge.

Osuna

1947   Códice Osuna. Reproducción facsimilar de la obra del mismo título, editada en Madrid, 1878. Mexico.

Porfirio Díaz (reverse)

1892   *In* Antigüedades mexicanas publicadas por la Junta Colombina. Homenaje a Cristóbal Colón. Atlas. Mexico.

Ramírez

1944   Códice Ramírez. Manuscrito del siglo XVI intitulado: Relación del origen de los indios que habitan esta Nueva España, según sus historias. M. Orozco y Berra, ed. Mexico.

CODICES—*continued*

Ríos
1900   *See* Codex Vaticanus A.

Selden 3135 (A.2)
1964   Interpretation of the codex by A. Caso, translated by J. Quirate, revised by J. Paddock, with a facsimile of the codex. Soc. Mex. Antr. Mexico.

Telleriano-Remensis
1830   *See* Kingsborough, 1830–48, vol. 1.
1899   Codex Telleriano-Remensis. Manuscrit mexicain. Loubat reproduction. Intro. by E. T. Hamy. Paris.

Tlaquiltenango (Mauricio de la Arena)
1926   M. Mazari, Códice Mauricio de la Arena. *An. Mus. Nac. Antr. Hist. Ethnog.*, ép. 4, 4: 273–78. Mexico.
1943   R. H. Barlow, The periods of tribute collection in Moctezuma's empire. *Carnegie Inst. Wash., Notes Middle Amer. Archaeol. Ethnol.*, no. 23.

Vaticanus A (3738)
1900   Il manoscritto Messicano Vaticano 3738, detto il codice Ríos. Loubat reproduction. Rome.

Vaticanus B (3773)
1896   Il manoscritto Messicano Vaticano 3773. Loubat reproduction. Rome.
1902   Codex Vaticanus nr. 3773 (Codex Vaticanus B). Eine altmexikanische Bilderschrift der Vatikanischen Bibliothek. Loubat ed. Berlin. (See Seler, 1902a).

Veytia
1944   *In* Veytia, 1944. Text, 2: 339–46; illustrations, *passim*.

Vindobonensis Mexicanus I
1963   Facsimile ed. O. Adelhofer, ed. Graz, Austria. (See Seler, 1902–23.)

Xólotl
1951   *See* Dibble, 1951.

COE, M. D.
1963   Cultural development in southeastern Mesoamerica. *In* Meggers and Evans, 1963, pp. 27–44.
1965a   The jaguar's children: pre-classic central Mexico. Mus. Primitive Art. New York.
1965b   The Olmec style and its distribution. *In* Handbook of Middle American Indians, R. Wauchope, ed., vol. 3, art. 29.
1965c   Archaeological synthesis of southern Veracruz and Tabasco. *Ibid.*, vol. 3, art. 27.
1965d   A model of ancient community structure in the Maya lowlands. *SW. Jour. Anthr.*, 21: 97–114.
1967   America's first civilization. New York.
1968a   *Idem*, another ed. Princeton.
1968b   San Lorenzo and the Olmec civilization. *In* Benson, 1968, pp. 41–78.
1969   The archaeological sequence at San Lorenzo Tenochtitlan, Veracruz, Mexico. Paper presented to 34th annual meeting of Soc. Amer. Archaeol.

——, R. A. DIEHL, AND M. STUIVER
1967   Olmec civilization, Veracruz, Mexico: dating of the San Lorenzo phase. *Science*, 155: 1399–1401.

COLECCIÓN DE DOCUMENTOS
1842–95 Colección de documentos inéditos para la historia de España. 112 vols. Madrid.
1864–84 Colección de documentos inéditos relativos al descubrimiento, conquista y organización de las antiguas posesiones españolas de América y Oceanía, sacados de los archivos del reino, y muy especialmente del de Indias. J. Pacheco, F. de Cardenas, and L. Torres de Mendoza, eds. 42 vols. Madrid.
1885–1932 Colección de documentos inéditos relativos al descubrimiento, conquista y organización de las antiguas posesiones españolas de ultramar. 25 vols. Madrid.

COLLIER, D.
1960   Aztec sculpture. *Bull. Chicago Natural Hist. Mus.*, 34 (6): 4–5.

——, A. E. HUDSON, AND A. FORD
1942   Archaeology of the upper Columbia region. *Univ. Washington Pub. Anthr.*, 9: 1–178.

CONFIRMACIÓN DE CALPAN
1578   Confirmación de las elecciones de Calpan. Manuscrit mexicain nr. 73, Bibliothèque Nationale. Paris.

CONQUISTADOR ANÓNIMO, EL

1858 Relación de algunas cosas de la Nueva España y de la gran ciudad de Temestitlán, México. *In* García Icazbalceta, 1858–66, 1: 368–98. (Other eds. 1556, 1563, 1606, 1838, 1938, and the following entries.)

1917 *Idem.* M. H. Saville, trans. *Cortés Soc.*, Pub. 1.

1941 *Idem.* L. Díaz Cárdenas, ed. Mexico.

CONTRERAS S., E.

1966 Trabajos de exploración en la zona arqueológica de Ixtlán del Río Nayarit. Inst. Nac. Antr. Hist. Mexico.

CONZATTI, C., AND OTHERS

1922 Flora y fauna de la región. *In* Gamio, 1922a, 1: 19.

COOK, S. F.

1949 The historical demography and ecology of the Teotlalpan. *Ibero-Amer.*, no. 33. Univ. California Press.

—— AND L. B. SIMPSON

1948 The population of central Mexico in the sixteenth century. *Ibid.*, no. 31.

COOK DE LEONARD, C.

1952a Cronología de la cultura teotihuacana: comparación de los sistemas Pedro Armillas and George Vaillant. *Tlatoani*, 1 (2): 11–16.

1952b Teotihuacán: notas del interior. *Ibid.*, 3 (4): 49.

1953 Los Popolocas de Puebla: ensayo de una identificación etno-demográfica e histórico-arqueológica. *In* Huastecos, Totonacos, pp. 423–45.

1956a Algunos antecedentes de la cerámica tolteca. *Rev. Mex. Estud. Antr.*, 14: 37–43.

1956b Dos atlatl de la época teotihuacana. *In* Estudios Antropológicos, pp. 183–200.

1957a El origen de la cerámica anaranjada delgada. MS. Tesis, Escuela Nac. Antr. Mexico.

1957b Excavaciones en la plaza no. 1, "Tres Palos," Teotihuacan. *Bol. Centro Invest. Antr. Mex.*, 4: 3–5. Mexico.

1959a [ed.] Esplendor del México antiguo. 2 vols. Mexico.

1959b Ciencia y misticismo. *In* her 1959a, 1: 127–40.

1959c La escultura. *In* her 1959a, 2: 519–606.

1967 Sculptures and rock carvings at Chalcatzingo, Morelos. *Contrib. Univ. California Archaeol. Research Facility*, 3: 57–84. Berkeley.

COON, C. S.

1931 Tribes of the Rif. *Peabody Mus. Harvard Univ., Harvard African Studies*, vol. 9.

1966 The living races of man. New York.

COOPER-CLARK, J.

1938 *See* Codex Mendoza, 1938.

CORONA NÚÑEZ, J.

n.d. Nayarit informes. MS filed at Inst. Nac. Antr. Hist. Mexico.

1952 El templo de Quetzalcoatl en Ixtlán, Nayarit. *An. Inst. Nac. Antr. Hist.*, ép. 6, vol. 4, no. 32. Mexico.

1954 Diferentes tipos de tumbas prehispánicas en Nayarit. Centro Invest. Antr. Méx. *Yan*, 3: 46–50.

1955 Tumba de El Arenal, Etzatlán, Jalisco. *Inst. Nac. Antr. Hist., Dir. Monumentos Prehispánicos*, Informe 3. Mexico.

1960a Exploraciones en El Ixtepete. *Eco*, 2. Inst. Jalisciense de Antr. Hist. Guadalajara.

1960b Investigación arqueológica superficial hecha en el sur de Michoacán. *In* Brand, 1960, pp. 366–403.

CORTÉS, H.

n.d. Cartas de Cortés. *In* Cartas de relación de la conquista de América. J. de Riverend, ed. Col. Atenea. Mexico.

1844 Carta del Marqués del Valle. . . . *In* Col. doc. España, 4: 193–201. Madrid.

1866 Cartas y relaciones de Hernán Cortés al emperador Carlos V. Paris.

1877 Cartas de relación. *Historiadores Primitivos de Indias*, 1: 1–153. Madrid.

1908 Letters of Cortés. F. A. MacNutt, ed. and trans. 2 vols. New York.

1942 Cartas de relación de la conquista de Méjico. 2 vols. Madrid.

1960 Cartas de relación. *Col. "Sepan Cuantos . . .,"* no. 7. Mexico.

CORTÉS, M.
1865 Carta de D. Martín Cortés, segundo Marqués del Valle, al rey D. Felipe II. *In* Col. doc. Indias, 4: 440–62.

COVARRUBIAS, M.
1942 Origen y desarrollo del estilo artístico olmeca. *In* Mayas y Olmecas, pp. 46–49.
1946 El arte "Olmeca" o de La Venta. *Cuad. Amer.*, 28: 153–79.
1948 Tipología de la industria de piedra tallada y pulida de la cuenca del Río Mezcala. *In* El Occidente de México, pp. 86–90.
1949 Las raices políticas del arte de Tenochtitlán. *México en el Arte*, vol. 8. Mexico.
1950 Tlatilco: el arte y la cultura preclásica del Valle de México. *Cuad. Amer.*, 51: 149–62.
1957 Indian art of Mexico and Central America. New York.

CRABTREE, R. H., AND R. J. FITZWATER
n.d. Test excavations at Playa del Tesoro, Colima, Mexico. Mimeographed. Dept. Anthr., Univ. California, Los Angeles.

CRANE, H. R., AND J. B. GRIFFIN
1958a University of Michigan radiocarbon dates, II. *Science*, 127: 1098–1105.
1958b University of Michigan radiocarbon dates, III. *Ibid.*, 128: 117–32.
1959 University of Michigan radiocarbon dates, IV. *Amer. Jour. Science, Radiocarbon Suppl.*, 1: 173–98.

CRUZ, J. DE LA
1571 Doctrina christiana en la lengua guasteca . . . compuesta por industria de un frayle de la orden del glorioso S. Agustín. Mexico.

CUEVAS, M. (S. J.), ed.
1914 Documentos inéditos del siglo XVI para la historia de México. Mexico.
1964 Prólogo. *In* Clavijero, 1964.

CUMMINGS, B. C.
1933 Cuicuilco and the archaic culture of Mexico. *Bull. Univ. Arizona*, vol. 4, no. 8.

CUSTER, J. L.
1951 Excavations at Culhuacan. Master's thesis, Univ. of the Americas. Mexico.

DAHLGREN DE JORDÁN, B.
1954 La mixteca: su cultura y historia prehispánicas. *Col. Cultura Mex.*, no. 11. Mexico.
1961 El nocheztli o la grana de cochinilla mexicana. *In* Homenaje Martínez del Río, pp. 387–99.
1963 Nocheztli: economía de una región. Nueva Biblioteca Mexicana de Obras Históricas. Porrúa. Mexico.

DANZEL, T.
1922 Mexiko. Schriften-Reihe: Kulturen der Erde. Material zur Kultur- und Kunstgeschichte aller Völker, Band 12, Mexiko, vol. 2. Hagen-Darmstadt.

DÁVALOS HURTADO, E., AND OTHERS
1965 Museo Nacional de Antropología. *Artes de México*, año 12, 2d ép., no. 66/67.

DECICCO, G.
1969 The Chatino. *In* Handbook of Middle American Indians, R. Wauchope, ed., vol. 7, art. 17.

DEEVEY, E. S., R. F. FLINT, AND I. ROUSE, eds.
1963 Radiocarbon. *Amer. Jour. Science*, 261: 1–349.

——, L. J. GRALENSKI, AND V. HOFFREN
1959 Yale natural radiocarbon measurements, IV. *Amer. Jour. Science, Radiocarbon Suppl.*, 1: 144–72.

DELGADO, H. S.
n.d. Archaeological textiles from Durango, Zacatecas, and Sinaloa. MS.

DESCRIPCIÓN DEL ARZOBISPADO DE MÉXICO
1905 *In* Paso y Troncoso, 1905–06, vol. 3.

DESCRIPCIÓN DE INDIOS
1912 *In* Codex Kingsborough, pp. 199–202.

DESCRIPCIÓN . . . PUEBLO DE GUAUCHINANGO
1948 Descripción del pueblo de Guauchinango y de otros pueblos de su jurisdicción, sacada de la relación hecha por el alcalde mayor de aquel pueblo en 13 de Mayo de 1609. *In* Toussaint, 1948, pp. 293–303. (Also in Col. doc. Indias, 9: 150–66).

DESCRIPCIÓN . . . PROVINCIA DE PÁNUCO
1948 Descripción de los pueblos de la provincia de Pánuco, sacada de las relaciones hechas por Pedro Martínez,

821

capitán y alcalde mayor de la provincia. *Ibid.*, pp. 271–81. (Also in Col. doc. Indias, 9: 150–66.

DESCRIPCIÓN . . . VILLA DE PÁNUCO

1948 Descripción de la villa de Pánuco, sacada de las relaciones hechas por Pedro Martínez, capitán y alcalde mayor de aquella provincia. *Ibid.*, pp. 261–70. (Also in Col. doc. Indias, 9: 133–49.)

DESCRIPCIÓN . . . VILLA DE TAMPICO

1948 Descripción de la villa de Tampico, sacada de las relaciones hechas por Pedro Martínez, capitán y alcalde mayor de aquella provincia. *Ibid.*, pp. 283–91. (Also in Col. doc. Indias, 9: 167–79.)

D'HARCOURT, R.

1948 Arts de l'Amérique. Paris.

1950 Primitive art of the Americas. Paris. (English trans. of his 1948.)

DÍAZ DEL CASTILLO, B.

1904 Historia verdadera de la conquista de la Nueva España. Mexico.

1927 *Idem.* M. Keatinge, trans. New York. (Reprinted from 1800 ed.)

1938 *Idem.* 4 vols. Herrerías, ed. Mexico.

1939 *Idem.* 3 vols. P. Robredo, ed. Mexico.

1942 *Idem.* 2 vols. Madrid.

1950 *Idem.* 3 vols. Mexico.

DÍAZ LOZANO, E.

1922 Rocas y minerales del Valle. *In* Gamio, 1922a, 2: 31–66.

DIBBLE, C. E.

1942 Códice en Cruz. Mexico.

1951 Códice Xolotl. *Univ. Nac. Autónoma Méx., Pub. Inst. Hist.*, 1st ser., no. 22. Mexico.

DIETSCHY, H.

1945 Alt-Mexiko. Führer durch das Museum für Völkerkunde. Basel.

1948 La coiffure de plumes mexicaines du Musée de Vienne: critique iconographique et notes ethno-psychologiques. *28th Int. Cong. Amer.* (Paris, 1947), Acta, pp. 381–92.

DIRECCIÓN DE MONUMENTOS PREHISPÁNICOS

1933 Monumentos arqueológicos de México. Pub. Sec. Educación Pública,

Depto. Monumentos Prehispánicos. Mexico.

DISSELHOFF, H. D.

1932 Note sur le résultat de quelques fouilles archéologiques faites à Colima (Mexique). *Rev. Inst. Etnol., Univ. Nac. Tucumán.* Tucumán, Argentina. (25th Int. Cong. Amer.)

DIXON, K. A.

1958 Two masterpieces of Middle American bone sculpture. *Amer. Antiquity*, 24: 53–62.

1959 Two carved human bones from Chiapas. *Archaeology*, 12: 106–10.

DOCKSTADER, F. J.

1964 Indian art in Middle America. Greenwich, Conn.

DOCUMENTOS:

16thC Documentos inéditos . . . México. *See* Cuevas, 1914.

16thC–17thC Documentos inéditos . . . Tampico. *See* Meade, 1939.

16thC–17thC Documentos . . . México colonial. *See* Scholes and Adams, 1955–61.

1842–95 Colección de documentos inéditos . . . España. *See* Colección de Documentos, 1842–95.

1858–66 Colección de documentos . . . México. *See* García Icazbalceta, 1858–66.

1864–84 Colección de documentos inéditos . . . Indias. *See* Colección de Documentos, 1864–84.

1885–1932 Colección de documentos inéditos . . . ultramar. *See* Colección de Documentos, 1885–1932.

1886–92 Nueva colección de documentos . . . México. *See* García Icazbalceta, 1886–92.

1897–99 Colección de documentos . . . San Luis Potosí. *See* Velázquez, 1897–99.

1897–1903 Colección de documentos . . . historia mexicana. *See* Peñafiel, 1897–1903.

1903–07 Documentos históricos de México. *See* García Pimentel, 1903–07.

DREWITT, B.

1966 Planeación en la antigua ciudad de

Teotihuacán. *In* Teotihuacán, pp. 79–94.

DRIVER, H. E., AND W. C. MASSEY
1957   Comparative studies of North American Indians. *Trans. Amer. Phil. Soc.*, 47 (part 2): 165–456.

DRUCKER, P.
1943a   Ceramic sequences at Tres Zapotes, Veracruz, Mexico. *Smithsonian Inst., Bur. Amer. Ethnol.*, Bull. 140.
1943b   Ceramic stratigraphy at Cerro de las Mesas, Veracruz, Mexico. *Ibid.*, Bull. 141.
1952   La Venta, Tabasco: a study of Olmec ceramics and art. *Ibid.*, Bull. 153.
——, R. F. HEIZER, AND R. J. SQUIER
1957   Radiocarbon dates from La Venta, Tabasco. *Science*, 126 (no. 3263): 72–73.
1959   Excavations at La Venta, Tabasco, 1955. *Smithsonian Inst., Bur. Amer. Ethnol.*, Bull. 170.

DRUCKER, S., R. ESCALANTE, AND R. J. WEITLANER
1969   The Cuitlatec. *In* Handbook of Middle American Indians, R. Wauchope, ed., vol. 7, art. 30.

DUPAIX, G.
1834   Antiquités mexicaines: relation des trois expéditions du Capitaine Dupaix, ordonnées en 1805, 1806, et 1807, pour la recherche des antiquités du pays, notamment celles de Mitla et de Palenque; accompagnés des dessins de Castañeda. . . . 2 vols. and atlas. Paris.

DURÁN, D.
1868–80 Historia de las Indias de Nueva España y islas de tierra firme. 2 vols. and atlas. Mexico.
1951   *Idem*, reprinted.
1967   *Idem*. Ed. paleográfica del manuscrito autógrafo de Madrid, con introducciones, notas y vocabularios de palabras indígenas y arcaicas. A. M. Garibay K., ed. 2 vols. *Biblioteca Porrúa*, 36. Mexico.

DU SOLIER, W.
1939a   Informe sobre la zona de Tuzapan, Veracruz, año de 1939. Inst. Nac. Antr. Hist., Archivo Técnico de Monumentos Prehispánicos. Mexico.

1939b   Una representación pictórica de Quetzalcoatl en una cueva. *Rev. Mex. Estud. Antr.*, 3: 129–41.
1943   A reconnaissance on Isla de Sacrificios, Veracruz, Mexico. *Carnegie Inst. Wash., Notes Middle Amer. Archaeol. Ethnol.*, no. 14.
1945a   La cerámica arqueológica de El Tajín. *An. Mus. Nac. Arqueol. Hist. Etnog.*, ép. 5, 3: 147–92.
1945b   Estudio arquitectónico de los edificios huastecos. *Ibid.*, 1: 121–46.
1946   Primer fresco mural huasteco. *Cuad. Amer.*, año 5, no. 6, pp. 151–59.
1947a   Cerámica arqueológica de San Cristóbal Ecatepec. *An. Inst. Nac. Antr. Hist.*, 3: 27–58.
1947b   Sistema de entierros entre los huastecos prehispánicos. *Jour. Soc. Amér. Paris*, n.s., 36: 195–214.
——, A. D. KRIEGER, AND J. B. GRIFFIN
1947   The archaeological zone of Buena Vista, Huaxcama, San Luis Potosi, Mexico. *Amer. Antiquity*, 13: 15–32.

DUTTON, B. P.
1955   Tula of the Toltec. *El Palacio*, 62: 195–251.

EASBY, D. T.
1957   Sahagún y los orfebres precolombino de México. *An. Inst. Nac. Antr. Hist.*, 9: 85–117.
1962   A man of the people. *Metropolitan Mus. Art Bull.* (December), pp. 133–40.

EKHOLM, G. F.
1939   Results of an archaeological survey of Sonora and northern Sinaloa. *Rev. Mex. Estud. Antr.*, 3: 7–10.
1942   Excavations at Guasave, Sinaloa, Mexico. *Amer. Mus. Natural Hist., Anthr. Papers*, 38: 23–139. New York.
1944   Excavations at Tampico and Panuco in the Huasteca, Mexico. *Ibid.*, 38: 319–512.
1945   A pyrite mirror from Queretaro, Mexico. *Carnegie Inst. Wash., Notes Middle Amer. Archaeol. Ethnol.*, no. 53.
1946   The probable use of Mexican stone yokes. *Amer. Anthr.*, 48: 593–606.
1948   Ceramic stratigraphy at Acapulco,

Guerrero. *In* El Occidente de Méxi-co, pp. 95–104.

1949 Palmate stones and thin stone heads: suggestions on their possible use. *Amer. Antiquity*, 15: 1–9.

1953 Notas arqueológicas sobre el valle de Tuxpan y areas circunvecinas. *In* Huastecos, Totonacos, pp. 413–21.

1958 Regional sequences in Mesoamerica and their relationships. *In* Willey, Vogt, and Palerm, 1958, pp. 15–24.

1959 Stone sculpture from Mexico. Mus. Primitive Art. New York.

EMMERICH, A.
1959 Savages never carved these stones. *Amer. Heritage*, 10: 46–57.

1963 Art before Columbus: the art of ancient Mexico, from the archaic villages of the second millennium B.C. to the splendor of the Aztecs. New York.

ENCISO, J.
1947 Sellos del antiguo México. Mexico.

ENGELS, F.
1884 Der Ursprung der Familie, des Privateigenthums, und des Staats.

EPISTOLARIO DE NUEVA ESPAÑA
1505–1818 *See* Paso y Troncoso, 1939–42.

ERBEN, H. K., U. ERBEN, C. COOK DE LEONARD, D. J. LEONARD, G. O'NEIL, N. O'NEIL
1956 Una contribución geológico-arqueológica al problema de niveles de lagos de la cuenca de México. *Rev. Mex. Estud. Antr.*, 14: 23–39.

ERNST, A.
1892 Notes on some stone yokes from Mexico. *Internat. Archiv für Ethnog.*, 5: 71–76. Leiden.

ESPEJO, A.
1945 Las ofrendas halladas en Tlatelolco. *Tlatelolco a través de los tiempos*, 4: 15–29.

1949 Fragmentos de vasijas de barro con decoración en relieve. Introduction to C. Seler-Sachs, 1913. *El México Antiguo*, 7: 96–104.

1953 Dos tipos de alfarería negro-sobre-anaranjado en la cuenca de México y en el Totonacapan. *Rev. Mex. Estud. Antr.*, 13: 403–12.

ESPLENDOR DEL MÉXICO ANTIGUO
1959 Esplendor del México antiguo. R.

Noriega and C. Cook de Leonard, eds. 2 vols. Centro Invest. Antr. Mex.

ESTRADA BALMORI, E., AND R. PIÑA CHAN
1948a Funeraria en Chupícuaro, Guanajuato. *An. Inst. Nac. Antr. Hist.*, 3: 79–84.

1948b Complejo funerario en Chupícuaro. *In* El Occidente de México, pp. 40–41.

ESTUDIOS ANTROPOLÓGICOS
1956 Estudios antropológicos publicados en homenaje al doctor Manuel Gamio. Soc. Mex. Antr. Mexico.

FAURÉ, E.
1931 Some observations on Aztec art. *California Arts and Architecture*, 40 (6): 21–22, 50. San Francisco.

FAY, G. E.
1959 Handbook of pottery types of Nayarit, Mexico. *Inst. Interamer., Misc. Papers, Archaeol. Ser.*, no. 1. Magnolia, Arkansas.

FELDMAN, L. H.
1967 Archaeological mollusks of west Mexico. MS.

FERGUSSON, G. J., AND W. F. LIBBY
1963 UCLA radiocarbon dates, II. *Radiocarbon*, 5: 1–22.

FERNÁNDEZ, J.
n.d. Escultura prehispánica de México. Mexico.

1954 Coatlicue: estética del arte indígena antiguo. Centro Estud. Filosóficos, Univ. Nac. Autónoma Méx.

1958 Arte mexicano de sus origines a nuestros dias. Mexico.

1959a El arte. *In* Esplendor del México Antiguo, 1: 305–22.

1959b Coatlicue: estética del arte indígena antiguo. 2d ed., augmented, of his 1954.

FERNÁNDEZ DE MIRANDA, M. T.
1961 Toponimia popoloca. *In* Homenaje Townsend, pp. 431–47.

FEWKES, J. W.
1907 Certain antiquities of eastern Mexico. *Smithsonian Inst., Bur. Amer. Ethnol.*, 25th ann. rept. (1903–04), pp. 221–96.

1919 Antiquities of the gulf coast of Mexico. *Smithsonian Inst., Smithsonian Misc. Coll.*, vol. 70, no. 2.

FLORES GUERRERO, R.
1958 Castillo de Teayo. *An. Inst. Invest. Estéticas*, 7 (27): 5–15. Univ. Nac. Autónoma Méx.
1962 Historia general del arte mexicano: época prehispánica. Mexico.

FONDO EDITORIAL DE LA PLÁSTICA MEXICANA
1964 Flor y canto del arte prehispánico de México. Mexico.

FONDS MEXICAIN 20
1891 *In* Boban, 1891, atlas, pl. 20. (Color reproduction in Caso, 1966c.)

FORD, J. A.
1944 Excavations in the vicinity of Cali, Colombia. *Yale Univ. Pub. Anthr.*, no. 31.
1954 The history of a Peruvian valley. *Sci. Amer.* (August), pp. 28–34.
1969 A comparison of Formative cultures in the Americas. *Smithsonian Inst., Smithsonian Contrib. Knowledge*, vol. 11.

—— AND C. H. WEBB
1956 Poverty Point, a late archaic site in Louisiana. *Amer. Mus. Natural Hist., Anthr. Papers*, vol. 46, pt. 1.

FOSHAG, W. F.
1957 Mineralogical studies on Guatemalan jade. *Smithsonian Inst., Smithsonian Misc. Coll.*, vol. 135, no. 5.

FOSTER, G. M.
1944 Nagualism in Mexico and Guatemala. *Acta Amer.*, 2: 85–103. Mexico.

FOURTH ANONYMOUS
1955 Memoria de los servicios que habia hecho Nuño de Guzmán, desde que fue nombrado gobernador de Pánuco en 1525. M. Carrera Stampa, ed. Mexico. Reproduces (pp. 93–128) Cuarta relación anónima de la jornada que hizo Nuño de Guzmán a la Nueva Galicia. (See also García Icazbalceta, 1858–66, 2: 461–83.)

FRANCO C., J. L.
1945 Comentarios sobre tipología y filogenia de la decoración negra sobre color natural del barro en la cerámica "Azteca II." *Rev. Mex. Estud. Antr.*, 7: 163–86.
1949 Algunos problemas relativos a la cerámica azteca. *El México Antiguo*, 7: 162–208.

1955 Sobre un molde para vasijas con decoración en relieve. *Ibid.*, 8: 76–84.
1956 Malacates del complejo Tula-Mazapan. *In* Estudios Antropológicos, pp. 201–12.
1957 Motivos decorativos en la cerámica azteca. *Mus. Nac. Antr., Ser. Cien.*, 5: 7–36. Mexico.
1958 Un oyohualli mixteco. *Bol. Centro Invest. Antr. Méx.*, 5: 13–15.
1960 Mezcala, Guerrero (I, II, III). *Ibid.*, 7: 4–6, 8: 1–5, 9: 8–12.

FRIEDMAN, I., AND R. L. SMITH
1960 A new dating method using obsidian. *Amer. Antiquity*, 25: 476–537.

FUHRMANN, E.
1922 Mexiko. Schriften-Reihe: Kulturen der Erde. Material zur Kultur- und Kunstgeschichte aller Völker, Band 13, Mexiko, vol. 3. Hagen-Darmstadt.

FURST, P. T.
1965a Radiocarbon dates from a tomb in Mexico. *Science*, 147 (3658): 612–13.
1965b West Mexico, the Caribbean, and northern South America: some problems in New World interrelationships. *Antropológica*, 14: 1–37. Inst. Caribe Antr. Sociol. de la Fundación La Salle. Caracas.
1965c West Mexican tomb sculpture as evidence for shamanism in prehispanic Mesoamerica. *Ibid.*, 15: 29–81.
1966 Shaft tombs, shell trumpets, and shamanism: a culture-historical approach to problems in west Mexican archaeology. Doctoral dissertation, Univ. California, Los Angeles.
1967 Tumbas de tiro y cámara: un posible eslabón entre México y los Andes. *Eco*, 26: 1–6. Inst. Jalisciense Antr. Hist. Guadalajara.

GALINDO, M.
1922 Bosquejo de la geografía arqueológica del estado de Colima. *An. Mus. Nac. Arqueol. Hist. Etnog.*, ép. 4, vol. 1. Mexico.

GALINDO Y VILLA, J.
1902 [ed.] Álbum de antigüedades indígenas que se conservan en el Museo Nacional de México.

1903 La escultura nahua. *An. Mus. Nac. Méx.*, ép. 2, 1: 195–234.

1904 Catálogo del departamento de arqueología del Museo Nacional. Part 1: Galería de monolitos. 4th ed. Mexico.

1921 Los yugos. *Mem. Soc. Cien. Antonio Alzate*, 39: 219–29.

GAMBOA, F., ed.

1963 Masterworks of Mexican art from pre-Columbian times to the present. Los Angeles County Mus. Art. Los Angeles.

GAMIO, M.

1910 Los monumentos arqueológicos de los inmediaciones de Chalchihuites, Zacatecas. *An. Mus. Nac. Arqueol. Hist. Etnog.*, ép. 3, 2: 469–92.

1913 Arqueología de Azcapotzalco, D.F., Mexico. *18th Int. Cong. Amer.* (London, 1912), Acta, pp. 180–93.

1917 Investigaciones arqueológicas en México, 1914–1915. *19th Int. Cong. Amer.* (Washington, 1915), Acta, pp. 125–33.

1920 Las excavaciones del Pedregal de San Angel y la cultura arcaica del Valle de México. *Amer. Anthr.*, 22: 127–43.

1921a Álbum de colecciones arqueológicas: texto. Pub. Escuela Internac. Arqueol. Etnol. Amer. Mexico. (See Boas, 1911–12, for photographs.)

1921b Una mascara falsificada. *Ethnos*, 1: 260.

1922a La población del valle de Teotihuacán. 3 vols. Sec. Agricultura y Fomento, Dir. Antr. Mexico.

1922b Las pequeñas esculturas. *In* his 1922a, 1: 179–86.

1924 Sequence of cultures in Mexico. *Amer. Anthr.*, 26: 307–22.

GARCÍA, E.

1918 Crónica de la provincia agustiniana del santísimo nombre de Jesús de México. Madrid.

GARCÍA COOK, A.

1967 Análisis tipológico de artefactos. *Inst. Nac. Antr. Hist., Ser. Invest.*, no. 12. Mexico.

GARCÍA CUBAS, A.

1907 Mis últimas exploraciones arqueológicas: excursión a Teotihuacán. *Mem. Soc. Cien. Antonio Alzate*, 24: 261–77.

GARCÍA GRANADOS, R.

1939 Mexican feather mosaics. *Mexican Art and Life*, no. 5, pp. 1–4. Mexico.

1946 El arte plumario. *In* Mexico Prehispánico, pp. 576–81.

1952–53 Diccionario biográfico de historia antigua de México. 3 vols. Inst. Historia. Mexico.

GARCÍA ICAZBALCETA, J., ed.

1858–66 Colección de documentos para la historia de México. 2 vols. Mexico.

1886–92 Nueva colección de documentos para la historia de México. 5 vols. Mexico.

1941 *Idem*, 2d ed.

GARCÍA PAYÓN, J.

n.d.,a Informes de los trabajos de exploración y conservación llevados a cabo en El Tajín, abarcan el período de 1938 a 1962. Inst. Nac. Antr. Hist., Archivo Técnico. Mexico.

n.d.,b Las artes menores de los Totonacos de Zempoala.

1938 La zona arqueológica de Tecaxic-Calixtlahuaca y los Matlatzincas. Part 2. 2 vols. Mexico.

1939 Exploraciones y comentarios sobre la zona arqueológica de El Tajín, temporada de 1938–1939. Inst. Nac. Antr. Hist., Archivo Técnico. Mexico.

1941a Estudio preliminar de la zona arqueológica de Texmelincan, estado de Guerrero. *El México Antiguo*, 5: 341–64.

1941b La cerámica del valle de Toluca. *Rev. Mex. Estud. Antr.*, 5: 209–38.

1942 Conclusiones de mis exploraciones en el Totonacapan meridional, temporada 1939. *27th Int. Cong. Amer.* (Mexico, 1939), Acta, 2: 88–96.

1943 Interpretación cultural de la zona arqueológica de El Tajín, seguida de un ensayo de una bibliografía antropológica del Totonacapan y región sur del estado de Veracruz. Univ. Nac. Autónoma Méx.

1944a Notas de campo.

1944b Un templo de Xolotl descubierto en

Zempoala, Veracruz. *El Dictámen*, Feb. 6.

1945a Notas de campo.

1945b Mausolea in central Veracruz. *Carnegie Inst. Wash., Notes Middle Amer. Archaeol. Ethnol.*, no. 59.

1946 Los monumentos arqueológicos de Malinalco, estado de México. *Rev. Mex. Estud. Antr.*, 8: 5–63.

1947a Sinopsis de algunos problemas arqueológicos de Totonacapan. *El México Antiguo*, 6: 301–32.

1947b Exploraciones arqueológicas en el Totonacapan meridional (región de Misantla). *An. Inst. Nac. Antr. Hist.*, 2: 73–111. Mexico.

1949a Arqueología de El Tajín. I: ensayo de interpretación del monolito con relieve del monumento V de El Tajín. *Uni-Ver*, 1: 299–305. Jalapa.

1949b Notable relieve con sorprendentes revelaciones. *Ibid.*, 1: 351–59.

1949c La zona arqueológica de Zempoala, I. *Ibid.*, 1: 11–19.

1949d Arqueología de Zempoala, II. *Ibid.*, 1: 134–39.

1949e Zempoala: compendio de su estudio arqueológico. *Ibid.*, 1: 449–76.

1949f Arqueología de Zempoala, III. *Ibid.*, 1: 534–48.

1949g La zona arqueológica de Oceloapan, Ver. *Ibid.*, 492–504.

1949h Arqueología de El Tajín. II: Un palacio totonaca. *Ibid.*, 1: 581–95.

1949i Arqueología de Zempoala, IV. *Ibid.*, 1: 636–56.

1950a Palmas y hachas votivas. *Ibid.*, 2: 63–66.

1950b Restos de una cultura prehispánica encontrados en la región de Zempoala, Veracruz. *Ibid.*, 2: 90–130.

1950c Castillo de Teayo: noticias sobre su arqueología. *Ibid.*, 2: 155–64.

1950d Exploraciones en Xiuhtetelco, Puebla. *Ibid.*, 2: 397–426, 447–76.

1950e Las tumbas con mausoleos de la región central de Veracruz. *Ibid.*, 2: 7–23.

1950f Notas de campo.

1951a La pirámide de El Tajín: estudio analítico. *Cuad. Amer.*, 10 (6): 153–77.

1951b La ciudad arqueológica de El Tajín. Contrib. Univ. Veracruzana, Reunión de Mesa Redonda Antr. Jalapa.

1951c Breves apuntes sobre la arqueología de Chachalacas. *Ibid.*

1951d La cerámica de fondo "sellado" de Zempoala, Veracruz. *In* Homenaje Caso, pp. 181–98.

1952 Totonacas y Olmecas: un ensayo de correlación histórico-arqueológica. *Univ. Veracruzana*, 3: 27–52.

1954 El Tajín: descripción y comentarios. *Ibid.*, año 3, 4: 18–63.

1956–57 Síntesis de las investigaciones en Tecaxic-Calixtlahuaca. *Rev. Mex. Estud. Antr.*, 14: 157–59.

1959–61 Ensayo de interpretación de los tableros del juego de pelota sur de El Tajín. *El México Antiguo*, 9: 445–60.

1963 Quienes construyeron El Tajín y resultados de las últimas exploraciones de la temporada 1961–1962. *Palabra y Hombre*, pp. 243–52. Jalapa.

1965 [ed.] Descripción del pueblo de Gueytlalpan (Zacatlán, Jujupango, Matlatlán y Chila, Papantla) por el alcalde mayor Juan de Carrion, 30 de Mayo de 1581. Jalapa.

1966 Prehistoria de Mesoamérica: excavaciones en Trapiche y Chalahuite, Veracruz, México, 1942, 1951 y 1959. *Cuad. Facultad Filosofía, Letras y Ciencias*, no. 31. Univ. Veracruzana. Jalapa.

GARCÍA PIMENTEL, L., ed.

1897 Descripción del arzobispado de México hecha en 1570 y otros documentos. Mexico.

1903–07 Documentos históricos de México. 5 vols. Mexico, Paris, Madrid.

1904 Relación de los obispados de Tlaxcala, Michoacán, Oaxaca y otros lugares en el siglo XVI. Mexico.

GARIBAY K., A. M.

1940a Llave del Náhuatl. Otumba, Mexico. (2d ed. 1961.)

1940b Poesía indígena de la altiplanicie. *Bib. Estudiante Universitario*, no. 11. Mexico. (3d ed. 1962.)

1943 Huehuetlatolli, Documento A. *Tlalocan*, 1: 31–53, 81–107.

1945 Épica Náhuatl. *Bib. Estudiante Universitario*, no. 51. Mexico. (Another ed. 1964.)

1953–54 Historia de la literatura Náhuatl. 2 vols. Mexico.

1958 Veinte himnos sacros de los Nahuas. *Informantes de Sahagún*, no. 2. Univ. Nac. Autónoma Méx., Inst. Hist., Seminario de Cultura Náhuatl.

1961 *See* his 1940a.

1962 *See* his 1940b.

1964a *See* his 1945.

1964b [ed.] Poesía Náhuatl. I: Romances de los señores de la Nueva España. Manuscrito de Juan Bautista de Pomar, Tezcoco, 1582. Univ. Nac. Autónoma Méx., Inst. Hist., Seminario de Cultura Náhuatl, Fuentes Indígenas de la Cultura Náhuatl. Mexico.

1965a Teogonía e historia de los mexicanos: tres opúsculos del siglo XVI. *Col. "Sepan Cuantos . . .,"* no. 37. Mexico.

1965b Poesía Náhuatl. II: Cantares mexicanos. Manuscrito de la Bib. Nac. Méx. Part 1. Mexico.

GAY, C. T. E.
1966 Rock carvings of Chalcacingo: bas reliefs add to knowledge of ancient Olmec culture in Mexico. *Natural Hist.*, 75: 57–61.

GENIN, A. M. A.
1928 Note sur les objets precorteziens nommés indûment yugos ou jougs. *22d Int. Cong. Amer.* (Rome, 1926), Acta, 1: 521–28.

GERHARD, P.
1964 Shellfish dye in America. *35th Int. Cong. Amer.* (Mexico, 1962), Acta, 3: 177–91.

GIBSON, C.
n.d. The pre-conquest Tepanec zone and the labor drafts of the sixteenth century. MS.

1952 Tlaxcala in the sixteenth century. *Yale Hist. Pub.*, Misc. no. 56.

1956 Llamamiento general, repartimiento, and the empire of Acolhuacan. *Hisp. Amer. Hist. Rev.*, 36: 1–27.

GIFFORD, E. W.
1950 Surface archaeology of Ixtlan del Rio, Nayarit. *Univ. California Pub. Amer. Archaeol. Ethnol.*, vol. 43, no. 2. Berkeley.

GILLMOR, F.
1949 Flute of the smoking mirror: a portrait of Nezahualcoyotl, poet-king of the Aztecs. Univ. New Mexico Press.

GLASSOW, M. A.
1967 The ceramics of Huistla, a west Mexican site in the municipality of Etzatlan, Jalisco. *Amer. Antiquity*, 32: 64–83.

GOGGIN, J. M.
1943 An archaeological survey of the Rio Tepalcatepec basin, Michoacan, Mexico. *Ibid.*, 9: 44–58.

GÓMEZ CAÑEDO, L. (O.F.M.)
1959 Nuevos datos acerca del cronista Fray Antonio Tello. *Estud. Hist.*, 1: 117–21. Guadalajara.

GÓMEZ DE OROZCO, F.
1945 Costumbres, fiestas, enterramientos y diversas formas de proceder de los Indios de Nueva España. Copy of part of text of Madrid Museo de América codex cognate with Codex Magliabecchiano. *Tlalocan*, 2: 37–63.

GONZÁLEZ, P. D.
1897 Algunos puntos y objetos monumentales antiguos del estado de Guanajuato. *11th Int. Cong. Amer.* (Mexico, 1895), Acta, pp. 149–59.

GRAHAM, J., ed.
1966 Ancient Mesoamerica: selected readings. Palo Alto.

GRIFFIN, J. B., AND A. ESPEJO
1947 La alfarería correspondiente al último período de ocupación nahua del Valle de México, I. *Mem. Acad. Mex. Hist.*, 6: 131–47. (Also Tlatelolco a través de los tiempos, 9.)

1950 La alfarería del último período de ocupación del Valle de México, II: Culhuacan, Tenayuca, Tenochtitlan y Tlatelolco. *Ibid.*, 9: 118–67.

GRIJALVA, J. DE
1624 Crónica de la orden de nuestro padre San Agustin en las provincias de la Nueva España. Mexico. (2d ed. 1924.)

GROSSCUP, G. L.

1961 A sequence of figurines from west Mexico. *Amer. Antiquity*, 26: 390–406.

1964 The ceramics of west Mexico. Doctoral dissertation, Univ. California, Los Angeles.

GROTH-KIMBALL, I., AND F. FEUCHTWANGER

1953 Kunst im alten Mexiko. Zurich-Freiburg.

1954 The art of ancient Mexico. English trans. of their 1953. London and New York.

GROVE, D.

1968 Chalcatzingo, Morelos, Mexico: a reappraisal of the Olmec rock carvings. *Amer. Antiquity*, 33: 486–91.

GUEVARA CALENDAR (TLAXCALTECA)

1901 *In* Chavero, 1901, 1: 31–38.

GUILLEMIN TARAYRE, E.

1869 Informe sobre las ruinas de la Quemada.

GUTIÉRREZ DE LIÉVANA, J.

1905 Relación de la villa de Tepuztlan. *In* Paso y Troncoso, 1905–06, 6: 237–50.

GUZMÁN, E.

1933 Caracteres fundamentales del arte antiguo mexicano: su sentido fundamental. *Univ. México*, 5: 117–55, 408–29.

1934 Los relieves de las rocas del Cerro de la Cantera, Jonacatepec, Morelos. *An. Mus. Nac. Arqueol. Hist. Etnog.*, 1: 237–51. Mexico.

1938 [ed.] Un manuscrito de la Colección Boturíni que trata de los antiguos señores de Teotihuacán. *Ethnos*, 3: 89–103.

1946 Caracteres fundamentales del arte. *In* Vivó, 1946, pp. 545–51.

1959 Huipil y máxtlatl. *In* Esplendor del México Antiguo, 2: 959–82.

HAGEN, V. W. VON

1945 La fabricación del papel entre los aztecas y los mayas. Nuevo Mundo. Mexico.

HAKLUYT, R.

1927 The principal navigations, voyages, traffiques and discoveries of the English nation. 8 vols. London, Toronto, New York.

HAMILTON, P.

n.d. Jade and two cultures. MS.

—— AND D. LEONARD

1966 There is native jade in Mexico. *Intercambio* (November). Mexico.

HAMMOND, G. P., AND A. REY, trans. and eds.

1928 Obregón's history. Los Angeles.

HAMY, E. T.

1897 Galerie américaine du Musée d'Ethnographie du Trocadéro. Paris.

1899 *See* Codex Borbonicus.

HANDBOOK . . . BLISS COLLECTION

1963 Handbook of the Robert Woods Bliss Collection of pre-Columbian art. Dumbarton Oaks. Washington. (See also Lothrop, 1956; Lothrop, Foshag, and Mahler, 1957.)

HASTINGS, W., ed.

1916 Encyclopedia of religion and ethics. 8 vols. New York.

HAURY, E. W.

1933 Maya textile weaves. MS.

1954 The problem of contacts between southwestern United States and Mexico. *SW. Jour. Anthr.*, 1: 55–74.

HAUSWALDT, J. G.

1940 Kurze Notiz über eine, im Tal von Mexiko gefundene "palma." *El México Antiguo*, 5: 202–03.

HEFLIN, A. A.

1961 Bone spindle whorls in the Valley of Mexico. *Bol. Centro Invest. Antr. Méx.*, 12: 9–12.

HEIZER, R. F., AND T. SMITH

1964 Olmec sculpture and stone working: a bibliography. *Contrib. Univ. California Archaeol. Research Facility*, 1: 71–87. Berkeley.

—— AND H. WILLIAMS

1965 Stones used for colossal sculpture at or near Teotihuacan. *Ibid.*, 1: 55–70.

——, ——, AND J. A. GRAHAM

1965 Notes on Mesoamerican obsidians and their significance in archaeological studies. *Ibid.*, 1: 94–103.

HENDRICHS PÉREZ, P. R.

1940 ¿Es el arco de Oztuma de construcción azteca? *El México Antiguo*, 5: 142–47.

1945 Por tierras ignotas: viajes y observaciones en la región del Río de las Balsas. Vol. 1. Mexico.

1946 *Idem*, vol. 2.

HERNÁNDEZ, FRANCISCO

1959 Obras completas: historia natural de Nueva España, 1571. Univ. Nac. Méx.

HERNÁNDEZ, FRANCISCO JAVIER

1959 El Museo Nacional de Antropología. Bib. Popular de Arte Mexicano.

HERNÁNDEZ RODRÍGUEZ, R.

1952 El valle de Toluca: su historia, época prehispánica y siglo XVI. *Bol. Soc. Mex. Geog. Estad.*, 74: 7–124.

[HERNÁNDEZ Y DÁVALOS, J., comp.]

1878 Noticias varias de Nueva Galicia, intendencia de Guadalajara. Guadalajara.

HERRERA, M.

1922 Esculturas zoomorfas. *In* Gamio, 1922a, 1: 187–96.

1925 Las representaciones zoomorfas en el arte antiguo mexicano. *Pub. Sec. Educacion Púb.*, 2: 8. Mexico.

1935 Estudio comparativo de las serpientes de la pirámide con los crótalos vivos. *In* Tenayuca, pp. 203–32.

HERRERA Y TORDESILLAS, A. DE

1934 Historia general de los hechos de los castellanos en las islas i tierra firma del mar océano. Madrid.

HESTER, J. A.

1953 Agriculture, economy, and population densities of the Maya. *Carnegie Inst. Wash.*, Year Book 52, pp. 289–92.

HICKS, F., AND H. B. NICHOLSON

1964 The transition from classic to postclassic at Cerro Portezuelo, Valley of Mexico. *35th Int. Cong. Amer.* (Mexico, 1962), Acta, 1: 493–506.

HIRTZEL, J. S. H.

1930 Le manteau de plumes dit de "Montezuma" des Musées Royaux du Cinquantenaire de Bruxelles. *23d Int. Cong. Amer.* (New York, 1928), Acta, pp. 649–51.

HISTORIA DE LOS MEXICANOS POR SUS PINTURAS

1941 Historia de los Mexicanos por sus pinturas. *In* García Icazbalceta, 1941, 3: 207–40.

1965 *Idem*. *In* Garibay K., 1965a, pp. 23–90.

HISTORIA TOLTECA-CHICHIMECA

1937–38 Die mexikanische Bilderhandscrift Historia Tolteca-Chichimeca. Die Manuskripte 46–58bis der Nationalbibliothek in Paris. K. T. Preuss and E. Mengin, eds. and trans. *Baessler-Archiv*, 20, Beiheft 9, 21: 1–66. Berlin.

1942 Historia Tolteca-Chichimeca. E. Mengin, ed. *Corpus Codicum Americanorum Medii Aevi*, 1. Copenhagen.

1947 Historia Tolteca-Chichimeca: anales de Quauhtinchan. H. Berlin in collaboration with S. Rendón, eds. Prologue by P. Kirchhoff. *Fuentes para la Historia de México*, 1. Mexico.

HISTOYRE DU MECHIQUE

1905 Histoyre du Mechique: manuscrit français inédit du XVIe siècle. E. de Jonghe, ed. *Jour. Soc. Amér. Paris*, n.s., 2: 1–41.

1961 Histoyre du Mechique. Retraducción del francés al castellano por Joaquín Meade, con notas de W. Jiménez Moreno. *Mem. Acad. Mex. Hist.*, 20: 183–210.

1965 *Idem*. *In* Garibay K., 1965a, pp. 91–120. (Spanish trans.)

HODGMAN, C. D.

1948 Handbook of chemistry and physics. 13th ed. Cleveland.

HOIJER, H.

1956 Language and writing. *In* Man, culture, and society, H. L. Shapiro, ed., pp. 196–223.

HOLLAND, W. R.

1964 Contemporary Tzotzil cosmological concepts as a basis for interpreting prehistoric Maya civilization. *Amer. Antiquity*, 29: 301–06.

HOLMES, W. H.

1895–97 Archaeological studies among the ancient cities of Mexico. *Field Columbian Mus., Anthr. Ser.*, vol. 1, no. 1. Chicago.

1916 Masterpieces of aboriginal American art. IV: Sculpture in the round. *Art and Archaeol.*, 3: 71–85. Washington.

1919 Handbook of aboriginal American antiquities. Part 1: The lithic industries. *Smithsonian Inst., Bur. Amer. Ethnol.*, Bull. 60.

HOLMES ANNIVERSARY VOLUME
1916 Anthropological essays presented to William Henry Holmes in honor of his seventieth birthday. Washington.

HOMENAJE BEYER
See Beyer, 1965 and 1969.

HOMENAJE CASO
1951 Homenaje al doctor Alfonso Caso. Nuevo Mundo. Mexico.

HOMENAJE GARCÍA GRANADOS
1960 Homenaje a Rafael García Granados. Inst. Nac. Antr. Hist. Mexico.

HOMENAJE MÁRQUEZ-MIRANDA
1964 Homenaje a Fernando Márquez-Miranda. Madrid and Seville.

HOMENAJE MARTÍNEZ DEL RÍO
1961 Homenaje a Pablo Martínez del Río en el XXV aniversario de la primera edición de Los Orígenes Americanos. Inst. Nac. Antr. Hist. Mexico.

HOMENAJE TOWNSEND
1961 A William Cameron Townsend en el vigésimoquinto aniversario del Instituto Lingüístico del Verano. B. F. Elson, ed. Mexico.

HOMENAJE WEITLANER
1966 *See* Pompa y Pompa, 1966.

HOWARD, A. M.
1957 Navacoyan: a preliminary survey. *Bull. Texas Archaeol. Soc.*, 28: 181–89.

HRDLIČKA, A.
1903 The Chichimecs and their ancient culture, with notes on the Tepecanos and the ruin of La Quemada, Mexico. *Amer. Anthr.*, n.s., 5: 385–440.

HUASTECOS, TOTONACOS
1953 Huastecos, Totonacos y sus vecinos. I. Bernal and E. Dávalos Hurtado, eds. *Rev. Mex. Estud. Antr.*, vol. 13, nos. 2 and 3.

HVIDTFELDT, A.
1958 Teotl and Ixiptlatli: some central conceptions in ancient Mexican religion. Copenhagen.

ICAZA, I. I. DE, AND I. R. GONDRA
1827 Colección de antigüedades mexicanas que existen en el Museo Nacional. Litografiadas por Federico Waldeck e impresas por Pedro Robert. Mexico. (Facsimile ed. 1927.)

INFORMANTES DE SAHAGÚN
See Codex Matritense, 1907.

INSTITUTO NACIONAL DE ANTROPOLOGÍA E HISTORIA
1946 Pre-Hispanic art of Mexico. Mexico.
1956 Guía oficial: Museo Nacional de Antropología. Mexico.
1967 *Idem*, another ed.

IRRIGATION CIVILIZATIONS
1955 *See* Steward, 1955.

IXTLILXOCHITL, F. DE A.
See Alva Ixtlilxochitl, F. de

IZUMI, S., AND T. SONO
1963 Andes 2: excavations at Kotosh, Peru. Univ. Tokyo Exped. to the Andes, 1960. Tokyo.

JACOBS-MÜLLER, E. F.
See Müller, E. F. J.

JENKINS, K. D.
1967 Lacquer. *In* Handbook of Middle American Indians, R. Wauchope, ed., vol. 6, art. 7.

JENNINGS, J. D.
1956 [ed.] The American southwest: a problem in cultural isolation. *In* Wauchope, 1956, pp. 59–127.

—— AND E. NORBECK, eds.
1964 Prehistoric man in the New World. Univ. Chicago Press.

—— AND E. K. REED
See Wauchope, 1956.

JIMÉNEZ MORENO, W.
1939 Origen y significación del nombre "Otomí." *Rev. Mex. Estud. Antr.*, 3: 62–68.
1941 Tula y los Toltecas según las fuentes históricas. *Ibid.*, 5: 79–83.
1942 El enigma de los Olmecas. *Cuad. Amer.*, 1: 113–45.
1945 Introducción. *In* Ruz Lhuillier, 1945, pp. 7–18.
1948 Historia antigua de la zona tarasca. *In* El Occidente de México, pp. 146–57.
1953a Historia antigua de México. Mimeographed. Soc. Alumnos de la Escuela Nac. Antr. Hist. Mexico. (2d ed. 1956.)
1953b Cronología de la historia de Veracruz. *In* Huastecos, Totonacos, pp. 311–13.

1954–55 Síntesis de la historia precolonial del Valle de México. *Rev. Mex. Estud, Antr.*, 14: 219–36.

1956 Historia antigua de México. (2d ed. of his 1953a.)

1959 Síntesis de la historia pretolteca de Mesoamérica. *In* Esplendor del México Antiguo, 2: 1019–1108.

1962a Etimología de toponímicos mixtecos. *In* F. de Alvarado, Vocabulario en lengua mixteca, 1593. Facsimile ed. Mexico.

1962b La historiografía Tetzcocana y sus problemas. *Rev. Mex. Estud. Antr.*, 18: 81–86.

1966 Mesoamerica before the Toltecs. *In* Paddock, 1966c, pp. 1–82.

—— AND S. MATEOS HIGUERA

1940 Códice de Yanhuitlán. Mexico.

JOHNSON, A. S.

1958 Similarities in Hohokam and Chalchihuites artifacts. *Amer. Antiquity*, 24: 126–30.

JOHNSON, I. W.

n.d. Tejidos de la Cueva de La Candelaria, Coahuila. MS.

1954 Chiptic cave textiles from Chiapas, Mexico. *Jour. Soc. Amér. Paris*, n.s., 43: 137–48.

1956 Análisis de un tejido de Tlatelolco. Tlatelolco a través de los tiempos, no. 12. *Mem. Acad. Mex. Hist.*, 15: 127–28.

1957a An analysis of some textile fragments from Yagul. *Mesoamer. Notes*, 5: 77–81. Mexico City College, Dept. Anthropology.

1957b Survival of feather ornamented huipiles in Chiapas, Mexico. *Jour. Soc. Amér. Paris*, n.s., 46: 189–96.

1958–59 Un antiguo huipil de ofrenda decorado con pintura. *Rev. Mex. Estud. Antr.*, 15: 115–22.

1959 Hilado y tejido. *In* Esplendor del México Antiguo, 1: 439–78.

1960 Un tzotzopaztli antiguo de la región de Tehuacán. *An. Inst. Nac. Antr. Hist.*, 11: 75–85.

1964 Copper preserved textiles from Michoacan and Guerrero. *35th Int. Cong. Amer.* (Mexico, 1962), Acta, 1: 525–36.

1966 Análisis textil del Lienzo de Ocotepec. *In* Pompa y Pompa, pp. 139–44.

1966–67 Miniature garments found in Mixteca Alta caves, Mexico. *Folk*, 8–9: 179–90. Copenhagen.

1967 Textiles. *In* The prehistory of the Tehuacan Valley, 2: 189–226.

1970 A painted cloth from Tenancingo, Mexico. Paper presented to 35th annual meeting, Society for American Archaeology, Mexico, 1970.

in press Textiles. *In* La minería prehispánica en la sierra de Querétaro. Sec. Patrimonio Nacional. Mexico.

—— AND J. L. FRANCO C.

1967 Un *huipilli* precolombino de Chilapa, Guerrero. *Rev. Mex. Estud. Antr.*, 21: 149–89.

JONES, J.

1963 Bibliography for Olmec sculpture. *Mus. Primitive Art. Primitive Art Bibliographies*, no. 2. New York.

1964 Sculpture from Mexico in the collection of the Museum of Primitive Art. *Mus. Primitive Art.* New York.

JOYCE, T. A.

1912 A short guide to the American antiquities in the British Museum. London.

1920 Mexican archaeology. London and New York.

1927 Maya and Mexican art. London.

JUÁREZ, T., AND P. VALENTÍN

1554 Tiburcio Juárez y Pedro Valentín, sobre tierras, 1554. MS. Archivo General de la Nación, ramo de Tierras, 13, exped. 4. Mexico.

KAPLAN, L., AND R. S. MACNEISH

1960 Prehistoric bean remains from caves in the Ocampo region of Tamaulipas, Mexico. *Bot. Mus. Leafl., Harvard Univ.*, 19: 33–56.

KATZ, F.

1956 Die sozialökonomischen Verhältnisse bei den Azteken im 15. und 16. Jahrhundert. *Ethnographische-archäologische Forschungen*, vol. 3, part 2. Berlin.

1958 The evolution of Aztec society. *Past and Present*, 13: 14–25.

1966 Situación social e económica de los

832

aztecas durante los siglos XV y XVI.
Univ. Nac. Mexico.

KELEMEN, P.
1943 Medieval American art. 2 vols.
New York.
1956 *Idem*, 2d ed. in 1 vol., slightly augmented. New York.
1969 *Idem*, 3d ed., slightly revised, paperback.

KELLEY, J. C.
1953 Reconnaissance and excavation in Durango and southern Chihuahua, Mexico. *Amer. Phil. Soc.*, Year Book (1953), pp. 172–76. Philadelphia.
1956 Settlement patterns in north-central Mexico. *In* Willey, 1956, pp. 128–39.
1960 North Mexico and the correlation of Mesoamerican and southwestern cultural sequences. *In* Wallace, 1960, pp. 566–73.
1963 Northern frontier of Mesoamerica. First ann. rept., Aug. 15, 1961–Aug. 15, 1962. A report of research under the auspices of the National Science Foundation (Grant 18586) and the University Museum and Mesoamerican Cooperative Research Program of the Southern Illinois University. Carbondale.
1966 Mesoamerica and the southwestern United States. *In* Handbook of Middle American Indians, R. Wauchope, ed., vol. 4, art. 5.

—— AND E. ABBOTT
1966 The cultural sequence on the north central frontier of Mesoamerica. *36th Int. Cong. Amer.* (Seville, 1964), Acta, 1: 326–37.

——, T. N. CAMPBELL, AND D. J. LEHMER
1940 The association of archaeological materials with geological deposits in the Big Bend region of Texas. *West Texas Hist. Sci. Soc.*, no. 10.

—— AND W. J. SHACKELFORD
1954 Preliminary notes on the Weicker site, Durango, Mexico. *El Palacio*, 61: 145–50. Santa Fe.

—— AND H. D. WINTERS
1960 A revision of the archaeological sequence in Sinaloa, Mexico. *Amer. Antiquity*, 25: 547–61.

KELLY, I. T.
1938 Excavations at Chametla, Sinaloa. *Ibero-Amer.*, no. 14. Univ. California Press.
1941 The relationship between Tula and Sinaloa. *Rev. Mex. Estud. Antr.*, 5: 199–207.
1944 West Mexico and the Hohokam. *In* El Norte de México, pp. 206–22.
1945a Excavations at Culiacan, Sinaloa. *Ibero-Amer.*, no. 25. Univ. California Press.
1945b The archaeology of the Autlan-Tuxcacuesco area of Jalisco. I: The Autlan zone. *Ibid.*, no. 26.
1945c Report on grant for study and analysis of a large collection of potsherds gathered during extensive surveys in the Sayula basin of west central Mexico. *Amer. Phil. Soc.*, Year Book (1944), pp. 209–12.
1947a An archaeological reconnaissance of the west coast: Nayarit to Michoacan. *27th Int. Cong. Amer.* (Mexico, 1939), 2: 74–77.
1947b Excavations at Apatzingan, Michoacan. *Viking Fund Pub. Anthr.*, no. 7.
1948 Ceramic provinces of northwestern Mexico. *In* El Occidente de México, pp. 55–71.
1949 The archaeology of the Autlan-Tuxcacuesco area of Jalisco. II: The Tuxcacuesco-Zapotitlan zone. *Ibero-Amer.*, no. 27. Univ. California Press.
1953 The modern Totonac. *In* Huastecos, Totonacos, pp 175–86.

—— AND B. BRANIFF DE TORRES
1966 Una relación cerámica entre occidente y la mesa central. *Bol. Inst. Nac. Antr. Hist.*, 23: 26–27.

—— AND A. PALERM
1952 The Tajin Totonac. Part 1: History, subsistence, shelter and technology. *Smithsonian Inst., Inst. Social Anthr.*, Pub. 13.

KIDDER, II, A.
1949 Mexican stone yokes. *Bull. Fogg Mus. Art*, 11: 3–10. Cambridge, Mass.

KIDDER, A. V.
1947 The artifacts of Uaxactun, Guatemala. *Carnegie Inst. Wash.*, Pub. 576.
——, J. D. JENNINGS, AND E. M. SHOOK
1946 Excavations at Kaminaljuyu. *Ibid.*, Pub. 561.

KING, E.
See Kingsborough, Lord.

KINGSBOROUGH, LORD [EDWARD KING]
1830–48 Antiquities of Mexico, comprising fac-similes of ancient Mexican paintings and hieroglyphics. 9 vols. London.
1964 Antigüedades de México, basadas en la recopilación de Lord Kingsborough. Palabras preliminares, Antonio Ortiz Mena. Prólogo, Agustín Yáñez. Estudio e interpretación, José Corona Núñez. 2 vols. Sec. Hacienda y Crédito Público. Mexico.

KIRCHHOFF, P.
1940 Los pueblos de la Historia Tolteca-Chichimeca: sus migraciones y parentesco. *Rev. Mex. Antr. Hist.*, 4: 77–104.
1943 Mesoamérica: sus límites geográficas, composición étnica y caracteres culturales. *Acta Amer.*, 1: 92–107.
1946 La cultura del occidente de México a través de su arte. *In* Arte Precolombino del Occidente de México, pp. 49–69.
1948 Etnografía antigua. *In* El Occidente de México, pp. 134–36.
1955 Quetzalcoatl, Huemac y el fin de Tula. *Cuad. Amer.*, 14: 163–96.
1956a Land tenure in ancient Mexico. *Rev. Mex. Estud. Antr.*, 14: 351–61.
1956b Composición étnica y organización política de Chalco según las relaciones de Chimalpahin. *Rev. Mex. Estud. Antr.*, 14: 297–302.
1961a Das Toltekenreich und sein Untergang. *Saeculum*, 12: 248–65.
1961b ¿Se puede localizer Aztlán? *Univ. Nac. Autónoma Méx., Anuario Hist.*, año 1, pp. 59–73.
1964 La aportación de Chimalpahin a la historia tolteca. *An. Antr.*, 1: 77–90.

KRICKEBERG, W.
1918 Die Totonaken: ein Beitrag zur historischen Ethnographie Mittelamerikas. *Baessler-Archiv*, 7: 1–55; 9: 1–75.
1933 Los Totonaca. Mexico.
1949 Felsplastik und Felsbilder bei den Kulturvölkern Altamerikas mit besonderer Beruck sichtigung Mexikos. I: Die Andenlander. II: Die Felsentempel in Mexiko. Berlin.
1956 Altmexikanische Kulturen. Berlin. (2d ed. 1966.)
1958 Bermerkungen zu den Skulpturen und Felsbildern von Cozumalhuapa. *In* Misc. Paul Rivet, 1: 495–513.
1960 Altmexikanischer Felsbilder. *Tribus*, 9: 172–84.
1961a Die Religionen der Kulturvölker Mesoamerikas. Die Religionen des Alten Amerika (Religionen der Menschheit, 7), pp. 1–89. Stuttgart.
1961b Las antiguas culturas mexicanas. Mexico. (Spanish trans. of his 1956; 2d ed. 1964.)
1966 Altmexikanische Kulturen (mit einem Anhang über die Kunst Altmexikos von G. Kutscher). Berlin. (2d ed. of his 1956.)
1968a Felsplastik und Felsbilder bei den kulturvölken Altamerikas Band II: Felsbilder Mexikos als historische, religiöse und Kunstdenkmäler. Aus dem Nachlass herausgegeben von K. Hahn-Hissink, M.-B. Franke und D. Eisleb. Berlin.
1968b Mesoamerica. *In* Pre-Columbian American religions, pp. 5–82. London. (English trans. of his 1961a.)

KRIEGER, A. D.
1951 Stephenson's "Culture chronology in Texas." *Amer. Antiquity*, 16: 265–67.

KROEBER, A. L.
1925 Archaic culture horizons in the Valley of Mexico. *Univ. California Pub. Amer. Archaeol. Ethnol.*, 17: 373–408.
1939–44 The historical position of Chicomuceltec in Maya. *Int. Jour. Amer. Linguistics*, 10: 159–60.
1948 Anthropology. New York.

KUBLER, G.
1943 The cycle of life and death in metropolitan Aztec culture. *Gazette des*

Beaux Arts, 23: 257–68.   New York.

1948   Mexican architecture of the sixteenth century.   2 vols.   Yale Univ. Press.

1954   The Louise and Walter Arensberg collection: pre-Columbian sculpture. Mus. Art.   Philadelphia.

1961   Chichén-Itzá y Tula.   *Estud. Cultura Maya*, 1: 47–80.

1962   The art and architecture of ancient America: the Mexican, Maya, and Andean peoples.   Pelican Hist. Art. Baltimore.

1967   The iconography of the art of Teotihuacan: the pre-Columbian collection, Dumbarton Oaks.   *Studies in Pre-Columbian Art and Archaeol.*, no. 4.   Washington.

—— AND C. GIBSON

1951   The Tovar calendar.   *Mem. Connecticut Acad. Arts and Sci.*, vol. 11. New Haven.

KUTSCHER, G.

1958   *Introduction   to*   Präkolumbische Kunst aus Mexiko und Mittelamerika. Munich.

LAMBERT, J. C., ed.

1961   Mexique précolombien.   *Art et Style*, Pub. 2.   Paris.

LANDERO, P. A. DE

1922   Rocas y minerales del valle: canteras. *In* Gamio, 1922a, 2: 67–79.

LAS CASAS, B. DE

1909   Apologética historia de las Indias. *Nueva Biblioteca Autores Españoles*, no. 13.   M. Serrano y Sanz, ed.   Madrid.

LEACH, E. R.

1966   Lévi-Strauss in the Garden of Eden: an examination of some recent developments in the analysis of myth. *In* Reader in comparative religion, W. Lessa and E. Z. Vogt, eds., pp. 574–92.   2d ed.

LEBRÓN DE QUIÑONES, L.

1945   Memoria de los pueblos de la provincia de Colima.   Mexico.

LEHMANN, H.

1948   Résultat d'un voyage de prospection archéologique sur les côtes du Pacific (nord de l'état de Guerrero et sur de l'état de Michoacán).   *28th Int.*

Cong. Amer. (Paris, 1947), Acta, pp. 425–39.

1960   L'art précolombien.   Paris.

LEHMANN, W.

1905   Die fünf im Kindbett gestorbenen Frauen und die fünf Götter des Südens in der mexikanischen Mythologie.   *Zeit. für Ethnol.*, 37: 848–71. Berlin.

1921   Altmexikanische   Kunstgeschichte: eine Entwurf in Unrissen. "Orbis Pictus": Weltkunst-Bucherei-Band, 8. Berlin.

1922   The history of ancient Mexican art: an essay in outline. "Orbis Pictus": the Universal Library of Art, vol. 8. New York.   (English trans. of his 1921.)

1938   *See* Anales de Cuauhtitlan, 1938.

1949   Sterbende Götter und christliche Heilsbotschaft: wechselreden indianischer Vornehmer und spanischer Glaubensapostel in Mexiko 1524. ("Coloquios y doctrina christiana" des Fray Bernardino de Sahagún aus dem Jahre 1564.)   Aus dem Nachlass herausgegeben von Gerdt Kutscher. Quellenwerke zur alten Geschichte Amerikas Aufgezeichnet in den Sprachen der Eingeborenen, Herausgegeben   von   der   Latein-Amerikanischen Bibliothek, III. Stuttgart.

1958   *See* Chimalpahin, 1958.

1966   Las cinco mujeres del oeste muertas en el parto y los cinco dioses del sur en la mitología mexicana.   *Soc. Mex. Antr., Traducciones Mesoamericanistas*, 1: 147–75.   (Spanish trans. of his 1905.)

LENZ, H.

1948   El papel indígena mexicano: historia y supervivencia.   Mexico.

LEÓN, M. DE

1611   Camino del cielo en lengua mexicana. Mexico.

LEÓN, N.

1903a   Familias lingüísticas de México.   *An. Mus. Nac. Méx.*, 7: 279–335.

1903b   Los tarascos.   *Ibid.*, ép. 2, 1: 392–505, 592.

1967   La pintura al aje de Uruapan (Michoacan). *Bol. Centro Invest. Antr. Méx.*, no. 14, pp. 1–15. (MS 1910?)

LEÓN-PORTILLA, M.
1956   La filosofía Náhuatl, estudiada en sus fuentes. *Special ed., Inst. Indigenista Interamer.*, Pub. 26. Mexico. (2d ed. 1959). English trans., Aztec thought and culture: a study of the ancient Nahuatl mind, 1963, Norman, Okla. (3d ed. 1966, Mexico.)
1958   Ritos, sacerdotes y atavíos de los dioses. Univ. Nac. Autónoma Méx., Inst. Hist., Seminario de Cultura Náhuatl, *Textos de los Informantes de Sahagún*, no. 1.
1961a Mythology of ancient Mexico. *In* Mythologies of the ancient world, S. N. Kramer, ed., pp. 443–72. New York.
1961b Los antiguos mexicanos a través de sus crónicas y cantares. Fondo de Cultura Económica. Mexico.
1967   El proceso de aculturación de los Chichimecas de Xolótl. *Inst. Hist., Estud. Cultura Náhuatl*, 7: 59–86.

—— AND A. M. GARIBAY K.
1959   Visión de los vencidos: relaciones indígenas de la conquista. *Bib. Estudiante Universitario*, no. 81. Mexico.

LEÓN Y GAMA, A.
1832   Descripción histórica y cronológica de las Dos Piedras que con ocasión del nuevo empedrado que se está formando en la plaza principal de México, se hallaron en ella el año de 1790. 2d ed., C. M. Bustamante, ed. Mexico.

LEWIS, O.
1951   Life in a Mexican village: Tepoztlan restudied. Univ. Illinois Press.

LEYENDA DE LOS SOLES
1903   Leyenda de los Soles, continuada con otras leyendas y noticias: relación anónima escrita en lengua mexicana el año 1558. F. del Paso y Troncoso, ed. and trans. *Bib. Náhuatl, 5: Tradiciones, Migraciones*, Cuad. 1, pp. 1–40. Florence.
1938   *See* Anales de Cuauhtitlan, 1938, pp. 322–88.
1945   *See* Anales de Cuauhtitlan, 1945, pp. 119–42.

LIBBY, W. F.
1951   Radiocarbon dates, II. *Science*, 114: 291–96.
1952   Radiocarbon dates, III. *Ibid.*, 116: 673–81.

LIENZO DE TLAXCALA
1892   Lienzo de Tlaxcala. *In* Antigüedades mexicanas publicadas por la Junta Colombina de Mexico. 2 vols.

LINDSAY, A. J., JR.
1968   Northern Mexico. *Amer. Antiquity*, 33: 122.

LINNÉ, S.
1934   Archaeological researches at Teotihuacan, Mexico. *Ethnog. Mus. Sweden*, n.s., Pub. 1. Stockholm.
1936   The expeditions to Mexico sent out in 1934–35 by the Ethnographical Museum of Sweden. *Ethnos*, 1: 39–48.
1938   Zapotecan antiquities and the Paulson collection in the Ethnographical Museum of Sweden. *Ethnog. Mus. Sweden*, Pub. 4. Stockholm.
1942   Mexican highland cultures: archaeological researches at Teotihuacan, Calpulalpan and Chalchicomula in 1934–35. *Ibid.*, Pub. 7.
1956   Treasures of Mexican art: two thousand years of art and art handicraft. Stockholm. A. Read, trans. Swedish-Mexican Exhibition Comm.
1960   The art of Mexico and Central America. *In* The art of ancient America: civilizations of Central and South America, pp. 13–134. New York.

LISTER, R. H.
1941   Cerro Oztuma, Guerrero. *El México Antiguo*, 5: 209–20.
1947   Archaeology of the middle Rio Balsas basin, Mexico. *Amer. Antiquity*, 13: 67–78.
1948   An archaeological survey of the region about Teloloapan, Guerrero. *In* El Occidente de México, pp. 107–22.
1949   Excavations at Cojumatlan, Michoacan, Mexico. *Univ. New Mexico Pub. Anthr.*, no. 5.
1955   The present status of the archaeology of western Mexico: a distributional study. *Univ. Colorado Studies, Ser. in Anthr.*, no. 5.

REFERENCES

—— AND A. M. HOWARD

1955 The Chalchihuites culture of north-western Mexico. *Amer. Antiquity,* 21: 122–29.

LITVAK KING, J.

1968 Excavaciones de rescate en la presa de La Villita. *Bol. Inst. Nac. Antr. Hist.,* 31: 28–30.

LIZARDI RAMOS, C.

1944 El chacmool mexicano. *Cuad. Amer.,* 14: 137–48.

1956–57 Arquitectura de Huapalcalco, Tulancingo. *Rev. Mex. Estud. Antr.,* 14 (part 2): 111–16.

1959 El calendario maya-mexicano. *In* Esplendor del México Antiguo, 1: 221–42.

LOMBARDO TOLEDANO, V.

1931 Geografía de las lenguas de la sierra de Puebla, con algunas observaciones sobre sus primeros y sus actuales pobladores. *Univ. México,* 2 (13): 14–96.

LONG, R. C. E.

1942 The payment of tribute in the codex Mendoza. *Carnegie Inst. Wash., Notes Middle Amer. Archaeol. Ethnol.,* no. 10.

LONG, S. V.

1965 Shaft-tombs and hollow figurines from the Magdalena lake basin of Jalisco, Mexico. Doctoral dissertation, Univ. California, Los Angeles.

1967 Form and distribution of shaft-and-chamber tombs. *Rev. Univ. de los Andes,* no. 1. Bogota.

—— AND R. E. TAYLOR

1966a Chronology of a west Mexican shaft tomb. *Nature,* 212 (5062): 651–52.

1966b Suggested revision for west Mexican archaeological sequences. *Science,* 154 (3755): 1456–59.

—— AND M. V. V. WIRE

1966 Excavations at Barra de Navidad, Jalisco. Inst. Caribe Antr. Sociol. de la Fundación La Salle. *Antropológica,* no. 18. Caracas.

LÓPEZ AUSTIN, A.

1961 La constitución real de México-Tenochtitlan. Univ. Nac. México.

1967 Cuarenta clases de magos del mundo Náhuatl. *Inst. Hist., Estud. Cultura Náhuatl,* 7: 87–117.

LÓPEZ DE GÓMARA, F. DE

1852 Primera y segunda partes de la historia general de las Indias. *Bib. Autores Españoles, desde la formación del lenguaje hasta nuestros días,* vol. 1. Madrid.

1943 Historia de la conquista de México. 2 vols. P. Robredo, ed. Mexico.

LÓPEZ DE MENESES, A.

1948 Tecuichpochtzin, hija de Moteczuma (¿1510?–1550). *In* Estudios cortesianos recopilados con motivo de la IV centenario de la muerte de Hernán Cortés (1547–1947), pp. 471–95. Madrid.

LORENZO, J. L.

1953 A fluted point from Durango, Mexico. *Amer. Antiquity,* 18: 394–95.

1964 Primer informe sobre los trabajos arqueológicos de rescate efectuados en el vaso de la presa de El Infiernillo, Guerrero y Michoacán. *Bol. Inst. Nac. Antr. Hist.,* 17: 24–31. Mexico.

1965 Tlatilco: artefactos. *Inst. Nac. Antr. Hist., Ser. Invest.,* 7. Mexico.

LOTHROP, S. K.

1923 Stone yokes from Mexico and Central America. *Man,* 23: 97–98. London.

1926 Pottery of Costa Rica and Nicaragua. *Mus. Amer. Indian, Heye Found.,* Contrib. 8. 2 vols. New York.

1927 The museum Central American expedition, 1925–1926. *Mus. Amer. Indian, Heye Found., Indian Notes,* 4: 12–33.

1952 Metals from the Cenote of Sacrifice, Chichen Itza, Yucatan. *Mem. Peabody Mus., Harvard Univ.,* vol. 10, no. 2.

1956 Indigenous art of the Americas: catalogue of the collection of Robert Woods Bliss. London. (See also Lothrop, Foshag, and Mahler, 1957; Handbook . . . Bliss Collection, 1963.)

1964 Treasures of ancient America: the arts of the pre-Columbian civilizations from Mexico to Peru. Geneva.

——, W. F. FOSHAG, AND J. MAHLER

1957 Pre-Columbian art: Robert Woods Bliss collection. New York. (See also Lothrop, 1956; Handbook . . . Bliss Collection, 1963.)

—— AND OTHERS

1961 Essays in pre-Columbian art and archaeology. Harvard Univ. Press.

LUMHOLTZ, C.

1902 Unknown Mexico. 2 vols. New York.

MCBRYDE, F. W.

1945 Cultural and historical geography of southwest Guatemala. *Smithsonian Inst., Inst. Social Anthr.*, Pub. 4.

MACCURDY, G.

1910 An Aztec "calendar stone" in Yale University Museum. *Amer. Anthr.*, 12: 481–96.

MACDOUGALL, T., AND I. W. JOHNSON

1966 *Chichicaztli* fiber: the spinning and weaving of it in southern Mexico. *Archiv für Völkerkunde*, 20: 65–73. Vienna.

MACNEISH, R. S.

1947 A preliminary report on coastal Tamaulipas, Mexico. *Amer. Antiquity*, 13: 1–13.

1948 Prehistoric relationships between the cultures of the southeastern United States and Mexico in light of an archaeological survey of the state of Tamaulipas, Mexico. Doctoral dissertation, Univ. Chicago.

1950 A synopsis of the archaeological sequence in the Sierra de Tamaulipas. *Rev. Mex. Estud. Antr.*, 11: 79–96.

1954a An early archaeological site near Panuco, Vera Cruz. *Trans. Amer. Phil. Soc.*, 44: 539–641.

1954b The Pointed Mountain site near Fort Liard, Northwest Territories, Canada. *Amer. Antiquity*, 19: 234–53.

1956 Prehistoric settlement patterns on the northeastern periphery of Meso-America. *In* Willey, 1956a, pp. 140–47.

1958 Preliminary archaeological investigations in the Sierra de Tamaulipas, Mexico. *Trans. Amer. Phil. Soc.*, 48: 1–209.

1961a Restos precerámicos de la Cueva de Coxcatlán, en el sur de Puebla. *Inst. Nac. Antr. Hist., Depto. Prehistoria*, Pub. 10. Mexico.

1961b First annual report of the Tehuacan archaeological-botanical project. Phillips Acad. Andover, Mass.

1961c Recent finds concerned with the incipient agriculture stage in prehistoric Meso-America. *In* Homenaje Martínez del Río, pp. 91–101.

1962 Second annual report of the Tehuacan archaeological-botanical project. Phillips Acad. Andover, Mass.

——, A. NELKEN-TERNER, AND I. W. JOHNSON

1967 Nonceramic artifacts. Vol. 2 of The prehistory of the Tehuacan Valley.

——, F. A. PETERSON, AND K. V. FLANNERY

1970 Ceramics. Vol. 3 of The prehistory of the Tehuacan Valley.

MANGELSDORF, P. C., R. S. MACNEISH, AND W. C. GALINAT

1956 Archaeological evidence on the diffusion and evolution of maize in northeastern Mexico. *Bot. Mus. Leafl., Harvard Univ.*, 17: 125–50.

MARGAIN, C. R.

1939 Escultura náhoa. *Artes Plásticas*, 1: 57–69.

1944 Zonas arqueológicas de Querétaro, Guanajuato, Aguascalientes, y Zacatecas. *In* El Norte de México, pp. 145–48.

1956 La habitación popular en el México prehispánico. Soc. Arquitectos Mexicanos, Colegio Nac. de Arquitectos de México, *Ciclo de Conferencias sobre Vivienda Popular*, no. 5.

1966 Sobre sistemas y materiales de construcción en Teotihuacán. *In* Teotihuacán, pp. 157–211.

1968 Sobre la policromía del llamado "Calendario Azteca." MS.

MARINGER, J.

1950 Contributions to the prehistory of Mongolia. *Sino-Swedish Exped.*, Pub. 34, no. 7. Stockholm.

MARINO FLORES, A.

1958–59 Grupos lingüísticos del estado de Guerrero. *Rev. Mex. Estud. Antr.*, 15: 95–114.

MARQUINA, I.

1951 Arquitectura prehispánica. *Mem.*

838

Inst. Nac. Antr. Hist., no. 1. Mexico. (2d ed., enlarged, 1964.)

1960 El Templo Mayor de México. Inst. Nac. Antr. Hist. Mexico.

1964 Arquitectura prehispánica. (2d ed. of his 1951.)

1968 Exploraciones en la pirámide de Cholula. *Bol. Inst. Nac. Antr. Hist.*, 32: 12–19.

MARTÍNEZ, M.

1936 Plantas utiles de México. Mexico.

1959 Plantas medicinales de México. Mexico.

MARTÍNEZ DEL RÍO, P.

1953 La cueva mortuoria de La Candelaria, Coahuila. *Cuad. Amer.*, 4: 177–204.

1954 La comarca lagunera a fines del siglo XVI y principios del XVII según las fuentes escritas. *Univ. Nac. Autónoma Méx., Pub. Inst. Hist.*, 1st ser., no. 30.

MASON, J. A.

1935 The place of Texas in pre-Columbian relationships between the United States and Mexico. *Bull. Texas Archaeol. Paleontol. Soc.*, 7: 29–46.

1937 Late archaeological sites in Durango, Mexico, from Chalchihuites to Zape. *Pub. Philadelphia Anthr. Soc., 25th Anniv. Studies*, 1: 117–26.

MASTACHE, A. G.

1966 Técnicas prehispánicas de tejido. Master's thesis, Esc. Nac. Antr. Hist. Inst. Nac. Antr. Hist. Mexico.

1970 Tejidos arqueológicos de una cueva seca de la región de Caltepec, Puebla. Paper presented to 35th annual meeting, Society for American Archaeology, Mexico, 1970.

MATEOS HIGUERA, S.

1948 La pictografía tarasca. *In* El Occidente de México, pp. 160–74.

MATOS MOCTEZUMA, E.

1968 Piezas de saqueo procedentes de Jerécuaro, Gto. *Bol. Inst. Nac. Antr. Hist.*, 33: 30–35.

MATRÍCULA DE HUEXOTZINCO

1560 Matrícula de Huexotzinco, manuscrit mexicain 387. Bibliothèque Nationale. Paris.

MATRÍCULA DE TRIBUTOS

1890 *See* Peñafiel, 1890, vol. 2, pls. 228–59.

MAUDSLAY, A. P.

1889–1902 Archaeology. Biologia Centrali-Americana. 5 vols. London.

MAYA AND THEIR NEIGHBORS, THE

1940 The Maya and their neighbors. C. L. Hay and others, eds. New York.

MAYAS Y OLMECAS

1942 Mayas y Olmecas. Rafael Pascacio Gamboa, ed. Segunda reunión de mesa redonda sobre problemas antropológicos de México y Centro América, Tuxtla Gutiérrez. Soc. Mex. Antr.

MAYER, B.

1844 Mexico: Aztec, Spanish and Republican. New York. (2d ed. 1953, Mexico.)

MAYER-OAKES, W. J.

1959 A stratigraphic excavation at El Risco, Mexico. *Proc. Amer. Phil. Soc.*, 103: 332–73.

MAZA, F. DE LA

1959 La ciudad de Cholula y sus iglesias. Inst. Invest. Estéticas. Mexico.

MEADE, J.

1939 Documentos inéditos para la historia de Tampico, siglos XVI y XVII. Mexico.

1940 ¿Fué la nación Maguage la misma que la Olive? *Divulgación histórica*, 2: 28–31. Mexico.

1942 La Huasteca: época antigua. Mexico.

1948 Arqueología de San Luis Potosi. Mexico.

1950 Fray Andrés de Olmos. *Mem. Acad. Mex. Hist.*, 9: 374–452. Mexico.

1953 Historia prehispánica de la Huasteca. *In* Huastecos, Totonacos, pp. 291–302.

MEDELLÍN ZENIL, A.

1950 Arqueología de Remojadas. MS in Archivo Inst. Antr. Veracruz. Jalapa.

1952a Distribución geográfica de la "Cultura de Remojadas": exploraciones arqueológicas de 1952. MS, *ibid.*

1952b Exploraciones en Quauhtochco. Gobierno del estado de Veracruz, Depto. Antr. Jalapa.

1953 Exploraciones en Los Cerros y Dicha Tuerta. MS in Archivo Técnico, Inst. Antr., Univ. Veracruzana. Jalapa.

1955 Exploración en la Isla de Sacrificios. Gobierno del estado de Veracruz. Jalapa.

1960a Cerámicas del Totonacapan: exploraciones arqueológicas en el centro de Veracruz. Jalapa.

1960b Nopila: un sitio clásico del Veracruz central. *Palabra y Hombre*, 13: 37–48.

1962 El monolito de Maltrata, Veracruz. *Ibid.*, 24: 555–62.

——, O. PAZ, AND F. BEVERIDE

1962 Magia de la risa. Mexico.

MEDINA DE LA TORRE, F.

1934 Monumentos arqueológicos en el oriente del estado de Jalisco. *Bol. Junta Auxiliar Jalisciense de la Soc. Mex. Geog. y Estad.* Guadalajara.

MEDIONI, G., AND M. T. PINTO

1941 Art in ancient Mexico. Collection of Diego Rivera. New York.

MEGGERS, B. J., AND C. EVANS, eds.

1963 Aboriginal cultural development in Latin America: an interpretative review. *Smithsonian Inst., Smithsonian Misc. Coll.*, vol. 146, no. 1. Washington.

MEIGHAN, C. W.

1959 New findings in west Mexican archaeology. *Kiva*, 25: 1–7.

1960 Prehistoric copper objects from western Mexico. *Science*, 131 (3412): 1534.

1961 Interrelationships of New World cultures: field activities of Project A (west Mexico), 1960–1961. Mimeographed. Dept. Anthr., Univ. California, Los Angeles.

MELGAREJO VIVANCO, J. L.

n.d.[1947] La provincia de Tzicoac. Jalapa.

1943 Totonacapan. Jalapa.

1950 Historia de Veracruz (época prehispánica). Jalapa.

MEMORIAL . . . TLACUPAN

1939–42 Memorial de los pueblos sujetos al señorio de Tlacupan, y de los que tributaban a México, Tezcuco y Tlacupan. *In* Paso y Troncoso, 1939–42, 14: 118–22.

MEN AND CULTURES

1960 *See* Wallace, 1960.

MENA, R.

1913 El trabajo de la obsidiana en México: ejemplares de la colección arqueológica de la Sociedad Mexicana de Geografía y Estadística. *Bol. Soc. Mex. Geog. Estad.*, 6: 203–11.

1924 Arqueología: monolitos. Cartillas de vulgarización del Museo Nacional de México.

MENDIETA, G. DE

1870 Historia eclesiástica indiana. J. García Icazbalceta, ed. Mexico.

1945 *Idem.* S. Chávez Hayhoe, ed. 4 vols. Mexico.

MENGIN, E.

1945 *See* Anales de Tlatelolco, 1945.

1952 Commentaire du Codex Mexicanus nrs. 23–24 de la Bibliothèque Nationale de Paris. *Jour. Soc. Amér. Paris*, 41: 387–498.

MÉXICO, DEPTO. DE MONUMENTOS

1935 *See* Tenayuca, 1935.

MÉXICO PREHISPÁNICO

1946 *See* Vivó, 1946.

MÉXICO Y LA CULTURA

1946 México y la cultura. Sec. Educación Pública. Mexico. (2d ed. 1961.)

MILLER, A. G.

1967 The birds of Quetzalpapalotl. *Ethnos*, 32: 5–17.

MILLON, R. F.

1954 Irrigation at Teotihuacan. *Amer. Antiquity*, 20: 177–80.

1957a Irrigation systems in the valley of Teotihuacan. *Ibid.*, 23: 160–166.

1957b New data on Teotihuacan I in Teotihuacan. *Bol. Centro Invest. Antr. Méx.*, no. 4, pp. 12–17.

1960 The beginnings of Teotihuacan. *Amer. Antiquity*, 26: 1–10.

1964 Valley of Teotihuacan chronology. Mimeographed chart, dated 1964, distributed during 11th Round Table meeting, Soc. Mex. Antr., 1966. Mexico.

1966a Cronología y periodificación: datos

estratigráficos sobre períodos cerámicos y sus relaciones con la pintura mural. *In* Teotihuacán, pp. 1–18.

1966b Décimaprimera mesa redonda de antropología. *Bol. Inst. Nac. Antr. Hist.*, no. 25.

1966c Extension y población de la ciudad de Teotihuacán en sus diferentes períodos: un cálculo provisional. *In* Teotihuacán, pp. 57–78.

1967 Teotihuacan. *Sci. Amer.*, 216: 38–48.

—— AND J. A. BENNYHOFF

1961 A long architectural sequence at Teotihuacan. *Amer. Antiquity*, 26: 516–23.

——, B. DREWITT, AND J. A. BENNYHOFF

1965 The Pyramid of the Sun at Teotihuacan: 1959 investigations. *Trans. Amer. Phil. Soc.*, vol. 55, part 6.

MIRAMONTES, F.

1936 Geografía económica agrícola del estado de Michoacán. *In* Cámara de Diputados, vol. 4. Mexico.

MISCELÁNEA PAUL RIVET

1958 Miscelánea Paul Rivet, octogenario dicata. 2 vols. Mexico.

MOEDANO KOER, H.

1941 Estudio preliminar de la cerámica de Tzintzuntzan: temporada III. *Rev. Mex. Estud. Antr.*, 5: 21–42.

1942 Estudio general sobre la situación de la fortaleza de Oztuma. *27th Int. Cong. Amer.* (Mexico, 1939), Acta, 1: 557–63.

1944a La diosa raptada. *Nosostros*, 1 (19): 24–26. Mexico.

1944b El octavo xiuhmolpilli. *El Nacional*, March 22, section 1, pp. 3–4.

1946 La cerámica de Zinapécuaro, Michoacán. *An. Mus. Michoacano*, ép. 2, no. 4, pp. 39–49.

1947 El friso de los caciques. *An. Inst. Nac. Antr. Hist.*, 2: 113–36. Mexico.

1948 Breve noticia sobre la zona de Oztotitlan, Guerrero. *In* El Occidente de México, pp. 105–06.

MOLINA, A. DE

1944 Vocabulario en lengua castellana y mexicana. *In* Colección de incunables americanos, siglo XVI, vol. 4. Ediciones Cultura Hispánica (facsimile ed. of 1571 ed.). Madrid.

MOLINS FABREGA, N.

1956 El Códice Mendocino y la economía de Tenochtitlan. Mexico.

MONTELL, G.

1937 Statens etnografiska museums expedition till Mexico 1934–35: de etnografiska undersökningarna. *Ethnos*, 2: 301–18. Stockholm.

MONTERDE, F.

1955 Teatro indígena prehispánico: Rabinal Achí. *Bib. Estudiante Universitario*, no. 71. Mexico.

MONZÓN, A.

1949 El calpulli en la organización social de los tenochca. *Univ. Nac. Autónoma Méx., Pub. Inst. Hist.*, 1st ser., no. 14.

—— AND A. ESPEJO

1945 Algunas notas sobre organización social de los tlatelolca. *Mem. Acad. Mex. Hist.*, 4: 484–89.

MORENO, M. M.

1931 La organización política y social de los aztecas. Univ. Nac. Autónoma Méx.

MORENO DE LOS ARCOS, R.

1967 Los cinco soles cosmogónicos. *Univ. Nac. Autónoma Méx., Estud. Cultura Náhuatl*, 7: 183–210.

MORGAN, L. H.

1878 Ancient society or researches in the lines of human progress from savagery through barbarism to civilization. New York.

MORIARTY, J. M.

1964 The influence of strand plain morphology on the development of primitive industries along the Costa de Nayarit, Mexico. Part 1. *Amér. Indígena*, 24: 365–97.

1965 *Idem*, part 2. *Ibid.*, 25: 65–78.

MORLEY, S. G.

1947 The ancient Maya. 2d ed. Stanford Univ. Press.

MORRIS, E. H.

1931 The Temple of the Warriors: the adventure of exploring and restoring a masterpiece of native American architecture in the ruined Maya city of Chichen Itza, Yucatan. New York.

——, J. CHARLOT, AND A. A. MORRIS

1931 The Temple of the Warriors at Chichen Itza, Yucatan. 2 vols. *Carnegie Inst. Wash.*, Pub. 406.

MOTA PADILLA, M. DE LA
1870   Historia de la conquista de la provincia de la Nueva Galicia. Mexico.

MOTA Y ESCOBAR, A. DE LA
1940   Descripción geográfica de los reinos de Nueva Galicia, Nueva Vizcaya, y Nuevo León. Mexico.
1945   Memoriales del obispo de Tlaxcala, fray Alonso de la Mota y Escobar. *An. Inst. Nac. Antr. Hist.*, 1: 191–306 (1939–40).

MOTOLINIA, TORIBIO (FRAY TORIBIO DE BENAVENTE)
1903   Memoriales. *In* García Pimentel, 1903–07, vol. 1.
1914   Historia de los indios de la Nueva España. Barcelona.
1941   *Idem.* S. Chávez Hayhoe, ed. Mexico.
1950   History of the Indians of New Spain. *In* Documents and narratives concerning the discovery and conquest of Latin America, n.s., no. 4. E. A. Foster, ed. and trans. Cortés Soc. Berkeley.

MUIR, J. M.
1926   Data on the structure of pre-Columbian Huastec mounds in the Tampico region, Mexico. *Jour. Royal Anthr. Inst.*, 56: 231–38. London.

MÜLLER, E. F. J.
1956–57 El valle de Tulancingo. *Rev. Mex. Estud. Antr.*, 14: 129–38.
1966   Instrumental y armas. *In* Teotihuacán, pp. 225–38.

MÜLLERRIED, F. K. G., AND H. VON WINNING
1943   El "Cerrito" al este de Tepotzotlán, México, en el Valle de México. *El México Antiguo*, 6: 131–39.

MUMFORD, L.
1952   Art and technics. 2d ed. Columbia Univ. Press.

MUÑOZ CAMARGO, D.
1948   Historia de Tlaxcala. Mexico.

MURDOCK, G. P.
1949   Social structure. New York.

MURIEL, J.
1948   Reflexiones sobre Hernán Cortés. *Rev. Indias*, año 9, pp. 229–45.

MUSÉE DE L'HOMME
1965   Chefs-d'oeuvre du Musée de l'Homme. Musée de l'Homme, Caisse Nationale des Monuments Historiques. Paris.

NADER, L.
1969   The Trique of Oaxaca. *In* Handbook of Middle American Indians, R. Wauchope, ed., vol. 7, art. 19.

NAZAREO, P., AND OTHERS
1940   Carta al rey don Felipe II . . . 17 de Marzo de 1566. *In* Paso y Troncoso, 1939–42, 10: 89–129.

NEBEL, C.
1839   Viaje pintoresco y arqueológico sobre la República Mexicana, 1829–1834. Paris.

NEPEAN, E.
1844   Letter to Samuel Birch upon the antiquities discovered in the Island of Sacrificios. *Soc. Antiquaries London, Archaeologia*, 30: 339–41. London.
1857   Excavations in the Island of Sacrificios. *Ibid.*, 30: 138–339.

NICHOLSON, H. B.
1955a Aztec style calendric inscriptions of possible historical significance: a survey. Mimeographed. Mexico.
1955b The temalacatl of Tehuacan. *El México Antiguo*, 8: 95–134.
1957   Topiltzin Quetzalcoatl of Tollan: a problem in Mesoamerican ethnohistory. Doctoral dissertation, Harvard Univ.
1958   An Aztec monument dedicated to Tezcatlipoca. *In* Misc. Paul Rivet, 1: 593–607.
1959a The Chapultepec cliff sculpture of Motecuhzoma Xocoyotzin. *El México Antiguo*, 9: 379–444.
1959b Los principales dioses mesoamericanos. *In* Esplendor del México Antiguo, 1: 161–78.
1960   The Mixteca-Puebla concept in Mesoamerican archeology: a re-examination. *In* Wallace, 1960, pp. 612–17. (Reprinted in Graham, 1966, pp. 258–63.)
1961a Interrelationships of New World cultures: Project A, central Pacific coast of Mexico. Mimeographed. Dept. Anthr., Univ. California, Los Angeles.

1961b Notes and news: Middle America. *Amer. Antiquity*, 26: 594–600.

1961c The use of the term 'Mixtec' in Mesoamerican archaeology. *Ibid.*, 26: 431–33.

1962 Notes and news: Middle America. *Ibid.*, 27: 617–24.

1963 Interrelationships of New World cultures: Project A, central Pacific coast of Mexico. 1961–62 season. *Katunob*, 4: 39–51.

1966 The problem of the provenience of the members of the "Codex Borgia group": a summary. *In* Pompa y Pompa, 1966, pp. 145–58.

1967 A "royal headband" of the Tlaxcalteca. *Rev. Mex. Estud. Antr.*, 21: 71–106.

1968 *Review of* Alfonso Caso, Interpretación del Códice Colombino. *An. Antr.*, 5: 280–87. Mexico.

—— AND J. SMITH

1960 Interrelationships of New World cultures: Project A, central and south Pacific coast, Mexico. 1960 season. Mimeographed. Dept. Anthr., Univ. California, Los Angeles.

NICHOLSON, I.

1967 Mexican and Central American mythology. London.

NICOLAU D'OLWER, L.

1952 Fray Bernardino de Sahagún (1499–1590). *Inst. Panamer. Geog. Hist., Comisión de Historia, Historiadores de América*, no. 9. Mexico.

NOGUERA, E.

1925 Las representaciones del buho en la cultura teotihuacana. *An. Mus. Nac. Méx.*, ép. 4, 3: 444–48.

1930 Ruinas arqueológicas del norte de México: Casas Grandes (Chihuahua); La Quemada, Chalchihuites (Zacatecas). Pub. Sec. Educación Pública. Mexico.

1931 Excavaciones arqueológicas en las regiones de Zamora y Pátzcuaro, estado de Michoacán. *An Mus. Nac. Arqueol. Hist. Etnog.*, ép. 4, 7: 89–103.

1932 Extensiones cronológico-culturales y geográficas de las cerámicas de México. Mexico.

1935a Antecedentes y relaciones de la cultura teotihuacana. *El México Antiguo*, 3 (5–8): 3–90, 93–95.

1935b La cerámica de Tenayuca y las excavaciones estratigráficas. *In* Tenayuca, pp. 141–201.

1936 Los petroglifos de Maltrata. *Mapa*, 3 (26): 39–41.

1937 El altar de los cráneos esculpidos de Cholula. Mexico.

1938 Guide book to the National Museum of Archaeology, History, and Ethnology. Popular Library of Mexican Culture. Mexico.

1940 Excavations at Tehuacan. *In* The Maya and their neighbors, pp. 306–19.

1942 Exploraciones en "El Opeño," Michoacán. *27th Int. Cong. Amer.* (Mexico, 1939), Acta, 1: 574–86.

1943 Excavaciones en El Tepalcate, Chimalhuacán, México. *Amer. Antiquity*, 9: 33–43.

1944 Exploraciones en Jiquilpan. *An. Mus. Michoacano*, ép. 2, 3: 37–54.

1946 La escultura. *In* Vivó, 1946, pp. 583–90.

1947 Cerámica de Xochicalco. *El México Antiguo*, 6: 273–98.

1948 Estado actual de los conocimientos acerca de la arqueología del noroeste de Michoacán. *In* El Occidente de México, pp. 38–39.

1954 La cerámica arqueológica de Cholula. Ed. Guaranía. Mexico.

1955 Extraordinario hallazgo en Teotihuacán. *El México Antiguo*, 8: 43–56.

1958 Tallas prehispánicas en madera. Ed. Guaranía. Mexico.

1960a La Quemada, Chalchihuites. Guía oficial del Inst. Nac. Antr. Hist. Mexico.

1960b Zonas arqueológicas del estado de Morelos. Guía oficial del Inst. Nac. Antr. Hist. Mexico.

1961 Últimos descubrimientos en Xochicalco. *Rev. Mex. Estud. Antr.*, 17: 33–37.

1962 Nueva clasificación de figurillas del horizonte clásico. *Cuad. Amer.*, no. 5. Mexico.

1965 La cerámica arqueológica de Meso-

843

américa. *Univ. Nac. Autónoma Méx., Inst. Invest. Hist.*, 1st ser., no. 86.

—— AND D. J. LEONARD

1957 Descubrimiento de la Casa de las Águilas, en Teotihuacán. *Bol. Centro Invest. Antr. Méx.*, 4: 6–9.

—— AND R. PIÑA CHAN

1956–57 Estratigrafía de Teopanzolco. *Rev. Mex. Estud. Antr.*, 14: 139–56.

NORTE DE MÉXICO, EL

1944 El norte de México y el sur de Estados Unidos. Tercera reunión de mesa redonda sobre problemas antropológicos de México y Centro América. Soc. Mex. Antr. Mexico.

NOWOTNY, K. A.

1959 Die Hieroglyphen des Codex Mendoza. *Mitteilungen aus dem Museum für Völkerkunde in Hamburg*, vol. 25. Hamburg.

1960 Mexikanische Kostbarkeiten aus Kunstkammern der Renaissance, im Museum für Völkerkunde Wien und in der Nationalbibliothek Wien. Mus. für Völkerkunde. Vienna.

1961 Tlacuilolli: die mexikanischen Bilderhandschriften, Stil und Inhalt: mit einem Katalog der Codex-Borgia-Gruppe. *Ibero-Amerikanischen Bibliothek, Monumenta Americana*, 3. Berlin.

NOYES, E.

1932 *See* A. Ponce, 1932.

NUEVOS DOCUMENTOS . . . CORTÉS

1946 Nuevos documentos relativos a los bienes de Hernán Cortés. Archivo General de la Nación. Mexico.

NUTINI, H. G.

1961 Clan organization in a Nahuatl-speaking village of the state of Tlaxcala, Mexico. *Amer. Anthr.*, 63: 62–78.

NUTTALL, Z.

1886 Terra cotta heads of San Juan Teotihuacan. *Amer. Jour. Archaeol.*, 2: 151–318.

1892 On ancient Mexican shields. *Internat. Archiv für Ethnog.*, 5: 34–53, 89. Leiden.

1903 *See* Codex Magliabecchiano, 1903.

1904 A penitential rite of the ancient Mexi-

cans. *Papers Peabody Mus., Harvard Univ.*, vol. 1, no. 7.

1909 A curious survival in Mexico of the use of the purpura shellfish for dyeing. *In* Putnam Anniversary Volume, pp. 368–84.

1910 The Island of Sacrifice. *Amer. Anthr.*, n.s., 12: 257–95.

1927 [ed.] El libro perdido de los pláticas o coloquios de los doce primeros misioneros de México, por Fr. Bernardino de Sahagún. *Rev. Mex. Estud. Hist.*, 1:101–39.

OCCIDENTE DE MÉXICO, EL

1948 El occidente de México. Cuarta reunión de mesa redonda sobre problemas antropológicos de México y Centro América. Soc. Mex. Antr. Mexico.

O'GORMAN, E.

1941 Noticia sobre los Indios guastecos de la provincia de Pánuco y su religión. Primer tercio del siglo XVII. *Bol. Archivo General de la Nación*, 12: 215–21. Mexico.

OKADA, F. E.

1951 Some characteristics of Mongolian-type lames. *Amer. Antiquity*, 16: 254.

OKLADNIKOV, A. P.

1959 Dalekoye proshloye primorya. [The remote past of the maritime province.] Vladivostok.

OLIVERA SEDANO, A.

1956 Cuitlahuac. *Rev. Mex. Estud. Antr.*, 14: 299–302.

O'NEILL, G. C.

1956–57 Preliminary report on stratigraphic excavations in the southern Valley of Mexico: Chalco-Xico. *Ibid.*, 14: 45–52.

ORDEN . . . TECUTLES

n.d. La orden que los yndios tenian en su tiempo para hacerse tecutles. MS. in Rich Collection, New York Public Library.

ORDÓÑEZ, E.

1922 Escultura: la labra de piedra. *In* Gamio, 1922a, 1: 164–68.

ORIGEN DE LOS MEXICANOS

1941 Origen de los mexicanos. *In* García Icazbalceta, 1941, 3: 256–80.

REFERENCES

OROPEZA, M.
1968 Teotihuacán: escultura. *Inst. Nac. Antr. Hist., Mus. Nac. Antr., Col. Breve*, no. 3. Mexico.

OROZCO Y BERRA, M.
1864 Geografía de las lenguas y carta etnográfica de México.
1877 El cuauhxicalli de Tizoc. *An. Mus. Nac. Méx.*, 1: 3–36.
1880 Historia antigua y de la conquista de México. 4 vols. and atlas. Mexico.
1960 *Idem*, 2d ed. Con un estudio previo de A. M. Garibay K. y biografía del autor más tres bibliografías referentes al mismo de M. León-Portilla. Mexico.

ORTEGA, M. F.
1940 Extensión y límites de la provincia de los Yopes a mediados del siglo XVI. *El México Antiguo*, 5: 48–53.

ORTELIUS, A.
1584 Theatrum orbis terrarum. Antwerp.

OSBORNE, D.
1943 An archaeological reconnaissance in southeastern Michoacan. *Amer. Antiquity*, 9: 59–73.

OVIEDO Y VALDÉS, G. F. DE
1851–55 Historia general y natural de las Indias, islas y tierra-firme del mar océano. J. Amador de los Ríos, ed. 4 vols. Madrid.

PADDOCK, J.
1966a Distribución de rasgos teotihuacanos en Mesoamérica. Mimeographed and distributed during 11th Round Table meeting, Soc. Mex. Antr. Mexico.
1966b [ed.] *Mesoamerican Notes*, 6–7. Dept. Anthr., Univ. of the Americas. Mexico.
1966c [ed.] Ancient Oaxaca: discoveries in Mexican archeology and history. Stanford Univ. Press.
1966d Mixtec ethnohistory and Monte Alban V. *In* his 1966c, pp. 367–86.
1966e Oaxaca in ancient Mesoamerica. *Ibid.*, pp. 83–242.
1967 Western Mesoamerica. *Amer. Antiquity*, 32: 422–27.
1968 Western Mesoamerica. *Ibid.*, 33: 122–28.

——, J. R. MOGOR, AND M. D. LIND
1968 Lambityeco, Tomb 2: a preliminary report. *Bol. Estud. Oaxaqueños*, no. 25. Mexico.

PADRONES DE TLAXCALA
n.d. Padrones de Tlaxcala del siglo XVI. *Mus. Nac. Méx., Archivo Histórico, Col. Antigua 377.*

PÁEZ BROTCHIE, L.
1940 La Nueva Galicia a través de su viejo archivo judicial. *Bib. Hist. Mex. Obras Inéd.*, no. 18. Mexico.

PALACIO, LICENCIADO
1864–84 Relación hecha por el Licenciado Palacio al rey Felipe II, en la que describe la provincia de Guatemala, las costumbres de los indios y otras cosas notables. *In* Col. doc. Indias, 1864–84, 6: 5–40.

PALACIOS, E. J.
1923a Otra ciudad desconocida en Hueyaltepetl. *Bol. Mus. Nac. Arqueol. Hist. Etnog.*, 2: 21–32. Mexico.
1923b Documentos relativos a la exploración de Hueyaltepetl. *Ibid.*, 2: 33–35.
1929 La piedra del escudo nacional de México. *Pub. Sec. Educación Pública*, vol. 22, no. 9. Mexico.
1943 Los yugos y su simbolismo: contribución al VI Congreso Mexicano de Historia, con sede en Jalapa, Veracruz. Mexico.
1945 Exploración en Tuzapan y zonas comarcanas. *An. Mus. Nac. Arqueol. Hist. Etnog.*, 3: 133–37. Mexico.

PALERM, A.
1953 Etnografía antigua totonaca en el oriente de México. *In* Huastecos, Totonacos, pp. 163–73.
1954 La distribución del regadío en el área central de Mesoamérica. *Pan Amer. Union, Cien, Sociales*, 5: 2–15; 6: 64–74. Washington.
1955 The agricultural bases of urban civilization in Mesoamerica. *In* Irrigation civilizations: a comparative study, J. H. Steward and others, eds., pp. 28–42.

—— AND E. R. WOLF
1956 El desarrollo del área clave del im-

perio texcocano. *Rev. Mex. Estud. Antr.*, 14: 337–49.

PALMER, E.
1888 Dr. Palmer's unpublished notes on the Coahuila caves.

PAPELES DE NUEVA ESPAÑA
See Paso y Troncoso, 1905–06.

PARRES ARIAS, J.
1962 Nuevas adquisiones del Museo de Arqueolgía. *Eco*, 12: 6–7, 12. Inst. Jalisciense Antr. Hist. Guadalajara.
1963 Cofradía: nueva zona arqueológica en Jalisco. *Ibid.*, 14: 5–6.

PARSONS, E. C.
1936 Mitla: town of the souls and other Zapotec-speaking pueblos of Oaxaca, Mexico. Univ. Chicago Press.

PASO Y TRONCOSO, F. DEL
1891 Informes a la Secretaría de Instrucción Pública acerca de sus exploraciones en la Villa Rica y Cempoala. *Diario Oficial* (April 18), vol. 24, no. 93. Mexico.
1893 Catálogo de los objetos que presenta la República de México en la Exposición Histórico-Americana de Madrid. 2 vols. Madrid.
1898 Códice del Palais Bourbon de París. Florence.
1903 *See* Leyenda de los Soles, 1903.
1905–06 [ed.] Papeles de Nueva España. Segunda Serie, Geografía y Estadística. 6 vols. Vol. 1: Suma de visitas de los pueblos de la Nueva España. Vol. 3: Descripción del Arzobispado de México, 1571. Vol. 4: Relaciones geográficas de la diócesis de Oaxaca, 1579–81. Vol. 5: Relaciones geográficas de la diócesis de Tlaxcala, 1580–82. Vol. 6: Relaciones geográficas de la diócesis de México, 1579–82. Vol. 7: Relaciones geográficas de la diócesis de México y de la de Michoacán, 1579–82. Madrid.
1912 *See* Codex Kingsborough, 1912.
1939–42 [ed.] Epistolario de Nueva España, 1505–1818. 16 vols. Bib. Histórica Mexicana de Obras Inéditas, 2d ser. Mexico.

—— AND F. GALICIA CHIMALPOPOCA, eds.
1897 Lista de los pueblos principales que pertenecían antiguamente a Tetzcoco. *An. Mus. Nac. Méx.*, 4: 48–56.

PEARCE, J. E., AND A. T. JACKSON
1933 A prehistoric rock shelter in Val Verde county, Texas. *Univ. Texas Bull., Anthr. Papers*, vol. 1, no. 3.

PEARL, R. M.
1961 Rocks and minerals. New York.

PEITHMAN, R. I.
1961 Cultural history and significance of Nayar white-on-red. Master's thesis, Dept. Anthr., Southern Illinois Univ.

PELLICER, C., AND OTHERS
1965 Anahuacalli: Museo Diego Rivera. *Artes de México*, año 12, ép. 2, no. 66/67.

PEÑAFIEL, A.
1885 *See* his 1967.
1890 Monumentos de arte mexicano antiguo: ornamentación, mitología, tributos y monumentos. 5 vols. Berlin.
1897–1903 Colección de documentos para la historia mexicana. 6 vols. Sec. de Fomento. Mexico.
1900 Teotihuacán. Mexico.
1903a *See* Anales de Tecamachalco, 1903.
1903b Indumentaria antigua: armas y vestidos guerreros y civiles de los antiguos Mexicanos. Mexico.
1904 *See* Cantares mexicanos, 1904.
1909 Ciudades coloniales y capitales de la República Mexicana. 2 vols. Mexico.
1910 Destrucción del Templo Mayor de México antiguo y los monumentos encontrados en la ciudad, en las excavaciones de 1897 y 1902. Mexico.
1967 Nombres geográficos de México: catálogo alfabético de los nombres de lugar pertenecientes al idioma 'Náhuatl': estudio jeroglífico de la Matrícula de los Tributos del Códice Mendocino. Guadalajara. (Original ed. 1885.)

PENDERGAST, D. M.
1960 The distribution of metal artifacts in prehispanic America. Doctoral dissertation, Univ. California, Los Angeles.

PEPPER, G. H.
1916 Yácatas in the Tierra Caliente, Mi-

choacan. *In* Holmes Anniversary Volume, pp. 415–20.

PERET, B., AND M. ALVAREZ BRAVO
1943 Los tesoros del Museo Nacional de México: escultura azteca. Mexico.

PETERSON, F. A.
1959 Ancient Mexico: an introduction to the pre-Hispanic cultures. London.

—— AND F. HORCASITAS
1957 Recent finds at Tlatilco. *Tlalocan*, 3: 363–65.

PIJOAN, J.
1946 Arte precolombiano, mexicano y maya. *In* his Summa artis: historia general del arte, vol. 10. Madrid.
1958 *Idem*, 3d ed.

PIMENTEL NEZAHUALCOYOTL, H.
1880 Sacado de un memorial dirigido al rey. . . . *In* Orozco y Berra, 1880, 2: 201–03.

PIÑA CHAN, R.
1952 Tlatilco y la cultura preclásica del Valle de México. *An. Inst. Nac. Antr. Hist.* (1949–50), ép. 6, 4 (32): 33–43.
1955a Chalcatzingo, Morelos. *Inst. Nac. Antr. Hist., Dir. Monumentos Prehispánicos*, Informe 4. Mexico.
1955b Las culturas preclásicas de la Cuenca de México. Fondo de Cultura Económica. Mexico.
1958 Tlatilco. Inst. Nac. Antr. Hist., Ser. Invest. 2 vols. Mexico.
1960a Algunos sitios arqueológicos de Oaxaca y Guerrero. *Rev. Mex. Estud. Antr.*, 16: 65–76.
1960b Mesoamérica. *Mem. Inst. Nac. Antr. Hist.*, no. 6. Mexico.
1960c Descubrimiento arqueológico en Xochicalco, Morelos. *Bol. Inst. Nac. Antr. Hist.*, 2: 1–4.
1963a Las culturas prehispánicas en Jalisco. *Eco*, 14: 3–4. Inst. Jalisciense Antr. Hist. Guadalajara.
1963b Excavaciones en el rancho "La Ventanilla." *In* Bernal, 1963, pp. 50–52.

PINTURA DE MÉXICO
1891 Pintura de México. *In* Alva Ixtlilxochitl, 1891, pp. 258–61.

PLANCARTE Y NAVARRETE, F.
1893 Archeologic explorations in Michoa-

can, Mexico. *Amer. Anthr.*, o.s., 6: 79–84.

PNE
See Paso y Troncoso, 1905–06.

POLANYI, K., C. M. ARENSBERG, AND H. W. PEARSON
1957 Trade and market in early empires. Glencoe.

POMAR, J. B.
1941 Relación de Tezcoco. *In* García Icazbalceta, 1941, 3: 1–64.
1964 *Idem*. *In* Garibay K., 1964b, 4: 149–228.

POMPA Y POMPA, A., ed.
1966 Summa anthropologica: en homenaje a Roberto J. Weitlaner. Inst. Nac. Antr. Hist. Mexico.

PONCE, A.
1873 Relación breve y verdadera de algunas cosas de las muchas que sucedieron al Padre Fray Alonso Ponce en las provincias de la Nueva España. 2 vols. Madrid. (Originally issued in Col. doc. España, vols. 57 and 58, Madrid, 1872).
1932 Fray Alonso Ponce in Yucatan, 1588. E. Noyes, ed. and trans. *Tulane Univ., Middle Amer. Research Inst.*, Pub. 4, pp. 297–372.

PONCE, P.
1953 Breve relación de los dioses y ritos de la gentilidad. *In* Tratado de las idolatrías, supersticiones, dioses, ritos, hechicerías y otras costumbres gentílicas de las razas aborígenes de México. *Ediciones Fuente Cultural*, 10: 371–80. Mexico. (1st ed. 1892, Museo Nacional de México.)
1965 Tratado de los dioses y ritos de la gentilidad. *In* Garibay K., 1965a, pp. 121–32.

PORTER, M. N.
1948a Pipas precortesianas. *Acta Anthr.*, 3: 130–251.
1948b Pottery found at Chupicuaro, Guanajuato. *In* El Occidente de México, pp. 42–47.
1953 Tlatilco and the pre-classic cultures of the New World. *Viking Fund Pub. Anthr.*, no. 19.
1956 Excavations at Chupicuaro, Guana-

juato, Mexico. *Trans. Amer. Phil. Soc.*, vol. 46, part. 5.

PREHISTORY OF THE TEHUACAN VALLEY
See Byers, 1967a; MacNeish et al., 1967, 1970.

PREUSS, K. T.
1904 Der Ursprung der Religion und Kunst. *Globus*, 86: 321–27. Brunswick.
1930 Mexikanische Religion. *In* Bilderatlas zur Religiongeschichte, H. Haas, ed., vol. 16. Leipzig.

—— AND E. MENGIN, eds.
1937–38 See Historia Tolteca-Chichimeca, 1937–38.

PRIETO, A.
1873 Historia, geografía y estadística del estado de Tamaulipas, Mexico.

PRIMERA RELACIÓN DE . . . GUZMÁN
1858–66 Primera relación anónima de la jornada que hizo Nuño de Guzmán a la Nueva Galicia. *In* García Icazbalceta, 1858–66, 2: 288–95.

PROCESOS DE INDIOS
1912 Procesos de Indios: idólatras y hechiceros. *Archivo General de la Nación*, Pub. 3. Mexico.

PROSKOURIAKOFF, T.
1946 An album of Maya architecture. *Carnegie Inst. Wash.*, Pub. 558.
1950 A study of classic Maya sculpture. *Ibid.*, Pub. 593.
1953 Scroll patterns (entrelaces en Veracruz). *In* Huastecos, Totonacos, pp. 389–401.
1954 Varieties of classic central Veracruz sculpture. *Carnegie Inst. Wash.*, Pub. 606, Contrib. 58.
1968 Olmec and Maya art: problems of their stylistic relation. *In* Benson, 1968, pp. 119–34.

PUENTE Y OLEA, M. DE LA
1889 Relación de la comarca y minas de Temascaltepec hecha en 1579 por D. Gaspar de Covarrubias. *Mem. Soc. Cien. Antonio Alzate*, 3: 203–14.

PUTNAM ANNIVERSARY VOLUME
1909 Putnam anniversary volume: anthropological essays presented to Frederic Ward Putnam in honor of his seventieth birthday. New York.

RADIN, P.
1920 The sources and authenticity of the history of the ancient Mexicans. *Univ. California Pub. Amer. Archaeol. Ethnol.*, vol. 17, no. 1.
1933 Notes on the Tlappanecan language of Guerrero. *Int. Jour. Amer. Linguistics*, 8: 45–72.

RALPH, E. K.
1965 Review of radiocarbon dates from Tikal and the Maya correlation problem. *Amer. Antiquity*, 30: 421–27.

RAMÍREZ DE FUENLEAL, S.
1866 Parecer de Don Sebastián Ramírez de Fuenleal. . . . *In* García Icazbalceta, 1858–66, 2: 165–89.
1870a Carta a su magestad del obispo de Santo Domingo. . . . *In* Col. doc. Indias, 13: 233–37.
1870b Carta a su magestad del obispo de Santo Domingo. . . . *Ibid.*, 13: 250–61.

RAMÍREZ FLORES, J.
1935 La arqueología en el sur de Jalisco. Bol. Junta Auxiliar Jalisciense, Soc. Mex. Geografía y Estadística, 4 (2): 41–56. Guadalajara.

RAMÍREZ VÁSQUEZ, P., AND OTHERS
1968 The National Museum of Anthropology, Mexico: art, architecture, archaeology, ethnography. New York.

RAMMOW, H.
1964 Die Verwandschaftsbezeichnungen im klassischen Aztekischen. Mus. für Völkerkunde und Vorgeschichte. Hamburg.

RAMÓN Y LLIGE, A.
n.d. Estudio de las puntas arrojadizas de la altiplanicie de México. Thesis, Escuela Nacional de Antropología. Mexico.
1959 Útiles de piedra. *In* Esplendor de México Antiguo, 2: 480–84.

RANDS, R. L., AND R. E. SMITH
1965 Pottery of the Guatemalan highlands. *In* Handbook of Middle American Indians, R. Wauchope, ed., vol. 2, art. 4.

RATTRAY, E. C.
1966a Teotihuacan chronology. [Chart.] *In* Paddock, 1966b.
1966b An archaeological and stylistic study

of Coyotlatelco pottery. *Mesoamerican Notes*, 7–8, pp. 87–211. Mexico.

RECINOS, A., ed.

1947 Popol Vuh: las antiguas historias del Quiché. Fondo de Cultura Económica. Mexico.

1950 Memorial de Sololá; Anales de los Cakchiqueles; Título de los señores de Totonicapan. Fondo de Cultura Económica. Mexico.

1953 Popol Vuh: las antiguas historias del Quiché. Fondo de Cultura Económica. Mexico.

1957 Crónicas indígenas de Guatemala. Guatemala.

—— AND D. GOETZ, trans.

1953 *See* Annals of the Cakchiquels, 1953.

REDFIELD, R.

1930 Tepoztlan, a Mexican village. Univ. Chicago Press.

RELACIONES:

Genealogía

1941 Relación de la genealogía y linaje de los señores. . . . *In* García Icazbalceta, 1941, 3: 240–56.

Metztitlán

1865 Relación de la provincia de Metztitlán, hecha por Gabriel de Chávez, alcalde mayor de esta provincia, por S. M. de orden del Virrey de Nueva España. *In* Col. doc. Indias, 4: 530–555.

1924 *See* Chávez, 1924.

Mexico

1905–06 Relaciones geográficas de la diócesis de México. *In* Paso y Troncoso, 1905–06, vol. 6.

Michoacán

1903 Relación de las ceremonias y ritos y población y gobierno de los indios de la provincia de Mechuacan (1541). Morelia.

1956 *Idem.* Facsimile reproduction. Madrid.

1958 Relaciones geográficas de la diócesis de Michoacán, 1579–80. 2 vols. Guadalajara. Cited as RGDM.

Ocopetlayuca

1905–06 Relación de Ocopetlayuca. *In* Paso y Troncoso, 1905–06, 6: 257.

RELACIONES—*continued*

Tecciztlan

1905 Relación de Tecciztlan. *See* Castañeda, 1905a.

Tepuztlan

1905 Relación de la villa de Tepuztlan. *See* Gutiérrez de Liévana, 1905.

Teutitlan

1905 Relación de Teutitlan del Camino. *See* Castañeda, 1905b.

Tezcoco

1964 Relación de Tezcoco. *See* Pomar, 1964.

Tlaxcala

1940 Relación del distrito y pueblos del obispado de Tlaxcala. *In* Paso y Troncoso, 1939–42, 14: 70–101.

Tuzantla

1965 The Relación Geográfica of Tuzantla, Michoacan, 1579. Ed. by H. F. Cline. *Tlalocan*, 5: 58–73.

Uexutla

1905–06 Relación de Uexutla. *In* Paso y Troncoso, 1905–06, 6: 183–92.

Zempoala

1949 Relación de Zempoala y su partido, 1580. *Tlalocan*, 3: 29–41.

RENDÓN, S., ed.

1965 Relaciones originales de Chalco Amaquemecan por Francisco de San Anton Muñón Chimalpahin Cuauhtlehuanitzin. Mexico and Buenos Aires.

REVISTA MEXICANA . . .

1956–57 Revista mexicana de estudios antropológicos. Vol. 14, part 2. Soc. Mex. Antr. Mexico.

RGDM

See Relaciones Michoacan, 1958.

RICKETSON, O. G., AND E. B. RICKETSON

1937 Uaxactun, Guatemala, Group E— 1926–1931. *Carnegie Inst. Wash.*, Pub. 477.

RILEY, C. L., AND H. D. WINTERS

1963 The prehistoric Tepehuan of northern Mexico. *SW. Jour. Anthr.*, 19: 177–85.

RIVET, P., AND G. FREUND

1954 Mexique précolombien. Coll. des Idées Photographiques, no. 8. Paris.

ROBELO, C. A.
1951 Diccionario de mitología nahoa. *Ediciones Fuente Cultural.* Mexico. (Other eds., 1905–08, 1911.)

ROBERTSON, D.
1959 Mexican manuscript painting of the early colonial period. New Haven.

1963a The style of the Borgia group of Mexican pre-conquest manuscripts. *In* Studies in western art, M. Meiss and others, eds., vol. 3 (Latin American art and the Baroque period in Europe), pp. 148–64. 20th Int. Cong. History of Art (New York, 1961).

1963b Pre-Columbian architecture. *In* The great ages of world architecture, G. Braziller, ed. New York.

1964 Los manuscritos religiosos mixtecos. *35th Int. Cong. Amer.* (Mexico, 1962), Acta, 1: 425–35. (English trans. in Paddock, 1966c, pp. 298–312.)

1968 The Tulum murals: the international style of the Late Postclassic. Paper presented to 38th Int. Cong. Amer. (Stuttgart, 1968).

ROJAS, G. DE
1927 Descripción de Cholula. *Rev. Mex. Estud. Antr.*, 1: 158–70.

ROMANCES DE LOS SEÑORES
1964 Romances de los señores de la Nueva España. *In* Garibay K., 1964b.

ROMERO, J.
1958 Mutilaciones dentarias prehispánicas de México y América en general. *Inst. Nac. Antr. Hist., Dir. Invest. Antr.*, no. 3. Mexico.

—— AND J. VALENZUELA
1945 Expedición a la Sierra Azul, Ocampo, Tamaulipas. *An. Inst. Nac. Antr. Hist.*, 1 (1939–40): 7–15. Mexico.

ROMERO FLORES, J.
1946 Historia de Michoacán. 2 vols. Mexico.

ROSADO OJEDA, V.
1948 Interpretación de la grada jeroglífica del Chanal, Colima. *In* El Occidente de México, pp. 72–73.

ROSS, V.
1939 Some pottery types of the highlands of western Mexico. Master's thesis, Yale Univ.

ROYS, R. L.
1933 The book of Chilam Balam of Chumayel. *Carnegie Inst. Wash.*, Pub. 438.

1943 The Indian background of colonial Yucatan. *Ibid.*, Pub. 548.

1957 The political geography of the Yucatan Maya. *Ibid.*, Pub. 613.

RUBÍN DE LA BORBOLLA, D. F.
1939 Antropología Tzintzuntzan - Ihuatzio: temporadas I y II. *Rev. Mex. Estud. Antr.*, 3: 99–121.

1941 Exploraciones arqueológicas en Michoacán: Tzintzuntzan, temporada III. *Ibid.*, 5: 5–20.

1944 Orfebrería tarasca. *Cuad. Amer.*, 3: 125–38.

1946 Arqueología del sur de Durango. *Rev. Mex. Estud. Antr.*, 8: 111–20.

1947 Teotihuacán: ofrendas de los templos de Quetzalcoatl. *An. Inst. Nac. Antr. Hist.*, 2: 61–72.

1948 Arqueología tarasca. *In* El Occidente de México, pp. 29–33.

1953 México: monumentos históricos y arqueológicos. Libro primero: México precolombino. *Inst. Panamer. Geog. Hist.*, Pub. 145. Mexico.

RUIZ, D.
1785 La pirámide de Papantla. *Gaceta de México*, 1: 349–51.

RUIZ, E.
1940 Michoacán: paisajes, tradiciones y leyendas. Mexico. (Other eds. 1891, 1900.)

RUIZ COLMENERO, J.
1903 Abstract of linguistic data, from Visita General of 1648–1649, made by A. Santoscoy. Published 1902 in *Diario de Jalisco*; reprinted by N. Léon in *An. Mus. Nac. Méx.*, 7: 309–11 and passim to p. 335.

RUIZ DE ALARCÓN, H.
1892 Tratado de las supersticiones y costumbres gentílicas que hoy viven entre los indios naturales de esta Nueva España. *An. Mus. Nac. Mex.*, ép. 1, 6: 123–224. (See later eds.)

1948 *Idem*, 2d ed.

1953 *Idem*, 3d ed. *In* Tratados de las

idolatrías, supersticiones, dioses, ritos, hechicerías y otras costumbres gentílicas de las razas aborígenes de México. *Ediciones Fuente Cultural*, 20: 17–180. Mexico.

RUZ LHUILLIER, A.

1945 Guía arqueológica de Tula. Inst. Nac. Antr. Hist. Mexico.

1953 Presencia atlantica en Palenque. *In* Huastecos, Totonacos, pp. 455–62.

1962 Chichen-Itza y Tula: comentarios a un ensayo. *Univ. Nac. Autónoma Méx., Estud. Cultura Maya*, 2: 205–20.

SÁENZ, C. A.

1961 Tres estelas en Xochicalco. *Rev. Mex. Estud. Antr.*, 17: 39–66.

1962a Exploraciones arqueológicas en Xochicalco, Morelos. *Bol. Inst. Nac. Antr. Hist.*, 7: 1–3.

1962b Xochicalco: temporada 1960. *Inst. Nac. Antr. Hist., Dir. Monumentos Prehispánicos*, Informe 11. Mexico.

1964 Últimos descubrimientos en Xochicalco. *Ibid.*, Informe 12.

1966a Cabecitas y figurillas de barro del Ixtepete, Jalisco. *Bol. Inst. Nac. Antr. Hist.*, 24: 47–49.

1966b Exploraciones en el Ixtepete, Jalisco. *Ibid.*, 23: 14–18.

1966c Exploraciones en Xochicalco. *Ibid.*, 26: 24–34.

1967 Nuevas exploraciones y hallazgos en Xochicalco, 1965–1966. *Inst. Nac. Antr. Hist., Dir. Monumentos Prehispánicos*, Informe 13. Mexico.

1968 Cuatro piedras con inscripciones en Xochicalco. *An. Antr.*, 5: 181–98.

1969 Exploraciones y restauraciones en Uxmal, Yucatan. *Bol. Inst. Nac. Antr. Hist.*, 36: 6–13.

SAHAGÚN, B. DE

1905–07 Historia general de las cosas de Nueva España. F. del Paso y Troncoso, ed. Edición parcial en facsímile de los Códices Matritenses en lengua mexicana que se custodian en las bibliotecas del Palacio Real y de la Real Academia de la Historia, vols. 5–8. (Florentine Codex illustrations, prepared during same period, bound and distributed by Mus. Nac.

Arqueol. Hist. Etnog., 1926, as vol. 5 of the entire [unfinished] work.) Madrid.

1926 *See* preceding entry and Florentine Codex, 1926.

1927 Einige Kapitel aus dem Geschichtswerk des Fray Bernardino de Sahagún. E. Seler, trans. Stuttgart.

1938 Historia general de las cosas de Nueva España. 5 vols. Mexico. Mexico.

1944–46 Paralipómenos de Sahagún. A. M. Garibay K., ed. and trans. *Tlalocan*, 1: 307–13; 2: 167–74, 235–54.

1946 Historia general de las cosas de Nueva España. M. Acosta Saignes, ed. 3 vols. Mexico.

1948 Relación breve de las fiestas de los dioses. A. M. Garibay K., ed. and trans. *Tlalocan*, 2: 289–320.

1949 Sterbende Götter und Christliche Heilsbotschaft; Wechselreden Indianischer Vornehmer und Spanischer Glaubensapostel in Mexiko 1524: "Coloquios y doctrina christiana" des Fray Bernardino de Sahagún aus dem Jahre 1564. W. Lehmann, ed. and trans. Quellenwerke zur Alten Geschichte Amerikas Aufgezeichnet in den Sprachen der Eingeborenen (Latein-Amerikanischen Bibliothek, Berlin), III. Stuttgart.

1950 Wahrsagerei, Himmelskunde und Kalender der Alten Azteken aus dem Aztekischen Urtext Bernardino de Sahagún's. L. S. Schultze-Jena, ed. and trans. *Ibid.*, IV.

1950–69 Florentine codex: general history of the things of New Spain. Tr. from the Aztec into English, with notes and illustrations, by A. J. O. Anderson and C. E. Dibble. Univ. Utah and School of American Research. Santa Fe. Book 1 (1950): The gods. Book 2 (1951): The ceremonies. Book 3 (1952): The origin of the gods. Book 4 (1957): The soothsayers. Book 5 (1957): The omens. Book 6 (1969): Rhetoric and moral philosophy. Book 7 (1953): The sun, moon, and stars, and the binding of the years. Book

8 (1954): Kings and lords. Book 9 (1959): The merchants. Book 10 (1961): The people. Book 11 (1963): Earthly things. Book 12 (1955): The conquest of Mexico.

1952 Gliederung des Alt-Aztekischen Völks in Familie, Stand und Beruf aus dem Aztekischen Urtext Bernardino de Sahagún's. L. S. Schultze-Jena, ed. and trans. Quellenwerke zur Alten Geschichte Amerikas Aufgezeichnet in den Sprachen der Eingeborenen (Latein-Amerikanischen Bibliothek, Berlin), V. Stuttgart.

1956 Historia general de las cosas de Nueva España. A. M. Garibay K., ed. and trans. 4 vols. Biblioteca Porrúa, vols. 8–11. Mexico.

1958a Ritos, sacerdotes y atavíos de los dioses. M. León-Portilla, ed. and trans. Univ. Nac. Autónoma Méx., Inst. Hist., Seminario de Cultura Náhuatl, *Textos de los Informantes de Sahagún*, no. 1.

1958b Veinte himnos sacros de los nahuas, los recogío de los nativos. A. M. Garibay K., ed. and trans. *Ibid.*, no. 2.

1961 Vida económica de Tenochtitlan, 1: Pochtecayotl (Arte de Traficar). A. M. Garibay K., ed. and trans. *Ibid.*, no. 3.

1963 Náhuatl proverbs, conundrums, and metaphors, collected by Sahagún. T. D. Sullivan, ed. and trans. *Inst. Hist., Estud. Cultura Náhuatl*, 4: 73–177.

1965 A prayer to Tlaloc. T. D. Sullivan, ed. and trans. *Ibid.*, 5: 39–55.

1966 Pregnancy, childbirth, and the deification of the women who died in childbirth: texts from the Florentine Codex, book 6, folios 128v–143v. T. D. Sullivan, ed. and trans. *Ibid.*, 6: 63–95.

1969 Augurios y abusiones. A. López Austin, ed. and trans. Univ. Nac. Autónoma Méx., Inst. Hist., Seminario de Cultura Náhuatl, *Textos de los Informantes de Sahagún*, no. 4.

SAHLINS, M., AND E. R. SERVICE, eds.
1960 Evolution and culture. Ann Arbor.

SALDÍVAR, G.
1943 Los Indios de Tamaulipas. *Inst. Panamer. Geog. Hist.*, Pub. 70. Mexico.

SALTZMAN, M., A. M. KEAY, AND J. CHRISTENSEN
1963 The identification of colorants in ancient textiles. *Dyestuffs*, vol. 44, no. 8. Allied Chemical Corp. New York.

SÁNCHEZ, J.
1887 Mapa de Tepechpan: historia sincrónica y señorial de Tepechpan y México. *An. Mus. Nac. Méx.*, ép. 1, vol. 3.

SANDERS, W. T.
1953 The anthropogeography of central Veracruz. *In* Huastecos, Totonacos, pp. 27–78.

1956 The central Mexican symbiotic region: a study in prehistoric settlement patterns. *In* Willey, 1956a, pp. 115–27.

1960 Prehistoric ceramics and settlement patterns in Quintana Roo, Mexico. *Carnegie Inst. Wash.*, Pub. 606, Contrib. 60.

1963 Teotihuacan valley project (1960–1961), Mexico. *Katunob*, 4: 24–38.

1966 Life in a classic village. *In* Teotihuacán, pp. 123–48.

SANTAMARÍA, F. J.
1959 Diccionario de Mexicanismos. Ed. Porrúa. Mexico.

SATTERTHWAITE, L.
1967 Radiocarbon and Maya long count dating of "Structure 10" (Str. 5D-52, first story), Tikal. *Rev. Mex. Estud. Antr.*, 21: 225–49.

SAUER, C. O.
1941 The personality of Mexico. *Geog. Rev.*, 31: 353–64.

1948 Colima of New Spain in the sixteenth century. *Ibero-Amer.*, no. 29. Univ. California Press.

—— AND D. D. BRAND
1932 Aztatlan: prehistoric Mexican frontier on the Pacific coast. *Ibid.*, no. 1.

SAVILLE, M. H.
1900 An onyx jar from Mexico in the process of manufacture. *Bull. Amer. Mus. Natural Hist.*, 13: 105–07.

1920 The goldsmith's art in ancient Mexico. *Mus. Amer. Indian, Heye Found., Indian Notes and Monogr.* New York.

1922 Turquoise mosaic art in ancient Mexico. *Contrib. Mus. Amer. Indian, Heye Found.*, vol. 6.

1925 The wood-carver's art in ancient Mexico. *Ibid.*, vol. 9.

1928 Bibliographic notes on Xochicalco, Mexico. *Mus. Amer. Indian, Heye Found., Indian Notes and Monogr.*, vol. 6, no. 6.

1929 Tizoc: great lord of the Aztecs, 1481–1486. *Contrib. Mus. Amer. Indian, Heye Found.*, vol. 7, no. 4.

SAYLES, E. B.
1935 An archaeological survey of Texas. *Medallion Papers*, no. 17. Gila Pueblo.

SCHOLES, F. V., AND E. B. ADAMS, eds.
1955–61 Documentos para la historia del México colonial. 7 vols. to date. Mexico.

1957 Información sobre los tributos que los indios pagaban a Moctezuma, año de 1554. *In* their 1955–61, vol. 4.

SCHÖNDUBE, O.
1968 Figurillas del occidente de México. *In* Colección breve, no. 8. Mus. Nac. Antr. Mexico.

SCHULLER, R.
1923–24 Die ehemalige und die heutige Verbreitung der Huaxteca Indianer. *Anthropos*, 18–19: 793–803. Vienna.

1925 La patria originaria de los Indios Mayas. *Ethnos*, ép. 3, 1 (3–4): 52–59. Mexico.

SEARS, P. B.
1951 Pollen profiles and culture horizons in the basin of Mexico. *In* Tax, 1951, pp. 57–61.

SEJOURNÉ, L.
1956a Estudio del material arqueológico de Atetelco, Teotihuacán. *Rev. Mex. Estud. Antr.*, 14: 15–23.

1956b Informe sobre el material exhumado en Ahuixotla. *Ibid.*, 14: 33–35.

1957 Pensamiento y religión en el México antiguo. *Breviarios del Fondo de Cultura Económica*, no. 128. Mexico. (English trans., Burning water: thought and religion in ancient Mexico, 1957, London.)

1959 Un palacio en la ciudad de los dioses, Teotihuacán. Inst. Nac. Antr. Hist. Mexico.

1961 El culto de Xochipilli y los braseros teotihuacanos. *El México Antiguo*, 9: 111–24. (Homenaje al Dr. Hermann Beyer.)

1963 Exploración de Tetitla. *In* Bernal, 1963, pp. 46–49.

1965 El Quetzalcóatl en Teotihuacán. *Cuad. Amer.*, año 1.

1966 El lenguaje de las formas en Teotihuacán. Mexico.

SELER, E.
1889–91 Altmexikanischer Schmuck und soziale und militärische Rangabzeichen. *Zeit. für Ethnol.*, 21: 69–85; 23: 114–24. (Collected Works, 2: 509–619, much enlarged.)

1892 L'orfévrerie des anciens Mexicains et leur art de travailler la pierre et de faire des ornements en plumes. *8th Int. Cong. Amer.* (Paris, 1890), Acta, pp. 401–52.

1894 Die grossen Steinskulpturen des Museo Nacional de México. *Ethnologisches Notizblatt*, 1: 19–31.

1899a Zauberei und Zauberer im alten Mexiko. *Veröffentlichungen aus dem Königlichen Museum für Völkerkunde*, VI. Band 2/4. Heft, Altmexikanische Studien II, 1: 29–57. Berlin.

1899b Die bildlichen Darstellungen der mexikanischen Jahresfeste. *Ibid.*, 2: 58–66.

1899c Die achtzehn Jahresfeste der Mexikaner (Erste Hälfte). *Ibid.*, 3: 67–204.

1900 Das Tonalamatl der Aubin'schen Sammlung. Eine altmexikanische Bilderhandschrift der Bibliothèque Nationale in Paris (Manuscrits mexicains nrs. 18–19). Berlin. (English trans. in his 1901a.)

1901a The Tonalamatl of the Aubin collection. A. H. Keane, trans. London. (English trans. of his 1900.)

1901b Codex Fejérváry-Mayer. Eine alt-mexikanische Bilderhandschrift der Free Public Museum in Liverpool (12014/M). Berlin. (English trans. 1901–1902, Berlin and London.)

1902a Codex Vaticanus Nr. 3773 (Codex Vaticanus B). Eine altmexikanische Bilderschrift der Vatikanischen Bibliothek. Berlin. (English trans. 1902–03, Berlin and London.)

1902b Die Tageszeichen der aztekischen und der Maya Handschriften und ihre Gottheiten. *In his* 1902–23, 1: 417.

1902–23 Gesammelte Abhandlungen zur Amerikanischen Sprach- und Alterthumskunde. 5 vols. Berlin. (2d ed. 1960–61, Graz, Austria.)

1904a Archäologisches aus Mexiko. 5: Altmexikanischer Schmuck und soziale und militärische Rangabzeichen. *In his* 1902–23, 2: 509–619. (Reprint of his 1889–91.)

1904b Alexander von Humboldt's picture manuscripts in the Royal Library at Berlin. *Smithsonian Inst., Bur. Amer. Ethnol.*, Bull. 28, pp. 123–229.

1904c Reprint of his 1892 *in his* 1902–23, 2: 620–63.

1904d Die alten Ansiedelungen im Gebiet der Huasteca. *In his* 1902–23, 2: 168–83. (Also in *Zeit. für Ethnol.*, 20 [1888]: 451–59.)

1904–09 Codex Borgia. Eine altmexikanische Bilderschrift der Bibliothek der Congregatio de Propaganda Fide. 3 vols. Berlin. (Spanish trans. 1963, Mexico.)

1908 Die alten Bewohner der Landschaft Michuacan. *In his* 1902–23, 3: 33–156.

1913 Similarity of design of some Teotihuacan frescoes and certain Mexican pottery objects. *18th Int. Cong. Amer.* (London, 1912), Acta, pp. 194–202.

1915 Die Teotihuacan-Kultur des Hochlands von Mexiko. *In his* 1902–23, 5: 405–585.

1916 Mexicans [ancient]. *In* Hastings, 1916, 8: 612–17.

1927 Einige Kapitel aus dem Geschichtswerk des Fray Bernardino de Sahagún aus dem Aztekischen übersetzt. Stuttgart.

1963 Comentarios al Códice Borgia. 3 vols. Fondo de Cultura Económica. Mexico and Buenos Aires.

SELER-SACHS, C.

1913 Die Reliefscherben von Cuicatlan und Teotitlan del Camino. *18th Int. Cong. Amer.* (London, 1912), Acta. (Spanish trans. 1949 in *El México Antiguo*, 7: 105–18.)

SERNA, J. DE LA

1955 Manual de ministros de Indios para el conocimiento de sus idolatrías, y extirpación de ellas. *In* Tratados de las idolatrías, supersticiones, dioses, ritos, hechicerías y otras costumbres gentílicas de las razas aborígenes de México. *Ediciones Fuente Cultural*, 10: 41–368. Mexico. (1st ed. 1892.)

SHEPARD, A. O.

1946 Technological notes. *In* Kidder, Jennings, and Shook, 1946, pp. 261–77.

SHOOK, E. M., AND A. V. KIDDER

1952 Mound E-III-3, Kaminaljuyu, Guatemala. *Carnegie Inst. Wash.*, Pub. 596, Contrib. 53.

SIMONS, B. B.

1968 Los mapas de Cuauhtinchán y la Historia Tolteca-Chichimeca. Inst. Nac. Antr. Hist. Mexico.

in press Un posible glifo de Cuauhximalpan en el mapa de Cuauhtinchan No. 2. *Rehue*. Concepcion, Chile.

SMITH, A. L., AND A. V. KIDDER

1951 Excavations at Nebaj, Guatemala. *Carnegie Inst. Wash.*, Pub. 594.

SMITH, B.

1968 Mexico: a history in art. New York.

SMITH, C. E., AND R. S. MACNEISH

1964 Antiquity of American polyploid cotton. *Science*, 143 (3607): 675–76.

SMITH, M. E.

1963 The Codex Colombino: a document of the south coast of Oaxaca. *Tlalocan*, 4: 276–88.

1966   Las glosas del Códice Colombino. Soc. Mex. Antr. Mexico.

SMITH, T.
1963   The main themes of Olmec art tradition. *Papers Kroeber Anthr. Soc.*, 28: 121–213.

SO LIVE THE WORKS OF MEN
1939   So live the works of men: seventieth anniversary volume honoring Edgar Lee Hewett. D. D. Brand and F. E. Harvey, eds. Univ. New Mexico and School Amer. Research.

SOBRE EL MODO DE TRIBUTAR
1958   Sobre el modo de tributar los indios de Nueva España a su majestad, 1561–1564. *In* Scholes and Adams, 1955–61, vol. 5.

SOLÁ, M.
1936   Historia del arte precolombino. *Artes Plásticas*, nos. 391, 392. Editorial Labor, sec. 4. Barcelona.

SOLECKI, R. S.
1955   Lamellar flakes versus blades: a reappraisal. *Amer. Antiquity*, 20: 393–94.

SOUSTELLE, J.
1937   La famille Otomi-Pame du Mexique central. *Inst. Ethnol., Travaux et Mem.*, no. 26. Paris.
1940   La pensée cosmologique des anciens Mexicains (representation du monde et de l'espace). Paris. (Spanish trans. 1959, Puebla.)
1953   La religion des Aztèques. *In* Histoire des Religions, 5: 7–30. Brussels.
1956   La vida cotidiana de los aztecas en vísperas de la conquista. Fondo de Cultura Económica. Mexico. (English trans. 1961.)
1959   Album de la vie quotidienne des Aztèques. Paris.
1961   The daily life of the Aztecs on the eve of the Spanish conquest. London. (English trans. of his 1956; 1st ed. 1955 in French.)
1966a L'art du Mexique ancien. Paris.
1966b Terrestrial and celestial gods in Mexican antiquity. *Diogenes*, 56: 20–50.
1967   Arts of ancient Mexico. E. Carmichael, trans. Photographs by C.

Arthaud and F. Herbert-Stevens. New York.

SPENCE, L.
1923   The gods of Mexico. New York.
1926   Witchcraft and sorcery in ancient Mexico. *Discovery*, 7: 47–50. London.
1930   The magic and mysteries of Mexico. London.

SPENCE, M. W.
1967   The obsidian industry of Teotihuacan. *Amer. Antiquity*, 32: 507–14.

SPINDEN, E. S.
1933   The place of Tajin in Totonac archaeology. *Amer. Anthr.*, 35: 225–70.

SPINDEN, H. J.
1911   An ancient sepulcher at Placeres del Oro, state of Guerrero, Mexico. *Ibid.*, 13: 29–55.
1913   A study of Maya art, its subject matter and historical development. *Mem. Peabody Mus., Harvard Univ.*, vol. 6.
1915   Notes on the archaeology of Salvador. *Amer. Anthr.*, 17: 446–87.
1917   Ancient civilizations of Mexico and Central America. *Amer. Mus. Natural Hist., Handbook Ser.*, no. 3. New York. (Other eds. 1922, 1928.)
1935   Indian manuscripts of southern Mexico. *Smithsonian Inst.*, ann. rept. for 1933, pp. 429–51.
1937   Huastec sculptures and the cult of apotheosis. *Brooklyn Mus. Quar.*, 24: 179–89.
1948   Chorotegan influences in western Mexico. *In* El Occidente de México, pp. 34–37.
1957   Maya art and civilization. Revised and enlarged with added illustrations. Part 1: A Study of Maya art. Part 2: The nuclear civilization of the Maya and related cultures. Indian Hills, Colo.

SPRANZ, B.
1964   Göttergestalten in den mexikanischen Bilderhandschriften der Codex Borgia-Gruppe. *Acta Humboldtiana, Ser. Geog. Ethnog.*, no. 4. Wiesbaden.

SPRATLING, W.
1932   Little Mexico. New York.

STADELMAN, R.
1940 Maize cultivation in northwestern Guatemala. *Carnegie Inst. Wash.*, Pub. 523, Contrib. 33.

Stanislawski, D.
1947 Tarascan political geography. *Amer. Anthr.*, 49: 46–55.

STARR, F.
1897 Little pottery objects from Lake Chapala, Mexico. *Dept. Anthr., Univ. Chicago*, Bull. 2.

STAUB, W.
1923 Beiträge zur Landeskunde des nordöstlichen Mexiko. *Zeit. Gesellschaft für Erdkunde zu Berlin*, nos. 5–7, pp. 187–211.
1924 Zur Kenntnis der Indianischen Orstnamen in der Huaxteca (ost Mexiko). *Ibid.*, Jahrgang 1924, pp. 215–34.
1926 Le nord-est du Mexique et les Indiens de la Huastèque. *Jour. Soc. Amér. Paris*, 18: 279–96.

STEPHENSON, R. L.
1950 Cultural chronology in Texas. *Amer. Antiquity*, 16: 151–57.
1951 Archaeological excavations at the Falcon Reservoir, Starr County. Smithsonian Inst., Texas report prepared by River Basin Surveys.

STEWARD, J. H.
1955 Theory of culture change. Univ. Illinois Press.

—— AND OTHERS
1955 Irrigation civilizations: a comparative study. *Pan Amer. Union, Social Sci. Monogr.*, no. 1. Washington.

STEWART, T. D.
1948 Distribution of the type of cranial deformity originally described under the name "tête trilobée." *In* El Occidente de México, pp. 17–20.

STIRLING, M. W.
1965 Monumental sculpture of southern Veracruz and Tabasco. *In* Handbook of Middle American Indians, R. Wauchope, ed., vol. 3, art. 28.

STREBEL, H.
1885–89 Archäologische Beiträge zur Kulturgeschichte seiner Bewohner. 2 vols. Hamburg and Leipzig.
1890 Studien über Steinjoche aus Mexiko und Mittel-Amerika. *Internat. Archiv für Ethnog.*, 3: 16–28, 49–61. Leiden.
1893 Nachtrag zu Studien über Steinjoche. *Ibid.*, 6: 44–48.

STRESSER-PÉAN, G.
1953a Les Indiens Huastèques. *In* Huastecos, Totonacos, pp. 213–34.
1953b Les Nahuas du sud de la Huasteca et l'ancienne extension méridionale des Huastèques. *Ibid.*, pp. 287–90.
1964 Première campagne de fouilles à Tamtok, près de Tamuín, Huasteca. *35th Int. Cong. Amer.* (Mexico, 1962), Acta, 1: 387–94.

——, A. ICHON, AND Y. GUIDON
1963 La première statue antique en bois découverte dans la Huasteca. *Jour. Soc. Amér. Paris*, 52: 315–18.

STRÖMBERG, E.
1942 Technical analysis of textiles recovered in Burial 1. *In* Linné, 1942, pp. 157–60.

STUIVER, M., E. S. DEEVEY, AND L. J. GRALENSKI
1960 Yale natural radiocarbon measurements, V. *Amer. Jour. Sci., Radiocarbon Suppl.*, 3: 49–61.

SUÁREZ DE PERALTA, J.
1878 Noticias históricas de la Nueva España. Madrid.

SUHM, D. A., A. D. KRIEGER, AND E. B. JELKS
1954 An introductory handbook of Texas archaeology. *Bull. Texas Archaeol. Soc.*, vol. 25.

SUMA DE VISITAS
1905–06 Suma de visitas de pueblos por orden alfabético. *In* Paso y Troncoso, 1905–06, vol. 1.

SUSIA, M.
1961 The Morett sequence. Mimeographed. Dept. Anthr., Univ. California, Los Angeles.

SWADESH, M.
1953 The language of the archaeologic Huastecs. *Carnegie Inst. Wash., Notes Middle Amer. Archaeol. Ethnol.*, no. 114.
1961 Interrelaciones de las lenguas mayas. *An. Inst. Nac. Antr. Hist.*, 13: 231–67.
1967 Lexicostatistic classification. *In* Handbook of Middle American Indi-

ans, R. Wauchope, ed., vol. 5, art. 4.

TABLADA, J. J.
1927 Historia del arte en México. Mexico.

TAMAYO, J.
1949 Geografía general de México. 2 vols. Mexico.
1962 Atlas geográfico general de México, con cartas físicas, biológicas, demográficas, sociales, económicas y cartogramas. 2d ed. Inst. Mex. Invest. Económicas. Mexico.

TAPIA ZENTENO, C. DE
1767 Noticia de la lengua huasteca . . . con catecismo y doctrina christiana . . . y copioso diccionario. Mexico.

TARAYRE, E. GUILLEMIN
See Guillemin Tarayre, E.

TAX, S., ed.
1951 The civilizations of ancient America. Selected papers of the 29th Int. Cong. Amer. Chicago.
1952 Heritage of conquest: the ethnology of Middle America. Viking Fund seminar on Middle American ethnology. Glencoe.

TAYLOR, W. W.
1948 A study of archaeology. Mem. Amer. Anthr. Assoc., no. 69.
1968 A burial bundle from Coahuila, Mexico. Papers Archaeol. Soc. New Mexico, 1: 23–56. Santa Fe.

TEEPLE, J. E.
1930 Maya astronomy. Carnegie Inst. Wash., Pub. 403, Contrib. 2.

TEILHARD DE CHARDIN, P.
1939 On the presumable existence of a world-wide sub-Arctic sheet of human culture at the dawn of the Neolithic. Bull. Geol. Surv. China, 19: 333–39. Peiping.

TELLO, A.
1650 Fragmentos de una historia de la Nueva Galicia escrita hacia 1650. In García Icazbalceta, 1858–66.
1891 Libro segundo de la crónica miscelánea. . . . Guadalajara.

TENAYUCA
1935 Tenayuca: estudio arqueológico de la Pirámide de este lugar. Sec. Educación Pública, Depto. Monumentos. Mexico.

TEOTIHUACÁN
1966 Teotihuacán. Onceava mesa redonda: El Valle de Teotihuacán y su contorno. Soc. Mex. Antr. Mexico.

TERMER, F.
1930 Über die Mayasprache von Chicomucelo. 23d Int. Cong. Amer. (New York, 1928), Acta, pp. 926–36.

TERNAUX-COMPANS, H., ed.
1837–41 Voyages, relations et mémoires originaux pour servir à l'histoire de la découverte de l'Amérique: recueil de pièces relatives à la conquête du Mexique. 20 vols. Paris.

TEZOZOMOC, H. A.
See Alvarado Tezozomoc, H.

THOMPSON, E. H.
1957 See Tozzer, 1957, pp. 194–96.

THOMPSON, J. E. S.
1934 Sky bearers, colors and directions in Maya and Mexican religion. Carnegie Inst. Wash., Pub. 436, Contrib. 10.
1939 The moon goddess in Middle America, with notes on related deities. Ibid., Pub. 509, Contrib. 29.
1941a Dating of certain inscriptions of non-Maya origin. Ibid., Theoretical Approaches to Problems, no. 1.
1941b Yokes or ball game belts? Amer. Antiquity, 6: 320–26.
1948 An archaeological reconnaissance in the Cotzumalhuapa region, Escuintla, Guatemala. Carnegie Inst. Wash., Pub. 574, Contrib. 44.
1950 Maya hieroglyphic writing: introduction. Ibid., Pub. 589.
1954 The rise and fall of Maya civilization. Univ. Oklahoma Press.
1957 Deities portrayed on censers at Mayapan. Carnegie Inst. Wash., Current Reports, no. 40.
1959 Systems of hieroglyphic writing in Middle America and methods of deciphering them. Amer. Antiquity, 24: 349–64.

TÍTULO DE TIERRAS . . . SANTA ISABEL TOLA
1897 Título de tierras del pueblo de Santa Isabel Tola. Manuscrito americano no. 4 de la Biblioteca Real de Berlin. In Peñafiel, 1897–1903, vol. 1.

TÍTULOS DE LA CASA IXQUIN-NEHAIB
1957 Títulos de la casa Ixquin-Nehaib, se-
ñora del territorio de Otzoyá. *In*
Recinos, 1957, pp. 71–94.

TOLSTOY, P.
1958 Surface survey of the northern Valley
of Mexico: the classic and post-classic
periods. *Trans. Amer. Phil. Soc.*,
vol. 48, part 5.

—— AND A. GUÉNETTE
1965 Le placement de Tlatilco dans le cadre du pré-classique du bassin de
Mexico. *Jour. Soc. Amér. Paris*, 54:
47–91.

—— AND L. PARADIS
1970 Early and middle preclassic cultures
in the basin of Mexico. *Science*,
167: 344–51.

TONALAMATL AUBIN
1900 Tonalamatl de Aubin. Collection de
M. E. E. Goupil. Loubat ed. Paris.
(See Seler, 1900.)

TORQUEMADA, J. DE
1723 Los veinte i un libros rituales i mo-
narchía indiana. . . . 2d ed. 3 vols.
Madrid. (1st ed. 1615, Seville.)
1943–44 *Idem*, 3d ed., facsimile of 1723.
Mexico.
1964 *Idem*, 4th ed. Bib. Estudiante Universitario. Mexico.

TORRE, E. DE LA
1960 El arte prehispánico y sus primeros
críticos europeos. *In* Homenaje García Granados, pp. 259–318.

TOSCANO, S.
1940 La pintura mural precolombina en
México. *Bol. Bibliográfico Antr.
Amer.*, 4: 37–51.
1944 Arte precolombino de México y de la
América Central. Univ. Nac. Autónoma Méx., Inst. Invest. Estéticas.
(2d ed. 1952.)
1946 El arte antiguo. *In* Mexico y la cultura, pp. 81–163.
1951 Codices Tlapanecas de Azoyu.
Cuad. Amer., 10: 4.
1952 Arte precolombino de México y de la
América Central. 2d ed., slightly
augmented. Mexico.

TOUSSAINT, M.
1931 Taxco: su historia, sus monumentos,

características actuales y posibilidades
turísticas. Mexico.
1942 Pátzcuaro. Mexico.
1948 La conquista de Pánuco. Mexico.

——, F. GÓMEZ DE OROZCO, AND J. FERNÁN-
DEZ
1938 Planos de la Ciudad de México, siglos
XVI y XVII: estudio histórico, urba-
nístico y bibliográfico. Inst. Invest.
Estéticas. Mexico.

TOVAR, J. DE
1944 Códice Ramírez. Manuscrito del siglo XVI intitulado: Relación del origen de los indios que habitan esta
Nueva España, según sus historias.
Mexico.

TOVAR CALENDAR
1951 *See* Kubler and Gibson, 1951.

TOZZER, A. M.
1921 Excavations of a site at Santiago
Ahuitzotla, D. F., Mexico. *Smithsonian Inst., Bur. Amer. Ethnol.*, Bull.
74.
1957 Chichen Itza and its Cenote of Sacrifice: a comparative study of contemporaneous Maya and Toltec.
Mem. Peabody Mus., Harvard Univ.,
vols. 11, 12.

TRIMBORN, H.
1959 Das alte Amerika. Stuttgart.

TROIKE, N. P.
1962 Archaeological reconnaissance in the
drainage of the Rio Verde, San Luis
Potosi, Mexico. *Bull. Texas Archaeol. Soc.*, 32: 47–55.

VAILLANT, G. C.
1930a Notes on the cultures of Middle
America. *23d Int. Cong. Amer.*
(New York, 1928), Acta, pp. 74–81.
1930b Excavations at Zacatenco. *Amer.
Mus. Natural Hist., Anthr. Papers*,
vol. 32, part 1. New York.
1931 Excavations at Ticoman. *Ibid.*, vol.
32, part 2.
1935a Excavations at El Arbolillo. *Ibid.*,
vol. 35, part 2.
1935b Early cultures of the Valley of Mexico: results of the stratigraphical project of the American Museum of Natural History in the Valley of Mexico,
1928–1933. *Ibid.*, vol. 35, part 3.
1935c Artists and craftsmen in ancient Cen-

tral America. *Amer. Mus. Natural Hist., Science Guide*, no. 88.

1938 A correlation of archaeological and historical sequences in the Valley of Mexico. *Amer. Anthr.*, 40: 535–73.

1939 An early occurrence of cotton in Mexico. *Ibid.*, 41: 170.

1941 Aztecs of Mexico. New York. (Rev. eds. 1950, 1962, 1966.)

1944 La civilización azteca. Fondo de Cultura Económica. Mexico.

1949 Artists and craftsmen in ancient Central America. 2d ed. New York.

1950 Aztecs of Mexico. Pelican ed., with supplementary material by C. A. Burland. Harmondsworth, England.

1962 *Idem.* Rev. by S. B. Vaillant. New York.

1966 *Idem.* Reprinted in Pelican ed. Harmondsworth, England.

VAILLANT, S. B., AND G. C. VAILLANT
1934 Excavations at Gualupita. *Amer. Mus. Natural Hist., Anthr. Papers*, vol. 35, part 1. New York.

VALENZUELA, J.
1945 La segunda temporada de exploraciones en la región de Los Tuxtlas, estado de Veracruz. *An. Inst. Nac. Antr. Hist.*, 1 (1939–40): 81–94.

VELÁSQUEZ GALLARDO, P.
1948 Toponimia tarasca. *In* El Occidente de México, pp. 125–26.

VELÁZQUEZ, P. F., ed.
1897–99 Colección de documentos para la historia de San Luis Potosí. 4 vols. San Luis Potosi.

1945 *See* Codex Chimalpopoca, 1945.

VERA, J. DE
1905 Relación de Acatlan y su partido. *In* Paso y Troncoso, 1905–06, 5: 55–80.

VERBA . . . TLACAUEPANTZI
1946 Verba sociorum domini Petri Tlacauepantzi. G. Rosas Herrera, trans. *Tlalocan*, 2: 150–62.

VETANCURT, A. DE
1870 Teatro mexicano. 4 vols. Bib. Histórica Iberia, vols. 7, 8. Mexico. (1st ed. 1698.)

VETCH, CAPTAIN
1837 On the monuments and relics of the ancient inhabitants of New Spain.

Jour. Royal Geog. Soc. London, 7: 1–11.

VEYTIA, M.
1907 Los calendarios mexicanos. Mexico.
1944 Historia antigua de México. 2 vols. Mexico.

VEYTIA CALENDAR WHEEL 4 (GEMELLI CARERI)
1907 *See* Veytia, 1907, pl. 4.
1944 *See* Veytia, 1944, vol. 1, pl. 4.

VEYTIA CALENDAR WHEEL 5 (SANTOS Y SALAZAR)
1907 *See* Veytia, 1907, pl. 5.
1944 *See* Veytia, 1944, vol. 1, pl. 5.

VILLAGRA CALETI, A.
1951a Las pinturas de Atetelco en Teotihuacán. *Cuad. Amer.*, 10: 153–62.

1951b Murales prehispánicos: copia, restauración y conservación. *In* Homenaje Caso, pp. 421–26.

1953 Teotihuacán y sus pinturas murales. *An. Inst. Nac. Antr. Hist.*, 5: 67–74.

1954 Pinturas rupestres: "Mateo A. Saldaña" Ixtapantongo, estado de México. *Caminos de México*, no. 9.

1956 Teotihuacán, la ciudad sagrada de Tlaloc. *Ibid.*, no. 21.

1959 La pintura mural. *In* Esplendor del México Antiguo, 2: 651–70.

VILLASEÑOR Y SÁNCHEZ, J. A.
1746–48 Theatro americano, descripción general de los reynos, y provincias, de la Nueva-España, y sus jurisdicciones. 2 vols. Mexico. Facsimile ed., 1952, Mexico.

VISITACIÓN . . . CORTÉS
1937 Visitación que se hizo en la conquista, donde fue por Capitán Francisco Cortés. *In* Nuño de Guzmán contra Hernán Cortés, sobre los descubrimientos y conquistas en Jalisco y Tepic, 1531. *Bol. Archivo General de la Nación*, 8: 556–72.

VIVÓ, J.
1946 [ed.] México prehispánico: culturas, deidades, monumentos.

1949 Geografía de México. Fondo de Cultura Económica. Mexico and Buenos Aires.

VOGT, E. Z.
1964 Ancient Maya concepts in contemporary Zinacantan religion. *6th Int.*

Cong. Anthr. Ethnol. Sci. (Paris, 1960), Acta, 2: 497–502.

WALLACE, A. F. C., ed.
1960 Men and cultures. Selected papers of the 5th Int. Cong. Anthr. Ethnol. Sci. (Philadelphia, 1956).

WARDLE, H. N.
1905 Certain clay figures of Teotihuacan *13th Int. Cong. Amer.* (New York, 1902), Acta, pp. 213–16.

WATERMAN, T. T.
1917 Bandelier's contribution to the study of ancient Mexican social organization. *Univ. California Pub. Amer. Archaeol. Ethnol.*, 12: 249–82. Berkeley.

WAUCHOPE, R.
1934 House mounds of Uaxactun, Guatemala. *Carnegie Inst. Wash.*, Pub. 436, Contrib. 7.
1938 Modern Maya houses: a study of their archaeological significance. *Carnegie Inst. Wash.*, Pub. 502.
1948 Excavations at Zacualpa, Guatemala. *Tulane Univ., Middle Amer. Research Inst.*, Pub. 14.
1950 A tentative sequence of pre-classic ceramics in Middle America. *Ibid.*, Pub. 15, pp. 211–50.
1956 [ed.] Seminars in archaeology: 1955. *Mem. Soc. Amer. Archaeol.*, no. 11.
1964 Southern Mesoamerica. *In* Jennings and Norbeck, pp. 331–86.

WEIANT, C. W.
1943 An introduction to the ceramics of Tres Zapotes, Veracruz, Mexico. *Smithsonian Inst., Bur. Amer. Ethnol.*, Bull. 139.

WEIGAND, P. C.
1968 The mines and mining techniques of the Chalchihuites culture. *Amer. Antiquity*, 33: 45–61.

WEITLANER, R. J.
1941 Chilacachapa y Tetelcingo. *El México Antiguo*, 5: 255–80.
1946 Paul Radin's "Classification of the languages of Mexico." *Tlalocan*, 2: 65–70.
1948a Exploración arqueológica en Guerrero. *In* El Occidente de México, pp. 77–85.

1948b Etnografía del estado de Guerrero. *Ibid.*, pp. 206–07.
—— AND R. H. BARLOW
1944 Expeditions in western Guerrero: the Weitlaner party, spring, 1944. *Tlalocan*, 1: 364–75.

WEST, R. C.
1948 Cultural geography of the modern Tarascan area. *Smithsonian Inst., Inst. Social Anthr.*, Pub. 7.
1961 Aboriginal sea navigation between Middle and South America. *Amer. Anthr.*, 63: 133–35.
1964 Surface configuration and associated geology of Middle America. *In* Handbook of Middle American Indians, R. Wauchope, ed., vol. 1, art. 2.
—— AND P. ARMILLAS
1950 Las chinampas de México. *Cuad. Amer.*, 2: 165–82.

WESTHEIM, P.
1948 Textilkunst in Mexiko. *Ciba Rundschau*, 78: 289.
1950 Arte antiguo de México. Mexico. (English trans. 1965, New York.)
1956 La escultura del México antiguo. *Univ. Nac. Autónoma Méx., Col. de Arte*, no. 1. (English trans. 1963, New York.)
1957 Ideas fundamentales del arte prehispánico en México. Fondo de Cultura Económica. Mexico and Buenos Aires.
1963 The sculpture of ancient Mexico. New York. (English trans. of his 1956.)

WEYERSTALL, A.
1932 Some observations on Indian mounds, idols and pottery in the lower Papaloapan basin, state of Veracruz. *Tulane Univ., Middle Amer. Research Inst.*, Pub. 5., pp. 27–67.

WHITAKER, T. W., H. C. CUTLER, AND R. S. MacNEISH
1957 Cucurbit materials from three caves near Ocampo, Tamaulipas. *Amer. Antiquity*, 22: 352–58.

WHITE, L. A.
1940 Pioneers in American anthropology: the Bandelier-Morgan letters, 1873–1883. 2 vols. Univ. New Mexico Press.

1959 The evolution of culture. New York.

—— AND I. BERNAL

1960 Correspondence de Adolfo F. Bandelier. Inst. Nac. Antr. Hist. Mexico.

WICKE, C. R.

1966 Tomb 30 at Yagul and the Zaachila tombs. *In* Paddock, 1966c, pp. 336–44.

WILLEY, G. R.

1956a [ed.] Prehistoric settlement patterns in the New World. *Viking Fund Pub. Anthr.*, no. 23.

1956b Problems concerning prehistoric settlement patterns in the Maya lowlands. *In his* 1956a, pp. 107–14.

1966 An introduction to American archaeology. Vol. 1: North and Middle America. Englewood Cliffs, N. J.

——, G. F. EKHOLM, AND R. MILLON

1964 The patterns of farming life and civilization. *In* Handbook of Middle American Indians, R. Wauchope, ed., vol. 1, art. 14.

—— AND P. PHILLIPS

1962 Method and theory in American archaeology. Phoenix Books, P88. Chicago. (1st ed. 1958, Univ. Chicago Press.)

——, E. Z. VOGT, AND A. PALERM, eds.

1958 Middle American anthropology. *Pan Amer. Union, Social Sci. Monogr.*, no. 5. Washington.

WINNING, H. von

1956 Offerings from a burial mound in coastal Nayarit. *Masterkey*, 30: 157–70. Los Angeles.

1958 Figurines with movable limbs from ancient Mexico. *Ethnos*, 23: 1–60. Stockholm.

1959 Eine keramische Dorfgruppe aus dem alten Nayarit im westlichen Mexiko. *In* Amerikanistiche Miszellen (Festband Franz Termer). *Mitteilungen aus dem Museum für Völkerkunde in Hamburg*, 25: 138–43.

1961a Two figurines with movable limbs from Veracruz, Mexico. *Masterkey*, 35: 140–46. Los Angeles.

1961b Teotihuacan symbols: the reptile's eye glyph. *Ethnos*, 26: 121–66. Stockholm.

—— AND A. STENDAHL

1969 Pre-Columbian art of Mexico and Central America. New York.

WINSHIP, G. P.

1896 The Coronado expedition, 1540–1542. *Smithsonian Inst., Bur. Amer. Ethnol.*, 14th ann. rept. (1892–93), pp. 329–637. (Reprinted 1964, Chicago.)

WITTE, N. DE

1913 Carta de Fray Nicolas de Witte a un ilustrísimo señor, Metztitlan 27 de Agosto de 1554. *An. Mus. Nac. Arqueol. Hist. Etnog.*, 3d ser., 5: 145–51. Mexico.

WITTFOGEL, K. A.

1957 Oriental despotism. Yale Univ. Press.

WOLF, E. R.

1959 Sons of the shaking earth. Univ. Chicago Press.

—— AND A. PALERM

1955 Irrigation in the old Acolhua domain, Mexico. *SW. Jour. Anthr.*, 11: 265–81.

WORMINGTON, H. M.

1957 Ancient man in North America. *Denver Mus. Natural Hist., Popular Ser.*, no. 4.

YÁÑEZ, A., ed.

1964 Mitos indígenas. Mexico.

ZANTWIJK, R. A. M. VAN

1963 Principios organizadores de los mexicas: una introducción al estudio del sistema interno del régimen azteca. *Inst. Hist., Estud. Cultura Náhuatl*, 4: 187–222.

1965 Introducción al estudio de la división en quince partes en la sociedad azteca y su significación en la estructura interna. *Jour. Soc. Amér. Paris*, 54: 211–22.

ZIMMERMANN, G.

1955 Das Cotoque, die Maya-Sprache von Chicomucelo. *Zeit. für Ethnol.*, 80 (1): 59–87. Brunswick.

1960 Das Geschichtswerke des Domingo de Muñón Chimalpahin Quauhtlehuanitzin. *Beiträge zur mittelamerikanischen Völkerkunde*, no. 5. Hamburg.

ZORITA, A. DE

1864 Breve y sumaria relación de los seño-
      res y maneras y diferencias que había
      de ellos en la Nueva España. *In*
      Col. doc. Indias, 2: 1–126.

1891 *Idem*. *In* García Icazbalceta, 1886–
      92, 3: 71–227.

1909 Historia de la Nueva España. *In*
      Col. libros y documentos referentes a

la historia de América, vol. 9. Madrid.

1941 Breve y sumaria relación. . . . *In*
      García Icazbalceta, 1941.

ZUAZO, A.

1858 Letter written to Fray Luis de Figue-
      roa, dated November 14, 1521. *In*
      García Icazbalceta, 1858–66, 1: 359.

INDEX

abogados: 409–410, 426, 430, 434

abstinence. SEE Bathing; Religious activities, fasting; Sexual abstinence

Acamapichtli, reign of: 378, 379, 383

Acaponeta phase: 700, 771, 795

Acapulco: 621–625, 627, 628, 630, 638, 645

Acatl. SEE Aztec, calendrics of

Acatlan (Puebla): 237, 244

Acaxee: 632

Acolhua: 465, 466, 472

Acolhuacan: 19, 42, 361, 366, 466, 467, 470, 471

Acolman: church construction at, 207; city-state of, 19, 22, 23; population figures for, 21 (Table 4), 22

acorns: 399

acrobat: 164 (fig. 6)

Acropolis, at Xochicalco: 32

"acropolis complex," of Maya: 45, 47, 69–72

Acxotec: 468, 469

adobe: 13, 34, 54, 58 (fig. 18), 63, 76, 90, 148, 153, 185, 189 (Table 1), 609, 615, 677, 704, 717, 751, 762, 779, 789, 797, 799

adobe bricks: in Chalchihuites architecture, 777, 783; at La Quemada, 775; on market lists, 27

adobe-makers: 206

adornment, architectural. SEE Architecture, adornment of

adornment, personal. SEE Anklets; Beads; Body paint; Bracelet; Breastplate; Ear pendant; Earplug; Earring; Headdress; Necklace; Nose ornament; Nose pendant; Nose ring; Pendant; Tattooing; Tooth blackening

adultery: 495, 614, 615

adze: 265, 285 (Table 4), 286–287 (fig. 5), 578, 579, 581, 590, 776

afterworld. SEE Heaven; Paradise; Underworld

agate: 291

agave: 219, 220–221, 222, 302 (fig. 3), 304 (fig. 8), 312, 575, 577, 589. SEE ALSO Maguey

agricultural crops. SEE by individual name

agriculture, pre-Hispanic: intensity of, 5, 6; on marginal lands, 6; technology of, 5–11. SEE ALSO Cultivation techniques; Irrigation; and by crop name

Ahuizotl: 259, 263, 380, 385, 388, 588, 608, 611 (fig. 7), 614, 628, 645, 646

Ajalpan: 176

aje oil: 220

al fresco: 139, 152, 153, 154, 200, 792. SEE ALSO Fresco decoration; Frescoes

alabaster: formation of, 210, 211 (Table 1); ornaments of, 631; vessels of, 210, 245, 676, 679, 680, 702 (fig. 3), 792

aldea. SEE Settlement patterns

Aljojuca: 237

alleys: 25, 35, 37. SEE ALSO Street

alligator: 143, 776, 780, 781, 782, 784, 785, 786

Almagre phase: 574, 576, 577, 580

almena. SEE Silhouette stone

alms-beggars: 424, following 432 (Table 4). SEE ALSO Beggars

Alta Verapaz: 210

Alta Vista: 777, 778, 780

Alta Vista phase: 771, 777, 778, 779, 781–783, 786, 787, 792, 793, 800, 801

altar: 26, 70, 94, 103 n. 7, 126, 139, 151 (fig. 28), 152 (fig. 29), 155 (fig. 33), 199, 438, 734, 771, 775, 777, 779, 781, 789, 795, 797

Altar of the Sculptured Skulls: 244

"Altars of Skulls": 126, 131, 133

alum: 220, 268, 312

Alvarado: 344, 345

Alvarado (Veracruz): figurines at, 521, 525; monument at, 570; pottery at, 518

amanteca. SEE Featherworkers

Amantla: 38, 39, 40, 42, 197, 264. SEE ALSO San Miguel Amantla

Amapa (Nayarit): 696, 698, 699, 702–712 (figs. 5–13), 717, 719, 727, 729, 747–752, 759, 765

Amapa phase: 709, 747, following 750 (Chart 1)

amaranth: cosmogonic origin of, 401; cultivation of, 8; gathering of, 577; ritual use of, following 432 (Table 4)

Amazons: 638–639, 642, 645, 695

ambassadors, in Moctezuma's palace: 28

amber: 260

amethyst: 260

amphora. SEE Pottery

amygdalin stone: 521

Anales de los Cakchiqueles: 383, 456, 457–458

Anales de Cuauhtinchan: 231

Anales de Cuauhtitlan: 323, 388, 396, 397, 475, 477 n. 2, 496. SEE ALSO Cuauhtitlan

Anales de México-Atzcapotzalco: 344, 345

Anales de Tecamachalco: 346

Anales de Tlatelolco: 344, 397

Anauac Mixtec: 460. SEE ALSO Mixtec

ancestor worship: 427

andesite: 54, 206, 207

animal effigies: 260–262, 267. SEE ALSO Effigy vessels; Zoomorphic shape

animal pens: 210

animal sacrifice. SEE Sacrifice, of animals

animal teeth: 175

animals, domesticated. SEE Chickens; Dog; Donkey; Izcuintli; Sheep; Turkey

animals, representations of: 77, 125, 128, 135, 148, 173, 174, 183, 188, 199, 213, 216, 243, 260, 315, 316, 324, 339, 564, 565, 625, 691, 707, 708 (fig. 11), 710, 716, 739, 740 (figs. 33, 34), 782. SEE

863

beads: of bone, 294, 684; of clay (pottery), 579, 671, 790, 794; of copper, 310, 628, 689, 764; of gold, 790; of iron oxide, 689; of jade, 212, 665, 667, 680; of jadeite, 581, 623; of metal, 684; of obsidian, 213; representations of, 143; of shell, 575, 631, 665, 706, 717, 734, 764, 780, 781, 782, 790; of stone, 213, 592, 625, 631, 706, 717; in Teotihuacan box, 180; of turquoise, 665, 780, 782

beams, architectural: 47 (figs. 3, 4), 56, 57 (fig. 16), 61 (fig. 22), 62 (fig. 23), 63, 65 (fig. 26), 66, 67, 264. SEE ALSO Master beam

beans: cosmogonic origin of, 401; cultivation of, 11, 577, 578, 579, 589, 615, 697, 779; divining with, 440 (fig. 53); gathering of, 575, 577; tribute payment of, 392

beggars: 28, 30. SEE ALSO Alms-beggars

behavior, of respect: 14

beheading. SEE Decapitation

Belen: 207

bell: of bronze, 590; of clay (pottery), 542, 590, 780, 782; of copper, 306 (figs. 11, 12), 310, 312, 313 (fig. 14), 628, 630, 679, 683, 689, 691, 702, 706, 733, 755, 764, 790, 797; of gold, 267, 628; of metal, 684; on warriors' belts, 595

belt: 154, 208, 312, 560, 564, 579, 595. SEE ALSO Sash

bench: 31, 183, 711

beryl: 180, 214, 783

beverage, from agave: 220. SEE ALSO Pulque

biological species, accurate representations of: 74, 129

bird bones: 211, 217, 293 (fig. 7), 294

birds: calendrical association of, 336; in captivity, 589; hunting of, 144, 218; raising of, 262; representations of, 74, 118 (fig. 46), 129, 144, 149, 170, 172, 173, 174, 175, 236, 260, 267, 324, 404 (fig. 4), 540, 542, 564, 568, 625, 739, 781, 782, 784, 785, 786, 790, 794, 795; sacred, 406 (fig. 6), 407. SEE ALSO Bats; Buzzard; Duck; Eagle; Hawk; Heron; Hummingbird; Macaw; Owl; Parakeet; Parrot; Quetzal bird

bitumen: 260

blade: 40, 212, 217, 243, 263, 265, 273–276 (fig. 1, Table 1), 295, 579, 580, 590, 595, 631, 671, 684, 729, 733, 764, 800. SEE ALSO Dagger; Knives

blanket: of maguey fiber, 297; of rabbit hair, 312; twined, 577. SEE ALSO Textiles

blood: on maguey spines, 131, 152, 433; offerings (sacrifice) of, 132, 400, 402, 406, 424, 425; representations of, 128 (fig. 62), 144, 149, 152, 324. SEE ALSO Heart, human; Sacrifice

bloodletting. SEE Self-mutilation

bloodstone: 180, 214

blowgun: 521

Boban Calendar: 343

body (face) paint: 72, 149, 151, 154, 301, 312, 437, 502 n. 19, 592, 596, 597, 598, 612, 714, 724

Bolaños-Juchipila culture: 769–774

bolas: 158, 173, 174, 289. SEE ALSO Timbrels

Bonampak murals: 72. SEE ALSO Murals

bone carving: from Chiapa de Corzo, 559; from Kaminaljuyu, 217, 559; from La Villita, 665; of Maya, 216; of Mixtec, 77

bone-collagen analysis: 726

"Bone of Tequixquiac": 216

bones: costume of, 154; dating techniques with, 726; of horse, 575; mosaics on, 260, 261; notched, 599; objects of, 216, 217, 261, 292–295 (Table 5, fig. 7), 301, 316, 590, 631, 671, 684, 689, 705, 734, 781; techniques of working, 217; rasps of, 216; statuette of, 217; tools of, 262, 263. SEE ALSO Bird bones; Crossbones; Human bones; Skeleton; Skull

books: Chilam Balam, 453, 456; contents of, 323–324; divinatory nature of, 323; of Maya, 453; pictorial style of, 119, 397; Popol Vuh, 453, 456, 457; ritual screenfold, 397. SEE ALSO Codices; Literature; Writing

borrow-pit: 36

boulder carving: 117, 131 (fig. 65)

boulder sculpture: 107

bouquet. SEE Flowers, representations of

bow and arrow: representations of, 144, 265, 280 (fig. 3)—in central Mexico, 281–282; of Chichimec, 465, 466, 468, 469; of Chontal, 609; of Cuitlatec, 615; of Huastec, 594; in Sinaloa, 755; in Tamaulipas, 580; of Tarascans, 646; of Yope, 613

bowl, atop incense burners: 96 (figs. 5, 6), 99 (fig. 11). SEE ALSO Pottery

box: for burial, 180; carving on, 125; painting on, 154; of pottery, 669, 722; of wood, 265; from Teotihuacan, 180

bracelet: of bone, 684; of mosaic, 259, 260; of Huastec, 591; of pottery, 729, 731; representations of, 154; of shell, 591, 631, 665, 689, 706, 717, 729; tribute payment of, 259

brachycephaly: 690. SEE ALSO Hyperbrachycephaly

braiding: 304, 305, 307, 319

braids. SEE Hair, representations of

branch: 143, 144, 152

brazier: of Huastec, 600; for perpetual fires, 438; from Tehuacan valley, 243; of Teotihuacan style, 99 (fig. 11), 141, 207, 208; of Tlaloc effigy, 240, 243. SEE ALSO Incense burner

bread, barrio specialization of: 28

breastplate: 154

bridge: 25, 26, 265, following 432 (Table 4)

British Honduras: Mixteca-Puebla influence in, 240

brocading, of cloth: 306, 309, 315, 318, 590

bronze: 590

brush, for painting: 135, 237, 262

bugle: 149. SEE ALSO Trumpet

bules. SEE Pottery

bultos: 137, 138 (fig. 5)

bundle. SEE Ceremonial bundle; Mummy bundle; Sacred bundle

burial: bolas outline, 174; in caves, 630; collective (multiple), 538, 665–666, 667, 690, 722, 743, 745, 751; grave goods in, 143, 157, 159, 173, 175, 180, 181, 190, 191, 193, 194 (fig. 10),

Cuextecatlichocayan: 587

Cuezala: 607

Cuicatec region: 245

Cuicuilco: 43, 49 (fig. 8), 50 (fig. 9), 51, 96, 135, 136 (fig. 2), 157, 158, 172, 173, 176, 185, 190 (fig. 5)

Cuitlahuac: 469

Cuitlatec: burials of, 678; location of, 614–615, 637, 644, 646, 657, 677; pottery of, 679; religion of, 615; subsistence of, 615

Culhua empire: 378

Culhuacan: chinampa agriculture in, 8; history of, 481, 488, 489, 502; place glyph for, 484 (fig. 3); pottery from, 236, 237, 254, 255 (fig. 24), 533, 535

Culiacan: Aztatlan complex at, 699–700, 761; burials at, 762; figurines from, 766 (fig. 10); locations of, 655; phases at, 710, 761–762; pottery from, 751, 764 (fig. 8), 765 (fig. 9)

"cult of capillas": 609

cult of the dead, at Monte Alban: 77

cult objects: 409–410, 437

cult themes: following 408 (Table 3), 410–430

cultivation techniques: barbecho, 8, 545, 547; burning, 7, 588; calmil, 7–8, 16; chinampa, 7–11, 16, 24, 25, 26, 38, 80, 223; crop rotation, 8; dry-farming, 10; fertilizing, 7; mixed cropping, 8; plantation, 545, 546, 553; with plow, 6, 10, 545, 552; rastreo, 10; Sahagún's description of, 10; slash-and-burn, 545–549, 551, 552, 553, 681; tlacolol, 7. SEE ALSO Irrigation

"Cultura de Los Cerros": 157

"Cultura Madre": 94

cuneiform decoration. SEE Pottery

cupola, on modern churches: 68

curers: 430, 439, 441

curing. SEE Sickness, curing of; Turpentine unguent

currasows: 98

curtain, of reed: 224

Curutaran phase: 676

"curved stones" (small yokes): 569

cycle, 52-year: of Aztec, 117, 122 (fig. 53), 131, 335, 347; in religion, 399, 400, 413, 434, 435; Tula chronology based on, 231. SEE ALSO Year-bundle stones

cycles, in calendrical system: 347–348

cylindrical stone, of Xochicalcoid style: 120 n. 18

dagger: 213, 556. SEE ALSO Blade; Knives

dais, sculptured: at Tula, 31

dance, god of: 266

dance court, at Tenochtitlan: 26

dancer: figurine of, 171 (fig. 16); representations of, 266; shells worn by, 216; special residence of, 28

dances: of Huastec, 599; in paradise, 143; representations of, 144, 527, 746. SEE ALSO Religious activities, dancing

dartpoints: 575, 577. SEE ALSO Atlatl points; Fluted points; Projectile points; Spearpoints

dart-thrower: 71

date glyphs. SEE Calendric symbols

date stones, carving of: 125

dating: of Aztec monuments, 116; of bone material, 726; obsidian-hydration technique of, 726, 737; in Tamaulipas, 574, 575, 576, 577, 578. SEE ALSO Radiocarbon dating; and under individual sites

day, Aztec: 345, 348

day names: divinatory function of, 322, 323, 338–339. SEE ALSO Calendrical system

day signs (tonalpohualli): 333–348, 398, 403–404 (figs. 3, 4), 405 (Table 1), 406 (fig. 6), 407, following 408 (Table 3), 417, 422, 430, 434, 435, 439

dead, disposal of. SEE Burial; Cremation; Shaft-tombs; Tombs; and under individual sites

death: causes of, 143, 404, 422, 423 (fig. 32), 442, 597, 598; of gods, 400, 402. SEE ALSO Auto-sacrifice; Decapitation; Heart, human; Paradise; Sacrifice; Suicide

death monster (tzitzimime): 422, 427, 428

death symbols: 71, 422, 428, 564, 565, 566, 569, 571, 597

decapitation: 71, 500, 595, 596, 598, 613, 627, 667 n. 1

deformation: of upper lip, 562, 563. SEE ALSO Head deformation

deer: 149, 241, 594, 781

deer bones: 175, 217, 292

deer skin: 216

deforestation: 56, 58, 287

deities: calendric names of, 132, following 408 (Table 3), 412, 413; clothing of, 263, 264, 402; description of, 395–445; household, 123, 127; representations of, 67, 68, 71, 77, 107, 127, 130, 132, 144, 149, 151, 175, 182, 183, 199, 241, 242, 256, 264, 266, 324, 334–348, 374, 408, 533, 540, 579. SEE ALSO Cosmogony; Cosmology; and by individual name

Delicias phase: 661, 674, 675

deme: 14, 16. SEE ALSO Kin groups

demographic data: for central Mexico, 3–5, 9, 12, 15–23 (Tables 3, 4), 25, 26, 29–32, 43, 80, 368, 369, 393; for Guerrero, 617; for Gulf Coast area, 546, 547, 549, 550, 551, 552, 557; for Nueva Galicia, 642, 695; for Sinaloa, 755. SEE ALSO Census figures; Population density

"demon": 67

density. SEE Population density

dental mutilation: 193, 217 (fig. 8), 218, 592, 630, 665, 689, 690

dentist: 206

Desert culture: 769, 800

Diablo Cave: 574

Diablo phase: 574, 575, 576

diadems. SEE Gold jewelry

dietary deficiency, at Teotihuacan: 203

dietary habits, vessel shape indicative of: 242, 250

digging stick: 545. SEE ALSO Coa

diopside-jadeite: 211

diorite: 89, 123, 175, 560

directions. SEE Cardinal points

disc: of clay, 578, 580, 781, 790; representations of, 139, 240–241; of stone, 289, 705 (fig. 6), 790,

fugitive slip. SEE Pottery
furniture: 224, 265, 299, 589

games: in paradise, 143; patron deities of, 419; representations of, 338, 746. SEE ALSO Ball game; Patolli; Pelota
gaming pieces: 289
gardeners: 30
gardens: 28, 438
garland, of flowers: 224 (fig. 15)
garrisons. SEE Military garrisons
gathering, subsistence based on: 462, 465, 575, 577, 578, 589
Gavilan phase: 709, 711, 719, 720, 747, following 750 (Chart 1), 771
genealogical codices, of Mixtec: 243, 478 (Table 1), 480 (Table 2)
genealogical tables, of Teotihuacan nobility: 203
geography: architecture influenced by, 45–49; of Mesoamerica, 3–4, 505, 543–545, 548–549, 558, 573, 583–584, 619–621, 657, 697, 768–769
giant, in cosmogony: 399
gift-giving, religious activity of: 435
gladiatorial platform: 26
gladiatorial sacrifice: 424 (fig. 36), 432, following 432 (Table 4), 469
gladiatorial stone (temalacatl): 114, 124, 125, 126
glue: birds caught by, 218; feathers attached by, 219, 263; in mosaic work, 260. SEE ALSO Paste, flour
glyphs: Aztec, 222 (fig. 13); meaning gold, 267; at Monte Alban, 96; meaning mountain, 241; meaning tribute payment, 259; at Tula, 108 (fig. 26). SEE ALSO Calendric symbols; Place glyphs; "Reptile's Eye" glyph
gobernador. SEE Officials
goblets. SEE Pulque, goblets for; Pottery, of goblet-form
"God M": 430
goddesses, colossal: 100–102 (fig. 16), 207
gold: beads of, 790; bells of, 267, 628; on bracelets, 259; figurine of, 628; on headdresses, 263; in literature, 449, 450; of Lord of Michoacan, 634; panning of, 267; shield of, 268; in Sinaloa, 755, 761; sources of, 267, 617, 628, 639, 677; Spanish acquisition of, 180, 207, 266, 268, 694; on statues, 207; techniques of working, 268; in Tenochtitlan market, 260; tribute payment of, 267, 603; value of, 268; vases of, 180
gold alloy: 268
gold dust: 180, 267
gold embroidery: 312
gold jewelry: 30, 259, 260, 266–268
gold leaf: 691
gold nuggets: 267
gold-plating technique: 690
goldsmiths: 15, 264
Goodman-Martínez-Thompson correlation: 201 (Table 3), 230, 232, 711. SEE ALSO Correlations, calendric; Spinden correlation
gouge: 577, 580
gourd: cloisonné on, 764; cultivation of, 575, 577, 578, 579, 589, 615; decoration on, 223, 764;

lacquer on, 223, 590, 594, 676, 680; representations of, 222–223, 437 (fig. 50). SEE ALSO Calabash; Squash
gourd-shaped vessels. SEE Pottery
governor of ward. SEE Officials
graffito, of bow and arrow: 283
Gran Canal: 4
granary, 13, 28, 609, 642
granite: necklaces of, 175; yokes of, 560
graphite slip, on pottery: 254
grasshopper: 118 (fig. 44), 129
grater bowls (molcajetes): 38, 237, 242, 248, 250, 251, 256, 580, 628, 629, 630, 674–675, 679, 681 (fig. 16), 682, 686, 688, 705, 717, 721, 736, 737, 743, 744, 790, 791, 792, 796
grave goods. SEE Burial
gravel, architectural use of: 59 (fig. 20), 62. SEE ALSO Rubble
graver: 135, 275, 575
Great Rebellion: 632, 643
Great Temple, Tenochtitlan: 82, 85
grid pattern. SEE Settlement patterns, Spanish grid; Streets
griddle. SEE Comal
grinding tools. SEE Disc, of stone; Mano; Metate; Mortar; Pestle
grooving: on deer scapula, 175; on marble vessel, 210; on pottery, 168, 199, 514, 519, 665, 709 (fig. 12), 795; of stone tools, 285 (Table 4), 287, 288, 289, 292, 294, 296, 631, 679, 706, 717, 729, 770, 776, 781, 793
Guadalajara: 653, 654
Guadalcazar Cave: 307
Guadiana Branch, of Chalchihuites culture: 787–801
Gualupita (Morelos): animal figures at, 174; earplugs at, 173; necklaces at, 174; Olmec influence at, 95, 159; pottery at, 245, 247, 254; stamps at, 173; timbrels at, 173; whistles at, 174
Guanajuato: ceramic tradition of, 167, 171; excavations in, 659, 668–673; figurines from, 171, 172 (fig. 18); pottery from, 668–673 (figs. 6–11), 742; timbrels at, 173
Guasave (Sinaloa): Aztatlan complex at, 699–700, 710, 717, 750, 761; basketry and matwork from, 298; burials at, 762; copper objects at, 764; dating of, 767; as Mesoamerican outpost, 766; Mixteca-Puebla influence at, 240; pipes from, 761 (fig. 5); pottery from, 727, 758 (fig. 3), 760 (fig. 4), 764, 797; textiles from, 308
Guasave phase: 700
Guatemala: Aztec campaigns into, 383; Aztec dominance in, 80; hachas from, 565 (fig. 9), 568 (fig. 13); Mixteca-Puebla influence in, 240; Olmec influence in, 95; settlement pattern in, 17; yokes from, 562 (fig. 4), 563. SEE ALSO Kaminaljuyu; Maya; Tikal; Uaxactun
Gucumatz, lineage of: 229–230
Guerra phase: 574, 576, 577, 578, 580
Guerrero: archaeological remains from, 619–631, 659, 666, 678 (fig. 15), 736, 737, 750; ethnohistory of, 603–618, 646, 647; gold from, 267, 617, 628; Inca traits in, 677; linguistic distribu-

891

7; raising of, 589; representations of, 568 (fig. 14), 721

turpentine unguent: 416, 430, 449

turquoise: beads of, 665, 780, 782; on clothing, 312; inlays of, 665, 676; mosaics of, 154, 175, 258–262, 630, 691, 782, 783, 790; necklaces of, 676; representations of, 259, 339; sources of, 259, 779

turtle: 129, 141, 152, 174, 224 (fig. 15), 691, 739, 774, 782, 784, 786, 790, 794

turtle shells: 217, 671

tutelary deity. SEE Abogados

Tututepec: 482, 483, 484, 485, 490, 493. SEE ALSO Tototepec

Tututepeque: 612

Tuxcacuesco (Jalisco): 696, 698, 727, 729–733 (figs. 27, 29), 736, 741, 742, 743, 746, 747, 749, following 750 (Chart 1), 751

Tuxpan phase: 709, 710, 711, 747

Tuzapan: 533

Tuztec: 608

tweezers: 628, 684, 691, 706 (fig. 7), 736

twill. SEE Basketry; Weaving techniques

twins, deity of: 418–419

"tying of years": 347. SEE ALSO Year-bundle stones

Tzacualli (Tzaqualli) phase: 42, 189–190, 201 (Table 3), 202

Tzakol phase: 192, 230

Tzapotlan: 485

Tzaqualli. SEE Tzacualli

Tzintzuntzan: 46 (fig. 2), 299, 306 (fig. 11), 310, 629, 636, 637, 640, 653, 657, 659, 661, 673, 689–692, 694

tzitzimime. SEE Death monsters

Tzompantli. SEE "Skull platform"

Uaxactun: architecture at, 45, 47, 69, 70; bone tools at, 294; dates for, 230, 231; marble vessels from, 210; projectile points at, 281

ultraviolet waves, for bone dating: 726

Ulua: 259

undertakers: 206

underworld: 400, 408, following 408 (Table 2), 419, 422, 428, 567

unguent. SEE Turpentine unguent

United States: Mixteca-Puebla style in, 241. SEE ALSO Hohokam; Mogollon; Southern Ceremonial Cult; Southwestern-Mexican contacts

universe: concept of, 335, 403–408, following 408 (Table 2), 447

urbanization: criteria of, 11, 26–27; environmental diversity effect on, 11–12; at Tenochtitlan, 24–29

urban-rural symbiosis: 11, 15, 29. SEE ALSO Symbiotic patterns

urn burials: 678, 680, 713, 764, 765. SEE ALSO Burial

Uxmal: 210, 229, 231

Valenzuela Cave: 574

Valladolid, Cholula comparisons with: 29

Valles de Morelos: 4

Valley of Mexico. SEE Mexico, valley of

varnish: 220

vase: 180, 213

vegetables: barrio specialization of, 28; representations of, 89, 119 (fig. 47)

veintena ceremonies. SEE Religious activities

veneer: 52, 60 (fig. 21). SEE ALSO Concrete; Plaster; Stucco

Venta Salada: 231–233, 237, 241–243, 306

ventilator: 791

ventriloquism, by diviners: 195

Venus: 149, 241, 230 n. 2, 347, 348, 426, 475, 479 (fig. 2)

Veracruz: archaeology of, 505–542; hachas from, 563–565 (fig. 6), 567 (fig. 12), 568 (fig. 13); influence on sculpture, 102, 120 (SEE ALSO Tajin tradition); linguistic distribution in, 506 (fig. 1); mirrors from, 569; Mixteca-Puebla influence at, 240; mosaics from, 259; palmas from, 565–568 (figs. 10, 12); rainfall in, 543–544, 545; sculpture in, 124; settlement patterns in, 543–557; yokes from, 558–563 (figs. 1–3)

vessel: for paint, 135; representations of, 139; of soapstone, 679; from Teotihuacan, 180, 181. SEE ALSO Pottery; Sacrificial vessel; Stone, vessels of

Vesuvio phase: 777, 783–784, 787, 796

vigas maestras. SEE Master beam

Viking Group mounds: 35, 37, 38, 189 (Table 1), 193

village. SEE Settlement patterns

village groups, clay models of: 715 (fig. 17), 719

voladores, clay model of: 715 (fig. 17)

Volátiles: 335, 336

volcanic ash: 669

volcanic tuff: 206

volcano: Cerro Gordo, 51; Iztaccihuatl, 4, 5; Matlalcueye, 470; Popocatepetl, 4, 5; as source of natural cements, 54; Xitle, 135

votive axe: 526, 528, 529, 532. SEE ALSO Axe

Votive Pyramid: 774, 775

wall construction: of adobe, 76, 148; of cobble stones, 711; of dry stone, 32, 781; earthquake factor influencing, 62; at La Quemada, 775; of rubble mortar (stone and mud), 63, 76; of stone, 32, 40, 59 (fig. 20), 78, 88 (fig. 38); at Teotihuacan, 57 (fig. 15), 59–61 (figs. 20–22), 62; of wattle-and-daub, 54

walls: carving on, 109; of ceremonial precincts (coatepantli), 131, 437; mosaics on, 260; painting of, 76, 127 (SEE ALSO Murals); stucco on, 34, 37, 56, 59 (fig. 20), 153, 221, 538, 626 (fig. 5)

"war of the stone men": 474–475, 476 (fig. 1), 477, 498 (fig. 7), 500, 501, 502 n. 19

war service, tribute payment of: 392–393

war symbol, sacred: 123

ward. SEE Settlement patterns

warfare: class mobility through, 15, 352, 354–355, 356–358, 371, 389, 593; cosmogonic origin of, 402; of Cuitlatec, 615; of Huastec, 594–596; of Maya-Toltec society, 71–72; philosophical doubts about, 448; representations of, 71, 72,